W9-AFE-377

Encyclopedia of
transnational crime & just

ENCYCLOPEDIA OF

Transnational Crime & Justice

ENCYCLOPEDIA OF
Transnational
Crime & Justice

MARGARET E. BEARE | EDITOR
YORK UNIVERSITY, TORONTO, CANADA

$SAGE reference

Los Angeles | London | New Delhi
Singapore | Washington DC

Los Angeles | London | New Delhi
Singapore | Washington DC

FOR INFORMATION:

SAGE Publications, Inc.
2455 Teller Road
Thousand Oaks, California 91320
E-mail: order@sagepub.com

SAGE Publications Ltd.
1 Oliver's Yard
55 City Road
London, EC1Y 1SP
United Kingdom

SAGE Publications India Pvt. Ltd.
B 1/I 1 Mohan Cooperative Industrial Area
Mathura Road, New Delhi 110 044
India

SAGE Publications Asia-Pacific Pte. Ltd.
3 Church Street
#10-04 Samsung Hub
Singapore 049483

Publisher: Rolf A. Janke
Acquisitions Editor: Jim Brace-Thompson
Assistant to the Publisher: Michele Thompson
Managing Editors: Joseph Golson,
                 Susan Moskowitz
Reference Systems Manager: Leticia M. Gutierrez
Reference Systems Coordinator: Laura Notton
Production Editor: Jane Haenel
Typesetter: Hurix Systems Pvt. Ltd.
Proofreader: Kristin Bergstad
Indexer: Wendy Allex
Cover Designer: Janet Kiesel
Marketing Manager: Kristi Ward

Copyright © 2012 by SAGE Publications, Inc.

Printed in the United States of America.

Library of Congress Cataloging-in-Publication Data

Encyclopedia of transnational crime and justice / editor, Margaret E. Beare.

p. cm.
"A SAGE Reference Publication."
Includes bibliographical references and index.

ISBN 978-1-4129-9077-6 (cloth)

1. Transnational crime—Encyclopedias. 2. Justice, Administration of—Encyclopedias. I. Beare, Margaret E.

HV6252.E53 2012
364.03—dc23   2011051788

12 13 14 15 16 10 9 8 7 6 5 4 3 2 1

Contents

List of Entries

Reader's Guide

Corruption

Bribery and Graft
Commissions and Payoffs
Corporate Influence Peddling
Corruption
Electoral Manipulation
Influence and Position
Political Influence Peddling
Politically Exposed Persons
Public Expenditure Tracking Systems (PETS)
Transparency International

Crimes and Criminal Markets

Accounting Fraud
Art and Antiquities: Fraud
Art and Antiquities: Plunder
Biopiracy
Black Market Peso Exchange
Capital Flight
Charity Fraud
Child Exploitation
Cigarette Smuggling
Cocaine
Computer-Generated Scams
Copyright Infringement
Counterfeit Currency
Counterfeit Goods
Diamonds and Jewelry
Draft Dodging
Drug Trade: Legislative Debates
Drug Trade: Source, Destination, and
    Transit Countries
Financial Fraud
Forgery
Gambling: Illegal
Gambling: Legal
Gender-Based Violence

Heroin
Human Smuggling
Human Trafficking
Identity Theft
Informal Value
    Transfer Systems
International Crimes
Internet Crime
Investment Crimes
Job Offer Scams
Marijuana or Cannabis
Money Laundering: History
Money Laundering: Methods
Money Laundering: Targeting
    Criminal Proceeds
Money Laundering: Vulnerable
    Commodities and Services
Nigerian Money Scams
Organ Trafficking
Pharmaceuticals
Piracy: Failed States
Piracy: History
Pollution: Air and Water
Pollution: Corporate
Pollution: Shipping-Related
Pornography
Price-Fixing
Pyramid Schemes
Sales Tax
Sex Slavery
Tariff Crimes
Tax Evasion
Telemarketing Fraud
Tobacco Smuggling
Toxic Dumping
Value-Added Tax Fraud
Weapons Smuggling
Wildlife Crime

Definitions, Changing Concepts, and Impact of Transnational Crime

Alien Conspiracies and Protection Systems
Communication Technologies
Disorganized Crime: Reuter's Thesis
Impact of Transnational Crime
Legal and Illegal Economies
Mafia Myths and Mythologies
Measuring Transnational Crime
Offenders or Offenses
Organized Crime: Defined
Profit-Driven Crime: Naylor's Typology
Risk Assessments
Technology
Terrorism: Defined
Transnational Crime: Defined

Geography of Transnational Crime

Australia
Central America
Complicity of the International Community
East Asia
Eastern Europe and Russia
Globalization
Middle East
North America
South America
South Asia
Southeast Asia
Terrorism Versus Transnational Crime
West Asia
Western Europe

Modes of Operation and Facilitators for Crime

Popular Support Mechanisms: "Enablers" of
    Criminal Activity
Violence: Intimidation
Violence: Protection
Violence: Uses

Policing and Intelligence Organizations

Crime Commissions
Egmont Group of Financial Intelligence Units
European Union
Europol
Financial Action Task Force

International Association of Chiefs of Police
International Criminal Court
International Monetary Fund
Internationalized Criminal Tribunals
Interpol
Policing: Domestic
Policing: National Security
United Nations
War Crimes Tribunals
World Bank
World Court

Sources of Data and Research on Transnational Crime

Data Sources: Empirical Data
Data Sources: Media Coverage
Data Sources: Police Data
Data Sources: Prosecution and Courts
Government Reports
Nongovernmental Organizations
Public Perceptions of Crime
Transnational Crime: Research Centers

The State as an Instigator of Crime

Failed States
Intelligence Agencies: Illegal Engagements
Legislating Morality
Legislation as a Source of Crime
Military Industries
Military-Political-Industrial Nexus

Strategies of Law Enforcement and Justice

Adjudicating International Crimes
Anticorruption Legislation
Antiterrorist Financing
Centralization
Civil Forfeiture: The Experience of the
    United States
Conventions, Agreements, and Regulations
Corporate Liability
Criminal Associations
Criminal Forfeiture and Seizure
Deportation
Executive Order 13581
Extradition
Harmonization

About the Editor

Margaret E. Beare holds the position of professor of sociology and law at York University. She served from 1996 to 2006 as the first director of the Nathanson Centre for the Study of Organized Crime and Corruption, located at Osgoode Hall Law School. Her career combines academic teaching with research and policy development. She worked in the area of police research for 11 years with the Department of the Solicitor General Canada and served two years as director of Police Policy and Research. She brings an international perspective to her work. Her previous publications include *Criminal Conspiracies,* *Organized Crime in Canada* (1996); *Major Issues Relating to Organized Crime* (with Tom Naylor); *Critical Reflections on Transnational Organized Crime, Money Laundering and Corruption* (edited, 2003); *Money Laundering in Canada: The Chasing of Dirty and Dangerous Dollars* (co-authored with S. Schneider, 2007); *Police and Government Relations: Who's Calling the Shots* (co-edited with Tonita Murray, 2007); and *Honouring Social Justice: Honouring Dianne Martin* (edited, 2009) in honor of a colleague at Osgoode Hall Law School.

List of Contributors

Justin Lewis Abold
Oxford University

Nahel N. Asfour
University of Vienna

Julie Ayling
Australian National University

Elena Azaola
Centro de Investigaciones y Estudios Superiores en Antropologia Social

Margaret E. Beare
York University

Marcel F. Beausoleil
Fitchburg State University

Michael Paul Beltran
United States District Court

Giulia Berlusconi
Università Cattolica/ Transcrime

Kiara A. Booth
Knox College

Sarah E. Boslaugh
Kennesaw State University

Paul Brienza
York University

Benjamin E. Brockman-Hawe
Independent Scholar

Thomas F. Brown
Virginia Wesleyan College

Francesco Calderoni
Università Cattolica/Transcrime

Stefano Caneppele
Università Cattolica/Transcrime

John R. Cencich
California University of Pennsylvania

John Martyn Chamberlain
Loughborough University

Jacqueline Suzanne Chavez
Mississippi State University

Silvia Ciotti
EuroCrime—Research, Training and Consultancy

Karen K. Clark
Independent Scholar

Rochelle E. Cobbs
Mississippi Valley State University

Gregory Cooper
University of Texas

John Coxhead
University of Derby

D. Larry Crumbley
Louisiana State University

Matthew C. Dahl
Independent Scholar

Marika Dawkins
Prairie View A&M University

Joseph F. C. DiMento
University of California, Irvine

O. Oko Elechi
Prairie View A&M University

Charles L. Fisk Jr.
Saint Leo University

Jennifer Fleetwood
University of Kent

Jason Friedman
Wasatch Academy

Trevor Fronius
WestEd

Angeles Garduño
Knox College

Gilbert Geis
University of California, Irvine

Camille Gibson
Prairie View A&M University

Angela R. Gover
University of Colorado, Denver

Kacper T. Gradon
University College London

Neil Guzy
University of Pittsburgh, Greensburg

Francis Frederick Hawley
Western Carolina University

Jason A. Helfer
Knox College

David C. Hicks
Independent Scholar

Livia Holden
Lahore University of Management Sciences

Jason R. Jolicoeur
Cincinnati State Technical and Community College

Kimberly Jones
Northeastern University

Christina-Vasiliki
Kanellopoulou
Independent Scholar

Robert M. Keeton
University of Tennessee

Guy Richard Kempster
Sheffield Hallam University

Paula Bridget Kenny
Institute of Technology, Sligo

Janine Kremlin
California State University, San Bernardino

Bill Kte'pi
Independent Scholar

Liam Leonard
Institute of Technology, Sligo

Kristine Levan Miller
Plymouth State University

Ben F. Linton II
Independent Scholar

Keith Gregory Logan
Kutztown University

Robert M. Lombardo
Loyola University, Chicago

Nicholas Lord
Cardiff University

Arthur J. Lurigio
Loyola University, Chicago

Georgia Lysaght
University of Wollongong

Rande W. Matteson
Saint Leo University

Glenn P. McGovern
Santa Clara County District Attorney's Office

Sharon A. Melzer
State University of New York, Plattsburgh

Nancy Ann Morris
Southern Illinois University

Travis Morris
Norwich University

Barry D. Mowell
Broward College

Giulia Mugellini
Università Cattolica/ Transcrime

Krishna Mungur
Solution Concepts Consulting

Tony Murphy
University of Westminster

Timothy J. O'Boyle
Kutztown University

David Orrick
Norwich University

Maria Pasqualetti
The Chicago School of Professional Psychology

Jessica Peake
University of Pennsylvania

Adam R. Pearlman
Independent Scholar

Mladen Pecujlija
University of Novi Sad, Serbia

Anthony Petrosino
WestEd

Wm. C. Plouffe Jr.
Independent Scholar

Carol J. Pretlow
Norfolk State University

Michael J. Puniskis
Middlesex University

Elizabeth Rholetter Purdy
Independent Scholar

John V. Rafferty
Villanova University

Blake M. Randol
Washington State University

Harry M. Rhea
Richard Stockton College of New Jersey

Juan R. Rivera
Central Intelligence Retiree Association

Pierre M. Rivolta
Sam Houston State University

Cliff Roberson
Kaplan University

Kelly Rodgers
Hamline University School of Law

Michael D. Royster
Prairie View A&M University

Gabriel Rubin
Montclair State University

Edward J. Schauer
Prairie View A&M University

Stephen T. Schroth
Knox College

Richard Severns
Sheffield Hallam University

Jeffrey Shantz
Kwantlen Polytechnic University

Martha L. Shockey-Eckles
Saint Louis University

Anne R. Siders
Independent Scholar

Alka Simlot
South Jersey Legal Services

Rupendra Simlot
Richard Stockton College of New Jersey

Alicia H. Sitren
University of North Florida

Thomas M. Southard
University of Delaware

Rachel Elizabeth Southworth
Cardiff University

Toine Spapens
Tilburg University

Peter Squires
University of Brighton

Leonard A. Steverson
South Georgia College

Victor B. Stolberg
Essex County College

Elizabeth A. Tomsich
University of Colorado, Denver

Marcella Bush Trevino
Barry University

Alejandro Varela
Knox College

Santiago Villaveces-Izquierdo
Independent Scholar

Mark V. Vlasic
Georgetown University

Robert F. Vodde
*Fairleigh Dickinson
University*

Debra Warner
*The Chicago School of
Professional Psychology*

Stan C. Weeber
McNeese State University

Rob White
University of Tasmania

Robert D. Williams
*United States Court of Appeals,
Fifth Circuit*

Tanya Wyatt
Northumbria University

Marisha D. Ziajor
*California State University, San
Bernardino*

Introduction

If there was a race between the forces of globalized economies and the capabilities of globalized governance, the economic factors rather than the regulatory mechanisms might be seen to be winning. Any market—for goods or services—can be exploited by criminals for profit, and the flow of commerce across borders adds to these criminal opportunities. The opening of trade in parts of the world that previously were closed and the movement of tourists and businesses around the globe, together with advances in technology and communication systems, have created unprecedented opportunities for legitimate entrepreneurs as well as those who are intent on using this openness for illicit gain. As the 2010 report of the United Nations Office on Drugs and Crime, *The Globalization of Crime*, confirms, "Organized crime has diversified, gone global and reached macro-economic proportions."

Certainly local criminality continues. However, the advantages gained by crossing borders and moving from one jurisdiction to another have been recognized by criminals and by those professionals who facilitate the criminal activities. The disadvantages have been recognized by those professionals who try to bring the transnational criminals to justice and those who try to secure justice for the victims of these transnational criminals. Criminals, criminal products, and criminal proceeds cross borders. Presenting a one-volume "picture" of transnational crime together with a review of some of the domestic and international mechanisms to counter these crimes is the objective of this encyclopedia. This task of creating an encyclopedia on transnational crime and justice has necessarily meant that decisions were made as to what to include and what to omit. The objective was to identify the key issues. In some cases, these decisions reflect the impact on societies in general, or the more individualized personal harm

that is entailed in certain illegal acts, or occasionally the timeliness of the controversies.

The term *transnational crime* rather than organized crime was used in the title. By definition, transnational crimes involve border crossings as an integral part of the criminal activity. They also include crimes that take place in one country with consequences that significantly affect other countries. This encyclopedia does include transnational organized crime (transnational crime carried out by organized crime syndicates), but there is an awareness that all sophisticated crimes that cross borders may not be "organized" in any manner that resembles classic, Mafia-type structures. The entries address the shifting perspective of scholars regarding the nature of these structured organized crime operations. Although these crimes are included, so are those criminal operations that more closely resemble what Peter Reuter has termed "disorganized" crimes. Likewise, there is also an awareness of the role that so-called legitimate businesses and professional individuals play in criminal enterprises. Topics such as money laundering require that one recognizes lawyers, accountants, bank officials, and border officers to be among those who are vulnerable to exploitation—or on occasion who are active participants in the criminality. In addition to a blurring of criminals and professionals, the essential linkages between the legal and illegal economies are explored.

The encyclopedia addresses the justice aspect as well as the criminal side of the equation. Not only does it define, describe, and chart the crimes and criminal activity; it also includes significant coverage of the policing of those crimes and their prosecution within domestic and international court systems. The mechanisms that are set up to "police" global criminals obviously must reach from the local and domestic agencies to the international regimes. As an indication of the continuum, the encyclopedia includes entries on domestic policing, intelligence agencies (including a sampling of national security agencies as well as international organizations such as the International Chiefs of Police, Interpol, and Europol), and recognition of the private enforcement work of contracted police and contracted military groups. In addition to the enforcement personnel, the adjudication systems stretch from the domestic to the international; the encyclopedia therefore covers the impact of the mega-trials of organized crime members or street gangs on court processes, diverse prosecution approaches, the International Criminal Court, war crime tribunals, and a bevy of nonstate bodies, such as the United Nations, World Bank, International Monetary Fund, Financial Action Task Force, and numerous conventions and protocols that have been signed and eventually ratified.

Why Is This Topic Important?

There has long been an interest in the exploits of high-profile "organized" mobsters—from historical accounts to the movies. Some of these high-profile individuals have risen above their crimes to take on mythic reputations, and in several cases, their funerals have assumed an aura of celebrity status. Meyer Lansky, Al Capone, the "Teflon Don" John Gotti, the rest of the notorious Five Families of New York, the Canadian Rizzutos, and mafiosi scattered around the world are the source of much media attention and massive law enforcement—with some significant arrests as recently as January 2011 for violations of the Racketeer Influenced and Corrupt Organizations (RICO) Act. To some extent, however, these violent hoodlums no longer dominate the current list of transnational concerns. With or without the Mafia, international drug, and human-trafficking operations, the exploitation of the environment for profit, the smuggling of both legal and illegal goods, the proliferation and illicit sale of weapons of all sorts, and some of the "oldest" crimes, including gambling, will continue. Rigid Mafia-type, structured criminal organizations have given way to more fluid networks of criminals, often revealing a complex interaction between legitimate professionals and those who are more permanently entrenched in crime.

As international scholarship and government policies shift slightly away from a preoccupation with traditional forms of organized crime to a greater appreciation of "harm" as a measurement of seriousness, the encyclopedia places a greater emphasis on those transnational crimes that can

- undermine economies, such as price-fixing, capital flight, tax evasion, and corruption;
- exploit gender, such as sex slavery, child exploitation, gender-based violence, and pornography; and
- bridge organized crime with terrorist activities, either in the sense of organized crimes that provide financial support for terrorist operations or in the sense of criminal acts that themselves serve to terrorize populations.

International businesses rely on certain protections that are violated by criminals; such violations include copyright infringement, corporate influence peddling, price-fixing, telemarketing frauds, and the blurred distinctions between the paying of commissions to secure contracts and payoffs or bribes.

Old notions of sovereignty are challenged. The refrain that "criminals cross borders, but police can't" must change. Laws and law enforcement must follow them across and through countries in order to combat transnational crimes and in order to make international justice regimes viable. At the same time that we recognize the need to open the borders to cross-border intelligence sharing and transnational policing—to compete with the increasing traffic by commerce, currency, and citizens—the border must simultaneously be strengthened to counter threats to security. Obviously, it is a difficult balance to maintain: an open border for business and enforcement, but closed to transnational criminality and terrorist threats. New collaborative working arrangements are being forged, with varying degrees of success. Mutual legal assistance treaties (MLATs) facilitate the gathering and sharing of police intelligence. The roles of Interpol and Europol continue to shift to meet some of the law-enforcement demands. Conventions and agreements encourage the "harmonization" of policies and legislation across nations.

Current Issues

While some topics may be prioritized differently depending on the jurisdiction, other topics appear to be nearly universal. Drug trafficking and the collateral damage caused by this industry continue to harm developing as well as developed countries. The encyclopedia includes entries that address legalization debates as well as specific entries on cocaine, heroin, cannabis (marijuana), and pharmaceuticals. Included as well are analyses of drug source countries, plus destination and transit routes. "Fighting" drug trafficking has lately consisted of going after the huge profits that are seen to be accrued by drug traffickers, and therefore the encyclopedia includes entries on anti-money-laundering efforts, civil and criminal forfeiture, joint-force policing initiatives, and an array of enforcement efforts against trafficking.

As the international community strives toward the harmonization of policies and laws, there is an increased need to have confidence in the direction in which those policies are moving. Some of the internationally advocated enforcement activities are not without controversy. Among the relevant conventions, the United Nations Convention Against Transnational Organized Crime plays a significant role in terms of its objective to "promote cooperation and combat transnational organized crime more effectively." Anti-money-laundering laws, policies, and mechanisms have garnered an often hysterical international response. Countries are encouraged to criminalize participation in an organized criminal group, criminalize the laundering of the proceeds of crime, and put in place all of the measures deemed necessary to combat money laundering. The Financial Action Task Force (FATF) has been particularly aggressive in encouraging compliance, backed up by blacklisting and punishing those countries that fail to meet FATF's expectations. The final partner in this effort against money laundering is the Egmont Group of Financial Intelligence Units (FIUs). Together these nonstate organizations exert a strong influence on policy and legislation globally. Critics may question this "harmonized" focus on criminal membership, given the simultaneous recognition of fluid and more open criminal operations. However, in order to provide full coverage of the anti-money-laundering issue, the encyclopedia looks at the policing of laundering via the focus on the proceeds of crime and the increasing use of forfeiture (both civil and criminal). Certain sectors of the economy that are the most vulnerable to exploitation by launderers are identified—as are the linkages between legal and illegal economies. Given the recent focus on terrorist financing, the underground banking of informal value transfer systems has merited scrutiny as well.

Frauds and scams, often perpetuated via the Internet, have become commonplace. We turn on our computers to be welcomed by an e-mail that invites us to make millions of dollars simply by sending a few dollars to Nigeria or elsewhere. There are too many of these schemes to cover, but the most typical and significant types are examined. Some frauds may target corporations or involve criminal behavior by corporations—such as copyright infringement, counterfeiting of goods or currency, forgery, financial fraud, accounting fraud, and price-fixing. As banks around the world have faced possible collapse with the worldwide recession that began in 2008, there has been a heightened concern over frauds of all types. Some of these frauds—such as massive pyramid schemes and accounting frauds—have left not just individuals but whole communities as victims and have even, to some extent, had an impact on the stability of entire economies.

Several of the topics of course overlap. Charities—so essential in many communities—can also be vehicles for fraud, and following the terrorist attacks of September 11, 2001, these have been recognized as potential sources of terrorist financing. Smuggling operations can involve more than one commodity, and in some cases different types of goods travel in each direction. Some of the enforcement agencies, such as intelligence agencies, that are essential in combating transnational crimes may themselves exploit criminal commodities to advance their own or their governments' objectives. Transnational criminals benefit greatly from the corruption of border officials, police, government officials, and white-collar professionals to assist with the hiding of their illicit proceeds.

All of these separate topics are covered in this encyclopedia. In short, there is an endless number of topics to be covered and all areas of the world to be considered. We have tried to cover the essential issues that are priority topics in the widest number of regions of the globe.

Margaret E. Beare
Editor

Chronology

1856

Great Britain, France, Russia, Austria, Prussia, and Sardinia sign the Declaration of Paris, agreeing that they will not engage privateers.

1898

The First Hague Convention adopts a number of principles regarding the laws of war and war crimes.

1900

The Lacey Act in the United States attempts to protect game species by prohibiting the sale or importation of plants, fish, and wildlife that have been taken illegally, as defined by the laws in the region where they were acquired.

1912

The International Opium Convention, the first international drug control treaty, is signed by the United States, Germany, France, China, the United Kingdom, Italy, the Netherlands, Portugal, Russia, Japan, and Thailand; it goes into force globally in 1919 as part of the Treaty of Versailles.

1915

The phrase "crime against humanity" is used in a statement by Britain, France, and Russia denouncing the Ottoman Empire's role in the Armenian genocide.

1918

The United States passes the Migratory Bird Treaty Act, which prohibits the hunting, capture, or sale of migratory birds or any part of them, such as eggs and feathers. The act currently lists more than 800 species that are thus protected. The United States will later enter into agreements with other nations, including Canada and Mexico, to expand these protections.

1919

Prohibition begins in the United States with passage of the Volstead Act and the Eighteenth Amendment to the U.S. Constitution, prohibiting manufacture, sale, and transportation of "intoxicating liquors." Ironically, one of Prohibition's effects is to strengthen organized crime and foster a culture of bootlegging across both national and state boundaries. Prohibition will be repealed in 1933.

1923

Interpol, the International Criminal Police Organization, is founded (as the International Criminal Police Commission) to promote cooperation among the law enforcement agencies of member countries.

1925

The Geneva Protocol prohibits the use of chemical and biological weapons.

1945

The London Charter of the International Military Tribunal establishes, in August, the procedures by which the Nuremberg trials will be conducted.

The United Nations charter establishes the International Court of Justice to settle disputes between nations; it begins work in 1946.

1946

The United Nations Commission on Human Rights (UNHCR), a subsidiary body of the UN Economic and Social Council, is established. It will be replaced in 2006 by the UN Human Rights Council.

The Commission on the Status of Women Within the United Nations is established; it and the United Nations Commission on Human Rights are the first two functional commissions established within the UN structure.

1948

The American Declaration of the Rights and Duties of Man is adopted in April at the Ninth International Conference of American Stages in Bogotá, Colombia, making it the first general international declaration of human rights.

The Universal Declaration of Human Rights is adopted by the United Nations General Assembly in 1948; it contains 30 articles setting out various points, such as the prohibition of slavery, the right to political and religious freedom, and social, economic, and cultural rights.

The United Nations Convention on the Prevention and Punishment of the Crime of Genocide defines genocide as acts intended to destroy a national, racial, ethnic, or religious group.

1951

The United Nations adopts the United Nations Convention Relating to the Status of Refugees, which defines who qualifies as a refugee, their rights, and the responsibilities of nations that grant them refuge.

1959

The Declaration of the Rights of the Child, adopted by the United Nations General Assembly in November, sets out 10 principles pertaining to all children, such as the right to education, food, medical care, and citizenship, as well as protection against exploitation or cruel treatment, including protection against being forced into work that pays less than a minimum wage.

1961

Amnesty International is founded by British lawyer Peter Benenson.

1963

The initial draft of the Convention on International Trade in Endangered Species of Wild Fauna and Flora (CITES) is drafted at a meeting of the World Conservation Union (IUCN).

The Convention on Offenses and Certain Other Acts Committed on Board Aircraft (the Tokyo Convention) is concluded; it comes into force in 1969 and is the first law recognizing the authority of the aircraft commander on international flights to restrain anyone believed to be committing or about to commit an offense endangering the safety of those onboard.

1967

The United Nations Commission on Human Rights (UNHCR) begins to investigate and report on human rights violations, in contrast to its former policy of restricting its activities to drafting treaties and promoting human rights in general.

The Popular Front for the Liberation of Palestine is founded.

1969

U.S. President Richard M. Nixon announces Operation Intercept in September, instituting increased surveillance of the U.S.-Mexican border and inspection of vehicles crossing the border in an attempt to prevent marijuana from Mexico from entering the United States. Operation Intercept is abandoned after less than a month because of the burden imposed on vehicles crossing the border.

1971

The 1971 Convention on Psychotropic Substances responds to a broadening spectrum of drugs by introducing controls over synthetic drugs.

1972

The Biological Weapons Convention supplants the 1925 Geneva Protocol and becomes the first multilateral disarmament treaty to ban an entire class of weapons.

At the Olympic Games in Munich, Germany, 11 members of the Israeli Olympic team (coaches and athletes) are taken hostage and murdered by the Palestinian terrorist group Black September.

1973

The final language of the Convention on International Trade in Endangered Species of Wild Fauna and Flora (CITES) is approved by representatives of 80 nations meeting in Washington, D.C.;

CITES will go into effect in 1975 and, as of 2010, will be accepted by 175 countries.

1976

The International Foundation for Art Research (IFAR) creates an art-theft archive and begins publishing the Stolen Art Alert. Ten years later, the archive will include more than 20,000 manual records.

1978

Helsinki Watch is founded to monitor the Soviet Union's adherence to the Helsinki Accords; today it is called Human Rights Watch and conducts advocacy and research into many aspects of human rights.

1981

The Chaos Computer Club, an organization of computer hackers, is formed in Germany.

1982

The United Nations Convention on the Law of the Sea (UNCLOS), an international agreement defining laws concerning the world's oceans, is concluded; it comes into force in 1994.

1984

The Court of Arbitration for Sport, an international body established to deal with disputes related to the Olympics, is established.

1986

The International Whaling Commission (IWC) establishes a moratorium on commercial whaling.

The U.S. Congress passes the Computer Fraud and Abuse Act, which makes it a crime to access (without authorization) computers used by the U.S. government, by financial institutions, or in foreign or interstate commerce, and to transmit a program or other code (such as a computer virus or worm) that causes damage.

1987

The United Nations Convention Against Torture and Other Cruel, Inhuman and Degrading Treatment or Punishment—adopted in 1984—comes into force. It includes provisions against the use of torture and against returning any individual to a state where he or she would be likely to be subjected to torture.

1988

The 1988 Convention Against Illicit Traffic in Narcotic Drugs and Psychotropic Substances is abroad in scope and includes provisions against money laundering.

Cornell University graduate student Robert T. Morris sends a computer worm across the ARPAnet (the predecessor to the Internet), and it eventually spreads to about 6,000 networked computers; Morris is sentenced to three years' probation and a fine of $10,000 and is dismissed from Cornell.

1989

The United States invades Panama during Operation Just Cause, in part to combat drug trafficking.

The Financial Action Task Force (FATF) is founded at the G7 Summit in Paris to combat money laundering and funding of terrorist organizations.

In *Soering v. United Kingdom*, the European Court of Human Rights declares that allowing extradition of a German national to the United States to face capital charges is a violation of the European Convention on Human Rights.

1990

International trade in ivory is banned by the Convention on International Trade in Endangered Species of Wild Fauna and Flora (CITES), in response to the rapid decline of the African elephant population in the previous decade. (Some estimate that in 1979 there were more than 1.3 million African elephants; by 1989, there were fewer than half that number.)

1991

The Art Loss Register (ALR) is created by the International Foundation for Art Research to combat the international trade in stolen art; by 2010, the ALR will have become the world's largest private database of lost and stolen art, collectables, and antiques.

1992

The Chemical Weapons Convention (CWC) outlaws the use and stockpiling of chemical weapons; as of

2010, 188 countries will have become party to the CWC.

The Maastricht Treaty (Treaty on European Union, or TEU) creates the European Union.

The United Nations Security Council passes Resolution 780, condemning widespread violations of international law in Bosnia and Herzegovina and providing a definition of the term *ethnic cleansing*.

Six international organizations join forces to create the International Campaign to Ban Landmines.

1993

The *Golden Venture*, a Chinese smuggling ship, is grounded in New York City's harbor with nearly 300 illegal immigrants aboard; an estimated six to 10 of the immigrants die while trying to swim to shore.

1995

The UNIDRIOT Convention on Stolen or Illegally Exported Cultural Objects creates regulations regarding the return of cultural objects stolen from member states.

1997

The Convention on the Prohibition of the Use, Stockpiling, Production and Transfer of Anti-Personnel Mines (the Ottawa Treaty) bans the use of anti-personnel landmines; 156 countries will be parties to the treaty by April 2010.

The Organisation for Economic Co-operation and Development's Convention on Combating Bribery of Foreign Public Officials in International Business Transactions calls for effective measures to deter, prevent, and combat the bribery of foreign public officials in connection with international business transactions, in particular the prompt criminalization of such bribery in an effective and coordinated manner.

1998

Physicians for Human Rights is founded in Cambridge, Massachusetts, to conduct research and investigation into potential human rights violations.

The Washington Conference on Nazi-Confiscated Art, involving 44 countries, is held and endorses 11 principles regarding art confiscated during the Holocaust.

The Rome Statute of the International Criminal Court is adopted in July and enters into force in July 2002; it establishes a permanent international tribunal to prosecute genocide and other serious international crimes; as of October 2009, 110 countries will be parties to the statute, but the United States and Israel will not.

1999

The World Anti-Doping Agency (WADA) is established in Lausanne to combat the use of performance-enhancing drugs in international sport, including the Olympics.

The International Labour Organization (ILO) adopts the Convention Concerning the Prohibition and Immediate Action for the Elimination of the Worst Forms of Child Labor; signatories agree to eliminate the worst forms of child labor, which are defined as slavery (including trafficking in children, debt bondage, forced or compulsory labor, and forced recruitment of child soldiers); commercial sexual exploitation of children (CSEC), including prostitution and pornography; and the use of children in commission of crimes, including drug trafficking and production.

Europol, the European Police Office, becomes fully operational.

The United Nations International Convention for the Suppression of the Financing of Terrorism specifies that it is a criminal activity to help finance terrorist activity, even if the person involved is not actually taking part in the violent action; nations that sign this treaty commit to freezing funds to be used for terrorist activity.

2000

The United Kingdom passes the Terrorism Act, which defines terrorism, proscribes a number of domestic and international organizations, and allows police special powers with regard to those suspected of terrorism (such as an extended period of time during which a person could be held without charge).

The United Nations Convention Against Transnational Organized Crime, adopted by the General Assembly November 2000, is the main international instrument in the fight against transnational organized crime. It opened for signature by member states at a high-level political conference convened for that purpose in Palermo, Italy, on December 12–15, 2000, and entered into force on September 29, 2003. The convention is further supplemented by three protocols that target specific areas and manifestations of organized crime: the Protocol to Prevent, Suppress and Punish Trafficking in Persons, Especially Women and Children; the Protocol Against the Smuggling of Migrants by Land, Sea and Air; and the Protocol Against the Illicit Manufacturing of and Trafficking in Firearms, Their Parts and Components and Ammunition. Countries must become parties to the convention itself before they can become parties to any of the protocols.

2001

A conference of East Asia Forest Law and Governance is held in Bali, Indonesia, to address issues related to forest policy and law enforcement, including illegal logging.

Following the September 11 terrorist attacks in the United States, the Financial Action Task Force (FATF) issues eight Special Recommendations on Terrorist Financing.

2002

The International Criminal Court (ICC) is created to prosecute individuals for war crimes, genocide, and crimes against humanity.

U.S. art and antiquities dealer Frederick Schultz is convicted of receiving antiquities stolen and smuggled out of Egypt; together with co-conspirator Jonathan Tokeley-Parry, an antiquities restorer (who was prosecuted in the United Kingdom), Schultz had smuggled more than 2,000 artifacts out of Egypt.

2003

Africa Forest Law Enforcement and Governance (AFLEG) holds a conference in Yaoundé, Cameroon, to address issues, including methods to combat illegal forest exploitation and trade associated with that practice.

The International Criminal Court issues arrest warrants for Joseph Kony, leader of the Lord's Resistance Army (LRA) in Uganda, as well as Vincent Otti, Raska Lukwiya, Okot Odiambo, and Dominic Ongwen, who also held leadership positions in the LRA.

International action against corruption progressed from general consideration and declarative statements to legally binding agreements. The United Nations Convention Against Corruption (UNCAC) deals with forms of corruption such as trading in official influence and general abuses of power, including a focus on the recovery of stolen assets, that had not been covered by many of the earlier international instruments.

The Financial Action Task Force (FATF) completely revises its 40 Recommendations (originally issued in 1990) in recognition of the continued evolution of techniques in money laundering.

2004

European and North Asian Forest Law Enforcement and Governance (ENAFLEG) holds a conference in Russia and agrees to the St. Petersburg Declaration on Forest Law Enforcement and Governance.

The United Kingdom passes the Human Tissue Act, specifying regulations regarding the handling of human tissues, partly in response to the Alder Hey organs scandal, during which medical personnel, without obtaining parental permission, harvested organs and other body parts from infants who had died at the Alder Hey Children's Hospital in Liverpool.

2005

The Fund for Peace, a think tank founded in Washington, D.C., in 1957, begins publishing the Failed States Index.

The National Consortium for the Study of Terrorism and Responses to Terrorism (START) is established at the University of Maryland, funded with a $12 million grant from the U.S. Department of Homeland Security, to study terrorism and society responses to it.

The United Kingdom passes the Prevention of Terrorism Act, which allows the home secretary (secretary of state for the Home Department) to restrict the liberty of individuals suspected of being involved in terrorism through the use of control orders that may affect their ability to travel, their right to choose their place of residence or employment, and other liberties.

2006

Thomas Lubanga is arrested under a warrant issued by the International Criminal Court for conscripting children under the age of 15 to serve in the Union of Congolese Patriots.

The J. Paul Getty Museum in Los Angeles, California, announces that it will return a Greek statue dating from the 6th century B.C.E. and a gold funerary wreath dating from the 4th century B.C.E. in response to claims by the Greek government that these artifacts were illegally excavated and removed from Greece.

2008

In January, an illegal organ-trafficking scheme is discovered in Gugaon, India, in which kidneys were obtained from poor Indians and sold to clients in the United States, Europe, and elsewhere.

In June, the International Criminal Court (ICC) issues an arrest warrant for Jean-Pierre Bemba, a former official of the Democratic Republic of the Congo, for crimes against humanity and war crimes in the Central African Republic; he is turned over to the ICC in July.

In July, Omar al-Bashir, president of Sudan, becomes the first sitting head of state to be indicted by the International Criminal Court (ICC) for war crimes and crimes against humanity.

2010

Ten American missionaries are charged with kidnapping for taking children out of Haiti in the wake of the January 2010 earthquake without proper authorization.

The labor recruiting firm Global Horizons, based in Los Angeles, is indicted for bringing Thai farm workers to the United States, then mistreating them and withholding their wages.

2011

A number of artifacts illegally removed from Iraq by U.S. Department of Defense contractors in 2004 are returned to Iraq.

2012

The International Criminal Court finds Thomas Lubanga, a Congolese military leader, guilty of kidnapping children to serve as soldiers.

The short film *Kony 2012* spreads rapidly over video-sharing Internet sites and draws attention to the alleged war crimes of Joseph Kony, head of the Ugandan guerilla group the Lord's Resistance Army.

Sarah E. Boslaugh
Kennesaw State University

ACCOUNTING FRAUD

Accounting fraud is an international problem touching all countries and most entities. Fraud affects companies of all sizes in a variety of industries. Transparency International is a global network whose goal is to fight fraud and corruption in the national arena by producing an annual Corruption Perceptions Index (CPI). Just some of the massive frauds within the past few years include those associated with Adelphia, Bernard Madoff (now serving a 150-year prison sentence), Cendant, Computer Associates, Dell, Enron, Harris Scarfé, HealthSouth, Livedoor, Parmalat, Qwest, Royal Ahold, Satyam, Siemens, Sir Robert Allen Stanford, SK Global, Tyco, Vivendi, Waste Management, WorldCom, and Xerox. In the United States, 20 percent of the locations of fraud companies' headquarters were in California, 10 percent in New York, and 8 percent in Texas and Florida.

A 2010 Committee on Sponsoring Organizations (COSO) study covering a 10-year period in the United States (1998–2007) found that fraudulent financial reporting results had significant negative consequences for executives and investors. The average cumulative misstatement or misappropriation amount for 300 companies was $397.68 million, while the median cumulative misstatement was $12.05 million. The frauds of the early 2000s skewed the 1998–2007 total and mean cumulative misstatements or misappropriations upward. The median fraud in this study was almost three times larger than the previous 1999 COSO study. For the purposes of this discussion, accounting fraud is defined, as stated by the American Institute of Certified Public Accountants (ACFE), as "any intentional act or omission designed to deceive others, resulting in the victim suffering a loss and/or the perpetrator achieving a gain." Coverage will emphasize financial statement fraud and not necessarily others, such as occupational fraud, white-collar crime, or computer fraud. For example, accounting fraud is the intentional manipulation of (rather than an error in) the recording of revenues (inflows) and expenses (outflows) in order to make the operating profit of an entity appear better. Typical examples would be overreporting of sales or revenue: Cendant Corporation created at least $500 million in fictitious revenues, and Barry Minkow created a $200 million corporation based upon fictitious sales.

Costs of Accounting Fraud

There have been some massive accounting frauds throughout the years, including the $11 billion WorldCom and $50 billion Madoff scandals. In an interview in the February 16, 2011, edition of the *New York Times*, Madoff spoke of the "willful blindness" of many hedge funds and banks that dealt with his investment advisory business: "They had to know. But the attitude was sort of, 'if you're doing something wrong, we don't want to know.'"

Financial scandals and their resulting fallout in the first few years of the 21st century in the United States drew comparisons with activities surrounding the stock market crash of 1929. Superstar companies such as Enron and HealthSouth were caught in

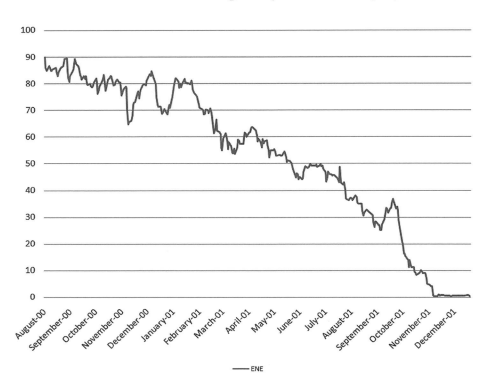

Charting Enron's stock dip from August 2000 to January 2002. Prior to companies such as Enron and HealthSouth being caught committing massive fraud, that type of fraudulent financial reporting would have seemed unimaginable to most people. (Wikimedia)

the fraudulent behaviors that seemed untenable for most investors and unfathomable for most people. The worldwide stock markets shook. One of the most respected, storied, and successful accounting firms, Arthur Andersen, became a casualty of the financial scandals.

Although there are no reliable statistics as to the cost of fraud, the 2010 Report to the Nations of the ACFE group reports that the typical organization loses 5 percent of its annual revenue to fraud. Based upon the estimated 2009 Gross World Product, this percentage translates to a total potential fraud loss of more than $2.9 trillion each year worldwide. Although asset misappropriation losses were the most common form of fraud (at $100,000 per scheme), financial statement frauds were the most costly (at $1,730,000 per scheme). Corruption schemes fell in the middle at $176,000 per scheme. Like a cold, it is hard to keep fraud from spreading.

With fraud there is often collusion. The president and chief financial officer of Continental Express established an insurance company with the same name in another state. The real company made payments to the fraudulent insurance company and the executives paid themselves multiple salaries.

Lee Seidler (as reported by George Mannes) says that "auditors will continue to miss fraud because much of their work is predicated on the assumption that separation of duties—say, one person holds the money and another person keeps track of it—prevents fraud." The equity funding scandal "shakes the foundations of auditing, in that so much is based on the assumption that people don't collude, or they wouldn't collude very long. But they do."

"Cooking the books" is often a collaborative effort. For financial restatements between January 1, 1997, and June 30, 2002, 45 percent were accused of securities fraud and subject to shareholder suits. An average of seven individuals were implicated, including chief executive officers, chief financial officers, chief operating officers, general counsels, directors, and, internal/external auditors. In the case of WorldCom, at least 40 people knew about the fraud but were afraid to talk. Chief financial officer

Scott Sullivan handed out $10,000 checks to seven individuals involved.

Joseph Wells, the founder of ACFE, says that the actual cost of fraud is unknown and unknowable. It is a concept the criminologists call "the dark figure." Unlike visible crimes, such as robbery, not all frauds are uncovered. Of those uncovered, not all are reported. No agency is tasked with compiling comprehensive data on fraud. More forensic techniques should become a part of both external and internal auditing. However (as reported by Eric Krell), Stephen Seliskar says that "in terms of sheer labor, the magnitude of effort, time and expense required to do a single, very focused (forensic) investigation—as contrasted to auditing a set of the financial statements—the difference is incredible." It is physically impossible to conduct a generic fraud investigation of an entire business.

Abusive Earnings Management

Financial statement fraud, fraudulent earnings management, or creative accounting has become an increasing concern to accounting regulators, especially in the post-Enron era (since 2002). The flexibility in generally accepted accounting principles (GAAP) gives management discretion to use its professional opinion to choose from a range of alternatives in selecting those standards that suit the needs of a company—such as "first-in, first-out" (FIFO) or "last-in, first-out" (LIFO) inventory methods. Different accounting methods result in different earnings and earnings per share, and most often management prefers to smooth earnings. Companies tend to use accounting techniques to try to smooth earnings from one period to the next. Under International Accounting Standards, management has even more discretion.

The U.S. Securities and Exchange Commission (SEC) defines abusive earnings management as an intentional and material misrepresentation of results. Nonfraudulent earnings management is accomplished within the GAAP framework, whereas fraudulent earnings management does not follow GAAP (such as recording fictitious sales). The National Center for Continuing Education even offers a seminar, "How to Manage Earnings in the Conformance with GAAP." Nothing, however, gives greater fear to a corporate officer or investor than when there is a rumor about "an accounting problem." Glass, Lewis and Co. indicated that between 200 and 500 publicly traded companies listed in the United States,

or about 5 to 12 percent of the total, have to restate their earnings each year.

Some motivations for fraudulent behavior are meeting external or internal expectations, concealing bad performance, preparing for a debt/equity offering, improving management compensation (for example, through stock options), and covering up fraud.

Abusive earnings management would include the following:

- Improper revenue recognition (such as bill and hold sales)
- Improper expense recognition
- Using reserves to inflate earnings in years with falling revenues (cookie-jar accounting)
- Shifting debt to a special-purpose entity (SPE)
- Channel stuffing
- Capitalizing rather than expensing marketing costs
- Extending useful lives and inflating salvage values
- Accelerating revenue from leasing equipment
- SPEs that are not consolidated

Early warning signs of earnings management include the following:

- Cash flows that are not correlated with earnings
- Receivables that are not correlated with revenues
- Allowances for uncollectible accounts that are not correlated with receivables
- Reserves that are not correlated with balance-sheet items
- Acquisitions with no apparent business purpose
- Earnings that consistently and precisely meet analyst's expectations

The 2010 COSO fraud report indicates that revenue recognition schemes are used 61 percent of the time to cook the books, followed by overstating assets (51 percent), understatement of expenses and liabilities (31 percent), and misappropriation of assets (14 percent).

Revenue Recognition Schemes

Companies use any of multiple methods to create fictitious revenues in order to inflate income on financial statements. A slightly different approach is simply to overstate income either by omitting elements that would lower actual revenues (such as returns of purchases) or by using mark-to-market accounting to make records of (future) income more "flexible."

One type of overstated-income scheme is the bill-and-hold transaction. The customer agrees to purchase goods and the seller invoices the customer but retains physical possession of the products until a later delivery date. Not all such transactions involve fraud, but the practice must be closely examined in light of accounting rules because it is open to abuse. Fraudsters may use this approach to count both sales and inventory on hand as revenue procedures. In a well-publicized scandal, Sunbeam created revenues in 1997 by using a bill-and-hold practice. The company sold products to customers but held onto the shipments with an agreement to deliver the goods later. Coca-Cola created income by loading up syrup trucks near the end of the year and driving the trucks outside the warehouse and parking them. After the end of the year, the trucks with spoiled syrup came back inside the warehouse and the inventory was written off.

Premature revenue recognition is a means of recording income as actual in order to inflate earnings totals when sales have not been completed, the products have not been delivered, or invoices have not been paid. In general, revenue from product sales should not be recognized on financial statements until it has been realized or realizable and earned. Based on the provisions of Staff Accounting Bulletin (SAB) 101, income should not be recognized under these circumstances because delivery has not actually occurred. Customers on the other side of early delivery schemes often return the unfinished product or demand more completion before payment is rendered.

Xerox, for example, overstated revenue for more than four years by accelerating the recognition of $3 billion in revenue and inflating earnings by $1.5 billion. It allegedly included the recognition of revenue on Xerox office copy equipment leases too early in the cycle. Parmalat, an Italian milk company, invented $620 million sales of powdered milk to Cuba. If the "sales" were true, Cuba would have been "swimming in milk." The company also used double invoicing: one real and one fake invoice. Both invoices were entered into the books, but only one was sent to the customer. U.S. Foodservice, Inc., was offered rebates from its vendors for volume purchases. The company recognized these vendor rebates as a reduction of cost of goods sold (thereby increasing income), which should not have been recognized.

Overstating Assets

Assets may be overvalued or expenses may be capitalized. Overvalued assets comprise property for which executives set prices that are unsupportable using standard business valuation approaches. These assets might be bought to essentially pay off parties to which the fraudsters are beholden, sold to artificially boost income, or simple held and recorded on statements at far more than their actual worth.

Gain-on-sale accounting is a technique enabling fraudulent executives to use special-purpose entities to purchase or sell overvalued ventures at unsupportable values, which are recorded by the corporation as massive losses/revenues.

Accounts receivables offer myriad opportunities for valuation schemes. GAAP require accounts receivable to be reported at net realizable value—the gross value of the receivable minus an estimated allowance for uncollectible accounts. Companies circumvent GAAP by underestimating the uncollectible portion of a receivable. Underestimating the value of the provision (the amount deemed uncollectible) artificially inflates the receivables value and records it at an amount greater than net realizable value. A related fraud is failing or delaying to write off receivables that have become uncollectible.

Inventory is another area ripe for earnings management and misclassification by manipulating the quantity or value. GAAP require that inventory be reported at the lower of replacement cost or market value (current replacement cost). Inflating inventory value achieves the same impact on earnings as manipulating the physical count. Fraudulent managers can accomplish this creative accounting simply by creating false journal entries that increase the balance in the inventory account. Another common way to inflate inventory value is to delay the write-down of obsolete or slow-moving inventory, since a write-down would require a charge against earnings.

Although GAAP require expenses to be recognized in the period in which they are incurred, Symbol Technologies, Inc., deferred $3.5 million of FICA expenses to a later year in order to boost its net income. WorldCom initially properly expensed its operating line costs. However, near the end of various quarters it would reverse these expenses by creating various huge assets. Parmalat had a nonexistent Bank of America account worth $4.83 billion. Apparently, the auditors Grant Thornton relied on a fake Bankers' Automated Clearing Services (BACS) confirmation prepared by Parmalat. No auditor took the time to call or e-mail the bank.

Understating or Omitting Liabilities and Expenses

Omitted liabilities are the mirror image of fictitious revenues and assets: Fraudsters hide debt or employ other off-balance-sheet financing to avoid having to include the negative picture on corporate financial statements. Special-purpose entities (SPEs) may be used to bury poorly performing assets because their transactions are not part of the corporate financial statements. Decreasing liabilities increase the net worth of the company.

By the time Enron declared bankruptcy in December 2001, it was reported to have hidden billions of dollars of off-balance-sheet debt using SPEs. Also, Enron entered into futures contracts with financing organizations such as J. P. Morgan that were thinly disguised loans not actually based on delivery of energy commodities. Enron also used prepaid swaps through its Delta subsidiary, wherein CitiGroup paid the fair value of its portion of the swaps, but Enron was allowed repayments spread over five years—in effect, obtaining loans. Enron never disclosed these transactions as such on its financial statements, accounting for the deals as "assets from price risk management" and as "accounts receivable."

Waste Management shifted current expenses to a later period by debiting rather than expensing asset accounts. In 1999, AMR Corporation changed the depreciation schedule from 20 years to 25 years on some planes, which reduced depreciation expense in 2000 by $158 million. Adelphia Communications omitted at least $1.8 billion of debt from its balance sheet.

Misappropriation of Assets

Misappropriation of assets is generally considered to be individual fraud by employees or outsiders. However, the Rigas family, who owned Adelphia Communications, a cable operator, was accused by the U.S. Department of Justice of looting Adelphia on a massive scale and using it as a personal piggy bank. This area involves situations where a manager misappropriates assets and then covers up the theft by manipulating the financial statements.

One problem fraudsters have is getting the assets into their pockets. Tyco solved this problem by granting large, interest-free loans to the officers ($8.71 million). The company then forgave the loans. Unauthorized bonuses also were given to the officers without the approval of the board of directors.

Chung Moung-koo, chairman of Hyundai Motors, South Korea's largest car maker, was sentenced to three years in prison in February 2007 for embezzlement, breach of trust, and secretively setting up slush funds. He embezzled about $100 million in company funds, although he owned only 5 percent of the company.

Other Fraudulent Financial Reporting Schemes

Companies can manipulate reserves by placing a contingency or liability on the balance sheet during a poor performance period (so-called cookie-jar accounting). In subsequent years, these reserves are reduced in order to pump up revenues. Alternatively, these reserves can be created in high-revenue years, and then fraudsters can dip into the cookie-jar reserves during difficult times. Both Xerox and Sunbeam engaged in cookie-jar accounting.

For example, a large Canadian telecommunications manufacturer, Nortel Network, was accused by the SEC of establishing more than $400 million in excess reserves. Eventually Nortel restated an excess of $2 billion in revenues. Cendant Corporation overstated acquisition-related reserves and then reversed portions back into earnings. In the early 1990s, W. R. Grace had earnings far exceeding estimates, so the company deferred some of its income by establishing and increasing reserves. Grace then released these reserves to report steady earnings growth in subsequent years. Freddie Mac understated its income from 2000 to 2002 by $5 billion using a tactic called wrong-way earnings management.

Related parties can be used to increase revenues and hide liabilities. The 2010 COSO report found that firms that engaged in fraud disclosed significantly more related-party transactions than no-fraud companies. CEC Industries Corp., a Nevada Corporation, created a substantial portion of its revenue as a result of an asset exchange transaction with a related party. Enron shifted a massive amount of liability to special-purpose entities. Tyco had undisclosed real estate transactions with related parties, and Adelphia moved debts to subsidiaries, which were not consolidated. Baptist Foundation of Arizona (BFA) set up subsidiaries owned by insiders to buy real estate (which had crashed in value) from BFA. Nikko Cordial (Japan) was fined for failure to consolidate a special-purpose entity that was 100 percent owned by its subsidiary.

Afinsa, a Spanish stamp company, controlled 72 percent of Escala, a U.S. stamp company. Escala said all sales to Afinsa took place at independent established prices. However, Escala's reported gross margin on stamp sales to Afinsa exceeded 44 percent, compared to less than 14 percent on those to U.S. clients. Therefore, Escala was manipulating the value of stamps sold to Afinsa in order to boost its own bottom line artificially. Escala's stock fell from $32 to $5 in five days after the May 8, 2006, arrests of seven executives. Police found $12.6 million behind one dealer's freshly plastered walls in his home.

Conclusion

Thomas Ray, chief auditor of the Public Company Accounting Oversight Board (PCAOB), says that a large number of financial frauds are accomplished by simply booking late entries. "It's the easiest way to commit fraud. It's the easiest thing to find." Nevertheless, Dell, Inc., cooked the books for four years, overstating profits by $50 million without Price Waterhouse Coopers' knowledge. Just as termites never sleep, fraud never sleeps, and just like termites, fraud can destroy the foundation of an entity.

D. Larry Crumbley
Louisiana State University

See also Charity Fraud; Financial Fraud; Investment Crimes; Money Laundering: Countermeasures; Money Laundering: Methods; Sales Tax; Tax Evasion; Value-Added Tax Fraud

Further Readings

American Institute of Certified Public Accountants. *Managing the Business Risk of Fraud: A Practical Guide*. 2008. http://www.acfe.com/uploadedFiles/ ACFE_Website/Content/documents/managing -business-risk.pdf (Accessed February 2011).

Beasley, M. S. et al. *Fraudulent Financial Reporting, 1998–2007: An Analysis of U.S. Public Companies*. New York: Committee on Sponsoring Organizations, 2010.

Blumenstein, Rebecca and Susan Pullian. "WorldCom Fraud Was Widespread." *Wall Street Journal* (June 10, 2003).

Crumbley, D. Larry. *Forensic and Investigative Accounting*. Chicago: Commerce Cleaning House, 2011.

Financial Week. "Auditors Told to Go Harder on Fraud." December 17, 2007. http://www.financialweek.com/ apps/pbcs.dll/article?AID=/20071217/REG/71214031 (Accessed February 2011).

Glass, Lewis and Co. "Trend Report: Restatements." March 19, 2009.

Henriques, D. B. "Madoff Said From Prison That Banks Had to Know." *The New York Times* (February 16, 2011).

Jones, M. *Creative Accounting, Fraud and International Accounting Scandals*. New York: Wiley, 2011.

Krell, Eric. "Will Forensic Accounting Go Mainstream?" *Business Finance Journal* (October 2002).

Mannes, George. "Cracking the Books II: Reliving Equity Funding." October 22, 1999. http://www.thestreet.com/ story/791614/cracking-the-books-ii-reliving-equity- funding-part-2.html (Accessed February 2011).

Tillman, Robert and Michael Indergaard. "Control Overrides in Financial Statement Fraud." http://www .theifp.org/research-grants/tillman_final_report.pdf (Accessed February 2011).

ADJUDICATING INTERNATIONAL CRIMES

Since the war crimes trials that followed World War II, the "law of nations" has become more widely understood and accepted throughout the world. As a result, an increasing number of individuals have been prosecuted and convicted for international crimes. Understanding the principles of effective administration of international criminal justice and the proper adjudication of international crimes begins with a review of the sources of international criminal law, followed by the various steps in the process. In general terms, these are the investigation, the indictment, the trial, and appeals.

The sources of international criminal law can be divided into two basic categories: international and state. References to state law in this context mean international law that has, in one way or another, been incorporated into the national, domestic, or municipal laws of a country. The sources of international law that are found beyond the borders of any given state include multilateral treaties such as the Geneva Conventions of 1949 and the Rome Statute of the International Criminal Court (ICC). International crimes also can be found in customary international law, which is viewed as generally accepted principles of law or customs, irrespective of whether they are codified into any particular convention, treaty, or legislation.

Regardless of the specific source of international law, the acts and offenses categorized as international crimes include, but are not limited to genocide, war crimes, and crimes against humanity, such as murder, extermination, enslavement, torture, forced prostitution, rape, forced sterilization, and forced disappearance when perpetrated in connection with an attack against a civilian population. It should be noted that the nexus between the attack against civilians and specific crimes is purely jurisdictional, and it is not an element of the crime that must be proved against a particular defendant.

International crimes that are specified in treaties, conventions, and other international instruments include the taking of hostages, apartheid, terrorist bombings, financing of terrorism, crimes against internationally protected persons and diplomatic agents, and slavery. For example, the Hague Convention on the Suppression of Unlawful Seizure of Aircraft (Hijacking Convention) requires each contracting state to take all necessary measures to establish criminal jurisdiction over offenses falling within the convention. Another example is the Geneva Conventions of 1949, particularly the Third Convention Relative to the Treatment of Prisoners of War and the Fourth Convention Relative to the Protection of Civilian Persons in Time of War. Both of these conventions codify grave breaches of the conventions, such as murder, rape, and torture, as international crimes.

Individual Criminal Responsibility

Contemporary prosecutions for violations of international criminal law are brought against individuals. As with most domestic criminal law, in order for a person to be held criminally responsible for a particular act, there must be a coexistence between the *actus reus*, or physical act, and the *mens rea*, or

"guilty mind." The *actus reus*, however, can take different forms, such as an omission or a failure to perform a legal duty. One very good example is a military commander's failure to prevent a crime from being committed by one or more subordinates if the commander reasonably should have known the crime was likely to occur. Alternatively, military commanders who fail to punish their subordinates after learning of their criminal activities, such as murdering prisoners of war or sexually assaulting civilians, also may be held individually criminally responsible for international crimes.

Historically, the idea of collective criminal responsibility—holding an individual criminally responsible merely for membership in a particular group—has drawn criticism, particularly when a specific criminal act (other than group membership or association) cannot be demonstrated. Participation in criminal conspiracies and criminal enterprises is an exception to this notion, although these concepts also have been criticized by some jurisdictions when holding one participant criminally responsible for the acts of another. As in many national jurisdictions, the crime of conspiracy may or may not be available relative to a particular crime under international law. For example, the International Criminal Tribunal for the former Yugoslavia (ICTY) has jurisdiction to adjudicate charges of conspiracy to commit genocide under Article 4 of the Statute of the ICTY, but conspiracy is not applicable to other crimes. However, the ICTY has ruled that the word *commit* under Article 7 of the statute includes committing crimes by indirect means, such as participating in an activity with a "common purpose" or a joint criminal enterprise (JCE) with a nexus to one or more of the crimes over which the tribunal has jurisdiction. Since the indictment of Slobodan Miloševi in 2001 for crimes alleged to have been committed throughout the Republic of Croatia, almost every major international criminal indictment has incorporated some aspect of the theory of the JCE. This was the first indictment at the ICTY that specifically charged the JCE, which was also based on an investigation premised upon this specific theory of individual criminal responsibility.

Investigation

Prior to the actual adjudication of an international crime, a criminal investigation must be conducted. The investigation of international crimes can be undertaken by international bodies such as the ICTY or the ICC, or by national authorities. Most investigations of international crimes pursued at the national level are undertaken by national-level investigative or law-enforcement agencies, as opposed to states, provinces, or other political subdivisions.

Investigations are led in a number of ways. They include the common-law method, led by senior investigating police officers; the civil-law method, by investigating judges or magistrates; and the grand-jury method, with a prosecutor providing overall direction that is carried out at the operational level by criminal investigations managers. At the ICTY, for example, during the earlier stages of the tribunal's work, police investigative managers, working closely with team legal advisers, carried out the overall supervision of the entire case until the time of indictment, when a senior trial attorney (STA) took over the case. During the later stages of the tribunal's work, officials believed that legal direction from the outset of the investigation was critical to the successful outcome of the case. Accordingly, a model roughly following the U.S. investigative grand-jury process was adopted, whereby overall direction from the inception of the investigation was directed by an STA with experience as a criminal prosecutor in a common-law country or an investigating judge in a civil-law country. Supervision of the investigative team and operational control in the field remained with the investigation manager.

Indictment

Following the investigation, the next step is formal indictment of the suspect. The prosecutor writes an indictment that informs judicial authorities of the charges alleged and provides, in one way or another, a minimal amount of evidence or a *prima facie* case to support the allegations. A judge reviews the indictment and the evidence and decides whether there is indeed sufficient evidence to warrant proceeding to trial. The judge may ask to speak to the prosecutor or the lead investigator during an *in camera* review, that is, a meeting in the judge's chambers. This is an *ex parte* proceeding in which the person named in the indictment is not present to give evidence in his or her favor. If the judge agrees that a trial is warranted, the judge will confirm the indictment by affixing his or her signature to the indictment. This process is relatively analogous to returning a "true bill" of indictment in many common-law countries.

If the judge believes there is insufficient evidence to proceed further, the indictment will be dismissed.

Initial Appearance

Once arrested or surrendered to the court of jurisdiction on the indictment, the accused will be brought before the judge without unnecessary delay. This is the stage where the accused is formally charged with the crime or crimes. The judge will ensure that the accused has legal counsel and, if the defendant is indigent, counsel will be arranged at no cost. The indictment then will be read to the defendant in a language he or she understands, and the accused will be called upon to enter a plea of guilty or not guilty. If the plea is not guilty, the case will be docketed for trial. If the accused fails to enter a plea or refuses to do so, the court automatically will enter a plea of not guilty on the defendant's behalf.

If the accused pleads guilty, the court will endeavor to ascertain two important facts: whether the plea was voluntarily and knowingly made and, if so, whether there is a sufficient factual basis for a finding that a crime within the court's jurisdiction indeed was committed and that the accused committed the crime.

Trial

From the outset, it must be noted that in the process of adjudicating international crimes, the objective of the criminal justice system is to provide internationally recognized standards in connection with the rights of the accused at every step of the judicial process. Article 14 of the International Covenant on Civil and Political Rights is of the utmost importance. This international instrument lays the groundwork for many of the defendant's rights, which are similar to those found in domestic criminal justice systems. These include the presumption of innocence, the burden of proof on the prosecution, and the standard of proof. Other international legal instruments incorporate the provisions of Article 14. For example, Article 66 of the Rome Statute provides for a presumption of innocence for an accused person, and Article 21 of the ICTY statute places the burden of proof on the prosecutor.

There are, however, some differences between the rights and processes of international and domestic courts. At international tribunals, for instance, hearsay evidence is more easily admissible. For example,

Article 69 of the Rome Statute of the ICC allows all probative evidence, that is, evidence that tends to prove an issue before the court. Another difference concerns the right to trial by jury. Unlike courts in the United States and other common-law countries, where a jury trial is provided by law, most international criminal trial courts consist of a panel of three judges, and judgments must be rendered by a majority of the judges.

At a minimum, the accused will be given adequate time and facilities to prepare a defense and will be tried without undue delay. Defendants will have the right to legal counsel of their own choosing, and if they are indigent, legal assistance will be provided at no cost. Defendants have the right to examine witnesses on their own behalf and to have the court compel the attendance of witnesses. Defendants also may not be compelled to be witnesses against themselves, and inferences of guilt cannot be drawn from their silence.

Defenses

Many of the traditional defenses seen in national courts, such as self-defense and mistake of fact, are provided for in connection with international crimes. Some defenses, however, may not be available. For example, the defense of duress for the killing of another and the defense of superior orders when the act was manifestly unlawful are not available. Moreover, even traditional defenses may not be available under some circumstances. For example, defenses such as legitimate military targets and collateral deaths associated with those targets are inapplicable to crimes against humanity. These defenses also may not be available to a defendant charged with war crimes if the military objective was criminal from the outset, since combatants may lose their lawful combatant immunity for their criminal acts.

Protective Measures

In order to ensure the proper administration of justice in international criminal tribunals, the court sometimes implements protective measures to protect the privacy of victims and witnesses. To maintain balance, these efforts must be consistent with the rights of the accused. Some examples of protective measures include preventing disclosure to the public, including the media, of the names, identities, and locations of victims and witnesses; using

pseudonyms for witnesses; and altering the voices or images of witnesses. The court also may hold certain closed sessions of the proceedings for this purpose.

Appeals

Like many domestic legal systems, international tribunals have due process safeguards that provide the right to appeal a negative decision of the trial court. The case typically moves to an appeals chamber of the court, which reviews the case on record for error of fact and error of law. This review may include the sufficiency of the evidence for a finding of guilt and the appropriateness of the sentence.

Unlike in the United States and many other states, the prosecutor has the right to appeal a finding of "not guilty" or the appropriateness of the sentence. This means that an accused who was found not guilty could face jeopardy a second time, a notion that is not entirely uncommon in many legal systems throughout the world. It must be noted that international criminal tribunals are often a hybrid of a number of legal systems, such as adversarial and inquisitorial models, and do not necessarily view one system as better than another.

National Prosecutions

Most of the discussion thus far has focused on the adjudication of international crimes by international tribunals, but as previously noted, national jurisdictions also can adjudicate international crimes. Indeed, many United Nations (UN) conventions and resolutions require member states to adopt relevant national-level legislation so that crimes can be prosecuted.

For example, Article 4 of the UN Convention Against Torture (CAT) requires state parties to enact legislation that criminalizes torture. In this sense, state prosecutions for violations of CAT can be had in national courts. This includes legislation that establishes jurisdiction over the offender by various means, including foreign nationals who are present in the state and nationals who are abroad. Such a prosecution incorporates the notions of extraterritorial jurisdiction over a state's own nationals and universal jurisdiction of crimes committed abroad by persons who are then in their states. Another example is the United States War Crimes Act, which codifies several instruments of international law. Section 2441 of Title 18 of the United States Code proscribes crimes against humanity, genocide, and grave breaches of the Geneva Conventions of 1949.

Other examples of national prosecutions related to international crime include Article 101 of the UN Convention on the Law of the Sea, which defines acts of piracy on the high seas, including theft, hostage taking, and other acts of violence or depredation. Directly related to this is the Convention for the Suppression of Unlawful Acts Against the Safety of Maritime Navigation and the International Convention Against Taking of Hostages. In spite of these conventions and the fact that piracy is an international crime under customary international law, jurisdiction to prosecute and adjudicate these crimes is often problematic, because various states have different laws under which the matter is approached, and some lack such laws altogether. The United States, however, pursuant to its authority under the Constitution and federal criminal laws, exercises "universal" jurisdiction over all acts of piracy on the high seas when the offenders are physically in or taken to the United States. Courts may impose strict punishment, including life in prison.

Enforcement of Sentences

Individuals found guilty of international crimes by an international criminal tribunal usually serve their sentences at a correctional or penal facility physically located within a state that has entered into an agreement for this purpose with the international court. The laws of the receiving state relating to pardons and commutation of sentences typically apply to international prisoners serving their sentences in that state. If that is the case, the state notifies the international tribunal, which makes the ultimate decision in this regard. The statutes that form the basis for the creation of an international criminal tribunal typically require member states to cooperate with the international tribunal.

Civil Adjudication of International Crimes

The International Court of Justice (ICJ), often referred to as the World Court, does not have jurisdiction to adjudicate international crimes committed by individuals. The ICJ has jurisdiction over disputes between states, some of which do indeed involve international crimes. Accordingly, the ICJ cannot find anyone guilty of a crime, nor can it sentence someone. In fact, its decisions sometimes are seen as nonbinding or, at the very least, unenforceable.

However, decisions of the ICJ often are very relevant and persuasive in national and international criminal courts when interpretation of the UN Charter or the application of domestic law in international criminal prosecutions is relevant.

Another example of civil adjudication of international crimes is the U.S. Alien Tort Claims Act (ATCA). The ATCA incorporates the Law of Nations into the domestic law of the United States, which provides a venue for U.S. district courts to hear claims under the act. Non-U.S. citizen victims of war crimes and crimes against humanity—including torture, cruel and inhuman treatment, forced disappearance, sexual assault, and other serious violent crimes—can seek damages against individuals who were acting pursuant to foreign "color of law" or private parties who were acting under foreign color of state authority or whose conduct violates a norm of international law that extends to private parties. The accused must be properly served within the borders of the United States in order for there to be jurisdiction in the case.

John R. Cencich
California University of Pennsylvania

See also Conventions, Agreements, and Regulations; Genocide; International Criminal Court; Policing: Transnational; War Crimes Tribunals

Further Readings

Abrams, Jason and Steven Ratner. *Accountability for Human Rights Atrocities in International Law—Beyond the Nüremberg Legacy.* Oxford: Oxford University Press, 2001.

Bassiouni, M. Cherif. *Crimes Against Humanity in International Criminal Law.* The Hague: Kluwer International, 1999.

Bassiouni, M. Cherif. *The Statute of the International Criminal Court.* Ardsley, NY: Transnational Publishers, 1998.

Bassiouni, M. Cherif et al. *International Criminal Law Documents Supplement.* Durham, NC: Carolina Academic Press, 2000.

Epps, Valerie. *International Law.* Durham, NC: Carolina Academic Press, 2005.

Ginsburgs, George and Vladimir Kudriavtsev, eds. *The Nüremberg Trial and International Law.* Boston: Martinus Nijhoff, 1990.

Hagan, John. *Justice in the Balkans: Prosecuting War Crimes in the Hague Tribunal.* Chicago: University of Chicago Press, 2003.

International Criminal Tribunal for the former Yugoslavia. *Basic Documents/Documents de Référence.* The Hague: Author, 1998.

Kittichaisaree, Kriangsak. *International Criminal Law.* New York: Oxford University Press, 2002.

Robertson, Geoffrey. *Crimes Against Humanity: The Struggle for Global Justice.* London: Penguin, 2002.

Van Sliedregt, E. *The Criminal Responsibility of Individuals for Violations of International Humanitarian Law.* The Hague: T. M. C. Asser Press, 2003.

AL QAEDA

When translated from Arabic, Al Qaeda simply means "the base." However, after September 2001, when the Pentagon and the World Trade Center were attacked by hijacked aircraft, Al Qaeda became known globally as the group responsible for the largest terrorist attack on U.S. soil. Al Qaeda's leader, Osama bin Laden, a Saudi and son of a wealthy construction magnate, instantly became the focus of international media. Ayman al-Zawahiri, bin Laden's ideological mentor and second in command, an Egyptian medical doctor and founder of Egyptian Islamic Jihad, also shared in the infinite media coverage. Bin Laden and Ayman al-Zawahiri created Al Qaeda to wage global jihad against the enemies of Islam because they both held beliefs that the world was corrupt, oppressive, and locked in a perpetual conflict of Muslims against non-Muslims. Al Qaeda professes a core message that it follows the original and pure manifestation of Islam with a strict adherence to Sharia (Islamic sacred law), that it adheres to the teachings of the Prophet Muhammad, and that it wages war against anything it deems pollutes its version of Islam. Al Qaeda's ideology is spread through propaganda via the media, the Internet, publications, training camps, and terrorist attacks in order to catalyze Muslims who are feeling discontented, humiliated, or frustrated in the fight against those responsible for belittling Islam. Al Qaeda as an organization was founded between 1988 and 1989 to purify Islam and the world from moral pollutants, and it has since evolved into three distinct phases in response to outside political and military intervention.

The first phase can be classified as Al Qaeda's formative stage. The early members of Al Qaeda were influenced by the 1979–89 war between the Soviet Union and the Afghani mujahedeen or holy freedom fighters. Independent of the Afghan-Soviet War, many of Al Qaeda's early membership had experience in political conflict in their own countries against established Muslim governments, most notably in Egypt, Saudi Arabia, Jordan, Syria, Yemen, and Algeria. In order to escape their domestic troubles, some early members followed the call to assist the Afghan mujahedeen in jihad. During the latter portion of the Afghan-Soviet War, the United States provided weapons and resources to the Afghan mujahedeen. After a full Soviet withdrawal from Afghanistan in February 1989, Al Qaeda was officially born. Its battle-hardened members and future recruits, who previously received aid from the United States in the Afghan-Soviet War, targeted the United States. The founding Al Qaeda members determined that the United States should be held responsible for humiliating the Arab and Islamic world, notably because of its support of Israel, its support of repressive Arab and Muslim regimes, and the presence of U.S. troops in the Middle East.

Creating a global army of trained jihadi fighters marks the second phase of Al Qaeda. Led by bin Laden and al-Zawahiri, Al Qaeda established a dozen training camps in Afghanistan, solicited economic funding, and carried out terrorist attacks in Africa and the Middle East. In August 1996, bin Laden issued a declaration of war against the United States. The declaration was preceded in November 1995 by bombing the Saudi-American base in Riyadh, followed by a June 1996 attack against the Khobar Towers in Saudi Arabia. Following the declaration of war, Al Qaeda members in August 1998 simultaneously bombed U.S. embassies in Nairobi, Kenya, and in Dar-es-Salaam, Tanzania. These attacks demonstrated Al Qaeda's ability to reach across national boundaries and maintain a sophisticated communication network. One year before the September 11, 2001, attacks, which was the culmination of this phase, Al Qaeda members attacked the USS *Cole*, which was docked in the port city of Aden in Yemen, in October 2000. This phase lasted until the American forces entered Afghanistan, resulting in the dispersal and killing of many members of Al Qaeda, sending them underground in a series of disconnected networks.

The U.S. invasion of Afghanistan pushed Al Qaeda into its present phase. This phase can reasonably be characterized as one in which the group Al Qaeda evolved into Al Qaedaism, an ideological franchise. Rather than attempting to attack the

United States on its soil, members of Al Qaeda relocated from Afghanistan, selected U.S. allies to attack, and focused on a decentralized strategy. As a result, Pakistan, Yemen, Saudi Arabia, Spain, Turkey, England, and Jordan all experienced medium-scale attacks between 2002 and 2005. Spanning the period between 2004 and 2006, a decentralized organizational structure facilitated the establishment of six branches dedicated to following Al Qaeda's ideology; they are Al Qaeda in Afghanistan, Al Qaeda in the Maghreb, Al Qaeda in Iraq, Al Qaeda in the Gulf, Al Qaeda in Europe, and Al Qaeda in Egypt. Al Qaeda in Iraq fought an active insurgency against U.S. and coalition forces, led by the Jordanian violent jihadist Abu Musab al-Zarqawi, before his death in 2006. Al Qaedaism as a franchise not only is marked by ideological agreement among groups but also displays Al Qaeda's methods, particularly (1) its evidentially substantial planning and preparation, (2) the signature high-profile and symbolic targets of its attacks, and (3) its emphasis on the systematic use of digital propaganda. Because Al Qaeda is now a franchised mythology that has evolved into a decentralized complex global network of trained fighters spread across the Middle East, Africa, Asia, and Europe, it will remain a significant threat for years to come.

Travis Morris
Norwich University

See also Jihad; Middle East; Narco-Terrorism

Further Readings

Atwan, B. A. *The Secret History of Al Qaeda.* London: Saqi Books, 2006.

Gunaratna, R. *Inside Al Qaeda: Global Network of Terror.* New York: Berkley, 2002.

Whelan, R. *Al-Qaedaism: The Threat to Islam, the Threat to the World.* Dublin: Ashfield Press, 2005.

Wright, L. *The Looming Tower: Al-Qaeda and the Road to 9/11.* New York: Knopf, 2006.

ALIEN CONSPIRACIES AND PROTECTION SYSTEMS

The Mafia as a criminal enterprise has garnered much interest over the years and has created much discussion about how it originated and developed in America. Although the concept of a mafia, in common parlance, may refer to "organized crime" as imported from different countries (particularly Russia, Japan, and Hong Kong), most scholars use the term to refer to activity by people who immigrated to the United States from Italy, specifically from the island of Sicily, located near the southern region of the country. The Sicilian Mafia, sometimes called La Cosa Nostra (or, less formally, the Mob), refers to a loosely knit group of organized crime syndicates. The fact that immigration and ethnicity are important factors in understanding the Mafia makes it more intriguing and open to various theoretical explanations. The "Mafia mystique" refers to how this criminal organization, with its distinct ethnic overtones, has captured the public imagination and has led to much public speculation as well as serious scientific inquiry. The early "alien conspiracy theories" and later "protection systems" perspectives are a result of that inquiry.

Many immigrants from Italy came to America in the middle and late 19th and early 20th centuries. Those from the more affluent north flowed into the new county in consistent numbers prior to the 1880s. After this decade, immigrants from the south entered in very large numbers to escape government oppression, poverty, and other undesirable social conditions. It is the immigration from the southern portion of Italy that has primarily become associated with criminal enterprises. Even prior to immigration, residents of northern Italy perceived of their southern counterparts as prone to deviance and criminality, a perspective that was continued in the United States.

In New York City as early as 1891, newspapers reported that some Italian Americans in the city were part of a crime syndicate called the Mafia and committed heinous crimes but had escaped prosecution. Fears of criminal networks, fueled by xenophobia created by recent waves of immigration, began to spread. Later, in the 1920s, the public image of gangsters in the style of Al Capone became closely connected with the Mafia and with Italian Americans generally. Persons of Italian descent who were found guilty of crimes were incarcerated, whereas those whose guilt was unproved were routinely rounded up and deported. These persons were considered foreign mobsters, although groups of other ethnic backgrounds, such as Irish Americans and American Jews, also had crime syndicates. The Federal Bureau of Investigation (FBI), under the direction of J. Edgar Hoover, targeted the Mafia in the 1920s and reported that the agency was successful in thwarting the syndicates' criminal activity; many scholars claim that Hoover used his media influence to amplify the extent of the Mafia's reach into the public sphere in order to showcase his agency's effectiveness. Similarly, in the 1930s Federal Bureau of Narcotics chief Harry Anslinger exaggerated the influence of the Italian networks to reflect his own agency's prowess in combating crime, specifically the nation's drug trade. The Mafia gangster image grew in American popular culture as a result of national Prohibition, enacted into law with the passage of the Volstead Act and the adoption of the Eighteenth Amendment to the U.S. Constitution. During this period (1920–33), people such as Capone and "Lucky" Luciano became household names. The image of the Mafia mobster could be found in newspapers, magazines, books, movies, and songs.

At mid-century, the Mafia received renewed media attention in the wake of the Kefauver Commission hearings, named after Tennessee senator Estes Kefauver. These televised hearings were conducted in

Most scholars use the term *Mafia* to refer to criminals who immigrated to the United States from the island of Sicily in Italy. The term *mafia mystique* refers to how this criminal organization has captured the public imagination and led to much speculation, depiction in films and literature, and as serious scientific inquiry. (Photos.com)

response to fears of the Mafia's criminal activity. The committee hearings concluded that organized crime syndicates, including the Mafia, were widespread and that corruption in law enforcement contributed to the growth of Mob activity. The imagery of the Mafia member as a public enemy of the state became solidified as many American television viewers learned about organized crime and the Mafia's role in it from the hearings. The public's connection of ethnic identity to criminal behavior, particularly with the gangsters' interesting (albeit violent) lifestyles, appealing style of dress, and intriguing and curious nicknames, became part of the national psyche.

Some theories of criminality of the 20th century were in some part influenced by the incoming peoples of various foreign nations. The idea of biological predisposition based on nation of origin provided a quick and easy explanation for criminal behavior. It not only created and reinforced racial and ethnic stereotypes but also created many foreign scapegoats, especially in times of high crime activity called "crime waves."

The idea that the Italians imported crime from their homeland to complex networks in the host country has been labeled the alien conspiracy theory. This theory posits that Italian immigrants with ties to organized criminal networks naturally created these networks in the United States after their arrival. If this were the case, however, people in the Mafia in Italy who immigrated to countries other than the United States would have established similar criminal operations there as well; this, however, did not happen. In addition, it was claimed by many people during the waves of Italian immigration that many of these Mafia members had escaped Italian justice to set up shop in the host country; this appears to be unfounded, since the well-connected Mafia bosses were normally protected from prosecution by corrupt agents of the Italian legal system.

The alien conspiracy theory has been deemed by many academics as an overly simplistic explanation for the Mafia's existence in America. Other theories evolved, such as the crooked ladder theory, which states that immigrants engage in criminality because of external, social factors such as unfamiliarity with the host culture, language barriers, xenophobia, lack of adequate job skills, and ignorance in navigating through bureaucratic organizations. In this model, discrimination occurs against the immigrants, and their failure to assimilate and better themselves occupationally and financially simply reinforces ideas of their innate inferiority. As biological and constitutional theories began to decline and acceptance developed for people of divergent backgrounds, the alien conspiracy theories have, for the most part, been discredited.

Another theoretical model that emphasizes environmental factors involves the Mafia's protection function. The Mafia has long been involved in many organized criminal endeavors, including illegal gambling, prostitution, extortion, drug activity, voting-related crime, and many others. It has been a hallmark of the Mafia to include violence in their activities. Some researchers have suggested, however, that protection is the primary duty of the Mafia. Also called the protection racket, this refers to when people pay for services to protect themselves or their possessions from some type of threat, such as theft or vandalism, which may be real or imagined. Sometimes the racketeers will intimidate anyone who presents a potential risk of harm to the person for whom they work. At other times they may extort from the person who is providing the payments for protection. Often racketeers have special geographic areas (such as a certain community or neighborhood) or specialties (such as gambling or prostitution) that they claim for themselves; violence often occurs when the racketeers attempt to defend their "turf." Not only businesses use the protection system; often individual criminals turn to the racketeers; they are unable to consult the police when victimized, since their activities are often criminal in nature. Since there is a naturally occurring distrust among those in criminal enterprises, it makes the protection more valuable, and in some cases necessary, for the criminal activity to continue.

According to the protection function perspective, it has been assumed, possibly in part because of media portrayals, that protection is simply an ancillary part of the Mafia's underground operation. This is incorrect; the Mafia often is not skilled in the business end of organized crime, such as the gambling or prostitution rackets. Its primary activity is protection services. Protection therefore has become an industry unto itself for groups engaged in underground activities. Violence is inherent in this form of activity, and a cultural viewpoint develops that accepts violence as a necessary part of the job. Adherents of the protection function model and other environmental perspectives claim that Mafia activities were not exported to America from southern Italy. Instead, the conditions in America in the early part of the 19th century, created by the Great Depression, Prohibition, and other social, political, and economic factors, produced the need for illicit protection services, a need that came to be filled by immigrants. This idea is quite different from earlier, more ethnocentric views that foreigners with natural inclinations for criminality simply retained and expressed those traits after moving to America.

Closely related to the concept of alien conspiracies is the idea of criminal conduct by people who have entered the United States illegally. A large debate has centered on this issue and has had significant political manifestations as certain states have passed stringent laws to curb illegal immigration and associated criminal activity. The fact that people enter a country illegally is in itself a crime, but many claim that gang activity and other deviant behavior, such as substance abuse, theft, and assault, are perpetrated by illegal immigrants perhaps more than other populations. Others believe that these claims are exaggerated and in many ways are racist and ethnocentric; they attribute the claims of immigrant criminality to social construction theory, the idea that if many people believe a certain way about a group, they will treat that group in a way that conforms with that belief, whether it is true or not.

Leonard A. Steverson
South Georgia College

See also Mafia Myths and Mythologies; Organized Crime: Defined; Organized Crime: Ethnic- Versus Market-Based

Further Readings

Finckenauer, James O. and Elin J. Waring. *Russian Mafia in America: Immigration, Culture, and Crime.* Boston: Northeastern University Press, 1988.

Gambetta, Diego. *Codes of the Underworld: How Criminals Communicate.* Princeton, NJ: Princeton University Press, 2009.

Gambetta, Diego. *The Sicilian Mafia: The Business of Private Protection.* Cambridge, MA: Harvard University Press, 1993.

Nelli, Humbert S. *The Business of Crime: Italians and Syndicate Crime in the United States.* Chicago: University of Chicago Press, 1976.

Smith, Dwight C. *The Mafia Mystique.* New York: Basic Books, 1975.

Varese, Federico. *Mafias on the Move: How Organized Crime Conquers New Territories*. Princeton, NJ: Princeton University Press, 2011.

ANTICORRUPTION LEGISLATION

Corruption—defined as abuse of public office for private gain—is one of the greatest challenges facing the world today. Bribery, fraud, vote buying, illegal political contributions, and misappropriation of funds are examples of this global phenomenon. Corruption is estimated to add 10 percent or more to the costs of doing business in many parts of the world; the World Bank estimates that bribery alone has become a $1 trillion industry. Moreover, corruptive behavior has become an increasing problem of world trade that disturbs international competition and erects major obstacles for economic and social development in many countries of the Southern Hemisphere. Corruption also appears to be embedded within complex structural social problems, such as human trafficking, organized crime, and terrorism.

Once tolerated as an unfortunate by-product of economic development in the developing world, Western governments appear to have given up their support for corrupt regimes in developing countries and have increasingly demanded good governance. Accordingly, there has been a strong challenge to corruption that includes voluminous numbers of anticorruption laws on the books in numerous countries as well as 21 international legal instruments now available to fight it. The world's first convention against corruption was the Organisation for Economic Co-operation and Development's (OECD's) Convention on Combating Bribery of Foreign Public Officials in International Business Transactions in 1997. Such initiatives culminated in the 2003 UN Convention Against Corruption (UNCAC).

OECD Convention

Signed in December 1997 and entered into force two months later, the OECD Convention committed all 38 parties to the convention to ensure that their parliaments would approve the convention and pass legislation necessary for its ratification and implementation as national law. The convention's breakthrough development was the movement toward adopting national legislation making it a crime to bribe foreign public officials; moreover, it provided a broad definition of bribery, requiring countries to impose dissuasive sanctions and committing them to providing mutual legal assistance.

The OECD Convention's first item of business was to recommend that member states criminalize the offense of bribery of foreign public officials. Each party to the convention was required to establish a criminal offense under its law for any person intentionally offering, promising, or giving any undue pecuniary advantages to a foreign public official in exchange for advantageous action or inaction on the part of the official.

Second, the convention required that the bribery of a foreign public official be punishable by dissuasive penalties that are appropriate in relation to the scope of the crime. The types of penalties ideally would be similar to those used by member countries to punish those who had bribed their own public officials and would include enough deprivation of liberty to enable mutual legal assistance and extradition. Additionally, each party was supposed to make arrangements so that the bribe and the proceeds thereof could be subject to seizure and confiscation.

The mandate in the convention's seventh article was that signatory parties that have made bribery of their own public officials a predicate offense for the purpose of the application of money-laundering legislation apply that same standard to the bribery of a foreign public official. The mandate applies regardless of the jurisdiction where the bribery occurred.

Article 8, which dealt with accounting, asserted that each signatory party shall do all possible to prohibit the establishment of off-the-books accounts, the making of off-the-books transactions, and the use of false documents for the purpose of bribing foreign public officials. Furthermore, it was expected that the signing nations would provide dissuasive penalties for offenses such as falsifying accounts, financial statements, records, and books.

Articles 9 and 10 concerned mutual legal assistance and extradition, respectively. Article 9 stated that each party would promise to provide legal assistance promptly and effectively to another state as needed for the purpose of any criminal investigations brought by another state relative to any of the offenses within the scope of the OECD Convention. The party that was being requested to supply information pledged to be cooperative with the requesting party and to serve up any additional information or documents needed to support the request for assistance. Article 10 specified that bribing a foreign public official become an extraditable offense under the domestic laws of the convention parties as well any extradition treaties between them.

UN Convention Against Corruption

UNCAC included preventive measures and provisions on international cooperation as well as effective legal strategies concerning money laundering and asset recovery. Its chapter on criminalization and law enforcement, however, was the heart of the convention. States were required to implement the provisions on bribery of national public officials (Article 15), bribery of foreign public officials (Article 16), laundering of proceeds of crime (Article 23), and obstruction of justice (Article 25).

Article 15 of UNCAC defined bribery as the granting of some kind of benefit that enables the grantor to exert undue influence upon an official action or decision. Article 15(a) prohibited "active bribery," thus criminalizing those who promise, offer, or give an undue advantage to a public official in exchange for the official's acting or refraining from acting in the exercise of his or her duties. Article 15(b) covers "passive bribery," making it a crime for public officials to solicit or accept, directly or indirectly, an undue advantage.

Article 16 transferred the legal goals outlined in Article 15 to the realm of foreign officials. It stipulated that each party to the convention make bribery of foreign officials, and also the bribery of officials of public international organizations, a crime. By doing the latter, the convention closed legal loopholes in criminal codes whose antibribery provisions covered only national and foreign public officials.

According to Article 23, each state was committed to adopt laws to make laundering a crime—that is, the conversion or transfer of property or assisting others in evading the legal consequences of their action, knowing that such property is the proceeds of crime. Specifically, it criminalizes concealing or disguising the nature, source, or location of such property. Additionally, the article criminalizes conspiracy to commit money laundering as well as aiding, abetting, facilitating, and counseling the commission of any offenses established relative to this article.

Article 25 criminalized any physical force, threats, or intimidation that might be used to induce false testimony or to interfere in any way with giving testimony relevant to any matter related to the convention's business. The article also makes it a crime to threaten force or actually use it in an attempt to interfere with the exercise of official duties by law-enforcement or justice officials.

Compliance With Provisions of the Two Conventions

The OECD Convention's enforcement provisions constituted a gold standard for follow-up and implementation work toward full compliance with the convention's original articles. This three-pronged effort included the 2009 antibribery recommendation, the recommendation on tax measures for further combating bribery of public officials, and the Working Group monitoring program.

The 2009 antibribery recommendation strengthened OECD's structure for fighting foreign bribery by calling on all parties to the convention to take the following actions: (1) adopt the best evidence-based practices for making companies liable for foreign bribery; (2) review policies on small facilitation payments as these are legal in some countries in order to expedite an administrative process; (3) do all possible to revamp and improve cooperation between countries for evidence sharing in investigations of foreign bribery; (4) provide effective channels for public officials to report suspected foreign bribery; and (5) work with the private sector to adopt more stringent controls and higher ethical standards that would have the effect of preventing and detective bribery.

A 2009 document titled "Recommendation of the Council on Tax Measures for Further Combating Bribery of Public Officials in International Business Transactions" suggested that parties to the OECD Convention explicitly and effectively disallow the tax deductibility of bribes to foreign public officials for all tax purposes. The document further extends such disallowance of tax deductibility to all criminally corrupt conduct as specified by the convention.

The actualization of these instruments is monitored strictly by the OECD Working Group on Bribery. Made up of representatives from all 38 signatory states, this group meets four times per year in Paris. The Working Group's peer-review monitoring process includes a thorough evaluation of each state's legislation, institutions, policies, and practices for complying with the instruments related to the convention. Then, the group makes on-site visits to the countries being evaluated. The subsequently produced country summary reports generated by the Working Group are published and uploaded onto the OECD Website in their entirety. They provide a summary of the findings as well as recommendations on how states should improve compliance with the convention. By continually failing to implement the OECD antibribery instruments, member countries run the risk of facing strong pressure by the Working Group to rectify the problem—up to and including such measures as sending a high-level mission to the country in question, or by issuing a formal public statement.

The UNCAC, for its part, established a Conference of the State Parties with a mission to promote and review the progress of the signatory countries in implementing the 2003 convention. At its first session, held in Jordan on December 10–14, 2006, this conference agreed that it was necessary to work toward a formal procedure for ensuring that the legislation agreed to at the convention was actually achieved; to that end, a pilot program was conceived. The Secretariat was enlisted to be available to assist any parties as they collect and provide information on their nation's progress and to relay the results of these self-assessments to the conference.

The 2006 Jordan Conference also adopted a resolution titled "Establishment of an Intergovernmental Working Group on Asset Recovery," which provided for an interim open-ended intergovernmental working group to assess progress in implementing the convention's mandate to return the proceeds of corruption. At the Qatar Conference in 2009, the assembly adopted a similar resolution, "Preventive Measures," that allowed the establishment of another interim working group, this one to advise and assist the conference in the following through on its mandate on preventing corruption.

Conclusion

The perceived high rates of corruption believed to exist worldwide could be interpreted positively as evidence that the global intention to fight corruption is brisk and that laws already on the books (or laws being enacted now) are working well to fight corruption, judging from the volume of current cases being prosecuted. Following up upon the mandates from the OECD Convention and UNCAC should also help in the battle against corrupt practices. At some future date, especially if preventive measures work, a worldwide decline in perceptions of corrupt behavior could be noted.

A more discouraging scenario may be discovered by reading the independent reports of monitoring groups such as Transparency International suggesting that, even among some of the signatory nations that agreed to the articles of the two conventions, compliance with anticorruption legislation is sluggish at the local level because of a lack of political will in individual countries to follow through with enforcement. Regulation is unlikely to be effective in terms of results unless robust enforcement mechanisms are put into place.

Stan C. Weeber
McNeese State University

See also Bribery and Graft; Conventions, Agreements, and Regulations; Corporate Influence Peddling; Extradition; Money Laundering: Countermeasures

Further Readings

Carr, Indira. "Corruption, Legal Solutions and Limits of Law." *International Journal of Law in Context*, v.3 (2007).

Harris, Robert. *Political Corruption: In and Beyond the Nation State*. London: Routledge, 2003.

Kubiciel, Michael. "Core Criminal Law Provision in the United Nations Convention Against Corruption." *International Criminal Law Review*, v.9 (2009).

Transparency International. *Transparency International Annual Report 2009*. Berlin: Author, 2010.

Transparency International. *Transparency International Progress Report 2010: Enforcement of the OECD Anti-Bribery Convention*. Berlin: Author, 2010.

ANTITERRORIST FINANCING

Antiterrorist financing measures involve efforts to monitor and thwart the flow of funds to known and suspected terrorist organizations. The money on which terrorists rely for the day-to-day operations of their organizations and to orchestrate violent attacks may come from any number of sources. In some cases, funds are channeled to terrorist organizations from legitimate business ventures, such as taxi companies and charitable organizations; in other cases, terrorists receive their funds from illegitimate activities, such as drug trafficking. Countries including the United States and the United Kingdom, which tend to drive global norms in the field of antiterrorist financing, view the interception of money flowing to dangerous terrorist groups as among their highest law-enforcement and national security priorities.

Terrorist organizations often use complex, transnational networks of financing to obtain the resources they need to sustain themselves. For example, Al Qaeda is financed by a global fund-raising network that includes charities, nongovernmental organizations (NGOs), mosques, Websites, financial institutions, and various intermediaries. Some donors know that their money will go to fund violent terrorism, while other contributors may believe that their donations will be used for humanitarian aid. The money is laundered through conduits in the international financial system, the Islamic banking system, or the informal value transfer system known as hawala. Funds are stored and transferred through investments in commodities (such as gold) as well as through traditional means such as cash smuggling.

The objectives of antiterrorist financing efforts are relatively straightforward. To the extent that terrorist organizations have less money with which to operate, this may weaken their efforts to recruit new members and stifle their ability to carry out violent attacks. It may also help to erode terrorist groups' levels of expertise with respect to coordinated violence and counterintelligence. Ultimately, the purpose of all antiterrorist financing activities is to save lives.

A number of methods are used to combat terrorist financing activities. For example, in the wake of the terrorist attacks of September 11, 2011, the United Kingdom enacted legislation allowing government authorities to confiscate money believed to be related to terrorist operations, regardless of whether prosecution of an offense has commenced. Where a non-U.K. person is believed to be a threat to the British economy or U.K. residents, the head of the U.K. Treasury may issue an order to seize that person's assets. For the order to continue in effect beyond 28 days from issuance, each house of Parliament must pass a resolution to that end. In addition, U.K. law-enforcement authorities may apply for open warrants, renewable after 90 days, that allow the state to conduct ongoing monitoring of individual accounts. The country has also formed an Asset Recovery Agency, in part to disrupt terrorist financing activity, that seeks to recover criminal assets and promote financial crimes investigations.

In many respects, the development of the antiterrorist financing legal regime in the United Kingdom has eschewed the criminal-law system in favor of civil-law standards for confiscation, which afford the government relatively greater flexibility. In civil forfeiture proceedings, for example, the presumption of innocence does not apply; moreover, the standard of guilt and the government's burden of proof are more relaxed than in criminal proceedings. The U.K. government has also adopted measures that heighten the internal record-keeping, reporting, and identification procedures of U.K. business entities in order help stem the tide of money laundering.

Like the U.K., the United States has implemented a number of statutory and regulatory strategies for thwarting the flow of funds to terrorist groups. Legislation dating back to the 1970s authorizes the president to designate individuals or organizations he or she considers a threat to national security and to freeze the assets of those entities or block transactions between them and U.S. persons. These powers are often carried out through a robust economic sanctions program operated by the Department of the Treasury's Office of Foreign Assets Control (OFAC). Additionally, U.S. financial institutions are generally obligated to file "suspicious activity reports" (SARs) with the Treasury Department's Financial Crimes Enforcement Network (FinCEN) when they observe suspicious transactions or become aware of criminal behavior.

U.S. law makes it a crime for persons to engage in transactions with the governments of states designated as state sponsors of terrorism. It is similarly a crime to provide "material support" to terrorism—a concept broadly defined to include the provision of money, training, weapons, shelter, and food. The U.S.A. Patriot Act, enacted shortly after the September 11, 2001 (9/11), terrorist attacks, increased criminal sanctions for U.S. persons and organizations that knowingly or purposefully provide material support to terrorism or foreign terrorist organizations. The act, along with other post-9/11 measures, increased due-diligence ("know your own customer") and reporting standards for financial intermediaries; encouraged data sharing among financial institutions to incentivize joint investigation of questionable transactions; provided broad authority to the Treasury Department concerning the identification of money launderers; authorized the government to freeze assets temporarily during investigations; and enhanced the legal protections for confidentiality of information utilized in such investigations—a provision designed in part to alleviate the risk of capital flight.

Under the United States' antiterrorist financing regime, a broad range of U.S. businesses are required to file SARs and currency transaction reports (CTRs) when engaging in transactions exceeding $10,000. United States law empowers the government to freeze the property and assets of people and organizations identified as terrorists or supporters of terrorism. Many of these anti-money-laundering and antiterrorist financing laws are subject to extraterritorial enforcement.

In addition to efforts by national governments such as those cited above, international organizations and multilateral arrangements—both formal and informal—provide a framework for international cooperation in the fight against terrorist financing. For example, the United Nations (UN) has developed model domestic laws for antiterrorist financing, many of which reflect norms influenced by the government policies outlined above. The Financial Action Task Force (FATF), which had 34 member jurisdictions and two regional organizations by 2011, is an intergovernmental body formed with the objective of developing and promoting policies to counter the use of the international financial system by criminals and terrorist groups. Among other coordinating tasks, the FATF issues recommendations that reflect best practices and international standards for dealing with money laundering and terrorist financing. Beyond seeking the counsel of such organizations, national governments invoke multilateral UN treaties, bilateral mutual legal assistance treaties, and cooperative relationships between intelligence agencies to help counter transnational terrorist financing activity.

These antiterrorist financing strategies have met with varying degrees of success and have generated both praise and criticism. There is little doubt, however, that these and other measures to target the financial networks on which terrorists rely will continue to play a critical role in global efforts to combat the transnational threat of terrorism.

Robert D. Williams
United States Court of Appeals, Fifth Circuit

See also Criminal Forfeiture and Seizure; Financial Action Task Force; Informal Value Transfer Systems; Money Laundering: History; Money Laundering: Methods; Money Laundering: Targeting Criminal Proceeds; Money Laundering: Vulnerable Commodities and Services; Mutual Legal Assistance Treaties; Sanctions and Blacklisting

Further Readings

Aufhauser, David D. "Terrorist Financing: The Privatization of Economic Sanctions." *Federal Lawyer*, v.56 (2009).
Donohue, Laura K. "Anti-Terrorist Finance in the United Kingdom and United States." *Michigan Journal of International Law*, v.27/2 (2006).
Financial Action Task Force. "About the FATF." http://www.fatf-gafi.org/pages/0,3417,en_32250379_32236836_1_1_1_1_1,00.html (Accessed February 2011).
O'Leary, Robert E. "Note: Improving the Terrorist Finance Sanctions Process." *New York University Journal of International Law and Politics*, v.42 (2010).

ART AND ANTIQUITIES: FRAUD

Both a criminal act and a civil wrong, art and antiquities fraud is one of the most significant types of transnational crime and an epidemic plaguing the art world. Accounting for an estimated loss of hundreds of millions of U.S. dollars annually, it extends to all deceptive activities involving, or relating to, works and items of artistic, ethnographic, archaeological, or historical value. These activities vary in complexity and sophistication, occasionally involving foreign jurisdictions and multinational criminal networks.

There are numerous definitions in respect of the meaning and scope of the word *art*. Classic accounts usually identify art with visual expressions of human creativity, such as paintings, drawings, prints, sculptures, photographs, and engravings. This notion takes various shapes and turns once it is incorporated into legal statutes. For example, U.S. tariff laws regulating duty-free exemptions on imported arts frequently associate arts with ornamental purposes, turning down any items that have utility or industrial purposes.

Antiquities, however, are mostly items of considerable age and historical or archaeological value, such as coins, medals, armor, vessels, bowls, and inscriptions. Classical accounts often identify antiquities with items of ancient cultures, such as the Greek, Roman, and Egyptian cultures. While most definitions limit the scope of antiquities to items up to late antiquity (the 5th century C.E.), some definitions—such as that of the Convention on the Means of Prohibiting and Preventing the Illicit Import, Export and Transfer of Ownership of Cultural Property (1970)—broadens the notion, embracing all historical items that are more than 100 years old.

Art and antiquities are considered ambassadors of goodwill. They enrich human existence and educate, encouraging mutual respect, acceptance, and appreciation of other peoples' heritage, history, and traditions. A nation's art and antiquities are the cultural property of the nation and an extension of its identity. Each nation strives to protect its cultural heritage from all sorts of criminal behavior, such as theft, smuggling, vandalism, illicit export, fraud, and forgery.

Considered one of most pressing problems in the art world, fraud extends to all intentional deceptions meant to induce a victim to part with his or her property or money and enrich the deceiver. Fraud takes various forms, such as the purchase of items with bad checks; defrauding banks when using items as collateral for loans by inflating value; scamming insurance companies with falsified value and theft faking; evading taxes and laundering money through value misrepresentation; making excessive profit selling artistic items while underpaying artists; selling bad titles; selling consigned items and failing to pay the owners; faking provenance documentation;

Antiquities are defined as objects of historical or archeological value, like coins, medals, armor, vessels, bowls, and inscriptions. Counterfeits, fakes, and forgeries are the leading form of art and antiquity fraud. (Photos.com)

and manipulating biddings and distorting competition in auctions.

The leading form of art fraud, however, is the trade in counterfeits, fakes, and forgeries. While preceding forms involve value misrepresentation and trust betrayal, this form also involves matters of authenticity and attribution. A fake is basically a duplicate or an imitation of an original work. Fakers copy valued pieces and pass them on as genuine. For example, works believed to have been by Vincent van Gogh, Salvador Dalí, Auguste Rodin, Maurice Utrillo, Joan Miró, Marc Chagall, and Pablo Picasso have frequently been reported as fakes. To educate the public and the art community, some institutions—notably the McIntosh-Drysdale Gallery (Washington, D.C.) in 1986 and the British Museum in 1990—have mounted exhibitions exclusively of fake art.

Unlike fakes, forgeries are new creations deceptively attributed to known artists. Forgers create such pieces by "borrowing" motifs, styles, ideas, colors, and signatures of other artists. They may complete an uncompleted work or assemble portions from different works to produce new ones. Sophisticated forgers carefully study the targeted artist, including his or her biography and works. They track down old materials and use similar ingredients to create the forged art. They imitate signs of age by pressing items, adding black spots, and heating or cracking the artwork.

Skilled forgers have attracted world attention, and some, such as Giovanni Bastianini (1830–69), Otto Wacker (1898–1970), and David Stein (1935–99), gained fame in their own right. Among those is Dutch forger Han van Meegeren. Van Meegeren created many forgeries of the famous Dutch artist Johannes Vermeer. One piece, titled *Christ and the Adulteress*, was sold during World War II to Nazi Reich Marshal Hermann Göring. Soon after the war ended, he was accused of collaborating with the enemy and selling national treasures. To evade these charges, van Meegeren stated the piece was a forgery, yet no one believed him. To prove his innocence, he painted a new piece while under police guard. The outcome was supportive of his claim and the heavy charges were dropped.

In spite of their sophistication, forgers are never able to commit a perfect crime. An artwork is not an isolated piece without reference to time or space. It is the output of the culture, style, and features of its era and place of creation. No forger is able to genuinely imitate or re-create those conditions, nor is it possible to fully hide the person behind the forgery. Art experts are occasionally employed to give their opinion on matters of authenticity and attribution, and scientific detection methods, such as chemical analysis, X-ray scanning, and digital analysis, aid in that regard. Nevertheless, some cases have not been resolved, as is the case with the Greek kouros of the J. Paul Getty Museum in Malibu, California.

A complex crime, art and antiquities fraud is not a one-person act. It frequently leans on national and international criminal networks to smuggle, distribute, and sell the illegal goods. Mafias, drug cartels, and shady dealers are the main vehicles in these activities. Some countries' growing art markets contribute to the problem, with massive numbers of counterfeits flowing across their borders, as is the case with China. Others, such as African countries, escalate the problem, with tribes counterfeiting their own ethnographic items. As African arts are usually anonymous, fakes are extremely hard to differentiate from originals; moreover, whereas Western communities identify authentic African items with those genuinely used in social and religious rituals, Africans treat both old and new items as equally authentic and their sale as a welcome source of income for poor African villages. Technological advances such as the Internet have exacerbated the problem: Multiple Websites, Internet auctions, and e-mails defraud surfers interested in art and antiquities yet unable to examine the pieces or their documentation physically.

In spite of its vast dimensions and growing complexity, art and antiquities fraud is barely treated with the care required by national authorities. Only a few police forces have squads and agents specially trained for art crimes. Among those are the United States' Federal Bureau of Investigation (FBI), the French Police Nationale (national police), the Art and Antiques unit of the English Metropolitan Police Service, and the Italian Comando Carabinieri Tutela Patrimonio Artistico (artistic heritage police unit). These agencies work closely with dealers, auction houses, and museums, gathering information from them regarding suspicious activities as well as learning innovative investigative skills.

National legislators deal with the crime solely within general antifraud statutes, such as 18 U.S.C. section 1341 or California Penal Code section 470. While demonstrating some success, these statutes are not fully adjusted to the level, complexity, and uniqueness of art and antiquities fraud today, and

many complain that they lack any real deterrent effect with their low imposed fines, compared to profits made from the crime. In addition, art and antiquities fraud convictions are rare, and many factors have contributed to this outcome. Dealers, auction houses, museums, and even collectors are unwilling to risk their reputations or shake the art market and thus are less willing to report crimes. Reported crimes do not always lead to arrests or allegations. Many cases are dealt with as private disputes and are settled outside court. In addition, numerous mature cases do not always meet the heavy burden of proving the fraudulent intent of the accused.

National customs services such as those of the United States and various European nations help combat smuggling and illegal transport of items across national borders. However, only a few international initiatives such as the International Criminal Police Organization (Interpol) and the International Foundation for Art Research (IFAR), a nonprofit organization with offices situated in different countries, have aided in the prevention of and struggle against art and antiquities fraud. Moreover, international treaties dealing with art and antiquities fraud are lacking. Current treaties focus instead on illegal international movement of supposedly genuine art and antiquities. Lacking also are registries and databanks for forgeries and counterfeits. Existing ones are partial and mostly centered on stolen art.

Art and antiquities fraud, a crime of transnational dimensions, is not just an infringement of the individual creator's economic and moral rights, it is a crime against a people: their culture, heritage, and national treasures. Greater efforts—such as more specialized police forces, closer cooperation, better databases, and greater public awareness—would go some way to solving this epidemic, thus protecting the public and true works of greatness.

Nahel N. Asfour
University of Vienna

See also Art and Antiquities: Plunder; Copyright Infringement; Counterfeit Goods; Forgery

Further Readings

Conklin, John. *Art Crime*. Westport, CT: Praeger, 1994.
DuBoff, Leonard and Christy King. *Art Law in a Nutshell*. Detroit, MI: Thomson-West, 2006.
DuBoff, Leonard, Michael Murray, and Christy King. *The Deskbook of Art Law*. New York: Oceana, 2006.

ART AND ANTIQUITIES: PLUNDER

Art and antiquities have been plundered on a transnational basis for millennia. Invading armies from time immemorial have seized prized objects as booty from conquered lands. For instance, a stele commemorating the 2250 B.C.E. victory of Naram-Sim of Akkad over the Lullubi was taken, about a thousand years after it was erected, as booty by the Elamites and transported to their capital in Susa, Iran. Rome, the seat of the Roman Empire, was decorated with looted art and antiquities from Greece and other conquered lands. The Napoleonic Wars brought troves of art and antiquities to the Louvre and elsewhere in France. The Nazi Third Reich, with bureaucratic efficiency, plundered millions of objects from private collectors and art museums across Europe. Restitution of works stolen from Jewish collectors by the Nazi machinery has been a difficult and, at times, very public enterprise, including notable works such as Marc Chagall's *The Rabbi*, Édouard Manet's *Portrait of Antonin Proust*, and Gustav Klimt's *Portrait of Adele Bauer-Bloch*. Unfortunately, many other plundered works have disappeared into the underground criminal black market, occasionally resurfacing as private collections come up for auction.

The trade in illicit art and antiquities is a widespread global problem. It has been estimated that between $3 billion and $14 billion in art and antiquities are plundered each year. This is frequently done with the assistance of corruptible government officials and the protection of organized crime syndicates, as well as with the compliance of unscrupulous art dealers. The Internet has helped looters get more connected to dealers and other markets for their illicit gains. On the other hand, the Internet has also helped law-enforcement agencies and others to monitor the trade in plundered objects. For example, a Nazi-era plundered art database of more than 20,000 pieces of stolen art is available through a joint initiative between the U.S. Holocaust Museum and the Conference of Jewish Material Claims Against Germany. It remains, however, immensely difficult to determine where plundered art and antiquities go.

Complex routes have been developed for the trade in plundered objects. For instance, in 2005 the Italian Culture Ministry raided an antiquities fair near Milan and recovered hundreds of plundered objects, including many Middle Eastern artifacts that had been smuggled into Italy by way of Thailand. Also in 2005, U.S. Immigration and Customs Enforcement agents seized hundreds of plundered artifacts taken from graves in Colombia and Peru that were in the possession of an Italian citizen selling them from the back of a van in Florida. The networks developed for smuggling drugs, weapons, and other contraband are often employed for the trade in plundered art and antiquities. This trade, accordingly, supports other criminal activity, including terrorist operations. Hezbollah in Lebanon, for example, appears to be taxing looted antiquities traveling through its areas of control.

The plundering of art and antiquities is particularly prevalent in poor and politically unstable areas. For example, burial mounds around Djenne in Mali are torn open and scavenged for terra-cotta pottery and figurines, many dating to the 13th century. Unauthorized excavation of archaeological sites in conflict zones is rampant. Looters are known to use heavy machinery and explosives to get to artifacts, destroying irreplaceable archaeological sites in the process. The destruction of an archaeological site not only destroys scientific evidence but also it blurs, if not erases, the cultural heritage of a people and nation. Even archaeological fieldwork performed with proper permits can be regarded as plundering, particularly by those who perceive themselves as descendants of ancient inhabitants; such cases include excavations of Native American grave sites or burials on tells in Israel.

Many of the world's leading museums hold art and antiquities whose origins are suspect. In 1816, the British Museum purchased and continues to display the Elgin Marbles, cut from the Parthenon. Berlin's Egyptian Museum exhibits the bust of Nefertiti, which the Egyptian Supreme Council of Antiquities claims was taken from Egypt in 1912. In 2010, the Louvre purchased fresco fragments that Egypt claims were plundered from the Valley of the Kings in the 1980s. Nevertheless, many museums have made efforts to return art and antiquities proven to be plundered. In 1993, the New York Metropolitan Museum of Art returned the Lydian Hoard, along with hundreds of artifacts looted from sites in Turkey, to Turkish authorities. The Michael Carlos Museum of Atlanta, Georgia, confirmed in 1999 by carbon-14 dating that a mummy thought to be that of Ramses I dated to the period and returned it to Egypt, where it is now placed in the Luxor Museum. It has been argued by museums that these artifacts are part of our universal human history, that they have curated and preserved items that would otherwise likely have been destroyed, and that their display and study promote knowledge and broaden cultural understanding.

Looters commonly take advantage of political instability to conduct their illicit activities. In 2003, for example, after the fall of Saddam Hussein's regime in Iraq, thousands of antiquities were looted from Baghdad's National Museum and other locations. A link has since been established between the smuggling of antiquities and Iraqi extremist groups. Apparently insurgents have been forcing payments from art and antiquities smugglers and may even have been involved directly in such illegal trafficking to help fund their own operations. During the January 2011 rioting in Cairo, looters broke into the Egyptian Museum, committing widespread vandalism, and some ancient objects were also taken.

International law efforts have endeavored to address the plundering of art and antiquities. One of the first comprehensive treaties was the 1954 Hague Convention for the Protection of Cultural Property in the Event of Armed Conflict, but it was concerned only with incidents resulting from warfare. The 1970 United Nations Educational, Scientific and Cultural Organization (UNESCO) Convention on the Means of Prohibiting and Preventing the Illicit Import, Export and Transfer of Ownership of Cultural Property forbids the illegal import or export of plundered artifacts within signatory countries, including the United States. This convention outlines an international policy for the protection of art and antiquities. In 1978, UNESCO created the Intergovernmental Committee for Promoting the Return of Cultural Property to Its Countries of Origin or Its Restitution in case of Illicit Appropriation; this body conducts bilateral negotiations to return plundered art and antiquities. In 1983, the U.S. Congress passed the Convention on Cultural Property Implementation Act to comply with its obligations under the 1970 UNESCO convention. The International Criminal Police Organization (Interpol) maintains a specialized unit to investigate crimes involving art and antiquities. Furthermore, the National Stolen Property Act grants the U.S. government the right to seizure and forfeiture of merchandise transported or sold that

is known to have been stolen or taken by fraud. A more recent attempt is the International Institute on the Unification of Private Law's Convention on Stolen or Illegally Exported Cultural Objects, but the United States has yet to agree to this convention.

Victor B. Stolberg
Essex County College

See also Art and Antiquities: Fraud

Further Readings

Feliciano, Hector. *The Lost Museum: The Nazi Conspiracy to Steal the World's Greatest Works of Art.* New York: Basic Books, 1987.

Miles, Margaret M. *Art as Plunder: The Ancient Origins of Debate About Cultural Property.* Cambridge: Cambridge University Press, 2008.

Waxman, Sharon. *Lost: The Battle Over the Stolen Treasures of the Ancient World.* New York: Times Books/Henry Holt, 2008.

AUSTRALIA

The nature of transnational crime in Australia is closely related to Australia's geography and demographics. As an island continent, Australia lacks any shared borders. Onshore smuggling of goods and people can occur only by air or sea. The inhospitality and infertility of much of Australia's sizable terrain has concentrated its small population of 22.7 million into mostly urban areas in the southeast and southwest and along the eastern seaboard. Policing of borders is difficult because of Australia's huge maritime jurisdiction, its long stretches of sparsely populated coastline, and its small workforce. Despite its location in Oceania, legally and politically Australia has strong Western roots, having begun as an English penal colony in the late 18th century. In 2010, it ranked second in the United Nations (UN) Development Programme's Human Development Index, making it an attractive destination for the peoples of neighboring regions. Australia's strong socioeconomic status and highly urbanized population ensure a strong demand for illicit goods and services, and the multicultural composition of its inhabitants means that transnational connections often already exist for, or are easily acquired by, organized criminal groups. Those groups include Australian crime families, outlaw motorcycle gangs and ethnic groups such as Italian mafias, Chinese triads, and Vietnamese, eastern European, and Middle Eastern gangs.

The primary activities of organized crime in Australia are the production, importation, and trafficking of drugs. High street prices for illicit drugs, as compared to North America and Europe, reflect the small market and the limited number of criminal groups. Cannabis remains the most popular drug, but importations (mainly of seed) are relatively low because of abundant domestic cultivation. The markets in both amphetamine-type stimulants (ATS), including MDMA (Ecstasy) and precursors, and cocaine are currently expanding. Seizure data collected by the Australian Crime Commission suggest that air and sea cargo and postal shipments (including letter-class mail) are the main method of importation of these drugs, rather than drug couriers. In 2008–09, the major embarkation points for larger shipments were China (including Hong Kong) for methamphetamine and other ATS (excluding MDMA) and Canada for MDMA. An emerging trend is the transshipment of methamphetamine through some Pacific islands. Importations of sassafras oil from Southeast Asia for use as an MDMA precursor are increasing. The cocaine used in Australia originates in South America and is brought in by Mexican, ethnic South American, and some West African criminal groups but transits through numerous countries (in 2008–09 embarkation countries numbered 46, more than double the number in 1999–2000). Most heroin arrives by parcel post and air cargo from Afghanistan and Myanmar via South Africa, Pakistan, and several countries in Southeast Asia. While seizures have recently increased, they are still relatively low compared to earlier in the decade. Growing markets in other drugs, including steroids and hormones, hallucinogens (such as LSD), anesthetics (such ketamine and GHB), synthetic cannabinoids, and counterfeit pharmaceuticals, are posing increasing challenges for Australian authorities. Seizures of these drugs were the highest on record in 2008–09.

The international laundering of Australian proceeds of drug trafficking and other serious crimes occurs in diverse ways, such as the smuggling of cash and bearer-negotiable instruments, alternative remittance systems such as hawala, and the manipulation of the regulated financial sector by delinquent professionals engaged by organized crime. Money laundering is complemented by identity theft and fraud and aided by ongoing advances in information technologies. The financial services and insurance sectors are the targets of choice for cybercriminals. Other forms of transnational cybercrime, such as phishing (the use of e-mails seemingly from legitimate businesses to obtain confidential information such as passwords) and the circulation of child pornography, are perpetrated both on and by Australians.

Australia is a destination country for persons trafficked for sexual and labor purposes. Victims come from Southeast Asia (particularly Thailand), East Asia (particularly China and the Republic of Korea), and to a lesser extent eastern Europe. Many come voluntarily on temporary work visas but are deceived about working conditions and exploited upon arrival, being forced into prostitution or into laboring in unsafe workplaces for low pay in sectors such as agriculture, hospitality, and construction. The traffickers are often small, highly sophisticated criminal networks with overseas family and business connections. The exact number of trafficking victims is unknown, but the U.S. Department of State suggests it is likely to be modest relative to the population. However, Fiona David has pointed out that

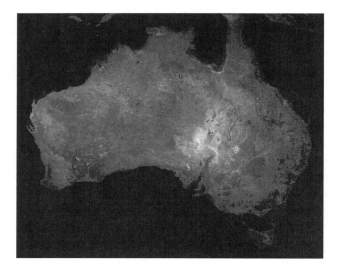

A composed satellite photograph of Australia. The nature of transnational crime in Australia is closely related to Australia's geography and demographics—policing Australian borders is difficult due to its huge maritime jurisdiction, long stretches of sparsely populated coastline, and its small workforce. (Wikimedia)

a significant degree of underreporting confounds attempts to estimate the level of the problem.

People smugglers bring into Australia paying customers, generally refugees from conflict-prone areas, in often dilapidated boats. By global standards, the number of unauthorized arrivals by sea is low. However, people smuggling has stimulated much debate in Australia, sparked by both Australia's mandatory detention processes and several instances in which these boats sank. People smugglers are generally not Australian citizens, so apprehending and prosecuting offenders can be difficult.

The trafficking of Australian flora and fauna is also significant. Abalone and shark fins are illegally extracted and smuggled to lucrative produce markets in China and Japan. High-value birds (such as parrots) and reptiles are exported in small shipments to collectors in the West, often accompanied by forged papers that suggest they are captive-bred. The risk of detection is low, but the profits are high; rare cockatoos, for example, can fetch up to US$30,000 per pair.

Responses to Transnational Crime

Australia is a party to the majority of international conventions relating to transnational crime, including the UN Convention Against Transnational Organized Crime (UNTOC), the UNTOC protocols on human trafficking and people smuggling, the UN Convention Against Illicit Traffic in Narcotic Drugs and Psychotropic Substances, the UN Convention Against Corruption, and the Convention on International Trade in Endangered Species of Wild Fauna and Flora (CITES). It is also a member of the Financial Action Task Force on Money Laundering. To implement these agreements, Australia has enacted large amounts of legislation. For example, Australia's Criminal Code criminalizes slavery, sexual servitude and deceptive recruiting, trafficking in persons, and debt bondage, with penal sanctions of 12–25 years for each offense. Legislation does not, of course, guarantee a high conviction rate. Despite a plethora of money-laundering offenses, convictions for money laundering are few. The existence of nine jurisdictions (six states, two territories, and the Commonwealth), each having its own policies, laws, and agencies for dealing with organized crime can hinder efficient enforcement. National institutions such as the Australian Crime Commission,

the national criminal intelligence agency, and AUSTRAC, Australia's financial intelligence unit, facilitate coordination between jurisdictions and with relevant agencies such as the Australian Customs and Border Protection Service.

Australia also strives to reduce its exposure to transnational crime by building capacity and improving cooperation on law-enforcement responses in the region. The Australian Federal Police's International Liaison Officer Network, comprising (in 2010) 85 officers in 30 countries, fosters collaboration and intelligence sharing with host countries' criminal justice agencies. Australia also enters into collaborative agreements and funds regional projects. For example, Australia cofounded and cochairs the Bali Process on People Smuggling, Trafficking in Persons, and Related Transnational Crime, designed to enhance cooperative efforts against people smuggling and trafficking in the region.

Julie Ayling
Australian National University

See also Cocaine; Financial Fraud; Heroin; Human Smuggling; Human Trafficking; Identity Theft; Informal Value Transfer Systems; Investment Crimes; Marijuana or Cannabis; Money Laundering: Methods; Technology; Wildlife Crime

Further Readings

Australian Crime Commission. *Illicit Drug Data Report 2008–09*. http://www.crimecommission.gov.au/publications/illicit-drug-data-report/illicit-drug-data-report-2008-09 (Accessed February 2011).

Australian Crime Commission. *Organised Crime in Australia*. http://www.crimecommission.gov.au/publications/organised-crime-australia/organised-crime-australia-2011-report (Accessed February 2011).

Australian School of Business. "Wildlife Smuggling: Could Legalising Trade Stop a Jumbo-Sized Problem?" *Knowledge@Australian School of Business*, http://knowledge.asb.unsw.edu.au/article.cfm?articleid=1303 (Accessed February 2011).

Choo, Kim-Kwang Raymond. "Cyber Threat Landscape Faced by Financial and Insurance Industry." In *Trends and Issues in Crime and Criminal Justice*, v.408 (2011).

David, Fiona. "Labour Trafficking." In *AIC Reports: Research and Public Policy Series*, v.108 (2010).

U.S. Department of State. "Country Narratives: Australia." In *Trafficking in Persons Report 2010*. Washington, DC: Author, 2010.

B

BIKERS AND MOTORCYCLE GANGS

Outlaw motorcycle gangs have been a constant feature of organized crime in North America. Traditionally, bikers were representative of a very American-style cultural model that emphasized the open road and a flagrant disregard for conventional or mainstream values. The roots of the biker culture can largely be traced to the post–World War II era. In the 1950s, biker culture, as well as the Beat generation, turned away from the traditional sources of male commitment to a mainstream lifestyle. Bikers were predominantly, if not exclusively, male. As a result, they represented the particular features of a particular male, a countercultural reaction to the dominant features of American middle-class existence. As the biker subculture developed, it tended to focus on a rejection of marriage, corporatized work, and mainstream morality. In fact, biker subculture has largely been premised on a rejection of anything considered conventional. The lifestyle itself is based on a proclivity toward a wandering or peripatetic lifestyle with an aversion to being tied to any particular locale. At the same time, bikers have long and established roots in certain towns, cities, and areas. The Hells Angels, for example, were founded in Fontana, California, and continue to have a dominant presence in the area.

In recent times, biker gangs have been able to spread globally while maintaining a uniquely American identity. Motorcycle enthusiasts can be divided between those who are simply interested in pursuing the joys of motorcycle ownership and those who actively engage in criminal activities. The criminal motorcycle gangs often refer to themselves as one-percenters. This brings to mind a comment made by the American Motorcyclist Association (AMA) in which it was claimed that 99 percent of motorcyclists were law-abiding citizens, implying that the remaining 1 percent were involved in criminal enterprises. Outlaw biker gangs have tended to focus on drug trafficking, prostitution, and arms dealing. Over time, these gangs have become more capable of cooperation and effective divisions of labor. However, rivalries and "wars" are still a prevalent feature of the biker gang lifestyle. In Quebec, Canada, for example, a long war between the Hells Angels and other gangs caused more than 150 murders over a two-decade period. The federal government has brought proceedings against the Hells Angels, Pagans, Outlaws MC, and Bandidos based on the Racketeer Influenced and Corrupt Organizations (RICO) Act. These outlaw biker gangs have come to dominate the sale and trafficking of methamphetamines and "crystal meth." They continue to be a threat to law enforcement and are able to renew and revive their membership with fresh recruits.

Criminal motorcycle gangs often refer to themselves as one-percenters, in reference to a statement by the American Motorcyclist Association that claimed that 99 percent of motorcyclists were law-abiding citizens, implying that the other 1 percent were involved in criminal activities. (Photos.com)

Features of Membership

Outlaw biker gangs have a tendency to be racially homogeneous. For example, gangs such as the Bandidos and the Mongols were created as a way for Latinos to form their own organizations outside the exclusive membership practiced by the more traditional clubs. Members largely come from working-class backgrounds. Occasionally, professionals such as doctors and lawyers may become members. This is most likely the case because such members can provide vital services to a clandestine criminal enterprise. The one-percenters are almost exclusively male and tend to exclude women from any important role in the organization. Occasionally, a member's "old lady" can attain a position of limited respect and authority. However, by and large women are often seen as property and are subject to gang rape and severe forms of punishment if they upset the male members. Women are often seen as "collective property" and are sexually passed around. Outlaw biker clubs do not have a set age cohort in terms of membership. Members usually join in their early 20s and many continue

to retain their membership well into their 50s and 60s. There is a clear hierarchy based on experience, status, and power or authority. However, these organizations do have a prevalent democratic orientation in that all members have some type of say in how the organization is run. Members have some rights combined with a clear set of responsibilities to the organization. Certain bylaws clearly lay out what an individual must do to become a member. According to the Hells Angels' bylaws, as described by Frank Reynolds, prospective members must own a motorcycle and they must be 21 years of age. A member must be voted in, and if only two members refuse, he will be denied entry. Furthermore, as James Francis Quinn notes, members are clearly expected to put "club affairs" before any type of personal obligation. If a member has a full-time job, for example, this would be considered as a possible source of interference with club dictates. As a result, members are expected to be open to criminal activities. To leave an outlaw biker gang can often be difficult and can result in severe punishment or even death. Membership is strongly centered on a perceived sense of loyalty between bikers and their organization. As a result, a good club member will never want for food, housing, alcohol, drugs, and bike parts. Most potential members must have a sponsor who is in good standing. This individual will bear responsibility for the conduct of the potential member. When sponsorship has occurred, the potential member attains prospective status. He will be treated with a certain distance, especially with regard to the inner workings of the criminal organization, and will have to go through a process of hazing. Next, the new member enters into a probationary phase. New protocols and secrets are revealed to the individual, which introduce him to "dangerous types of knowledge" that could pose a problem if he decides to leave the organization. He will perform the more menial tasks of the organization and will be expected to wait for up to two years for full membership. Finally, the potential member will have to go through an initiation ceremony. These ceremonies are often kept very secret but may involve such rituals as the wearing of new badges or symbols as well as an initiatory "symbolic fight" with the chapter enforcer or "sergeant-at-arms." Once accepted, the new member will don distinctive emblems and badges meant to express his status and place within the organization. Moving up in the organization is often based on criminal entrepreneurial skill, loyalty, and, in some cases, the ability to fight and commit violence with ease.

Paul Brienza
York University

See also Mega-Trials; United Nations: Typologies of Criminal Structures

Further Readings

Barker, Tom. "One Percent Bikers Clubs: A Description." *Trends in Organized Crime*, v.9/1 (2005).

Finlay, Tom and Catherine J. Matthews. *Motorcycle Gangs: A Literature Search of Law Enforcement, Academic and Popular Sources: With a Chronology of Canadian Print News Coverage*. Toronto, ON: University of Toronto, Centre of Criminology, 1996.

Marsden, William and Julian Sher. *Angels of Death: Inside the Bikers' Global Crime Empire*. London: Hodder & Stoughton 2006.

Quinn, James Francis. *Outlaw Motorcycle Clubs: A Sociological Analysis*. Master's thesis. University of Miami, Coral Gables, FL, 1983.

Reynolds, Frank. *Freewheelin' Frank*. London: New English Library, 1967.

BIOPIRACY

Biopiracy is the stealing of biological materials or traditional knowledge. Such theft creates conflict between transnational corporations and indigenous people who are unable to challenge the rich companies' claims of ownership or the powerful intellectual property regimes. The source of the biological materials is the biological diversity, or biodiversity, located predominantly within the territories of developing nations in the South, which could benefit both economically and socially from this vast resource. Generations of indigenous people have been relying on and cultivating the properties of many plant and animal species contained within these diverse ecosystems for food and medicine. Both the species making up the diversity and the accumulated knowledge about them, however, have remained somewhat unknown to the West. Whereas historically it has been argued that biodiversity is part of the larger global commons—a resource shared by all, especially those living in proximity to it—biotechnology companies have altered the value of this diversity

by making it the material basis for new corporate endeavors where they claim ownership of their new "discoveries."

Biopiracy results in the unauthorized commercial use of these biological resources. Transnational biotechnology corporations, usually based in the West, seek out plants (or other natural resources) in these environmentally diverse areas and claim ownership and control over seeds, plants, and their properties through legal systems in their home countries. In addition to the pirating of the plant materials, biopiracy can be the theft of the traditional knowledge of indigenous people in regard to these materials. This stolen knowledge leads to the patenting and therefore property rights of so-called inventions or even of commercially valuable genes. Biopiracy and the resulting patents take from the South the accumulated indigenous knowledge about the environment and turn that into a profit for companies in the North without compensating those in the South or sharing the profits with those from whom the information was obtained. This sort of exploitation is not new and has been argued to be an extension of colonial expropriation; the conquering empire has been replaced by the biotech firm.

One example of biopiracy out of the many is described by John Vidal and comes from the actions of the "biopirate" Dr. Conrad Gorinsky. Gorinsky is an ethnobotanist who has traveled the world in search of plant materials with commercial potential. In one instance, he successfully obtained a patent in the United States for a chemical protein found within the greenheart tree, found in the South American country of Guyana. Gorinsky in his patent application claimed that the protein was useful in the prevention and suppression of fever with further possible uses in the treatment of malaria, cancer, and perhaps even acquired immune deficiency syndrome (AIDS). The Amazonian people with whom Gorinsky spent his time in Guyana, the Wapishana tribe, showed Gorinsky how they used derivatives from the greenheart tree to stop hemorrhaging, prevent infections, and perform as a contraceptive. Gorinsky's "invention" or "discovery," then, is based on the local resources and knowledge of these indigenous people. Understandably, the Wapishana are against the patenting of their natural resources and traditional wisdom in the United States for the profit of one scientist and a transnational corporation.

As is evident, biopiracy, or bioprospecting as supporters call it, is part of the larger discussion surrounding free trade and globalization. Whereas opponents of biopiracy argue that the actions of these transnational companies constitute theft and exploitation of Third World knowledge and resources, advocates of bioprospecting see the "discovery" and wide distribution of products made from these materials as integral to competition in the global market. This leads to the knowledge stemming from generations of indigenous people's relationship with their surroundings being monopolized and owned by transnational corporations.

As stated above, the properties of plants from which Western corporations reap profits have been known to the local people where these plants have originated and where they have been used for possibly thousands of years. Historically, these plants have been freely traded between the farmers and villagers of the region. With corporate ownership comes the loss of control for the indigenous communities over their own natural resources. The cost to the corporation for obtaining highly profitable products is minimal, yet the local people lose a much-needed source of income because the patent holder is entitled to all profits arising from the new product. Additionally, modern synthesis of chemical compounds removes the need for the traditional cultivation of the plants with these chemicals. This practice could have been undertaken by indigenous communities to earn money. Through international trade systems, such as the World Trade Organization and international property laws, transnational corporations have commoditized nature and threatened the basic rights of indigenous people and their relationship to their environment by challenging their sovereignty. What was once indigenous knowledge has become, through biopiracy, Western intellectual property.

Intellectual property regimes do not recognize indigenous or non-Western knowledge systems. Plants whose properties have been cultivated by indigenous people for generations are taken from these countries by Western transnational corporations without permission; then, after minimal alterations in a laboratory, these companies receive patents for their inventions based on the plants' compounds and other properties. Pirated products protected by intellectual property statutes provide evidence that indigenous knowledge is unvalued and can be seen as a violation of indigenous people's rights.

Biopiracy is a transnational intersection where differing cultural beliefs pertaining to knowledge and property, including ownership and privatization of the environment, come into conflict. Economic interests and powerful Western legal and trade systems are pitted against thousands of years of indigenous knowledge of the plants and animals in their environment and the belief that nature is a global commons. As the economy shifts from the current sole reliance on fossil fuels and extracted natural resources toward increased utilization of biological and genetic materials, biopiracy is bound to increase in frequency and spark more conflicts.

Tanya Wyatt
Northumbria University

See also Pharmaceuticals; South America

Further Readings

Mgbeoji, I. *Global Biopiracy: Patents, Plants and Indigenous Knowledge.* Vancouver: University of British Columbia Press, 2006.

Shiva, V. *Biopiracy.* Boston: South End Press, 1999.

South, N. "The 'Corporate Colonisation of Nature': Bio-Prospecting, Bio-Piracy and the Development of Green Criminology." In *Issues in Green Criminology: Confronting Harms Against Environments, Humanity and Other Animals*, by P. Bierne and N. South. Cullompton, UK: Willan, 2007.

Vidal, J. "Biopirates Who Seek the Greatest Prizes." *The Guardian* (November 15, 2000).

White, R. *Crimes Against Nature: Environmental Criminology and Ecological Justice.* Cullompton, UK: Willan, 2009.

BLACK MARKET PESO EXCHANGE

Today, it is estimated that in excess of US$14 trillion in deposited funds are held in offshore financial institutions, such as Panama, Luxembourg, and other offshore tax havens with reputations for being popular banking centers. The original sources for these funds have been laundered through various mechanized schemes. This is exacerbated by the fact that the world has evolved into a electronically connected transnational global network consisting of business and social links equivalent to a vastly unregulated electronic underground.

In the 1980s, The Black Market Peso Exchange was developed in Colombia as a result of the illicit drug trade, as a way to conceal monies and avoid detection by government officials. The Black Market Peso Exchange offers a full range of economic opportunities to engage in a variety of corrupt business practices and has the potential to benefit and undermine private and public sectors while arguably creating a series of financial opportunities. Today, the Black Market Peso Exchange has evolved into a global electronic underground full of moneymaking opportunities. As a result of the success of the Black Market Peso Exchange system, the scheme is a widely accepted practice found in other regions of the world.

Digital masked bandits and sophisticated money launderers lurk in cyberspace as the new electronic predators hiding behind all sorts of legitimate and illegitimate businesses. The entrepreneurial spirit of these actors offers its willing participants unlimited opportunities to engage in many diverse and complex financial and commercial schemes. Some of these schemes include concealment, omission, and misrepresentation combined with the intent to defraud individuals or to facilitate business ventures for individuals, corporations, and governments by promoting an organized and systematic schema of false information.

These savvy and educated global facilitators offer a real challenge for others to understand their world. To enter the Black Market Peso Exchange game, government and private-sector officials need to develop knowledge and special skill sets for the 21st century in order to understand these complex schemes. This recommendation would include designing ways to intercede at the various axes' choke points of these monetary and commercial pathways, developing enforcement tools and exchanging information among interested officials.

Simply speaking, the Black Market Peso Exchange is commonly referred to as a method to transfer and conceal valuable global commerce through a series of complex laundering schemes. The Black Market Peso Exchange includes the Informal Funds Transfer Systems (IFTSs) and the Informal Value Transfer Methods (IVTMs) models. Generally speaking, these methods both support the overall Black Market Peso Exchange system by providing additional means to conceal money and trade finance schemes to defraud. Today, the sophisticated transnational criminals who deal in diverse business crimes include all kinds of smugglers, commodity traffickers, and copycat pirates, to name a few.

The Black Market Peso Exchange, developed in Colombia in the 1980s, is a method of transferring and concealing valuable global commerce through a series of complex money laundering schemes. (Photos.com)

Definitions and Methods

Since ancient times, underground networks of people developed clever schemes to conceal and avoid disclosing sources of income and revenue to government officials. The Black Market Peso Exchange is reported to have its developmental roots in Colombia and was formed to conceal illegal funds tied to clandestine drug smuggling. The enormous amounts of cash generated from the illegal drug business presented an economic problem: how to conceal and reinvest (cleanse or launder) those proceeds without detection. This would require assistance from a variety of facilitators, including bankers and government officials. Ancillary to this is the question of how much these activities distort official economic statistics, since the underground economy is left out of them. Overall, economists would tend to agree that economic inequality and monopoly power and inadequate information tend to cause market failure.

Today, aided by the use of technology, the modern Black Market Peso Exchange enterprise is a popular method of transferring funds and assets internationally to avoid detection and evade the payment of commerce trade duties and taxes and, importantly, of providing investment capital to purchase high-demand (tariff-cost-prohibitive) U.S. goods to import and sell in Latin American markets. However, one of the key concerns is that, by following the money trail, authorities could uncover serious violations of the law and link those activities to organized criminal cartels. The old notion of the participant is that tax avoidance and repayment plans can be far less life-changing events than a conviction and incarceration linked to other serious offenses. However, U.S. laws on money laundering and other serious crimes today carry severe penalties.

The Black Market Peso schematic generally involves proceeds from an illegal or legal enterprise that are deposited into a friendly financial institution. The funds are then moved around to conceal their original bank depositor, and then, once cleansed, investment brokers offer these funds (investment capital) to purchase commerce. The targeted commerce is then purchased, transferred to various Latin American ports of entry, and then ultimately sold to the Latin American consumer via a network of brokers and facilitators, who often are corrupt. As noted previously, in the overall scheme, the reasons for concealment could include tax avoidance (linked to illegal activity), concealing proceeds from creditors, and establishing "untraceable funds" for use later on.

The Black Market Peso Exchange funds may be held in foreign investment accounts and then dispersed and moved around to launder and/or conceal and cleanse the original source. In the process, corrupt officials and unregulated government oversight programs are secured to assist in the movement and concealment methods. After the funds are determined to have been sufficiently laundered through the institutional transfers, the foreign source offers the funds as capital to investors, who are generally commodity importers. From this point on, the shadowy network becomes more complex, and following the various actors into the international commerce landscape becomes more difficult. These complexities make the scheme popular, since they lessen the potential for detection by authorities.

The original investment monies are then used by those importers to purchase and pay for various products using the currency of the host country's financial institutions—in this example, the peso. The money is repaid in the same currency, the peso. The commodities are then shipped to the Caribbean or another location in the Americas and end up being smuggled into the country of choice by the importer to evade the payment of duty and related taxes and applicable exchange tariffs.

The Black Market Peso broker earns a fee-based commission on each aspect of the laundering process. The monies are used to purchase U.S. goods, and those are considered instrumentalities of the illegal money laundering scheme. In essence, the investor becomes a principal coconspirator to criminal conduct.

Probable Criminal Violations Under U.S. Law

During a Black Market Peso Exchange scheme, a number of key U.S. federal laws are potentially violated in U.S. Code Title 18 (crimes and criminal procedure), including Sections 371 (conspiracy to commit an offense or to defraud the United States), 1000 (false statements or entries generally), 4 (misprision of a felony), 1956 (laundering of monetary instruments), 1341 (frauds and swindles), 1342 (fictitious name or address), 1951–1968 (racketeering, in violation of the Racketeer Influenced Corrupt Practices Act violations), as well as Title 15, Section 78 (based on the Foreign Corrupt Practices Act) and Title 26 (federal criminal tax violations).

An example would include the transnational criminal drug cartels, with partnerships between Colombia and Panama. In the early 1980s, the Medellín Cartel, composed of Carlos Escobar, Carlos Lehder, and the Ochoa brothers, faced the daunting task of having to move U.S. dollars from the United States to Colombia without attracting attention from U.S. and Colombian authorities. To solve their problem, they turned to the *casas de cambio* (exchange houses), a black market, largely unregulated system of currency exchange in Colombia (Latin America). The Colombian money brokers, acting as full-service bankers, would use their electronic monetary system and links to international entities as fronts to launder the drug traffickers' dollars. The scheme became a large part of the Black Market Peso Exchange.

The Colombian money brokers would advertise that they had dollars available for the purchase of U.S. products. Colombian importers, businesses, and private individuals would pay for their goods in pesos in Colombia, and the peso brokers would place purchase orders on their behalf in the United States. The system would appeal to the importers because, in addition to obtaining access to dollars at favorable exchange rates, they would evade government controls and payment of import tariffs. The drug traffickers would receive their money untainted by its origin in the drug trade, and the peso brokers would derive a hefty commission for their role in the scheme.

U.S. and Colombian authorities began to assert greater controls over the purchase of U.S. products as they became cognizant of the Black Market Peso Exchange scheme. To get around these controls, drug lords developed an elaborate system composed of legal and business entities in multiple countries.

The Republic of Panama and its de facto leader, former strongman General Manuel Antonio Noriega, became key elements in the scheme. The strong business and political ties between the United States and Panama made the use of Panama propitious for this purpose. However, most significant was the fact that Panama's leader, General Noriega, had facilitated the use of Panama for evasion of U.S. economic embargos. Among others, General Noriega had given the Cuban government, the Farabundo Martí National Liberation Front of El Salvador, and the Sandinistas of Nicaragua access to the U.S. economic system. Actually, in Panama under its leader General Noriega, Colombian drug traffickers found an ideal vehicle and a natural ally for their money-laundering scheme.

Summary

This scheme produces more opportunities for corruption, provides for lower-cost investment capital, encourages the supply in commodity diversion, skews international commerce and trade data, and impacts a series of other macro- and microeconomic opportunities, including having a negative impact on wholesale distribution of U.S. goods and loss of American jobs.

The Black Market Peso Exchange scheme has grown considerably since the early days and is now a much larger and more intricate global enterprise. In the 2010 criminal investigation of the Angel Toy Company in Los Angeles, California, the method of concealment of laundered-structured proceeds and investment capital was linked to Chinese businessmen operating in concert with Colombia and Mexican counterparts under the auspices of the Black Market Peso Exchange model.

Rande W. Matteson
Saint Leo University
Juan R. Rivera
Central Intelligence Retiree Association
Charles L. Fisk Jr.
Saint Leo University

See also Cigarette Smuggling; Informal Value Transfer Systems; Money Laundering: Targeting Criminal Proceeds; Underground Banking Regulations

Further Readings

Passas, N. "The Genesis of the BCCI Scandal." *Journal of Law and Society*, v.23/1 (1996).
Passas, N. "The Mirror of Global Evils: A Review Essay on the BCCI Affair." *Justice Quarterly*, v.12/2 (1995).
Passas, N. "Structural Sources of International Crime: Policy Lessons From the BCCI Affair." *Crime, Law and Social Change*, v.20/4 (1993).
Richards, J. *Transnational Criminal Organizations, Cybercrime and Money Laundering: A Guide for Law Enforcement Officers, Auditors and Financial Investigators*. Boca Raton, FL: CRC Press, 1999.

Bribery and Graft

Bribery and graft are both closely linked with corruption and are punishable as felonies. They have increasingly become the object of national and international anticorruption laws that have expanded their definitions to include interference not only with the judicial process (judiciary, jurors, witnesses, and laypersons) but also with public employees and some classes of private and commercial transactions. Bribery is now defined as any promise or undertaking to give money, goods, property, advantage, privilege, or emolument with a corrupt intent to induce or to influence the actions, votes, or opinions of persons in any public or official capacity. Bribery can also be a gift, not necessarily of pecuniary value, bestowed to influence the conduct of the receiver. Graft has been defined as the fraudulent obtaining of public money or any other undue advantage of a public position or a position of trust for personal gain.

A consensus has grown around the idea of a direct link between the rule of law that prohibits the misuse of public office for private gain and the integrity of the state and development. In most legislation the term *corruption* is technically restricted to those practices by state officials (and some private transactions) that deviate from or undermine the rule of law by substituting personal goals for the goals and rules of the organization; in such cases, the integrity of governing institutions is broken, and bribery and graft become widespread and will directly hamper development. The gradual assertion of a broader definition of corruption as drawing on moral criteria but having a direct impact on development has caused a drastic change in the regulation of investments within the financial landscapes of global economies. Until the 1990s, many companies used to factor in bribery in some international transactions when engaging in business partnerships in some geographic areas but found themselves at risk of violating anticorruption laws in their own countries.

Since 1975, following the public disclosure of the "Lockheed model" (according to which corporate officers paid bribes to government officials overseas), the United States started to play a central role in the fight against bribery and graft. Investigations of companies' accounts brought striking evidence of the pervasive violation of American laws by American companies that paid bribes abroad to circumvent disadvantages they would otherwise sustain when adhering to their home country's regulations. This prompted a massive campaign by the American government for multilateral cooperation against bribery and graft, aiming at two principal changes: the criminalization of bribes of foreign officials and the elimination of a bribery tax deduction that some other governments seemed to have adopted. It took almost two decades to see tangible results. The first attempts to reach international consensus at the level of the United Nations (UN) as well as with the Organisation for Economic Co-operation and Development (OECD) were unsuccessful because of the difficulties in bridging the differences among the various countries' legal systems. However, in 1996 the OECD Council approved the recommendation to eliminate tax deductibility, and in 1998 it was agreed that all member states would act for the criminalization of bribery of foreign officers.

After much negotiation led by the United States, the fight against corruption was included within the global framework of good governance, to be achieved through programs aiming at transparency in public management and the strengthening of tax laws and customs. On November 21, 1997, the Convention on Combating Bribery of Foreign Public Officials in International Business Transactions defined bribery as the act to "offer, promise or give any undue pecuniary or other advantage, whether directly or through intermediaries, to a foreign

Bribery itself was defined by the UN Global Compact Leaders Summit as "any kind of advantage granted to or coming from any person as inducement to do something illegal, dishonest, or constituting a breach of trust in the conduct of the enterprise's business." (Photos.com)

public official, for that official or for a third party, in order that the official act or refrain from acting in relation to the performance of official duties, in order to obtain or retain business or other improper advantage in the conduct of international business" (Article 1). The convention clearly made it an offense for citizens of signatory countries to bribe foreign officials, thereby targeting bribery instead of graft.

As a result of the United States' massive strategy, the OECD recommendations were reiterated and supported at the G7 countries meeting in 1996. As a consequence, in 1997, the resolution on Action Against Corruption was adopted by the UN almost at the same time as the Framework Convention Against Corruption signed by the European Union. Until that time, however, the stress was put on the bribe giver. The Manila Declaration on the Prevention and Control of Transnational Crime (1998) listed bribery and graft in international commercial transactions as among the factors that undermine democracy, morality, and ultimately social, economic, and political development.

The fight against pervasive graft has often stemmed from the breakdown of state-owned banks of certain countries that have given loans and undue benefits to political elites without adequate security. In the years preceding the massive student protests in the wake of the financial crisis in Indonesia, the World Bank reported 20–30 percent graft in a project financed by the state bank. In 1998, the International Monetary Fund and the World Bank intervened to refinance the bank system, but President Suharto was urged to step down because of charges of nepotism and graft. On June 24, 2004, the UN Global Compact Leaders Summit adopted the 10th principle in the areas of human rights, labor, the environment, and anticorruption that enjoys universal consensus: "Businesses should work against corruption in all its forms, including extortion and bribery." The purpose of this 10th principle was to include the private sector in the fight against corruption and thereby elicit the cooperation of private companies and governments in the fight against corruption, as broadly defined by Transparency International as "the abuse of entrusted power for private gains." Hence the definition of bribery itself was broadened to include any kind of advantage granted to or coming from any person as inducement to do something illegal, dishonest, or constituting a breach of trust in the conduct of the enterprise's business. Bribery and graft ceased to be confined to the state sector and thus became targets not only of state legislation but also of corporate policies within organizations and businesses operations. Moreover, private implementation of anticorruption policies is controlled through regular reports and consultation with industry peers.

The progressive shift from the public sector moved the definition of bribery with a stress on the act of receiving (graft) to an encompass a broad definition of bribery within the global framework of the anticorruption fight for better governance and created a corresponding shift in trade practices. After the adoption of international anticorruption laws worldwide, bribery and graft are fought against irrespective of their actual impact on the success of the trade. Furthermore, the engagement in anticorruption policies became valuable in itself for both the public and the private sectors.

However, investing companies still find it difficult to observe the requirements of the bribery laws of their countries of residence when doing business in countries whose legislation is less strict. The main obstacle to the successful implementation of anticorruption legislation has been the definition of bribe and graft as involving only money or favors and other benefits. Hence there is a need for a balance between a strict approach, likely to unduly criminalize a wide range of legislative and executive agreements, and a restrictive approach, in which the corrupt purpose of the unlawful transaction must be proved.

The World Bank plays a central role in the implementation of anticorruption policies in the private sector within the conceptual framework that sees the fight against corruption as strictly linked with good governance aiming at the alleviation of poverty. The Partnering Against Corruption Forum went as far as to place the private sector in the position of guiding governments and international organizations in the fight against bribery and graft. Several private initiatives have been adopted to locate, monitor, and report companies and individuals demanding bribes. BRIBEline uses an online secure system of anonymous reporting on a multilingual Website that compiles data on who is demanding bribes, where are bribes demanded, and under what circumstances.

However, sociological studies on corruption that, significantly, have expanded considerably since the 1990s, point out, on one hand, that bribery and graft are not absolute indicators of a lack of development and, on the other, that the rule of law has itself been used to legitimate plunder. These studies have often argued for the need to contextualize the practices of bribery and graft in order to avoid the failure of anticorruption policies drafted on universalistic assumptions. The reasons for this sudden sociolegal interest in the local modalities of bribery and graft are explained by the evolution of these concepts within the post-1990s global legal framework. Funding agencies have invested in applied research to implement anticorruption policies whose conceptual core is the need for strong states through good governance that is achieved by fighting corruption.

Besides conventional trends upholding global anticorruption policies, it has also been argued that graft and bribery serve at times as critical elements of informal institutions of state control. Contrary to the conventional view, such informal institutions of the state can complement, rather than undermine, the formal institutions for securing compliance with political objectives. In particular, graft, combined with systematic surveillance, blackmail, and the selective enforcement of laws, is a means that can be employed by political leaders to exert control over their subordinates and to expand their authority into areas where its exercise is formally prohibited.

In certain circumstances, pervasive graft may signify not the breakdown of the state but instead the existence of an alternative state acting alongside or behind the façade of formal legal institutions. The global consensus on anticorruption policies headed by Transparency International and the World Bank was criticized for its orientalist undertones—targeting the South and the East as the main areas for the global fight against corruption. Recent sociolegal studies have focused on the modalities of anticorruption policies and have pointed out that this global action by multinational corporations and international organizations is not necessarily more transparent to citizens and consumers. Hence, some have postulated that the Western initiatives to identify bribery and graft as punishable crimes undergirds an imperialistic ideology that imposes the rule of law by so-called democratic institutions as a façade that legitimizes plunder and ultimately hampers economic progress.

Livia Holden
Lahore University of Management Sciences

See also Anticorruption Legislation; Corporate Influence Peddling; Corporate Liability; Corruption; Failed States; Impact of Transnational Crime; Influence and Position; Informal Value Transfer Systems; Measuring Transnational Crime; Money Laundering: History; Money Laundering: Methods; Money Laundering: Targeting Criminal Proceeds; Money Laundering: Vulnerable Commodities and Services; Political Influence Peddling; Sanctions and Blacklisting; South Asia; Tax Evasion; World Bank

Further Readings

Gruetzner, Thomas, Ulf Hommel, and Klaus Moosmayer, eds. *Anti-Bribery Risk Assessment: A Systemic Overview of 151 Countries*. Portland, OR: Hart, 2011.

Haller, Dieter and Chris Shore, eds. *Corruption: Anthropological Perspectives*. London: Pluto Press, 2005.

Mattei, Ugo and Laura Nader. *Plunder When the Rule of Law Is Illegal*. Malden, MA: Blackwell, 2008.

Nuijten, Monique and Gerhard Anders, eds. *Anthropology of Corruption and the Secrets of Law*. Aldershot, UK: Ashgate, 2007.

C

Capital Flight

The term *capital flight* generally refers to the movement of large amounts of capital out of a country. This phenomenon sometimes occurs as a result or in anticipation of an economic shock such as rapid currency devaluation or sovereign default. Investors may become fearful of perceived country-specific risks to their assets (such as political instability, sovereign debt burden, or nationalization of private industry), and consequently they move their securities or cash out of that country in search of higher returns on their investments elsewhere. When it is intended that the money disappear from financial records in the country of origin, or when the entity making the cross-border transfer of funds does not properly record the transaction on its books, capital flight is usually illegal. This entry focuses primarily on the issue of illegal capital flight.

Illegal capital flight takes place when proceeds of economic activity—whether legally or illegally obtained—move across national borders in violation of law. This type of activity is also sometimes referred to as "illicit financial flows" and can take the form of tax evasion, embezzlement of public funds, or money laundering. For example, a corrupt government official who receives a bribe for a government contract, license, or other benefit may seek to move the bribe money abroad in order to evade prosecution or detection in his home country. There are two primary mechanisms through which illegal capital flight takes place: (1) use of the international banking system to transfer money across borders and (2) trade misinvoicing, or the intentional misreporting of financial trade data, commonly in order to overstate imports and understate exports. Earnings on illegal flight capital—for example, interest or appreciation of stock values—often do not return to the country of origin.

The consequences of capital flight can be severe. Particularly in small, developing countries, the rapid movement of capital across borders can disturb normal financial activity and affect interest rates through sudden changes in currency exchange rates. Investors may lose confidence in the financial stability of the reference country and lower their valuations of assets within that country as the value of its currency declines. Capital flight thus can lead to significant erosion of wealth within an affected country.

Challenges involving the availability and reliability of relevant data make it difficult to approximate the full extent of illicit capital flight. Economists use a number of different metrics to do so, including the hot money model, the World Bank residual model, and the trade misinvoicing model. The hot money (narrow) model limits its analysis to the net errors and omissions in a country's external accounts, thereby reflecting unrecorded capital flows in a country's balance of payments. By contrast, hot money 3 is a model that focuses on records of short-term capital flows in the private sector. The World Bank residual model compares a country's capital inflows to its outflows in an attempt to capture unaccounted-for sources of capital. The trade misinvoicing model scrutinizes a country's reported data for imports and exports with a particular partner country, comparing these statistics to the same trade data reported by the partner country. After adjusting for transaction costs such as transportation and insurance, any discrepancies in the reported statistics may reflect over- or underinvoicing, and thus could signal illegal capital movements.

A study conducted in 2008 concluded that illegal capital flight is growing rapidly and steadily and that poor countries are among the most severely affected. The study conservatively estimated that, as of 2006, developing countries were losing about $850 billion to $1 trillion per year to illegal capital flight. It estimated that about half of the global share of illegal capital flight comes from Asia, including a disproportionate share from the People's Republic of China.

Although widely used, the expressions "capital flight" and "flight capital" (the former referring to the phenomenon and the latter to the capital itself) have been criticized as implicitly suggesting that the responsibility for the problem that these phrases identify is entirely the responsibility of the developing countries from which capital is disappearing. Critics suggest that using this terminology improperly deemphasizes the important role that industrialized nations have played in the facilitation of illicit financial flows.

Robert D. Williams
United States Court of Appeals, Fifth Circuit

See also Bribery and Graft; Financial Fraud; Legislation as a Source of Crime; Money Laundering: Targeting Criminal Proceeds; Tax Evasion; World Bank

Further Readings

Ajayi, Simeon Inidayo and Mohsin S. Khan. *External Debt and Capital Flight in Sub-Saharan Africa*. Washington, DC: International Monetary Fund, 2000.

Kar, Dev, Devon Cartwright-Smith, and Ann Hollingshead. *The Absorption of Illicit Financial Flows From Developing Countries: 2002–2006*. Washington, DC: Global Financial Integrity, 2008.

Lessard, Donald R. and John Williamson. *Capital Flight: The Problem and Policy Responses*. Washington, DC: Institute for International Economics, 1987.

McLeod, Darryl. "Capital Flight." *The Concise Encyclopedia of Economics*. http://www.econlib.org/library/Enc1/CapitalFlight.html (Accessed February 2011).

Central America

A significant problem throughout the developing world, transnational crime has long been a concern in Central America in the form of the illicit narcotics trade. In an increasingly globalized economy, transnational crime has been on the rise throughout the region. The production of cocaine takes place principally in South American countries, but much of it is trafficked through Central America en route to the United States or Europe, as is the heroin manufactured in Colombia. Migrant smuggling is also huge business: About 2.7 million Latin Americans, including Central Americans, are illegally brought across the U.S. border every year, for about $7 billion in monies paid to smugglers. Another $20 billion is sent back from the United States in remittances; in Honduras, remittances from expatriates account for a staggering 21 percent of the national gross domestic product (GDP)—nearly as much as industry.

In the 21st century, transnational gang violence has become a serious problem in Central America, where violent crime in general and homicide in particular are both on the rise. Youth gangs called *maras* are active in Guatemala, Honduras, El Salvador, and southern Mexico, with ties to the United States. Some of these *maras* have established elaborate criminal networks, which typically emphasize the narcotics trade and supplement it with migrant smuggling and human trafficking, kidnapping and extortion, arms dealing, robbery, violence against other gangs and against law enforcement, contract killing, and even random acts of violence against the general public. In 2004, the Mara Salvatrucha gang, also known as MS-13, is believed to have met with a representative of Al Qaeda in order to offer their services for sale, and the gang is known to operate an extensive network of drug, arms, and human smuggling. Like other *maras*, MS-13 operates in multiple countries, with customers and suppliers in still more, and consists of loosely connected groups scattered throughout the operating region.

The *maras* have roots in the gangs that formed in Los Angeles and along the U.S.-Mexican border in the 1980s and 1990s, when refugees from Guatemala, Honduras, and El Salvador relocated to poor Los Angeles neighborhoods with a population of mixed nationalities and a strong Mexican street gang presence. MS-13 formed in large part because its Los Angeles rival, M-18 or the 18th Street Gang, allowed only full-blooded Mexican immigrants into the gang—leaving no route to gang power for the Central Americans in the mixed Latino community. MS-13 filled that void while at the same time paying homage to the Mexican Mafia—M is the 13th letter in the alphabet—which is a powerful force in the southern California prison system. Ties to the Mexican Mafia helped MS-13 grow, and in the 21st century the Department of Justice estimates that in the United States alone there are 8,000 to 10,000 members with activities in 33 states. The numbers are much larger in Central America. Clashes with M-18 led MS-13 to develop a reputation for violence quickly; gang members are known for their use of the machete.

As gang members returned home, either voluntarily or as a result of deportation (particularly after the aggressive deportation of illegal immigrants from American prisons beginning in 1996), they established an MS-13 presence in their home countries, and the gang's power expanded. Gang members return from the United States with a more sophisticated understanding of guns, smuggling, and the narcotics trade, as well as connections in the supply chain, and use this knowledge to establish new gangs, culturally connected to the other MS-13 gangs. Many of these gangs have monopolies over the drug trade in their local towns. Over time, MS-13 became as elaborate and widespread a network as an American restaurant franchise, and the model was followed by other gangs.

Central American governments have taken a zero-tolerance approach to the growing problem of *maras*, at the same time being implicated in many of the social problems that encourage the gangs' growth. New policies, popularly supported by voters, allow the police in many Central American countries to arrest young people who fit a particular profile, such as association with convicted gang members, loitering in particular neighborhoods, or possessing gang affiliation tattoos. Critics have argued that these *mano dura* (hard hand), tough-on-crime policies have made the violence worse; the homicide rate in El Salvador, which has the highest per capita rate of murders in Central America, has steadily increased since the adoption of such policies, and in Honduras an MS-13 attack on a passenger bus resulted in 28 civilian fatalities when gang members opened fire on

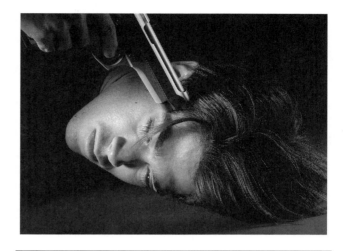

Youth gangs from Guatemala, Honduras, El Salvador, and southern Mexico called *maras* have ties to the United States and have established elaborate criminal networks, primarily dealing in the drug trade. *Maras* are also involved in human trafficking, kidnapping and extortion, contract killing, and random acts of violence. (Photos.com)

the bus with automatic rifles. The attack has been seen as the gang's way of "protesting" Honduras's *mano dura* policies. Key to the significance of the attack, and of the voting public's support of *mano dura* policies, is that the bus was chosen randomly; none of the passengers had any known connection to the gangs or the government.

Transnational gangs like the *maras* and their analogues in southeastern Asia and eastern Europe are sometimes called third-generation gangs, in contrast to the simple (first-generation) street gangs concerned mainly with protecting local turf and the well-connected but still locally focused (second-generation) gangs that operate supply chains across multiple cities. This third generation of gangs thinks globally, not expanding into international business from a domestic base but immersed in international business from the start. Transnational gangs are not simply gangs that enjoy connections to international cartels, such as MS-13 when it first started; they are international in their own right. Violence and bribery are tools they use to undermine weak states, and the line between criminal activity and insurgency can sometimes be blurred. MS-13's meeting with Al Qaeda, for instance, and its attack on the passengers in Honduras make the gang sound like a terrorist organization, but despite the means, the motive remains profit. Political agendas are often nonexistent or focused only on expressing displeasure with policies that make the criminal work more difficult. The problem is at its worst in Central America because the governments there are weaker than those in North and South America and because without the domestic drug production such as is found in South America, the heroin and cocaine cartels were not as thoroughly entrenched in Central American crime and government. Weak local governments have made it easy for the *maras* to dominate entire towns or suburbs, in which they are the most powerful, wealthiest, and best-armed organization. The Latin American maxim *plata o plomo*—cash (silver) or bullets, referring to the two ways of dealing with government officials—is older than the *maras* but is one to which they adhere. The threat of violence and the *maras*' violent reputation make bribery easier and easily rationalized by officials, whether they are working in a small town where they are effectively powerless to stop the gangs anyway, or they are working in a large city where they are cogs in an already corrupt system. The extent of corruption by the *maras* is always unclear; every scandal seems to confirm the worst suspicions. Rumors claim that in some countries entire ministries are "owned" by the gangs, and more stable states might actually be easier to corrupt: In Brazil, the *mara*-like gang called the PCC has sent many of its members with clean records to take civil service exams, placing gang members throughout the government in order to influence and inform on it.

Transnational gangs benefit from the same global arms trade as political insurgents and have exploited globalization's softening of national borders. Many of the *maras*, and all of the largest ones, are extremely well organized despite the looseness of their connections. A top tier of leaders overseeing at the transnational level direct the leaders at the national and regional levels, and individual gang members are typically tasked with specific duties such as recruiting, arms procurement, enforcement, intelligence, and even propaganda. Roles potential gang members can fill range from a young teenage lookout to a prostitute gathering intelligence (even if she is in the employ of some other criminal organization) to ex-cons, mercenaries, and former soldiers used as muscle. Some *maras* even have legal, surveillance, and business divisions, the latter of which manages the gangs' investments and money

laundering. Central American gangs are highly tech-savvy, coordinating assassinations by cell phone and text message; using the Internet for recruiting, organizing, research, and propaganda; and keeping imprisoned members in the loop by e-mail and telephone.

Some argue that the violence of the *maras* is unprecedented in character. Rivals are not just killed; they are in some cases tortured, beheaded, or burned to death. MS-13 has left decapitated bodies in the street as a warning. The violence is not so much random as it is indifferent to the sanctity of life; that is, the media may often characterize attacks such as that on the bus in Honduras as random in the sense that the passengers did nothing to provoke the attack. However, the attack had the definite, nonrandom purpose of demonstrating the power and ferocity of MS-13; the appearance of randomness stems from the gang's indifference to the identities of those who needed to die for that message to be conveyed. While the Mafia in the United States has long been associated with symbolic acts of violence, it has also made a point of keeping most of its murders quiet; no such attempt seems to be made by the *maras*, which at times almost seem as though they are in competition to see who can be the wildest. However, organization and level-headedness are still at the heart of the network: In El Salvador and Guatemala, gangs have established free zones where the local authorities have been intimidated to such an extent that they simply are no longer present; in these zones, drug and arms sales can be conducted in the open and "taxes" are collected through extortion. There are strong parallels between the *maras*' free zones and the liberated zones of the politically motivated insurgents of the 1970s—just as in the 1970s many saw in those insurgents parallels to gangs and thugs.

Combating transnational gangs has required the cooperation of multiple agencies in Central America and North America, including a multiagency task force in the United States first formed by the Federal Bureau of Investigation in response to the expansion of MS-13 out of California.

Bill Kte'pi
Independent Scholar

See also Adjudicating International Crimes; Conventions, Agreements, and Regulations; Drug Trade: Source, Destination, and Transit Countries; Globalization; South America

Further Readings

Liddick, Donald. *The Global Underworld: Transnational Crime and the United States.* Westport, CT: Praeger, 2004.

Reichel, Philip, ed. *Handbook of Transnational Crime and Justice.* Thousand Oaks, CA: Sage, 2005.

Shanty, Frank and Patit Paban Mishra. *Organized Crime: From Trafficking to Terrorism.* Santa Barbara, CA: ABC-CLIO, 2008.

CENTRALIZATION

This entry seeks to examine the concept of centralization as it applies to transnational crime. As a broad category, centralization encompasses a wide range of issues that relate both to the nature of crime itself and to the various state and nonstate reactions to crime. Centralization occurs in two main guises. First, criminal organizations develop global networks that allow them to move illegal goods across borders. This increases the profitability of the various enterprises and extends their influence beyond the traditional borders of the nation-state. As a result, the local street gang is no longer purely local but is tied into an international set of illegal trade initiatives. Second, state and nonstate actors have had to respond to these new criminal enterprises across local national boundaries. Nonstate actors, such as Interpol, have emerged as active responses to borderless criminal activities. In addition, the rise of greater arenas of jurisdiction for the International Criminal Court and the prosecution of war crimes has created a new zone of interstate criminal law enforcement.

Some of the earliest reflections on crime in modern society can be traced to the work of the Chicago School. Its importance cannot be underestimated in the general history of criminology, for the Chicago School established many of the conceptual and research parameters that are still in use today. As a result, it is important to explore the general features of this work and determine how it might have a significant influence on the concept of centralization. Frederic Thrasher built upon the ideas of Robert E. Park, Ernest Burgess, and others, creating a framework for understanding the urban phenomenon of crime. Thrasher's particular focus was the "street gang." Park and Burgess had argued that the urban environment presented social researchers with a new human ecology. This new ecology was bound to have an inestimable effect on how social relations were formed. The city, for example, was characterized by a general social anonymity and distance. At the same time, the local site became ever more important in determining the formation of modern problems. Thrasher, like his Chicago School associates, argued that the urban spaces of a city were crucial. His analysis focused on the formation and significance of the local street gang as a natural part of the urban ecology. Suffering from social anonymity and distance combined with boredom and a lack of parental guidance, young men tended to drift into a life of deviance and eventual criminality. They were largely of working-class and immigrant backgrounds and this contributed to their disenfranchisement from mainstream society. These youth were able to establish surrogate networks of support and, in many ways, the gang became a new family. Street gangs, according to Thrasher, formed organically in and through street-level interaction. Because of their proximity, youths formed locally grounded social networks. Crime was embedded in a local context, and it was through the understanding of this local context that one was able to grasp the essence of modern crime. To an extent, the process of centralization was already present because these gangs, as they moved into criminal activities, accepted a local hierarchy that centralized the profits and scope of action. This centralization was a local one, however, as each street gang remained irredeemably tied to the "street." That is, gangs worked to protect and maintain areas of influence and territory. Clifford R. Shaw and Henry D. McKay examined the general topographical structure of crime in the city of Chicago and determined that crime was the product of a "disorganized community." These were largely working-class and transitory communities with a lack of political organization. All these early works of the Chicago School focused on an ethnographic account of crime. As a result, the concept of centralization did not play a significant role in early criminological understandings. In fact, what the Chicago School could not see was the development of a new type of criminal organization.

Organized crime, in many ways, developed from the street gang. However, Thrasher, Shaw, and McKay did not anticipate that these gangs would become viable national structures. Even in the 1920s, however, former street gangs were becoming powerful sources of coordinated and centralized criminal activity. Al Capone and his criminal enterprise were able to run a large syndicate that established smuggling links between the street-level speakeasy and the crossing of international boundaries. In this particular case, alcohol was moved across the Canadian border; alcohol was still in demand, despite (some would say because of) Prohibition. On one hand, Capone and his gang were able to use their newfound riches to attract members and coercively dominate, through explicit violence and corruption, the criminal underworld. On the other hand, the mass wealth created was an attraction to the "legitimate society" of politicians. As a result, centralized and transnational criminal enterprises were established because of their ability to exploit niche demands combined with their capacity to extort and corrupt legitimate society. Prohibition, and the criminality to which it gave rise, definitively turned the local street-level gang into a highly organized form of illegal activity. In the 1930s and later, figures such as Lucky Luciano, Bugsy Siegal, and others were able to refashion the disorganized nature of street-level crime into an organized "national syndicate." This national syndicate was able to coordinate the activities of a wide array of criminal gangs. The national syndicate was founded upon the recognized need for centralization.

As a result of Prohibition, organized crime became capital-rich and was able to invest its proceeds in expansion. Whether it was prostitution, gambling, or illegal drugs, organized crime was able to reinvest its profits in new illicit markets and manipulation. Racketeering and union control were examples of this newfound power and influence. Luciano and his associates also cultivated cross-oceanic links based on ethnic affiliation and shared profit. As a result, centralization was seen as a beneficial and profitable strategy. Over time, street gangs had emerged from the local level to become organized and sophisticated outlets of criminal management. In fact, criminal centralization could be seen as part of a wider trend known as bureaucratization. This trend affected business and government as much as crime. Therefore, "centralization in crime" was subject to broader sociological and political forces.

Today, criminal enterprises are fully centralized. Even the traditionally locally bound street gang relies on a wide array of international trade networks to establish its community dominance. Street gangs such as MS-13 have extended their influence from the small East Los Angeles neighborhoods in which they began to include widespread drug-smuggling networks as well as immense amounts of control in Central America. In fact, the average source of local street gang profit, the sale of drugs, cannot even be conceived without global networks of smuggling that belie the simplicity of the local drug dealer. Drugs such as cocaine, marijuana, and heroin are not grown locally but are smuggled across borders, thus immediately linking the local dealer and gang member to a sophisticated international set of networks. As a result, the local gang must respond to these centralized networks with a managed centralization of its own. Organization and international linkages make those who use these strategies more successful. Centralization is, therefore, an intricate and necessary part of modern crime.

Law enforcement and government are not strangers to the trend of centralization. However, issues of jurisdictional precedence and control have persistently hampered law-enforcement agencies. Local police forces, for example, often come into jurisdictional conflict with the Federal Bureau of Investigation (FBI) or Drug Enforcement Administration (DEA), as well as other governmental agencies. These jurisdictional issues can often result in a lack of information exchange and labor coordination. This was seen in the case of the September 11, 2001, terrorist attacks. It was not the case, according to the National Commission on Terrorist Attacks Upon the United States (the 9/11 Commission), that the government was completely unaware of the possibility of an impending attack. The scale of the attacks and their sources were attested to through the examination of the intelligence collected by the CIA and the National Security Agency (NSA). However, the ability and desire to share and coordinate this knowledge with local action was not taken advantage of. As a result, the new threat posed by terrorism brought with it a new and pressing need for centralization.

The creation of the Department of Homeland Security as an organized body with the goal of coordinated intelligence and action at the global, national, and local levels was a response to this demand for a new form of centralization. Another important new level of centralization is to be found in and through the demand to prosecute war crimes. The creation of the International Criminal Court (ICC) in 1998 has resulted in a new series of indictments and convictions. This new level of global criminal prosecution is meant to keep a critical eye on the actions of states. Heads of states have become criminal defendants in a transnational forum. All of these activities speak to the state and "trans-state" response to the greater need for centralization.

Paul Brienza
York University

See also Disorganized Crime: Reuter's Thesis; Organized Crime: Defined; Organized Crime: Ethnic- Versus Market-Based; UN Convention Against Transnational Organized Crime

Further Readings

Beare, Margaret. *Critical Reflections on Transnational Organized Crime, Money Laundering and Corruption.* Toronto, ON: University of Toronto Press, 2003.

Park, Robert E. *Human Communities: The City and Human Ecology.* New York: Free Press, 1952.

Shaw, Clifford R. and Henry D. McKay. *Juvenile Delinquency and Urban Areas.* Chicago: University of Chicago Press, 1969.

Thrasher, Frederic. *The Gang: A Study of 1,313 Gangs in Chicago.* Chicago: University of Chicago Press, 1963.

CHARITIES AND FINANCING

Charitable organizations of all sizes are involved in financial crimes: transnational crimes centered on the solicitation, management, investment, and use of financial resources. Charities are the victims as well as the perpetrators of financially oriented crimes. Factors that have all increased such organizations' vulnerability to transnational financial crimes include the growing international outreach of many charitable organizations; the use of computers, the Internet, and online banking; and the reliance on outside commercial fund-raising companies. The link between charitable organizations and the financing of terrorist organizations has come under increasing scrutiny since the September 11, 2001 (9/11), terrorist attacks. Charitable organizations' roles in transnational financial crimes have resulted in increased regulatory scrutiny and demands for public accountability.

Charity Fund-Raising

The financing of charitable organizations through individual and corporate fund-raising efforts has come under increased scrutiny for fraudulent or unethical practices. Vulnerability to such fraudulent fund-raising practices increased with the worldwide economic downturn that began in 2008, as government, corporate, and individual donations dropped while competition among charitable organizations and requests for assistance rose. Many charities rely on outside professional and commercial fund-raising organizations that utilize outsourced labor, which decreases their oversight, increases their administrative costs and vulnerability to fraudulent practices, and fosters a negative image among the public.

Internationally based charitable contribution scams allow the perpetrators to operate in countries with lax government oversight. The spread of telemarketing and Internet-based charitable fund-raising has increased both instances of charity fraud involving sham charitable organizations and misrepresentations on behalf of legitimate charitable organizations. Common misrepresentations include overstating the percentage of donations that go directly to charitable causes versus administrative and other indirect costs and promotion schemes involving prizes for donors. Fraudulent charity fund-raising schemes frequently target vulnerable populations such as the elderly.

Charitable organizations are also the targets of crimes by outside perpetrators with no direct association. The use of computers and credit card donations has increased the possibility of identity theft, as computer hackers break into an organization's records to steal and sell credit card numbers. Another common crime involves fraudulent mail-order businesses, which obtain and sell lists of charitable foundations, misrepresenting their purposes by promising easy aid. Listed foundations are then inundated with individual requests for assistance.

Another common source of crime involving charities and financing are the employees of the organizations themselves, many of whom are volunteers even at the highest financial responsibility levels. Common employee financial crimes include asset theft, accounting fraud, check forgery, money laundering, diversion of funds for personal use, overstating the value of gifts and donations, embezzling, mail and wire fraud, and stealing and selling donors' credit card numbers. The rise of online banking has facilitated electronic financial crimes such as employee theft. Accounting fraud is one of the least common but costliest of employee crimes.

Many charitable organizations lack sufficient internal precautions against employee crimes, such as background checks on employees as well as local and international business partners, internal auditing practices, the use of multiple employee systems for donation logging and check authorization, and insuring employees with key financial responsibilities. Many charitable organizations are unwilling to criminally prosecute employees who commit financial crimes. Prosecution increases negative public exposure, and many organizations believe that the resulting backlash could include a significant loss of donations by an untrusting public. Small to midsize charitable organizations are more often the victims of employee crimes, but large organizations are not immune.

Charity Financing and Transnational Crimes

Globalization has extended the international reach of many charitable organizations. For example, many U.S.-based charitable organizations solicit donations in the United States and then transfer the money raised to international investments or charitable programs. Some of these funds are either purposely or inadvertently funneled to transnational criminal activities. Notable examples of the diversion of charitable funds to illicit activities include the actions of African Christian Relief and its executive director, Charles Williams. The organization diverted discounted pharmaceuticals meant for humanitarian distribution to the illicit U.S. drug market, subsequently laundering the profits. Williams was also later suspected of being connected to the illicit trade in conflict diamonds from Angola.

Natural disasters and other mass tragedies that result in an outpouring of global charitable contributions also create criminal opportunities for unscrupulous charities and individuals. International scandals include the use of internationally raised charitable donations for the bribery and corruption of government officials in the wake of the devastating Haiti earthquake of 2010. Tragedies that occur in countries where the national or local governments do not welcome international aid workers or openly account for the use of international relief financing lead to questions of government corruption and illicit use of such funds, which keeps such funds from reaching their intended recipients.

The links between charitable financing and international terrorism emerged as a key concern in the late 20th and early 21st centuries. Charities have directly and indirectly, willingly and unknowingly funneled financial support to terrorist organizations and operations. The same lax internal controls and external regulations that make charitable organizations vulnerable to fraud make them appealing to terrorists, as does the public trust they engender. Many international charities also operate in the areas of conflict, instability, and economic distress where terrorists base their operations.

Charities have been accused of laundering funds raised by terrorist activities as well as providing financing for the same through legitimately raised donations. Terrorist organizations have also used sham charities to hide their financial sources and assets. Charitable funds are diverted to terrorist organizations and activities both willingly and without the knowledge of charitable organizations' officers or donors. Even those charities or donors who willingly funnel money to terrorist organizations are unlikely to face prosecution. U.S. government investigations following the September 11, 2001, terrorist attacks played a vital role in publicizing the links between the terrorists and charitable financing.

Since the War on Terrorism launched by the Bush administration, the U.S. government has frozen the assets of multiple charitable organizations globally that are known or suspected of financial ties with terrorist organizations such as Al Qaeda. Results of such publicity include a more careful attitude among donors and an increased demand that charities follow ethical practices when investing their money. Others argue that charities must instead focus on obtaining the highest possible investment returns.

Charities are also vulnerable to financial victimization through fraudulent investment schemes, many of which also have international effects. Two of the more well-known examples are the pyramid or Ponzi schemes perpetrated by John G. Bennett Jr.'s Foundation for New Era Philanthropy in the 1990s and the 21st-century scheme of Bernard L. Madoff Investment Securities. In both cases, philanthropists, charities, and other nonprofit organizations lost hundreds of millions of donation and investment funds.

Public scandals over charity organizations' financial involvement in transnational criminal activities and the bad publicity of losing donation money to financial crimes has resulted in a public backlash, loss of trust in charitable organizations, and increased demands for openness and accountability in terms of charitable organizations' financial activities. Prosecution of such fraud often occurs at the local or national level, through groups such as the U.S. Federal Trade Commission (FTC). Tactics include injunctions from further solicitation, frozen assets, and the publication of percentages of donations that go directly to charitable activities.

Grassroots and government initiatives have publicized the links between charities and transnational criminal activities. Groups such as Charity Navigator use the Internet to publicize their ratings of charity organizations, which consider such factors as the percentage of revenue that goes directly to charitable programs and their financial strength. For example, the Campaign Against Arms Trade names charitable organizations that have made investments that finance the international arms trade to warn potential donors. Other groups have created "clean" investment opportunities such as common interest funds (CIFs), charitable investment funds that often utilize various screening tools for questionable investments such as arms trading, human trafficking, pornography, environmental degradation, and other transnational crimes.

Marcella Bush Trevino
Barry University

See also Charity Fraud

Further Readings

Falk, Gerhard. *Fraud: Deceit Among Scientists, Academics, Writers, and Philanthropists.* Lanham, MD: University Press of America, 2007.

Napoleoni, Loretta. *Modern Jihad: Tracing the Dollars Behind the Terror Networks.* Sterling, VA: Pluto Press, 2003.

Wolverton, Brad. "Fighting Charity Fraud." *Chronicle of Philanthropy* (August 7, 2003).

Zack, Gerard M. *Fraud and Abuse in Nonprofit Organizations: A Guide to Prevention and Detection.* Hoboken, NJ: Wiley, 2003.

CHARITY FRAUD

International charity fraud most often refers to charitable organizations or individuals claiming to be charitable organizations defrauding donors by taking monetary donations intended to be used for charitable purposes. This type of fraud is typically used to take advantage of large-scale disasters but can also be unrelated to those issues. It is typically perpetrated by counting on the willingness of people to help others but can offer a personal incentive to the defrauded individuals.

In the past, charity fraud was often executed over the phone. Callers would introduce themselves as representatives of charitable organizations—sometimes real organizations and sometimes made-up organizations with convincing missions and stories. They would ask for a donation. The donation would often be taken by credit card over the phone, but in some documented cases, a check was sent or the caller agreed to drop by in person and pick up cash. As the Internet and e-mail became more popular, it became easier for frauds to be performed from a distance, often internationally. E-mail spoofing—altering the header of an e-mail to make it appear as if the e-mail comes from a different source—became much more popular. It has become quite simple to send an e-mail that seems as if it came from a different, legitimate e-mail address. Publishing fake Websites, often patterned exactly after legitimate Websites, also became easier for scammers to do. These sites will often give incorrect information; collect money or bank account and credit card information; and direct individuals to send their friends and family to the site to the donate.

After the 2004 tsunami in south Asia and the 2005 hurricanes in the Gulf Coast region of the United States, an unprecedented number of cases of fraud came to light. Humanitarian organizations were seeking donations from individuals, organizations, and companies from around the world. Fraudulent organizations and individuals posing as legitimate charity organizations would request donations, typically of money but sometimes of supplies. In the haste to donate to these needy areas, few donors checked the legal status of these organizations. In fact, it is believed that many people who were defrauded still do not know they gave to an illegitimate organization or individual.

Oxfam International and World Vision UK are two of the charities hit hardest by charity fraud. They are large, international organizations; Oxfam coordinates other nongovernmental organizations to fight poverty and injustice, while World Vision UK advocates for international justice, focusing on developing communities. They are both often named as the senders of e-mails or letters and as the recipients of donated money and materials. Both are highly respected internationally, and it is much easier for fraudulent individuals to gain credibility by posting as these organizations.

Studies have found that smaller organizations rarely have to deal with charity fraud. Typically, the organizations having their names misappropriated are larger, international organizations, with no central office that is easily reachable by phone. The organization is typically headquartered in a country different from that of the victims of the fraud. There is no statistical difference in the number of frauds committed in the names of secular or religious organizations.

Mismanagement has become a large part of international charity fraud. United Nations (UN) officials from various agencies, including peacekeeping forces, the Office for Project Services, and United Nations Children's Fund (UNICEF), have faced charges of fraud and mismanagement of funds, often dealing with requesting and accepting bribes from partner organizations or for-profit companies seeking to work in that area or bid on contracts, theft of funds, and charging unreported management fees on top of contracts. In these examples, the projects being carried out are typically of such high importance that the upper management is removed, new leaders are hired, grants to those organizations continue, and the work goes on. International frauds of this type are easily performed, as there are rarely checks and balances in place to oversee the process.

In 2009, a syndicate stealing credit card numbers began charging large amounts as donations to international charities, with smaller amounts being charged to shell companies that would later turn the proceeds over to the syndicate. They operated under the belief credit card companies would be reluctant to quickly act on suspected thefts if most of the charges are going to charitable organizations.

Another common fraud is the job offer for a charitable organization. An e-mail will be sent from a fraudulent individual, posing as a large nongovernmental organization. It will offer a job position, often claiming it found the defrauded person on a career/job Website. It will offer a position, but will require a "registration fee" to be transferred to a certain bank account.

Charity fraud can often come in the form of a Nigerian money came (419 scam). In the past, some have asked for a processing fee for winning a charity raffle. Others have announced to the recipient that they have received a grant from a charitable foundation, but that a percentage must be returned immediately. Still others have asked for assistance in bringing refugees to the recipient's home country.

A growing type of charity fraud is one that focuses on tax evasion. Fraudulent organizations will offer donors the opportunity to evade taxes by giving a charitable deduction and then returning the funds. In most countries, some type of tax incentive for giving exists, typically through a tax credit or tax deduction. Many countries give that incentive to donors to charitable organizations outside that country, as long as it goes to a charitable cause. The organization will offer the donor the opportunity to make a donation to the charity. Once the donor has claimed the deduction on his or her tax return, the organization claims it will return the funds. Donors are typically reluctant to report these events, as they have committed tax evasion, and would most likely face some penalty in their own country.

International charity fraud has an impact on those who are defrauded but also on the charitable sector as a whole. A decline in public trust led to calls from the public for more transparency and more regulation. It can also lead to decreased donations to charitable organizations.

The International Criminal Police Organization (Interpol) General Secretariat has created a list of recommendations to protect donors and donations: (1) ask charity collectors for proof of identity as well as written permission to collect money in the name of their organization; (2) in suspicious cases, note the identity details of the collector and immediately inform local police; (3) follow donation advice from governmental institutions or national and international charity organizations published in the press and media and/or directly contact charity organizations to obtain details on how to make donations; and (4) use direct bank remittances from your account to the account of charity organizations instead of cash donations.

Thomas M. Southard
University of Delaware

See also Nigerian Money Scams; Nongovernmental Organizations

Further Readings

Cordery, C. J. and R. F. Baskerville. "Charity Transgressions, Trust and Accountability." *Voluntas: International Journal of Voluntary and Nonprofit Organizations*, v.22/2 (2011).

Gaskin, Katharine. "Blurred Vision: Public Trust in Charities." *International Journal of Nonprofit and Voluntary Sector Marketing*, v.4/2 (May 1999).

Greenlee, Janet, Mary Fisher, Teresa Gordon, and Elizabeth Keating. "An Investigation of Fraud in Nonprofit Organizations: Occurrences and Deterrents." *Nonprofit and Voluntary Sector Quarterly*, v.36/4 (2007).

CHILD EXPLOITATION

Child exploitation has an extensive history not just in the United States but globally as well. Cultural differences and citizens' beliefs in both the dominant religious doctrine and laws set forth by the reigning government in any given country account for a vast array of differences when defining the exploitation of children on a global level. Simply defined, exploitation is any act or behavior committed with the intent to preserve the positions of those already in power while harming the less powerful. According to American standards, a harmful act committed *with intent* and in violation of the law constitutes a crime—an act that victimizes both the injured party and society as a whole. Hence, according to the rights and rules set forth by those who originally drafted the Constitution and its Amendments and established and defined the role of the criminal justice system, a crime against one is viewed as harmful to all in society. Hence, when one is victimized within the United States, it is the state that brings charges against and prosecutes the alleged offender. However, a relatively new criminal act—both widespread and heinous in nature—has appeared on the global scene, demanding collaboration and action from international officials.

The History of Child Exploitation

The media expose the viewing audience to the plight of children in underdeveloped countries: those living in poverty, devoid of proper nutrition, medical care, and sanitary living conditions. Wrapped in the cocoon of middle- and upper-class America, most are ill prepared to comprehend the very real fact that these portrayals show only those children who are visible to the outside world. They do little to shed light on the nameless and faceless victims who remain invisible to the general public—the women and children who are bought and sold transnationally by those engaged in human sex trafficking.

In reality the exploitation of children has a long-standing history based largely in capitalism as wealthy entrepreneurs exploited youth as just one of many profit-making mechanisms. During the late 19th century and extending into the early 1900s, developing countries and forward-thinking profiteers embraced industrialization. So, too, did those who bought into the promise of lucrative employment as a result of burgeoning workplaces unavailable until the Industrial Revolution. Thus, the changing nature of America's cities brought with it an influx of immigrants hoping to achieve the American Dream.

Armed with little more than the hope of achieving lucrative employment, those who left their homelands were ill prepared for the realities of life in American cities. The American Dream was, for the most part, elusive to those seeking a better life. Rather than achieving economic success, the hardworking immigrants were segregated in neighborhoods mired in squalor, earning salaries far less than expected, and forced to put all family members to work—including those as young as three years of age. Eventually this exploitation resulted in the passage of U.S. child labor laws, contributed to the emergence of social work as a discipline unto itself, and led to the creation of the juvenile justice system. Just as children were exploited in the early 20th century, so too do they remain victims of those seeking to profit from their desirability as sex slaves

Child sex trafficking is the recruitment, harboring, transport, or sale of people under the age of 18 with the intent of placing them for sale in the commercial sex industry. U.S. children and adolescents are the most likely nationality to be abducted when visiting foreign countries. (Photos.com)

in the underground economy. It has been argued by some that the contemporary exploitation of today's youth has its roots in the industrialization occurring in the late 19th and early 20th centuries. While the victimization of children in earlier years bears little resemblance to the exploitation of today's youth, the outcome is the same: childhood lost.

Children for Sale: Human Sex Trafficking

Only recently have the media turned their attention to the global phenomenon of human sex trafficking. The selling of humans who will serve as sex slaves for their owners compels many to revisit the time in U.S. history when African Americans and blacks in other nations were little more than commodities to be bought and sold on the open market. They, too, were trafficked globally, with many sold to U.S. citizens who exploited their physical work abilities, their human sexuality, and even their very sense of personhood. Most in America prefer to think of slavery as an act that was abandoned as a result of its legal abolishment following the Civil War. Many are stunned to learn the transnational sale of individuals into slavery, albeit different from the form it took during the Civil War era, is alive and well. Even more incomprehensible to many laypersons is the very real fact that the egregious act of selling children into slavery for purposes of sexual exploitation is occurring worldwide. Efforts by the media have begun to bring this reality to the forefront of the American psyche. As a result of these efforts, only recently have many—academicians, lawmakers, practitioners, and laypersons alike—begun to speak out in opposition to the presence of a global marketplace that exploits children while lining the pockets of those who serve as entrepreneurs in the global market of human sex trafficking.

History is rife with examples of child exploitation; however, discussions of past abuses pale in comparison to the atrocities exacted on many contemporary youth. These are the children—often as young as four years old—who are most often drawn, through coercion, into the world of child sex trafficking. Human sex trafficking is a highly lucrative enterprise, bringing in approximately $9.5 billion annually to those who profit from the sale of humans on a global level. Much of this profit comes from the sale of an estimated 1.2 million children and preadolescents trafficked annually.

Child sex trafficking is defined as the recruitment, harboring, transport, and sale of those under the age of 18 with the intent of placement in the commercial world of sex for sale. Key to this process is the coercion used in order to abduct those who will serve as sex slaves for the masters who have purchased them. As the world's second largest organized crime, human sex trafficking, especially as it relates to children, brings irreparable harm to those victimized at the hands of both those who sell and who purchase these youth. Still, precisely because so little is known or documented about the human sex-trafficking industry, any estimates or claims made about the sellers and buyers are questionable at best. Likewise, little is known about the futures of those sold for the purpose of satiating the needs of the consumers. Perhaps most unsettling is the fact that the United States, considered to be the most highly civilized country in the world, boasts the highest rates of purchasing children via the black market. Sadly, U.S. children and adolescents are also the most likely to be abducted when visiting foreign countries, eventually being sold into slavery by those who continue to profit from the exploitation of mere children.

Needed Reform

Reform is needed if the global industry of human sex trafficking is to be eradicated. This reform must be transnational in nature, requiring both cooperation and collaboration between multiple countries in order for any efforts aimed at ending the sexual exploitation of both adults and children. Efforts to inhibit, if not eradicate, human sex trafficking were first fully addressed in the United Nations' (UN's) 2000 Protocol to Prevent, Suppress, and Punish Trafficking in Persons, Especially Women and Children, which is designed to stop those who continue to sustain and maintain the underground market promoting the sale of women, children, and men. While laudable in its own right, in reality this protocol did little to inform the global public about the practice of selling individuals into what constitutes little more than slavery for whatever purpose the purchaser desires. Following the protocol's adoption, increased legislation emerged. However, in the absence of public awareness, education, and action, little can be achieved to stop the lucrative organizations that sell hundreds of thousands of individuals on an annual basis.

Following the United Nations' 2000 response to the scope of, and harm done by, the transnational enterprise in human sex trafficking, other organizations followed suit. Organized in 2003, the contemporary organization working to eliminate human sex trafficking through standardized legislation is the Organization for Security and Co-operation in Europe (OSCE). An intergovernmental agency that operates under the auspices of the UN Charter, the OSCE introduced its landmark proposal, Action Against Trafficking in Human Beings, at the Council of Europe's convention. The OSCE bill was signed by 41 member states and ratified by 26. As a result, both legal and international attempts to end human trafficking have begun. Unfortunately, the goal of ending human sex trafficking will demand much more than transnational legislation. It will call for diligent enforcement, the eradication of corruption in many global law-enforcement agencies (including in the United States), and a collaborative commitment to ending the atrocities enacted on women and children on a global level.

Many claim it will take time to get all nations educated about and on board with efforts to put an end to a black market that risks the well-being, self-worth, and very survival of those who spend much of their lives fulfilling the sexual needs of their purchasers. Time, however, is the one commodity those attempting to end human trafficking claim we do not have. Across the United States and globally, nonprofit organizations have emerged that share the common goal of ending human sex trafficking and the exploitation of children through education, raising awareness, and pressuring the U.S. government to assume a bold stance against the practice and, in so doing, pressure other countries to join the fight against the evils faced by too many individuals—primarily children—worldwide. It has been said it takes a village to raise a child. In this instance, it takes much more than a village to protect, not merely raise, the world's children.

Martha L. Shocy-Eckles
Saint Louis University

See also Human Smuggling; Human Trafficking; Sex Slavery; Violence: Protection

Further Readings

Batstone, David. *Not for Sale: The Return of the Global Slave Trade—and How We Can Fight It*. New York: HarperOne, 2007.

Clemmit, Marcia. "Prostitution Debate: Should the United States Legalize Sex Work?" *QC Researcher*, v.18/19 (May 23, 2008).

DeStefano, Anthony M. *The War on Human Trafficking: U.S. Policy Assessed*. New Brunswick, NJ: Rutgers University Press, 2008.

Farr, Kathryn. *Sex Trafficking: The Global Market in Women and Children*. New York: Worth, 2005.

Kerschner, Art, Jr. "Child Labor Laws and Enforcement." In *Report on the Youth Labor Force*. Washington, DC: Bureau of Labor Statistics, 2000. http://www.bls.gov/opub/rylf/pdf/chapter2.pdf (Accessed February 2011).

Skinner, E. Benjamin. *A Crime so Monstrous: Face-to-Face With Modern-Day Slavery*. New York: Free Press, 2008.

Smith, Linda A., Samantha Healy Vardaman, and Melissa A. Snow. "The National Report on Domestic Minor Sex Trafficking: America's Prostituted Children." *Shared Hope International* (May 2009).

Cigarette Smuggling

Cigarettes are one the world's most taxed and smuggled goods. Each state or country imposes different levels of taxation on the product. The differences create a financial opportunity that criminals, including terrorists, often exploit. Cigarette smuggling has become a sizable revenue stream for illicit actors. The global cigarette black market accounts for 8 to 10 percent of all cigarettes sold worldwide and annually costs governments between US$40 billion and US$50 billion in lost tax revenues.

The illegal market contains counterfeit and contraband cigarettes. Criminals produce counterfeit cigarettes—usually containing substandard, unregulated ingredients with increased levels of toxins such as arsenic, cadmium, lead, and thallium—and then package them to imitate well-known and trademarked cigarette brands, such as Marlboro. Contraband cigarettes are cigarettes produced by legitimate manufacturers who produce genuine cigarettes according to corporate and government standards. Because manufacturers do not sell directly to the end user, cigarettes pass through a system of wholesalers and distributors. Cigarettes become contraband when appropriate taxes are not paid. "Cigarette diversion" is another name for this practice.

Smugglers use various methods to avoid paying all or part of the taxes on contraband cigarettes. Smuggling schemes vary, but most can fall into one of two categories: large-scale smuggling organizations and bootlegging. Bootleggers are smaller-scale, mom-and-pop schemes or small networks of individuals. Typically, they buy a few cartons or cases of cigarettes in a jurisdiction with no tax (such as duty-free areas or Native American reservations) or a lower tax rate, sell them in a jurisdiction with a higher tax rate, and keep the difference. Smugglers conceal cigarettes in personal vehicles, luggage, boats, buses, or mailed packages. This type of smuggling is popular both in the United States and throughout the world. The difference between pre- or low-tax prices and the retail price in jurisdictions with higher tax rates can yield significant profits.

Large-scale smugglers follow the same concept, except that instead of moving a carload of cigarettes, they are moving shipping containers or tractor-trailer loads of contraband or counterfeit cigarettes. These schemes tend to be more sophisticated, take advantage of free trade zones, may involve legitimate manufacturers and distributors, and require the commission of other crimes, such as fraudulent documents and money laundering. These schemes can yield millions in profits. Some large-scale smugglers steal cargo containers of cigarettes and sell them in the black market. In other cases, the tobacco companies have played a role. Numerous countries have filed lawsuits against tobacco companies because of their participation in large-scale smuggling operations or failing to do the required due diligence. Cigarette smuggling was a key component of the Black Market Peso Exchange, which was a popular method of laundering Colombian drug money. However, not all large-scale schemes directly involve well-known and legitimate tobacco manufacturers.

The illicit cigarette market also deals with counterfeit or illegally manufactured cigarettes. Cigarette counterfeiters combined constitute the world's fifth largest tobacco "company." The level of counterfeit manufacturing sophistication varies, especially among different countries. Some operations are small scale; workers hand-roll each cigarette, assemble the packs, and glue them by hand. These "factories" are often in isolated or hidden locations. Other operations are large scale, using the same machinery as legal factories and operating openly. Illegal counterfeit factories operate in China, Iraq, Iran, Turkey, Russia, Romania, the Czech Republic, the tri-border region of South America, and several other countries. Counterfeiting is not limited to the

The international cigarette black market comprises 8 to 10 percent of all cigarettes sold worldwide. The U.K. Border Agency found more than 1 million Chinese-made cigarettes hidden inside concrete blocks during a search in October 2010. (U.K. Home Office via Wikimedia)

cigarettes and their packaging but also includes tax stamps. Smugglers affix counterfeit tax stamps to both counterfeit cigarettes and contraband cigarettes to hide their illegality.

Cigarette smuggling becomes even more attractive when offenders consider the low likelihood that the criminal justice system will detect, prosecute, and punish them or their conspirators. In general, authorities detect a small percentage of smuggled cigarettes. When authorities do discover cases, the punishments are lax or are dramatically more lenient than for smuggling in drugs.

Cigarette smugglers can belong to small or family based smuggling operations, established organized crime groups, legitimate companies, and terrorist organizations. In the early and mid-20th century, cigarette smuggling provided a significant revenue source for the Italian Mafia. These groups can operate domestically, regionally, or internationally, and there are numerous examples of cigarette smuggling converging with terrorist cells and other crimes. Cigarette smuggling is a top fund-raising activity used by terrorist groups. Law-enforcement agencies have identified terrorist organizations throughout the world, including Hezbollah, Hamas, the Irish Republican Army, and the PKK (Kurdistan Workers' Party), as participants in this illicit trade.

Cigarette smuggling has been linked to illegal drugs, weapons, political crimes, and other serious crimes. During the Balkan Wars, Serbia and

Montenegro's government openly supported cigarette smuggling and used the profits to help finance the wars and governments. American law-enforcement agencies and the Royal Canadian Mounted Police conducted joint operations concerning counterfeit cigarettes, counterfeit cash, Ecstasy, methamphetamine, and weapons trafficking. American law-enforcement agencies detected another ring involving more than $8 million in cash and significant amounts of Ecstasy, cigarettes, counterfeit cigarette tax stamps, and a murder-for-hire case. Officials from the European Union and the United States investigated a case involving an American who purchased cigarettes in Panama, processed the cigarettes in Miami and disguised the shipments as home improvement products, and then shipped them to various European ports without paying the required $6.5 million in duties and taxes. The profits allegedly supported the IRA's (Irish Republican Army) terrorist attacks and criminal actions. The convergence between cigarette smuggling and serious crimes illustrates the importance of this illicit market.

Sharon A. Melzer
State University of New York, Plattsburgh

See also Tobacco Smuggling

Further Readings

Beare, Margaret. "Organized Corporate Criminality: Tobacco Smuggling Between Canada and the U.S." *Crime, Law and Social Change*, v.37 (2002).

International Consortium of Investigative Journalists. "Tobacco Underground." http://www.publicintegrity .org/investigations/tobacco (Accessed September 2010).

LaFaive, Michael, Patrick Fleenor, and Todd Nesbit. *Cigarette Taxes and Smuggling: A Statistical Analysis and Historical Review*. Midland, MI: Mackinac Center for Public Policy, 2008.

Shelley, Louise and Sharon Melzer. "The Nexus of Organized Crime and Terrorism: Two Case Studies in Cigarette Smuggling." *International Journal of Comparative and Applied Criminal Justice*, v.31 (2008).

CIVIL FORFEITURE: THE EXPERIENCE OF THE UNITED STATES

Civil forfeiture is a legal proceeding that forces obedience to the law by transferring ownership of property that has been used in violation of the legal code.

What is unique about civil forfeiture is that it is not necessary to prove that the owner of the property committed the crime. The prosecution is against the property, not the owner. Such forfeitures are based upon the "relation back" doctrine, which transfers title of property to the government at the moment a criminal act is committed. Seizure and formal proceedings simply confirm the forfeiture that has already taken place.

Seizure proceedings also provide property owners with an opportunity to be heard as required by the due process clauses of the Fifth and Fourteenth Amendments to the U.S. Constitution. Innocent parties are protected by remission procedures and in some instances by statute. Those who own or purchase property subject to forfeiture, but who do not have knowledge of the prohibited activity or tainted nature of the property, may petition the government to pardon the property. The filing of a petition for remission of forfeiture does not deny that the property was involved in a violation of law but asks the pardon of the property because of the involvement of innocent parties.

Civil forfeiture actions are *in rem* proceedings against property that are used to determine ownership. This is in contrast to criminal forfeitures, which are *in personam* and refer to actions directed against individuals to determine their obligations and liabilities. Unless a forfeiture statute expressly requires a conviction, it is considered a civil action against property, totally independent of any criminal action against the owner. Even an acquittal on a related criminal charge will not bar the forfeiture. Civil forfeiture differs from criminal forfeiture in that punishment is not the intention of the law. The purpose of civil forfeiture is to return property to its rightful owner. If Congress passes a law that makes property used in violation of a statute forfeitable, once the crime is committed the property no longer belongs to the defendant, but to the government.

Property is seized upon the government's demonstration that there is probable cause to believe that the property was used illegally. This probable cause is the same probable cause used to effect an arrest. It exists when the facts and circumstances lead a person of reasonable caution to conclude that the property was used to violate the law. However, a determination of proof beyond a reasonable doubt is necessary for the actual forfeiture of the seized property. A seizure warrant is used when the property is not in police custody, such as money held in a bank or real property. Although forfeiture proceedings are civil in form, they are quasi-criminal in nature. The exclusionary rule does apply and evidence obtained in violation of an individual's constitutional rights cannot be considered in establishing probable cause. The fact that there is illegally obtained evidence, however, does not preclude forfeiture of the property if there is other evidence to prove that the violation occurred.

Civil forfeitures in the United States generally stem from drug investigations at both the state and federal levels, although there are other crimes that have forfeiture provisions. For example, the U.S. Controlled Substances Act provides for the seizure of money and property that are the "proceeds" of the illicit drug trade or are used to "facilitate" a drug crime. The word *proceeds* refers to property derived from money directly exchanged for drugs: that is, the profits of drug trafficking. *Facilitation* of a drug crime means that property (such as an automobile used to deliver drugs) is used to make a violation of law easier. It is not the intention of the law, however, to take real property from people merely because an offense was committed on the premises. In the case of real property, courts have interpreted facilitation to mean a significant connection between the property and an offense such as the recovery of multiple kilograms of heroin. Some states have added presumptions to their forfeiture statues. For example, in Illinois any money found in close proximity to drugs or drug paraphernalia is "presumed" to be the proceeds of drug trafficking and automatically subject to seizure without additional probable cause.

Some forfeitures are done administratively. Administrative forfeiture is the process by which property may be forfeited without judicial involvement. The forfeiture is conducted by the seizing agency. Administrative forfeiture, however, has a dollar threshold and cannot be used to forfeit real property. Essentially, administrative forfeiture is used to forfeit uncontested property. A court date is granted if the property owner wishes to contest the seizure.

An important aspect of civil forfeiture is that property seized by local and state officers in the United States can be transferred to a federal agent, who can in effect "adopt" the seizure just as though it had originally been seized by him or her. State and local officers may thus benefit from the power of federal statutes when their state does not permit civil forfeiture or when state law is more restrictive than

federal law, as in those states that prohibit the forfeiture of real property.

The ability to seize property without an arrest or criminal conviction has caused civil forfeiture to be the subject of an ongoing controversy within the legal community. Although often criticized as in violation of the Due Process Clause of the Fourteenth Amendment, civil forfeiture has continually withstood constitutional challenges and provides an important tool in the war against crime by denying criminals the proceeds of their illegal conduct.

Robert M. Lombardo
Loyola University, Chicago

See also Criminal Forfeiture and Seizure; Drug Trade: Legislative Debates; Executive Order 13581; Heroin; Money Laundering: History; Money Laundering: Vulnerable Commodities and Services; Recovery of Stolen Assets

Further Readings

Boister, Neil. "Transnational Penal Norm Transfer: The Transfer of Civil Forfeiture From the United States to South Africa as a Case in Point." *South African Journal of Criminal Justice*, v.16/1 (2003).

Boudreaux, Donald J. and Adam C. Pritchard. *Civil Forfeiture as a "Sin Tax."* Oakland, CA: Independent Institute, 1996.

Civil Asset Forfeiture Reform Act of 2000. Public Law 106–185, 106th Congress (2000).

Controlled Substance Act. Title 21 U.S.C. Section 881 Forfeitures (1970).

Edgeworth, Dee. *Asset Forfeiture: Practice and Procedure in State and Federal Courts.* Chicago: American Bar Association, Criminal Justice Section, 2008.

Drug Asset Forfeiture Procedure Act. Illinois Revised Statutes. Chapter 725 ILCS 150/7 (2005).

Goldsmith, Michael. *Civil Forfeiture: Tracing the Proceeds of Narcotics Trafficking.* Washington, DC: U.S. Department of Justice, Office of Justice Programs, Bureau of Justice Assistance, 1992.

Young, Simon N. M. *Civil Forfeiture of Criminal Property: Legal Measures for Targeting the Proceeds of Crime.* Northampton, MA: Edward Elgar, 2009.

Cocaine

Contemporary availability of cocaine worldwide is the result of centuries of transnational trade, both legal and illegal. Like tobacco and opiates, coca made its journey to the global northwest on the back of European colonialism. In more recent years, globalization has accelerated the movement of people, goods, and technologies around the globe, facilitating both licit and illicit trade. The international cocaine trade is of particular importance to scholars of transnational crime and justice. In addition to being one of the largest forms of transnational crime, it is also one of the most politically important.

History, Uses, and Effects

Cocaine is an alkaloid that is typically taken through insufflation (sniffed) or smoked in the form of freebase (known commonly as crack cocaine). Less commonly it is injected, sometimes in combination with heroin. It is a stimulant. Effects include feeling awake, feelings of euphoria, having increased confidence, and having an increased heart rate. Health issues are associated with long-term or heavy use.

Cocaine is the refined product of the coca plant, native to Latin America. Archaeological evidence has shown that coca has been used in its natural form for at least 4,000 years across most of Central and South America. Spanish conquistadores banned coca use initially; however, once it was discovered that it allowed slaves to work long days with little rest, its use was allowed to continue. Coca is still used in indigenous communities in the Andean region, particularly in Bolivia, where it has an ambiguous legal status. Evo Morales, president of Bolivia and president of the Bolivian union of *cocaleros* (coca growers), has campaigned for the recognition of coca is a legitimate crop. He famously declared, "I am not a drug trafficker. I am a coca grower. I cultivate coca leaf, which is a natural product. I do not refine [it into] cocaine, and neither cocaine nor drugs have ever been part of the Andean culture."

In indigenous cultures in the Andes, coca is popularly consumed in the form of the tea *mate de coca* or chewed with lime, which may be mixed with spices and cane sugar. Reported effects include a feeling of alertness more similar to caffeine than cocaine, as well as reduced feelings of hunger and numbness in the mouth. Coca is also taken as a medicine for pain relief; leaves may be applied directly to wounds to aid healing, and it may also counteract the effects of altitude sickness. Although the effects bear some resemblance to those of cocaine, habitual users do not report negative effects upon withdrawal.

Coca was brought back to Europe by the Spanish conquistadores and in the 19th century chemists across Europe experimented with it as a potential medicine. Albert Neimann isolated the active alkaloid (cocaine hydrochloride) in 1860 while studying for a Ph.D. Cocaine was initially employed as a therapeutic drug for alcoholism and depression (famously proselytized by Sigmund Freud). It was also used in "tonics" such as Coca-Cola (hence the "coca" in Coca-Cola), although that is no longer the case. Thus, the international cocaine trade has its roots in the 19th and early 20th centuries, when it was produced on an industrial scale. The largest producers were Dutch, German, and Japanese pharmaceutical firms, which processed cocaine from leaves grown on plantations in colonial empires such as Java. At the beginning of the 20th century (at the height of the legal trade), more cocaine was grown in Asia than in South America. In the United Kingdom, cocaine (as well as heroin) was eventually outlawed in the 1920 Dangerous Drugs Act, which was prompted by public alarm at the numbers of soldiers who returned home from World War I with drug addictions.

The history of crack cocaine is much shorter. It was not until the 1970s that crack cocaine was refined from cocaine. In the United States, use was first reported among stockbrokers and investment bankers. In the 1980s, its use spread into impoverished inner-city neighborhoods, prompting moral panic and punitive sanctions. Predictions of a similar crack epidemic in the United Kingdom were unfounded. Although reported deaths from crack

The success of the cocaine trade is dependent on avoiding detection, making it difficult to measure the size and scope with any accuracy; yet available data suggest that the cocaine trade is significant and thriving. (Photos.com)

cocaine have increased since 1995 in the United Kingdom, most drug-related deaths there are a result of opiate use (often in combination with alcohol), and the numbers of drug-related deaths are dwarfed by the number of deaths related to alcohol and tobacco. Unlike cocaine, crack cocaine has never been legal. Crack cocaine is almost entirely processed in destination rather than source countries. As such, there is no international crack cocaine trade, only an international cocaine trade.

Size and Scope of the International Cocaine Trade

The contemporary illegal trade in cocaine first emerged in the late 1960s in response to demand from the global Northwest and has continued to grow since. As an illegal phenomenon, the success of the cocaine trade depends on remaining hidden. This makes it notoriously difficult to measure with any accuracy. Furthermore, collating data gathered in different nations is complex, because different tools of measurement, categories, or terminology may be used. Additionally, measuring the cocaine trade and the effectiveness of antidrug interventions is an intensely politicized field because nations (particularly those in the global South) are under pressure to demonstrate that they are actively combating the drug trade. The most significant documentation on the international cocaine trade is the *World Drug Report*, published by the United Nations Office on Drugs and Crime (UNODC), which brings together research on the international cocaine trade annually.

In spite of the difficulties, available studies concur that the international cocaine trade is significant in scope and size. Cocaine markets can now be found in all industrialized nations and in many developing ones. Despite efforts to curb the drug supply internationally, all available data suggest that the cocaine trade remains buoyant. There is debate about whether the amount of coca being cultivated has changed in the 21st century in response to eradication efforts. All the world's coca is grown in the Andean region, mainly in Colombia but also in Peru and Bolivia. According to the *World Drug Report*, cocaine production in the Andean region decreased by 28 percent between 2000 and 2010; however, estimates from the United States maintain that the trade remains the same size or has grown slightly. It is also possible that, while cultivation

may have decreased, methods of processing may have become more efficient to produce higher yields from less coca.

Coca is refined into cocaine exclusively in Latin America (not only in Colombia, Bolivia, and Peru but also in Brazil, Ecuador, and Venezuela). Once processed, cocaine is then exported to the rest of the world. Transport routes are constantly changing in response to law-enforcement efforts. Although cocaine can be found across the globe, most is destined for the United States and Europe. According to UNODC, the United States is the largest market (consuming 40 percent of the world's cocaine). The second largest market is Europe. The United Kingdom and Spain together consume half of the cocaine that reaches the European continent. Some cocaine travels directly to the countries where it is used; however, much will pass through several countries on the way. Because almost all countries in Latin America serve as export points to the rest of the world (to a greater or lesser extent), cocaine is trafficked within Latin America. As of 2010, the Caribbean served as an important transit destination, along with nations in West Africa (mainly in response to interception efforts in the Caribbean). This is commonly referred to as the "balloon effect": Where the cocaine trade is combated in one area, it will expand into another area.

Cocaine is trafficked along a number of international routes, which, more often than not, parallel legal transit routes for goods and people. For example, cocaine is often concealed in legitimate products being exported from Latin America, such as fish or fruit, which are sent as cargo. Surprisingly large consignments of drugs can be concealed this way. In 2009, the Mexican navy intercepted a ton of cocaine that was concealed in 20 frozen shark carcasses. Larger quantities of cocaine are often concealed in commercial or leisure boats in the hold or behind false paneling.

Methods of concealment have become increasingly sophisticated in response to detection efforts. Whereas drugs could simply be concealed compressed in double-bottomed suitcases or strapped to bodies, sophisticated chemical processes are now employed to camouflage the drug chemically. The European Monitoring Centre for Drugs and Drug Addiction reports that cocaine may be incorporated into plastic, clothing, fertilizers, guano, or beeswax. When the concealed cocaine enters Europe, it is processed back into cocaine in "secondary extraction" laboratories. In 2008, 38 such laboratories were seized across the European Union. Chemical camouflage techniques such as these may also be used to send medium-sized quantities through freight either over sea or by air. Smaller quantities are also sent by post or accompanied by a person known as a drug mule. Mules can typically swallow up to 1.5 kilos of cocaine. Larger quantities (of up to around 6 kilos) can be concealed in luggage. Drug mules are employed by someone else to carry drugs for a fixed fee. Recent research has found that some, although not all, mules carry drugs as a result of coercion. Not all those arrested at borders with drugs are mules.

Drug traffickers are a diverse group. In contrast to media images of cocaine traffickers as cartels, recent years have seen a diversification toward temporary, flexible groups. Although "professional" groups may dominate the trade, research has found that the cocaine trade is nowhere nearly as well organized as might be expected. Thus, cocaine is also trafficked by individuals who may work alone (solo entrepreneurs) or small collectives of just two or three people. Such collectives may traffic cocaine only once or may do so several times over a period of years.

Policing the International Cocaine Trade

Drug trafficking is illegal in all countries worldwide as a result of the 1961 Single Convention on Narcotic Drugs, which replaced previous international treaties. Drug trafficking is punished with criminal sanctions including life imprisonment and the death penalty, punishments previously reserved for violent and dangerous offenders. Drug-trafficking offenses are met with mandatory minimum sentences in most of the global Northwest. "Mandatory minimums" originated in the United States in the 1980s and are now employed in the United Kingdom, Europe, and Latin America; indeed, the United States has assisted in drawing up drug laws in some countries in Latin America. In the United States, traffickers are usually dealt with at a federal level. The minimum sentence (for a first offense) for trafficking between 500 and 4,999 grams of cocaine is five years. For more than five kilos of cocaine, the minimum sentence is 10 years. In England and Wales, maximum rather than minimum penalties exist. The recommended maximum sentence for importing between 500 grams and five kilos of a Class A drug (both cocaine and heroin) is 10 years' imprisonment. For quantities greater than five kilos, the sentence rises to 14 years.

The average sentence for those caught importing a Class A drug into the United Kingdom is seven years.

Nations in the developed world have attempted to stem the supply of cocaine to the global Northwest at its source in Latin America. As demand has increased and the trade has grown, the business of policing the cocaine trade has expanded considerably. Governments worldwide invest millions of dollars each year in an attempting to halt the flow of drugs. This quantity dwarfs the amount spent on reducing demand and treating those with drug addictions. This is largely achieved through the increased securitization of borders and through drug eradication programs in Latin America. Experts in the area disagree as to whether crop eradication programs have been successful. Although it is generally agreed that there is less coca grown in Colombia now than there was 15 years ago, it is also agreed that production has increased in Bolivia and Peru. Although many tons of cocaine are seized worldwide each year, the availability and use of cocaine in the United States and the United Kingdom have not decreased. Despite this, some experts in the area contend that the reduced purity of the drugs sold in these markets is a sign that less cocaine is getting through.

It is important to remember that the drug trade and antidrug interventions are intricately intertwined. Without prohibition, there would be no international trade in drugs as it is today, since prohibition ensures that the profit margins remain high. Without probation, there would be no drug traffickers and there would also be no mules. No legal forms of business ship commodities in the luggage or in their bodies. Thus, it should not be forgotten that prohibition maintains and shapes the international drug trade in significant ways.

Human Rights Issues in Policing the International Cocaine Trade

While the international cocaine trade produces a variety of harms (such an environmental damage from cultivating coca, violence as a result of conflict within the trade, and even deaths of mules who swallow cocaine), attempts to stem the supply of drugs from the Third World have produced countless kinds of "collateral damage." In *Drugs and Democracy in Latin America*, Coletta Youngers and Eileen Rosin bring together information from across Latin America about the collateral damage done. The collateral effects of efforts to eradicate cocaine are clearly illustrated in the case of Colombia, where coca crops have been sprayed with herbicides in an attempt to eradicate the crop. Since crop-dusting planes are the targets of gunfire, they have to fly at much higher altitude than commercial crop-spraying planes. They are also more likely to fly in zigzag patterns to avoid being hit. As a result, herbicides drift over a much larger area, which includes water sources, legal crops, and populated areas. A number of health problems have been reported, including stomach upsets and rashes, particularly in children. Herbicides in water sources have also resulted in environmental damage to rain forests. Aerial spraying near the Ecuadorian border has exacerbated political tensions in the area. Finally, a number of Colombians from the area either have become refugees in Ecuador or are internally displaced within Colombia. A variety of collateral damage can be found across Latin America and the Caribbean. This includes increased militarization of the region, restriction of civil liberties, political instability, and compromises of the democratic process, particularly in the area of criminal justice.

Jennifer Fleetwood
University of Kent

See also Criminal Associations; Drug Trade: Source, Destination, and Transit Countries; Globalization; Impact of Transnational Crime; Measuring Transnational Crime; Money Laundering: History; Money Laundering: Methods; Money Laundering: Targeting Criminal Proceeds; Money Laundering: Vulnerable Commodities and Services; Organized Crime: Defined; Transnational Crime: Defined

Further Readings

European Monitoring Centre for Drugs and Drug Addiction. *Cocaine: A European Union Perspective in the Global Context.* The Hague: Europol, 2010.

United Nations Office on Drugs and Crime. *World Drug Report.* Vienna: Author, 2010.

Youngers, C. and E. Rosin. *Drugs and Democracy in Latin America.* Washington, DC: Washington Office on Latin America, 2005.

COMMISSIONS AND PAYOFFS

In relation to transnational crimes, commissions and payoffs are forms of potentially corrupt activities that involve the giving, offering, receiving, or soliciting of bribes or inducements, most often in the context of international business transactions, especially in relation to the granting of contracts or permissions to trade. These transactions usually occur between companies (private bribery) and/or between companies and public officials (public corruption), but individuals may also be convicted without corporations being charged, even in those countries that have corporate criminal liability on their statutes. Such commissions and payoffs therefore involve the giving or offering of an advantage to induce a service or a specified action or omission. These desired services, actions, and/or omissions can be for legal activities (such as public contracts) or illegal activities (such as drug smuggling), and inducements usually involve monetary payments but can take the form of gifts, loans that may never need to be repaid, fees, services (including sexual services), and donations.

The scale and scope of inducements can vary. Low-level, one-off, small "transaction" or "facilitation" payments may be intended not to change decisions, but rather to ensure or accelerate the performance of the receiver in the course of the receiver's formal duties—for example, to accelerate an application process for a permit or a license. Such payments are currently permitted under U.S. law. However, high-level, often systematic bribe-paying, which may be in the millions of dollars U.S., that aims to ensure anticompetitive and/or unlawful behavior by officials, such as inappropriately allocating public contracts, are illegal. Differing cultural and normative frameworks throughout the world shape the (il)legality of these actions in different countries. However, the extrajurisdictional reach of the U.S. Foreign Corrupt Practices Act of 1977 (FCPA) and the United Kingdom's Bribery Act of 2010 render multinational companies liable for such high-level international transactions, even if the country where the bribe or extortionist lives does not criminalize the behavior or does not act in practice against it.

Commissions usually take the form of a percentage of the money received for a given transaction or as a sum to the responsible agent or intermediary. They provide financial incentives in numerous legitimate business settings, although they are not universally permitted. Commissions in public arms contracts in India are prohibited, for example, in order to reduce their appeal to corrupt intermediaries and agents. However, commissions may also be used illegally to disguise illegal bribes, inducements, and payoffs in transnational business transactions and therefore knowingly or with "willful blindness" provide funds for illicit behavior. When conducting business overseas, companies may appoint agents or intermediaries to act on their behalf to assist in winning or extending business contracts. Illegal commissions, usually in cash or valuable considerations such as businesses, real estate, or securities, may be used to aid this and may involve written contracts that appear to be lawful. For example, company A in the United States may provide agent B, who is based in developing country C and who has local knowledge and expertise, with US$5 million in commissions to acquire and "negotiate" contracts. Agent B may then pay staff at state-owned company D or government official E in order to win or maintain such contracts. Agent B has acted under the instruction of U.S. company A, which authorized the commission fees paid to the agent. Commissions, then, can be used by legitimate organizations to create opportunities for bribes and payoffs. If there is a subsequent investigation, the proportionality of such payments may be an issue in guiding the extent of individual or corporate knowledge of what would be done with the funds.

"Payoffs" can be used by agents and intermediaries to corrupt and pay off overseas officials in order to induce favorable actions or omissions. They may be taken from large commission fees paid to the third party as outlined above, may be regular payments to encourage officials to turn a blind eye to illegal activities (such as the smuggling of drugs, people, or minerals), or may be stand-alone, one-off payments for a specific act or omission. The purpose of the payoff may sometimes go beyond the inducing of, or acceleration of, a specific act or omission and intend to acquire the official for an extended period of time. Synonyms of *payoffs* include kickbacks, grease-money, and baksheesh. For example, client Z, the briber, offers or gives an advantage as an inducement for an action to state agent Y, the receiver. In this arrangement, client Z receives a service or other form of advantage to which client Z has no entitlement, such as a tax rebate or public contract, and which constitutes an illegal or unethical action or breach of trust. An example of this process would be a company paying off an official in order to be included in a list of qualified bidders. "Ad hoc" funds and "slush funds" may also be created to enable both one-off payoffs to especially influential people (if and when such requirements should arise) or to enable systematic payoffs or bribes to

predetermined organizations and individuals. Such payoffs can be made on behalf of organizations or for individual private gain, although the latter usually accompanies the former.

The company, the intermediary, and the bribe receiver can be held liable for prosecution in various jurisdictions. This depends on the legal provisions in the countries where the company is based and where the bribe is paid, as well as the extrajurisdictional reach of other anticorruption legislation. The U.S. FCPA and the U.K. Bribery Act enable agencies in these countries to investigate and prosecute companies that, while not based in their jurisdictions, nonetheless conduct business there. Prosecution can lead to criminal and civil sanctions, including fines, individual incarceration, and company debarment.

Nicholas Lord
Cardiff University

See also Anticorruption Legislation; Bribery and Graft; Corporate Liability; Corruption

Further Readings

Lambsdorff, Johann Graf. *The Institutional Economics of Corruption and Reform: Theory, Evidence, and Policy.* Cambridge: Cambridge University Press, 2007.

Reisman, Michael W. *Folded Lies.* New York: Free Press, 1979.

Rose-Ackermann, Susan. "The Political Economy of Corruption." In *Corruption and the Global Economy*, Kimberly Ann Elliot, ed. Washington, DC: Institute for International Economics, 1997.

COMMUNICATION TECHNOLOGIES

Criminals and crime networks have taken advantage of technological developments and improved global communications to expand their scope of activities. Criminals have always been able to transcend national borders. Global high-speed digital networks have significantly changed myriad criminal activities. The communication revolution has created new opportunities for criminals and new challenges for justice systems and professionals. The impacts of such international criminal activities substantially affect worldwide commerce and security. Although it is considerably challenging to afford adequate and effective protections domestically, it is even more daunting in a global context. In the setting of the global information infrastructure of the Internet, with its digital distribution systems, nation-based (let alone subnational) enforcement agencies and approaches are increasingly irrelevant. The enormous economic potential of information superhighways has, not surprisingly, attracted the attention of the criminally inclined. Many significant privacy and security issues are related to global communications factors; moreover, there is an expanding realm of cybercrime.

Historical Background

Telecommunications infrastructures were under development long before electronic computers became a pervasive technology. Samuel Morse's first telegraph transmission in May 1844 crossed the threshold into the "wired world." Seven years later, the first undersea cable was stretched beneath the English Channel, while the first transatlantic cable began transmitting messages in 1866. The introduction of the telegraph created expectations of global peace and harmony, but criminal elements soon began to utilize this and subsequent technological developments, including the telephone and radio.

In the 1950s, the United States became a wired nation with the pervasive presence of television sets in homes across the country. This phenomenon eventually overtook the rest of the planet. There were accompanying sociopolitical changes. In the 1960s and 1970s, developments in computing led to the linking of computers through the Advanced Research Projects Agency Network (ARPANET), allowing geographically dispersed users to access powerful computer systems. Computer-networking developments progressed throughout the 1970s and 1980s, eventually spawning the formation of the Internet. Although Americans became more libertarian domestically in the 1980s, particularly as a result of the Reagan administration, they became more activist globally, aided in part by global communications factors. The end of the Cold War aided criminal organizations in expanding their horizons and attaining global reach. Technological innovations of the 1990s, such as those in Silicon Valley, gave the United States substantial economic surpluses to use to expand its influence globally. As the War on Drugs escalated at a time when the United States military had moved to an all-volunteer force, there was, of necessity, an increasing reliance upon the use of private contractors; much of their operations

depended on global communications technologies. The nature and scope of global communications technologies have expanded exponentially, along with the growth of the Internet and the World Wide Web, and these factors have altered many aspects of everyday life across the planet.

The Internet, the network of networks, and other global communication structures enabled the germination and flourishing of globalization. The forces of cyberspace and globalization reciprocally fueled each other. Information delivery increased in importance as more users regularly accessed global communications systems. Cybernetics and communications theories recognized that the flow of information was altering social relations; criminals have recognized new opportunities as well. Privacy and security issues became significant areas of concern in an era of electronic networking. Since cyberspace is borderless and makes it exceedingly difficult to relate illegal activities to actual physical locations and jurisdictions, fundamental challenges have arisen with regard to how to regulate criminal activity conducted within it.

Privacy and Security Issues

Security is a core human value, whereas privacy, although important to many Americans and others, is not necessarily a universal concern. A filter, for instance, is a technological tool that permits users to control the type of incoming information that a Web browser can display. Governments can and have blocked material to which they object from being available to users in their territories; China, for example, has been a flagrant user of this type of technology. A larger concern for many individuals and organizations, however, is with outgoing information. Cookies are small data files that many Websites use to identify you every time you visit their site; other technologies attempt to collect much more information, without intentionally trying to inform you about the process. Immense quantities of transaction-generated information raise serious questions about individual control over the release of personal information. Theft of proprietary information and assaults on electronic money management systems have become rampant, given the nature of global communication networks.

Hacking and cracking are specific types of security concern. A hacker or cracker breaks into computers and attempts to steal files and other information.

Techniques to do so include the use of authentication bypassing, buffer overflows, password cracking, session hijacking, and spoofing. Many governmental organizations, such as the United States' Central Intelligence Agency (CIA), National Aeronautics and Space Administration (NASA), and Department of Justice, have had their Websites hacked. Espionage has become far easier with the openness of global communication networks. Various models for secure interconnection of global communications networks suggest that common ethics should serve as the basis for legal, managerial, and operational procedures; of course, other layers of technical and administrative protection should be considered as well.

Computer crime, much of which is characterized as cybercrime, has become a reality. Attacks on computers, networks, Websites, and files can come from many sources. These include pranksters, financial thieves, and terrorists; attacks can consist of denial of service or take far more subversive forms. The Internet Fraud Complaint Center has been established to serve as a clearinghouse to collect and review complaints about these sorts of crimes. Extortion, harassment, or threats can be perpetrated readily and relentlessly, given the far-flung reach of cyber stalking.

The increased number of people online has created a tremendous pool of potential victims of cybercrimes. Many fraudulent and misleading Internet-based scams have been perpetrated as purported financial investment schemes. There has been, for example, a plethora of money scams coming from Nigeria. Identity theft and profiling are two other rapidly growing areas of cybercrime that have received the attention of the U.S. Federal Trade Commission (FTC). Online advertising of prostitution services (via Craigslist, for example), solicitation of minors, child pornography, and related activities have expanded because of the power of global communication networks.

Privacy advocates have battled against any efforts to enhance the capacity of law enforcement to conduct electronic surveillance activities. Nevertheless, changes in global communications and computer technologies have yielded great opportunities for electronic surveillance techniques. However, this clearly raises a host of practical and legal problems. Digital networks carry not only telephone traffic but also immense amounts of e-mail, text messaging, instant messaging, voice-over Internet protocols, videoconferencing, and other communication formats. The problem of monitoring the immense volume of electronic communication was highlighted with the Federal Bureau of Investigation's (FBI) use of Carnivore, a controversial Internet wiretapping system. The immense volume of contemporary global communication raises daunting challenges to law enforcement.

Cryptography applications based on algorithms have been developed with the hope of maintaining privacy for those on the Internet. However, there is an encryption conundrum for American software developers, as the U.S. government has imposed very severe export restrictions on encryption technology. Nevertheless, encryption software is readily available, such as Pretty Good Privacy (PGP), a freely available encryption program that can help protect the privacy of e-mail and other transmitted files. The points at which individuals directly interface with global communications networks appear to be the most vulnerable in terms of security. Biometrics may offer some assistance in authenticating user identities. Cybercriminals, however, have been very industrious in finding ways to counter encryption technologies.

Information warfare is thought to cost the United States an estimated $300 billion each year through criminal activities such as counterfeiting, industrial espionage, data eavesdropping, hacker attacks, code breaking, and viruses. Computer viruses that can infiltrate and harm hardware and data have been around for some time. Web servers need to be protected from information harvesting by robots, automated programs that recursively follow links. Technological protections, such as firewalls, packet filtering, and proxying solutions, can be configured to offer a modicum of security within the desired state of greater Internet accessibility. Computer emergency response teams (CERTs) are coordinated through the Forum of Incident Response and Security Teams (FIRST) to monitor the Internet continually for security incidents and to develop responsive advisories.

Cybercriminals

Cybercriminals are harder to trace and prosecute than are more standard types of criminals. One variant specializes in breaking the security of computer systems; they then transmit unauthorized program files, rifle accounts, and steal government or company secrets. Cybercriminals can participate as disguised individuals in virtual communities. It must also be recognized that the information and intelligence networks of some criminal organizations have been far superior to those of law enforcement. An array of weapons is used by cybercriminals who engage in these types of activities, such as distributed denial-of-service attacks, logic bombs, masquerades, Trojan horses (such as BackOrifice), viruses, war dialers, and worms. Various techniques have been developed to detect these diverse approaches. Computer viruses, for example, can be detected by using pattern scanners, integrity checkers, and behavior blockers. Organizations such as the CIA, the FBI, and the Institute for the Advanced Study of Information Warfare study this type of information theft. Many of the initial instances of cybercrime were reported in the United States, but it has since spread around the globe as telecommunications systems have been adopted across the planet. Electronic data, which may be both directly and indirectly accessible, represent completely new types of assets that are subject to new forms of fraud, theft, and unauthorized use. Electronic information can easily be taken and moved across both physical and virtual borders, posing even greater challenges for law-enforcement efforts than in the past.

Cybercriminals infringe on copyrights by downloading and copying intellectual property such as movies and music without paying royalties or other appropriate forms of remuneration. Copyright infringement, along with privacy violations and piracy concerns, is pursued by the U.S. Department of Justice's Computer Crime and Intellectual Property Section.

The detection of cybercrime has become a major problem. Most instances of such crimes are discovered by accident. Sometimes considerable time may have elapsed since the crime occurred and when it was discovered; this, of course, hampers effective investigation and prosecution efforts. Even when such a cybercrime is discovered, whether by local, regional, or national authorities or by those in the private sector, there is frequently a reluctance to report the crime, often from fear of adverse publicity as well as a loss of public trust. However, any findings and evidentiary materials should be submitted to law enforcement and, if appropriate, corporate investigators.

Law Enforcement

For many law-enforcement agencies, the Internet and other global communications infrastructures enabled major advances in availability and accessibility of information. Websites are open 24 hours a day, seven days a week, affording individuals and organizations increased access to information, as well as a certain degree of interaction with authorities, such as via e-mails. Interagency cooperation and access to criminal justice databases and other resources have substantially enhanced efficiency and expediency of many law-enforcement endeavors.

Law-enforcement agencies are looking into better ways to provide services to more citizens online. This has fostered a citizen-oriented service approach with more fluid communication between agencies and systems. Many law-enforcement agencies operate with a wide selection of forms, which can now be completed online or downloaded and completed at will. Organizational barriers have been breached somewhat by these types of developments, although there is some resistance, which is not unexpected. While it is conceivable that some of these organizational barriers will evaporate under the force of the existence of global networks, difficulties will need to be resolved by means of cooperation and agreement between law-enforcement departments, other agencies, and the private sector. Interoperability difficulties need to be addressed to permit greater access to electronic public law-enforcement-related services from computerized and other applications.

Law enforcement has acquired myriad communication devices for sending, receiving, and storing messages from varied sources through an array of devices and channels. However, communicative and analytical technologies are still somewhat underused by law enforcement; the complex and rich potential of these technologies has yet to be fully utilized. The varied media can be mined in many ways. For instance, evidence of global criminal activity, such as smuggling, can be obtained from communication records, like mobile cell phone logs or computer data files, which can be incidental to criminal activity but still of high evidentiary value. Communication technologies will no doubt continue to evolve rapidly through phases of stability and instability. Advances in smart objects, variants of pervasive computing, intelligent software, and so forth will certainly present new challenges for crime prevention and other law-enforcement efforts as criminals create new strategies. Furthermore, developers of global communication networks must adopt measures that will make their media less attractive to criminals and others who promote crime, including terrorist organizations.

Summary

Communication technologies can be both targets and instruments of crime. Criminals and crime networks have taken advantage of technological developments and improved global communications; law enforcement has as well. The nature of transnational crime has changed as communication technologies have altered the environments and methods of crime. Greater attention must be paid to concerns of privacy and security of communication systems, and new techniques of auditing and tracking of data are also necessary. Consequently, law-enforcement professionals need additional training and resources to deal with these larger spheres of operation.

Victor B. Stolberg
Essex County College

See also Computer-Generated Scams; Copyright Infringement; Globalization; Nigerian Money Scams; Technology; Telemarketing Fraud

Further Readings

Koherti, Nir. "Pattern of Global Cyber War and Crime: A Conceptual Framework." *Journal of International Management*, v.11/4 (2005).

Kovacich, Gerald L. *High-Technology-Crime Investigator's Handbook: Working in the Global Information Environment.* Burlington, MA: Elsevier, 2000.

Mansell, Robin and Brian S. Collins, eds. *Trust and Crime in Information Societies.* Northampton, MA: Edward Elgar, 2005.

Stephenson, Peter. *Investigating Computer-Related Crime: A Handbook for Corporate Investigators.* Boca Raton, FL: CRC Press, 2000.

COMPLICITY OF THE INTERNATIONAL COMMUNITY

The phrase *complicity of the international community* has come to mean the inaction or silence of foreign governments during episodes of civil war or conflict that result in many deaths of civilians, sometimes bordering on genocide. The limits of international law govern foreign intervention, whether by the United Nations, or unilaterally from the United States or some other exterior power. The international community has been labeled complicit in several atrocities from the conflicts in former Yugoslavia to as recently as in Syria, where the opposition leadership in 2011 accused the international community of complicity due to inaction during the civil protests against the Syrian regime and the resulting brutal crackdowns. But one instance stands out as defining the concept of complicity of the international community and that is the Rwandan Civil War.

The Rwandan Civil War, which culminated in the 1994 Rwandan Genocide, began in 1990 when the Rwandan Patriotic Front (RPF) invaded Rwanda from Uganda. The civil war was a continuation of a conflict between the country's two most prominent ethnic groups, the Tutsis and the Hutus, which dates at least to colonial times, when Belgian colonialists elevated the Tutsi minority—whom they believed may have had some European ancestry—to a greater position of power than the Hutu majority. By the time Rwanda gained independence, Belgium had changed its allegiance, supporting the Hutu activists who demanded an end to the Tutsi monarchy. The Hutus' greater numbers allowed them to easily gain control of the government in Rwanda's first general elections, and the Tutsis became an oppressed minority. Further, in nearby Burundi—which had become separate from Rwanda in 1962—the Tutsis were able to retain power, and in 1972 conducted a campaign of genocide against the Hutus who had attempted to overthrow them, making the Tutsi/Hutu conflict one that spanned several countries.

The Rwandan Patriotic Front consisted of Tutsis who had fled Rwanda over the previous 30 years, and had formed in 1987 with the goal of returning Rwandan refugees to Rwanda by force, and to return Tutsis to power. Many of them were soldiers and officers in the Ugandan Army. The invasion increased support in Rwanda for stricter Hutu control of the country and its media, and for the ideology of Hutu Power, which portrayed Tutsis as a threat that must be contained or resisted. When President Habyarimana was assassinated in April 1994, months after the ceasefire he initiated in response to international pressures, the Hutus retaliated with mass killings of both Tutsis and "collaborationist" Hutus.

One of the central figures in the story of the Rwandan Genocide is Lieutenant-General Roméo Dallaire, the Force Commander of UNAMIR, the United Nations Assistance Mission for Rwanda, between 1993 and 1994. Dallaire (b.1946 in the Netherlands) had served in the Canadian Army since 1963, and in 1993 received his commission as UNAMIR's Force Commander. UNAMIR was deployed to assist Habyarimana's Hutu government in implementing the Arusha Accords, which had been signed in August 1993. The Arusha Accords established a Broad-Based Transitional Government (BBTG) that shared power among the Rwandan Patriotic Front and the five political parties that had made up the temporary government since 1992. The rebel RPF was allowed to participate in the national assembly, and soldiers from the RPF were integrated into the Rwandan army. Under the Accords, the BBTG would last for 22 months, to be followed by general elections.

On January 11, 1994, Dallaire received a fax from a former member of Habyarimana's security staff, alerting him to an upcoming attack on the Tutsi faction. A paramilitary organization backed by the Hutu government, the Interahamwe ("those who stand together"), had arranged a shipment of weapons and ammunition that would arrive in the capital city of Kigali, to be used against the Tutsis after forcing a Belgian withdrawal. Dallaire contacted the United Nations but was told that, because the shipment of weapons and ammunition predated the signing of the Arusha Accords, seizing it or otherwise intervening was outside his mandate.

Dallaire's fax would appear later in an article by journalist Philip Gourevitch, which was developed into a book titled *We Wish to Inform You That Tomorrow We Will Be Killed With Our Families*. The book, published in 1998, demonstrates that the Hutu genocide had clearly been planned, that the necessary information had been disclosed to peacekeeping forces, and that the international community had remained inactive. Three months after Dallaire sent the dispatch to the United Nations, on April 26, 1994, Habyarimana was shot coming back from Tanzania, and the Tutsis were immediately blamed. Despite the fact that Dallaire had ordered 10 Belgian soldiers to protect the prime minister, Agathe Uwilingiyimana, she was killed along with her husband and the Belgian soldiers. Dallaire pleaded to the United Nations for the reinforcement of troops and more logistic support, but again the United Nations refused in spite of the fact that the international media were reporting that this was not the usual civil war between rival ethnic groups, but had progressed to genocide.

A number of factors combined to secure the inaction of the Security Council. The United States,

one of the five permanent members of the United Nations, argued that the Rwandan conflict was not different from any other tribal war that would subside without the need of an armed intervention. The Clinton administration's policy was that Rwanda was to be left to its fate. Second, U.S. peacekeeping forces sent into Somalia had only recently been unsuccessful at achieving their objectives, and the public reaction was that undue deaths had been caused in the absence of major stakes. Third, Rwanda was at the time a temporary rotating member of the Security Council, and its representative argued against intervention. France, which had provided the weapons in the Kigali shipment, supported Rwanda's argument.

The Security Council's decision was to take no action, in spite of ample media coverage of the genocide. It was not until the end of May, six weeks after the mass killings began, that the United States acknowledged that genocide was occurring. The United Nations originally had 1,500 troops in Rwanda, but the Belgians withdrew their troops after Uwilingiyimana's assassination. The Bangladeshi troops were also soon withdrawn, leaving fewer than 500 troops in the country. The United Nations continued to resist diplomatic and economic pressures to deny the legitimacy of the Rwandan government and take action against the ongoing genocide. Over 100 days, an estimated 800,000 people were killed, ending with the RPF takeover of Kigali and the establishment of a new Tutsi-dominated government. Refugee camps were set up all along the Rwandan borders to accommodate some of the million and a half people fleeing the country.

Livia Holden
Lahore University of Management Sciences

See also Genocide; United Nations; United Nations: Typologies of Criminal Structures/Operations

Further Readings

Dellaire, R. *Shake Hands With the Devil: The Failure of Humanity in Rwanda*. New York: Random House, 2003.

Khan, Shaharyan M. *The Shallow Graves of Rwanda*. London: Tauris, 2001.

Raymont, P. *Shake Hands With the Devil: The Journey of Roméo Dallaire*. Documentary. Montreal, QC: National Film Board of Canada, 2004.

COMPUTER-GENERATED SCAMS

Computer-generated schemes and scams usually begin with a potential victim receiving unsolicited contact by telephone or e-mail. There are significant transnational concerns over such scams, given the proliferation of global digital communication and a popular interest in preserving the economic, social, and political prospects of services, sales, and social networking online. Cyberspace facilitates easy contact with persons in most corners of the world. This, plus the posting of personal details once deemed private in online databanks available worldwide, means that scammers in one country can victimize a citizen in another country rapidly, in a faceless manner, using information that is publicly available or naïvely rendered.

Beyond public access information on the Internet, data might be obtained by creating a fake Website that solicits the information (for example, a fake loan or credit card application Website) through a process called phishing. If necessary, the scammer may go further by embedding malware, such as the Zeus Trojan, in e-mails sent to business or personal e-mail addresses. If the e-mail is opened, the malware is planted and then captures personal information stored on the victim's computer.

In 2010, 60 persons, mostly based in eastern Europe, were prosecuted for a Zeus Trojan attack that resulted in the theft of $4 million from persons in the United States. The Zeus/Zbot Trojan is a type of Bredolab malware. Another case involved a variant of the Bredolab out of Ukraine that was sent to a business in an e-mail response about a job posting. When the unsuspecting person opened the e-mail, the malware was planted. It captured private company financial data that the scammers used later to steal funds. Adware or cookie surveillance might also be used to capture a person's online activity. Information might also be obtained when persons are tourists overseas or by many other means while people are traveling: dumpster diving in personal or business trash, skimming information on credit or debit cards, looking over a person's shoulder when the person is entering a password, using a keystroke logger (which captures what the person types on a computer keypad), stealing a person's purse or wallet, breaking into a person's lodging, or eavesdropping.

Scammers in one country can use computer-generated schemes to anonymously victimize a citizen in another country, using information that is publicly available or carelessly given when requested by any number of scams involving phony lotteries, prizes, and charities, among other gimmicks. (Photos.com)

Common computer-generated scams include phony lotteries, phony raffles or other prizes, charities, dating services, adoptions, housing deals, auctions, job offers, business communications, inheritance announcements, and computer virus claims requiring immediate action. In the phony lottery, persons are told via e-mail that they have won a foreign lottery. To claim the prize, fees and a bank account number will be required. The scammers will then empty the victim's account. The victim is left with little recourse because it is illegal for U.S. citizens to engage in foreign lotteries. With phony raffles or prizes, the person is told that he or she won something, often in Europe. He or she might even be invited to select a prize from various options. Funds are then required to remit the prize, which the victim is told may take some time to arrive from overseas. A worthless gift or nothing is eventually sent.

In charity scams, a fake Website or unsolicited contact will solicit personal financial information for a charity or cause. The scams proliferate after a major tragedy such as a hurricane. In dating-service scams, people are asked to pay in advance to obtain a visa and other fees to date foreign, often "attractive

Russian women." Photographs of supposedly interested women are sent to the victim and phony e-mail communications with the women might go on for a while to encourage the victim's making the required payments. In other dating scams, persons receive e-mails that their profile has been viewed online. Next, these persons are directed to a Website to see who is interested in their profile—but to see it a fee is required.

In adoption scams, a woman who may or may not be pregnant will place ads online offering her baby for adoption. The scammer might agree to give the child to multiple couples, each unaware of the others. During the course of the pregnancy, the supposed mother will request funds to take care of the baby—to eat well, for rent, to pay for doctor's appointments, and so on. Shortly before the supposed baby is due, the scammer will cut off communication.

In housing scams, the scammer might send a fake check in excess of the rent or deposit required and request that the change is remitted to him or her. Another housing scam involves the scammer's using an advertisement for housing that is altered to show the scammer's contact information. Interested parties are then told to send their housing rent or deposit to an address overseas where the "owners" are on business or vacation.

In auction or retail scams, high-priced products are advertised at bargain prices. The scammer might tell the victim that he or she cannot receive payment by PayPal, so the money should be wired via Western Union or sent directly to a specific bank account. Some retail scams focus on offering a subscription to adult materials. To prove that the person is old enough to subscribe, personal information is required, plus credit card information to subscribe. Once this information is given, the person is charged a surprisingly large fee. Efforts to cancel the subscription or to obtain a refund are futile. The victim then absorbs the loss out of embarrassment. With online auctions, the scammer might create fake accounts and act as a shill (someone who bids merely to drive up legitimate bids). Once payment is sent, what is delivered is not what was promised, or nothing is delivered.

In job offer scams, persons are sent a fake check in excess of what was owed for some task performed or to be performed and are then asked to send back the extra funds. In some cases, the victim is asked for his or her banking information so that advance payment might be deposited directly into the victim's bank account. Other job offer scams emphasize the possibility of working from home and making a lot of money. Some of these e-mails might be sent from the hacked e-mail address of someone whom the potential victim knows with a message that endorses the opportunity. The e-mail will often direct the target to a Website with fake testimonials by persons who supposedly live in the target's ZIP code area. If the potential victim expresses interest, funds are required to obtain a starter kit for this promising opportunity. Of course, the opportunity does not prove to be real.

In business communications, an e-mail is sent to the target claiming to be from a business that the person utilizes, asking for information to rectify a problem such as access to an account. The scam might even direct the target to a phony Website on which to enter the information. In inheritance scams, such as the Nigerian 419 scam (419 is Nigeria's criminal code for the offense), persons receive e-mails stating that to receive a large inheritance, some funds are required or bank account information is needed to send the inheritance. In computer virus scams persons receive e-mails that their computer is infected and that they need to buy something to address the problem right away. In all of these schemes and scams, if they succeed, the victim loses.

Other computer-generated schemes include Websites where schemers offer fake diplomas, fake scientific journals, and fake medicines or medications that make false claims. Some persons have created Websites with domain names very similar to those of legitimate Websites and include a payment section in the hope that people will mistakenly enter personal financial information.

Efforts to prevent individuals and groups that are motivated to commit computer-generated schemes and scams are limited. Thus, much of the prevention focus is on public awareness and warnings to maintain privacy and avoid deals that are too good to be true. One offensive technique is called reverse scamming or scam baiting, whereby persons engage the scammers with the aim of frustrating them by causing the scammers some expense and time. There have also been laws that address the international aspects of the problem and changes in the nature of policing toward capturing perpetrators. In the 1990s, the G8 nations—Canada, France, Germany, Italy, Japan, Russia, the United Kingdom, and the United States—crafted a cybercrime plan in accordance with the Council of Europe Convention on Cybercrime. The aim was to make both substantive and procedural laws compatible across nations to facilitate the prosecution of computer crimes across national borders and to develop the capacity of investigators. The efforts began in 2004.

Camille Gibson
Prairie View A&M University

See also Adjudicating International Crimes; Charity Fraud; Counterfeit Goods; Eastern Europe and Russia; Telemarketing Fraud

Further Readings

Bocij, Paul. *The Dark Side of the Internet: Protecting Yourself and Your Family From Online Criminals.* Westport, CT: Praeger, 2006.

Grabosky, Peter. *Electronic Crime.* Upper Saddle River, NJ: Pearson/Prentice Hall, 2007.

Jewkes, Yvonne and Majid Yar. *Handbook of Internet Crime.* Cullompton, UK: Willan, 2009.

Maras, Marie-Helen. *Computer Forensics: Cybercriminals, Laws, and Evidence.* Sudbury, MA: Jones and Bartlett, 2012.

CONVENTIONS, AGREEMENTS, AND REGULATIONS

A series of international instruments enable nations to cooperate and coordinate their efforts to combat transnational organized crime. Such cooperation is necessary to track perpetrators, victims, and illicit proceeds across national borders and jurisdictional lines and to make the most effective use of limited resources.

The United Nations (UN) and regional organizations have enacted a multitude of international instruments to address transnational organized crime. Each instrument is unique in its scope and its approach to joint action, but such instruments have several common features. Often nations are required to create legislation that criminalizes both primary crimes, such as human trafficking, and enabling activities, such as money laundering. Instruments also regularly include a mechanism for financial assistance and a framework for mutual cooperation in law enforcement, extradition, information exchange, capacity building, and training. The UN

Convention Against Transnational Crime, which entered into force in 2003, is the most extensive of the international instruments to date. It provides a flexible framework under which nations pledge to pursue cooperative activities through detailed regional and topical instruments. This flexible structure permits international and regional organizations to adapt international cooperation agreements to address the changing and expanding nature of transnational organized crime.

UN Convention Against Transnational Organized Crime

The UN Convention Against Transnational Organized Crime was intentionally crafted to be flexible in its scope and its requirements so that it might better respond to changes in the nature of transnational organized crime and so that it might be implemented by a wide range of nations with varying national legal requirements. The convention is unusual in two respects: It encompasses transnational crime worldwide rather than in a single region, and it targets the mechanisms that enable transnational organized crime rather than an individual or a set of transnational crimes. By contrast, most instruments are limited to a single geographic region or an individual crime.

The convention was signed in Palermo, Italy, and is therefore sometimes called the Palermo Convention. It is the result of early efforts at the 1994 World Ministerial Conference on Organized Transnational Crime, where more than 142 nations recognized the need for an overarching convention on transnational crime and unanimously adopted the Naples Political Declaration and Global Action Plan against transnational crime.

The convention does not contain a list of transnational organized crimes, either crimes organized criminal groups might commit or crimes nations may wish to combat. Drafters of the convention were concerned that it would prove too difficult to gain political support for a long list of crimes and that the types of activities in which organized crime groups were likely to participate would change too quickly for the convention to remain relevant if it were limited to a list of specified crimes. Instead, drafters limited the convention to serious crimes committed by organized criminal groups. An organized criminal group is defined as one with three or more members who join together for an extended time with the intent to engage in multiple criminal activities for illicit gain. A serious crime is one punishable by a maximum of four years' imprisonment or more. By limiting the convention to serious organized crimes, the drafters restricted the scope of the convention while retaining ample flexibility for nations to combat a range of criminal activities.

As the nature of these serious organized crimes is changeable, the convention focuses on preventing activities that enable transnational crimes and on building the capacity of less developed nations to combat transnational crimes. The convention does so in three ways: by criminalizing activities that enable transnational crime, by facilitating law-enforcement cooperation, and by developing new frameworks for financial assistance. The convention requires nations to create legislation that criminalizes money laundering, corruption, obstruction of justice, and participation in an organized criminal group. The decision to include participation in a criminal organization represents a particularly significant step in the prosecution of organized criminal groups. The provision represents a compromise between states that wished to criminalize mere membership in a criminal group and those, such as the United States, whose domestic law requires an act in support of a criminal conspiracy in order to establish liability. The corruption provision was included so as to note its important connection to transnational crime, but the drafters, recognizing the complex nature of corruption, left detailed definitions and enforcement requirements for later, more specific instruments. This method of drafting gives the convention concrete goals and the flexibility to adapt to national legislative requirements and political pressures.

The convention demonstrates similar flexibility in its provisions on law-enforcement assistance. Rather than require nations to take specific actions, the convention recommends areas for improvement and requires states to pursue further bilateral and regional agreements as appropriate. For example, the convention mentions extradition as an important component of international assistance, but it leaves the specifics as to when extradition is appropriate to national legislation and bilateral treaties. The convention similarly promotes mutual legal assistance, the transfer of criminal proceeds, the exchange of information regarding organized criminal groups, and the exchange of information and technology for modern investigative methods. The need for and extent of such cooperation are then left to nations to determine on a bilateral or regional basis.

Increased law-enforcement efforts can be resource-intensive, which presents a challenge for those developing nations where criminal organizations are most prevalent. The convention therefore contains provisions for financial assistance that cover the development of training programs for law enforcement as well as the financing of cooperative and capacity-building programs. Financial assistance may occur at a bilateral level or through the UN.

UN Efforts Against Transnational Crime

Beyond the Convention Against Transnational Organized Crime, the majority of UN efforts has focused on particular transnational crimes rather than on the problem as a whole. As a result, numerous new international instruments have been required to adapt to changes in the nature of transnational crime. Of particular note are treaties addressing corruption, drug trafficking, human trafficking, and terrorism.

Corruption is a pervasive problem that has only recently been addressed in connection with organized crime. It was included in the Convention Against Transnational Organized Crime but, because of the complex nature of the problem, was not completely addressed. Instead, the UN enacted a separate and more comprehensive Convention Against Corruption (UNCAC), which entered into force in 2005. UNCAC focuses primarily on prevention of corruption, and it includes model policies for increasing transparency in election financing and implementing anticorruption mechanisms in both public and private sectors. UNCAC also promotes international cooperation in the form of legal assistance, the gathering and transfer of evidence, extradition, and the recovery of illicit proceeds. It was a progressive step to include asset recovery as a fundamental principle of UNCAC, but it was important for many developing nations whose limited resources have been plundered by corrupt officials with access to foreign markets.

Illegal drug trafficking has long been a source of concern for the UN, although the types of drugs and the methods of regulation have changed over the years. The 1961 Single Convention on Narcotic Drugs is limited in scope to narcotics, but it aims to combat drug abuse generally through intervention and control of the substances. It limits drug trade to exclusively medical and scientific purposes and promotes international law-enforcement cooperation. The 1971 Convention on Psychotropic Substances responded to a broadening spectrum of drugs by introducing controls over synthetic drugs. The 1988 Convention Against Illicit Traffic in Narcotic Drugs and Psychotropic Substances is even broader in scope and includes provisions against money laundering and the purchase of precursor chemicals. It also promotes cooperation on controlled delivery of legal drugs and extradition of offenders.

Historically, the UN has regarded human trafficking as a matter of women's and children's rights. The UN included provisions against trafficking in the Convention on the Elimination of All Forms of Discrimination Against Women (CEDAW) and the Convention on the Rights of the Child (CRC). It also adopted measures against the forced sale of children and the exploitation of the prostitution of others. An increased awareness of human trafficking of men for forced labor has resulted in new and broader trafficking instruments. The Convention Against Transnational Organized Crime was adopted simultaneously with two protocols on trafficking: the Protocol to Prevent, Suppress, and Punish Trafficking in Persons, Especially Women and Children, and the Protocol Against the Smuggling of Migrants by Land, Sea, and Air. These protocols expand protections against trafficking to men, women, and children trafficked for a wide range of illicit purposes.

Terrorism is sometimes considered a new form of transnational organized crime, but it has long been a focus of the UN. Between 1963 and 1999, the international community adopted several instruments relating to the prevention of terrorism. Difficulty in defining the nature of terrorism resulted in a series of instruments that protect potential targets. As the realm of possible targets has expanded, so has the list of antiterrorism conventions protecting those targets, including aircraft (1963), civil aircraft (1971), airports serving civil aviation (1988), internationally protected persons (1973), hostages (1979), nuclear material (1980), maritime navigation (1988), fixed platforms on the continental shelf (1988), and public places (1997). Two conventions that broke from this pattern, criminalizing activities by terrorists, are the Convention Against the Making

of Plastic Explosives (1991) and the International Convention for the Suppression of the Financing of Terrorism (1999). In addition, the Protocol Against the Illicit Manufacturing of and Trafficking in Firearms (2005) supports the Convention Against Transnational Organized Crime and addresses the important connection between arms trafficking and terrorism.

In 2006, the UN General Assembly broke away from its piecemeal approach to counterterrorism and adopted a Global Counter-Terrorism Strategy. The plan of action includes measures to prevent the spread of terrorism by addressing the conditions conducive to it, to prevent and combat terrorism, to build state capacity, to strengthen the role of the UN, and to ensure fundamental human rights as a basis for the fight against terrorism. This plan evinces a new approach to counterterrorism insofar as it promotes the prevention of terrorism through increased economic prosperity and social stability rather than through law enforcement or military means alone. The plan also demonstrates recognition that the nature of organized terrorist groups changes too rapidly to make target-based regulation effective. Instead the plan supports counterterrorism efforts that address the causes and enablers of terrorism and that remain flexible enough to adapt in response to organized criminal groups.

Regional Instruments Against Transnational Organized Crime

In addition to the UN's worldwide efforts against transnational crime, many regional organizations dedicated to economic development, security, and regional stability have adopted multilateral instruments to address transnational organized crime within their geographic areas. The following examples are by no means comprehensive, but they illustrate the common goals of criminalization, financial assistance, and mutual cooperation in law-enforcement activities, and they also demonstrate the use of regionally specific adaptations.

The South Asian Association for Regional Cooperation (SAARC) and the Association of Southeast Asian Nations (ASEAN) have both issued numerous conventions and declarations relating to transnational crime. These include efforts to prevent human trafficking of women and children, trafficking for prostitution, drug trafficking, and terrorism.

In addition, SAARC has issued a broad Convention on Mutual Assistance in Criminal Matters to promote legal enforcement across borders on a variety of topics. ASEAN has an overarching framework for cooperation in the Manila Declaration on the Prevention and Control of Transnational Crime (1998), which built on an earlier declaration by the same name and expanded the scope of the fight against transnational crime. The Manila Declaration remains one of the few regional instruments to address transnational crime broadly rather than focus on a particular crime.

The basic purposes of the Organization of American States (OAS), as articulated in the Constitutive Charter, are to strengthen the security of the continents; to promote democracy; to provide for common defense; to solve political, juridical, and economic problems among member states; and to promote the development of its members. To this end, OAS has issued several conventions to increase cooperation against drug trafficking, trafficking in minors, and terrorism. Of particular note, the Inter-American Convention Against the Manufacture and Illicit Trafficking of Firearms, Munitions, Explosives, and Related Materials (CIFTA, 1998) was the first convention to successfully negotiate a mutually acceptable definition of the term *firearm* and to recognize the important connection of arms trafficking to transnational crime.

The African Union (AU), in addition to adopting instruments for the prevention of human trafficking, drug trafficking, corruption, and terrorism, has taken an unusual approach by choosing to combat transnational organized crime under the auspices of the African Charter on Human and Peoples' Rights. The AU has also developed a set of cooperative instruments that cover crimes specifically relevant to Africa: advanced fee and Internet fraud, diamond smuggling, cigarette smuggling, and oil smuggling. The AU Strategic Plan 2009–12 with regard to Peace and Security specifically calls for the development of new policies toward combating transnational organized crime, and some of these new policies will no doubt promote cooperation to address new areas of concern, such as maritime piracy.

In Europe, the Council of Europe and the European Union (EU) have followed a similarly unusual approach to combating transnational crime. The Council of Europe has certainly enacted conventions governing corruption, migrant worker status, counterterrorism, human trafficking, money laundering, and the return of illicit proceeds. However, the Council's European Court of Human Rights has also prosecuted transnational criminals for violations of the European Convention on Human Rights, particularly with regard to human trafficking. This uncommon but effective use of international human rights law to enforce international criminal law is possible only because of the unusual cross-border power the Council of Europe has given to the Court. In a similarly uncommon move, the EU has promoted cooperative efforts among members of the EU not by establishing numerous instruments but by using its existing framework. The EU has promoted cooperation under two of its founding pillars: common foreign and security policy, and police and judicial cooperation in criminal matters. In addition, the EU has recognized its need to cooperate beyond its limited membership and has established the means to cooperate with some non-EU neighbors through the Pre-Accession Pact on organized crime. This use of existing frameworks centers the fight against transnational crime at the core of the EU mission and lends additional credibility to its continuing struggle against transnational organized crime.

Anne R. Siders
Independent Scholar

See also Extradition; Mutual Legal Assistance Treaties; United Nations

Further Readings

Berdal, M. and M. Serrano. *Transnational Organized Crime and International Security: Business as Usual?* New York: Lynne Rienner, 2002.

Hauck, P. and S. Peterke. "Organized Crime and Gang Violence in National and International Law." *International Review of the Red Cross*, v.92 (2010).

Jojarth, C. *Crime, War, and Global Trafficking: Designing International Cooperation.* Cambridge, UK: Cambridge University Press, 2009.

McClean, D. *Transnational Organized Crime: A Commentary on the UN Convention and Its Protocols.* Oxford, UK: Oxford University Press, 2007.

Schloenhardt, A. "Transnational Organized Crime and International Law: The Palermo Convention." *Criminal Law Journal*, v.29 (2005).

COPYRIGHT INFRINGEMENT

Copyright infringement can be defined as the exercising of any of the exclusive rights of a copyright holder without the express authorization of said holder, or as excused by an exemption or other defense, such as fair use. Substantial similarity to a copyrighted work is sufficient to prove infringement, even if none of the words, musical notes, brushstrokes, or other media-relevant criteria are identical. The holder of a copyright has certain exclusive rights, such as the right to sell or reproduce specific material, violation of which is infringement.

Historical Background

The beginnings of copyright law followed the emergence of printing. The church and sovereign governments attempted to control the production of printers. In 1501, Pope Alexander VI issued a papal bull against the unlicensed printing of books. Early copyright privileges were often given by royalty of a country as monopolies granting the exclusive privilege of printing for a specific time period. Consequently, the history of copyright infringement began primarily as a transnational activity as printers, mainly in other countries, would copy works without permission of or remuneration to the copyright holder. These works were then often smuggled across borders and sold illegally. The first copyright statute was enacted by Great Britain in 1709 and was known as the Statute of Anne; its full title was "An Act for the Encouragement of Learning, by vesting the Copies of Printed Books in the Authors or purchasers of such Copies, during the Times therein mentioned." It limited the term of copyright to 14 years. Copyright laws initially applied only to the copying of books but were expanded to cover an array of works, including translations, maps, paintings, photographs, sound recordings, movies, and computer programs.

A watershed historical moment in international copyright infringement concerns was the September 9, 1866, conclusion of the Berne Convention for the Protection of Literary and Artistic Works. This convention established minimum standards, which were subsequently revised five times, of copyright protection and created a national treatment standard whereby Berne member nations had to afford as much copyright protection to works of those outside their borders as they did to those of their own nationals. Copyright laws generally do not have any extraterritorial jurisdiction. Protection against infringement in a particular country depends mainly on the national laws of that country. Nevertheless, many countries afford protection of foreign works under restricted conditions, most of which are in accord with international copyright treaties and conventions. The use of a copyright notice is recommended even in transnational contexts, because it may help negate a claim of innocent infringement.

Common-law countries, mainly following Anglo-American traditions, have copyright systems that encourage the creation of new works for the public benefit by maintaining protections for the economic rights of created works. This is understood as part of the social contract between individuals and the state. This theory is manifest in Article 1, Section 8, Clause 8 of the U.S. Constitution. Civil-law countries, such as France, typically protect not only the economic rights of creators of copyrighted works but also their moral rights; this distinction is maintained in the Berne Convention.

The United States did not sign the Berne Convention until 1988, and it took effect on March 1, 1989. Copyright infringement became a greater area of concern to the United States when it changed from being a net importer of copyrighted works to the largest global net exporter. However, there was a jurisdictional concern with respect to copyright infringement in a transnational context. There are doctrinal and policy difficulties in applying U.S. laws regarding copyright beyond U.S. borders; this expansion raises territorial questions on the validity of such measures outside U.S. domain. Similarly, how are U.S. courts to deal with foreign copyright protections and laws? Considerable deliberation was needed to determine whose copyright laws apply where. This problem was largely resolved under the Agreement on Trade Related Aspects of Intellectual Property, which subsumed major international copyright obligations under the World Trade Organization's Dispute Settlement System. This process can result in the imposition of trade sanctions on nations, which strongly encourages addressing copyright infringement within areas of their purview. International norms must now be considered in crafting copyright laws. The ability of electronic works to easily evade national regulations has increased the need to harmonize disparate national copyright laws. Furthermore, U.S. courts now assume jurisdiction over foreign activities that result in copyright infringement within the United States.

Control Measures

The Universal Copyright Convention was developed by United Nations Educational, Scientific and Cultural Organization (UNESCO) in 1952 at Geneva. This convention was intended to serve as an alternative to the Berne Convention mainly for developing countries and the former Soviet Union, which felt the Berne Convention overly benefited developed Western, copyright-exporting countries.

The Online Copyright Infringement Liability Act (Public Law 105-304) was passed in the United States in 1988 as Section 512 of the Digital Millennium Copyright Act; it was enacted in order to implement the World Intellectual Property Organization Copyright Treaty and Performances and Phonograms Treaty, to which the United States became a signatory in 1996. The Online Copyright Infringement Liability Act creates conditional safe harbors for online service providers, including Internet service providers and Internet intermediaries, by shielding them from potential liability for copyright infringement, whether direct or indirect. In exchange for this protection, online service providers must fully comply with respective national copyright laws; must implement infringement-preventative measures; must adopt a policy of expeditiously terminating the accounts of repeat infringers; and must also not interfere with standard technical measures. Furthermore, notices of copyright infringement must be sent to a designated agent. Similar laws outside the United States include the European Union's Electronic Commerce Directive, Article 14, which has notification and takedown provisions; the Digital Economy Law of France; and Sections 102 and 103 of the Copyright Law of Korea.

The Office of the U.S. Trade Representative coordinates activities with other U.S. agencies, including the Justice Department, the Department of Commerce, the State Department, and Homeland Security, in combating intellectual property violations. Each year, the U.S. Trade Representative conducts a Special 301 process to identify countries that lack adequate protection for intellectual property. There are several tariff preference programs managed by the U.S. Trade Representative, such as the Generalized System of Preferences. International antipiracy agreements and other initiatives are crafted by the U.S. Trade Representative frequently through collaboration with the World Trade Organization. The U.S. Trade Representative initiates dispute resolution proceedings through the World Trade Organization against foreign governments and institutions. The membership application for the World Trade Organization now encourages more stringent intellectual property laws for prospective member nations.

Criminal infringement of copyright was traditionally that done for the purpose of private financial gain or commercial advantage. However, the No Electronic Theft Act of 1997 made the reproduction or distribution of copyrighted works a felony, even if not done with profit intent. This criminalizing of noncommercial infringement was deemed necessary because it is so easy to infringe copyrighted works with the Internet and its tools. Commercially motivated infringers can receive greater punishments, with respect to both prison and fines.

The European Commission, on April 23, 2010, held a public hearing on the governance of collective rights management in the European Union (EU) to examine relationships between copyright owners, collecting societies, and commercial users of copyright. A recommendation was made on the management of online rights for musical works; recommendations were also made for EU-wide licensing of copyright for online services.

Some organizations concerned with copyright infringement include the International Intellectual Property Alliance, the Federation Against Software Theft, the Canadian Alliance Against Software Theft, the Business Software Alliance, the Motion Picture Association of America, the Recording Association of America, and the World Intellectual Property Organization. The World Intellectual Property Organization was created in 1967, and almost all members of the UN are members.

Copyright owners can sue not only those who directly infringe but also those who are facilitators of infringement, such as Napster, Aimster, and Fonovisa. Industry estimates are that the inadequacies of copyright and similar protection costs about $15 to $17 billion annually.

Victor B. Stolberg
Essex County College

See also Communication Technologies; Sanctions and Blacklisting; Technology

Further Readings

Austin, Graeme W. "Domestic Laws and Foreign Rights: Choice of Law in Transnational Copyright Infringement Litigation." *Columbia Journal of Law and the Arts*, v.23 (1999).

Ginsburg, Jane C. "Copyright Without Borders? Choice of Forum and Choice of Law for Copyright Infringement in Cyberspace." *Cardozo Arts and Entertainment Law Journal*, v.15 (1998).

Lemley, Mark A. and R. Anthony Reese. "Reducing Digital Copyright Infringement Without Restricting Innovation." *Stanford Law Review*, v.56 (2004).

CORPORATE INFLUENCE PEDDLING

Corporate influence peddling occurs when corporate agents or their designees use their influence with persons in political authority to obtain favors or preferential treatment for their corporations, usually in return for payment. Within the United States, examples of corporate influence peddling include illegal campaign contributions to office seekers and domestic commercial bribery, both of which have a long and sordid history. Corporations have also made payments to foreign government officials in order to obtain or to retain business, reduce political risks, avoid harassment, reduce taxes, and induce official action. Innovative payment methods were justified as normal practices in the country where the business was being transacted. It was realized that such practices might invoke opprobrium at home, so elaborate concealment strategies were established to hide the bribes from U.S. regulators. Disclosure of the payments often resulted in public scandals in America and abroad and a reduction in citizens' trust in big business in general.

More than 450 large corporations based in the United States, mostly Fortune 500 companies, ultimately disclosed to the Securities and Exchange Commission during the late 1970s and early 1980s illegal or questionable payments abroad, totaling more than $1 billion and paid either as direct bribes to foreign government officials or through corporate "sales agents" or other intermediaries. The list of guilty corporations included ITT Corporation, McDonnell Douglas, Northrop Grumman, Textron, American Cyanamid, Xerox, Exxon, Lockheed, Gulf, and Pfizer. Thirty-two firms had each given bribes totaling more than $1 million over the years, and many individual corporations made bribes totaling $10 million or more.

Bribes from multinationals were distributed to a variety of foreign recipients, as each target was deemed important in accomplishing corporate objectives in a given situation. The recipients included major government officials (legislative, executive, or judicial); minor government employees; employees of government owned corporations; political organizations; candidates for government office; politically affiliated news media; and agents, finders, consultants, or representatives.

Many businessmen defended the foreign payments, and evidence suggested that the payoffs proceeded with the full knowledge and consent of high-ranking corporate officials. Standard arguments were that such expenditures were simply "confidential commissions," that they were normal business practice in certain countries and therefore not really harmful, and that they were infinitesimal in comparison to sales totals—generally involving less than 1 percent of sales volume. Moreover, some corporations claimed that bribery was necessary to economic survival, that without bribery international markets could not be expanded, and that without such expansion corporate enterprises would collapse. Despite such rationalizations, payments were rarely made openly and directly.

Foreign subsidiaries of large corporations were involved in the payoffs in two ways. Either payments were made to maintain the effectiveness of the subsidiary's operations, with little control by the parent corporation—thereby making it difficult to trace the payment back to the parent corporation—or the subsidiary was used to handle a foreign payoff by the parent corporation. In the latter case, the parent corporation retained control of the money until it was passed to the individual. The parent firm could also disguise the payment as an expenditure for goods or services never actually delivered to the subsidiary.

Payoffs were also funneled through dummy corporations—corporations set up by the parent firm with no purpose other than to serve as a funnel for illegal transactions. In this method, the parent paid sales commissions to the dummy corporation and the latter then passed the payments on to independent agents for distribution as payoffs.

The most common method of channeling foreign payoffs, however, was through a sales agent. Many multinational corporations found it too expensive, as well as unnecessary, to establish an office in each country in which they operate; instead, they used sales agents, who are often already well established in a particular country. These sales agents were able to facilitate marketing arrangements, which were maintained through special favors. Examples of such favors included overbilling of sales with kickbacks to the buyers, gifts of property, gifts of services, payment of travel and entertainment expenses, provision of unsecured loans that were never collected, putting relatives on payrolls as "consultants," providing scholarships and educational expenses for children of customers, contributions to charities of the payee's choice, purchasing property from the payee at inflated prices, and selling property to the payee at deflated prices.

Corporations that bribed foreign officials were not violating any laws until 1977. There were violations only in cases where the corporation concealed the payment by failing to report it in their financial statements to the Internal Revenue Service or the Securities and Exchange Commission. Passage of the U.S. Foreign Corrupt Practices Act of 1977 allowed for the first time for charges to be brought against corporate officers; these officials could be jailed for up to five years for bribing foreign officials. Corporations could receive fines up to $1 million. This law had overwhelming public and congressional support. However, the Reagan administration made a concerted attempt to dilute it. The administration argued that (1) the criminal penalty was too severe and (2) U.S. corporations were suffering losses because they could not compete fairly. In 1988 Congress retained the original legislation though in a watered-down form that made convictions more difficult.

Public disclosure of the bribes had potentially serious and far-reaching effects on American foreign relations. For example, Lockheed's payment of $1.6 million to Prime Minister Kakuei Tanaka of Japan and $1.1 million to Prince Bernhard of the Netherlands resulted in the criminal prosecution of Tanaka and almost brought down the Royal House of Orange in the Netherlands.

Interest in investigating corporate influence peddling was rekindled in the 2000s amid disclosures of questionable or illegal activities by Enron, Halliburton, WorldCom, and other companies. For example, in 2009 six former employees of Control Components of California were indicted by the Justice Department. The indictment alleged that the employees made at least 236 payments to win contracts in more than 30 counties. In 2010, the German conglomerate Siemens AG paid $800 million in U.S. fines to settle a bribery investigation. The inquiry discovered that Siemens made payments to government officials around the world to win infrastructure contracts. In 2010, Kellogg Brown and Root (KBR) and its former parent, Halliburton, were charged by the United States with bribery of Nigerian officials. KBR agreed to pay a total of $579 million to settle the charges.

Corporate bribery has tarnished the image of U.S. democracy abroad, especially among the developing nations, and threatened the political stability of the targeted nations. Bribery also undercut fair competition among corporations by rigging the market with bribes and allowing inferior, higher-priced products to win contracts. Perhaps most damaging of all, bribery has eroded the ethos of fairness and a level playing field that once surrounded corporate competition. The foreign payoffs rendered such an ethos to be more myth than substance.

Stan C. Weeber
McNeese State University

See also Anticorruption Legislation; Bribery and Graft; Corruption; Influence and Position; Political Influence Peddling

Further Readings

Clinard, Marshall. *Corporate Corruption*. New York: Praeger, 1990.

Clinard, Marshall and Peter Yeager. *Corporate Crime*. New York: Free Press, 1980.

Roebuck, Julian and Stan Weeber. *Political Crime in the United States*. New York: Praeger, 1978.

Ross, Jeffrey Ian. *Dynamics of Political Crime*. Thousand Oaks, CA: Sage, 2003.

CORPORATE LIABILITY

A corporation may be considered to be a separate entity from its constituent parts. Others would argue that corporations are nothing more than a collection of individuals. In law, it is possible to differentiate between a "legal" and "natural" person whereby a corporate entity can be considered a "legal person" but constituted of "natural" persons, such as directors and board members. However, corporations as legal entities may be held accountable under criminal and civil law for the acts of their employees if those acts are carried out in the course and scope of their employment and with the intention of benefiting the corporate entity. This is a form of vicarious liability that also renders corporations accountable for the actions of third parties and intermediaries and that requires no proof of *mens rea*.

A corporation may therefore be held liable even in cases where directors and senior managers were unaware of or did not participate in the acts and even if the corporation's policies and protocols prohibited the act. There may be grounds for legal defense in some jurisdictions if the company can demonstrate due diligence in its procedures. A corporation may also be liable for the collective knowledge of several of its employees even if no single employee intended to commit an offense. In common-law (and some civil-law) jurisdictions, corporate criminal liability exists in three forms: agency (vicarious or strict), identification (direct), and organizational (corporate culture). The type of liability varies for different offenses and is contrary to the traditions of different countries. A director may be held criminally and/or civilly accountable depending on the law invoked and the evidential requirements and availability. Directors sometimes act against their duties to the corporation, making the corporation the victim.

Directors are the fiduciary agents of a corporation who, individually or as part of a board, shape a corporation's governance and policy through interaction with shareholders, managers, and employees. Board structures vary under different legal and cultural frameworks. For example, a two-tier board system exists in Germany, unlike the unitary board system in the United States and the United Kingdom. Directors and employees may be held criminally accountable and face personal liability if they are found to have acted negligently or if evidentially they can be found to have behaved culpably. In these instances, the "corporate veil" does not protect the individual from criminal liability and the director can be separately or jointly charged with the corporation. In cases involving civil law, directors of limited companies are not usually personally liable for the tortious acts or omissions of the company. Determining individual accountability is complex and problematic, and numerous factors shape this determination. The size and scope of a corporation influences director accountability, as devolved decision-making processes, issues of implied consent, "corporate cultures" and various other structural complexities within large multinational corporations make links between a corporation's and director's actions difficult to detect and prove, unless there are "smoking guns" such as e-mails, faxes, or recordings. Links between the directors of small and medium-sized enterprises and their company's actions may be more easily determined. In addition, transnational crimes, given their multijurisdictional, multicultural, and cross-border nature, render director accountability even more difficult to ascertain.

Cultural and legal frameworks in different jurisdictions shape the extent to which a corporation can be held liable, criminally or civilly. The example of transnational bribery illustrates this. Since the U.S. Foreign Corrupt Practices Act was established in 1977, corporate criminal liability has been easier to establish, as legal entities (including corporations) in the United States can be held liable for the acts and omissions of individual directors, managers, employees, and third parties (although this was rarely used before 2005). Such laws, in line with the *Federal Sentencing Guidelines Manual* for organizations, dictate that corporations, while they cannot be incarcerated, can be fined, sentenced to probation, ordered to make restitution and issue public notices of conviction to their victims, and be exposed to applicable forfeiture statutes. Frequently, corporate entities and prosecutory agencies negotiate plea bargains incorporating various civil solutions, but the prosecution of natural persons often accompanies this. In comparison, courts in the United Kingdom have traditionally had to locate the corporate mind for purposes of assessing *mens rea* as a necessary condition for criminal liability, with English judges traditionally finding the "company's mind" in the minds of persons who could be "identified" with the company for legal purposes. The United Kingdom's Bribery Act of 2010, however, renders companies potentially criminally liable for failing to prevent the corrupt actions of their third parties and subsidiaries.

Conversely, in Germany liability may be imposed on corporations by state authorities only for administrative offenses, or *Ordnungswidrigkeiten*; this is largely because in Germany a corporation cannot "act" as a "natural person" is able to and therefore has no criminal responsibility. As a result, what a corporation does cannot be interpreted as an "act" in German penal law. Sanctions involve a maximum fine of 1 million euros and unlimited confiscation of profits that were made from the unlawful act. The extrajurisdictional reach of the U.S. and U.K. laws, however, render any corporation that conducts all or part of its business in their jurisdictions liable for criminal prosecution, creating *potential* need for international agreements between prosecutors. Differences in legal frameworks in cases of transnational crimes such as bribery and corruption may create difficulties for investigation and prosecution. Mutual legal assistance, for example, may be hampered if a corporation's actions come under criminal law in one country but civil law in another.

Nicholas Lord
Cardiff University

See also Anticorruption Legislation; Bribery and Graft; Commissions and Payoffs; Corruption

Further Readings

Pieth, Mark et al., eds. *The OECD Convention on Bribery: A Commentary*. New York: Cambridge University Press, 2007.

Pinto, Amanda and Martin Evans. *Corporate Criminal Liability* (2nd ed.). London: Sweet and Maxwell, 2008.

U.S. Federal Sentencing Guidelines for Organizations. http://www.ussc.gov/Guidelines/Organizational_Guidelines/index.cfm (Accessed February 2011).

Wells, Celia. "Corporate Crime: Opening the Eyes of the Sentry." *Legal Studies*, v.30 (2010).

CORRUPTION

As a general matter, before any topic can be adequately understood, it must be defined. There are many different ways of defining a term, which include explaining it, providing a demonstration of it, or experiencing it. In most academic fields, explanation is the most common way to define a concept, except, of course, the natural sciences, where the preferred method is demonstration through experimentation. Furthermore, the context within which a term is being defined may significantly influence or alter the understanding of that term. *Corruption* is one of those terms.

In the dictionary, corruption is generally defined as something that is evil or wicked or something involving dishonesty, bribery, or illegality. This is a very broad definition and can include almost any act and, as a general matter, includes any and all criminal acts. Indeed, it likely includes any number of acts that, although dishonest, may not be crimes. In the context of transnational crime and justice, it can, likewise, have almost any number of applications.

In the context of criminal activity, corruption is usually not used for the common generic crimes, such as murder, rape, kidnapping, arson, battery, assault, robbery, burglary, or simple theft, although such crimes would be encompassed in a broad definition of corruption. The term *corruption* can be and frequently is applied to certain crimes that involve the violation of a trust or a fiduciary relationship. These crimes usually involve embezzlement, bribery, extortion, insider trading, and malfeasance or abuse of office. Embezzlement is usually defined as the crime of theft by a person who holds a position of fiduciary responsibility, such as a banker or a trustee. Bribery is usually defined as the payment of money to a person in a position of trust, such as a government official or a corporate officer, to influence that person's behavior in his or her official capacity in a particular manner. The crime of extortion is frequently defined as the demand for money by a government official in exchange for performing a certain act. Insider trading is a crime involving stocks and bonds whereby a person with confidential knowledge, not available to the participants in the free market, uses that information to profit from the sale or purchase of such securities. Malfeasance or abuse of office occurs when a government official intentionally engages in some activity for his or her own or another's personal gain or purposes, such as the harm of another person, even if the act was technically legal. Malfeasance is not a crime in some jurisdictions and may constitute only a civil offense.

Bribery is officially illegal in the United States—the Foreign Corrupt Practices Act of 1977 was installed to prohibit American corporations from bribing foreign government officials. (Photos.com)

Corruption is also used when describing unethical activities, such as conflicts of interest, to include nepotism and cronyism, which might not constitute crimes. Nepotism is the employment of a relative rather than hiring the most qualified person for a job. Cronyism is the hiring of people based on their personal or professional contacts rather than their qualifications. Some political entities have laws against nepotism, but cronyism is usually not illegal, even though it is generally recognized as not fair or equitable; indeed, it is even widely accepted in political systems that allow for "political spoils" to be awarded to a prevailing political figure or party. Conflicts of interest usually involve situations in which a government official might have a personal or financial interest in a matter before that official. Many political entities have laws or regulations that prevent some of the more blatant conflicts of interest.

Corruption also can be viewed as a government-based phenomenon, including political corruption, or as a private act, such as the acts of a corporation or an individual. In either perspective, the corrupt act can be prosecuted if it constitutes a crime. However, corruption by government officials tends to be viewed as more serious, at least in certain democratic nations. Moreover, political corruption can include activities by a government that suppress or oppress the citizenry for the enrichment and benefit of government officers and powerful private entities. Political corruption would also include tampering with elections or improperly influencing the creation or selection of a political system or leader. Of course, the view of such activities must be interpreted through the nature and philosophy of the political system present in the country in question. What might be corrupt in one country (such as capitalism in a communist regime) might not be corrupt in a country holding different political values. Regardless of the political perspective of a nation, political corruption can and does have transnational consequences. Transnational political corruption occurs when one government interferes in the internal affairs of another government. A primary example of transnational political corruption occurred when the United States interfered with the internal political affairs of Chile in 1973, which resulted in the assassination of President Salvador Allende.

This does not mean that corruption involving corporations or individuals is not common or unimportant. Corporations, as artificial entities, are not easily prosecuted for crimes, but they can engage in lawful activities that can have a serious detrimental effect on people that can be viewed as corruption. For example, the Enron debacle in the United States during 2001 led to serious economic harm to the economy and the company's thousands of employees. Although many of the activities of Enron were not criminal and few people were prosecuted, there are few people who would say that activities of Enron's corporate officials that led to the collapse were not corrupt. The fact that corporations frequently have an immense amount of power makes it very difficult to hold them accountable for acts and results for which an individual person would be jailed. This problem is aggravated by the fact that many corporations are transnational, having operations in many different countries. Indeed, the Bhopal disaster in 1984, where a Union Carbide Corporation pesticide plant had a leak resulting in the deaths of thousands and the injury of hundreds of thousands of people, has yet to be completely settled. There is little doubt that some form of the term *corruption* can be applied to corporations in both of these examples and that such corruption had transnational effects.

Internationally, one of the more frequent forms of corruption is bribery involving corporations and governments. Bribery, in many nations, is de facto, if not de jure, an accepted practice. Bribery, at least officially, is illegal in the United States. The United States enacted the Foreign Corrupt Practices Act of 1977, prohibiting American corporations from bribing foreign government officials.

In conclusion, it is difficult to provide a bright-line definition of what is corruption, especially in the context of transnational crime and justice. There is little doubt that transnational crime is a form corruption. However, the use of the term *corruption* is more appropriately limited to those acts that concern some violation of public trust.

Wm. C. Plouffe Jr.
Independent Scholar

See also Bribery and Graft; Corporate Influence Peddling; Military-Political-Industrial Nexus; Political Influence Peddling

Further Readings

Ackerman, Susan. *Corruption and Government: Causes, Consequences, and Reform.* New York: Cambridge University Press, 1999.

Ackerman, Susan. "Governance and Corruption." In *Global Crises, Global Solutions*, Bjørn Lomberg, ed. (pp. 301–362). New York: Cambridge University Press, 2009.

Korten, David C. *When Corporations Rule the World.* West Hartford, CT: Kumarian Press, 2001.

Nichols, Philip M. "Outlawing Transnational Bribery Through the World Trade Organization." *Law and Policy in International Business*, v.28 (1997).

Noonan, John T., Jr. *Bribes.* New York: Macmillan, 1984.

Schlegel, Kip and David Weisburd, eds. *White-Collar Crime Reconsidered.* Boston: Northeastern University Press, 1992.

Wong, James. *Corporate and Government Corruption.* San Clemente, CA: LawTech, 2005.

COUNTERFEIT CURRENCY

Counterfeiting was especially problematic when banks issued their own currency prior to the adoption of a national currency in 1863, and it poses a unique challenge to officials in the United States and abroad. Unfortunately, the implementation of a national currency did little to curtail the efforts of counterfeiters and their crimes. Shortly after the adoption of the national currency, the Secret Service was given the task of detecting and punishing counterfeiting in the United States. At its inception in 1865, the Secret Service estimated that counterfeit currency represented approximately one third of all currency in circulation. Counterfeiting poses a unique problem to the government and law-enforcement officials because of the fact that so much of it is manufactured outside the United States in other countries. The U.S. Treasury's Bureau of Engraving and Printing (BEP) was established during the U.S. Civil War in an effort to reduce counterfeiting. Since that time, the primary focus of U.S. currency design has been counterfeit deterrence. In 1993, the National Research Council's (NRC's) Committee on Currency Design explored the various features of currency in order to evaluate various methods to deter counterfeiting. One of the first criteria the committee considered was "visual and tactile recognizability," which was deemed an important aspect of currency in order for U.S. citizens to recognize U.S. currency by its look and feel. The NRC's Committee on Next-Generation Currency Design noted that the perfect currency should be extremely difficult to duplicate, aesthetically pleasing to the public eye, easily recognizable to the public, durable and tough, easy to produce at a low cost, machine-readable, nontoxic, and nonhazardous. Nonetheless, studies have shown that the public is often unaware of the many security features present in U.S. currency. Despite these new measures, the Secret Service seized more than $295 million worth of counterfeit currency in the United States between 2003 and 2008.

To deter counterfeiting, the process of evaluating currency redesigns has historically focused on technological advancements to which counterfeiters have access. Therefore, in order to deter counterfeiting, those who redesign currency must take into account the advancements in color copying, scanning, and printing that have become widely available. Currency in the United States contains a variety of security features that were implemented in the hope of deterring counterfeiting. These features include security threads that glow under UV light, various watermarks, embedded fibers, color-shifting ink, and microprinting. There are also numerous machine-readable features that vary by denomination. It has been reported that low-quality counterfeited currency is recognizable by its low optical image quality, lack of magnetic and infrared ink, or incorrect paper fluorescence. However, higher-quality counterfeits may be detectable only by their magnetic, infrared, or ultraviolet signatures.

Before the advent of low-cost, high-quality digital technology, now seen in our computers, printers, and copiers, counterfeiters usually needed a high level of skill in order to produce realistic counterfeit currency. In addition, counterfeiting was often committed by multiple individuals in criminal networks through contacts that made it possible to obtain access to the various equipment needed for the task. However, there are also less advanced methods of counterfeiting that are easier to detect. The raised note method does not require any form of technology and is therefore an easy process for offenders. With the raised note method, an offender attempts to alter the value of genuine currency by using scissors and glue to transform lower denominations into higher denominations.

Although the process of counterfeiting was once considered a highly sophisticated and often expensive offense, technological advancements have made the process of counterfeiting considerably easier over time. Despite the anticounterfeiting measures used in U.S. currency, counterfeiting occurs and works to undermine the public's confidence in currency. In addition, counterfeiting has been linked to providing financial support to various domestic

When currency is redesigned, attention is paid to which technological advancements counterfeiters have access to, taking into account the improvements in color copying, scanning, and printing that have become widely available. (Photos.com)

and international criminal organizations. The Secret Service estimates that counterfeiting will most likely increase despite recent advancements in the security features of U.S. currency. These predictions are based on the availability of computer printing, the quality of the printing, and the increasing number of individuals who are able to understand and use the available technology needed for counterfeiting.

Manufacturing counterfeit currency or altering genuine currency to increase its value is a violation of Title 18, Section 471 of the United States Code and is punishable by a fine and/or imprisonment for up to 15 years. The crime of counterfeiting U.S. currency has long remained problematic in the United States and abroad. As technological advancements in printing and scanning continue, considerable attention must be paid to the security features of U.S. currency in the hope of deterring these crimes both domestically and internationally.

Jacqueline Suzanne Chavez
Mississippi State University

See also Counterfeit Goods

Further Readings

Chia, T. and M. Levene. "Detection of Counterfeit U.S. Paper Money Using Intrinsic Fluorescence Lifetime." *Optics Express*, v.17/24 (2009).

Morris, R. G., H. Copes, and K. Perry-Mullis. "Correlates of Currency Counterfeiting." *Journal of Criminal Justice*, v.37/5 (2009).

Williams, M. and M. Anderson. "Currency Design in the United States and Abroad: Counterfeit Deterrence and Visual Accessibility." *Federal Reserve Bank of St Louis Review*, v.89/5 (2007).

COUNTERFEIT GOODS

The term *counterfeiting of goods* implies a series of actions, aimed at reproducing copyrighted or patented goods, that violate intellectual property rights (IPRs) and supplying those goods to consumers who may be either aware or unaware that they are counterfeit. The IPR concept, as specified by the World Trade Organization (WTO) under the 1994 Agreement on Trade Related Aspects of IPRs (TRIPS), includes counterfeiting of both trademarked goods (goods bearing, without authorization, a trademark that is identical or very similar to the original) and copyrighted goods (copies made without consent, such as pirated compact discs).

Economic motivation is the driver of counterfeiting. Profits are usually increased as a result of not bearing the following costs: expenses for research and development (R&D) activities, because the good copied by the counterfeiter already incorporates the R&D content of the original; advertising expenses, because the counterfeiter exploits the advertising campaigns for the original, which often represent well-known brands; production costs, because usually the quality of raw materials of counterfeited goods is lower than that of original items; labor costs, because usually counterfeiters exploit illegal workers; and taxes, because no duties are paid, as counterfeiting is an illegal activity occurring on the black market.

Counterfeiting is not a new practice. In the Middle Ages, with the development of world trade, special marks were used by manufacturers to distinguish high-quality products from others. However, today, thanks to the globalized market, counterfeiting has a strong transnational dimension that covers all six continents and has more serious economic and social consequences. Globalization of trade and reduced trade barriers, the Internet, the existence of powerful worldwide brands, high tariffs and customs taxes, the expansion of channels and markets, and specifically economic delocalization in Asia seem to have facilitated counterfeiting and its diffusion. New criminal opportunities have been generated by the transfer of knowledge and technology from the West to the East. In many Asian countries (but also in Western ones), legislative and criminal justice systems have not been fully prepared to protect IPRs and, in the name of economic development, have been much more oriented toward supporting production without examining whether IPRs—an issue closer to Western culture—are being respected. On the other hand, even where legislation provides severe sanctions for counterfeiters, law-enforcement agencies are not capable of complying effectively with the law. In addition, world consumers' demand for original (and fake) goods has continued to grow. As a result, the number of counterfeit goods has rapidly increased.

Since the 1990s, the market for counterfeit goods has dramatically grown not only in volume but also in the variety of fakes and in the complexity and professionalism of the counterfeit goods. The illicit nature of the phenomenon limits the accuracy of statistics in the field. Some tentative estimates have been provided by international organizations in order to give an account of the economic impact of the phenomenon. In 2001, the International Chamber of Commerce estimated that the counterfeit goods market accounted for US$350 billion globally. The Organisation for Economic Co-operation and Development (OECD) adopted a conservative metrics system and recalculated the estimates, on the basis of customs seizure data. According to the OECD's figures, the counterfeit and pirated goods market constantly increased over the period 2000–07, accounting for $250 billion in the last years examined and, in percentage terms, for 1.95 percent of world trade. The most recent economic estimates, provided by an organization called Havocscope (using published open sources, newspaper and government reports), assess the market value of counterfeit goods at more than $566 billion. According to these estimates, the most significant counterfeit goods are pharmaceuticals (with a market value of $200 billion), followed by electronics ($100 billion), videos ($60 billion), software ($51.4 billion), and auto parts ($45 billion). The counterfeit clothes and shoes markets accounted for $12 billion each.

As already mentioned, the estimates provided can be seriously criticized for the methodologies used and for the limited reliability of the sources of information. However, nobody contests the fact that the phenomenon exists and should be fought for at least three main reasons. From an economic point of view, counterfeiting goods damages the official brand owner by generating losses and, as a consequence, puts at risk the very existence of legitimate firms. From a cultural point of view, fake goods threaten innovation because they reduce legitimate revenue and can deter new investments. From a social point of view, the existence of a counterfeit goods market represents a danger for society itself, because it deprives the public of taxes, it sometimes distributes unhealthy or unsafe goods, and in the long term it results in job losses. In addition, the counterfeit goods market enriches organized criminal groups and terrorists, although for the latter the connection with counterfeiting is not yet widely proven.

The counterfeit goods market is complex, and its functioning is similar to a legitimate market of products with a supply chain involving manufacturers, brokers, importers, distributors, and retailers, who operate jointly in order to make a profit and sometimes play a double game in the licit and illicit arenas. Market routes are also similar to the legitimate ones. Fake goods are mainly produced in Asia (especially in China), which actually produces the majority of the goods for the world's licit market as well. More than in the past, an increasing quota of the counterfeit goods stays on the continent for the domestic market and is sold by street vendors, in retail outlets, or in shopping districts devoted to counterfeit goods. Another quota is shipped by Western or Eastern importers to European and American consumers. A residual part moves to Africa, which seems to be the main destination for counterfeit pharmaceutical products.

The most difficult activity of a counterfeiter's job is importing fake goods in developed countries. The techniques adopted by counterfeiters in order to pass customs controls became more sophisticated once the controls increased at the borders of Western-developed countries. The techniques available range from corruption of customs officials to fraudulent schemes that also exploit free trade zones and free ports to "launder" the suspicious origins of cargoes. Among the fraudulent schemes, the most common involve hiding counterfeit products in cargoes with licensed products or unfaithfully reporting the content of the cargoes, declaring something that is completely different from what the cargo actually contains. Other schemes include importing with different cargoes different parts of the counterfeit goods, which will later be assembled in laboratories that operate in the developed country (or in the free trade area). Counterfeiters also may disguise the country of origin of goods in order to avoid inspections, moving cargoes across several destinations.

Generally, it should be noted that importers of counterfeit goods operate rationally. They maximize their benefits (avoiding goods confiscation), selecting the most vulnerable countries as entry points for their trafficking. This is especially problematic for free trade zones (such as Dubai in the United Arab Emirates) and the free-market area in the European Union (EU). In fact, despite customs controls operated at the EU border, considerable differences in legislation and law-enforcement control exist across member states. This situation increases the EU's permeability to fake products.

The Internet has also become a powerful tool for selling fake goods. Its anonymity and flexibility turn the Web into a perfect virtual marketplace where counterfeiters can advertise their products at relatively cheap cost, addressing a huge audience of buyers without any significant risk of being caught by law-enforcement agencies. This is particularly true for the pharmaceutical sector: according to the World Health Organization (WHO), purchasing medicines online without the required prescription results in counterfeit products in more than 50 percent of cases.

Undoubtedly, some types of goods are more exposed to counterfeiting than others. L. Jacobs, A. Coskun, and T. Jedlik divided products at risk into four categories: (1) highly visible, high-volume, low-tech products with well-known brand names, such as toothpaste, candies, chocolates, and cigarettes; (2) high-priced, high-tech products, such as computer games, audio or video entertainment products, and auto and airplane parts; (3) exclusive, prestige products such as well-known apparel and accessories as well as perfumes and other expensive gift items; and (4) intensive R&D, high-tech products, such as pharmaceuticals.

The role of consumers in such counterfeiting is widely discussed. Today it is unanimously acknowledged that a significant number of buyers are fully aware of the counterfeit nature of what they are buying. However, they still insist on purchasing counterfeit goods because they do not perceive this practice as unethical or risky for the economic system or for their own safety.

This brings us to the issue of policing the counterfeit goods market. In recent years, a growing set of initiatives have been adopted, especially by the U.S. government and the European Commission. These include training police officers, prosecutors, and customs officials in the most exposed countries (such as China, Korea, and Brazil) to increase their capacity to prosecute IPR violations; strengthening U.S. and EU customs controls and coordinating joint inspections; changing legislation and setting a minimum standard of enforcement of IPR regulations at the EU level; implementing sting operations against Internet piracy; promoting closer cooperation and regular information exchange with the private sector; developing, together with the private sector, a practical guide for customs; and promoting stronger partnerships and cooperation with multilateral and international organizations such as TRIPS in the WTO, the World Intellectual Property Organization (WIPO), the OECD, the World Customs Organization, and the International Criminal Police Organization (Interpol).

Private firms can also act autonomously in order to protect their IPRs through different initiatives. The most advanced have adopted technological systems (equipped with radio-frequency identification or other "taggants") capable of marking products, ensuring their unique identification and tracking their movements. These new systems facilitate other actions that aim at reducing the permeability of the licit market to the counterfeit goods, such as educating, monitoring, and sanctioning suppliers, distributors, and retailers. To this end, investigations are often carried out by an ad hoc company enforcement team, which tends to cooperate with local law-enforcement authorities. In addition, private companies are used to support international organizations and research studies in order to stress the seriousness of the phenomenon and receive stronger protection from policy makers.

However, the issue of an effective deployment of public resources remains. D. S. Wall and J. Large have suggested that, in the counterfeit fashion market, public resources should be reoriented toward a more effective approach that focuses solely on highly deceptive products. In fact, this type of product accounts for the majority of sales losses and, when the quality is low, for reputational damage. A priority should be placed on policing counterfeit goods acknowledged to be safety-critical, such as automobile parts and pharmaceutical products, because of the potentially hazardous impact that the distribution of these counterfeit goods could have on society.

Stefano Caneppele
Università Cattolica/Transcrime

See also Copyright Infringement; Counterfeit Currency; Measuring Transnational Crime

Further Readings

Chaudhry, P. and A. Zimmerman. *The Economics of Counterfeit Trade: Governments, Consumers, Pirates, and Intellectual Property Rights.* Berlin: Springer, 2009.

Eisend, M. and P. Schuchert-Güler. "Explaining Counterfeit Purchases." *Academy of Marketing Science Review*, v.12 (2006).

Havocscope. "Havocscope Black Markets: Counterfeit Goods." http://www.havocscope.com/black-market/counterfeit-and-piracy (Accessed February 2011).

Jacobs, L., A. Coskun, and T. Jedlik. "The Nightmare of International Product Piracy: Exploring Defensive Strategies." *Industrial Marketing Management*, v.30 (2001).

Organisation for Economic Co-operation and Development. *The Economic Impact of Counterfeiting and Piracy.* Paris: Author, 2008.

Organisation for Economic Co-operation and Development. "Magnitude of Counterfeiting and Piracy of Tangible Products: An Update." 2009. http://www.oecd.org/document/23/0,3746,en_2649_34173_44088983_1_1_1_1,00.html (Accessed February 2011).

Staake, T. and E. Fleish. *Countering Counterfeit Trade Illicit Market Insights, Best-Practice Strategies, and Management Toolbox.* Berlin: Springer, 2009.

Staake, T., F. Thiesse, and E. Fleish. "The Emergence of Counterfeit Trade: A Literature Review." *European Journal of Marketing*, v.43 (2009).

United Nations Interregional Crime and Justice Research Institute (UNICRI). "Counterfeiting: A Global Spread, a Global Threat." 2007. http://www.unicri.it/news/2007/0712-3_counterfeiting_crt_foundation (Accessed February 2011).

Wall, D. S. and J. Large. "Jailhouse Frocks: Locating the Public Interest in Policing Counterfeit Luxury Fashion Goods." *British Journal of Criminology*, v.50 (2010).

World Health Organization. "Medicines: Counterfeit Medicines." http://www.who.int/medicines/services/counterfeit/impact/ImpactF_S/en/ (Accessed February 2011).

CRIME COMMISSIONS

Crime commissions are governmental organs mostly created in the wake of mass atrocity, but they may also be formed to address or combat large-scale and potentially ongoing criminal activities at a local or national level that do not necessarily involve elements of transnational or international law, such as New York City's Commission to Combat Police Corruption or the Australian Crime Commission, which has jurisdiction over organized crime and related multijurisdictional investigations in that country. The commissions chartered in response to large-scale human rights violations, which constitute the focus of this entry, are meant to help transition a country back to the rule of law and civil society by emphasizing truth telling, and psychosocial healing and reconciliation. These commissions are an alternative to, although not mutually exclusive from, criminal prosecutions. They are generally perceived as a middleground between tribunals and general amnesty for past crimes, simultaneously serving as historical and archival bodies with an aim toward creating the most complete and accurate record of the events they are chartered to investigate and study. Often called "truth commissions" or "truth and reconciliation commissions," these crime commissions, in various forms, have been experimented with by more than 20 countries to address past wrongdoing.

Often commissions are created in the wake of large-scale human rights violations committed by a former controlling regime against its own people, although they may also examine the actions of nonstate actors (domestic groups opposed to the former regime that engaged in violent acts or guerrilla warfare). The first such body, Argentina's National Commission on the Disappearance of Persons (NCDP), was created in 1983 to investigate forced disappearances during Argentina's Dirty War. The commission took more than 7,000 statements from survivors and others during its nine months of operation, eventually concluding that 8,960 disappearances took place during military rule from 1976 to 1983, based on the information it obtained. The commission nevertheless estimated that the real numbers were much higher: between 10,000 and 30,000, attributing the disparity to nonreporting by people too afraid or otherwise unwilling to be interviewed by commission staff, and to the military government's destruction of records that could have revealed the true scale of the atrocities and the role of the chain of command.

Although five generals from Argentina's junta government were prosecuted in the 1980s based on information gathered by the NCDP, the commission was meant to serve as an alternative to a Nüremberg-like tribunal, exercising what some have called a "restorative justice" model that emphasizes victims' psychological healing through therapeutic testimony and historical recording of offenders' acknowledgments of their wrongdoings, rather than retributive justice, which has as its chief goal prosecution and punishment.

Throughout the 1990s, at the same time that the United Nations' (UN's) two International Criminal Tribunals for Yugoslavia and Rwanda were beginning their operations to investigate and adjudicate violations of International Humanitarian Law, more crime commissions were created in various countries around the world, usually rooted in principles derived from international human rights law. These commissions varied widely in their respective mandates, structures, and procedures. Some were created by domestic mechanisms, others by international means such as UN missions independent of the operations of the criminal tribunals. Although all of the commissions made their ultimate reports public, some featured public hearings, while others (generally the earlier commissions) did not. The process of appointing commission members also differed greatly in each instance.

Often thought to be the most famous and successful example of a crime commission is South Africa's Truth and Reconciliation Commission (TRC). Chartered by statute in 1995 and chaired by Archbishop Desmond Tutu, the TRC was charged with investigating, documenting, and promoting national recovery from the apartheid regime. The TRC was divided into three committees: the investigative Human Rights Violations Committee; the Repatriation and Rehabilitation Committee, charged with developing rehabilitation policy and victim assistance initiatives; and the Amnesty Committee. Of the 7,112 applications filed with the TRC for amnesty, 849 were granted. Despite the thousands of applications for amnesty that were denied, few trials were held to prosecute those wrongdoers who did not qualify for amnesty under the statute.

Another notable commission, the Commission for Reception, Truth and Reconciliation in East Timor, was created by the UN in 2001 to examine human rights violations during the lengthy civil war in that country, which lasted from April 1974 to October 1999. This commission operated simultaneously with the UN-backed Special Court.

The Sierra Leone Truth and Reconciliation Commission was created by a provision in the Lomé Peace Accord in 1999 that aimed to end the country's civil war, which by that time had continued for nine years. Opposition forces finally disarmed in 2001, and the commission began operations in November 2002, filing its report with the government of Sierra Leone and the UN Security Council in 2004. Although the report names perpetrators of human rights violations, the Lomé Peace Accord included an amnesty provision that prevented prosecution of all but the most serious violations of international humanitarian law: genocide, war crimes, and crimes against humanity.

Other countries that have experimented with a form of crime commission, with widely varying degrees of success, include Canada, Chile, El Salvador, Fiji, Ghana, Guatemala, Liberia, Morocco, Nigeria, Panama, Peru, the Philippines, the Solomon Islands, South Korea, Sri Lanka, Uganda, and Uruguay. Still other countries have created similarly titled bodies that serve chiefly as policy-making or executive agencies. For example, although Rwanda created its constitutionally chartered National Unity and Reconciliation Commission to supplement the UN criminal tribunal, it is not a truth commission that receives testimony itself, but rather a policy organ that promotes and coordinates educational programs and community-based initiatives to achieve greater reconciliation in postgenocide Rwanda.

The promulgation of crime commissions is not without controversy. Many critics question their effectiveness in achieving their stated goals, especially in the instances of commissions that offer amnesty from prosecution for certain crimes in exchange for testimony. Not only does the prospect of granting human rights violators immunity from prosecution for their crimes rile critics, but many speculate that even guaranteed amnesty to those individuals does not ensure complete truth telling. Some also question whether policy makers and commission staff pay enough attention to the complexities of reconciliation in transitional countries, as involving both individual and systemic factors that range from the psychological and sociological to the economic and bureaucratic. In other instances, such as Sri Lanka's Lessons Learnt and Reconciliation Commission, shortcomings have been attributed to lack of protection for would-be witnesses.

Adam R. Pearlman
Independent Scholar

See also Adjudicating International Crimes; Crimes Against Humanity; Genocide; Government Reports; Impact of Transnational Crime; International Criminal Court; Prosecution: International; War Crimes Tribunals

Further Readings

Pearlman, Adam Ross. "Digging for Truth, Justice, or the Humanitarian Way: Priorities in Post-Genocide Transitional Justice and Exhumations of Mass Graves." http://papers.ssrn.com/sol3/papers.cfm?abstract_id=1322155 (Accessed February 2011).

Sarkin, Jeremy. "Achieving Reconciliation in Divided Societies: Comparing the Approaches in Timor-Leste, South Africa and Rwanda." *Yale Journal of International Affairs* (Summer 2008).
South Africa Truth and Reconciliation Commission. "Truth and Reconciliation Commission Report." http://www.justice.gov.za/trc/report/index.htm (Accessed February 2011).
Steiner, Henry J. and Philip Alston. *International Human Rights in Context: Law, Politics, Morals* (2nd ed.). New York: Oxford University Press, 2000.
Waldman, Ellen. "Healing Hearts or Righting Wrongs? A Meditation on the Goals of 'Restorative Justice.'" *Hamline Journal of Public Law and Policy*, v.25 (2004).

CRIMES AGAINST HUMANITY

Crimes against humanity have a long history. In what is often cited as the first prosecution by an international tribunal, Peter von Hagenbach was prosecuted in the 15th century by the Holy Roman Empire for violating "the laws of God and man." This is evidence that there were offenses that were considered violations of the laws of man that could be prosecuted as crimes. In May 1915, the phrase *crimes against humanity* was officially used for the first time in a warning issued by the British Empire, France, and Russia to the Young Turks governing the Ottoman Empire. During World War I, the Young Turks implemented deportation laws to rid the Ottoman Empire of certain religious and ethnic minority groups, including Armenian Christians. The multinational threat warned the Young Turks that they would answer for their "crimes against humanity and civilization."

When the hostilities of World War I ended, the British Empire, France, and Russia attempted to make good on their threat to impose retribution on the Young Turks as well as the former German emperor, William II, for initiating the war. At the Paris Peace Conference, a 15-member commission was establish to decide which states were responsible for initiating the war and to recommend an appropriate tribunal to prosecute and punish those responsible. The commission was officially named the Commission on the Responsibility of the Authors of the War and on Enforcement of Penalties. Most members of the commission urged the creation of an international criminal tribunal to prosecute the former German emperor for violating the laws of war and "the laws and principles of humanity." The United States and Japanese representatives on the commission disagreed with the prosecution of violations of the laws of humanity, since there was no law and no legal precedent for the prosecution of such crimes. In its memorandum of reservations to the commission's recommendations, the United States said that "the laws and principles of humanity vary with the individual, which, if for no other reason, should exclude them from consideration in a court of justice, especially one charged with the administration of criminal law." The U.S. position prevailed, and William II was not arraigned for violating the laws and principles of humanity. William II was publicly arraigned for a supreme offense against international morality and the sanctity of treaties but was never prosecuted, because he was provided sanctuary in the Netherlands. Crimes against humanity were not mentioned in the Paris Peace Treaty of 1919; however, most states that participated on the Commission on the Responsibility of the Authors of the War and on Enforcement of Penalties agreed that there were laws of humanity. Therefore, it can be inferred that a general agreement was established that if the laws of humanity were violated, such acts may be categorized as crimes against humanity.

In June 1945, the four Allied victors of World War II—the United States, the United Kingdom, the Soviet Union, and France—gathered in London to negotiate creating an international court to prosecute major Nazi war criminals. At the London Conference, the issue of crimes against humanity was picked up from the post–World War I negotiations that had considered violations of the laws of humanity. The Allied victors agreed to establish the International Military Tribunal and to include the charge of crimes against humanity within the tribunal's jurisdiction.

Article 6(c) of the Charter of the International Military Tribunal defined crimes against humanity as "namely, murder, extermination, enslavement, deportation, and other inhumane acts committed against any civilian population, before or during the war, or persecutions on political, racial or religious grounds." The major Nazi war criminals were the first to be prosecuted for committing crimes against humanity. The definition went beyond traditional war crimes by including crimes "against any civilian population," enabling the four Allied victors

In 1909, Young Turk revolutionaries (the "Young Turks" governing the Ottoman Empire) are pictured entering Istanbul. The phrase *crimes against humanity* was used for the first time as a warning sent by the British Empire, France, and Russia to the Young Turks that were deporting certain religious and ethnic minority groups. (Wikimedia)

to prosecute Nazi officials for crimes committed against their own people. The jurisdiction of the International Military Tribunal was limited to World War II. Crimes against humanity, however, were included in the Nüremberg Principles of 1950 as a crime under international law.

In 1993, the United Nations (UN) Security Council created the International Criminal Tribunal for the former Yugoslavia (ICTY). Under Article 5 of the ICTY Statute, crimes against humanity were defined as certain acts, including murder, extermination, and torture, "committed in armed conflict, whether international or internal in character, and directed against any civilian population." The ICTY's definition, like the International Military Tribunal's definition 50 years prior, had to be connected to a certain armed conflict.

In 1994, the UN Security Council created the International Criminal Tribunal for Rwanda (ICTR). Article 3 of the ICTR Statute defined crimes against humanity as certain acts, including murder, extermination, and torture, "when committed as part of a widespread or systematic attack against any civilian population on national, political, ethnic, racial or religious grounds." Like the International Military Tribunal's definition, the ICTR's definition is limited to attacks on categorical grounds. However, for the first time crimes against humanity did not have to be committed in connection to an armed conflict.

Appropriately, since humanity exists outside armed conflicts, it became possible that crimes against humanity could be committed during peacetime. Furthermore, the ICTR's definition excluded individual instances and required that attacks against civilians be either widespread or systematic. This meant that a rape during peacetime was the crime of rape, whereas a rape of a civilian during war was a war crime. However, widespread or systematic rapes of civilians during either war or peace were crimes against humanity.

On July 17, 1998, the Rome Statute of the International Criminal Court was adopted, and, after its 60th ratification, it entered into force on July 1, 2002. Under Article 7, crimes against humanity are certain acts "when committed as part of a widespread or systematic attack directed against any civilian population, with knowledge of the attack." The Rome Statute expanded on the ICTR's definition of crimes against humanity in several ways. First, it extensively expanded the list of acts from any previous list of crimes against humanity. Second, under Article 7(2), the Rome Statute defines every act included in the list of crimes. Previous statutes and charters failed to define such acts. Finally, the Rome Statute's definition of crimes against humanity, in addition to requiring attacks against a civilian population to be widespread or systematic, requires that each perpetrator participating in the attack have knowledge that the attack is part of a larger, widespread or systematic attack. Without this knowledge, it is possible that an individual instance of rape is coincidentally occurring at the same time as civilians are being systematically raped.

The Rome Statute of the International Criminal Court is the most authoritative international criminal code. It was adopted with 120 countries voting in favor, seven voting against, and 21 abstentions. The United States was one of the seven countries that voted against the adoption of the Rome Statute, since the International Criminal Court is independent of the UN Security Council, which is responsible for responding to breaches of the peace. On December 31, 2000, the United States signed the Rome Statute, but it has remained reluctant to ratify it. Currently, out of the five permanent members on the Security Council, France and the United Kingdom have ratified the Rome Statute, and the United States, China, and Russia have not.

The concept of crimes against humanity has traveled a long path. Under the Rome Statute, the definition of crimes against humanity is comprehensive, and when such attacks on civilians occur, all members of the human family are victimized. The Rome Statute can be amended every seven years at a review conference. In 2008, the prosecutor charged the president of Sudan, Omar al-Bashir, with crimes against humanity in Darfur and in 2011 the prosecutor was in the process of charging the president of Libya, Muammar al-Qaddafi, with crimes against humanity against Libyan rebels. However, Muammar al-Qaddafi was killed in October 2011.

Harry M. Rhea
Richard Stockton College of New Jersey

See also Genocide; International Criminal Court; War Crimes

Further Readings

Bassiouni, M. Cherif. *Crimes Against Humanity: Historical Evolution and Contemporary Application.* New York: Cambridge University Press, 2011.
Jones, Adam. *Crimes Against Humanity: A Beginner's Guide.* Oxford: Oneworld, 2008.
May, Larry. *Crimes Against Humanity: A Normative Account.* New York: Cambridge University Press, 2006.
Robertson, Geoffrey. *Crimes Against Humanity: The Struggle for Global Justice.* New York: New Press, 2006.

CRIMINAL ASSOCIATIONS

Transnational crimes either can involve crossing country borders as an integral or central part of the criminal activity or can include crimes that take place in one country with significant consequences in another country. Criminal associations, also known as transnational criminal organizations (TCOs) or international criminal organizations (ICOs), are the groups of people who are committing these crimes. Criminal associations are significant to the transnational playing field, posing a major threat to the security of individuals, nations, and international relations. Dealing with criminal associations is an enormous task for any government or agency.

The UN Convention Against Transnational Organized Crime (2000, in force 2003) defined an organized crime group to mean a structured group with three or more persons, existing for a period of time and acting in concert to commit serious crimes or certain designated offenses. Together with this definition is the idea that "others" may be involved in facilitating or enabling the criminal operations. Hence the focus is now placed internationally on those criminals who are "associated" with organized criminal operations. The number of criminal associations that have come into play on a transnational scale has rapidly increased in the wake of specific historic events, such as the collapse of the Soviet Union; the growth of capitalism in China; the enactment of the North American Free Trade Agreement; the lowering of European customs, currency, passport controls; and other, lesser events. Those lesser events include increased interdependence between nations with regard to international travel and communications, the permeability of nations' borders, and the vast and incredible increase in transnational activity—the movement of information, money, physical objects, people, and other tangible or intangible items across borders.

With the globalization of trade and growing consumer demand for products, it is only natural that criminal organizations and crime would also become more transnational as these gangs of criminals begin to take advantage of new and growing markets. With ever-growing transnational activity and global markets, it has been easier for criminal associations to hide illicit transactions, because law-enforcement agencies and customs officers are unable to inspect more than a small proportion of the cargoes and people that are moving between nations. Furthermore, criminal associations are now able to transfer profits from their illegal transactions with greater speed and ease. Their operations are made more efficient by the increasing tendency for them to operate as loose networks rather than rigidly structured membership organizations.

Criminal organizations operate outside the existing structure of law and power and have developed and continually changed strategies for circumventing the law or evading governmental control in particular countries, as well as worldwide. Transnational criminal organizations vary in many different ways. They come in all shapes and sizes, allowing for different associations to be involved in different areas of crime; more often, they are involved in more than one area of crime. For example, some criminal associations are involved strictly in drug trafficking, while others engage in a broad range of criminal activities, such as extortion, fraud, prostitution, and drugs. These rather advanced associations are also diverse in structure, outlook, and membership. However, in order to be "successful" as a criminal association, they must be mobile and adaptable, thus allowing them to operate transnationally with great ease. In order to increase their ability to operate transnationally, they must create alliances with one another. Despite the fact that there is little definitive proof of these alliances, they do exist. They must exist in order to allow these associations to survive in a world of ever-changing and growing markets. Criminal associations find it easier to operate together if they are not constantly worried about competition with other organizations. Furthermore, not only can illegal and illicit businesses profit from engaging in alliances; alliances also allow the TCOs to more easily evade law-enforcement and governmental agencies, as well exploit different markets. The fact that TCOs have been increasingly working in alliances has only created more problems and hurdles for governmental agencies determined to stop the illegal transnational activity.

Not only are these organizations operating globally and forming strategic alliances with one another; they are working with rogue governments and terrorist organizations as well. Criminal associations and their ever-growing alliances are a dominant problem that local, national, and international law enforcement must face. The United Nations (UN) has listed 18 different areas in which criminal associations are involved, and this list is not exhaustive: money laundering, illicit drug trafficking, corruption and bribery of public officials, infiltration of legal businesses, fraudulent bankruptcy, insurance fraud, computer crime, theft of intellectual property, illicit traffic in arms, terrorist activities, aircraft hijacking, sea piracy, hijacking on land, trafficking in persons, trade in human body parts, theft of art and cultural objects, environmental crimes, and other offenses committed by organized crime groups. These areas become more dangerous when more associations are working together in each of these specific areas.

While there has been a move away from a focus on "ethnic-based" categories, the following "types" of criminal associations are continually mentioned: the Traditional Big Five and the now known Big Six; a second tier of smaller yet highly organized criminal associations; and finally terrorist groups. The Traditional Big Five transnational criminal organizations are the Italian criminal enterprises (including the Sicilian and American Mafia families), the Russian Mafiya, the Japanese Yakuza, the Chinese triads, and the Colombian cartels. Recently added to the Traditional Five, making it the Big Six, are the Mexican drug cartels, known collectively as the Mexican Federation. The second tier of criminal associations consists of groups with certain criminal specialties that work with and for the Big Six. This type of criminal organization works similarly to the way a franchise would work for its parent company. This second tier includes groups based all over world—for example, in Nigeria, Panama, Jamaica, Puerto Rico, and the Dominican Republic. Finally, the third tier of criminal associations is made up of terrorist groups, which often deal in contraband, narcotics, smuggling, and other crimes as a means to gain the financing to carry out their political agendas.

Many organized crime groups share common characteristics. For instance, the following have been identified:

- *Corruption:* The use of illicit influence, exploitation of weaknesses, and the blackmail of public and prominent figures.
- *Discipline:* The enforcement of obedience to the organization through fear and violence.
- *Infiltration:* The continued effort to gain a foothold in legitimate institutions to further profits or gain a level of protection from detection.
- *Insulation:* The protection of the organization's leaders by separating them from the soldiers.
- *Monopoly:* The control over certain criminal activities within a geographic area with no tolerance for competition.
- *Subversion:* The subversion of society's institutions and legal and moral value systems.
- *History:* Past events that have allowed the entrenchment and refinement of criminal activities and practices.
- *Violence:* Violence used without hesitation to further the criminal aims of the organization.
- *Sophistication:* The use of advanced communication systems and financial controls and operations.
- *Continuity:* The plans for future growth and succession that, as in a corporation, allow the organization to survive the individuals who created it.
- *Diversity:* The variety of illicit activities that insulate the organization and keep it from depending on one criminal activity.
- *Bonding:* The solidarity that emerges from bonding between individuals and between individuals and the organization, which leads to interdependence and protection, often through complex initiation rites.
- *Mobility:* A disregard for national and jurisdictional boundaries.

Criminal associations rely on these characteristics to be successful when carrying out transnational crimes. As previously stated, the growth of industrial economies and rise of consumer markets have thus increased and encouraged the growth of organized crime.

Criminal associations operate and are created for one main reason: economic benefit of their members at any expense to others. Some may believe that criminal organizations do not pose a threat because some of their profits are pushed back into the national and global economies. However, transnational criminal organizations pose many threats to the security of all nations in which they operate, as well as to the nations their illegal activities affect. There are other costs associated with international criminal operations. In certain nations, such as Italy and Colombia, TCOs have been more than willing to use force and violence against the nation and its law-enforcement agencies. As a result, some criminal associations have become more destabilizing than revolutionary or terrorist groups. This is because the associations have created a very effective authority structure, operating under their own laws, with their own populations and armed forces, on their own territory. Furthermore, the large profits these associations reap from their illegal activities make it easier for them to accomplish their goals. Therefore, by their nature, criminal associations undermine civil societies, destabilize domestic politics, and undercut any sort of law in place.

Governments competing with transnational criminal organizations are up against a significant challenge. Generally, there are not enough funds or time for government enforcement agencies to tackle the problem of the criminal associations appropriately. These problems are compounded by changing administrations with different ideas of what problems should be a priority for the nation to fix. As a result, even though one administration may work very hard and spend significant resources to extinguish criminal associations or at least diminish their effects on society, in a few short years a new administration with a different agenda may take over. Therefore, a concerted effort to form a unified and continuous policy is a high priority for nations if they are to see progress in stemming the activities of criminal organizations.

Kelly Rodgers
Hamline University School of Law

See also Al Qaeda; Cocaine; Heroin; Human Smuggling; Impact of Transnational Crime; Mafia Myths and Mythologies; Money Laundering: History; Money Laundering: Methods; Money Laundering: Targeting Criminal Proceeds; Money Laundering: Vulnerable Commodities and Services; Narco-Terrorism; Organized Crime: Defined; Sex Slavery; Violence: Uses

Further Readings

Arquilla, John and David Ronfeldt. *In Athena's Camp: Preparing for Conflict in the Information Age.* Santa Monica, CA: RAND, 1997.

Huntington, Samuel. "Transnational Organizations in World Politics." *World Politics*, v.25/3 (April 1973).

Kelly, R. J. "Criminal Underworlds: Looking Down on Society From Below." In *Organized Crime: A Global Perspective*, R. J. Kelly, ed. Totowa, NJ: Rowman & Littlefield, 1986.

Liddick, Donald R., Jr. *The Global Underworld: Transnational Crime and the United States.* Westport, CT: Praeger, 2004.

Richards, James R. *Transnational Criminal Organizations, Cybercrime, and Money Laundering: A Handbook for Law Enforcement Officers, Auditors and Financial Investigators.* Boca Raton, FL: CRC Press, 1999.

CRIMINAL FORFEITURE AND SEIZURE

Asset forfeiture is a term that commonly refers to the legal process through which government agencies are able to target illegally obtained financial resources, personal property, and other items of value for confiscation and seizure. Two broad types of asset forfeiture procedures are commonly recognized: criminal asset forfeiture and civil asset forfeiture. *Criminal forfeiture* refers to the process whereby the government attempts to seize illegally obtained proceeds or property in conjunction with, or subsequent to, a directly related criminal prosecution or conviction. In cases of criminal forfeiture, the individual is the actual target of the governmental action and the proceeds or items targeted for

seizure are subject to confiscation in conjunction with the action brought against the individual. In essence, the individual's criminal prosecution and conviction are thought to provide both proof of the illegal means whereby the property or resources in question were obtained and a justification for the state to seize those assets. Civil forfeiture, which is a much more controversial procedure, refers to the seizure of assets that are believed to have been obtained illegally without an accompanying criminal charge or conviction. In this type of forfeiture action, the assets or property being sought, rather than the individual criminal offender, become the primary focus of the governmental action. The processes and legal standards associated with civil forfeiture have led some to question its merits and justifications.

Criminal asset forfeiture is based on the underlying assumption that it is inherently wrong for criminal offenders to benefit financially from the fruits of their criminal activities or from the suffering that these activities caused their victims. As a result, both the individual offender and any proceeds associated with the offender's illegal actions become a concern for governmental authorities and a worthwhile target for their ongoing enforcement efforts. Advocates of criminal asset forfeiture have identified a number of potential benefits that are thought to accrue from the seizure process. First, it is believed that the seizure of profits obtained through criminal activity will ultimately undermine one of the primary motivations for criminal involvement. More specifically, it is believed that there is a profit motive upon which criminal behavior is predicated and that the elimination of financial incentives will result in both a decrease in criminal motivation and a corresponding reduction in crime rates. Second, it is commonly assumed that confiscating the financial resources, property, and equipment of criminals and criminal organizations will make it more difficult for these individuals and organizations to engage in ongoing criminal activity. Criminals and criminal organizations depend upon the capital and tools that they need to carry out their illegal activities, and they will no longer be capable of functioning effectively if they are deprived of these items. Third, it is believed that the assets seized from criminals and criminal organizations can ultimately be used to help further efforts to fight crime and improve local communities. Financial resources that are seized through asset forfeiture proceedings are frequently channeled to local law-enforcement agencies that use them to fund their ongoing crime suppression and enforcement activities. Seized funds can also be used to acquire the resources and fund the activities that are thought to be necessary to improve the quality of life for residents of the communities in which the seizures originally took place.

While advocates promote the benefits that are commonly associated with criminal asset forfeiture proceedings, critics have pointed to a number of concerns that have been identified. One commonly held concern pertains to how the desire to seize assets can ultimately skew law-enforcement priorities. Critics contend that the financial incentives inherent in existing asset forfeiture laws have encouraged law-enforcement agencies to shift their attention and enforcement focus to those types of offenses and offenders that offer the greatest hope of providing substantive financial seizures. Another concern regarding criminal asset forfeiture proceedings relates to the potential threat that these procedures may pose to civil liberties and individual due process protections. More specifically, concerns have surfaced regarding the degree to which subjecting an individual offender to both criminal prosecution and asset forfeiture proceedings amounts to a violation of that individual's Fifth Amendment protections against double jeopardy. While the courts have not supported this contention to date, ongoing concerns remain regarding the degree to which asset forfeiture laws threaten individual rights and liberties. Additionally, some have challenged the core ideas upon which asset forfeiture laws are based. More specifically, critics have questioned whether financial gain is really one of the primary motivations for involvement in the types of criminal offenses that have historically been the target of asset forfeiture proceedings. Finally, questions have also arisen regarding whether asset forfeiture proceedings are conducted with the frequency necessary to influence the cost-benefit calculations that are made by would-be offenders. If not, critics have contended that there is no reason to expect asset forfeiture proceedings to exert a limiting affect on criminal behavior.

Laws pertaining to criminal asset forfeiture exist at both the federal and state levels. There are a number of similarities and differences in the procedural and substantive applications of the various asset forfeiture laws that currently exist. While criminal asset forfeiture laws could conceivably be applied to any type of crime, they have typically been used to target only certain types of offenses. In the last several decades, criminal asset forfeiture laws have increasingly been used in the War on Drugs to confiscate the financial resources of organizations responsible for the trafficking of illicit drugs. However, these are not the only types of criminal offenses that have become the focus of asset forfeiture proceedings. In the past, criminal and civil asset forfeiture laws were used in conjunction with the Racketeer Influenced and Corrupt Organizations (RICO) Act in an attempt to seize the wealth of organized crime groups. At other times, asset forfeiture laws have been used to target offenses as diverse as gambling, selling counterfeit goods, and investment fraud. Today, criminal asset forfeiture remains an important part of the U.S. government's coordinated response to criminal activity. At the same time, efforts have also been undertaken to reform asset forfeiture laws in an attempt to control or eliminate some of their most controversial features.

Jason R. Jolicoeur
Cincinnati State Technical and
Community College

See also Civil Forfeiture: The Experience of the United States; Counterfeit Goods; Criminal Associations; Drug Trade: Source, Destination, and Transit Countries; Gambling: Illegal; Investment Crimes; Organized Crime: Defined; Racketeer Influenced and Corrupt Organizations Act

Further Readings

Casella, Stefan. *Asset Forfeiture Law in the United States.* Huntington, NY: JurisNet, 2007.

Edgeworth, Dee. *Asset Forfeiture: Practice and Procedure in State and Federal Courts* (2nd ed.). Chicago: American Bar Association, 2008.

Gurule, Jimmy et al. *The Law of Asset Forfeiture.* Newark, NJ: LexisNexis, 2004.

Levy, Leonard. *A License to Steal: The Forfeiture of Property.* Chapel Hill: University of North Carolina Press, 1995.

Williams, Howard. *Asset Forfeiture: A Law Enforcement Perspective.* Springfield, IL: Charles C Thomas, 2002.

Worrall, John and Tomislav Kovandzic. "Is Policing for Profit? Answers From Asset Forfeiture." *Criminology and Public Policy*, v.7/219–244 (2008).

Data Sources: Empirical Data

In general, criminology is a scientific approach to the study of criminal behavior. One of the first scientific approaches in criminology was the work of Cesare Beccaria in 1764 related to torture and the death penalty. Quantitative methods based on empirical data in criminology were developed in the 19th century by sociologist Émile Durkheim in his famous research project titled *Suicide*, which was published in 1897 and considered suicide rates across different populations.

According to R. K. Schutt and R. Bachman (2008), those interested in the study of criminology and criminal justice have at their disposal a wide range of research methods. Deciding which of the particular research methods to use is entirely contingent upon the question being studied. Research questions typically fall into four categories of research: descriptive, exploratory, explanatory, or evaluative. Descriptive research attempts to define and describe the social phenomenon under investigation. Exploratory research seeks to identify the underlying meaning behind actions and individual behavior. Explanatory research seeks to identify the causes and effects of social phenomena. Evaluative research seeks to determine the effects of an intervention on individual behavior. These four areas of research are not mutually exclusive; rather, they are designed to be used interactively in order to gain a deeper understanding of the question under investigation. All these types of research deal with empirical data.

The term *empirical* was originally used to refer to certain ancient Greek practitioners of medicine who rejected adherence to the dogmatic doctrines of the day, preferring instead to rely on the observation of phenomena as perceived in experience. Later, *empiricism* referred to a theory of knowledge in philosophy that adheres to the principle that knowledge arises from experience and evidence gathered specifically using the senses. In scientific use, the term empirical refers to the gathering of data using only evidence that is observable by the senses or using calibrated scientific instruments. What early philosophers described as empiricist and empirical research have in common is the dependence on observable data to formulate and test theories and come to conclusions.

The term *data* refers to qualitative or quantitative attributes of a variable or set of variables. Data are typically the results of measurements and can be the bases of graphs, images, or observations of a set of variables. Data are often viewed as constituting the lowest level of abstraction, from which information and then knowledge are derived.

According the *American Heritage Dictionary of the English Language*, the word *empirical* denotes information gained by means of observation or experiments, so we can say that empirical data are data produced by an experiment or observation. Criminologists more often gather data by observation, but they also may perform experiments.

When we are talking about empirical data in criminology, we always have to talk about quantitative methods in criminology. Quantitative methods in criminology use empirical data to support the mathematical research methods for studying the distribution and causes of crime in open cases and closed cases, as well as patterns in crimes. Quantitative methods provide numerous ways to obtain data that are useful to many aspects of society. The use of quantitative methods—such as survey research, field research, and evaluation research—helps criminologists to gather reliable and valid data helpful in the field of criminology. The data can be, and often are, used by criminologists and other social scientists in making causal statements about variables being researched.

Observation

Criminologists take several approaches to gathering quantitative data. First, observation uses several research designs: participant observation, intensive interviewing, focus groups, and case studies and life histories. At its most basic level, participant observation involves a variety of strategies in data gathering in which the researcher observes a group by participating, to varying degrees, in the activities of the group. There are four different positions on a continuum of roles that field researchers may play in this regard: complete participant, participant as observer, observer as participant, and complete observer. Complete participation takes place when the researcher joins in and actually begins to manipulate the direction of group activity. In the participant-as-observer strategy, the researcher usually makes him- or herself known and tries to observe the activities of the group objectively. The observer-as-participant strategy is very much like a one-visit interview, where the interviewees are also short-term participant observers. Typically, these interviews are conducted with individuals who are known to participate in a designated activity. Finally, the complete-observer strategy relies solely on observation, without any participation from the researcher. Intensive interviewing consists of open-ended, relatively unstructured questioning in which the interviewer seeks in-depth information on the interviewee's feelings, experiences, or perceptions. Unlike the participant-observation strategy, intensive interviewing does not require systematic observation of respondents in their natural setting. Typically, interviewing sample members, along with identification and interviewing of more sample members, continues until the saturation point is reached, the point when new interviews seem to yield little additional information.

Focus groups are groups of unrelated individuals that are formed by a researcher and then led in group discussions of a topic. Typically, the researcher asks specific questions and guides the discussion to ensure that group members address these questions, but the resulting information is qualitative and relatively unstructured.

Offender Surveys and Victim Surveys

In an attempt to combat the problems posed by the "dark figure of crime," new methods of identifying and recording criminal behavior, such as offender surveys (often known as self-report studies) and victim surveys, have been developed. Victim surveys substantially changed the definition of crime and the nature of the information available on crime events. The events defined as crime and the information collected on these events were shaped by the needs of police organizations. The surveys had a different set of limitations related to the survey enterprise. Police record systems available at the time included only those events reported and recorded by the police, collected data on a selected subset of crime, and presented data as aggregate counts of crimes. Victim surveys included events that were reported to the police as well as those that were not. They included extensive information on victims and the social context of the crime and made those data available on an incident or victim basis. These surveys gathered data from victims and nonvictims.

Offender surveys and victim surveys have become increasingly popular methods of criminological research. In order to analyze their success, it is important to look at them individually. Self-report studies consist of a series of questions directed at particular groups, usually youths, asking them to provide information on their involvement in criminality and rule breaking. According to Schutt and Bachman, Thornberry argues that "the introduction of the self-report method has had a greater impact on theory and research than any other single innovation and it has led to fundamental shifts in how delinquent behavior is described and explained." However, there are a number of criticisms of this method. First, they do not make use of a representative sample of society, often examining only the delinquent behavior of juveniles. Also, they are reliant on the honesty of those being surveyed, who may be inclined to embellish their criminal behavior. In spite of this, offender surveys offer useful insights into youth culture and particular youth crimes such as vandalism and recreational drug use. Coleman and Moynihan, as noted by Schutt and Bachman, put forward that "there is little doubt that self-report studies have contributed much in documenting some of the omissions in official data . . . making clear that offending behavior is far more widespread in the population than was once supposed, and that the offender cannot be so clearly distinguished as a minority with certain key characteristics as was once thought." Although self-report studies have compensated for the deficiencies of official statistics to some degree by offering insight into the nature and extent of juvenile offending and minor offenses, they have been largely unsuccessful in providing an indication or an understanding of more serious crimes and adult offending behavior. Also, self-report studies have done little to redress official crime statistics' failure to identify certain types of hidden crimes, such as white-collar crime and domestic violence. Many criminologists argue that victimization surveys can compensate for the problems relating to official statistics and successfully highlight the expanse of the "dark figure of crime."

Using Data That Have Already Been Obtained

Crime is very hard to measure, so it is often best to combine many of these methods in order to get the most valid data for measurement. The quality of data must be evaluated, and in this analysis process it helps to have access to both raw data and published data. This comparison can be more telling than simply referring to the published data, because there can be no bias in the comparison. Another valuable tool in research is the ability to compare newly collected data (secondary data) with previously collected data (primary data). There are two ways in which this approach can help: First, primary data can confirm newly found data, and second, differences in the data can point out problematic areas.

Data exchange can occur between nations. Data of this type are typically census data or other governmentally collected data. Exchange can also occur between regions, states, and municipalities to improve social problems or just display differences. Temporal data analysis is vital to our understanding of the world we live in and where we are headed. Data collected over time can provide researchers with infinite amounts of data that can aid in an equally large number of studies. Of course, there are challenges associated with measuring data in criminology. A number of variables influence police to record a crime or make an arrest. For example, an assault between people who know each other will less likely be recorded than a fight between two strangers. Also, there will be times when the victim will urge the police not to press charges on the offender or even not arrest that person. Another measurement challenge results from when laws change. There are different laws in effect in different jurisdictions, and laws often vary from country to country.

Measuring and Categorizing Data

Empirical data can be measured or categorized. If we measure data, we are assigning them quantities related to their attributes (attitudes); if we categorize them, we put them in the same or different categories with respect to a given attribute (classification). The research objects in criminology are usually people, their acts, or sometimes physical objects and people's relationships to them.

When we are talking about attributes, we are thinking about some particular feature of research objects (prisoner intelligence, material status, or educational level, for example). It is important to make clear distinctions between an object and its attributes. In criminology, an object can be prisoners, for example, but an attribute concerns relations among objects on a particular dimension—intelligence, for example. It is important to consider the nature of an attribute very carefully. The processes of measurement and categorization require a process of abstraction; some people fail to abstract a particular attribute from the whole object—for example, some people find it difficult to understand that a criminal and a law-abiding citizen can be equally intelligent.

Levels of Measurement

There are several levels of measurement. The first level is nominal and involves rules for deciding whether two objects are the same or not in the process of categorizing them. That means that two objects in the same category will have some attribute in common—for example, two criminals who are both males may be categorized as male. Nominal measurement results in series of categories with their own frequencies. Common categories are race, ethnicity, and gender. A category does not show any specific quantitative relationship; it just shows whether some object belongs to it or not. This measurement level allows us to describe basic operations among objects: equality versus inequality and showing categories' frequencies.

The second level is ordinal and involves rules for deciding whether objects that are not equal to one another are greater than the others or less than the others with respect to a given attribute. Investigators lump objects' scores into a smaller number of successive categories. Offenders' family incomes can be measured in this way. This approach is often used for data presentation. Also our empirical data may be ranked. Likert-scale items are common examples used in criminology for attitude measurement, in which subjects describe their intensity of feeling toward an item. For example, prisoners might be asked whether they strongly agree, agree, are indifferent, disagree, or strongly disagree with the statement, "I feel uncomfortable asking guards something." Rank ordering is basic to higher forms of measurement, and this measurement level allows us to identify such basic relationships among objects as greater than versus less than, as well as more sophisticated statistical procedures: median, percentile, and order statistics.

The third measurement level is the interval. It reflects operations that define a unit of measurement and deciding, as well as greater than, equal to, and less than. Intelligence is often subjected to this method of measurement. We have a unit of measurement but we do not have true zero. Deviations from any mean can be calculated without actually knowing how far anyone is from a true zero point (here, zero intelligence). We can decide whether somebody's IQ score is greater than, equal to, or less than someone else's IQ score, but if person A has an IQ of 71 and person B an IQ of 142, we cannot say that person B is "twice as" intelligent as person A. All we can say is that person B's IQ score is higher than person A's IQ score by 71 units. Hence, the rank ordering of objects on an attribute is known, the distances among objects on the attribute are known, but the absolute magnitude of the attribute is unknown. Interval measurements allow us to perform statistical procedures on obtained data: arithmetic mean, variance, and Pearson correlation.

The fourth measurement level is the ratio level. On this level, we have measurement units and we have a true zero. The ratio level allows the use of all four fundamental operations of mathematics: addition, subtraction, division, and multiplication. A true zero means real absence of the attribute. It is very difficult to define absolute zeros for most criminological attributes except height, weight, and similar attributes.

One important factor in all research is that methods will continue to change, improving the strength, diversity, scope, and effectiveness of data collected through research. Criminologists, like all other researchers, will use advancements in other fields of research to help improve their own.

Mladen Pecujlija
University of Novi Sad, Serbia

See also Data Sources: Media Coverage; Data Sources: Police Data; Data Sources: Prosecution and Courts; Measuring Transnational Crime; Money Laundering: History; Money Laundering: Methods; Money Laundering: Targeting Criminal Proceeds; Money Laundering: Vulnerable Commodities and Services

Further Readings

Nunnally, J. and I. H. Bernstein. *Psychometric Theory*. New York: McGraw-Hill, 1994.

Piquero, Alexis Russell and David Weisburd. *Handbook of Quantitative Criminology*. New York: Springer, 2010.

Riedel, Marc. *Research Strategies for Secondary Data: A Perspective for Criminology and Criminal Justice*. Thousand Oaks, CA: Sage, 2000.

Schutt, R. K. and R. Bachman. *Fundamentals of Research in Criminology and Criminal Justice*. Thousand Oaks, CA: Sage, 2008.

DATA SOURCES: MEDIA COVERAGE

There has been long-standing interest in the description and explanation of global terrorism trends in academics. Reviews of the transnational terrorism literature indicate that much of the evidence is based on open-source data sets that use media reports of terrorism. For example, in Schmid and Jongman's (1988) interviews of several leading terrorism scholars, 90 percent of those surveyed reported using data gathered from media and news services. Similarly, Silke's (2005) review of terrorism studies published between 1995 and 1999 in two leading terrorism journals, *Terrorism and Political Violence* and *Studies in Conflict and Terrorism*, indicates that more than 80 percent of terrorism research is based on open-source media reports. Although data collected using media reports are less frequently relied upon in traditional international research on violence and crime, media sources provide a valuable source of data for those interested in transnational terrorism. The reliance on the media as a source of terrorism data is so prominent that Schmid (1982) has stated that "terrorism and mass communication are linked together. Without communication there can be no terrorism."

This entry highlights the role of media sources for transnational terrorism research. The first section of the entry reviews conceptual and measurement issues associated with the study of transnational terrorism at the country level. The difficulties of obtaining cross-national data on transnational terrorism incidents through traditional data sources have led to increasing reliance on media sources for transnational terrorism data. Given the strong connection between the purpose of terrorism and the purpose of the mass media, it is likely that media-based reports have several advantages for the study of transnational terrorism. This entry reviews the advantages and limitations of using media-based reports of transnational terrorism and provides potential approaches for increasing the validity and reliability of media sources of transnational terrorism.

Defining and Measuring Transnational Terrorism

Defining terrorism has been a notoriously problematic and complex task for researchers. Although there is general agreement regarding the concept of terrorism broadly, defining and measuring terrorism have been done inconsistently within the literature. Schmid and Jongman examined more than 100 definitions of terrorism and found that violence/force was reflected in approximately 83.5 percent of definitions; 65 percent emphasized political motivation, 51 percent emphasized fear or terror, and 47 percent mentioned the use of threat. Thus, despite substantial variation in the precise conceptualization and measurement of terrorism, common elements are reflected across most operational definitions.

Common definitions of terrorism include Hoffman's "calculated use of unlawful violence or threat of violence to inculcate fear, intended to coerce or intimidate governments or societies in the pursuit of goals that are generally political, religious, or ideological objectives." Similarly, Enders and

Terrorism suspects are posted in a Federal Bureau of Investigation (FBI) Most Wanted Terrorist Composite that was widely seen on television and in other media. Media sources can provide a valuable source of data in international research on violence and crime. (U.S. Federal Bureau of Investigation)

Sandler (1999) define terrorism as "the premeditated use, or threat of use, of extra-normal violence or brutality to obtain a political objective through intimidation or fear directed at a large audience." Transnational terrorism is further distinguished from other types of terrorist events as those acts involving a national or a group of nationals from one country crossing international borders and attacking targets in another country. Transnational terrorism is distinguished from international terrorism when there are offenders from more than one country that attack victims from another country. Terrorism is further classified according to various elements of the incidents. For example, whereas some researchers have defined terrorism as acts of violence by nonstate actors perpetrated against civilian populations, other researchers have included state-sponsored terrorist acts. Some definitions include acts that involve only threat, while other definitions require acts beyond the threat of force. Definitions also vary by motivation, with some focusing solely on political motivation and others being more inclusive, incorporating religions and social motivations for violence.

Collecting country-level data on transnational terrorism events is a daunting task given the problems associated with collecting valid and reliable international crime data, and they are arguably amplified in the study of transnational terrorism. Traditionally relied-upon sources of data in cross-national criminology include official-record data, such as data taken from the International Criminal Police Organization (Interpol), the United Nations (UN) crime surveys, and the World Health Organization (WHO). Although containing valuable information on cross-national crime and violence more generally, these data sets are problematic for the study of terrorism because they lack data on terrorist events entirely, are not made publicly available, or are not distinguished from homicides more generally. Additionally, many countries do not collect their own systematic criminal history data on the arrest and conviction of terrorist suspects, or they are collected by intelligence agencies that do not make the data available to the public. Finally, many terrorist suspects are prosecuted under nonterrorism-related criminal offenses. Other traditional sources of cross-national crime data also have limitations, such as self-reports of terrorist victimization or involvement.

International surveys of self-reported victimization, such as the International Crime Victimization Survey (ICVS), also tend to lack data on transnational terrorism victimization and, according to LaFree and Dugan (2007), are "almost entirely irrelevant to the study of terrorist activities." One disadvantage of using victimization surveys centers on its poor ability to capture relatively rare events in the general population. Crime victimization is a relatively rare event in the larger population, and victimization via a transnational terrorism attack even more so.

Offending reports of terrorist involvement are also relatively rare and tend to take a case-study approach with relatively small sample sizes. Targeted sample selection of potential or suspected terrorists is also problematic because many active terrorists are reluctant to provide information about their activities. Nonetheless, several researchers have collected self-report terrorist offending data from interviews with known terrorists and by reviewing related documents and artifacts. An alternative to these traditional sources of criminological data are media-based databases of transnational terrorism incidents, often referred to as open-source or media-derived databases. (Open-source data sets refer to those secondary databases that are created using publicly available data; often open-source databases consist of data largely culled from media sources.

However, open-source databases may also contain publicly available data from government agencies or documents or from other private agencies.)

Researchers in international relations and comparative politics have traditionally used media sources as means to create event databases when traditional sources are unavailable. Open-source media-based data sets are arguably the best existing type of data on transnational terrorism at the country level.

Media-Based Data Sets of Transnational Terrorism

Terrorism has been inextricably linked to the onset of mass communication, primarily because acts of terrorism are viewed as acts of communication. One primary difference between traditional violent crime and terrorism is that the latter seeks to transmit a message to a broader audience, as opposed to focusing solely on the victims. Acts of terrorism are acts of violence and communication; thus, many scholars have argued that modern terrorism is closely linked to the rise of modern media. The implication of such a viewpoint is that terrorist groups act in such a way as to capture the attention of the media and generate international publicity. The infamous phrase "terrorism is theater" reflects this sentiment. Open-source media-based reports of terrorism have been used to create both offender and incident-level data sets. Similarly, law enforcement and the general public also appear to rank media-based sources as important sources of information on terrorism.

Researchers have used media reports to create incident-level data sets on domestic terrorism within countries over time, such as the United States Extremist Crime Database (ECDB). The *Preliminary Report*, based on the ECDB, contains information on extremist right-wing terrorist incidents occurring in the United States from 1990 to 2008. Media reports have also been used to create data sets that focus on collecting self-report information from terrorist offenders. Importantly for researchers interested in transnational crime and violence, there are also several existing data sets containing cross-national data on transnational and domestic terrorism events. One recently available open-source data set compiled using primarily media sources is the Global Terrorism Database (GTD). Additional open-source media-based databases include data from

RAND, the Memorial Institute for the Prevention of Terrorism (MIPT), and International Terrorism: Attributes of Terrorist Events (ITERATE).

The GTD is of special interest because it contains considerably more terrorism events over a longer time span, compared to other extant media-derived data sets. The GTD is a product of ongoing data collection that began with the acquisition of media-derived data from Pinkerton Global Intelligence Services (PGIS). The data were acquired by researchers at the University of Maryland in 2001, at which the point the data were electronically recoded and verified; complete electronic coding of the original PGIS data was completed in 2005. Since 1997 the data have been maintained and updated by a team of researchers at the National Center for the Study of Terrorism and Responses to Terrorism (START), a U.S. Department of Homeland Security (DHS) Center of Excellence, and are referred to as GTD2.

PGIS was a private risk assessment organization that collected data on more than 67,000 domestic and transnational terrorist attacks between 1970 and 1997. Since that time, the GTD has been expanded to include terrorism events after 1997. For example, the GTD now covers approximately more than 200 countries, nations, and territories from 1970 to 2007 and contains incident-level information for more than 80,000 events. Defining *terrorism* as "the threatened or actual use of illegal force and violence to attain a political, economic, religious or social goal through fear, coercion or intimidation," trained researchers collected incident-level terrorist information using several media sources as well as government-based resources.

A number of U.S.- and foreign-based media sources are used to compile data in the GTD. Researchers consult media-based accounts from Reuters, the Associated Press, the British Broadcasting Corporation (BBC), and the Foreign Broadcast Information Service (FBIS). Additionally, the GTD has relied upon a wide variety of U.S. and foreign media sources, including *Diario*, the *New York Times*, the *Washington Post*, *El Tiempo*, *El Mercurio*, *Ha'aretz*, *The Times* of India, *An Phoblacht*, the *Jakarta Post*, and the *Bangkok Post*. Internet media sources are also heavily relied upon. Researchers conduct daily examinations of general news-based databases, such as LexisNexis and Opensource.gov, and have produced thousands of potential events for each day of searching. The process employed by the GTD researchers is similar to those used by other researchers constructing media-based reports of terrorism events.

One advantage of using media-based databases is the widespread availability of this type of data and the relative unavailability of alternative sources of incident-level transnational data. The practical and logistical benefits of open-source media reports of terrorism, combined with the strong conceptual and historical evidence linking the importance of the media for transmitting terrorist-based messages to the general public, indicate that media reports of terrorism are sufficient for estimating country-level patterns of transnational terrorism. In spite of this suitability, there are caveats that must be noted when using media reports of terrorism events.

Woolley discusses several limitations of media-based data for studies in politics, and many of these limitations also more generally apply to the study of transnational terrorism. His review of the literature indicates that media-derived data may suffer from bias arising from differences in media processes by region or urban versus rural areas and the reporting of larger versus smaller events. Prior evidence indicates that regional variation in media reporting of certain events may occur because of variations in media resources. This may be especially problematic for transnational terrorism researchers who seek accurate country-level counts of terrorist events, as media resources vary considerably by region.

Selection bias because of high profile cases is also a possibility, as media reports tend to include those events that are extremely high-profile and exclude those events that are less newsworthy. Chermak and Gruenewald examined media coverage for 412 known incidents of U.S. domestic right-wing extremist terrorism and found that 55 percent had received coverage in the *New York Times*; however, they also found that 80 percent of all published terrorism stories referred to only 15 of the total known incidents. Similarly, a recent study that compared incidents from several media-derived databases of extremist right-wing domestic terrorism found that high-profile incidents were most likely to be included across all sources, such as the Oklahoma City bombing, the series of bombings attributed to Eric Rudolph, and the Ruby Ridge incident. Although it is promising that identical cases were found across different databases, incidents identified most consistently across the various data sources represent less than 6 percent of all known right-wing terrorist incidents. High-profile incidents, such as those with large numbers of fatalities, may not be generalizable to all terrorism attacks.

Woolley suggests that media-generated event databases use multiple media sources to guard against selection biases arising from differing media processes (regional bias, extreme events) and be attentive to the possibility of "censored samples" of events. Many media-derived databases, such as those of the GTD, ITERATE, and RAND, have implemented this suggestion, using multiple media outlets and venues (print and electronic) to gather data. The primary sources of media include not only major national entities but local country-specific entities as well. Moreover, not all evidence of the validity of media-based data is as pessimistic. Importantly, there is substantial evidence to indicate that reporting of objective acts (event counts rather than interpretations of events) and "large and violent events" are more likely to be reported without bias and more reliably. The unique event characteristics of transnational terrorist events may increase the validity with which they are reported in the media, as compared to other types of conflict-based events. This bodes well for studies of transnational terrorism events, as prior research indicates that they are often orchestrated for media attention. Future transnational terrorism studies can address these potential limitations by exploring the effects of differential validity in media reports of high- versus low-profile events by examining differences in the distribution and correlates of media-based reports of fatal (high-profile) attacks versus nonfatal (low-profile) attacks.

Another limitation is that often media reports of terrorist events increase following the occurrence of a high-profile event, leading to what is called an "echo effect." Suggestive evidence from the ECDB indicates that media reporting of extremist events increased following the Oklahoma City bombing, specifically, the number of separate sources reporting extremist homicides increased from 2.3 sources during 1990–94 to 3.54 sources during 1995–99.

Changes in the prominence of certain events in the media may also change over time; this is likely to occur after high-profile incidents, such as the aforementioned domestic terrorism events and transnational terrorism events (the attacks of September 11, 2001, being a prime example). A possible way to address this limitation is to create an additional variable to capture the prominence of the event in time or adjust for changes resulting from changes in recording practices.

In summary, suggestions for reducing measurement error and bias in media reports of transnational terrorism include increasing the number of media sources to include a wide variety of regional and national outlets, as well as increasing the search net that is cast (such as both print and Internet searches). Several scholars have cross-validated media-derived databases with similar databases as well as non-media-derived databases. Another important issue to explore in future research is the extent to which there is bias in media reporting; in particular, there may be greater, more thorough coverage of highly democratic countries as compared to less industrialized countries. Given the variation in definitions and measurement of terrorism across data sets, an alternative approach is to focus on replicating studies estimating the distribution of transnational terrorism country-level patterns using separate media-based databases. Existing literature within comparative politics indicates that media reports of events are valid under certain conditions; using these studies as a starting point, future research in transnational terrorism should also examine the validity and reliability of open-source media-based reports of terrorism.

Conclusion

Although the media are not a traditional source of data used within criminology, increasing interest in the distribution and explanation of transnational terrorism patterns has led to more research using the media as a primary source for transnational terrorism data. Media-based sources of data have provided valuable information of worldwide country-level patterns of transnational terrorism, overcoming the limitations of traditional criminological data. Media reports will undoubtedly continue as prominent sources of information for examining transnational terrorism. In line with this growing tendency is the heightened scholarly trend toward examining the reliability and validity of media-based sources of data. Existing evidence suggests that although there are limitations and biases associated with media-based data, there are advantages for using such data for the creation of event-based data sets of cross-national transnational terrorism. Given the strong link between terrorism and mass communication, media sources of information are useful alternatives to traditional forms of data for illuminating the descriptive and causal processes associated with transnational terrorism.

Nancy Ann Morris
Southern Illinois University

See also Data Sources: Empirical Data; Data Sources: Police Data; Data Sources: Prosecution and Courts; Measuring Transnational Crime

Further Readings

Burgoon, B. "On Welfare and Terror: Social Welfare and Political-Economic Roots of Terrorism." *Journal of Conflict Resolution*, v.50/2 (2006).

Chermak, S. M. and J. Gruenewald. "Domestic Terrorism and the Media." *Justice Quarterly*, v.4 (2006).

Enders, W. and T. Sandler. "The Effectiveness of Anti-Terrorism Policies: A Vector-Autoregression Intervention Analysis." *American Political Science Review*, v.87 (1993).

Enders, W. and T. Sandler. "Transnational Terrorism in the Post-Cold War Era." *International Studies Quarterly*, v.43/1 (1999).

Franzosi, R. "The Press as a Source of Socio-Historical Data: Issues in the Methodology of Data Collection From Newspapers." *Historical Methods*, v.20 (1987).

Freilich, J. D. and S. M. Chermak. "Preventing Deadly Encounters Between Law Enforcement and American Far-Rightists." *Crime Prevention Studies*, v.25 (2009).

Freilich, J. D. and S. M. Chermak. *United States Extremist Crime Database (ECDB), 1990–2008: Preliminary Results*. Washington, DC: Department of Homeland Security University Network Research and Education Summit, 2009.

Gartner, R. "Methodological Issues in Cross-National Cultural Large Survey Research on Violence." *Violence and Victims*, v.8/3 (1993).

Handler, J. "Socioeconomic Profile of an American Terrorist." *Terrorism*, v.13 (1990).

Hewitt, C. *Understanding Terrorism in America: From the Klan to Al Qaeda*. New York: Routledge, 2003.

Hoffman, B. *Inside Terrorism*. New York: Columbia University Press, 2006.

Horgan, J. "Interviewing Terrorists: A Case for Primary Research." In *Terrorism Informatics: Knowledge Management and Data Mining for Homeland Security*, H. Chen et al., eds. New York: Springer, 2008.

Jenkins, B. M. "International Terrorism: A New Mode of Conflict." In *International Terrorism and World Security*, D. Carlton and C. Schaerf, eds. London: Croom Helm, 1975.

LaFree, G. "A Summary and Review of Cross-National Comparative Studies of Homicide." In *Homicide: A Sourcebook of Social Research*, M. D. Smith and M. A. Zahn, eds. Thousand Oaks, CA: Sage, 1999.

LaFree, G. and L. Dugan. "Introducing the Global Terrorism Database." *Terrorism and Political Violence*, v.19 (2007).

LaFree, G. and L. Dugan. "Tracking Global Terrorism, 1970–2004." In *To Protect and to Serve: Police and Policing in an Age of Terrorism*, D. Weisburd et al., eds. New York: Springer, 2009.

LaFree, G., N. A. Morris, and L. Dugan. "Cross-National Patterns of Terrorism." *British Journal of Criminology*, v.50 (2010).

Leiken, R. S. and S. Brooke. "The Quantitative Analysis of Terrorism and Immigration: An Initial Exploration." *Terrorism and Political Violence*, v.18 (2006).

McAdam, D. *Political Process and the Development of Black Insurgency 1930–1970*. Chicago: University of Chicago Press, 1982.

Mullins, C. W. and J. Young. "Cultures of Violence and Acts of Terror: Applying a Legitimation-Habituation Model to Terrorism." *Crime and Delinquency*, v.20/10 (2009).

Neapolitan, J. L. "Cross-National Crime Data: Some Unaddressed Problems." *Journal of Criminal Justice*, v.19 (1996).

Reid, J., A. Sinai, A. Silke, and B. Ganor, eds. *Terrorism Informatics: Knowledge Management and Data Mining for Homeland Security*. New York: Springer, 2008.

Ross, J. I. "Research Note: Contemporary Radical Right-Wing Violence in Canada: A Quantitative Analysis." *Terrorism and Political Violence*, v.4/3 (1992).

Sageman, M. *Understanding Terror Networks*. Philadelphia: University of Pennsylvania Press, 2004.

Sandler, T. and W. Enders. "Applying Analytical Methods to Study Terrorism." *International Studies Perspective*, v.8 (2007).

Schmid, A. P. *Violence as Communication: Insurgent Terrorism and the Western News Media*. London: Sage, 1982.

Schmid, A. P. and A. J. Jongman. *Political Terrorism: A New Guide to Actors, Authors, Concepts, Databases, Theories and Literature*. Amsterdam: North-Holland, 1988.

Silke, A. "Children, Terrorism and Counterterrorism: Lessons in Policy and Practice." *Terrorism and Political Violence*, v.17 (2005).

Smith, B. L. *Terrorism in America: Pipe Bombs and Pipe Dreams.* Albany: State University of New York Press, 1994.

Smith, B. L. and K. R. Damphousse. "Terrorism, Politics and Punishment: A Test of Structural-Contextual Theory and the 'Liberation Hypothesis.'" *Criminology,* v.36/1 (1998).

Smith, M. D. and M. A. Zahn, eds. *Homicide: A Sourcebook of Social Research.* Thousand Oaks, CA: Sage, 1999.

Stamatel, J. P. "Overcoming Methodological Challenges in International and Comparative Criminology: Guest Editor's Introduction." *International Journal of Comparative and Applied Criminal Justice,* v.33/2 (2009).

Surette, R. "Media Echoes: Systematic Effects of News Coverage." *Justice Quarterly,* v.16/3 (1999).

Synder, D. and W. R. Kelly. "Conflict Intensity, Media Sensitivity, and the Validity of Newspaper Data." *American Sociological Review,* v.42 (1977).

Woolley, J. T. "Using Media-Based Data in Studies of Politics." *American Journal of Political Science,* v.44/1 (2000).

Data Sources: Police Data

Police data are data gathered and recorded by uniformed officers, detectives, and police staff in the course of their police duties and stored within police information systems. The main types of police data that are recorded are calls for service, incident data, and criminal intelligence. The main types of police data that are regularly reported publicly are crime statistics. While police data provide the most systematic coverage of reported crime available, they are susceptible to errors in recording, inconsistencies in format, and incomplete entries. Police data also are limited; typically they include only crime reported to the police or detected by them through the use of law-enforcement intelligence. For scholars of transnational crime, police data provide a valuable source of information but may be limited by current national crime reporting standards.

Types of Police Data

There are three main types of police data recorded by almost every police organization: calls for service data, incident data, and criminal intelligence. Data on calls for service are generated whenever a member of the public calls the police to ask for assistance. Calls for service are often recorded by a dispatch center. Incident data are generated whenever the police respond to a call for service or initiate contact with the public. Incident data are generally recorded by the responding officer, either on scene or later, back in the office, through the filing of official reports. Criminal intelligence is often considered the most sensitive data and is gathered by police surveillance, undercover officers, and confidential informants.

In addition to the three main types of police data, a number of emerging types of police data are growing in importance and in the number of jurisdictions making use of them. One type is closed-circuit television (CCTV) images. CCTV cameras are a growing part of the police's strategy for monitoring public places for disorder and for gathering data that can later be used to investigate crime. Another growing form of police data are Automatic Number Plate Recognition (ANPR) data. ANPR cameras automatically read license plate numbers as cars drive by and record the time and location. The results can be monitored in real time to track the movements of specific license plates.

Police Data Systems

In many jurisdictions, each of the main types of police data is stored in its own specialized police database. Sometimes these databases are accessible to officers when they are in the field, through computers mounted in their patrol cars. Often the information in the police data systems is accessible only in headquarters and access is limited to particular police officers and police staff. This complicates the ability of police officers to make use of the data. The police also often have difficulties sharing information between jurisdictions. In countries such as the United States, Belgium, and the United Kingdom, this complicates efforts to work collaboratively across jurisdictional lines. Many countries have attempted to improve the ability to share information between police organizations by developing national police databases. In the United States, for example, the National Crime Information Center (NCIC) is a computerized database of criminal justice information such as criminal records, stolen property, missing persons, and fugitives. In the United Kingdom, the Police National Computer (PNC) maintains information on wanted individuals, stolen property (including stolen vehicles), and stolen or lost firearms. These databases contain information entered by jurisdictions across those countries. These national police databases make it possible for one jurisdiction to see if another jurisdiction has entered information on a person, place, or thing of interest to it.

Limits of Police Data

Regardless of the source, all police data are limited by the same factors: lack of attention to detail, inconsistent recording practices, and incompleteness. Police data are often recorded under challenging field conditions, where time and attention are scarce. As a result, police forms are often filled out with partial attention to detail. As a result, the data fields may be only partially completed or even completed incorrectly. Moreover, because police data are recorded by many different individuals, it is difficult to maintain consistency in the way in which data are recorded. For example, two officers responding to a report of a radio being stolen from a car might record the incident with using different codes, one denoting "theft" and "theft from vehicle." Such inconsistencies complicate efforts to analyze and account for similar crime incidents. Police data also are often incomplete. When a member of the public makes a call for service, he or she may not report all relevant details, either intentionally or unintentionally. A police officer on the scene may forget to record some aspect of a criminal incident or the information, such as the time or date of the incident, may not be available. For example, a victim might report a burglary that took place when she was on vacation, but it might be impossible to tell the specific date and time of the event.

Another limitation of police data is that they typically underreport incidents of crime. Based on victimization surveys, scholars conclude that there is a significant amount of crime that goes unreported and undetected and is therefore not reflected in official police data. Some police jurisdictions attempt to mitigate the limits of police data by conducting their own victimization surveys. They survey a representative sample of citizens in their jurisdiction and ask them about their experiences of crime. This practice is not widespread, however, because of the cost of conducting these surveys and the expertise required to conduct them. Although there is a consensus that police data tend to underreport incidents of crime, most jurisdictions and nations continue to rely on police data as the most authoritative source of information on crime rates.

Publicly Available Police Data

The main type of police data reported publicly is incident data. Crime statistics typically provide a breakdown of all the incidents reported to, and recorded by, the police by type of crime. Many countries require all their police jurisdictions to report their local crime statistics to a national office that then compiles them on behalf of the national government. For example, crime statistics are reported officially in the United States as part of the Federal Bureau of Investigation's Uniform Crime Reporting (UCR) program; in the United Kingdom, police data and crime surveys are combined and reported by the Home Office; and in Canada, Statistics Canada presents information based on the Uniform Crime Reporting Survey of all crime substantiated by the police. Crime statistics may also be made public on a police organization's Website. Sometimes they are displayed both in chart format and on a map, showing where crimes took place. In some jurisdictions, calls for service are also made public, again often on the police organization's Website. Criminal intelligence is almost never made available to the public, although some jurisdictions do publish assessments based on criminal intelligence. In doing so, they "redact" (meaning remove or obscure) the most sensitive criminal intelligence and present their findings more generally to avoid compromising their intelligence informants and their technical intelligence-gathering methods.

The police also often publish their own assessments of public safety and security issues based on police data. Police organizations often have in-house research units that analyze topics of interest for police leadership and in response to statutory requirements for public reporting. In Germany, for example, the Bundeskriminalamt (BKA) publishes situation reports on the trafficking of human beings and organized crime. In the United States, the National Drug Intelligence Center (NDIC) publishes national drug assessments and national gang assessments. In Canada, the Royal Canadian Mounted Police puts its assessments on human trafficking, organized crime, missing children, and juvenile crime on its public-facing Website. Its security service counterpart, the Canadian Security Intelligence Service (CSIS), publishes *Commentary*, a journal written by its Intelligence Assessments Branch about topics from climate change to China and the Internet to human immunodeficiency virus/acquired immune deficiency syndrome (HIV/AIDS) and the security sector in Africa.

Privacy and Police Data

A growing concern about police data is their potential to have a negative impact on privacy and civil liberties. Many jurisdictions gather and retain data not only about crime incidents, offenders, and victims but also about the citizens with whom they have come in contact. Additionally, data on citizens are often available to the police in a multitude of government and commercially provided databases. Privacy advocates fear that the police may combine their own databases with this additional information and use them to attempt to identify potential offenders without probable cause. Civil liberties advocates worry that the combination of police data, CCTV images, and commercial data such as credit card transactions is creating a "surveillant assemblage" that makes it possible for the state to know where its citizens are at all times. They are concerned that the state may use this knowledge to control its citizens and impede their individual freedoms.

Police Data and Transnational Crime

Police data are a useful source of information to aid in the study of transnational crime because, despite their limitations, they reflect the most reliable data available on crime incidents. International criminal justice organizations such as the United Nations Office on Drugs and Crime (UNODC), the International Criminal Police Organization (Interpol), and the European Police Office (Europol) as well as national organizations such as the U.S. National Drug Intelligence Center and the U.K. Home Office make use of police data to publish in-depth assessments of transnational crime. These assessments represent one of the best sources of data for studying the official understanding of transnational crime. At the same time, one of the challenges of using police data to study transnational crime is that many types of transnational crime are not captured in the typical national crime reporting standards. For example, specific forms of transnational crime such as credit card fraud, human trafficking, and environmental crime may be subsumed under larger categories in national crime-reporting programs. Other types of transnational crime may go unreported because the victim is either unaware of the crime (for example, identity theft) or unable to report the crime (as might be the case in sex trafficking). These factors make it difficult to obtain accurate figures on specific types of transnational crime. One of the ways that organizations like UNODC try to overcome this obstacle is through specialized data calls to member nations about particular types of transnational crime.

Justin Lewis Abold
Oxford University

See also Data Sources: Empirical Data; Data Sources: Prosecution and Courts; Measuring Transnational Crime

Further Readings

Ericson, Richard and Kevin Haggerty. *Policing the Risk Society*. Toronto, ON: University of Toronto Press, 1997:

Manning, Peter. *The Technology of Policing: Crime Mapping, Information Technology and the Rationality of Crime Control*. New York: New York University Press, 2008.

Philippe, Robert, et al. *Comparing Crime Data in Europe: Official Crime Statistics and Survey Based Data*. Brussels: VUB Press, 2009.

DATA SOURCES: PROSECUTION AND COURTS

Records on prosecution and courts are a source of information on the process starting from the identification of a suspected offender by law-enforcement authorities to the decision of a judge at a criminal court. These sources also provide data on the staffs of prosecuting and court authorities. Notwithstanding the particular situations in specific countries, *input data* of prosecution and courts statistics refers to all cases of criminal offenses that are passed to the prosecuting authority for disposal; *process data* refers to persons prosecuted; and *output data* refers to convicted offenders. Data sources on prosecution and courts are publicly available, mainly at the country and international levels.

Prosecution data sources address information regarding the decision whether or not to initiate or confirm a formal criminal charge against an individual and the decision whether or not a case should be brought before a criminal court. Statistical records included in prosecution data sources typically refer to cases against an individual person; however, the counting unit may change from country to country according to the different statistical procedures and counting systems of the national criminal justice (hereinafter CJ) systems in question. *Input prosecutorial statistics* refers to all cases of criminal offenses that are passed to the prosecuting authority for disposal in a reference year. They refer to "person-cases initiated," when the focus is on the person, and "charges initiated," when the focus is on the criminal case. *Output prosecutorial statistics* refers to all disposals made (person-cases disposed) by prosecutors in a reference year. Different categories of disposals can be identified in prosecution data sources, mainly depending on the discretionary power of prosecutors in each country; cases can be disposed by being brought before a court; by a sanction imposed by the prosecutor (which may or may not lead to a formal verdict and count as a conviction); by conditional disposals; or by dropping the proceeding (in combination with a cautioning of the suspect, unconditionally because of lack of public interest or for efficiency measures, for legal or factual reasons, or because the offender remains unknown).

Court data sources record information on individuals entering a criminal court in order to face one or several charges. They also provide information on the persons convicted and acquitted and on the types of sanctions and measures imposed on offenders. Local courts, the basic reporting institutions of the data-collection systems for courts statistics, generally open a new file for each new case initiated. The information contained in each file forms the basis of data collection on courts' activities. A court case is usually intended as all of the charges against one offender; therefore, the unit of count is generally the offender who enters the court system. *Input courts statistics* refers to all cases or persons brought before the criminal court (or any legal body authorized to pronounce a conviction under national criminal law), whether the person is finally acquitted or convicted. More specifically, input courts statistics refer to "person-cases initiated," when the focus is on the person, and "charges initiated" or "appeals initiated," when the focus is on the case. *Output courts statistics* refers to persons convicted and acquitted.

Prosecution and court data sources providing both input and output statistics make it possible to calculate estimated "response/attrition rates." These rates are considered important indicators for assessing the workload and performance of a specific CJ system and can be calculated at a number of points within a CJ system (such as when comparing persons prosecuted or persons convicted/acquitted to persons brought into initial formal contact with the police, or when comparing persons convicted/acquitted to persons prosecuted or to persons brought before the criminal court). There are two main methods to calculate "attrition rates" in crime and criminal justice statistics, depending on the use or not of an integrated file number (IFN) to track an accused individual through each component of the criminal justice system. Where an IFN is used, attrition rates can be calculated directly following a "cohort" of individuals through the system, as the ratio of X persons arrested to those who were prosecuted, or as the ratio of X persons prosecuted to those who were convicted/acquitted. Where an IFN is not present, "attrition rates" may be calculated comparing the number of persons arrested in a specific year and the number of persons prosecuted in the same year or the number of persons prosecuted in a specific year and the number of persons convicted/acquitted in the same year. This calculation is less reliable than the former one, as it does not involve the same individuals at each stage and cannot take account of delays in the proceedings regarding cases at prosecution and courts level.

At the country level, data sources on prosecution and courts usually differ according to the forms of government of the specific country: national or federal.

In countries with a national form of government, the main source of data on the activities of the criminal justice system is usually a single government agency (where criminal justice agencies are subordinated to a single ministry of justice) or different agencies within the major components of the criminal justice system. These agencies coordinate the collection of statistics at the national level from local responsible authorities. At the prosecution level, these local authorities may be composed of public prosecutors at various levels of government, public defenders or private defense systems. At the courts level, these may range from local courts to general trial courts, appellate courts, and courts with specialized jurisdictions, such as tax courts, juvenile courts, and admiralty courts.

There are three main types of central agencies that can be responsible for criminal justice statistics in a given country and that act as main data sources on prosecution and courts: criminal justice statistics offices within national ministries; a criminal justice statistics office within an existing national statistical office; and a national criminal justice statistics office independent of the agencies responsible for the operations of the criminal justice system.

In countries with federal forms of government, the primary data sources on prosecution and courts, as well as on the other components of the criminal justice system, are statistical services at various levels of government or in various subnational entities. In addition to these subnational agencies, there may also be a central criminal justice statistics bureau producing nationwide statistics.

At the international level, the main data source on prosecution and courts statistics is the United Nations (UN) Survey of Crime Trends and the Operations of Criminal Justice Systems (UN-CTS). The main aim of this crime data collection is to provide reliable and comparable measures of crime and justice cross-nationally. To do so, the UN-CTS provides standard operational definitions of the phenomena under investigation and requires countries to adapt their national-level statistics to fit the standard categories of crime and justice and to indicate potential deviations from these standard definitions.

The UN-CTS is the oldest quantitative cross-national data source on prosecution and courts. The first wave started in 1978. Eleven surveys had been completed by 2011, representing data from 1976 to 2008 and covering all CJ components: police, prosecution, courts, and prisons. The UN-CTS records prosecution and courts statistics using the "person" as the unit of count. With regard to prosecution statistics, it collects data on persons (adults and juveniles) prosecuted by gender and by specific crime types. Persons prosecuted are operationalized as "alleged offenders prosecuted by means of an official charge, initiated by the public prosecutor or the law-enforcement agency responsible for prosecution." With regard to courts statistics, the UN-CTS records data on (1) persons brought before the criminal courts; (2) persons (adults and juveniles) convicted by gender, citizenship, and specific types

of crime; and (3) persons acquitted. Metadata about the organization of prosecution and courts statistics and the specific system of count in each country have also been covered since 2008.

At the European level, the *European Sourcebook of Crime and Criminal Justice Statistics* (hereinafter the *European Sourcebook*) collects data on 40 European countries with the same objectives and almost the same methodology adopted by the UN-CTS. The *European Sourcebook* started in 1990, from an initiative of the Council of Europe. Four publications have been released so far, representing data from 1990 to 2007. With regard to prosecution statistics, the *European Sourcebook* collects data using the "case" as the unit of count, intended as proceedings relating to one person only. In this sense, one case may combine several offenses and one offense may lead to several cases. Data are provided on (1) criminal cases handled by the prosecuting authorities, distinguishing the percentage of cases by different types of disposal; (2) persons whose freedom of movement was restricted, distinguished by different types of restrictions (police custody, pretrial detention, bail, and electronic monitoring); and (3) staff of the prosecuting authority, distinguishing between the total number of employees and the number of prosecutors. With regard to courts statistics, the *European Sourcebook* focuses only on persons who have been convicted and the sanctions and measures imposed on them. Data are provided on (1) persons convicted by crime type; (2) number of females, minors, and aliens among convicted persons, by crime type; (3) type of sanctions and measures imposed upon adults, by crime type; (4) number of convictions by length of unsuspended custodial sanctions and measures imposed upon adults, by crime type; and (5) persons held in pretrial detention (at least temporarily) among persons convicted, by crime type.

In the United States, the *Sourcebook of Criminal Justice Statistics* collects data on many aspects of criminal justice, including prosecution and courts statistics (section 5 is on judicial processing of defendants). This data collection, funded by the U.S. Department of Justice, Bureau of Justice Statistics, brings together data from more than 200 sources since 1973.

To enhance harmonization of crime and criminal justice statistics across different countries, international standards and the EU acquis (European law, comprising legislation, legal acts, court decisions) suggest that the basic minimum statistic to be covered by prosecution and courts data sources should be the person-case initiated (the number of persons prosecuted) and the number of persons convicted, possibly both by gender and by crime type.

The information collected by prosecution and courts data sources, at both national and international levels, presents some major problems of reliability and validity given the nature of the data collected by the agencies of the criminal justice system. Crime and criminal justice statistics, and especially prosecution and courts statistics, are produced mainly by government institutions to meet administrative bookkeeping needs and not with the purpose of measuring the actual level of crime in a specific country. This issue is strictly related to the problem of the "dark number," intended as the difference between the number of crimes committed in a given society and the number of crimes recorded in administrative statistics. In this regard, considering crime and criminal justice statistics as a funnel, starting from the offenses recorded by the police and concluding with prisoners received in penal establishments, the more one advances through this funnel, the more one moves away from the number of crimes committed in societies. In this sense, prosecution and courts statistics are considered worse measures of the actual level of crime than police statistics. Crimes known to the police offer more comprehensive data in their coverage of types of crime and include information on the incidents, even when the offender has not been identified.

Besides these problems of reliability and validity, data sources on prosecution and courts at the international level have to face comparability problems. Cross-national comparisons of crime and criminal justice statistics are hampered by three main factors: substantive, legal, and statistical. Substantive factors depend on the likelihood of citizens' reporting offenses to the police, on the propensity of police to record the reported crimes, and on the actual level of crime in different countries. Legal factors refer to the different ways in which crime is defined in each country and to the characteristics of its legal procedures. Statistical factors refer to different methods whereby statistics are elaborated—to the different statistical counting rules used to collect crime data across countries. With regard to prosecution and courts statistics, differences across countries are caused mainly by different input information and variations in output information. These are basically determined by the powers that the prosecution authorities themselves possess in different countries.

Awareness of these problems does not, however, constitute an obstacle to considering and using prosecution and courts statistics as proxies or indicators of the crime situation in a specific country.

Giulia Mugellini
Università Cattolica/Transcrime

See also Data Sources: Empirical Data; Data Sources: Police Data; Measuring Transnational Crime; Prosecution: International

Further Readings

Aebi, Marcelo F. et al. *European Sourcebook of Crime and Criminal Justice Statistics 2010*, 4th ed. The Hague: Wetenschappelijk Onderzoeken Documentatiecentrum, 2010.

Aromaa, Kauko and Markku Heiskanen. "Measuring the Influence of Statistical Counting Rules on Cross-National Differences in Recorded Crime." In *Crime and Criminal Justice Systems in Europe and North America, 1994–2005*. Helsinki: European Institute for Crime Prevention and Control, affiliated with the United Nations, 2008.

Jehle, Jörg Martin. "Prosecution in Europe: Varying Structures, Convergent Trends." *European Journal on Criminal Policy and Research*, v.8 (2000).

Smit, Paul. "Prosecution and Courts." In *Crime and Criminal Justice Systems in Europe and North America, 1994–2005*. Helsinki: European Institute for Crime Prevention and Control, affiliated with the United Nations, 2008.

United Nations Department of Economic and Social Affairs, Statistics Division. *Manual for the Development of a System of Criminal Justice Statistics*. New York: United Nations, 2003.

United Nations Office on Drugs and Crime. *Developing Standards in Justice and Home Affairs Statistics: International and EU Acquis*. Vienna: United Nations, 2010.

U.S. Bureau of Justice Statistics, U.S. National Criminal Justice Information and Statistics Service, Criminal Justice Research Center, and Michael J. Hindelang Criminal Justice Research Center. *Sourcebook of Criminal Justice Statistics*. Washington, DC: U.S. Department of Justice, Bureau of Justice Statistics, 2005. http://www.albany.edu/sourcebook (Accessed February 2011).

DEPORTATION

Deportation refers to the forced removal of people, either individuals or collectives, from a specific geographic area, typically a region, country, or nation. Deportations in the modern period have been initiated and carried out usually by nation-state bodies, such as ministries of immigration or citizenship or through agencies of border security. All modern states reserve for themselves the right and capacity to determine residency and citizenship, and as part of this right they assert the right to deport noncitizens, even those who have maintained long-term residency. Often the subjects of deportation have no recourse, with limited access to evidence, trials, hearings, or appeals. Such rights are denied on the basis of the subject's lack of citizenship and, therefore, lack of citizenship rights within the country from which they are being deported.

In addition to external deportation, whereby people are forcibly removed from one national territory or country into another, there is also internal deportation. Internal deportation has been an extensive feature of colonization. In the Americas, indigenous peoples have been subjected to internal deportation, forced from their traditional lands into typically less habitable, resource-deprived parts of colonized territory. Notorious cases include the infamous deportation of the Cherokee, Muscogee, Choctaw, and Seminole peoples from their traditional lands to what is now part of the state of Oklahoma in 1838–39. Tens of thousands of indigenous people died during this forced migration, which is known infamously as the Trail of Tears. Practices such as these, carried out against indigenous peoples, are now recognized as acts of genocide.

Deportation is a long-standing practice of ruling authorities, whether monarchies or constitutional governments. Examples can be seen in various periods of human history. In ancient Assyria, mass deportations were used as a mechanism to put down rebellions during the 13th century C.E. Regular deportations were carried out by Assyrian authorities through the 9th century C.E. Peter Christensen (1993) notes the mass deportation of around 292,000 people (citizens as well as slaves) by King Khosrau I of Persia around 542 C.E.

In European contexts, Romani and Jewish people have been subjected to deportation and expulsion from various countries on the continent over the course of centuries. One might refer to the expulsion of Jews from Spain in 1492 as an example from the period before capitalist modernity. Following the conquest of Ireland by English forces and the Act of Settlement of 1652, Irish Catholics were subjected to mass deportations, with nearly 100,000 forcibly resettled as servants and slaves in the colonies. Following the American War of Independence, many Loyalists and indigenous allies of England were forced from the new republic and fled to Canada.

In the period of capitalist modernity, mass deportations became a feature of state repression against political opponents and social reformers in Western liberal democracies such as Canada and the United States. Following the Winnipeg General Strike of 1919, the Canadian government passed the Alien Sedition Act, which targeted migrants and the descendants of migrants as foreign agitators and provided the federal government a mechanism to round up, detain, and deport people on the basis of national origin (or parental origin). Thousands were deported on this basis. The government argued that radical ideas, such as anarchism and Marxism, were imported to Canada from southern and central Europe. Similar practices were carried out during the first Red Scare of 1919 in the United States. During the so-called Palmer raids, named for Attorney-General Mitchell Palmer, thousands of labor organizers and political activists, including Alexander Berkman and Emma Goldman, were deported from the United States as a means to break union and political organizing.

Prior to World War II, there were no formal prohibitions against deportation, and the Hague Conventions of 1907 did not explicitly identify the practice as one deserving proscription. Under the Nazi regime, deportation became a regular aspect of state terrorism and domination of invaded and occupied territories. It is suggested that nearly 12 million non-Germans were deported to Germany to work as forced labor within German war industries. The Nazis also engaged in widespread practices of internal deportation. More than 1 million Poles were deported from western regions of the country. The Nazi process of Germanization of occupied territories involved the mass deportation of local populations, either to Germany or from one to another region within the territory, and the transfer of German people into the evacuated areas.

In the 21st century, customs departments, ministries of immigration or citizenship, or border security agencies generally carry out orders of deportation. Modern nations reserve the right to grant residency and citizenship and the right to deport noncitizens, even those with long-term residency. (Photos.com)

Such practices are forbidden by the Fourth Geneva Convention of 1949.

In the wake of the horrors of World War II, individual and mass deportations for political or economic purposes, or as part of war, came to be identified as crimes against humanity as an outcome of the Nüremberg Tribunals. Under the Fourth Geneva Convention, deportations under conditions of war came to be defined as war crimes. Article 49 states, "Individual or mass forcible transfers, as well as deportations of protected persons from occupied territory to the territory of the Occupying Power or to that of any other country, occupied or not, are prohibited, regardless of their motive." It goes on to specify, with reference to occupations, "The Occupying Power shall not deport or transfer parts of its own civilian population into the territory it occupies." In the second half of the 20th century, deportation came to be viewed as an act of genocide in cases where there is mass loss of life and where people have been targeted for injury or death on the basis of national, religious, racial, or ethnic identity or group membership. The so-called ethnic cleansing of Bosnian Muslims and their deportation from Bosnia during the Serbian invasion from 1992 to 1995 is a recent example.

Despite the proclamations against deportation as an effect of political or economic policy, there have been growing concerns about the uses of deportation as a political mechanism within liberal democracies within the period of neoliberal corporate globalization. This concern and concerns over the targeting of people from specific national, ethnic, and religious backgrounds have grown in the wake of the so-called War on Terrorism following September 11, 2001. In Canada, migrants have been arrested, detained, and deported under so-called security certificates that allow the federal government to hold someone indefinitely without charge, withhold all evidence in the case against them, and remove them from Canada with return to their country of origin after a closed hearing before a single adjudicator (who is the only person with full access to information in the case). Critics have noted that this is a violation of acceptable legal standards, including the right to habeas corpus, presumption of innocence, and the right to disclosure.

A 1996 U.S. law mandated the detention and deportation of all immigrants, including longtime lawful residents, if they have committed a crime punishable by a minimum carceral term of one year. This law, applicable retroactively, has led to deportations committed before the law was established. In the United States, despite government claims that the priority is to remove noncitizens engaged in violent crimes, almost three quarters of the nearly 897,000 immigrants deported between 1997 and 2007 had been convicted only of nonviolent, often minor, offenses. Among the crimes that have led to deportation are driving while under the influence of alcohol.

Jeffrey Shantz
Kwantlen Polytechnic University

See also Central America; Crimes Against Humanity; Intelligence Agencies: Illegal Engagements; International Crimes; Prosecution: International; War Crimes

Further Readings

Christensen, Peter. *The Decline of Iranshahr: Irrigation and Environments in the History of the Middle East, 500 B.C. to A.D. 1500*. Copenhagen: Museum Tusculanum Press, 1993.
Gutman, Roy. "Deportation." In *Crimes of War 2.0*, Anthony Dworkin, Roy Gutman, and David Rieff, eds. New York: W. W. Norton, 2007.

Human Rights Watch. *Forced Apart (by the Numbers): Non-Citizens Deported Mostly for Nonviolent Offenses.* Washington, DC: Human Rights Watch, 2009.

Shantz, Jeff. *Racism and Borders: Representation, Repression, Resistance.* New York: Algora, 2010.

Shantz, Jeff, ed. *Racial Profiling and Borders: International, Interdisciplinary Perspectives.* Lake Mary, FL: Vandeplas, 2010.

DIAMONDS AND JEWELRY

The illicit trafficking in diamonds, gemstones, and jewelry represents a large segment of the transnational criminal market. Diamonds, gemstones, and jewelry appeal to international criminal organizations because of their high value, the difficulty of identification by law-enforcement officials, the lack of strong international regulations, and the high demand for them in the developed world, notably North America. The illicit market in diamonds, gemstones, and jewelry is also linked to money laundering and the financing of other transnational crimes. The best-known example is the use of conflict diamonds to finance internal civil wars in African nations such as Angola and Sierra Leone. International regulatory efforts against illicit diamond and jewelry trafficking include United Nations (UN) sanctions and the development of the Kimberley Process Certification Scheme.

Transnational Illicit Trade

The illicit international trade in gemstones and minerals includes diamonds, garnets, bauxite, rubies, and gold. Areas where illicit diamond, gemstone, and gold mines are most prevalent include Africa and Central and South America. Illegal mining is an appealing alternative to workers who face long hours, poor pay, and harsh working conditions in the legal mining industry. Some miners participate in both, working for but at the same time stealing from a legitimate mining company.

Illegal miners are often subjected to forced labor, harassment, violence, and other human rights abuses. Families who live on land in which valuable gemstones or minerals are located also face threats and violence as well as illegal land and gemstone or mineral seizures. Illegal mining operations are not subjected to government inspections or environmental regulations, linking such operations with pollution, natural resource degradation, and other environmental offenses. The absence of miners from their families causes social disruptions.

The illicit trade in so-called conflict or blood diamonds is an area of particular international concern within the broader black market in diamonds. Conflict diamonds are rough diamonds mined in areas controlled by rebel forces that engage in the illicit diamond trade to raise funds. These illicit funds are then used to support their efforts to overthrow the government in power, often against the decisions of the United Nations (UN) or international community.

Conflict diamonds are frequently linked with other types of international conflict-related crimes, such as illegal weapons trafficking using diamonds as payment and the use of child soldiers. These problems lead to social and family disruptions and large-scale refugee problems, as local populations are forced to flee the violence, often across international borders or into environmentally sensitive areas. The illicit trade also interferes with the legitimate diamond trade, which also interferes with the maintenance of peace and successful development of the economy.

Key origins of conflict diamonds include war-torn African countries such as Angola and Sierra Leone, where illegal diamond funds raised by the National Union for the Total Independence of Angola (UNITA) and the Revolutionary United Front (RUF) have been blamed for prolonging civil conflicts that often cross borders. International investigations have also linked the government of the neighboring nation of Liberia with facilitating the RUF's involvement in conflict diamonds in Sierra Leone.

Illicit mining operations have benefited from the lack of government regulation of the mining industry and the participation of corrupt governments and military forces in such operations. National governments such as that of Zimbabwean president Robert Mugabe and his party, the Zimbabwe African National Union-Patriotic Front (ZANU-PF), have been accused of using their control of the military to gain political campaign funding through the illicit sale of diamonds mined under military control. International human rights groups have also accused the Marange diamond mine, where the stones are quarried, of utilizing forced labor and violence. Mugabe has denied all such allegations.

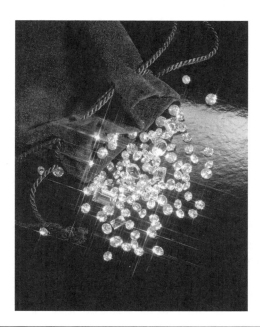

Illicit diamonds and gemstone mines are most prevalent in Africa and Central and South America. The resulting gemstones may be shuttled through one or more countries on their way to areas of high demand like North America. (Photos.com)

Diamonds and gemstones mined in Africa and other areas are then trafficked into high-demand areas such as North America. Many pass through one or more countries during the journey from the country of origin to the country of destination.

Jewelry sold on the illicit international market often has its origins in street-level criminal activities, such as residential burglaries and the robbery of retail jewelry stores in developed nations including the United States, where jewelry comprises one of the largest categories of stolen goods in terms of value. Criminals use such tools as under- or overvaluing diamonds and jewelry, false descriptions, and pawnshops to aid in such crimes as tax evasion, money laundering, smuggling, trafficking, and funneling illicit diamonds and jewelry into legitimate markets.

Transnational Prevention and Justice Responses

The high value, ease of concealment, and difficulty of identification have made diamonds, gemstones, and jewelry increasingly popular avenues for the financing of other criminal activities or money laundering among all levels of transnational criminals, criminal organizations, and terrorists. Agents working for large transnational crime organizations purchase the products of illegal mining and sell or trade them at large profits in urban areas or across borders, where they then enter the international market. Because diamonds and gemstones are small, they are easy to conceal and smuggle. Once the gemstones are polished and sold on the international market, their origins are obscured.

Prevention and prosecution measures against transnational crimes involving diamonds and jewelry have encountered a number of difficulties. Many law-enforcement officials do not have the background or training to aid in the difficult work of identifying illicit diamonds or jewelry—for example, the carat, color, clarity, and cut used to value diamonds. Diamonds and jewelry are among the least often recovered types of stolen property. Once criminal activity is detected, there are not enough specific national and international laws to aid in capture and prosecution as well as to act as deterrents.

Internationally, the UN has begun to address these problems. UN actions have included a 2000 General Assembly resolution to work toward developing effective methods of ending the illicit sale of rough diamonds to finance armed conflicts, such as a standardized certification system to mark those diamonds legally obtained from government-controlled mining areas and sanctions against noncompliance. The UN has sanctioned groups that have profited from the illicit conflict diamond industry, including UNITA in Angola and the RUF in Sierra Leone. The UN also helps broker peace in areas where illicit diamond trafficking is funding conflicts.

The industry has also taken measures to stop the illicit activities that harm its reputation and impact legitimate businesses, as publicity has increased buyer awareness and avoidance of conflict diamonds or other illicit jewelry. International diamond industry groups such as the General Assembly of the World Federation of Diamond Bourses (WFDB), which holds a World Diamond Congress every two years, are also developing measures to stop the international sale of conflict diamonds. Many jewelry distributors and retail outlets have responded to public awareness by offering so-called peace diamonds obtained from legitimate sources. Countries of origin, governments, nongovernmental organizations (NGOs), and the diamond industry have also worked together to stop the proliferation of the transnational illicit diamond and jewelry market. One example is the 2002 adoption of a regulatory process, commonly known as the Kimberley Process.

The international Kimberley Process import-export certification scheme, which took effect in 2003, targets the illicit trafficking of conflict diamonds. Participating nations, which are responsible for the implementation and enforcement of the process, establish domestic government certification programs for rough diamonds that ensure their legitimate origins. Member nations may trade only with other member nations. Member NGOs and diamond industry members act as observers and consultants. The UN and more than 70 nations around the world support the Kimberley Process. The Kimberley Process has reduced the numbers of conflict diamonds reaching the international marketplace.

Marcella Bush Trevino
Barry University

See also Legal and Illegal Economies; Money Laundering: Vulnerable Commodities and Services

Further Readings

Brittain-Catlin, William. *Offshore: The Dark Side of the Global Economy.* New York: Farrar, Straus and Giroux, 2005.

Campbell, Greg. *Blood Diamonds: Tracing the Deadly Path of the World's Most Precious Stones.* Boulder, CO: Westview Press, 2002.

United Nations. "Conflict Diamonds: Sanctions and War." http://www.un.org/peace/africa/Diamond.html (Accessed February 2011).

Zoellner, Tom. *The Heartless Stone: A Journey Through the World of Diamonds, Deceit, and Desire.* New York: St. Martin's Press, 2006.

DISORGANIZED CRIME: REUTER'S THESIS

Peter Reuter's work has been crucial in the promotion of the disorganized crime thesis. His controversial thesis on crime continues to be both influential and contested by academics. Reuter studied illegal markets in New York, focusing on such activities as drug dealing, loan-sharking, and illegal gambling rings. He sought to explore, and then dispel some of the myths concerning organized crime: "organized crime and illegal markets have been too long the source of myths. The truth may be less entertaining but it is certainly reassuring." One such myth concerns the extent of Mafia involvement in illicit markets and Mafia domination of such markets. Reuter discusses how criminal groups are less organizationally unified than that which is often portrayed in the media and by law enforcement groups. Reuter's work has had a profound influence via the disorganized crime thesis, and more widely within the study of organized crime and illicit markets.

Literature on organized crime groups traditionally viewed such groups as organizationally cohesive and having tight control over illicit markets. Such connections can be made; however, it is the extent of those connections that has fuelled debate. Many authors have argued that an overly simplistic notion of organized crime groups had been presented by academics, politicians, the media, and law enforcement agencies. Such an unrealistic view is unhelpful if we are to better understand such groups and ultimately tackle the problem of organized crime. Research began to assess taken-for-granted notions, Reuter's contributions to the discourse were pioneering, and his 1983 text *Disorganized Crime: The Economics of the Visible Hand* won him the Leslie Wilkins Award for the best book of the year in criminology and criminal justice.

Reuter is an economist by training, having obtained an M.Phil. and Ph.D. in economics from Yale University, which enabled him to utilize an economist's analysis within his research. Reuter wields the analogy of the "invisible hand" of the market, as employed by economist Adam Smith, to explore the role of market forces in shaping illicit economies. Such forces are played off against those of the "visible hand" of Mafia violence and intimidation. Reuter obtained data from a range of sources, including police documents and interviews involving informers and police. He applies these data against an industrial organization paradigm in order to consider the extent of organization across illicit markets, and therefore criminal groups. From this, he is then able to argue that taken-for-granted ideas concerning the role of the Mafia in illicit markets are at odds with reality. Reuter's methodology

Illegal gambling was just one the subjects Peter Reuter, an economist, focused on in his 1983 text *Disorganized Crime: The Economics of the Visible Hand.*

can be questioned on some counts, yet not enough to dismiss his findings.

Reuter argues that the illicit activities he studied were not particularly informed by central coordination and control. Nor were they subject to a limited set of goals and aims, as one might expect if such activities were tightly governed. He notes that such activity is disorganized, as opposed to organized. This is because of the lack of structure across such markets and the apparent fragmentation of objectives across such activities, contrary to what one would expect within organized and tightly administered markets. For Reuter, we cannot see such activity as fitting with an industrial organization paradigm, such as that described by Scherer. If such activity did deserve the title of "organized crime," then it could be reconciled with such a schema.

The notion of the visible hand of Mafia corruption, direct influence, and violence, had been assumed to play a vital role in suppressing competition within illicit markets. However, Reuter notes that in reality, market forces are very important in shaping those illicit activities. The forces of the visible hand are still relevant, but they are in conflict with those of the invisible hand, and they are often less important. Thus, rather than those illicit markets of loan-sharking and gambling rings providing large revenue streams for the Mafia, these markets are instead occupied by many small firms and operations. Such activities involve "a network characterized by complex webs of relationships." There is relative ease with which such enterprises can come and go. Access into those markets and failure forcing exit from them is not difficult when the Mafia exerts tight control over them. This demonstrates that competition thrives within such markets; "the magic of the market-place" is alive. The Mafia is not able to suppress competition.

The Mafia does have a role to play; often this is linked to "arbitration" (possibly involving violence). However, this is not particularly coordinated, and Mafia groups are not homogeneous. This means that there are often conflicting interests at work. Thus, Reuter remarks that the link between illicit markets and organized crime within America is over-played, noting how illicit markets are disorganized as opposed to organized. The extent to which the thesis accounts for different illicit markets in other contexts is subject to debate, yet Reuter's work continues to be important.

Tony Murphy
University of Westminster

See also Data Sources: Empirical Data; Gambling: Illegal; Mafia Myths and Mythologies; Organized Crime: Defined

Further Readings

Michael, K. *The Paradigm Shift in Transnational Organised Crime.* 2008. http://works.bepress.com/cgi/viewcontent.cgi?article=1194&context=kmichael&sei-redir=1#search=%22peter%20reuter%20disorganized%20crime%201983%22 (Accessed September 2011).

Reuter, P. *Disorganized Crime: The Economics of the Visible Hand.* Cambridge: MIT Press, 1983.

RAND Drug Policy Research Center. http://www.rand.org/multi/dprc.html (Accessed October 2011).

Scherer, Frederic M. *Industrial Market Structure and Economic Performance.* Chicago: Rand McNally & Co., 1970.

Wright, A. *Organized Crime.* Cullompton, UK: Willan Publishing, 2006.

DRAFT DODGING

For every draft (formally known as conscription), there will always be draft dodgers. Refusing military induction and fleeing military service mid-commitment are both considered criminal offenses. While this crime is domestic, it can become a transnational issue. For example, during the Vietnam War foreign havens—particularly Canada—quickly became a popular destination of those fleeing the U.S. military draft. Canada (and other nations) provided a refuge from prosecution and made resistance against military conscription during the Vietnam War an issue of international crime.

As a matter of terminology, it is important to clarify what draft dodging entails. The term is misleading. *Dodging*, or employing legal means to avoid service, allowed young men to elude service without risk of prosecution or conviction. These men found legal loopholes to avoid induction into the military. If a draftee exhausted his legal solutions (or was unaware they existed), he had two remaining options. He could either accept induction and serve his country or illegally evade the draft. *Resister* is a broader category that includes those who refused induction but also those who broke military law (notably deserters). Thus, when most scholars refer to draft dodging, they are usually referring to resisting. However, over time the term has become synonymous with anyone who resists or avoids military service.

Regardless of definitions, those Americans who evaded military service during the Vietnam War era found Canada to be an ideal location for Americans to hide in exile while avoiding both service and prosecution for fleeing. Geographically Canada is close, especially for the preponderance of resisters who left the northeastern United States to the American exile ghetto in Toronto. Culturally, Canada and the United States are similar, particularly in the Anglophone provinces such as Ontario. Americans could blend in, to a significant extent, could resume their U.S. lifestyles. Perhaps even more integral to the viability of Canada as a haven is that Canada had not had a draft since World War I. Quebecois protests and other political factors had prompted Canada to abandon conscription as a means to procure military personnel. As a result, draft resistance was not a crime. Additionally, by the late 1960s the Canadian government disapproved of the American prosecution of the war.

All this together meant that Americans could easily flee to Canada. Border crossings had an air of "don't ask, don't tell": Americans did not volunteer that they were fleeing military service, and Canadian border agents did not ask. Furthermore, by definition, Canada is outside the jurisdiction of the American government and for most of the Vietnam War the Royal Canadian Mounted Police did not pursue Americans in exile. Once in Canada, Americans generally found support from Canadians, especially from various religious and pacifist groups. (Much of the amicability of the Canadian government, however, dissipated after 1970 in the wake of the crisis involving the Front de Libération du Québec.)

Overall, scholars conclude that tens of thousands of Americans fled to Canada to escape from America and the Vietnam War. Their fate would be partially resolved in the 1970s, when U.S. presidents Gerald Ford and Jimmy Carter offered reconciliation measures for resisters. Ford's 1974 clemency program allowed men to return and perform alternative service to fulfill their commitment to the government. Three years later, Carter pardoned draft dodgers. His pardon did not cover other military resisters. Ultimately these Americans took advantage of the proximity and similarity of Canada and turned a domestic crime into an international issue.

Jason Friedman
Wasatch Academy

See also Extradition; North America; Policing: Domestic; Prosecution: International

Further Readings

Baskir, Lawrence and William A. Strauss. *Chance and Circumstance: The Draft, the War, and the Vietnam Generation.* New York: Alfred A. Knopf, 1978.

Emerick, Kenneth Fred. *War Resisters Canada: The World of the American Military Political Refugees.* Knox: Pennsylvania Free Press, 1972.

Foley, Michael S. *Confronting the War Machine: Draft Resistance During the Vietnam War.* Chapel Hill: University of North Carolina Press, 2003.

Friedman, Jason. "Reconciling the Vietnam War: Draft Dodgers, Resisters and the Debate Over Amnesty." In *Our Way Home 2007 Conference Proceedings.* Ottawa, ON: National Research Council of Canada Press, 2009.

Hagan, John. *Northern Passage: American Vietnam War Resisters in Canada.* Cambridge, MA: Harvard University Press, 2001.

Hayes, Thomas Lee. *American Deserters in Sweden: The Men and Their Challenge.* New York: Associated Press, 1971.

Jones, Joseph. *Contending Statistics: The Numbers for U.S. Vietnam War Resisters in Canada.* Vancouver, BC: Quarter Sheaf, 2005.

Kohn, Stephen M. *Jailed for Peace: The History of American Draft Law Violators, 1658–1985.* Westport, CT: Greenwood Press, 1986.

Maxwell, Donald. "Religion and Politics at the Border: Canadian Church Support for American Vietnam War Resisters." *Journal of Church and State,* v.48/4 (2006).

DRUG TRADE: LEGISLATIVE DEBATES

U.S. President Richard Nixon established the first War on Drugs in 1971, and President Ronald Reagan expanded the policy in 1986. Since that time, the United States has spent billions of dollars—exact estimates are difficult to calculate—and the number of incarcerated drug offenders has catapulted incarceration rates in the United States to the highest of all nations in the world. Although federal spending on drug enforcement has been maintained and arrests for drug offenses have risen to more than 1.5 million per year, the overall rate of illegal drug use in America has remained relatively stable. During this same period, violence related to the illicit drug trade has been a consistent problem for many communities where drug activity is present. The violence associated with the illicit drug trade is not limited to the United States, however. Drug-related corruption and violence in Central and South American countries are well documented, as is the connection between drug trafficking and terror organizations.

Many familiar with the drug issue have suggested that drug prohibition is the source for these problems and advocate changes in the legal status of controlled substances. They argue that the only way to address the problem of drug abuse effectively is to focus efforts on drug treatment and education for users rather than on criminal enforcement. Others argue that inconsistent policies and relaxed enforcement efforts in the United States have undermined any successes that drug-war policies have

accomplished. Although mainstream society does not appear to be in support of massive changes in the drug laws, some jurisdictions have been rethinking their approach to the drug problem. In addition to pushes to decriminalize simple possession of marijuana, several states have adopted laws permitting the use of marijuana for medical purposes. These localized efforts are in contradiction with federal policy that continues to prohibit any legal possession of controlled substances, and policy makers are generally resistant to changing these policies.

The history of American drug policy began in 1842 with the passage of a tariff on imported opium that was intended to control the use of the drug by Chinese immigrants. Various other policies were adopted throughout the remainder of the 19th and early 20th centuries that were intended to control the drug supply and make obtaining the drug more difficult. In 1914, the United States passed the Harrison Narcotics Tax Act, which served as perhaps the most significant piece of drug legislation in the nation's history. The law did not expressly prohibit any substances, but it heavily regulated "every person who produces, imports, manufactures, compounds, deals in, dispenses, distributes, or gives away opium or coca leaves or any compound, manufacture, salt, derivative, or preparation thereof." Although the act appeared only to regulate the transfer of these substances without a physician's prescription, the law was interpreted to prohibit prescribing drugs to individuals to maintain a drug habit, thus essentially prohibiting the possession and transfer of cocaine and heroin for recreational use. The Marijuana Tax Act of 1937 prohibited the private possession or transfer of any form of cannabis. The Controlled Substances Act (CSA), which was passed in 1970, ultimately superseded all of these regulations. The CSA currently serves as the foundation for federal drug policy in the United States and trumps state legislation as a result of the Supremacy Clause in Article 6 of the U.S. Constitution. States that have adopted less stringent laws can therefore find themselves at odds with the federal government. This conflict can be seen in states that have adopted medical marijuana policies.

One of the main criticisms of drug-war policy is that it criminalizes what many consider to be behaviors better addressed as public health issues. Many drug policy experts, including the former head of the Office of National Drug Control Policy, Barry

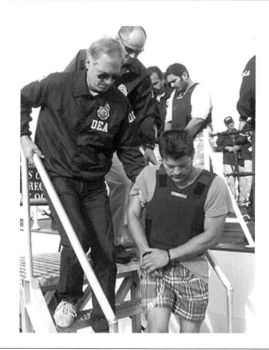

Mexican drug lord and leader of the Tijuana Cartel Francisco Javier Arellano Félix is arrested by the U.S. Drug Enforcement Administration. Some debate that although billions of dollars have been spent on drug prohibition, illegal drug use and violence continue and that the prohibition criminalizes behaviors that may be better addressed as public health issues. (U.S. Drug Enforcement Administration)

McCaffrey, agree that the answer to the drug problem is to shift money away from interdiction and criminal prosecution and toward drug treatments and specialized drug courts. Others argue that the enhanced attention given to the illicit drug trade that erupted in the 1980s cannot be explained by the overall patterns of drug use in society that had peaked in the early 1970s and had leveled off by 1986, when President Reagan and other politicians called for an enhanced War on Drugs. Rather than being a response to any significant shift in patterns of overall drug use, the War on Drugs became an extension of preexisting social, political, and economic interests that reacted to the growth in crack cocaine use in urban ghettos. Critics have suggested that drug-enforcement efforts disproportionately target African Americans and low-income residents, a contention that is supported by data on incarceration rates. One study found that although blacks make up between 15 and 20 percent of all drug users, they account for 50 to 65 percent of drug arrests, the majority of which are for nonviolent drug offenses.

The clandestine nature of the illicit drug trade creates a multitude of challenges for law enforcement in efforts to control the production, transportation, sale, and consumption of controlled substances. As the drug trade moves further underground, law-enforcement officers must employ more invasive and creative methods to detect and apprehend offenders. This has opened the door for police corruption that goes beyond the more blatant cases of police misconduct associated with bribery and drug-related criminal acts committed by the officers themselves. Instead, officers engage in a subtler form of police misconduct that Edwin Delattre and others refer to as "noble cause corruption," which is essentially the employment of unethical tactics in pursuit of a "greater good," necessitating acceptance of the notion that "the ends justify the means." Officers, who are strongly encouraged to make drug arrests, may employ questionable tactics in gathering the required burden of proof to stop an individual, conduct a search, or make an arrest. Officers may also engage in a practice of falsifying facts in official reports in order to ensure that their case is not thrown out in court for due process violations or lack of evidence.

The use of civil forfeiture in drug cases also created a situation in which law-enforcement officials can seize an individual's property on suspicion that it is related to, or has been purchased with money from, the illicit drug trade. Since 1989, the U.S. government alone has seized more than $10 billion in assets, which illustrates the lucrative nature of this drug-war tactic. Because the asset forfeiture process is a civil proceeding, the standard of proof required is much lower than the threshold of "proof beyond a reasonable doubt" in a criminal proceeding. An individual can be found not guilty of a drug crime but still lose his or her property in the civil forfeiture proceeding. Some have criticized the asset forfeiture process as little more than a way for law-enforcement agencies to extort money from low-income residents and minority groups that likely do not have the time or financial resources needed to fight the forfeiture in court. Researchers have also found that agencies became far more aggressive in their drug enforcement efforts when the possibility of boosting agency budgets through asset forfeiture became a reality. One interpretation of this finding is that agencies began to enforce drug laws because these laws served as a source of revenue rather than a means of furthering public safety. Others argue that the availability of revenue from drug seizures simply provides much-needed funding that allows agencies to focus more attention on drug crime.

Critics of current drug policy also point to the social unrest, violence, and corruption associated with eradication efforts in countries where illegal drugs are produced or that function as pipelines for the transportation of trafficked drugs. This is a very problematic issue given the complex social, economic, and political factors that influence policy between the United States and these foreign nations. One major hurdle for these eradication efforts is the reality that illegal drug production forms the backbone of many local economies and typically also contributes heavily to the overall economic prosperity of the national economies in these countries as well. The United States has "exported" the drug war and the tactics it employs to nations that are part of the international drug network. Many nations, including Colombia, Peru, Afghanistan, and Mexico, rely heavily on U.S. funding, equipment, weapons, and training for their domestic drug interdiction efforts, which are often conducted in response to American pressure. This infusion of American funding further embeds the drug war in the local economies of these nations. Critics point to this aspect of the drug war as proof that prohibition is a flawed policy. This perspective argues that if prohibition were successful in the United States, it would negate the need for any eradication efforts elsewhere in the world, because the need for imported drugs would cease.

In short, the United States has exported the drug war and its associated problems to nations where the consequences are graver. Afghanistan serves as an example of this problem. Although the United States has worked with the Afghan government to eradicate poppy production, United Nations (UN) data reveal that opium production in that nation remains virtually unchanged since 2004. In 2009, the UN estimated that 366,500 Afghan households cultivated opium, which provided an annual gross income of $1,997 per household, as compared to 2004, when 356,000 households cultivated opium to earn an annual gross income of $1,700 per household.

The 2009 report also points out that in response to stepped-up eradication efforts, growers have become more skilled and are now able to extract more opium per hectare of land than other opium-producing nations in the Golden Triangle. The current total value of exported opium is estimated at $730 million, which is 7 percent of the nation's GDP. It is unlikely that the nation's citizens are willing to adjust to the loss of income that total opium eradication would cause. The UN also found that the eradication efforts have resulted in the creation of narco-cartels similar to those found in nations such as Colombia and Mexico.

Although few dispute the harmful nature of drug use, the current approach to controlling it has been met with criticism from researchers, policy makers, and private citizens. The debate continues to rage as more states consider the adoption of medical marijuana laws and the decriminalization of small amounts of certain controlled substances. At the same time, many question the logic of reducing drug-enforcement efforts in the face of growing threats from clandestine methamphetamine production and unlawful use of prescription drugs such as Oxycontin. This debate is one that has become a central issue in American society, and it is an issue with literally billions of dollars at stake for those involved on all sides. It is unlikely that this debate will be settled in the near future, but the issue is clearly one that will remain at the forefront of criminal justice policy for some time to come.

Robert M. Keeton
University of Tennessee

See also Antiterrorist Financing; Bribery and Graft; Central America; Civil Forfeiture: The Experience of the United States; Cocaine; Criminal Forfeiture and Seizure; Drug Trade: Source, Destination, and Transit Countries; Heroin; Marijuana or Cannabis; Money Laundering: Countermeasures; Narco-Terrorism; South America; Stings and Reverse Stings; Violence: Uses

Further Readings

Bewley-Taylor, Dave, Chris Halam, and Rob Allen. "The Incarceration of Drug Offenders: An Overview." *The Beckley Foundation Drug Policy Programme, Report 16.* London: University of London International Centre for Prison Studies. http://www.idpc.net/sites/default/files/library/Beckley_Report_16_2_FINAL_EN.pdf (Accessed February 2011).

Cooper, Mary H. "Drug Policy Debate: Is There Too Much Emphasis on Law Enforcement?" *CQ Researcher*, v.10/26 (July 28, 2000).

Delattre, Edwin. *Character and Cops: Ethics in Policing*, Rev. ed. Washington, DC: Rowman & Littlefield, 2011.

Druglibrary.org. "Harrison Narcotics Tax Act of 1914." http://www.druglibrary.org/schaffer/history/e1910/harrisonact.htm (Accessed February 2011).

Gerber, Jurg and Eric L. Jensen, eds. *Drug War American Style: The Internationalization of Failed Policy and Its Alternatives.* New York: Garland, 2001.

Huggins, Laura E., ed. *Drug War Deadlock: The Policy Battle Continues.* Stanford, CA: Hoover Institution Press, 2005. http://www.hoover.org/publications/books/8307 (Accessed February 2011).

United Nations. "Afghanistan Opium Survey: Summary Findings." http://www.unodc.org/unodc/en/drugs/afghan-opium-survey.html (Accessed February 2011).

DRUG TRADE: SOURCE, DESTINATION, AND TRANSIT COUNTRIES

The global illicit drug trade is transnational by nature. It generates more than $400 billion a year, which represents almost 1 percent of the world's economy. The importance of this global illicit drug market is of concern, so much so that member countries of the United Nations (UN) have called for a global eradication of production by year 2019. Despite successful efforts in recent years by governments to reduce production, and thus availability of drugs, analyses of long-term trends show that global potential production of drugs is increasing. For instance, the UN Office on Drugs and Crime (UNODC) reports that opium production has increased worldwide by about 80 percent between 2000 and 2010 and that global cocaine production increased by about 5 percent. The marijuana market remains strong, and younger markets, such as the market for amphetamine-type stimulants (ATS), have developed rapidly.

The number of people who had used illicit substances at least once in 2008 ranged between 155 and 250 million, which corresponds to 3.5 to 5.7 percent of the population aged 15–64. This population has remained quite stable over the past decade. Among those, cannabis consumers represent the largest share, with 129 to 190 million, followed by users of amphetamines and other stimulants (13.7 to 52.9 million), cocaine (15 to 19.4 million), and opiates (22.8 to 21.9 million).

When considering the global illicit drug market, it is essential to explore each drug market separately. Two classes emerge as the biggest transnational drugs: cocaine and opiates. Other widely used illicit drugs, namely cannabis and ATS, are of less concern in terms of transnational crime, because they are for the most part produced locally. Nonetheless, their manufacture and trafficking often transcend borders as well.

Cocaine

Trends in cocaine production, trafficking, and consumption have shifted substantially over time. The majority of the world's cocaine is produced in South America, with a global production in 2008 of 865 tons. The three main producers of cocaine have been and remain Colombia (450 tons in 2008), Peru (302 tons), and Bolivia (113 tons). Increased eradication has had a strong impact on production in Colombia—results of an effort of the Colombian government to take greater control over its territory, with cultivation decreasing by as much as 58 percent over the last decade. Meanwhile, the cultivation of coca increased in Peru by about 38 percent, and more than doubled in Bolivia (up 112 percent).

Sharp contrasts are also seen in patterns of consumption. In the United States, the demand for cocaine has been declining for more than two decades, with an estimate of 5.3 million as of 2008, in contrast to 10.5 million in 1982. In Europe, an inverse trend has been observed, with an estimated 4.1 million cocaine users in 2008, twice as many as in 1998. The European market has therefore become almost as valuable as the North American market ($34 billion versus $37 billion), and the total value of the global market is estimated at $88 billion. The North American and European markets represent about 70 percent of demand and 85 percent of total value, thus contributing heavily to the valuation of the market. The 30 percent of demand that remains represents 2.7 million users in South and Central America and the Caribbean.

Shifts in production and consumption of cocaine have had a tremendous impact on trafficking patterns, creating many constraints on transit countries. For instance, the decreased production and increased enforcement efforts in Colombia have forced traffickers to rely more heavily on transit countries such as Venezuela and Ecuador. Mexico was long used for transit of cocaine shipments with destinations in North America (predominantly the United States); originally this distribution was under the control of Colombian cartels, with the Mexican cartels taking over in the mid- to late 1990s. However, drug enforcement efforts by the Mexican government have forced traffickers to rely on other Central American and Caribbean countries, such as the Bahamas, for transit. The European market has been supplied through the West African route since the mid-2000s. It is important to keep in mind that the markets remain fluid, and transit countries are the most vulnerable to those forces.

The North American market accounts for 40 percent of the global using population, which represents a demand of about 200 tons. In order to supply this demand, UNODC estimates that more than 300 tons must have been shipped from the South American producing countries (to account for seizures, consumption along the way, and purity).

The European market—world's second largest—has been growing at a fast pace in the past decade. Within Europe, the largest demand comes from the United Kingdom (23 percent), followed closely by Spain (21 percent), Italy (19 percent), Germany (9 percent), France (5 percent), and the other European countries (23 percent). It is estimated that, to supply the 120 tons of cocaine consumed in the European market, approximately 212 tons left the Andean region heading toward Europe. Whereas most of the cocaine supplying the U.S. market comes from Colombia, a greater share of the cocaine supplying the European market is produced by Peru and Bolivia. Cocaine is supplied to the European market through two major routes. The most popular route includes former colonies and overseas territories for the European countries as transit platforms. The route through West Africa increased in popularity in the mid-2000s, but its use declined toward the end of that decade. Spain and the Netherlands remain the two major ports of entry for the European market.

Opiates

Heroin is the most widely consumed illicit opiate in the world. In the 21st century, the production of opium increased without precedent, growing from more than 4,500 tons to reach 8,890 tons in 2007. The production then declined, reaching 7,754 tons in 2009. At the same time, the global demand remained stable at about 5,000 tons.

Heroin is currently produced in four different areas of the world: the Golden Triangle, the Golden Crescent, Mexico, and South America. The Golden Triangle (located in Southeast Asia) once was the world's largest source of heroin. Producing countries included Thailand, Burma (Myanmar), Laos, and Vietnam. Heroin was transported to the United States by ethnic Chinese and Asian criminal groups (triads and tongs). Currently, the largest supply of heroin comes from the Golden Crescent, which comprises Pakistan, Afghanistan, Turkey, and Iran. Mexico occupies the third position among the world's top heroin suppliers. The main producer of heroin in South America is Colombia. Most of the heroin available on U.S. illicit markets comes from South America. Transportation routes are aerial for the majority, usually through carriers (mules), who transport the drug aboard commercial flights from Colombia to U.S. international airports such as those in Miami, Atlanta, and New York.

Afghanistan is the world's greatest producer of illicit opiates, with an annual production of 6,900 tons of opium in 2009 (about 90 percent of the world's total production)—an almost total monopoly on production. The rest of the market is split between Myanmar (Burma), the second largest producer, with 330 tons, and Latin America (Mexico and Colombia in particular). Mexico currently holds third place, with a production of 325 tons. UNODC estimates that close to 380 tons of heroin were produced (of 430 tons potentially produced) from Afghan opium in 2008, in order to supply the majority of the 340 tons consumed that year.

The two largest heroin consumption markets are western Europe (88 tons) and the Russian Federation (70 tons), which, together, represent close to half of the world's heroin consumption. Other heroin consumers include China (45 tons), Africa (24 tons), North America (22 tons), Pakistan (19 tons), and India, Iran, and the Southeast Asian countries (17 tons each). Within the western European market, the largest consumer is the United Kingdom (21 percent), followed by Italy (20 percent), France (11 percent), and Germany (8 percent), the rest of Europe accounting for the remaining 40 percent.

A little less than 40 percent of Afghan heroin (about 140 tons) is transported to western Europe along the Balkan route, which includes Pakistan, Iran, and Turkey as major transit countries. A great majority of heroin is seized along the way. About 25 percent of Afghan heroin (about 95 tons) is trafficked to the Russian Federation along the northern route, exiting Afghanistan through Tajikistan,

Uzbekistan, and Turkmenistan and then transiting through Kyrgyzstan and Kazakhstan. Most of the seizures occur in the Russian Federation, and increased levels have been seen in Uzbekistan and Kazakhstan. Pakistan has become a trafficking hub for a large portion of the heroin and morphine produced in Afghanistan, with heroin transiting to Iran (through the Balkan route), Asia, Africa, the United Arab Emirates, and Europe, for a yearly total of 150 tons.

Amphetamine-Type Stimulants (ATS)

The amphetamine-type stimulants (ATS) encompass all synthetic substances that are analogous to amphetamines and Ecstasy. ATS have become increasingly prevalent and popular over the past decade, resulting in an increased share of the global illicit drug market. It is relatively difficult to estimate global trends in this market, because of the decentralization of the production. For instance, UNODC reports that as much as a third of its member states have reported production activity in recent years. Upper estimates of usage show that this market is likely to become more important than opiate and cocaine markets combined, in terms of number of users.

In 2008, 31 countries reported the existence of close to 8500 clandestine laboratories, which represented an increase of 20 percent compared to 2007. Put into perspective, the number of ATS laboratories reported to UNODC had steadily increased from about 7,400 in 1999 to reach a sky-high 18,874 in 2004 and then sharply decreased to about 7,000 in 2007. Note that methamphetamines constitute close to 95 percent of the substances produced by those laboratories. Countries that reported the largest numbers of laboratories include the United States, the Czech Republic, Australia, China, Slovakia, New Zealand, the Netherlands, Canada, and Mexico.

It is important to consider that different types of ATS create different drug problems in various regions of the world. Ecstasy, for instance, was at first limited to Anglophone countries—Europe at first, then North America and the South Pacific area, as it was associated with the dance club scene. It later spread to Asia. Methamphetamine has been a common problem in North America, East and Southeast Asia, as well as Oceania since the early 2009s. Amphetamines, originally found in Europe, spread to the Middle East in recent years. Like other drug markets, the ATS markets are subject to shifting trends. The European Ecstasy market is regressing; the demand for methamphetamines in the United States is shifting from the West to the East Coast and suffering losses through increased seizure and tighter control of precursors. Note that the ATS market is versatile in the type of products it offers. In recent years, a new trend has developed toward the use of ketamine, a veterinary anesthetic. Record seizures demonstrate the extent of this new fad.

Marijuana

Cannabis is the world's most popular illicit drug. Similar to ATS, and in contrast to cocaine and opiates, it is less subject to a transnational market because it is most often produced within the country of distribution. Two types of markets must be considered when it comes to cannabis: the market for cannabis resin and the market for herbal cannabis. Cannabis resin production is concentrated around two international exporters, Afghanistan and Morocco. Together, these two countries produce between 2,500 and 3,500 tons per year. Note that the production has decreased sharply in recent years, accentuated by increased seizures. The Afghan authorities reported the largest seizure of cannabis resin in history, with nearly 240 tons of recovered product.

By contrast to outdoor production of cannabis resin in Afghanistan and Morocco, the most important trend in cannabis production in recent years is that of indoor cultivation, particularly in North America, western Europe, and Australia, where hydroponic cultures have provided illicit enterprises with lucrative profits.

Impact on Transit Countries

The international community is becoming increasingly concerned with the impact of illicit drug trafficking on political instability. Reports indicate that drug trafficking is associated with violence and corruption, particularly in transit countries such as in Latin America (Brazil, Venezuela, and particularly Colombia), the Caribbean, and West Africa.

According to UNODC, political stability can be threatened by the illicit drug trade in two ways. First, organized crime groups and other insurgency movements are often involved in the production, trafficking, and smuggling of drugs, particularly in transit countries, and make profits out of taxation or service provision. Second, drug traffickers may gain sufficient power through increased violence and state-level corruption that the government may be threatened. Transit countries are often the first impacted by sudden shifts in drug trends, because they constitute an important source of revenue for local criminals.

Pierre M. Rivolta
Sam Houston State University

See also Cigarette Smuggling; Cocaine; Heroin; Marijuana or Cannabis; Narco-Terrorism; Tobacco Smuggling

Further Readings

Arnold, Guy. *The International Drugs Trade*. New York: Routledge, 2005.

Godhse, Hamid. *International Drug Control Into the 21st Century*. Burlington, VT: Ashgate, 2008.

United Nations Office on Drugs and Crime. "World Drug Report 2010." http://www.unodc.org/unodc/en/ data-and-analysis/WDR-2010.html (Accessed February 2010).

E

EAST ASIA

Even as most countries around the world become more concerned about both the domestic and the international impact of the rising incidence of transnational crime, leaders of Asian countries continue to give the issue a low priority on national agendas. They insist that their immediate needs involve dealing with traditional crimes, such as extortion, gambling, loan-sharking, prostitution, debt collection, and violence. Western allies are particularly concerned about the incidence of transnational crimes committed in East Asia involving drug and arms smuggling and human trafficking, both because of the impact on their own national interests and because of their ability to affect regional, national, and international stability. Those concerns are due in large part to the fact that certain East Asian countries, notably China and North Korea, serve as points of origin for illicitly transporting drugs and humans to western Europe. Other transnational crime activities in the area involve illegal logging, timber smuggling, and wildlife smuggling. There is also a flourishing black market in ozone-depleting substances that have been banned in most countries. In its Declaration on Transnational Crime, the Association of Southeast Asian Nations (ASEAN) identified all of these activities as matters of grave concern. The failure to prioritize transnational crime issues is partly a result of mixed policy signals and partly a consequence of experts in East Asian nations being excluded from high-level decision making on responses to transnational crimes.

East Asian crime groups are a blend of traditional and modern crime groups made up of secret societies, tongs, triads, gangs, drug cartels, and newer transnational crime groups. Experts in transnational crime, including the U.S. Federal Bureau of Investigation (FBI), have identified the Eurasian area as one of the world's hot spots for transnational crime activities. The problem, they say, has been exacerbated by the collapse of the Soviet Union, rampant government corruption, and civil wars in the area. The United Nations (UN) has identified a number of transnational crime activities that are common within East Asia, including human trafficking, forced labor, sexual exploitation, and money laundering. At the beginning of the 20th century, many criminal-minded immigrants from China, Korea, Japan, Thailand, and the Philippines came to the United States and continued to engage in criminal activities. Those activities expanded throughout the century in response to globalization, the introduction of sophisticated technologies such as the Internet, and the liberalization of trade and immigration policies.

In the early 21st century, Chinese officials were continuing to insist that transnational crimes were often committed by Chinese Americans, making it a problem for the United States rather than China. They offer as examples the so-called snakeheads, who have smuggled thousands of illegal immigrants into the United States at $20,000 a person. Internationally, East Asians involved in transnational crimes have posed serious problems because of their sophistication, their ability to speak several languages, and the large financial resources backing their activities. Many of these criminals have entered the world of legitimate business, using their companies as fronts for crimes such as racketeering, extortion, murder, kidnapping, illegal gambling, and prostitution. In some East Asian countries, local authorities are believed to be actively involved in transnational crimes by virtue of providing protection for criminals through a practice known as *baohusan*, which means they provide a "protecting umbrella." At the transnational level, East Asian crime groups have been involved in the smuggling of illegal immigrants, the manufacture and trafficking of heroin and methamphetamine, the theft of automobiles and computer chips, and the counterfeiting of credit cards, computer chips, clothing, and entertainment items. Many of these groups have also been linked to terrorist groups, including Al Qaeda.

Traditional organized crime as well as transnational crime is a major problem in Taiwan, where the *jao pho* (godfathers) have infiltrated the world of business, often serving as chief executive officers of business conglomerates. Their presence has been documented in 39 of Taiwan's 76 provinces. The business practices of the *jao pho* are far from legitimate, and these astute criminals have expanded their activities to include bid-rigging, waste disposal, construction, cable television network ownership, telecommunications, stock trading, and entertainment. Many of these individuals have successfully sought political office in order to prevent their becoming targets of clean-up efforts by reformers. By some estimates, at least a third of elected deputies in Taiwan are gangsters or have been identified as such in the past. Members of crime networks continue to engage in traditional crimes, and kidnapping for ransom has become so common that many legitimate businesses have left Taiwan out of safety concerns.

Hong Kong has something of a split personality among the nations of East Asia. It was under British control for a century but returned to Chinese control in 1997. Hong Kong continues to exercise a certain amount of autonomy and is self-governing. Throughout its history, Hong Kong has been home to Asian triads, despite government efforts to eradicate their criminal activities, which involve both domestic and transnational crimes. The triads currently exercise control of bus routes, fish markets, street markets, wholesale markets, entertainment centers, parking services, and the sale of counterfeit VCDs as well as prostitution, gambling, and

Transnational crime activities in the East Asia include drug and arms smuggling, illegal logging, and timber and wildlife smuggling. Pandas, found only in China, are legally protected to the degree that capital punishment can be imposed on killing a panda in the nation, although this does not protect the rare animals from illegal smuggling. (Photos.com)

extortion. Triads also exercise considerable control in the former Portuguese colony of Macau, which has become a tourist mecca as a result of easy access to casinos, prostitutes, and illegal drugs. While Japan is the most Westernized of all East Asian countries, the notorious Yakuza are extremely traditional in nature. The Yakuza are involved in gambling, prostitution, and human and drug trafficking. The Yakuza have also become expert at victimizing legitimate Japanese businesses. Many Chinese immigrants living in Japan have entered into organized criminal activities, and these individuals are considered highly dangerous and to be avoided whenever possible.

Drugs and Human Trafficking

Historically, human trafficking has been considered chiefly the province of Asian countries. That perception changed to some extent after the dissolution of the Soviet Union in 1991 opened the door to the trafficking of Russian and Ukrainian women to various parts of the world. The collapse of the Soviet bloc and the loosening of borders in China resulted in large numbers of illegal immigrants entering other countries as criminals or as victims of those trafficking in persons. In the early 21st century, East Asia continued to be heavily associated with human trafficking as well as with the production and trafficking of illegal drugs. Transnational criminals involved in human trafficking have always been aware that it is a highly profitable enterprise. Eluding detection is also easier because most countries consider catching human traffickers a lower priority than catching traffickers in illegal drugs. Even when caught, those who traffic in persons are likely to receive lighter sentences than those convicted of drug-trafficking offenses.

No other country in East Asia is more heavily involved in human trafficking than China, which has the largest population in the world, estimated at 1.33 billion by the end of 2010. The government's inability to provide an adequate standard of living for the 21.5 million people living below the absolute poverty line and for the 35.5 million who live on the fringe of poverty makes many Chinese desperate for economic opportunities. Thus, they are easy prey for traffickers. Partially because of this, China serves as a source as well as a transit and destination point for human trafficking. Much is known about human trafficking in China because of a large-scale investigation conducted by the United States. Officials were able to follow the day-to-day activities of trafficking networks from the recruitment stage to final delivery of victims. Financial records indicated that the profit margin from the illegal venture was 90 percent. That money was dispatched straight to China via wire transfers. A simultaneous investigation by French authorities revealed that chief perpetrators of the crime were raking in $750,000 a day.

Women, men, and children are trafficked for the purposes of sexual exploitation and forced labor. Although much of the trafficking involves transporting people from one location inside China to another, many victims are transported to other countries in Asia and to Africa, Europe, Latin America, the Middle East, and North America. Large numbers of Chinese females volunteer to leave their homes, hoping for gainful employment in other countries only to find themselves forced into prostitution in Taiwan, Thailand, Malaysia, and Japan. In this two-way enterprise, women and children from Mongolia, Myanmar, North Korea, Russia, and Vietnam are trafficked into China for the purposes of forced marriage, prostitution, and forced labor. Since 2006, China has been identified as a Tier 2 Watch List country by the U.S. State Department because it has failed to show progress in combating human trafficking. The Chinese government

has also been censured for its practice of deporting North Korean trafficking victims, forcing them to return to what the Central Intelligence Agency (CIA) has identified as "horrendous conditions." China's proximity to the Golden Triangle of Southeast Asia and its failure to check transnational crime have created an environment in which methamphetamine and heroin are widely produced, and synthetic drugs and heroin freely flow into China from the countries of Southeast and Southwest Asia.

The government of North Korea, another communist country, has strong links to both organized and transnational crime communities. North Korea is a major trafficking point for both humans and drugs. Because of their lack of economic opportunities, North Korean women are easy prey for traffickers, intent on transporting them to China, where they are forced into marriage, prostitution, or labor. North Korea is a Tier 3 country as a result of its refusal to comply with even minimum standards for combating trafficking. There is evidence from at least 50 separate incidents linking the North Korean government to international drug trafficking, and several North Korean diplomats have been arrested while engaged in this activity. The governments of Japan and Taiwan have produced evidence linking North Korea to the trafficking of both heroin and methamphetamine and to organized counterfeiting rings.

Malaysia is frequently a receiving nation for women and children who are trafficked for the purposes of sexual exploitation. Men, women, and children are also transported into the country for the purpose of participating in forced labor. Many of them voluntarily leave their homes in South and Southeast Asia only to become enslaved by employers seeking domestic, agricultural, construction, plantation, and industrial workers. Some Malaysian women, particularly those who are ethnically Chinese, are trafficked to other countries to be sexually exploited. Malaysia is ranked as a Tier 3 country because of its unwillingness to adequately combat human trafficking. There is considerable evidence to suggest that government employees engage in the trafficking and extortion of Burmese refugees. While the government has made some progress in combating drug trafficking, Malaysia has a serious problem with synthetic drugs such as Ecstasy and methamphetamine, which are produced for both domestic and export markets.

While other nations of East Asia have been more successful than China, North Korea, and Malaysia at combating human trafficking, those nations continue to deal with drug trafficking and other transnational crimes to varying degrees. Despite strong ties to the West, Japan has been identified as a major destination for trafficking victims from Thailand, the Philippines, Colombia, China, and Korea. The Yakuza are known to be involved in trafficking Japanese women outside the country for the purposes of sexual exploitation. Japan is considered a Tier 2 country. In Hong Kong, heroin, methamphetamine, and various synthetic drugs continue to be produced for transport to other parts of Asia and the world, and money laundering is an ongoing problem. Macau serves as a transshipment point for drugs to China, and there is a growing domestic problem with opiates and amphetamines. Taiwan serves as a producer of opium, marijuana, and heroin, which is channeled through Thailand from Myanmar and Laos on its way to international markets. Drug money is often laundered in Thai banks. Methamphetamine production is a problem in Thailand, the Philippines, Taiwan, and Indonesia. Marijuana is produced in rural areas of the Philippines, and Taiwan serves as a transit point for drugs channeled into Japan.

Elizabeth Rholetter Purdy
Independent Scholar

See also Al Qaeda; South Asia; Southeast Asia

Further Readings

Ceccarelli, Alessandra. "Clans, Politics and Organized Crime in Central Asia." *Trends in Organized Crime*, v.10/3 (September 2007).

Central Intelligence Agency. "China." *World Factbook*. https://www.cia.gov/library/publications/the-world-factbook/geos/ch.html (Accessed February 2011).

Central Intelligence Agency. "Korea, North." *World Factbook*. https://www.cia.gov/library/publications/the-world-factbook/geos/kn.html (Accessed February 2011).

Elliott, Lorraine. "Transnational Environmental Crime in the Asia-Pacific: An 'Un(der)securitized' Problem?" *Pacific Review*, v.20/4 (December 2007).

Emmers, Ralf et al. "International Arrangements to Counter Human Trafficking in the Asia Pacific." *Contemporary Southeast Asia: A Journal of International and Strategic Affairs*, v.28/3 (December 2006).

Finckenauer, James O. and Ko-Lin Chin. *Asian Transnational Crime*. New York: Nova Science, 2007.

Hesterman, Jennifer L. *Transnational Crime and the Criminal-Terrorist Nexus*. Maxwell Air Force Base, Montgomery, AL: Air University Press, 2005.

Smith, Paul J., ed. *Terrorism and Violence in Southeast Asia: Transnational Challenges to States and Regional Stability*. Armonk, NY: M. E. Sharpe, 2005.

Stoecker, Sally and Louise Shelley, eds. *Human Trafficking and Transnational Crime*. Lanham, MD: Rowman & Littlefield, 2005.

U.S. Department of State. "Tier Placements: Trafficking in Persons Report 2009." http://www.state.gov/g/tip/rls/tiprpt/2009/123132.htm (Accessed February 2011).

Van Schendel, William and Itty Abraham, eds. *Illicit Flows and Criminal Things: States, Borders, and the Other Side of Globalization*. Bloomington: Indiana University Press, 2005.

EASTERN EUROPE AND RUSSIA

The United Nations (UN) has identified 10 countries as forming eastern Europe: Belarus, Bulgaria, the Czech Republic, Hungary, Moldova, Poland, Romania, Russia, Slovakia, and Ukraine. Since the dissolution of the Union of Soviet Socialist Republics in 1991, there has been an increase in organized and transnational crime in the region, as criminals and would-be criminals in eastern Europe have taken advantage of unguarded borders, inexperienced police, and lax laws. They formed alliances with groups outside the region to supply demands for illicit goods and services. Some persons with law-enforcement experience, having worked previously for regional governments, have taken advantage of large financial gains that became available through participation in organized crime. Thus, the region's criminal justice systems' priorities have included combating growing violence, human trafficking, cybercrime, money laundering, terrorism, and organized crime related to drugs, arms, and goods (including fish, caviar, fruit, specific timber species, cotton, automobiles, and radioactive materials). Much of the crime is facilitated by syndicates or cartels that operate covertly to maximize profits through diverse criminal enterprises.

One transnational crime that has received substantial attention is human trafficking. In the Victims of Trafficking and Violence Prevention Act (or Trafficking Victims Protection Act, TVPA) of 2000, the U.S. Congress defined severe forms of trafficking in persons to clearly distinguish human trafficking from human smuggling. The TVPA definition of severe forms of human trafficking includes two classifications: The first is sex trafficking in which a commercial sex act is induced by force, fraud, or coercion or in which the person induced to perform such an act has not attained 18 years of age; the second is the recruitment, harboring, transportation, provision, or obtaining of a person for labor or services, through the use of force, fraud, or coercion, for the purpose of subjection to involuntary servitude, peonage, debt bondage, or slavery.

Until the 1980s, when cocaine became a part of the crime scene, drug trafficking in eastern Europe largely involved heroin. To a much lesser extent, the trade included synthetic drugs, marijuana, and LSD. Heroin passed through Europe from its source in Southeast Asia (the Golden Triangle), facilitated by French criminals even to destinations in the United States. This supply-and-demand relationship has commonly been referred to as having a "French connection." Eastern Europe in particular has been significant as a supplier of ingredients such as PMK (3,4 methylenedioxyphenyl-2-propanone), necessary for the manufacture of synthetic drugs. A demand for illicitly provided goods and services, unemployment, and inadequate enforcement efforts hinder efforts to diminish the social deviance in the global economy.

Russia has been among the states of greatest concern in transnational crime, given the rapid rise of organized crime within that nation. Rather loosely structured crime groups within the Soviet Union fortified their connections after the 1991 dissolution. Key players have been politicians and successful businesspersons. As a result, Russian cartels benefit from both legitimate (real estate, banking, casino gambling, hotels, restaurants, nightclubs, aluminum, and transportation) and illegitimate enterprises, as well as embezzlement from the government. Russian criminals have alliances with Colombian, Chinese, and Japanese drug dealers. Starting as a mere transshipment point, Russia has emerged as a major player in illicit drug supply. Much of Russia's illicit gains are laundered overseas. Weapons trafficked through eastern Europe have been found in places as distant as Mexico. Weapons have even been traded for diamonds. Criminal prosecution of Russian crime groups has been rare, given the political power and wealth of key players and the influence they wield over government officials, law enforcement, and the media. Investigators, for example, are routinely subject to bribes.

Russia is the source or origin country for more trafficked women than is any other country. Other members of the newly independent states (NIS) of the former Soviet Union tend to produce trafficked women and girls at high per capita rates when compared with other origin countries of the world. Russia and other NIS countries also serve as destination countries for humans trafficked for cheap labor, and as transition countries for both sex trafficking and labor trafficking.

The chief destination country, for women and children who are trafficked for purposes of sexual exploitation, is Germany. The United States follows closely as the second destination nation for sex-trafficked women and children. Many North Americans remain unconscious of the trafficked women from the NIS, eastern Europe, and Russia who perform sex acts to enrich those who hold them in debt bondage. However, the signs that read "The Russians Are Coming," displayed in the windows and on the marquees of the exotic dancing emporiums of New Jersey in the first decade of the 21st century, emphasized the reality and human pathos of this trafficking and commercial sexual exploitation.

Other major destination countries for women and children who are trafficked from eastern Europe and Russia for purposes of sexual exploitation are Italy, the Netherlands, Japan, Greece, India, Thailand, and Australia. After Russia, the other major source countries for sex trafficking are Ukraine, Thailand, Nigeria, Moldova, Romania, Albania, China, Belarus, and Bulgaria. Thus, of the top 10 source countries for sex-trafficked women and children, seven are located in eastern Europe and were part of the Soviet bloc of nations.

Estimating the extent of trafficked human beings is difficult: First, because the sex-trafficking enterprise is clandestine; second, because trafficked women often return to their countries of origin or are moved from one destination to another, so counting is difficult; and, third, too often the organizations doing the predicting have a stake in the outcome of those predictions. Annual predictions by the U.S. government have shrunk considerably since the TVPA of 2000. Furthermore, although predictions of nonprofit organizations, international agencies, and human rights organizations tend to be liberal, investigative reporters and social scientists visiting

NIS countries paint a picture of the human condition that is bleak indeed: For example, it has been reported that some small villages in rural Moldova have lost so many women to trafficking that there are in essence no women between the ages of 14 and 35 still living in them. It is surmised that women are lured into slavery by recruiters as poverty and marginalization lead to desperation in rural areas.

Adaptability is one of the chief qualities of criminal sex traffickers; they are highly organized, deal in high-volume and continuous supply, and handle the victims with extreme violence. Laws change slowly, and it takes time for police to be trained to recognize human trafficking and the techniques of the traffickers, yet the plasticity, diversification, and adaptability of the trafficking and commercial sexual exploitation industry keep traffickers not only coping with the legal establishment but also thriving in spite of their opposition.

As is true elsewhere in the world, trafficking in eastern Europe and Russia has been linked to money laundering, to document fraud, and to the illegal international trade in illicit drugs and arms. The currently held belief is that human trafficking is a more lucrative illegal international enterprise than is the illegal trading of arms.

Women from NIS countries tend to be especially vulnerable to the false promises of traffickers: While women who are sex-trafficked from eastern Europe tend to be better educated than their counterparts from Africa, Asia, or South America, their vulnerability is caused by similar factors. Many believe that all victims of sex trafficking worldwide are poor and uneducated, but this is a misunderstanding. Often, women trafficked from eastern Europe and Russia have college degrees, and many are high school graduates. The strong tradition among these women is to support their families and improve their lives through education.

The causal factors for women's victimization in the NIS from trafficking and sexual exploitation include gender inequality or blatant sex discrimination, as well as a lack of employment opportunity. Additionally, their countries of origin suffer from political and economic instability. Most of them, on their own, cannot afford to travel and migrate to countries of western Europe, Australia, or North America, where they feel they have better opportunities for employment and marriage; therefore, they tend to rely upon smugglers or traffickers to pay their way. In 2000, Donna M. Hughes noted that women from eastern Europe, including Russia, were so commonly exploited in the commercial sex industry in Israel and Turkey, that in those countries, sex workers/prostitutes were often called "Natashas." While historically, sex-trafficking victims tended to be Asian, since the fall of the Soviet Union, which left in its wake many NIS's with weak economies, large populations of women in eastern Europe and Russia have been left highly susceptible to sex-trafficking scams.

The Czech Republic is another eastern European country of concern, particularly for drug trafficking, human trafficking in women, pornography, prostitution, money laundering, commodity smuggling, weapons, auto theft, art and endangered plants smuggling, and white-collar crimes such as tax evasion. The Czech Republic is sometimes tagged as a "crossroads of crime" because, as researcher Miroslav Nozina explained, criminals in the Czech Republic include persons from former Soviet Union countries who have been successful in their criminal partnerships with persons in the Middle East, Latin America, Italy, Asia, sub-Saharan Africa, and the Balkans. Markedly, drug trafficking was virtually unknown in the Czech Republic until the 1990s, given the previous tight governmental controls. With a more globalized world in recent decades, licit and illicit financial operations have become closely intertwined. Eastern Europe emerged as a transit area for drugs heading to western Europe. Often the Balkan route has been utilized by Albanian criminals to move drugs. As in Russia, in the Czech Republic the line between licit and illicit businesses is difficult to detect. In the early 1990s, the region also had a surge in Nigerian drug couriers, but increased customs diligence curtailed Nigerian courier activities. Chinese and Vietnamese are also involved in drug trafficking in the region.

Bulgarian criminals have garnered a reputation for violence in the smuggling and exploitation of illegal immigrants into eastern Europe. In recent times, their focus has shifted from running sex clubs to providing prostitutes to establishing brothels. For decades, Bulgarian organized crime has been involved in extortion. Ukrainian crime groups are also known for violence associated with racketeering, human trafficking, bank robberies, and auto thefts. Nozina has revealed that Slovakian crime groups network with crime groups in other countries, depending on the goods of interest; for example, persons in Scandinavia, Germany, the Netherlands, Albania, Bulgaria, Turkey, Romania, and countries in Asia and Latin America facilitate drug trafficking; Romanians move stolen automobiles; and some Germans, Spanish, and Dutch facilitate the trafficking of women.

In Belarus and Moldova, cybercrime is fairly common. In Belarus, this includes identity theft, Nigerian-type scams, and false advertisements for overseas brides; throughout Moldova, cybercrime is likely the result of the use of skimmers and cameras that record secret credit card passwords. Many of the illicit drugs that originate in Moldova are consumed domestically, but the country is also a transshipment point for drugs heading to western Europe and Russia. In Hungary, one transnational crime concern is the radical hate group called Magyar Garda, which targets Roma and Jews. Despite the group's efforts to project a new service image, it is commonly perceived as a domestic terrorist threat.

The justice systems in the region have responded to increasing organized crime with changes in laws, including some restrictions on immigration and more active prosecutions. There are also efforts to curtail the demand for illicit goods and services and to encourage victims to make complaints. The judicial system, however, is understaffed and slow. Where violations are overt, progress is more evident than with more covert offenses, which require international cooperation to achieve successful prosecutions of offenses such as financial fraud and cybercrime.

Edward J. Schauer
Camille Gibson
Prairie View A&M University

See also Child Exploitation; Drug Trade: Source, Destination, and Transit Countries; Human Trafficking; Money Laundering: History; Money Laundering: Methods; Money Laundering: Targeting Criminal Proceeds; Money Laundering: Vulnerable Commodities and Services; Sex Slavery

Further Readings

Fijnaut, C. and L. Paoli. *Organized Crime in Europe: Concepts, Patterns, and Control Policies in the European Union and Beyond.* Dordrecht, Netherlands: Springer, 2004.

Henderson, K. *The Area of Freedom, Security and Justice in the Enlarged Europe.* New York: Palgrave Macmillan, 2005.

Hughes, D. "The 'Natasha' Trade: The Transnational Shadow Market of Trafficking in Women." *Journal of International Affairs*, v.53/2 (2000).

Hughes, D. *Trafficking for Sexual Exploitation: The Case of the Russian Federation.* Geneva: International Organization for Migration, 2002.

Pettman, J. J. "On the Backs of Women and Children." In *Beyond Borders: Thinking Critically About Global Issues*, P. S. Rothenberg, ed. New York: Worth Publishers, 2006.

Schauer, E. and E. Wheaton. "Sex Trafficking Into the United States: A Literature Review." *Criminal Justice Review*, v.31/1 (2006).

Segrave, M., S. Milivojevic, and S. Pickering. *Sex Trafficking: International Context and Response.* Portland, OR: Willan, 2009.

U.S. Department of Justice, Office on Violence Against Women. *Victims of Trafficking and Violence Prevention Act of 2000.* Washington, DC: Author, 2000.

Van Duyne, P., Klaus von Lampe, M. van Dijck, and J. L. Newell. *The Organized Crime Economy: Managing Crime Markets in Europe.* Nijmegen, Netherlands: Wolf Legal Publishers, 2005.

Wheaton, E. M., E. J. Schauer, and T. V. Galli. "Economics of Human Trafficking" (Special Issue on Human Trafficking). *International Migration*, v.48/4 (2010).

Egmont Group of Financial Intelligence Units

The Egmont Group of Financial Intelligence Units is a global network of domestic financial intelligence units that aims to expand and systematize international cooperation in the fight against money laundering, terrorist financing, and other financial crimes. Established in 1995 as an informal forum, the Egmont Group was named after the Egmont-Arenberg Palace in Brussels, where the first meeting was held. Membership in 2011 stands at 120 financial intelligence units from countries across the globe. A financial intelligence unit (FIU) is defined by the Egmont Group as a central, national agency within a given jurisdiction that is responsible for receiving (and, as permitted, requesting), analyzing, and disseminating, to the competent authorities, disclosures of financial information. Disclosure obligations, such as suspicious activity reports, are usually imposed on financial institutions and the designated FIU as part of the national legislative or regulatory anti-money-laundering framework.

Recognizing that FIUs sit at the operational heart of any jurisdiction's anti-money-laundering (AML)/counter-financing of terrorism (CFT)

regime, the key role of the Egmont Group is to foster and facilitate the reciprocal exchange of information and intelligence between FIUs. This is complicated by the fact that some (such as the United States' Financial Crimes Enforcement Network, or FinCEN) are administrative bodies that do not access law-enforcement information, whereas others—such as the United Kingdom's Serious Organised Crime Agency (SOCA)—sit alongside already existing law-enforcement systems (the judicial, law enforcement, and hybrid models). Egmont Group members commit to the "Principles of Information Exchange" found in the Egmont Statement of Purpose. In some jurisdictions, by law, the type of information that FIUs collect can be shared only with another FIU. Communication between FIUs is enhanced via the application of a secure and encrypted Internet facility—the Egmont Secure Web (ESW). This online portal provides access to sanitized case typologies, the minutes and documents from meetings, and member FIU contact information. The aim is to strengthen both national and combined law-enforcement efforts in the fight against transnational, organized crime. The Egmont Group promotes operational autonomy but also encourages coordination between the operational divisions of member FIUs, recognizing the need to enhance mutual assistance and build institutional capacity. The Egmont Group also offers training and promotes the exchange of personnel between FIUs in order to increase effectiveness, expertise, and capability and to overcome barriers to cross-border information sharing between different FIUs. The Egmont Group promotes the establishment and development of FIUs in the small number of jurisdictions where a national AML/CFT program is not in place or where it is in the early stages of development.

Mr. Boudewijn Verhelst was appointed chair of the Egmont Group of Financial Intelligence Units in June 2010. The operating structure of the Egmont Group includes a governing body known as the Head of FIUs (HoFIUs). The HoFIUs makes decisions, via consensus, regarding the structure and membership of the Egmont Group, its budget, and principles. The membership application process follows a specific procedure before acceptance can be granted by the HoFIUs. This involves identification of sponsor FIUs, monitoring, an onsite visit, and attendance at the Egmont annual plenary as observer or candidate. FIUs can be suspended if

The Egmont Group was established in 1995 as an informal forum and was named after the Egmont-Arenberg Palace in Brussels, Belgium, where the first meeting was held. Today Egmont Palace is the home of the Belgian Ministry of Foreign Affairs. (Wikimedia/Michel Wal)

they are judged to be seriously noncompliant: For 2009–10, El Salvador was suspended, although it was later reinstated.

The head of the Egmont Group Secretariat, the executive secretary, is appointed by the HoFIUs and reports to that body via the Egmont Committee. The Secretariat was established in July 2007 and is based in Toronto, Canada. It provides administrative and other support to the overall activities of the HoFIUs. The committee oversees the work of the Secretariat and five working groups. The structure of the committee includes permanent and regional members; a chair; two vice-chairs; chairs of the five working groups; regional representatives from Africa, Asia, Europe, the Americas, and Oceania; a representative of the host of the Egmont Secure Web (the Financial Crimes Enforcement Network, or FinCEN); and the executive secretary. The committee acts as a consultation mechanism for the HoFIUs and the working groups, assisting with internal coordination and representation at other international forums. Administration is supported by six reference groups.

Five working groups meet periodically (some with subgroups) and report their activities to the HoFIUs:

1. The Legal Working Group (LWG) deals with all legal aspects and matters of principle within Egmont, including the cooperation between FIUs and the candidacy of potential members.

2. The Outreach Working Group (OWG) promotes the Egmont philosophy globally to enhance the FIU network. The OWG identifies potential candidates for membership and works with FIUs to ensure that they comply with the Egmont Group standards.

3. The Training Working Group (TWG) identifies training needs and opportunities for FIUs and their personnel and conducts training seminars for both non-Egmont members' and Egmont members' jurisdictions.

4. The Operational Working Group (OpWG) brings FIUs together to work on long-term strategic analytical projects and the development of typologies.

5. The IT Working Group (ITWG) examines new software applications that can facilitate analytical work and provides advice and technical assistance to new and existing FIUs in order to develop, enhance, and/or redesign their IT systems.

Egmont Group member FIUs meet via annual events and regular workshops and meetings to exchange information and share best practices and expertise. Egmont products include annual reports, newsletters, and a white paper on enterprise-wide sharing of suspicious transaction reports (STRs). The Egmont Group works collaboratively with other AML/CFT global partners, including the Financial Action Taskforce (FATF), providing operational perspectives on AML/CFT policy, implementation, and evaluation for the FATF review work on mutual evaluations. A joint survey was also completed with the World Bank on FIU governance arrangements.

Rachel Elizabeth Southworth
Cardiff University

See also Antiterrorist Financing; Financial Action Task Force; Intelligence Agencies: Collaboration Within the United States; Money Laundering: Countermeasures; World Bank

Further Readings

Egmont Group. "Egmont Group Statement of Purpose." 2010. http://www.egmontgroup.org/library/egmont -documents (Accessed February 2011).

Egmont Group. *Information Paper on Financial Intelligence Units and the Egmont Group.* 2010. http://www .egmontgroup.org/library/egmont-documents (Accessed February 2011).

International Monetary Fund. *Financial Intelligence Units: An Overview.* Washington, DC: Author, 2004. http:// www.imf.org/external/pubs/ft/FIU/fiu.pdf (Accessed February 2011).

ELECTORAL MANIPULATION

Transnational crime networks depend on favorable local conditions at the production and distribution ends of their markets. Generating environments that guarantee both a minimum exposure to risks and an optimization of profit starts by ensuring some degree of local control over territories and governance structures. Electoral processes open a window of opportunity for transnational crime networks to gain influence and control over state administrations and decision makers, justice, governance, and public resource allocation. Through electoral manipulations, transnational crime networks protect and promote their interests by establishing or consolidating links to the state through the distortion of political competition in order to keep functional alliances with local, regional, and/or national political leadership. While all democracies are exposed to different degrees of electoral manipulation by transnational crime, the most acute cases occur when bureaucracies, including government and political structures, are embedded in predatory networks in which power holding is organically tied to corruption and illegality.

Nonetheless, in all cases, manipulating the different phases within an electoral process is an expedient vehicle for transnational crime networks to minimize risks and guarantee high returns. Understanding the different forms of electoral manipulation available for transnational crime networks needs to start by acknowledging the relationships that these networks establish with political parties. Criminal networks may seek political parties as much as political parties may seek criminal networks; in both of these cases, the drive for establishing a relationship stems from loyalties, protection, agreements, and/or financial opportunities. In any of these cases, the independence of political actors or political groups is hampered and translates into opening the field for various forms of distortions of political competition. Overall, transnational crime networks engage, during the period prior to election day, in actively endorsing and financing political candidates functional to their interest and by spearheading armed political, intimidation, and assassination campaigns aimed at those candidates who are resistant to their interests. The forms that shape this preelection manipulation are determined by the type of control that transnational crime networks exert over a territory.

An initial stage, often referred as predatory in specialized literature, is characterized by an overwhelming use of force and guided by a drive to ensure territorial presence and control. In such cases, the boycotting of elections becomes the extreme recourse of organized crime to create power vacuums and assert its territorial dominance. Boycotting elections is achieved through an overwhelming armed presence accompanied by the incapacity of the state to secure the territory, by the capacity of transnational crime networks to mobilize local populations, or by a combination of both. In any case, the inability of the state to mobilize the necessary voting infrastructure (ballots, registration points, etc.), as well as its inability to guarantee the safety of electoral administrators, results in the physical impossibility of holding the political contest.

When territorial control is still contested, transnational crime networks enter into what specialized literature refers to as a parasitical stage, characterized by a lessening of extended intimidation and coercion and an increase in collusion with local power elites. In this stage, preelectoral manipulation is structured around illicit financing of campaigns, targeted intimidation of opposing parties, electoral base manipulation, vote buying, and capture of voter education campaigns. In such stages, transnational crime networks manipulate political contests through campaigns of intimidation and violence against political party candidates, thus reducing electoral competition and favoring candidates with whom the networks have an established alliance—or triggering intimidation and violence campaigns against potential voters, thus creating political displacements that drastically change electoral behavior. In both cases, political parties that are resilient to organized crime are weakened, whether by the retrieval of candidates or by low turnout in elections of their

constituencies. Transnational crime networks often combine intimidation and violence campaigns with false voter registration lists, manipulating voter registration processes by discouraging qualified voters from registering and by registering unqualified voters, thereby misleading qualified voters by impeding the free and fair circulation of election information, disrupting the freedom for candidates from resilient political parties to campaign. It is worth highlighting that the effectiveness of these forms of tampering with the preelectoral process is boosted and on occasion guaranteed by the level of collusion between organized crime with local bureaucracies and state authorities.

The last stage of territorial control of transnational crime networks is characterized by an organic collaboration with political structures in which both transnational crime and politicians use each other for their own advantages. In these cases, transnational crime boosts the building of social bases for the dominant political faction, facilitates the deepening of patron-client relations, and ensures that the majority of voters are indeed aligned with the interest of the dominant political faction. This stage is characterized by the total capture of politics by criminal interests as result of the ability of transnational crime networks to infiltrate all levels of local and regional political, social, and economic structures, or as the result of local and regional political elites resorting to transnational crime networks as additional guarantors of their retaining control over power structures. Notwithstanding these characteristics, the forms of preelectoral manipulation present in the former two stages are also used, perhaps with a less overt display of sheer intimidation and violence and through more sophisticated and long-term manipulations of political and legal processes.

During the electoral days, the manipulation of the political contest depends as well on the stages of territorial control that transnational crime networks have. In general, the continuation of campaigns of intimidation throughout this time is sustained, while new forms of tampering are also used, including the establishment of fictitious polling stations, the blocking of access by qualified voters to legitimate polling stations, the coopting or intimidation of polling officials, the buying of voter behavior (through either financial or material compensation in exchange for a vote for the endorsed candidate), or the buying of abstentions or paying of voters to remain home. When collusion or symbiosis between transnational crime networks and local political and bureaucratic structures is deeper, the manipulation of the political contest often involves the falsification of official documents that announce electoral results (including the falsification of election returns, of the statement of votes, or certificates of canvass, at the local level, or the statement of votes or certificates of canvass at the regional level). As a result, voters may "vote" more than once, ballots may be miscounted, the content of ballot boxes through the use of fake ballots may be altered, ballot boxes may be replaced, and ballot boxes may even be destroyed.

Finally, manipulation of the political contest may also occur after elections and once results are already made official. The likelihood of this happening depends on the extent to which transnational crime networks have established relationships with state bureaucracies and political actors. Such forms of manipulation range from blocking candidates' right to appeal through independent corroboration of results to intimidating and extorting candidates who intend to resort to appeals.

In general, transnational crime networks will use a variety of manipulative techniques to tamper with the electoral process—in the preelectoral phase, during the electoral campaigns, on election day, and after election results are announced. The spectrum and use of such methods will depend on the stages of territorial control that these networks have, as well as the extent of the relationships—whether economic, social, or political—that these networks establish with state bureaucracies and political actors.

Santiago Villaveces-Izquierdo
Independent Scholar

See also Anticorruption Legislation; Bribery and Graft; Charities and Financing; Charity Fraud; Financial Fraud; Gender-Based Violence; Legal and Illegal Economies; Legislation as a Source of Crime; Money Laundering: Countermeasures; Money Laundering: History; Money Laundering: Methods; Money Laundering: Targeting Criminal Proceeds; Money Laundering: Vulnerable Commodities and Services; Political Influence Peddling; Politically Exposed Persons

Further Readings

Allum, F. and R. Siebert, eds. *Organized Crime and the Challenge to Democracy.* London: Routledge, 2003.
Briscoe, I. *The Proliferation of the "Parallel State."* Working Paper 71. Madrid: Fundación Para las Relaciones Internacionales y el Diálogo, 2008.
Fundación Para las Relaciones Internacionales y el Diálogo. "Organized Crime, the State and Democracy: The Cases of Central America and the Caribbean." Conference Report, May 2007.
Lupsha, P. "Transnational Organized Crime Versus the Nation-State." *Transnational Organized Crime,* v.2/1 (Spring 1996).
Porta, D. and A. Vannucci, eds. *Corrupt Exchanges: Actors, Resources and Mechanisms of Political Corruption.* New York: Aldine de Gruyter, 1999.

European Union

The European (EU) Union was established by the Maastricht Treaty in 1993, with origins in earlier supranational institutions, such as the European Economic Community and the European Coal and Steel Community. Under the principle of supremacy, the national courts of EU member states are required to enforce treaties for those member states that have ratified them and uphold the laws established therein, with certain exceptions when there is a conflict with the member state's constitution. The treaties that established the EU confer upon it the power to enact legislation affecting member states, as well as legal personality—the capacity to sign international treaties and agreements that likewise bind its member states.

The EU thus has a unique ability and responsibility to deal with transnational crime involving those member states. Various agencies have been formed in order to enforce EU laws and coordinate EU actions in the areas of crime and justice: the European Police Office (Europol), the criminal intelligence agency; Eurojust, an agency for prosecutors and magistrates dealing with organized and transnational crime; and Frontex, coordinating border security efforts. In 2004, member states agreed to expand the EU's authority in criminal matters in order to deal with increases in cross-border crime that had resulted from the new porousness of intra-European borders. Eurojust's powers have been increased in an attempt to strengthen its counterterrorism abilities and in response to the nearly 30 percent increase in cross-border crimes from 2006 to 2007. The EU also works with the United Nations (UN), the G8 nations, and other international organizations, as well as with the agencies of source or destination countries involved in transnational crime.

Organized crime has been a major concern of the EU's justice agencies. The European Commission's

Directorate-General of Home Affairs identifies human trafficking, the sexual exploitation of children, narcotics trafficking, money laundering, cybercrime, and counterfeiting as the principal areas of concern. The introduction of the euro has made money laundering an even more significant problem in Europe. Euros are preferred to other currencies for a number of reasons. First, the euro is a strong currency (or, at least, it was until 2011 when the financial crises challenged its strength), and the number of 500 euro notes in circulation makes it easy to carry large amounts of cash without a lot of volume, making it a useful currency when transporting cash in bulk or making cash payments. Second, tremendous quantities of euros cross borders all the time legitimately—not only because of the size and quantity of member states of the European Union but also because of the active encouragement of the legitimate use of the euro in developing countries in Africa, the Middle East, and the Balkans. Third, because the euro is in use in so many places, the euro is considered "prewashed." That is, because it is used in so many places, it is harder to tie to a crime than a national currency is; decades ago, depositing large amounts of German marks in French banks might have raised attention. When only one currency, the euro, is involved, nothing out of the ordinary appears to be going on.

The need to deal with euro money laundering has led to regulations requiring more robust anti-money-laundering measures at European banks. Cloud computing services analyze banking activity, profiling transactions and accounts in search of suspicious activity.

Organized crime in Europe comes from native transnational crime syndicates such as those based in Italy, Belgium, the United Kingdom, and the Netherlands; from the violent gangs formed in the Albanian, Chinese, Turkish, Moroccan, and Russian immigrant communities in EU member states, with their capacity to intimidate local police and judges; and from the highly organized motorcycle gangs that maintain chapters in the EU, including the Hells Angels, the Outlaws, and the Bandidos. After drug trafficking, financial scams have become the most common kind of transnational crime in the EU, the fastest-growing since the EU's inception. Again, the porous borders and shared economic community of the eurozone make finance crime easier or more profitable than before, and the Internet has enabled

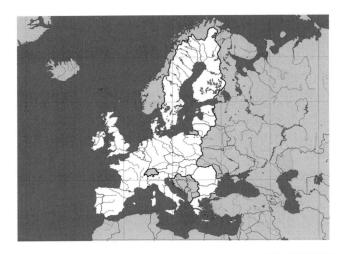

Money laundering is a growing problem in Europe since the establishment of the European Union (depicted in the map as the white areas). It is also increasingly used in developing countries in Africa, the Middle East, and the Balkans. Because it is used in so many nations, it is easier to pass large amounts through a laundering system. (Wikimedia/David Liuzzo, Radoslaw Botev)

a new generation of criminals. The Yahoo Boys, a criminal group that has plagued Europe's banks since the 1990s, operate in Nigeria's Internet cafés, while Russian cybercrime lords operate from the comfort of their own homes. Enormous amounts of money can be extorted under threat of distributed denial-of-service attacks, as banks are more willing to pay a criminal group off to stop the attack than to suffer the loss of profits and reputation if the attacks continue. The Russian mafia is also deeply involved in credit card fraud, as specialist carders collect credit card details by scanning or "harvesting" unprotected wireless Internet connections and using other methods; the information is then used for online transactions or even to manufacture counterfeit credit cards.

Occasionally, the legitimacy of identifying a group as criminal has been called into question. In 2010 and 2011, the EU dealt with the France-Roma controversy. After the death of a young Frenchman in a riot started by Roma travelers in July 2010, French president Nicolas Sarkozy ordered the police to close down the country's Roma camps (most of which were illegal but historically overlooked) and deport the Roma from the country. Many of the Roma were legally citizens of Romania or Bulgaria, permitted to enter the country but required to possess a residency visa if they stay more than 3 months. Typically the Roma will travel in groups from place to place, often quickly enough that they do not violate such visa requirements. French officials offered the Roma money to leave voluntarily—300 euros per adult and 100 per child—and deported those who refused. Much of the rhetoric of politicians supporting Sarkozy's actions characterized the Roma as criminals, as sexually violent, as baby-stealing "Gypsies." The EU Justice Commissioner, invoking the treatment of Roma, Jews, and refugees during World War II, announced her intention of taking France to the EU Court of Justice on charges of ethnic discrimination.

The issue came down to the definition of a criminal group and whether Sarkozy and the French government were targeting criminal behavior or an ethnic group. The EU does not permit ethnic discrimination, but ironically the porousness of EU borders and the introduction of greater numbers of immigrants to European countries have led to a rise in racism, nationalism, and chauvinism in political rhetoric throughout Europe. No easy solution presented itself; the Council of the European Union formally defined "itinerant criminal group" in a 2010 meeting in the wake of the controversy, declaring them as "mobile groups that are mainly active in . . . burglaries, skimming, organized shoplifting, organized pick-pocketing . . . cargo thefts, metal thefts, and thefts on construction sites," but it remains unclear whether Sarkozy was within his rights.

Bill Kte'pi
Independent Scholar

See also Conventions, Agreements, and Regulations; Eastern Europe and Russia; Europol; Intelligence Agencies: Collaboration Within the United States; International Criminal Court; International Monetary Fund; Interpol; UN Convention Against Transnational Organized Crime; United Nations; War Crimes; Western Europe; World Court

Further Readings

Anderson, Malcolm et al. *Policing the European Union.* New York: Oxford University Press, 1996.

Calderoni, Francesco. *Organized Crime Legislation in the European Union.* New York: Springer, 2010.

Elvins, Martin. *Anti-Drug Policies of the European Union: Transnational Decision-Making and the Politics of Expertise.* New York: Palgrave Macmillan, 2003.

Europol

Formally known as the European Police Office, Europol is the nonexecutive police agency of the European Union (EU) established to improve cooperation and intelligence sharing between authorities in member states in order to help combat a range of organized and transnational crimes. Priority is given to fraud, currency and commodity counterfeiting, money laundering, intellectual property theft, and trafficking of human beings, drugs, and radioactive materials; in January 2002, these priorities were expanded to include terrorism and other forms of international organized crime. Other crimes of interest include child pornography, stolen vehicles, and other offenses with transnational dimensions. As a type of information clearinghouse, Europol helps to facilitate information and intelligence exchange between liaison officers and law-enforcement agencies. Europol also provides operational, investigative, and technical support as well as expertise and training in intelligence and crime analysis, strategic research, and investigative techniques.

In order to improve security in Europe after growing criticism of the International Criminal Police Organization (Interpol), the idea for a Europe-wide police agency was proposed in 1991 by German chancellor Helmut Kohl, founded with a structure similar to that of the Bundeskriminalamt (German Federal Criminal Police). In 1993, the Maastricht Treaty then instituted Europol with limited operations commencing in January 1994 in The Hague, the Netherlands, as the Europol Drugs Unit, which focused solely on international drug crimes. In July 1995, the Europol Convention was drafted in Brussels and on October 1998 was ratified by all member states to allow Europol to commence full operations on July 1, 1999. The Europol Convention also requires each member country to establish a national office, staffed with officers seconded from home police agencies, and limits the power of Europol to intelligence and investigative support. Therefore, Europol officers not hold police powers.

With field offices in each member country of the EU, staffs of two to eight seconded officers have access to a number of information and intelligence databases, which can be shared with Europol officers in other countries. Europol offices are intended to serve as points of contact to enhance communication and cooperation with foreign police agencies. However, they are limited by language barriers, reluctance among member states to share information, and the fact that the operation of these offices is arranged by each country rather than Europol itself. Other challenges include the need for national police agencies to revise organizational structures and staffing to accommodate Europol field offices and thus look beyond their national borders, working together with other countries to adopt more modern practices and open-minded thinking. Europol also maintains relations with the Federal Bureau of Investigation (FBI), Interpol, and many other police agencies outside the EU and actively works to establish closer relations with eastern European states, such as Russia, including states seeking membership in the EU.

The directorate that governs Europol includes a director and three deputy directors appointed by the EU Council of Ministers for Justice and Home Affairs, for five-year and four-year terms, respectively; both terms are renewable once for a four-year period. The council serves as the regulatory body for Europol and allocates a budget and provides a yearly report to the European Parliament

The Europol headquarters at the Hague employs more than 600 staff members and is concerned with all 27 member states of the European Union. Formally known as the European Police Office, it was established to improve cooperation between authorities in member states and to help combat organized and transnational crimes. (Wikimedia)

documenting Europol's activities. Internally, a management board comprising a representative from each member state convenes annually to discuss these activities, finances, strategy, and future directions of Europol. Further management and guidance are provided by representatives from other national police bodies and supervisory boards, the European Police Chiefs' Task Force, and individual heads of Europol national units.

The events of September 11, 2001, brought about many changes in Europol in terms of size and scope. An operations center working 24 hours a day, seven days a week was immediately created in order to ensure rapid exchange of time-sensitive information. These additional demands resulted in a 50 percent budget increase for 2002. Although terrorism was part of Europol's mandate since 1998, the Council of Ministers for Justice and Home Affairs adopted various new counterterrorism measures shortly after on September 20, which helped establish the Counter-Terrorism Task Force on November 15, 2001, at Europol headquarters. With a combination of Europol staff along with experts and analysts seconded from member states, this unit is responsible for overall collection and analysis of information and intelligence pertaining to terrorism in the EU, including assessments of threats, terrorist modi operandi, and consequences of a terrorist attack. Terrorism intelligence is organized into two kinds of files: one exclusively for Islamic-related terrorism groups and activities, and a second called "Dolphin" for all other terrorist groups and activities. Previously, this division also included Europol's Serious Crime Department, which became a separate entity following the March 2004 Madrid bombings. Europol was criticized for being unable to prevent this incident and the July 2005 London bombings, despite making counterterrorism a priority area.

According to Europol's 2008 annual report, the organization operates with a 66.61 million euro budget (compared to 5.6 million euros in 1997) and consists of 605 personnel, compared to only 53 personnel at Europol's inception in 1994. Positions within Europol are highly competitive, with only 111 new staff appointed from 2,719 applications received. Operations in 2008 helped lead to 338 arrests. Europol also produces a number of other official publications, such as the *EU Terrorism Situation and Trend Report* (TE-SAT), *EU Organised Crime Report, European Organised*

Crime Threat Assessment, drug information bulletins, overviews of various serious crimes, policy briefs, and an anniversary publication detailing the history and achievements of Europol between 1999 and 2009. Each annual report also describes the activities and achievements of each of Europol's national offices.

Michael J. Puniskis
Middlesex University

See also Interpol

Further Readings

Deflem, Mathieu. "Europol and the Policing of International Terrorism: Counter-Terrorism in a Global Perspective." *Justice Quarterly*, v. 23/3 (2006).
European Police Office. "Annual Report 2008." In *Europol Review: General Report on Europol Activities*. The Hague: Author, 2008.

EXECUTIVE ORDER 13581

On July 24, 2011, President Barack Obama signed Executive Order 13581, "Blocking Property of Transnational Criminal Organizations." In the order, the president found that "the activities of significant transnational criminal organizations [TCOs] . . . have reached such a scope and gravity that they threaten the stability of international political and economic systems." Those organizations, defined in the order as persons or groups that engage in "an ongoing pattern of serious criminal activity involving the jurisdictions of at least two foreign states . . . that threatens the national security, foreign policy, or economy of the United States," are determined to "constitute an unusual and extraordinary threat to the national security, foreign policy and economy of the United States," making them subject to sanctions under the International Economic Emergency Powers Act (IEEPA).

IEEPA authorizes the president to declare a national emergency and regulate or seize "any property in which any foreign country or a national thereof has any interest" to counter "any unusual or extraordinary threat, which has its source in whole or substantial part outside the United States, to the national security, foreign policy, or economy of the United States" (50 U.S. Code, Sections 1701–1707). Passed in 1977, IEEPA powers have previously been

invoked via executive order by President Jimmy Carter, to block Iranian assets during the hostage crisis in Iran in 1979; by President Ronald Reagan, to block trade and travel with Libya in 1986; and by President Bill Clinton, to block transactions to Middle East terrorists and the Taliban. President George W. Bush also invoked IEEPA shortly after the terrorist attacks of September 11, 2001, when he promulgated Executive Order 13224, "Blocking Property and Prohibiting Transactions With Persons Who Commit, Threaten to Commit, or Support Terrorism."

The present order purports to provide the U.S. government with "new tools to break the economic power of transnational organized crime and protect financial markets." It blocks all property in the United States and interests in such property of designated groups, and it prohibits making any contributions to such groups and receipt of any contributions from them. The order calls upon the secretary of the Treasury to determine what persons, groups, and supporters of those persons and groups are subject to the sanctions laid out in the order, similar to how the secretary of state may designate foreign terrorist organizations (FTOs) under the Anti-Terrorism and Effective Death Penalty Act of 1996 (AEDPA). The order itself designates four such groups: the Brothers' Circle in eastern Europe and Asia, the Camorra in Italy, the Yakuza of Japan, and the Los Zetas drug cartel in Mexico. Los Zetas had already been designated as a sanctionable foreign narcotics trafficker by the secretary of the Treasury under the Foreign Narcotics Kingpin Designation Act of 1999. Because of the parallels between FTO and TCO designations, and because IEEPA violations are criminally enforceable felonies, this executive order has been compared to criminal statutes regarding material support of terrorism, governed by laws such as sections 2339A, 2339B, and 2339C of Title 18 of the United States Code.

According to national security law scholar Professor Robert Chesney, "There are few topics more slippery—and more emblematic of the current age—than the intersection of transnational organized crime, narcotics, illicit arms, and violent nonstate actors." The National Intelligence Council determined in January 2010 that TCOs "are threatening U.S. interests by forging alliances with corrupt government officials, destabilizing political institutions in fragile states, undermining competition in key world markets, perpetrating extensive cybercrimes and sophisticated frauds, [and] expanding their narco-trafficking and illicit smuggling networks" and that "terrorists and insurgents use criminal networks for logistical support and funding." The National Security Strategy, issued in May 2010, also acknowledged the growing threats of transnational criminal networks. In that vein, the White House released a new national strategy document simultaneously with the executive order, as well as a proclamation suspending the entry into the United States of aliens subject to IEEPA sanctions and United Nations (UN) travel bans, under authority granted by the Immigration and Nationality Act and international law. The Strategy to Combat Transnational Organized Crime: Addressing Converging Threats to National Security seeks "to build, balance, and integrate the tools of American power to combat transnational organized crime and related threats to national security."

This strategy identifies several ways in which TCOs harm American interests and pose threats to national and international security. These include bribery and corruption of foreign officials, subverting legitimate markets, and funding terrorism, drug trafficking, human smuggling, human trafficking, weapons trafficking, intellectual property theft, and cybercrime activity. The strategy lays out five broad policy objectives: protecting Americans and others from the harms TCOs inflict, promoting transparency and combating corruption in governments abroad, breaking the economic power of TCOs, attacking TCOs' infrastructures to prevent their facilitation of criminal and terrorist activities, and building partnerships to defeat TCOs. Those policy goals are to be achieved by a collection of 56 specified actions, including initiatives to enhance intelligence and information sharing among U.S. government agencies and between federal, state, and local agencies; monitoring strategic and emerging markets for signs of criminal activity (including cybercrime and intellectual property theft); and leveraging law-enforcement resources to investigate and prosecute persons involved with transnational organized crime activities. A series of legislative proposals was expected to follow the issuance of the executive order and the accompanying strategy to provide further statutory bases to combat TCOs.

Adam R. Pearlman
Independent Scholar

See also Adjudicating International Crimes; Antiterrorist Financing; Criminal Associations; Criminal Forfeiture and Seizure; Globalization; Measuring Transnational Crime; Money Laundering: Countermeasures; Organized Crime: Defined; Terrorism Versus Transnational Crime

Further Readings

Chesney, Robert et al. "Category Archives: Transnational Criminal Organizations." In *Lawfare: Hard National Security Choices*. http://www.lawfareblog.com/category/transnational-criminal-organizations (Accessed August 2011).

National Intelligence Council. "The Threat to U.S. National Security Posed by Transnational Organized Crime." http://www.dni.gov/nic/NIC_toc.html (Accessed August 2011).

U.S. Department of the Treasury. "Fact Sheet: New Executive Order Targets Significant Transnational Criminal Organizations." July 25, 2011. http://www.treasury.gov/press-center/press-releases/Pages/tg1255.aspx (Accessed August 2011).

White House. "Executive Order 13581." *Federal Register*, v.76/144 (July 27, 2011).

White House. "Strategy to Combat Transnational Organized Crime: Addressing Converging Threats to National Security." July 2011. http://www.whitehouse.gov/administration/eop/nsc/transnational-crime (Accessed August 2011).

EXTRADITION

Extradition is a legal process under which by treaty or other arrangement a country agrees to consider a request by another to return to it a person who is suspected of having committed a crime and then having fled to hide in another jurisdiction. In the United States, extradition can involve states seeking the return of alleged criminal perpetrators who are located in other states. Detective novels abound in episodes in which lawbreakers seek to determine what nation does not have an extradition treaty with the one where they are sought.

Roman Polanski

Almost invariably, especially in intrastate instances in the United States, a suspect voluntarily agrees to be extradited because he or she appreciates that the chances of successfully challenging the request are daunting. However, there are exceptions. A much-publicized extradition episode involved Roman Polanski, a highly regarded Polish-born French citizen and Oscar-winning motion-picture director. Polanski had been charged in California in 1977 with sexual intercourse with a 13-year-old girl he had allegedly plied with champagne and methaqualone (Quaaludes). His legal team negotiated a plea of guilty to a lesser charge than rape, under which he was to undergo psychiatric assessment in a hospital for 90 days and then be "voluntarily" deported. He was released after 42 days as perfectly sane and believed that now he was free. However, rumors arose that the judge intended to have Polanski serve the remaining 48 days of the 90-day sentence in jail. Polanski jumped bail and fled to France, which has a policy against extraditing its citizens. The French government indicated that if the entire file in the case were given to it, prosecution of Polanski would take place on French soil. American authorities would not agree to this arrangement.

Polanski subsequently lived in various European countries for 32 years, making films, and he traveled widely (including trips to Switzerland from 2006 onward) until in 2009 the Los Angeles district attorney's office asked the American government to request that the 76-year-old Polanski be extradited from Switzerland, where he had gone to receive a lifetime achievement award. He was arrested in the Zurich airport and ultimately was allowed to remain under heavy bail on house arrest and electronic monitoring in a Swiss chalet that he owned.

The Swiss Federal Department of Justice and Police announced in July 2010 that the request for Polanski's extradition had been rejected. Polanski had earlier made a financial settlement with the victim, who now advocated dropping the charge. Most important, the Swiss judges were influenced by the fact that American authorities refused to provide a transcript of a confidential hearing involving the prosecutor of the Polanski case, a hearing in which it might have been agreed that the accused need not serve jail time.

Robert Vesco

The success of Robert Vesco, a crooked financier, in avoiding extradition to the United States illustrates that the process is far from foolproof. On November 27, 1972, the Securities and Exchange Commission filed a complaint against Vesco, charging him with manipulating assets and securities that he controlled in violation of antifraud laws. Vesco had gained illegal control of more than $200 million, which he had secreted in offshore accounts in numerous banks around the world.

Facing arrest, Vesco in 1973 boarded a company jet and fled to Costa Rica, where he had stashed large sums of money. He bribed José Figueres Ferrer, the country's president, to have the government enact the "Vesco law," a statute that allowed Figueres unilaterally to grant political asylum to anyone he chose. Vesco was so designated. Sarcastically, the media labeled him "the undisputed king of fugitive financiers."

In 1977, a new government repealed the Vesco law, and Vesco moved first to the Bahamas, where he formed a business alliance with a cocaine-trafficking kingpin. The next destination was Antigua. In that Caribbean retreat, Vesco tried to purchase Barbuda, an island that is part of Antigua, in order to turn it into a sovereign state. That plan failed, and Vesco moved to Cuba on the promise that he could aid the Cubans in dodging the embargo that kept American goods from coming into the country. Vesco became involved with the Castro brothers and Donald Nixon Jr., a nephew of President Richard Nixon, in a scheme to market a product called Trioxidal, said to be a miracle drug that could cure arthritis, cancer, and a mélange of other ills. Tests failed to support the therapeutic claims for Trioxidal, and Cuban prime minister Fidel Castro became disenchanted with Vesco. Vesco was arrested, and a three-judge panel sentenced him to 13 years' imprisonment for fraud. He was released early and settled under the name Tom Adams in a Havana suburb. Vesco died two years later of lung cancer, having successfully avoided extradition for a third of a century.

Later Developments

The most significant recent development in the realm of extradition has been the growing focus on human rights issues. In the past, generally only the charge was considered, although countries that do not have the death penalty have refused to extradite a person if it appears likely that the suspect, if convicted, might be executed. There also has been less likelihood that a request for extradition will be granted if the person is being charged with a nonviolent political crime, and the country being asked to extradite generally must be convinced that there is a reasonable likelihood that the person is guilty as charged.

Gilbert Geis
University of California, Irvine

See also Anticorruption Legislation; Conventions, Agreements, and Regulations; Draft Dodging; Extraordinary Rendition; Globalization; Intelligence Agencies: Illegal Engagements; Interpol; Mutual Legal Assistance Treaties; Prosecution: International

Further Readings

Ain-Krupa, Julia. *Roman Polanski: A Life in Exile*. Santa Barbara, CA: Praeger, 2010.

Herzog, Arthur. *Vesco: From Wall Street to Castro's Cuba: The Rise, Fall, and Exile of the King of White Collar Crime*. New York: Doubleday, 1987.

Nicholls, Clive, Clare Montgomery, and Julian B. Knowles. *The Law of Extradition and Mutual Assistance*. New York: Oxford University Press, 1987.

Pyle, Christopher H. *Extradition, Politics, and Human Rights*. Philadelphia: Temple University Press, 2001.

Sambei, Avinder and John R. W. D. Jones. *Extradition Law Handbook*. New York: Oxford University Press, 2008.

EXTRAORDINARY RENDITION

The term *extraordinary rendition* as used in the realm of American criminal justice relates to the practice of government agents, usually employed by the Central Intelligence Agency (CIA), seizing a person believed to have ties to terrorist activities and transporting him (it invariably has been a man) to another country where he will be tortured. The reason for the adjective "extraordinary" is not clear. Perhaps it connotes the use of the practice when it was first employed, during the presidential administrations of Ronald Reagan and Bill Clinton, when it was rarely invoked. Since September 11, 2001, however, extraordinary rendition has been much more customary. Given its secret nature, there are no reliable numbers regarding its extent. However, an analysis of the logs of flight paths of airplanes leased from private firms by the CIA suggests that there may have been several hundred incidents of extraordinary rendition. The practice possesses an aura of legitimacy based on ancient common-law doctrine that a criminal court will not question how a person came before it, whether voluntarily, by a legal arrest, or as a result of kidnapping. The only concern is that the accused is present in person.

The most memorable illustration of this doctrine involves the capture of Nazi war criminal Adolf Eichmann by the Mossad, the Israeli intelligence agency, on May 11, 1960, in a suburb of Buenos Aires. Eichmann was kept briefly in a safe house and then flown to Dakar in Senegal and on to Israel. He was dressed in the uniform of an El Al employee and heavily sedated. Eichmann had served as a leading figure in the Nazi regime's "final solution," which had resulted in the killing of six million Jews, mostly in concentration camps. His show trial sought to revivify the horrors of the Holocaust. Eichmann was sentenced to death after having been found guilty by a three-judge tribunal in Jerusalem on 15 charges, including crimes against humanity. He was hanged just before midnight on May 31, 1962.

Abu Omar

A prominent case of extraordinary rendition took place in Milan, Italy, when a team of CIA operatives, working in conjunction with the Italian police, on February 17, 2003, seized 42-year-old Hassan Mustafa Osama Nasr. The prey, a Muslim imam from Egypt commonly known as Abu Omar, was on his way to his mosque for noontime prayers. He was driven to an Italian airfield, flown to Ramstein Air Base in Germany, and then transported to Egypt, where he was brutally tortured. The torture included electric shock to his genitals, being hung upside down, being bombarded with loud noises, and being moved from a hot sauna to a refrigerated cell. Abu Omar had gained political asylum in Italy. He had once been a government spy for the Albanian intelligence agency, and there was some belief that the Americans wanted him to play the same role in Italy in regard to possible Muslim terrorists.

The kidnapping operation was surprisingly sloppy. The American agents left behind credit card and hotel tabs, and had used cell phones indiscriminately to call CIA headquarters in Virginia and family members. An independent Italian prosecutor, Armando Spataro, issued warrants against 23 Americans (22 CIA operatives and one U.S. Air Force colonel), charging them with kidnapping.

They were convicted in absentia, but the Italian government, which undoubtedly was complicit in the rendition, refused to seek extradition. Had it done so, it is extremely unlikely that the United States would have returned the CIA agents to Italy to face prosecution and possible long jail terms.

Khalid El-Masri

Khalid El-Masri, born in Lebanon but a German citizen, was on vacation in the Balkans when he was removed from a bus at a border crossing and removed to Macedonia on New Year's Eve in 2003. It would later turn out that he had been mistaken for a member of the Hamburg Al Qaeda with a similar name. He believed his captors were members of a CIA team. He was flown to Kabul in Afghanistan, where he was placed in solitary confinement for nearly five months. He received meager food rations and putrid water. When he was released, he was dropped off in a desolate region in Albania. A Council of Europe investigation of American rendition practices concluded that El-Masri's allegation that he was beaten, drugged, and sodomized was substantially accurate. He filed a suit in an American court charging that the United States had contravened the international prohibition against subjecting a person to procedures that shock the conscience and that punish an individual without legal process.

A U.S. court of appeals held that security concerns dictated that El-Masri's case had to be dismissed because the government's actions could not be determined fully. The ruling was based on a state secrets doctrine that provides a daunting challenge to adjudication of claims involving extraordinary rendition. The El-Masri court relied on *United States v. Reynolds* (345 U.S.1, 1953), which traced the origin of the doctrine to the 1807 treason trial of Aaron Burr. Left unaddressed was the question regarding who, if not the judiciary, had the authority to rein in executive excesses. Critics of the El-Masri decision argued that the camouflage of the state secrets doctrine was often employed to avoid embarrassment and to handicap political opposition. For his part, El-Masri claimed that his experience with the Americans led him to conclude that the United States was no democracy but something of a dictatorial regime. He claimed that freedom and justice are disrespected, as are basic morals and values.

Maher Arar

Syrian-born Maher Arar had lived in Canada for 17 years. In September 2002, during a layover at John F. Kennedy Airport in New York en route to Montreal from Tunis, he was seized by U.S. Federal Bureau of Investigation (FBI) and immigration agents and held in a detention for 20 days. After that, he was transported to Syria, where he was placed in a "grave"— a cell 6 feet long, 7 feet high, and 3 feet wide. The cell was damp, cold, and infested with rats. Cats would urinate on Arar through an opening in the ceiling. He claimed that he was beaten with a two-inch-think shredded cable and was threatened with electric shocks and with placement in a spine-breaking chair. He lost 40 pounds during his ten-month period of captivity.

To alleviate the torture, Arar said he falsely confessed that he had trained with terrorists in Afghanistan, although he had never been in the country. He was released on October 10, 2003, with no charges having been made against him. Arar filed a lawsuit in the United States. The Appellate Court for the Second Circuit dismissed his suit on the grounds that, as a noncitizen, Arar lacked standing to make a claim under the Torture Victims Protection Act. Again, state security was invoked to keep Arar from litigating his claims. A commission of inquiry in Canada supported Arar's allegations, and the government awarded him 10 million Canadian dollars as compensation for his suffering.

The Law and Extraordinary Rendition

The case studies described above highlight the legal hurdles that confront victims of extraordinary rendition practices. Directly bearing on the legal issue is the United Nations (UN) Convention Against Torture and Other Cruel, Inhuman and Degrading Punishment and Treatment, adopted by the General Assembly in 1984 and entered into force in mid-1987. About 149 countries, including the United States, had ratified the convention by the end of 2010. It obliges signatories to prohibit and to punish torture as well as cruel, inhuman, and degrading treatment under all circumstances. The convention compels ratifying governments to investigate all allegations of such behavior and to provide remedies for victims. The phrase "all circumstances" is further specified as referring to any situation whatsoever, whether war or a threat of war, internal instability, or any other public emergency.

Portions of the Geneva Conventions are also relevant. These include Geneva III and the Convention Relevant to the Protection of Civilian Persons in Time of War. They both address treatment of individuals who are caught up during military activities.

International humanitarian law distinguishes "lawful combatants" from other fighters and from civilians. "Unlawful combatants" are said to be belligerent persons who do not enjoy the privileges given to the armed forces of a sovereign state under the terms of international treaties. The term commonly is applied to a person taking direct part in an international conflict without being entitled to do so.

In the United States, supporters of extraordinary rendition classify those they designate as "terrorists" as falling outside the boundaries of the protections specified by the conventions. However, there are additional treaties that, according to some commentators, make extraordinary rendition illegal. The International Covenant on Civil and Political Rights of 1966 states in Article 7 that no one shall be subjected to torture or cruel, inhuman, or degrading treatment or punishment.

There are also international norms that represent shared understandings on the part of nations regarding acceptable standards of behavior. The obligation regarding what is called nonrefoulment prohibits states from sending refugees to countries where they face torture. The United States, as a government, has consistently taken the position that the various human rights treaties are limited in their applications to treatment on American soil. The second Bush administration maintained that Guantánamo detainees were exempt from the mandates of domestic and international law because where they were imprisoned outside domestic U.S. territory. Critics insist that the Cuban garrison, located on a U.S. military base, is intrinsically part of American territory.

Torture

The legal situation in regard to extraordinary rendition involving torture is complicated by the fact that there is a widespread absence of respect for international law among American attorneys and legal scholars. Another element lies in the intensity and the depth of the reaction in the United States to the September 11, 2001, catastrophe. In addition, torture is subject to controversial definitions. One viewpoint is that brutal techniques beyond what is permissible under the *Army Field Manual* (*AFM*) guidelines constitute torture. Others maintain that neither the AFM nor international law establishes the limits of what are acceptable activities. Waterboarding, a simulated drowning procedure, has both advocates and opponents. There is no doubt, however, that the international reputation of the United States has suffered severely from the use of extraordinary rendition and torture. Once known for compassion and human decency, the country is now reviled overseas for what is seen as a "cowboy" frontier agenda.

The U.S. Torture Victims Protection Act defines torture as any act whereby severe pain or suffering, whether physical or mental, is inflicted on an individual in order to obtain information or a confession either from that person or from a third party. During the Bush administration several internal documents addressed the matter of torture. A prominent memorandum argued that the Geneva Convention did not apply to terrorists and that the president, as commander in chief, could authorize violations of the Torture Victims Protection Act if he believed an emergency existed that made it important do so. It was said that when Congress authorized the invasion of Iraq, it also authorized all means deemed necessary by the president to pursue that mission. It was claimed that the president could not violate the Constitution when acting under the umbrella of war powers.

The debate regarding the efficacy of torture to secure useful information constitutes an important element in an appraisal of extraordinary rendition. The evidence on this issue is inconclusive. There is no question that torture can be an effective tactic, presuming that the person being manhandled has something important to disclose. On the other hand, many persons who have been tortured testify later that they sought to determine what their interrogators wanted to hear and that they fabricated tales, willing to say anything to end their pain. The most persuasive evidence of the falsity of confessions is found in the annals of witchcraft prosecutions on the European continent (torture was not common in English witchcraft trials). Hundreds of persons, mostly women, confessed to having committed acts that we know they could not conceivably have done, such as flying through the air to attend conventicles presided over by the devil.

Political and ethical considerations underlie the varying assessments of the use of torture by American operatives. A sample of such positions can be found in statements of candidates who sought the presidency during the 2008 campaign regarding what euphemistically has come to be called "enhanced interrogation." Republican and former New York mayor Rudolph Giuliani urged that people who do the interrogation should be permitted to use any method they choose. Republican senator John McCain, who had been subjected to torture as a prisoner during the Vietnam War, wondered how anybody could condone the forms of torture reported to be in use. Republican governor of Massachusetts Mitt Romney declared that the better part of wisdom was to leave the issue ambiguous rather than advocate one or another view. Democratic senator and later U.S. secretary of state Hillary Clinton thought it a presidential right to decide whether or not to adhere to international treaties. Democratic senator John Edwards thought that not to torture would protect U.S. troops from similar kinds of retaliation. During his time as a Democratic senator, Barack Obama said that no administration should permit torture.

The Obama Administration

Supporters of President Obama were surprised and displeased when his Department of Justice declined to end extraordinary rendition, although it stressed that it would loosen the stranglehold of the state secrecy doctrine in the future. Conservatives were likely to regard the president's position as an endorsement of an approach that they considered essential in the campaign against terrorism.

Extraordinary rendition issues continue to appear in the courts. The U.S. Supreme Court in the autumn of 2010 agreed to decide a case involving a suit against Jeppesen, a Boeing aircraft subsidiary that allegedly arranged extraordinary rendition flights. The Court is expected to look closely at the state secrecy explanation for the government's unwillingness to allow such cases to proceed to trial.

The practice of extraordinary rendition and the recourse to torture force many people to consider fundamental moral and legal issues regarding permissible actions and what principles should guide state policies. It also brings into play questions concerning necessity, provides a context for examination of national values, and raises important concerns regarding priorities and means-end considerations.

Gilbert Geis
Joseph F. C. DiMento
University of California, Irvine

See also Extradition; International Criminal Court; Military Forces: Private or Contracted

Further Readings

Arendt, Hannah. *Eichmann in Jerusalem: A Report on the Banality of Evil*, Rev. ed. New York: Viking, 1965.
DiMento, Joseph F. C. and Gilbert Geis. "The Extraordinary Condition of Extraordinary Rendition: The CIA, the D.E.A., Kidnapping, and the Rule of Law." *War Crimes, Genocide, and Crimes Against Humanity*, v.2 (2006).
Mayer, Jane. *The Dark Side: The Inside Story of How the War on Terror Became the War on American Ideals*. New York: Doubleday, 2009.
Mazigh, Monia, Patricia Claxton, and Fred A. Reed. *Hope and Despair: My Struggle to Free My Husband, Maher Arar*. Toronto, ON: McClelland and Stewart, 2008.

FAILED STATES

Though there is no single agreed-upon definition of what a failed state is, failed states are generally considered to be nation-states that cannot provide basic services to their people. States that do not provide security for their people and whose governments do not have monopolies over the use of legitimate violence in their territories are viewed as failed or collapsed states. These states typically suffer from weak political, social, and economic institutions leading to some or all of the following conditions: lax law enforcement, poor infrastructure, government violence against citizens, high levels of corruption, civil war, rising inflation, falling life expectancy, and food shortages.

Somalia is the top-ranked state on The Fund for Peace and *Foreign Policy* magazine's Failed States Index. The Failed States Index ranks states on a number of factors, including demographic pressures, human flight, factionalized elites, human rights, security apparatus, and public services. According to the Failed States Index, the top five failed states in 2010, starting with the worst, were Somalia, Chad, Sudan, Zimbabwe, and the Democratic Republic of the Congo, all in Africa. Afghanistan, Iraq, and Pakistan were among the top 10 failed states on the index.

The paradigmatic failed state is Somalia. Somalia's central government has little power even over its capital, Mogadishu. Somaliland, in Somalia's northwest, declared independence in 1991 and has a functioning government but is not recognized as a state by most of the world. Punt, in Somalia's northeast, is a less well-functioning "state" within Somalia. The interior of the country has been overrun by civil war ever since the rule of the vicious Mohamed Siad Barre.

One factor many failed states have in common is that they were ruled by kleptocratic dictators who raided them of their resources. Eventually the people responded with protesting, violence, or rioting, and the state deteriorated. This process has been happening for years under the rule of Robert Mugabe in Zimbabwe, where hyperinflation has taken hold and where two thousand people die of acquired immune deficiency syndrome (AIDS) every week. Protests overtaking the Middle East and North Africa in 2011 threatened to yield more failed states, as corrupt dictators such as Libya's Muammar al-Qaddafi seemed likely to leave mere husks of a state in their wake.

Although transnational crime and terrorism can occur in weakly ruled regions of developed states, failed states are particularly pernicious because they are recognized as sovereign states in the international system. For this reason, other states cannot legally intervene in their affairs. The shield of sovereignty provides particularly strong protection for criminals who infiltrate these states. Failed or failing states were viewed as humanitarian catastrophes by policy experts in previous decades, which led to efforts such as the U.S. military intervention in Somalia and the proposed intervention into Haiti in the early to mid-1990s.

The September 11, 2001 (9/11), terrorist attacks on the United States brought failed states and their connection to terrorism and transnational crime into sharp focus. Since the 9/11 attackers had been trained in a failed state, Afghanistan, the issue of shoring up failed states gained great momentum. Politicians and policy experts began to see failed states as safe havens for organized crime and terrorism. There is some debate on whether or not failed states are ideal training grounds for terrorists and criminals. After all, the weak financial institutions and tenuous rule of law in collapsed states can make life difficult even for criminals.

Still, there is strong evidence that terrorists prosper from state failure. First and foremost, terrorists use failed states as safe havens that provide them with the ability to operate in a zone essentially free of law enforcement. Osama bin Laden spent much of his adult life in Afghanistan and the Sudan, two failed or failing states that provided him with combat experience, access to weapons, recruitment pools, and staging grounds for his Al Qaeda organization. In Afghanistan, he formed his Al Qaeda army from among the foreign Muslim fighters that poured into the country in order to fend off the Soviet Union in the mid- to late 1980s. After the Soviet withdrawal from Afghanistan, bin Laden was welcomed in Sudan, where international terrorists and organized criminals the world over were making their home. Other failed or failing states, such as Yemen and Pakistan, have been critical to the ascension of Al Qaeda.

The most important aspect of a failed state, from a terrorist group's perspective, is that it offers such groups the ability to operate with impunity within its borders. The training camps that Al Qaeda formed in Afghanistan when it was under Taliban rule are a case in point. Without these training camps, where the 9/11 hijackers, for instance, practiced for their mission by slitting the throats of livestock, Al Qaeda's assault on America at the beginning of the millennium probably would have been greatly muted.

Although there is some debate about whether failed states are ideal for terrorist operations, studies such as James Piazza's have shown a statistically significant connection between failed states and the incidence of terrorism. Failed states are both a staging ground for international terrorism and a target for internal attacks. Civil wars erode the state while also making it an ideal territory for international terror groups.

For this reason, Iraq since the American invasion has been viewed as an acute problem for international security. The American invasion stripped away the strong rule of Iraqi dictator Saddam Hussein, leaving a state with virtually no public services, intermittent electrical power, and almost no rule of law. De-Baathification of the military created a security vacuum that was quickly filled by both militias and international terrorists. Abu Musab al-Zarqawi led Al Qaeda in Mesopotamia until his death in 2006. His attacks on the United Nations (UN), Shia holy sites, and American workers fueled the Sunni-Shia civil war that overtook Iraq in the mid-2000s. This was a clear case of state failure leading to a huge rise in terror attacks, as Iraq was virtually terrorism-free under Saddam Hussein's rule.

The great fear of the American government, as explicated in the 2004 debates between President George W. Bush and Senator John Kerry, is of nuclear states collapsing completely, leading to terrorists or criminals controlling nuclear weapons. This scenario is possible in Pakistan and North Korea, two states that have nuclear weapons, where public services have been eroded; both rank in the top 20 on the Failed States Index.

Terrorism is not the only type of transnational crime that state failure engenders. Failed states are hubs of counterfeiting, piracy, organized crime, human trafficking, the trafficking of nuclear and radiological material, money laundering, and the drug trade. The lack of effective law enforcement makes all of these activities easier to perform in states that have collapsed. Failed or failing states may not have nuclear weapons, but many serve as transit points in the huge illegal small arms trade.

Criminal organizations are attracted to the corruption endemic in failed and weak states. They use poorly paid government officials to help them traffic drugs, weapons, and people. Failed states can also serve as money-laundering sites for organized criminals, though they often lack the financial institutions to attract major money-laundering operations.

The drug trade in particular is centered on failed states. Afghanistan, for example, produces about 90 percent of the world's heroin. Burma (Myanmar), another state in the top 20 on the Failed States Index, is the second-largest producer of opium worldwide and an important supplier of methamphetamines. Areas of Colombia controlled by the Revolutionary Armed Forces of Colombia (FARC), where the state has little or no reach, are key producers of cocaine.

State failure, according to Robert Rotberg, leads to private entrepreneurship. In other words, people have to take their lives into their own hands. As a result, failed and failing states are hubs of the narcotics trade, the trade in counterfeit drugs, and human trafficking. Increasing reports of piracy off the coast of Somalia are a case in point. There local pirates have become highly successful in extracting goods and money from their victims. Like drug dealers in inner cities, Somali pirates can be seen as people who have turned to crime because they lack other options.

Some criticisms of the thesis that links failed states to crime are that these arguments provide cover for rich countries to intervene in poor ones and that weak states provide better sanctuaries for criminals than failed ones. The first criticism contends that governments in the global North declare states in the global South as weak or failed as a precursor to invading them or otherwise intervening in their affairs. This criticism draws evidence from America's involvement in Somalia, Haiti, Afghanistan, Iraq, and Pakistan's Khyber Pakhtunkhwa (formerly the North-West Frontier Province). The second criticism holds that activities such as financial crimes and counterfeiting are more easily perpetrated in weak states, where there is some rule of law, modern technology, and institutional structure. This argument points to South Africa, Nigeria, and Mexico's large organized crime syndicates as evidence.

Failed states serve as a nexus for many of the world's most pressing problems: terrorism, transnational crime, disease, war, genocide, and starvation. There is strong evidence that international terrorists, particularly those in Al Qaeda, thrive in failed and failing states. The drug trade and maritime piracy, as well as other transnational crimes, are also rampant in these states. Although a single definition of state failure is not agreed upon, failed states are those whose governments and official armies have little reach or power, where public services are nearly nonexistent, and where the rule of law is weak.

Gabriel Rubin
Montclair State University

See also Bribery and Graft; Impact of Transnational Crime; Military Forces: Private or Contracted; Piracy: Failed States; Piracy: History; Southeast Asia; Terrorism Versus Transnational Crime; Weapons Smuggling; West Asia

Further Readings

Foreign Policy and the Fund for Peace. "2010 Failed States Index." http://www.foreignpolicy.com/articles/2010/06/21/2010_failed_states_index_interactive_map_and_rankings (Accessed February 2011).

Huria, Sonali. "Failing and Failed States: The Global Discourse." *IPCS Issue Brief*, v.75 (July 2008).

Patrick, Stewart. "Weak States and Global Threats: Fact or Fiction?" *Washington Quarterly*, v. 29/2 (Spring 2006).

Piazza, James A. "Incubators of Terror: Do Failed and Failing States Promote Transnational Terror?" *International Studies Quarterly*, v.52 (2008).

Reidel, Bruce. *The Search for Al Qaeda: Its Leadership, Ideology, and Future*. Washington, DC: Brookings Institution Press, 2008.

Rotberg, Robert I. "Failed States in a World of Terror." *Foreign Affairs*, v. 81/4 (July/August 2002).

U.S. Department of State. "Transnational Organized Crime: A Growing Risk to U.S. and Global Interests." September 10, 2010. http://www.state.gov/j/inl/rls/fs/146966.htm (Accessed February 2011).

FINANCIAL ACTION TASK FORCE

The Financial Action Task Force (FATF) is a nonpermanent intergovernmental policy-making body with a ministerial mandate to develop and promote international standards to combat money laundering and terrorist financing. These standards are known as the FATF (40+9) Recommendations. The aim of the FATF is to enhance global compliance and oversee national implementation in order to reduce the risks that money laundering and terrorist financing pose. Progress is reviewed by the members of FATF and FATF-style regional bodies (FSRBs) at plenary sessions, where typology reports on money laundering and terrorist methods, trends, and techniques are also presented and discussed. The impact of these measures on crime is not well understood. In 2011, the FATF reviewed the relevance of the Recommendations in response to the proliferation of finance and corruption.

The FATF was convened in 1989 at the G7 summit in Paris. The original 40 "Recommendations on Money Laundering" were published in 1990. They were later revised in 1996 and in 2003 to expand the range of predicate offenses from drug offenses to all "serious crimes," to reflect evolving thinking about money-laundering controls. The original mandate to focus on money laundering was extended in October 2001 when eight additional "Special Recommendations on Terrorist Financing" were published, and the ninth was added in October 2004. FATF membership stood at 36 in 2011, with 34 jurisdictions and two regional organizations (the Gulf Cooperation Council and the European Commission). Member jurisdictions include Argentina, Australia, Austria, Belgium, Brazil, Canada, China, Denmark, Finland, France, Germany, Greece, Hong Kong, Iceland, India, Ireland, Italy, Japan, Kingdom of the Netherlands (the Netherlands, Aruba, Curaçao and Saint Maarten), Luxembourg, Mexico, New Zealand, Norway, Portugal, Republic of Korea, Russian Federation, Singapore, South Africa, Spain, Sweden, Switzerland, Turkey, the United Kingdom, and the United States. Associate Members and Observers of FATF also include 27 international and regional organizations that participate in FATF work. The FATF Secretariat, which supports the task force and president, is housed at the Organisation for Economic Co-operation and Development (OECD) headquarters in Paris. The presidency of FATF is a one-year post, held by a senior official from an FATF jurisdiction. Luis Urrutia Corral of Mexico began his term as president in July 2010.

The FATF 40+9 Recommendations are intended to be implemented at the national level through legislation and other legally binding measures, and they provide enough flexibility to respect different constitutional frameworks. The standards range from the criminalization of money laundering and terrorist finance and the ability to confiscate the proceeds of crime to the implementation of mechanisms to facilitate cooperation and coordination of international and domestic anti-money-laundering/counter-financing of terrorism (AML/CFT) efforts. Establishing a financial intelligence unit (FIU) to receive and disseminate suspicious transaction reports from financial institutions and other designated professions is required, as is the implementation of effective measures by financial institutions to detect and prevent money laundering and terrorist financing. This includes measures such as customer due diligence (identity verification), record keeping, and suspicious activity reporting. Such institutions should also bear the threat of sanctions for noncompliance. It is the role of FATF to monitor members' progress in implementing such AML/CFT measures and to seek to generate political will to bring about national legislative and regulatory reforms, where necessary.

Although the FATF Recommendations have no binding effect, there are sanctions for members who fail to comply. Compliance with the standards is assessed via the mutual evaluation process, a form of multilateral peer review to which members of the FATF and the FSRBs are committed. Evaluations are conducted by a team of experts from financial, legal, and law-enforcement areas and from the FATF Secretariat. The process includes a two-week, on-site visit to the jurisdiction and comprehensive meetings with government officials and the private sector. The product is a mutual evaluation report, which in time is available on the FATF Website and provides a detailed description of the jurisdiction's systems and a rating for effectiveness. In a bid to promote fairness and consistency, the FATF has developed detailed assessment criteria and procedures in order to conduct mutual evaluations. These exist in the form of a "Methodology for Assessing Compliance with the FATF 40 Recommendations and the FATF 9 Special Recommendations" and a *Handbook for Countries and Assessors*.

In June 2009, the FATF's International Co-operation Review Group (ICRG) adopted new procedures to publicly identify high-risk jurisdictions with strategic deficiencies in their AML/CFT regimes. In February 2010, 31 jurisdictions were identified as posing a risk to the international financial system. The onus is placed on these jurisdictions to offer a high-level political commitment to address these deficiencies through implementation of an action plan developed with the FATF. The FATF can urge members to apply countermeasures to protect their financial sectors against both high-risk and noncooperative jurisdictions. By "naming and shaming" such jurisdictions via public statements, the FATF can create international pressure for countries to comply. For example, between 2000 and 2006, the FATF kept a list totaling 23 noncooperative countries and territories (NCCTs). Only once adequate progress had been made would jurisdictions be removed from public identification. In 2011, the FATF considered a modified version of this.

Rachel Elizabeth Southworth
Cardiff University

See also Antiterrorist Financing; Money Laundering: Countermeasures

Further Readings

Financial Action Task Force. *FATF 40 Recommendations*. 2003. http://www.fatf-gafi.org/dataoecd/7/40/34849567 .PDF (Accessed February 2011).

Financial Action Task Force. *FATF IX Special Recommendations*. 2001. http://www.fatf-gafi.org/ dataoecd/8/17/34849466.pdf (Accessed February 2011).

Financial Action Task Force. "An Introduction to the FATF and Its Work." http://www.fatf-gafi.org/dataoecd/48/11/ 45139480.pdf (Accessed February 2011).

FINANCIAL FRAUD

Accounting fraud involves an attempt by insiders at a company to manipulate the company's financial results to achieve an objective. The most common techniques used to manipulate the company's financial results include accelerating or deferring revenue or expenses. For example, in the WorldCom scandal of 2002, one of the techniques used was to "capitalize" expenses. In this process, expenses that should have been recorded in one accounting period were instead spread over many accounting periods, resulting in better performance of the company in the short run. Companies may attempt to do the reverse as well. In an accounting period when performance is particularly good, they may record additional expenses or defer revenue in order to improve performance during a later accounting period, when those expenses can be avoided or the revenue can be recorded. This is referred to as cookie-jar accounting. The temptation to manipulate a company's financial results may come from a number of sources. Company officials may want to improve a company's short-term performance in order to gain credit for good management of the company and increase share prices in order to sell their holdings. Company officials wishing to ensure against possible adverse developments in the future might understate the company's performance (using cookie-jar accounting) in the current period in order to overstate performance (through increased revenues or decreased expenses) at a later date. Company officials might also understate the company's performance to depress the stock price in order to allow a party with which they have an arrangement to take over the company at a bargain price.

Check kiting involves a scheme in which an individual writes a check for which there are insufficient funds in his account. The individual then deposits a check from a second account, for which there are also insufficient funds, into the first account in order to cover the shortfall. The bank immediately credits the account with the funds, which allows the first check to clear. This process can be repeated several times, with each check clearing because of a credit from a subsequent bad check. The result is to allow the check kiter to access money to which he or she is not entitled. In some instances, the individual never covers the funds, resulting in a loss to the financial institution. In other instances, the individual finally deposits genuine funds and the result is that the individual has effectively received an interest-free loan. However, the scheme continues only for the period of time between the crediting of the account and the presentation of the check for payment from the account it is written on. Repetition of the process can prolong the scheme, but eventually the money must be covered or the scheme will be detected. Recent decreases in the processing time for checks have impaired check-kiting schemes. Check kiting is not particularly effective, because it is difficult to sustain the scheme for any length of time.

Ponzi (also called pyramid) schemes involve investment programs promoted by a confidence man or woman. The confidence person promises a high and consistent rate of return to investors. The initial investors in the scheme are repaid with high rates of return and are encouraged (1) to reinvest and (2) to tell others about the investment opportunity in order to induce subsequent investments. If the original investors reinvest their money and subsequent investors also invest, the scheme can be continued indefinitely and the confidence person can keep control of a large sum of money. As long as the investors requesting the return of their money and profits are counterbalanced by new investors enticed by the scheme's apparent success, a casual observer will be unable to detect the fraud. The actual operation

Company insiders wishing to manipulate corporate financial results via accounting fraud can attempt to accelerate or defer revenue or expenses. (Photos.com)

of the investment program is usually described in grandiose and vague terms and kept secret by the confidence person so that investors and potential investors are unable to verify the scheme's success. In many instances, there is no investment scheme at all, and money is simply taken in from new investors and paid out to older investors. The most famous Ponzi scheme of all was the fraud perpetrated by Bernard Madoff, who defrauded investors out of an estimated over $50 billion. Madoff's scheme was ultimately uncovered with the economic collapse of 2008. Investors whose financial positions were impaired by the downturn attempted to liquidate their investments with Madoff. Because the many investors seeking to liquidate their investments counterbalanced new investors, Madoff was unable to sustain the scheme. Ultimately any Ponzi scheme ends when (1) the confidence person absconds with the proceeds, (2) investors lose confidence in the scheme or the flow of new investors slows for some other reason, or (3) investors decide for some other reason, such as a bad economy, to withdraw their funds.

The advance-fee fraud, also known as the Nigerian scam or Spanish prisoner scheme, involves a confidence man or woman who claims to have a large amount of money in a foreign location. The claim is that that he or she needs assistance to transfer the money. Once the victim agrees to help to transfer the money, the confidence person reports that financial assistance is necessary to complete the transfer. The confidence person may claim that he or she has to bribe a bank official to execute the transfer, that a person necessary to the transaction has been imprisoned and needs funds to secure his release (hence the name Spanish prisoner scheme), or that a wire fee is needed. The confidence person may request financial assistance based on pretext after pretext until the victim realizes that he or she has been defrauded. Frequently these schemes are perpetrated from Third World locations (thus the name Nigerian scam), and victims who have attempted to investigate or pursue the confidence person are usually unsuccessful. Many persons who involve themselves in such schemes may fail to report them because of the unsavory nature of the acts in which they have participated before recognizing the fraud.

Tax avoidance schemes involved attempts by individuals and corporations to hide assets or income from tax collectors. One type of scheme involves the use of offshore accounts in jurisdictions with bank secrecy laws. Investors place their money in accounts in those jurisdictions, invest it, and then fail to report the income to their home countries. One scandal involving Swiss accounts held at UBS unraveled when the bank agreed to provide information about U.S. clients to American law-enforcement authorities. The use of offshore accounts presents the challenge of funneling money to the offshore account without being detected and of repatriating the money when the funds are needed, but investors have found a number of ways of meeting this challenge.

Trading Offenses

There are a number of potential ways for an unscrupulous individual to gain an unfair advantage over fellow market participants. The schemes discussed here represent only a subset of the panoply of schemes that have been devised (and exposed).

Insider trading occurs when an individual makes a trade based on nonpublic information about a company's prospects. For example, a company executive who receives news of an unfavorable development and sells his shares has committed insider trading if he executes his trade before the news has been released to the general public and if the news has a material impact on the company's value. The executive's position puts him at an unfair advantage relative to other investors, because he has superior knowledge of the market.

Critics of the securities laws point out that insider trading actually helps average investors even if they end up losing money on their investments. To use the example of the company executive from the previous paragraph, the investor on the buy side of the transaction buys shares not because the executive is selling them but because he has otherwise decided to purchase shares in the company. The fact that the company executive is selling his shares because of the undisclosed bad news drives the market price down, resulting in a more favorable price for the buyer. Although the buyer will ultimately lose money when the undisclosed bad news is made public, he will have purchased his shares at a lower price and the loss will be less severe. The fallacy of this argument, of course, is that if the executive is not allowed to trade based upon the undisclosed information, he will have more incentive to disclose the information (which will benefit the buyer to a greater extent than the sale and resulting lower price). Moreover, a financial system that allowed insider trading would encourage insider chicanery and discourage ordinary investors, who would perceive the system as rigged. Foreign countries that historically have taken a lax approach to insider trading enforcement have stepped up their efforts in recent years.

One particularly pernicious form of insider trading is front-running. A front-runner learns of the intention of a large investor to execute a substantial trade in a particular security. Such a trade is likely to impact the value of the security. The front-runner then executes a trade before the large investor can execute its trade in an attempt to profit from the price move. A broker told to make a substantial purchase on behalf of a large investor might, for example, purchase shares for his or her own account prior to executing the client's trade. Once the client's trade is executed, the shares may have increased in value and the broker can sell the recently acquired holdings at a profit. The broker's previous trade may have increased the price at which all or a portion of the large investor's order was executed, to the disadvantage of the client. Other individuals who may be in a position to execute a front-running

transaction include insiders at institutional investors and persons to whom they might provide information about upcoming trades. The arguments in favor of normal insider trading do not apply to front-running, because front-running pushes prices in a direction unfavorable to the party from whom the front-runner received the information.

Cornering occurs when a large investor buys up a large position in a publicly traded asset. Investors who have previously speculated on a decrease in the asset's value by shorting the asset are forced to purchase the asset at a premium in order to cover their position. This technique is effective only for an asset for which there is a relatively small market (because any individual investor's resources would be insufficient to corner the market in a widely traded asset) with low liquidity and lax disclosure requirements. Corners are ineffective in U.S. securities markets, for example, because a liquid market is maintained and because investors acquiring more than 5 percent of the outstanding shares of a particular company are required to disclose their holdings to the Securities and Exchange Commission (SEC). For that reason, corners are frequently seen in the international commodities markets; tin, copper, and cocoa have been subject to corners and attempted corners in recent years.

Market timing and late trading occur when a mutual fund allows favored investors to make trades on more favorable terms than other investors. Market timing occurs when a mutual fund allows a large or otherwise favored investor to trade more frequently than the fund prospectus and rules allow. Such investors gain an advantage over other investors in the fund because they can exit and enter the fund strategically in order to maximize their return. This causes a loss to the fund (and therefore other fund investors) because of increased transaction costs and the fact that the market-timing investors gain a greater return than regular investors.

Late trading occurs when a favored investor is allowed to make trades based on outdated prices. In the United States, mutual fund share prices are set at 4:00 P.M. daily based on the then-prevailing value of their holdings, and orders placed after 4:00 P.M. the previous day are settled at that price. Late traders are investors who place an order after 4:00 P.M. but are still allowed to trade based upon that day's price rather than waiting until the close of trading the next day. Investors engaging in late trading are able to trade based on additional information (for example, developments in overseas markets that may impact the value of the fund) and are therefore at an unfair advantage relative to investors required to place their orders before 4:00 P.M. in order to receive that day's price.

Stock options backdating occurs when stock options are issued to company executives with strike prices based on prior low prices. Stock options issuance has become commonplace at many publicly traded companies because stock options are a tax-favored form of compensation and because stock options are believed to give executives an incentive to manage the company effectively in order to profit from the use of their options. Stock options are normally issued with a strike price equivalent to the price prevailing in the market at the time the options are issued. However, when a company decides to issue options but bases the strike price on a prior (lower) market price and claims to have issued the options on that earlier date, the executives gain an advantage because their options are already "in the money" and can be profitably exercised even if the executives do not manage to increase the stock price. In these instances, the company may not acknowledge for financial reporting purposes those benefits gained by the executive. This practice therefore understates (1) the company's executive compensation expense and (2) the executives' tax liability. Investors in the company are prejudiced because their holdings are diluted by the issuance of additional shares at below-market prices to executives.

Michael Paul Beltran
United States District Court

See also Accounting Fraud; Charities and Financing; Charity Fraud; Financial Action Task Force; Investment Crimes; Money Laundering: Countermeasures; Money Laundering: History; Money Laundering: Methods; Money Laundering: Targeting Criminal Proceeds; Money Laundering: Vulnerable Commodities and Services; Nigerian Money Scams; Pyramid Schemes; Sales Tax; Tax Evasion; Value-Added Tax Fraud

Further Readings

Block, Alan A. and Sean Patrick Griffin. "Transnational Financial Crime: Crooked Lawyers, Tax Evasion, and Securities Fraud." *Journal of Contemporary Criminal Justice*, v.18/4 (2002).

Blum, Jack A. *Enterprise Crime: Financial Fraud in International Interspace*. Washington, DC: National Strategy Information Center, 1997.

Fisher, Kenneth L. and Lara Hoffmans. *How to Smell a Rat: The Five Signs of Financial Fraud*. Hoboken, NJ: Wiley, 2009.

Rezaee, Zabihollah and Richard Riley. *Financial Statement Fraud: Prevention and Detection*. Hoboken, NJ: Wiley, 2010.

Turner, Jonathan E. *Money Laundering Prevention: Deterring, Detecting, and Resolving Financial Fraud*. Hoboken, NJ: Wiley, 2011.

Van Duyne, P. C. et al. *Cross-Border Crime in a Changing Europe*. Huntington, NY: Nova Science Publishers, 2001.

FORGERY

Forgery is the crime of producing something false with the purposeful intent of deceiving someone. Forgery is a type of fraud that has been utilized in many ways by those involved with transnational crime, as well as by more traditional types of criminals. For example, forged tax stamps are necessary for certain forms of tobacco smuggling typically conducted by large transnational organized crime organizations. Forged documents, such as passports, visas, licenses, and assorted permits, are employed in many types of transnational criminal activities. Many variations of Internet money scams, such as the infamous Nigerian money scam, rely upon forged items such as cashier's checks, money orders, bank statements, and shipping labels. As transnational criminal activities have evolved, forgery methods have kept pace. In fact, new techniques of forgery have even spawned new arenas of transnational criminal activity.

Historical Background

A substantial number of old and ancient documents are now considered by experts to be of doubtful authenticity; some have been innocently but mistakenly attributed to noted authors, particularly philosophers and religious figures, but other works are certainly intentional forgeries of purportedly ancient or classic texts. During the Middle Ages, forgery was widespread, with limited means of detection available; thus, common social responses to forgery included admiration, amusement, fascination, and scorn, as the typical belief, as promoted by the medieval church, was that truth resided in the mind of God and not in actual earthly phenomena. Ancient Roman law, dating from around 80 B.C.E., prohibited the falsifying of documents pertaining to the passing of land to heirs. In 1562, during the reign of Queen Elizabeth I of England, a forgery statute known as An Act Against Forgers of False Deeds and Writings prohibited forgeries of documents bearing an official seal and pertaining to land titles. In 1729, the Parliament of Great Britain passed An Act for the More Effectual Preventing and Further Punishment of Forgery, Perjury, and Subornation of Perjury, which made certain acts of forgery capital offenses. Consequently, through the early 19th century in Great Britain, forgers could be pilloried, fined, imprisoned, and even put to death. In 1823, the U.S. Congress passed An Act for the Punishment of Frauds Committed on the Government of the United States.

Forgery has long been part of the arsenal of transnational criminals but has taken on a more dominant role within their operations as we have moved into the Information Age. For prosecution of forgery in Anglo-American courts, it is necessary to consider three key elements: the making of a false document, the writing of something that alters an individual's public or private rights, and the intention to defraud. It should be noted that it is not necessary for there to be an actual financial gain obtained in order to convict someone of forgery; forgery may be proved based on evidence that demonstrates the intention to gain.

Modern Concerns

One of the most common targets of forgery is the personal signature. The handwritten signature is widely accepted as a form of identity authentication and is commonly targeted by transnational and other criminal elements. A handwriting expert examines samples of handwriting, including signatures, to determine the idiosyncrasies of an individual's handwriting in order to distinguish one individual's handwriting from another's. Handwriting can be influenced by myriad factors, including the material used, the conditions under which the handwriting was produced, the writer's mood, physical and mental states, and substance use. An impostor signature provider is essentially an opportunistic forger who presents an array of challenges to dynamic signature verification, many of which are influenced by the relationship, if any, between the forger and the genuine signature producer. One strategy of signature verification and forgery detection is based on fuzzy modeling, where signature samples are binarized and resized to a standard window size, then thinned using horizontal density approximation by means of the uniform portioning approach to determine a proper fuzzification function with structural parameters essential for signature verification or complete forgery detection. An additional concern is that handwriting biometrics appear to be susceptible to forgery attacks, which may be either human-generated or machine-based. Furthermore, the digital revolution has fostered serious security vulnerabilities that place digital signatures and documents at considerable risk of forgery. Unfortunately, appropriate security mechanisms have yet to be developed to protect these types of materials.

The threat of sophisticated forgeries has escalated as a result of advances in office-related technologies, such as digital scanners and full-color laser copiers linked to computers with digital photography capabilities. As a consequence of these technological factors, organizations such as banking institutions, social security offices, border-control agencies, and

Forged passports are regularly used to enable human trafficking, and stolen or altered passports are often purchased by those who intend to commit crimes in other countries. New technologies in desktop publishing and printing have aided forgers. (Photos.com)

immigration services have had to expand their forgery analysis capabilities. These include the forensic use of ultraviolet light to detect fluorescent qualities, such as chemical eradication, bleaching, and printing attributes; use of infrared radiation to analyze inks; electrostatic examination of latent impressions; and examination via high magnification microscopy for erasure or substitution.

The American Law Institute prepared the Model Penal Code, which recommended that some of the technical limits contained in many forgery laws be removed. Because of traditions going back to English common law, restrictions were maintained in many U.S. statutes that did not include acts such as uttering and counterfeiting under forgery laws. The Modern Penal Code specifically defined forgery and suggested an expansion of the scope of what could be prosecuted as forgery. For instance, it was suggested that the unauthorized changing of a piece of writing be included under the area of forgery. Furthermore, the definition of what could constitute a written document was expanded considerably in the Modern Penal Code to include any form of recording information as well as any form of money, credit instruments, trademarks, and all symbols of identification, privilege, right, or value.

There are myriad ways that transnational criminals use forgery to achieve a dishonest financial advantage or otherwise accomplish their objectives. Chinese crime organizations, for example, have been implicated in schemes to sell forged, counterfeit credit cards, manufactured mainly in Hong Kong, to organized crime groups in Australia. Skimmers, which are handheld devices used to record data on legitimate credit cards, are commonly used by these crime groups to generate forged credit cards. One particular Chinese crime group operating out of a restaurant in Rome, Italy, was especially prolific in the forging of passports, which are regularly used in human trafficking, until they were arrested and prosecuted. In Thailand, passport-forging gangs routinely steal passports from tourists. The stolen passports are then altered and often delivered to transnational organized crime groups. Other stolen and altered passports are sometimes sold to foreigners who intend to commit crimes in other countries. Some of these altered passports have apparently been obtained and used by members of terrorist organizations,

such as that involved in several terrorist attacks carried out by extremist groups in Madrid, Spain.

Transnational organized crime groups have created the demand for an array of forgery cottage industries around the world, such as those involved in the forgery and falsification of assorted documents, including those related to identity, import, export, end-user, and customs procedures. Sophisticated forgery techniques that utilize information technology and desktop publishing have aided those involved in the trafficking of myriad illicit commodities, as well as those who deal in such illegal goods in various markets scattered across the globe in both developing and in developed countries.

Transnational organized crime organizations have also been very flexible and have adapted many new technologies to expand the repertoire of their criminal operations. These developments have made it possible for forgery to go high-tech. For example, computer systems can be hacked and data files can easily be manipulated, such that documents digitally stored can, without much difficulty, be fraudulently altered and then, with the aid of digital color laser copiers, be printed. The reproduction quality of such documents makes it extremely difficult to identify them as forgeries. In fact, many companies, as well as law-enforcement agencies, have had to develop computerized detection systems in order to discriminate sufficiently between genuine and forged documents. Accordingly, a considerable proportion of transnational organized crime operations now involve the relatively new area of cybercrime. This particular development has necessitated the transformation of many law-enforcement approaches; new, often costly, technologies have had to be acquired by law-enforcement agencies around the globe, and personnel have had to be trained in the use of such technologies. Laws have had to be changed and updated in many cases, or at least interpreted more broadly, in order to account for these incursions into the realm of newer technologies by transnational criminals and increasingly by local criminals as well.

Summary

Forgery is a component of many aspects of transnational crime. For example, human trafficking typically involves conspiracy and the forging of many types of documents, such as passports, visas, entry cards, and work permits. The rampant use of forgery by transnational organized crime groups has resulted in the proliferation of forgery-detection units by law-enforcement agencies around the globe.

Victor B. Stolberg
Essex County College

See also Counterfeit Currency; Counterfeit Goods; Technology

Further Readings

Ballard, L., D. Lopresti, and F. Monrose. "Forgery Quality and Its Implications for Behavioral Biometric Security." *IEEE Transactions*, v.37/5 (2007).

Cheddad, Abbas, Joan Condell, Kevin Curran, and Paul McKevitt. "A Secure and Improved Self-Embedding Algorithm to Combat Digital Document Forgery." *Signal Processing*, v.89/12 (2009).

Davis, D. "Forensic Handwriting Analysis: The Key in Fighting Forgery." *International Security Review*, v.12 (1981).

Kelly, Jan Seaman and Brian S. Lindblom. *Scientific Examination of Questioned Documents*. Boca Raton, FL: CRC Press, 2006.

Nickell, Joe. *Detecting Forgery: Forensic Investigation of Documents*. Lexington: University Press of Kentucky, 2005.

G

Gambling: Illegal

Ever since the authorities decided to restrict gambling, criminals have offered gamblers the opportunity to play illegally. At the end of the 19th century, illegal gambling also became one of the favored activities of organized crime. Until fairly recently, illegal gambling operations, such as gambling dens, betting rings, and numbers games, were largely organized locally or regionally. In the mid-1990s, however, the Internet truly globalized illegal gambling. How to control online games of chance is now by far the most important policy question in this field.

Gambling has existed throughout history, and so have restrictions on gambling, albeit usually imposed locally and only for short time periods. The main concern was the threat that gambling presented to public order, in large part because of the conflicts that arose from cheating. Not until the late 19th century did moral concerns over the impact of gambling gain the upper hand. Restrictions aside, the demand for gambling remained, and so did those who offered gambling as a service. In the 17th century, for instance, traveling artists offered street games during markets and fairs, mainly with the intention of conning naïve locals. Although such scams were usually the work of individuals, records also mention itinerate groups whose male members committed burglaries and robberies and whose female members ran gambling and pickpocketing activities. A classic example of an illegal street game is the shell game, which can still be found in some European cities today, for example in Stockholm.

The game originates in the Arabian world and in the 19th century, and traveling *bons vivants* spread it throughout Europe. In the 1970s, Yugoslavian groups reintroduced the shell game in western European cities. At the time, there was an entire network of such groups, apparently controlled by a boss living in Belgrade. Persons running games intended to con players cannot stay in one place for too long, because they risk violent retribution by the victims.

The scale of illegal gambling increased during the Industrial Revolution. One explanation for this is the rapid urbanization that took place during this period, and the effect it had on the social lives of Europeans and North Americans. Alcohol abuse, prostitution, and gambling were endemic in the fast-growing cities of the era. Second, technological advances also pushed gambling as a pastime. The establishment of the telegraph network in the United States, for example, enabled patrons to bet on horse races in cities other than their own, and illegal operators quickly set up "wire rooms" where bets could be placed.

A large-scale illegal gambling activity usually requires a complex, coordinated process. A betting operation or a numbers game, for example, involves an organization consisting of "runners" who take bets or sell tickets, "clerks" who administer wagers, and a bank or a bookmaker to calculate the odds and keep track of everything. Criminal groups grew in size as a result. Clandestine gambling operations also call for continuity and therefore require a relatively stable organization. Illegal games of chance involving a substantial number of players are also

Illegal gambling activity usually requires a complex, coordinated process and a relatively stable organization. In 2011, many Hollywood celebrities were named as participants in an unlicensed Texas Hold'em poker gambling ring. (Photos.com)

almost impossible to hide. Consequently, it became necessary to bribe or threaten law-enforcement officials or policy makers to prevent "disturbances." The increasing scale of illegal gambling thus led to the emergence of criminal groups with the characteristics usually associated with organized crime. The notorious Al Capone, for example, is known mainly for bootlegging, but he also operated gambling dens where punters could not only bet on horse races but also play roulette, craps, and cards. Documents recently released by the U.S. Internal Revenue Service reveal that his famous conviction for tax evasion actually stemmed from his illegal gambling activities. In 1951, the U.S. Senate Special Committee to Investigate Organized Crime in Interstate Commerce (popularly known as the Kefauver Committee) concluded that gambling profits had developed "into the principal support of big-time racketeering and gangsterism" after Prohibition was repealed in 1933. Today, illegal gambling is still an important organized criminal activity in the United States. According to the U.S. National Gambling Impact Study Commission, approximately $80 billion to $380 billion of illegal sports bets alone were made

in 1999. The commission estimated that 92 percent of the earnings from sports betting found its way into the pockets of organized crime groups. A recent assessment by the Federal Bureau of Investigation (FBI) revealed that La Cosa Nostra still largely controls illegal bookmaking activities in the United States.

Apart from the United States, illegal gambling operations are also an important criminal activity in most Asian countries. In mainland China, for example, the lottery is the only legal type of gambling, and casino gaming, sports betting, and slot machines are all forbidden. In most other Asian countries, only lotteries and betting on horse racing are legal. Not surprisingly, there is a substantial illegal market for casino gaming and sports betting. The police believe that organized crime groups are closely involved in this, although their operations are thought to be predominantly local in scope. The authorities consider the involvement of organized crime in illegal gambling a major problem in Macau, Japan, the Philippines, and Thailand, and a medium-priority problem in Cambodia, Taiwan, and Hong Kong.

In western Europe, governments chose to decriminalize all or most types of gambling from the 1950s onward. The size of the gambling market is controlled through a system of licensing, in order to minimize the social costs. The effect is that illegal gambling is no longer a key activity for organized crime groups, although niches still exist. One example can be found in France, where slot machines in public places are still prohibited. Only electronic gambling machines that offer credits to earn extra rounds or free games are legal. Illegal operators, however, may circumvent such restrictions by paying out the credits in cash. The machines must be fitted with a "knock-off" switch that makes it possible to reset the credits to zero after payout. Organized crime groups are believed to control the placing of these machines, particularly in the south of the country.

In Europe, the former Eastern Bloc countries are a specific case. The socialist regimes prohibited most games of chance, but after the fall of the Iron Curtain in 1989, the new governments lifted most restrictions. Because of growing addiction problems, policies have now shifted toward tighter control of the market. Russia took a particularly radical approach by deciding to move virtually all gambling activities to a limited number of gambling zones, mainly located in distant areas such as Siberia. As a result, new opportunities for illegal operators have arisen, and it is presumed that they already run hundreds of establishments housing illegal casinos and slot machines.

By far the most important development related to illegal gambling is the Internet. Since the establishment of the first gambling Website in 1996, online gambling quickly grew into a multibillion-dollar business. It also created new opportunities for criminals to enter the gambling market and helped to modernize existing illegal operations. In 2008, for example, a group running a sports-betting ring in the United States had partly replaced the traditional street bookmakers with Websites that punters could enter with a password in order to place their bets.

The Internet also allowed for the introduction of new types of electronic gaming machines that no longer require internal gambling software. These machines are usually placed in bars, restaurants, and Internet cafés. To the uninitiated customer, it is just a terminal offering access to the World Wide Web. The bartender, however, can easily change it into a gambling machine by remote control. Technically, the terminals are highly sophisticated and often equipped with hardware encoders offering secure communication with the main data center, and with a mechanism that automatically erases all the gambling software in case the terminal is tampered with or improperly disconnected. Although Internet gambling machines require local representatives, usually known criminals, to "promote and manage" placing the terminals, the data center and games management can be located anywhere in the world. Consequently, it is next to impossible for the police to find and identify the core operators. Internet gambling machines can be found in the United States and Europe, but there is still little information on who is actually running the operations in the background.

In terms of turnover, however, the primary problem is probably gambling Websites that now offer a wide range of games of chance. Because such Websites are accessible 24 hours a day, seven days a week, they undermine the carefully designed regulatory regimes now in effect in many countries. Although operators of gambling Websites usually hold a license in one specific country or self-governing territory, it is illegal for them to offer their services to people living elsewhere. The Internet, however,

knows no boundaries. Moreover, the "domestic" market is usually small. In some cases—for example, in Malta—the authorities do not even allow operators to target the inhabitants of the country in which they are legally based.

Apart from the risk of addiction, one of the major concerns of the authorities is the possibility of criminals owning gambling Websites. Most jurisdictions hosting the Websites scarcely screen the backgrounds of applicants for operating licenses, if at all. Persons with a criminal history thus have little problem acquiring a license and generating income with virtually no risk of apprehension and prosecution. In addition, they also gain access to players' credit card data and other information, which they can use to skim customers' bank accounts and to commit identity fraud, although there is no hard evidence that this has actually happened. There are, however, concrete indications that operators do manipulate the gaming software to their own advantage. Even in online poker rooms, the provider can introduce a "virtual player of the house" into the game—a computer program that can steer the outcome at will—without the human players noticing.

The U.S. government in particular has tried to take action against online gambling, notably by targeting the Achilles heel of gambling Websites: the fact that payment via the Internet usually involves banks that *do* fall under the jurisdiction of the player's country of residence. To this end, the U.S. government adopted the Unlawful Internet Gambling Enforcement Act (UIGEA) in 2006. As a result, bona fide gambling Websites immediately stopped taking bets from U.S. customers. Nonpublicly traded Websites continued to accept U.S. players. As of mid-2010, not one of these had been indicted.

Toine Spapens
Tilburg University

See also East Asia; Eastern Europe and Russia; Gambling: Legal; Money Laundering: Vulnerable Commodities and Services; Responsibilization

Further Readings

Meyer, G., T. Hayer, and M. Griffiths, eds. *Problem Gambling in Europe: Challenges, Prevention and Intervention*. New York: Springer, 2009.

National Gambling Impact Study Commission. *Final Report*. 1999. http://govinfo.library.unt.edu/ngisc/reports/fullrpt.html (Accessed January 2011).

Reuter, P. *Disorganized Crime, Illegal Markets and the Mafia.* Cambridge: MIT Press, 1983.

Spapens, T., A. Littler, and C. Fijnaut, eds. *Crime, Addiction and the Regulation of Gambling.* Boston: Martinus Nijhoff, 2008.

GAMBLING: LEGAL

Gambling is one of the classic activities of organized crime, and criminals—who are often pathological gamblers themselves—remain attracted to it even if authorities decide to decriminalize the market and allow licenses to bona fide operators. Generally, three main crime problems related to legal gambling can be distinguished.

First, there is the risk of criminal groups obtaining permits for legal gambling operations and using these to generate a legitimate source of income or to gain illegal money by "skimming" taxes or by scamming the players. Second, criminals may misuse games run by official operators for money laundering. Third, criminals may "fix" sports matches and then wager substantial amounts of money on the outcome with legitimate betting companies. Since the emergence of online gambling in the mid-1990s, particularly the latter developed into a global problem.

The most notable example of criminal organizations involved in legal gambling operations is the Italian American Mafia in Las Vegas. La Cosa Nostra succeeded in obtaining licenses for a number of casinos in the 1940s and the 1950s. Tax evasion was endemic in the Mafia casinos. On one occasion, the state was able to prove that, between 1960 and 1967, an average of $4.5 million a year did not go through the books in one casino, out of an annual turnover of $36 million. In the 1950s, the Mafia also got involved in casinos in Cuba. Cuban law did not outlaw gambling, and American tourists visiting the island, who were more than willing to try their luck, often fell victim to fraudsters. The regime brought in American gangsters to professionalize operations and—contradictory as it sounds—to clean up the games.

The party in Cuba was cut short when Fidel Castro took power. The situation in Las Vegas gradually changed after 1955, when controls on applicants for licenses and investors were tightened. Henceforth they would be subject to thorough background checks. Furthermore, the famous businessman and

Hong Kong spectators await the beginning of a horse race. Even legal gambling can be linked to crime: a good way of explaining sudden wealth and laundered money is to say that it was won while gambling. (Photos.com)

movie star Howard Hughes appeared in town in 1966 and succeeded in buying six casino hotels in just a couple of years. His investments helped boost the city's image, which led to a substantial increase in casino tourism and attracted other bona fide investors. In later years, larger and larger investments had to be made in new casino hotels to keep drawing in the crowds. This, in combination with effective screening of investors, eventually led to organized crime being sidelined. Las Vegas is but one example of criminals entering the legal gambling market. Such cases stress the importance of effective screening of applicants for gambling licenses.

Next, legal gambling may be associated with money laundering. Because in gambling a big prize can be won with a small stake, it is a good way of explaining sudden wealth. One can launder money only through legal gambling activities. Money won through illegal gambling is still "black." In theory, several options exist, although there is little information about the extent to which such channels are actually used.

First, running a legal gambling operation offers the opportunity to inflate turnover artificially. After taxes, the remaining profit is then legitimate. A second option is to place large wagers on sports contests whose outcomes are relatively predictable. The fact that the proceeds are low is not important, as the aim is not primarily to win money. A third option is to use a lottery. One crude method is to buy a large number of tickets and collect the prize money.

A variant is to buy lottery tickets from real winners for a higher price. A fourth option is to use a casino. A criminal may, for instance, divide a sum of black money between two or more accomplices, who then play a game together. In the end, one of them wins, and this part of the original sum is thus laundered. All of these methods, however, are relatively complex and will undoubtedly attract attention when large sums of money are involved or when the same trick is repeated regularly.

Finally, match fixing, coupled with betting on the outcome, is a classic method for criminals to generate money. Bets may be placed either with illegal operators or with official betting companies. Since the emergence of online sports betting, opportunities for match fixing have greatly increased. Online betting companies now offer the opportunity to gamble on a large number of sports matches, in different competitions, and punters from all over the world may wager. According to representatives of the Dutch Football Pool and Lotto Association, Asian gamblers nowadays wager 50 million euros on average on any official match in even the lowest amateur divisions of the Dutch football (soccer) competition, for example. Theoretically, amateurs are much more vulnerable to bribery than the well-paid players in the top leagues are.

Match fixing was particularly endemic in Asia in the 1990s and compromised entire competitions. Corruption scandals in China, for instance, caused a major loss in confidence in the football competition. Nowadays, there is also considerable concern in Europe about the integrity of football competitions. There have been recent allegations of match fixing related to gambling in football in the Netherlands, Finland, Portugal, Italy, Poland, Austria, the Czech Republic, Turkey, and Romania. In response, the Union of European Football Associations has set up its own intelligence unit to track signs of manipulation, for instance by analyzing the patterns of bets placed on specific matches. In 2007, it investigated 26 suspect matches.

The basic method of match fixing is to bribe a number of players into throwing the game or to pay the referee to ensure that a particular side loses or wins the game. In the case of spread betting, which is common in the United States, "point shaving" may be an option. In spread betting, the theoretical strength of two teams is translated into a points difference with which it is assumed the better team will win the game (known as the "line"). Only when the difference is greater is there a win in gambling terms. In such a case, criminals may pay players not to win with a margin that exceeds the line. Sports-betting Websites have widely increased the opportunities for match fixing. Patrons can place bets on the outcome of not only a match but also, for instance, in football, on the exact score and on events occurring during the game, such as the first team to get a free kick or a penalty. In theory, criminals may try to ensure the outcome of any of those events. This also lowers the threshold for players' level of cooperation, because they are not necessarily required to lose the game. In any case of match fixing, manipulation is almost impossible to prove.

Toine Spapens
Tilburg University

See also East Asia; Eastern Europe and Russia; Gambling: Illegal; Money Laundering: Vulnerable Commodities and Services; Responsibilization

Further Readings

Hill, D. *The Fix, Soccer and Organized Crime*, Toronto, ON: McLelland and Stewart, 2008.

Meyer, G., T. Hayer, and M. Griffiths, eds. *Problem Gambling in Europe. Challenges, Prevention and Intervention*. New York: Springer, 2009.

Skolnick, J. *House of Cards: The Legalization and Control of Casino Gambling*. Boston: Little, Brown, 1978.

Spapens, T., A. Littler, and C. Fijnaut, eds. *Crime, Addiction and the Regulation of Gambling*. Boston: Martinus Nijhoff, 2008.

GENDER-BASED VIOLENCE

According to data collected and analyzed by the World Health Organization (WHO), approximately one third of all women become victimized by gender-based violence (GBV) at least once in their lifetimes. GBV derives primarily from a variety of gender-role ideologies that subordinate women, connotations of masculinity that imply degradation of women, and acquired social norms, especially when associated with conflict. Such activities become reinforced through blaming the victim, communal shunning of the victim, instilled fear of retaliation, and a lack of administered justice from law enforcement, especially for poor women.

Refugees or displaced persons are more vulnerable because their environments are less secure. Practices such as foot binding, wife beating, and female genital mutilation have tradition and custom as their basis, despite the persistent pain and health risks involved. Throughout history, women's bodies have been used as either the spoils of war or a means of causing terror.

Studies from the Asia Foundation and WHO indicate that gender-based violence ranks as one of the leading causes of death for women and girls worldwide. Nearly all GBV survivors face post-traumatic stress disorder. Additional problems associated with GBV include the increased risk of acquiring sexually transmitted diseases, permanent physical injuries, and mental and physical health problems associated with alienation from family and community.

Foot Binding

For approximately one thousand years, Chinese women had their feet bound as a requirement for securing a "proper marriage" and an external sign of honor to their families. The tradition dates back to the Sung Dynasty (960–1279), when it was practiced solely by members of the imperial palace and then spread to the lower social classes. By the time of the Ming Dynasty (1368–1644), foot binding was customary throughout the empire. Typically, the process resulted in women being disabled and homebound, a status symbol for the husband, proving that the husband could provide without relying on the labor of the wife for economic survival. Their disabled condition prevented women from participating in civil society and left them isolated from the public sphere, which supposedly ensured their fidelity.

In the old Chinese culture, small feet were considered attractive and were desired by men. Foot binding was best performed on young girls with pre-bone cartilage. In older children it would become necessary first to break the bones and then to bind the feet. Beyond pain, the girls faced the risk of paralysis and gangrene. The procedure was banned by law in 1912 by the Nationalist Revolution after approximately a billion women had been victimized. Despite the longevity of the tradition, the practice ceased rather quickly, within a generation.

Wife Beating

Although the practice of wife beating exists globally, several less industrialized nations structurally condone such behaviors. Grounds for wife beating include the woman's arguing, neglecting the children, leaving the residence without first consulting with the husband, failing to prepare food to the husband's satisfaction, and refusing to have sex upon the husband's demand. As of 2010, the United States has marital rape laws in all but a few states. All 50 states have laws against domestic violence, spousal abuse, and battering. Despite the frequent occurrence of such crimes in the United States, society collectively disapproves of the behavior.

Female Genital Mutilation

The practice of female genital mutilation (FGM) functions as a rite of passage and a sign of cultural identity in some societies but has both short-term and long-term psychological and physical effects. Different types of FGM include *sunna*, which involves puncturing the prepuce of the clitoris, and clitoridectomy, which entails the removal of the clitoris entirely. Excision and infibulation may form part of the clitoridectomy, including the additional removal of surrounding flesh such as the labia minora and possibly also the labia majora. The experience has been described as acute and prolonged torture, because the "surgical tools" for cutting include scissors, sharpened rocks, broken glass, or even teeth. Usually FGM occurs without the use of anesthesia, antiseptics, or antibiotics.

Infibulation is both the severest and most common form of FGM. Following the procedure, the girl typically faces several weeks of limited mobility as she lies with her legs tied together. The physical aftereffects linger for years. The women and girls subjected to this procedure face increased risk of developing keloid scars, pelvic infections, urinary retention, urinary infection, tetanus, infertility, and menstrual fluid accumulation that can lead to toxic shock syndrome. In the context of marriage, sexual intercourse becomes extremely painful, such that it can take up to two years before penetration can become possible. In the case of impregnation after the procedure, women have an increased risk of miscarriage or giving birth to brain-damaged or still-born infants. Often the delivery requires an introcision, which involves additional FGM by cutting into the vagina in order to allow passage of the infant, followed by resewing the genitalia and affected surrounding area.

In addition to suffering the pain and health complications from such risky and unhygienic methods, a high percentage of women and girls who have undergone the procedure have reported suffering from post-traumatic stress disorder. Despite the physical and psychological consequences associated with undergoing FGM, the procedure has been socially justified on the grounds that it deters acts of fornication prior to marriage and provides a visible proof of virginity upon marriage.

War and Rape

One unintended consequence of globalized gender inequality is that women are placed in subordinate positions, such that they become overly dependent on men. This subjection becomes acute in times of war and economic crisis, with their attendant famines, natural disasters, and political dissent. Poor women tend to be especially hard hit by such conditions, because during times of war, men of lower socioeconomic classes, their spouses, and their family members are more likely to enlist in the military to survive. When large sectors of the male population are captured or killed, their women partners become increasingly subject to violence.

Women have often been considered as spoils of war. For example, during the Crusades (11th–13th centuries), when European Christians invaded the Middle East in an attempt to retake the "holy land," women were regarded as a prize of war, and provisions were given to use them sexually. Raping the enemy's women served as a symbol of defeating the enemy, demonstrating that the opponents were unable to protect their women. During the Hundred Years' War between England and France (1337–1453), honors were bestowed upon those who protected women against enemy rape. During the American Revolutionary War (1775–83), however, George Washington issued a death sentence to a soldier for having committed rape. In 1914, at the start of World War I, German soldiers marched through Belgium

and resorted to rape, shooting civilians, and burning and looting as collective acts of terror. During World War II (1939–45), the Japanese used rape against the Chinese in order to achieve dominance. As a result of the Nanjing Massacre (often called the Rape of Nanjing, 1937–38), approximately 20,000 Chinese women were raped.

Shortly before the Vietnam War (1959–73), rape became classified as a crime according to international law. Under the Geneva Convention, such crimes could result in a maximum penalty of death and an automatic sentence of imprisonment. The deterrence effect of such new laws, however, was minimal, because rape and sexual assault were common. Court-martial records have revealed that more than 80 cases of rape or sexual assault have been filed against U.S. soldiers. More than half have been convicted. Allegedly rape-related crimes, including attempted rape, have historically been underreported, and sentences have usually been minimal, despite the Geneva Convention mandates.

During the mid-1990s, as part of the attempted genocide in Rwanda, Tutsi women and girls endured torture and public gang-rape to incite chaos, prior to their murder by Hutu soldiers. According to estimates made by the United Nations Human Rights Commission (UNHCR), between a quarter million and a half million rapes occurred. Under the threat of death, Tutsi boys were forced to rape their mothers, which had devastating effects, albeit in qualitatively different ways, on both the boys and the women involved.

Also in the 1990s, while residing in concentration camps, a multitude of Croatian and Muslim women endured ongoing rape by Serbian soldiers. Mass rapes with the intention of forced pregnancy served as a genocidal tactic by affecting the genetic imprint of the offspring in large numbers.

In addition to the physical trauma of forced or coerced penetration, radical feminist theory raises the hidden issue of rape as a violation of a "woman's sexual wholeness," such that future consensual sexual contact of any sort becomes emotionally linked to the horrific event. Unenlightened persons are unable to understand the woman's perspective in rape cases. However, victimized women often fail to realize that they have been raped to the extent that it can be proven legally. Abused persons may actually fear their mates so much that they consent to sexual intercourse because of perceived potential harm. The radical feminist theoretical perspective explains the underreporting of rape, and all forms of GBV, as attributable to a patriarchal legal system with covert sexism deeply embedded in the fabric of society.

Internal Conflicts

El Salvador has faced multiple waves of internal conflicts of varying severity. In some sectors of Salvadoran society, GBV is associated with male machismo, a hyperandrocentric ethic that places women in servitude in all areas of life. Machismo manifests itself as the denial of women's rights and individuality by maintaining male dominance through verbal reprimands backed by physical force. Feminist theory explains the practice as rooted in the broad societal acceptance of the belief in gender inequality that favors men. Through the socialization process, boys become implicitly indoctrinated with the ideology of women as inferior, which in turn supports and rationalizes the use of GBV, wife beating, and other forms of physical coercion as legitimate.

Mass oppression against the Salvadoran poor occurred during the Salvadoran Civil War (1980–92) under a regime supported by their military, guerrillas, and a host of paramilitary groups. Often innocent children were abducted, several clergy were assassinated, and the death toll reached an estimated 60,000. Terror tactics included beating, mutilating, and raping women. There were cases of pregnant women having their unborn children torn from their wombs. As a result, massive migration and a large-scale protest emerged from the mid-1970s to the late 1980s. By the late 20th century, poverty in El Salvador had become so severe that the average family was forced to survive on less than $2.00 per day, while one in every four children born died before age the age of 5.

Prior to the massive 2010 earthquake in Haiti, GBV threatened much of the Haitian female population. Economic deprivation has resulted in women having sex to obtain money to feed their children. Such actions have a consensual appearance, resulting in difficulty in classifying the acts as rape. Since the earthquake, however, sexual violence against women and girls has escalated. The mass displacement of more than 1 million earthquake survivors created conditions of increased vulnerability for all, but especially for women and girls, leading to their victimization by sexual predators. The earthquake scattered families and communities that previously had functioned as a support network. With communities dispersed and divided, it became easier not only to perpetrate rape but also to hide from the law; victims face immense challenges in seeking justice, often because they are unable to identify their assailants. That problem is compounded by fear of retaliation, the threat of social shunning (due to the stigma borne by rape victims), and the perception of law enforcement as favoring the affluent while unresponsive to the masses.

Based only on reported rape cases in Haiti, victims' ages have ranged from 5 to 60 years, with the vast majority being less than 18 years old. In several cases, women and girls have endured beatings and stabbings followed by gang rape. The assailants typically used physical force, knives, guns, or physical strength, especially in cases where multiple participants are involved in the attack. Psychological evaluations have been given to some of these rape and sexual assault victims, with results ranging from nightmares and post-traumatic stress disorder to suicidal tendencies. The physical effects endured by the victims include vaginal infections, human immunodeficiency syndrome/acquired immune deficiency syndrome (HIV/AIDS), and prolonged physical pain.

Similarly, Cambodia has a history of widespread, prolonged, and absolute deprivation, such that even 30 years after the Khmer Rouge regime, the remaining postconflict members of society collectively endure such life-threatening poverty that an estimated quarter of the population have died. Internal and external social conditions have resulted in human trafficking of women and girls in significant numbers. Typically, the vast majority of the affected females are ages 6 through 18 and engage in begging, domestic work, prostitution, or other occupations in the sex industry. Women or girls sold in the sex trade become subject to abuse by their owners.

Refugee and Displacement Settings

In the violence-prone displacement camps of Darfur and refugee camps in Chad, some police officers and fellow male residents have used extortion by coercing women to have sex as the means of exchange for protection. Other areas where women have been victimized by sexual violence in large numbers include camps in Liberia, Sierra Leone, and the Democratic Republic of the Congo, especially in the eastern provinces.

North American slavery from 1619 to 1865 provided a legally sanctioned context and structural incentive for GBV. Slave owners valued young, fertile women for their ability to produce more slaves to meet labor demands and increase revenue through trading slave children to other masters. Slave women were sexually exploited against their will for the gratification of the owner and were forced to reproduce more slaves. Early laws in the American legal system (such as the Virginia Slave Laws of 1662) gave slave status to children whose mothers were slaves even when the children were biologically fathered by white slave owners. A slave was considered to be property rather than a human being; hence, owners had the legal right to beat, mutilate, force-breed, overwork, rape, and whip slaves, including enslaved pregnant women. In 1808, the U.S. Congress banned the importation of slaves. Such legal changes increased the value of those slaves already resident in the United States and led to favorable conditions for massive forced breeding, at the physical and psychological expense of slave women.

Violence Against Men

Sexual violence in the context of war, displacement, or postwar transitional conflict tends to position women as subjects and men as assailants. However, men have not been exempt from victimization. Men have been anally raped and forced at gunpoint to perform fellatio on soldiers and fellow detainees. Such activities have been reported globally in conflicts occurring in China (the Sino-Japanese wars), Burundi, Iraq-Kuwait, Northern Ireland, Turkey, Guatemala, and Argentina, among other countries.

A select group of male slaves with exceptional physical features, such as height or muscle tone, were regarded as "stockmen." Such men were exploited as breeders and were forced against their will to reproduce genetically favorable slaves. In essence, stockmen were coerced into the active role of sexually exploiting slave women. Despite the significant qualitative differences between the sexual exploitation of the male and female slaves, both suffered GBV in uniquely different forms.

Michael D. Royster
Prairie View A&M University

See also Child Exploitation; Human Smuggling; Human Trafficking; Pornography; Sex Slavery; Women and Transnational Crime

Further Readings

Almeida, Paul. *Waves of Protest: Popular Struggle in El Salvador 1925–2005*. Minneapolis: University of Minnesota Press, 2007.

Barstow, Donald G. "Female Genital Mutilation: The Penultimate Gender Abuse." *Child Abuse and Neglect*, v.23/5 (1999).

Busza, Joanna. "Sex Work and Migration: The Dangers of Oversimplification, a Case Study of Vietnamese Women in Cambodia." *Health and Human Rights*, v.7/2 (2004).

Davis, Patricia H. "The Politics of Prosecuting Rape as a War Crime." *The International Lawyer*, v.34/4 (2002).

Fisher, Siobhan K. "Occupation of the Womb: Forced Impregnation as Genocide." *Duke Law Journal*, v.46/1 (1996).

Haffajee, Rebecca L. "Prosecuting Crimes of Rape and Sexual Violence at the ICTR: The Application of Joint Criminal Enterprise Theory." *Harvard Journal of Law and Gender*, v.29 (2006).

Lang, Kanika and Fenella Porter. "Resources on Working on Gender With Marginalised Peoples." *Gender and Development*, v.14/2 (2006).

Lim, Louisa. "Painful Memories for China's Footbinding Survivors." *Listen* (March 19, 2007). http://www.npr.org/templates/story/story.php?storyId=8966942 (Accessed January 2012).

Mackie, Gerry. "Ending Footbinding and Infibulation: A Convention Account." *American Sociological Review*, v.61/6 (1996).

MacKinnon, Catharine A. "Sex and Violence: A Perspective." In *Feminism Unmodified*. Cambridge, MA: Harvard University Press, 1987.

Madrigal, Larry J. and Walberto V. Tejeda. "Facing Gender-Based Violence in El Salvador: Contributions From the Social Psychology of Ignacio Martin-Baro." *Feminism and Psychology*, v.19/3 (2009).

Mohanty, Chandra Talpade. "Under Western Eyes: Feminist Scholarship and Colonial Discourses." *Feminist Review*, v.30 (Autumn 1988).

Parrot, Andrea. *Forsaken Females: The Global Brutalization of Women*. Lanham, MD: Rowman & Littlefield, 2006.

Roberts, Dorothy. *Killing the Black Body: Race, Reproduction, and the Meaning of Liberty*. New York: Vintage, 1997.

Sivakumaran, Sandesh. "Sexual Violence Against Men in Armed Conflict." *The European Journal of International Law*, v.18/2 (2007).

Terry, Geraldine and Joanna Hoare. *Gender-Based Violence*. Oxford: Oxfam Publishing, 2007.

GENOCIDE

For individual persons, in the context of criminal behavior, murder is considered the worst possible crime in those criminal justice systems that rank human life as having the most important value. In conjunction with this belief, genocide is probably the most heinous crime recognized by the civilized nations of the world, as it involves the mass murder of people for no legitimate reason. However, defining genocide is not simple. Indeed, there are many different definitions of genocide.

One aspect almost all definitions of genocide have in common is that the genocidal efforts are usually directed against one or more specific, identifiable groups of people. The United Nations (UN) Convention on the Prevention and Punishment of Genocide provides a definition of genocide as any of the following acts committed with intent to destroy, in whole or in part, a national, ethnic, racial, or religious group:

- Killing members of the group
- Causing serious bodily or mental harm to members of the group
- Deliberately inflicting on the group conditions of life calculated to bring about its physical destruction in whole or in part
- Imposing measures intended to prevent births within the group
- Forcibly transferring children of the group to another group

This convention was signed in 1948 and marked the first time in history that the crime of genocide was defined.

The date of the signing of the UN Convention on the Prevention and Punishment of Genocide is important. World War II had just ended in 1945. It was in World War II that probably the most horrible example witnessed by human history of genocide occurred: the Holocaust. As every schoolchild learns, the Holocaust was the systematic extermination by Germany's National Socialist (Nazi) regime of the Jewish people. More than six million Jews in Europe were killed by the Nazi regime until its defeat in 1945. However, it must be realized that the Nazis were not only interested in exterminating Jews; they also sought to eliminate many other

Skulls of victims of the Rwandan genocide can be seen at the Rwanda Genocide Memorial. The Rwandan military and Hutu militia groups killed between 500,000 and 1 million people of the minority Tutsi people, with the intent of destroying the ethnic group. (Photos.com)

classes of people the Nazis considered inferior or undesirable: homosexuals, people with disabilities, religious groups, and people with opposing political beliefs. Thus, many millions more people were slain by the Nazis. In the aftermath of World War II, the nations of the world formed the UN and enacted the UN Convention on the Prevention and Punishment of Genocide so that, at least in theory, recurrence of such genocide could be prevented.

The Convention limits genocide to national, ethnic, racial, and religious groups. Interestingly, however, it does not prohibit genocide based on political beliefs. The reason for this omission is that during the writing of the convention, the Soviet Union and several other nations objected to a prohibition of extermination of people based on political beliefs.

History of Genocide

Genocide, unfortunately, has a long and infamous reign in the history of humankind. Accurate historical records of genocide in ancient history simply do not exist, except as vague references to numerous episodes. However, modern history provides a horrifying litany of genocides, and some of them are briefly discussed below to demonstrate the prevalence of the phenomenon. It is depressing to note that such a universally condemned crime is so often repeated in human history.

One of the first genocides that is well established in history is a religious crusade. In the early part of the 13th century, the Catholic Church mounted the Albigensian or Cathar Crusade against the Cathars of southern France. The Cathars preached a doctrine of peace the held that the physical world was evil and that there were two gods, one good and one evil. The Catholic Church instituted a crusade and an inquisition to eliminate the heresy. It is estimated that more than 1 million people were slain.

In America, the treatment of the Native Americans since the landing of Christopher Columbus in 1492 is considered by many to constitute genocide, although some authorities argue that the decimation of the Native Americans was not an intentional, planned campaign and thus does not fall within the scope of a true genocide. However, the results are indisputable: Millions of Native Americans were exterminated by Europeans entering the Americas, both through military slaughter and by transfer of diseases, such as smallpox, against which the indigenous peoples had no immunity.

During World War I, the Turks of the Ottoman Empire engaged in the genocide of the Assyrian people. It is estimated that 750,000 Assyrians were killed or deported. During and after World War I, the Turks of the Ottoman Empire engaged in the genocide of the Greek people. It is estimated that several hundred thousand Greeks died. Also during World War I, the Turks of the Ottoman Empire engaged in the genocide of the Armenian people. It is estimated that approximately one and a half million Armenians were slaughtered or deported. The Turkish government denies that these historical events constitute genocide.

After World War I, the Bolsheviks, during the Russian Civil War, engaged in the genocide of approximately half a million Cossacks. Although it can be argued that it was a political act, the Cossacks were an identifiable ethnic group, so genocide would apply.

During 1932–33, the Soviet Union engaged in the confiscation of the entire harvest in Ukraine, which resulted in the deaths of more than 10 million people in the Soviet Union, 7 million of them in Ukraine. Many authorities considered this intentional act by the Soviet Union to constitute genocide, and in fact on January 13, 2010, a Ukrainian court found that Soviet premier Joseph Stalin and his supporters in this event were guilty of genocide.

In the late 1930s, in Turkish Kurdistan, the Turks engaged in the genocide of approximately 65,000 to 70,000 Kurds. The Turkish government denies this historical event was genocide.

The most famous genocide in modern history was the attempt by Nazi regime in Germany to eradicate the Jewish population prior to and during World War II. The war ended with Germany's defeat in 1945. By then, more than 6 million Jews had perished through persecution, starvation, and outright extermination in concentration camps across Germany and German-held territory. Many Nazi leaders were convicted of war crimes in connection with their treatment of the Jews.

In 1947, Pakistan separated from India to form a sovereign nation. Pakistan was primarily Islamic and India was primarily Hindu. Massive violence occurred before and after the creation of the Pakistani state. Unfortunately, millions of Hindus, Muslims, and Sikhs were massacred depending upon on which side of the border they resided at the time of the partition. As the slaughter was based on the religion of the people, genocide applies to this historic event.

During the 1960s in Africa, Nigeria enforced a policy of starvation in certain regions, which ultimately resulted in the declaration of independence of the nation of Biafra. Nearly 1 million people are estimated to have died as a result of this event.

Also in Africa, the nation of Burundi obtained its independence in 1962. In 1972, Burundi's Hutu people were subject to genocide by the Tutsis; in 1993, the Tutsis suffered genocide at the hands of the Hutus.

In the late 1970s, in the nation of Cambodia, the political group known as the Khmer Rouge engaged in genocide that resulted in the deaths of more than 1.5 million people. Cambodian society was essentially destroyed by this historical event.

In the 1990s, after the breakup of the former Yugoslavia into several smaller nations, numerous acts of genocide were committed involving nations such as Bosnia and Serbia. A special tribunal was established by the UN in The Hague to prosecute the people responsible for the genocide.

In 1994, the genocides of Rwanda occurred involving the Hutu and Tutsi peoples. More than 800,000 people were slain. As noted above, other incidents of genocide had occurred between the Hutus and the Tutsis. The genocide was so horrific that the UN established a special tribunal to prosecute the persons responsible for the genocides.

The foregoing list of modern examples of genocide is incomplete, representing only a brief review to demonstrate that genocide occurs in all cultures, religions, and political systems.

Causes of Genocide

There are several theories of the causes of genocide. One theory, presented by Leo Kuper, lists five reasons: (1) the need for a scapegoat on which to blame economic or social troubles (which is how the Nazi regime rose in Germany prior to and during World War II), (2) the need to advance colonial interests (as happened in colonial America), (3) the need to justify political positions or policies (as the Soviet Union did during the Great Famine), (4) the need to justify government actions on biological grounds (again, as Nazi Germany did), and (5) the need to advance political or belligerent actions on religious grounds (as the Catholic Church did during the Cathar and other Crusades). Although these reasons might explain why genocide occurs, they can never justify it.

Genocide is firmly established in international law as a crime. There are a number of examples of genocide being prosecuted by special tribunals, usually established by the UN. Despite the universal acceptance of the categorization of genocide as a serious crime, it still occurs.

Wm. C. Plouffe Jr.
Independent Scholar

See also Conventions, Agreements, and Regulations; Crimes Against Humanity; Deportation; War Crimes; War Crimes Tribunals

Further Readings

Chalk, Frank and Kurt Jonassohn. *History and Sociology of Genocide.* New Haven, CT: Yale University Press, 1990.

Gellately, Robert and Ben Kiernan. *The Specter of Genocide: Mass Murder in Historical Perspective.* New York: Cambridge University Press, 2003.

Horowitz, Irvin Louis. *Genocide: State Power and Mass Murder.* New Brunswick, NJ: Transaction, 1970.

Kuper, Leo. *Genocide: Its Political Use in the 20th Century.* New York: Penguin, 1981.

Staub, Ervin. *The Roots of Evil: The Origins of Genocide and Other Group Violence.* New York: Cambridge University Press, 1992.

GLOBALIZATION

Globalization refers to the interdependence of countries, illustrated in transactions of goods, services, and technology. Economic globalization has grown at a fast pace, creating openness in communication and trade. Globalization is also illustrated in the increasing mobility of both goods and people traveling between countries, and, as a result, transnational crime is both a new and growing form of crime.

For centuries, smugglers and pirates have sought to undermine local law enforcement, but globalization means that criminal activity is no longer primarily a local phenomenon. To facilitate both trade and travel, boundaries between nation-states have become less rigid, and even when a criminal group is based predominantly in one country, the criminals' reach can be extended to an international level. Transnational crime arguably has grown more quickly than transnational law enforcement, because the growth of economic globalization has outstripped formal governance arrangements—that is, markets have expanded without controls keeping pace. Reflecting this market globalization, the complexity of criminal activity across states, nations, and continents makes it difficult for local investigative and criminal justice processes to coordinate and have ownership.

In this entry, we will look at the effects of globalization in the growth of transnational crime but also what organized crime groups are as well as typical forms of transnational criminal activity. The entry explores this topic first through broad themes and then points to specific illustrations in order to expose the distinctive elements that define what we know as transnational crime.

Given such a broad topic, one way of beginning is with the United Nations' (UN's) 2010 identification of serious transnational criminal markets. The UN highlighted drug cartels in Central America and West Africa; slavery in eastern Europe and Southeast Asia; cybercrime threatening security infrastructures globally; counterfeit goods undermining legitimate trade; and money laundering, which corrupts trusted banking processes. These examples illustrate that transnational crime is not only highly complex but also, perhaps more significantly, one of the fastest-growing and most profitable global economies.

Although types of transnational crime are fluid and adaptive, key trends are identifiable. First, transnational crime is market-driven and hence undergoes constant entrepreneurial development. Understanding the criminal markets reveals both the motivations for and operations of both serious and organized crime. In many ways, criminals first assess potential markets, and it therefore follows that, in order to understand their activity and motivations, researchers need to understand their markets as well. In a crude sense, a general rule is that transnational crime is motivated by profit.

The distinct trends within the markets can be explored in various ways: for example, by looking at geographic patterns, crime type portfolios, and varying market types. In Europe, specific trends have been identified in the use of money laundering, violence, and corruption linked to loan-sharking, gambling, and drug dealing. Recent patterns have emerged wherein migrant smuggling is occurring from eastern to western Europe, particularly involving the Roma people. The exploitation of vulnerable groups, desperate for improved living conditions, often creates invisible victims who are reluctant to seek the help of law enforcement if they are criminally exploited.

Another type of market is in commodity provision, including the selling of firearms. Firearms trafficking can be linked to two markets: for criminal and political use. Weapons from North America to Mexico tend to be for criminal gang use, whereas eastern European markets supplying weapons to Africa are more predominantly for political insurgencies.

Drug markets are different from firearms markets. Whereas firearms are durable and can be used repeatedly, even though they might need to be replaced or refreshed as a result of new technology, drugs are consumed and require a constant source of replenishment. Drug markets vary as well, having a number of submarkets. Heroin, for example, comes primarily from Afghanistan, which supplies Europe. Cocaine stems mainly from South America and finds markets in North America and Europe.

Another category of a market-driven crime is cybercrime. Cybercrime is perhaps the most truly global type of transnational crime. A complex topic in itself, cybercrime includes hacking into data systems, phishing (fraud), the dissemination of illegal images (such as child pornography), and the distribution of counterfeit products that undermine copyrights. A prevalent and growing form of cybercrime fraud is identity theft.

A significant tool in the cybercriminal's arsenal is malware, software that is installed on the computers of unwitting users through their access to the Internet; these programs secretly steal the user's private information by allowing a cybercriminal to undermine the victim's security protection. The *Symantec Global Internet Security Threat Report* of 2008 found that credit card information was the largest criminal market within the category of cyberfraud. Cybercrime identity theft alone is estimated to be worth $1 billion annually. Cybercrime exploits market opportunities where there is a lack of global legal governance. In addition to identity theft, pornography is another market arena exploited by cybercriminals. The network to distribute and sell pornography represents a form of "desire" market akin to virtual human trafficking. The Canadian Centre for Child Protection in 2009 found that commercial child pornography Websites were having their greatest impact in the United Kingdom, Spain, Germany, and the United States. Much of the frustration of law enforcement with fighting such cybercrimes concerns legal jurisdiction restrictions. A Web host in one country may be able to have a global reach without any local legal accountability.

These various examples of global markets for criminally trafficked goods and services demonstrate the need for law enforcement that extends beyond local or even national jurisdictions. As a result, law enforcement has adapted to the growing complexity of transnational crime by challenging its own previously localized boundaries.

Various international enforcement agencies do exist, including Europol (formally known as the European Police Office) and the International Criminal Police Organization (Interpol), that seek to investigate transnational crime specifically. Europol, for example, acts as a European clearinghouse for intelligence exchange, operational intelligence analysis, and support for transnational operations from member states of the European Union (EU). Within law enforcement, much expertise has been developed in the counterterrorism effort. Europol, although founded in 1999, was not adopted by all EU member states until after the terrorist attacks of September 11, 2001 (9/11). This event gave impetus to a political will to facilitate information exchange and apply counterterrorist techniques to international crime fighting generally.

A network of liaison officers helps the flow of intelligence and links with North American support for extradition agreements and joint investigation teams. This development, again following 9/11, effectively created an EU-USA criminal justice relationship.

Judicial cooperation is important to prosecute transnational crime effectively. In Europe, a judicial network was established in 1998 to spread mutual assistance across states. The creation of EuroJust, designed to work in parallel with Europol, recognized the need to harmonize sanctions and judicial decision making. Again, the events of 9/11 accelerated these developments by providing a universal mandate for states to cooperate to meet an international need.

In summary, it is clear that globalization has created market opportunities for transnational crime. In turn, law enforcement has also changed in order to adapt to these new developments and react to transnational criminals. Although transnational organized crime trends have variations, their fluidity is underpinned by universal, profit-driven market forces, and their sustainability is ensured by organized crime structures. Coincidentally, arrangements for policing and judicial cooperation have improved significantly following the impetus created by the events of 9/11. For the future, combating transnational crime will require greater sophistication and the strategic development of transnational law enforcement and crime prevention methods, organizations, and instruments. It can be argued that these developments may become part of a widening global cooperation, diplomacy, and governance that might one day lead to a world state.

John Coxhead
University of Derby

See also Communication Technologies; Criminal Associations; Extradition; Impact of Transnational Crime; Influence and Position; International Criminal Court; International Monetary Fund; Interpol; Networks; Policing: Transnational; Terrorism Versus Transnational Crime; Transnational Crime: Research Centers; United Nations; World Bank; World Court

Further Readings

Andreas, Peter and Ethan Nadelmann. *Policing the Globe: Criminalisation and Crime Control in International Relations.* New York: Oxford University Press, 2006.

Beare, Margaret. "Structures, Strategies and Tactics of Transnational Criminal Organisations." Transnational Crime Conference, AIC, March 9–10, 2000.

Bruinsma, Gerben and Wim Bernasco. "Criminal Groups and Transnational Illegal Markets." *Crime, Law and Social Change*, v.41 (2004).

Edwards, Adam and Peter Gill. "Crime as Enterprise? The Case of 'Transnational Organized Crime.'" *Crime, Law and Social Change*, v.37 (2002).

Godson, Roy and Oliver Williams. "Strengthening Cooperation Against Transnational Crime." *Survival*, v.40/3 (1998).

Grabosky, Peter. "Crime in Cyberspace." In *Combating Transnational Crime*, Phil Williams and Dimitri Vlassis, eds. London: Frank Cass, 2001.

Lewis, Chris. "International Structures and Transnational Crime." In *Handbook of Criminal Investigation*, Tim Newburn et al., eds. Devon, UK: Willan, 2007.

Sheptycki, James. "Global Law Enforcement as a Protection Racket: Some Sceptical Notes on Transnational Organised Crime as an Object of Global Governance." In *Transnational Organised Crime: Perspectives on Global Security*, Adam Edwards and Peter Gill, eds. New York: Routledge, 2006.

Urbas, Gregor et al. *The Worldwide Fight Against Transnational Organised Crime: Australia.* Canberra: Australian Institute of Criminology, 2004.

GOVERNMENT REPORTS

Transnational crime occurs when criminal activity begins in one nation and crosses one or more national boundaries. Alternative forms of transnational crime consist of criminal activity with agents in multiple countries working in collusion. Direct human victimization includes: slave trade, illegal sweatshop laborers, kidnapping for ransoms, and human trafficking. Transnational environmental crimes include: wildlife trafficking, unauthorized hazardous waste dumping, trading illegal biohazards, and smuggling illegal timber and precious metals. Transnational monetary crimes include: sea piracy, drug trafficking, smuggling unauthorized medicines, money laundering, and bribery. High geographical dispersion of organized crime contributes to the difficulty in identifying informants and collecting reliable data. Great geographic distances between the national borders of the criminal activity require governmental reporting of such crimes, which frequently relies on biased secondary data in lieu of primary sources. Reporting faces further challenges when great geographical distances exist between the national borders in which the criminal activity occurs, because increased investigative sophistication and financial resources become essential.

By fusing sensationalism with facts, media have the power to manipulate emotions, resulting in crises construction. In the case of transnational drug-related organized crime, the press has vested professional interest in appealing to fear and panic in order to sell their narratives. However, the frequency in exaggerating accounts presented as factual and unbiased empowers skepticism and an overall distrust for reports, regardless of their authenticity and credibility. Consequently, transnational organized crime reports covering a range of mass offenses from smuggling narcotics to human trafficking become regarded as less frivolous. Such offenses pose an international security threat.

Ethnocentricity plays a significant role in Western international criminal reporting, because propaganda associates the Third World with drug trade, while North America receives a more favorable narrative. The ideology produced by such narratives lies at the heart of border control legislation. For example, the International Committee of the Red Cross (ICRC) reported to the U.S. government their inspection team's findings of detainee abuse at Guantanamo Bay in Cuba. The ICRC account indicated the U.S. interrogation methods as "tantamount to torture." A Department of Defense spokesperson denied such claims.

Drug-Related International Crime

In 1997, the United Nations International Drug Control Program reported an estimate of $400 billion as the annual profit from the global narcotics trading industry. Alan Dupont, director of the Asia-Pacific Security Program, highlighted that the estimate lacked reliability due to the nature of such underground industries. First, the narcotics industry consists of a complex bureaucracy with multiple levels of distribution, wholesale, retail, secondary retail, and beyond before the products reach the consumer. Second, the global economy has caused commodities such as regional supplies of crude oil to become part of a common market; however, such estimates inaccurately assume that

the narcotics market functions similarly. Certain regions of the world, primarily Latin America and East Asia, receive a disproportionate amount of attention when monitoring the drug trade, which helps less-suspected drug trafficking centers to avoid detection. Finally, the industry thrives on evading disclosure.

With the Golden Triangle of Thailand, Burma, and Laos having the reputation as the world's leading heroin producers, a flawed local law enforcement and banking system compounded with national corruption have functioned as contributing factors for Asian organized crime since the cold war. Since the 1949 Chinese Revolution, narcotic consumption has been relatively low. However, during the 1990s and early 2000s, China emerged as a new target market for heroin consumption, due to a surge in addictions correlated to the geographical proximity of its production.

During the 1990s, the African drug industry rapidly emerged as a significant contributor to the global market. However, Chris Allen acknowledges the flaws in the primary sources regarding reports on Africa and the international drug trade. Police reports lack reliability because of political instability and corruption. The press and non-officials face difficulty in obtaining such reports. The underreporting of African drug trafficking prevailed due to enforcement agencies focused on Europe and the United States as "consumer countries."

Corruption

According to the U.S. Drug Enforcement Administration (DEA), foreign government corruption ranks as the primary means of obstruction to curtailing international drug trafficking. DEA agents in Latin American and Caribbean countries rely on diplomacy and significant political leverage to navigate between the relative permissiveness in terms of foreign drug enforcement institutions and demands resulting from high consumption in the United States. Data from interviews conducted by the United States DEA reveal that the U.S. demand for psychoactive drugs exceeds the ability of international drug enforcements and the U.S. government's ability to seize control of drug trafficking and the industry as a whole. Because the United States DEA has been commissioned to make high-security charges and has been entrusted with sensitive information, it faces an increased risk of appearing to be in collusion with corrupt foreign government officials. The interviews also expose the source of corruption during the 1990s in countries such as El Salvador, Guatemala, Peru, and Columbia as attributed to limited power from the executive level. Furthermore, Panama's and Paraguay's powerful leaders lacked interest in direct intervention or cooperative investigation.

Economic decline and the destabilization of central government add a significant amount of corruption. Such combined factors affect the state's capacity to enforce existing laws and regulate legitimate business and civic activity with the intent to prevent cross-border crime. On a national level, diminished fiscal resources leave fewer funds for the military, multiple levels of law enforcement, and border security. Bank deregulation creates conditions favorable for money laundering to occur without restraint.

The Observatoire Geopolitique Report des Drogues (OGD) contains a series of left-leaning accounts regarding the relationship between African governments and drug enforcement actions apart from public policy. A 1998 OGD report portrays Gambian government officials as protecting the interests of the elite at the expense of petty criminals and the masses of the extremely impoverished. The report's tone portrays the police as following a conservative posture of appearing "tough on drugs" by destroying cannabis fields, and mass arrest of the petty users and growers. The report further exposes how major cannabis growers and distributors successfully escaped retribution through bribery. Furthermore, the OGD report sympathizes with the impoverished masses on the island of Djinack, who depend on marijuana cultivation for their minimal economic sustenance. A 1999 OGD report references Kenya as free of money-laundering laws as a means for creating a favorable business climate. The report entails a public announcement that international money-launderers have a "safe haven" for investing. Nevertheless, revenues from such investments tend not to benefit the non-elite natives.

Human Trafficking

Adolescent girls and young women serve as targets for human trafficking in the U.S.-Mexican borderlands. However, women in general, regardless of age, face a degree of vulnerability. In such cases, smugglers would appeal to their desperation due to poverty and use deception followed by coercion into the underground economy of prostitution. In one case in San Antonio, Texas, federal courts revealed that five years of prostitution functioned as a form of smuggling-fee debt payment. Death threats deterred the victims from attempting to escape. According to U.S. Justice Department records, between 2001 and 2005, approximately 100 human trafficking cases per year have been examined by federal prosecutors. Such offenses primarily include varying degrees of forced labor, child sex slaves, and childhood prostitution.

Effective on October 1, 2007, the U.S. Department of Defense incorporated Article 120 of the Uniform Code of Military Justice in order to make "patronizing prostitutes" a military offense. The article sought to prevent members of the U.S. military from becoming human trafficking participants in vulnerable areas such as the vicinity of U.S. bases. Arguments surrounding the amendments include safeguarding the U.S. military image and reacting to multiple cases of rape and forced prostitution in the Balkans and South Korea. Ultimately, the amendment aims to prevent collective guilt upon the U.S. military in the case of future offenses.

Michael D. Royster
Prairie View A&M University

See also Drug Trade: Source, Destination, and Transit Countries; Human Trafficking; Intelligence Agencies: Collaboration Within the United States; Money Laundering: Methods

Further Readings

Allen, Chris. "African Drug Trade." *Review of African Political Economy*, v.26/79 (1999).

Contreras, Guillermo. "Details Emerge in Human Trafficking Case in San Antonio." Express-News. www.madebysurvivors.com (Accessed May 2011).

Dupont, Alan. "Transnational Crime, Drugs, and Security in East Asia." *Asian Survey,* v.39/3 (1999).

Jelinek, Pauline. "Anti-Prostitution Rule Drafted for U.S. Forces." *Washington Post* (September 22, 2004).

Lewis, Neil A. "Red Cross Finds Detainee Abuse in Guantanamo." *New York Times* (November 30, 2004).

Mestrovic, Stjepan G. *The Trials of Abu Ghraib: An Expert Witness Account of Shame and Honor.* Boulder, CO: Paradigm Publishers, 2005.

Nadelmann, Ethan A. "The DEA in Latin America: Dealing With Institutionalized Corruption." *Journal of Interamerican Studies and World Affairs,* v.29/4 (1988).

HARMONIZATION

Harmonization refers to attempts to provide uniformity across diverse jurisdictions. The strengths and limitations of harmonization can be ascertained by examining the pitfalls and benefits associated with such trends. Separate jurisdictions frequently have different laws, policies, and law-enforcement practices. Attempts to harmonize laws, regulations, and practices are increasingly evident in countries with federal systems of governance (as in the states and territories of Australia, with their standardized laws, polities, and practices), in regions striving for improved forms of integration (for example, across the member countries of the European Union), and in relation to attempts to create global consensus around issues such as international terrorism, the illicit drug trade, and cybercrime—through, for example, the adoption of common definitions and protocols within the context of United Nations (UN) agencies.

The impetus toward harmonization generally stems from a concern that there is often significant variation in cross-jurisdictional roles, strategies, and practices in relation to specific types of crimes. For transnational crimes such as terrorism, illegal arms trading, and human trafficking, harmonization aims to improve capacity and to ensure that police and other law-enforcement officials are responding in similar fashion across the globe. In a nutshell, harmonization, at the global level, is informed by the observation that criminal networks operate with little concern for boundaries and borders, form relationships necessary to carry out crimes, and have the ability to act fluidly and adapt to external influences, including enforcement activity. By contrast, law-enforcement agencies generally operate strictly within regional or national boundaries, do not communicate effectively with one another, and take years to adapt to developing crime trends both tactically and legislatively.

Harmonization of legislation is viewed as a way of overcoming these types of enforcement limitations. It is also perceived as central to a consistent conceptualization of transnational crime, to effective levels of cooperation among participating states, and to a uniform legal framework. Perceived advantages include reducing complexity, increasing efficiency, and ensuring a consistent approach to particular criminal activities across jurisdictions.

However, several other factors simultaneously need to be acknowledged and addressed as part of the debate over harmonization. For example, there is the criticism that harmonization can, in effect, mean "Americanization" of policing via the dominance of particular models of policing. This criticism generally includes reference to an undue emphasis on paramilitary policing and the dominance of U.S. policy approaches to issues such as drug-law enforcement and the War on Terror. In essence, it is argued that a one-size-fits-all approach seldom works, and where implemented this approach has tended to be skewed to the advantage of particular groups and the exclusion of other possible policy directions.

Other critiques of harmonization include loss of flexibility and disconnection from local conditions, the imposition of an overwhelming and monolithic model (via legislation and standardized approaches), and great variation in the capacity of national police services to adhere to and enforce standards devised elsewhere. Not all countries, for example, have the resources and capacity to enforce uniform legislation; the question then becomes how this might affect implementation nationally and across borders.

Establishment of uniform laws is only one approach to harmonization endeavors. Such a legal approach may be accompanied by disputes over the content of substantive legislation and by difficulties in the administration and complexity of delivery based upon the legislation. Accordingly, at a practical level, a more productive strategy for harmonization is to focus on consistency in accomplishing regulatory and enforcement tasks rather than focusing on uniform legislation as such.

For instance, international networks of law-enforcement officers, such as the International Criminal Police Organization (Interpol) and the International Network of Environmental Enforcement and Compliance, provide invaluable forums for the exchange of information and knowledge transfer about "best practices" and "what works" in given situations. Participation in common training programs and attendance at conferences and workshops provide opportunities to enhance overall law-enforcement capabilities as well as contributing to shared understandings and values in regard to specific types of criminal activity. The use of regional case studies and reference to local experiences both reaffirm the importance of acknowledging specific jurisdictional differences as well as creating opportunities for the adoption of a more balanced view of what constitutes the most productive law-enforcement approaches and strategies.

Rob White
University of Tasmania

See also Conventions, Agreements, and Regulations; Mutual Legal Assistance Treaties

Further Readings

Andreas, P. and E. Nadelmann. *Policing the Globe: Criminalization and Crime Control in International Relations.* Oxford, UK: Oxford University Press, 2006.
Broodman, M. "The Myth of Harmonization of Laws." *The American Journal of Comparative Laws,* v.39/4 (1991).
U.S. Congress, House of Representatives, Standing Committee on Legal and Constitutional Affairs. *Harmonization of Legal Systems: Within Australia and Between Australia and New Zealand.* Canberra: Commonwealth of Australia, 2006.

Heroin

A discussion of the transnational trafficking of heroin should begin with a brief history of its immediate predecessors, particularly its fundamental precursor, opium. Since the late 1700s, the processing, use, and products of the opium poppy have been perceived to pose a transnational drug problem of the highest order. Some states have sought to control its use, while other states and/or criminal groups have tried to force its production on less powerful countries whose market they controlled.

The use of opium as an analgesic in antiquity is firmly established, but it was not commonly used in European and American medicine until the 1800s. It was used in Asia, particularly in China, for a wide variety of purposes but was not regarded as a problematic drug until the 1800s. The British, however, after winning the Opium Wars (1839), forced the Chinese to accept it as a normal import and did not end that trade until 1913. Chinese laborers imported opium smoking to the United States during the late 1840s and it was adopted by American cowboys, prostitutes, underworld denizens, and manual laborers. Opium began to be viewed as part of a growing menace, and newspapers and politicians linked it with the racist "yellow peril" propaganda of the period. Moreover, in the United States, the lack of governmental controls and heavy marketing by both British and American mercantile interests caused its use to mushroom in the mid-1800s. After the Civil War (1861–65), its use was supplanted by one of its products, morphine. This drug, often injected with the newly invented hypodermic syringe, was 10 times stronger than opium. Heavily used by people of all classes in the last part of the 19th century, it was especially popular with soldiers injured in that war. As many as 300,000 Americans were addicted, more than half of them women. These drugs, sometimes dissolved in strong solutions of alcohol and mixed with cocaine, often appeared in patent medicines of that era, which gave opiates in general a patina of respectability. Opiates provided

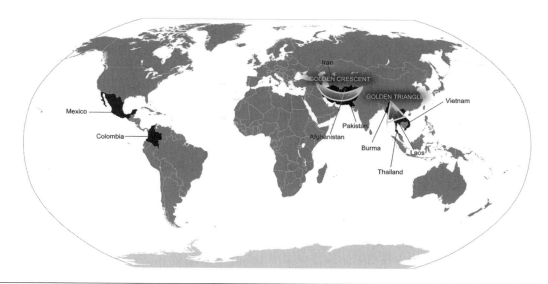

A map details the locations of the world's primary opium/heroin producers. Opium, the root of heroin, has been used since 3400 B.C.E. when it was cultivated in lower Mesopotamia. It was introduced in China by Arab traders in the 5th century and was used in Asia for centuries until the emperor Kia King banned opium trade and poppy cultivation. (Photos.com)

swift relief from pain, trauma, "female problems," and (because of their constipating effects) dysentery, and they were popular in Europe as well. The popular use of opium, in eclipse since the introduction of morphine, declined further with the introduction of heroin, marketed by the Bayer company, in 1898. This drug is three times stronger than morphine, has extremely euphoric effects when compared to other opiates then extant, and has a faster onset of action. Its addicting potential was not immediately recognized, as it was often used in very small dosages, as a substitute for codeine in cough medicine. From 1900 until the implementation of the Harrison Act in the years between 1915 and 1920, heroin, along with its opiate predecessors, was easily obtainable at general stores, at pharmacies, and by mail order (catalogs offered it at minimal cost to the user). Although use of heroin began to grow, it did not supplant morphine as the opiate of choice until the late 1920s. However, its use was viewed as problematic by moral crusaders and legislators.

The 1920s and 1930s

All opiates were put under potentially tight controls by the Harrison Act in 1914. This law required all users to get prescriptions from doctors. During the 1920s, government agents harassed and arrested doctors who prescribed opiates to addicts, and special clinics that were created to help addicts were shuttered by government action. Doctors had to change their philosophy of maintaining addicts on opiates in the face of ongoing government action. U.S. Supreme Court decisions in following years were confusing but had the effect of narrowing the addict's legal avenues for obtaining the drug. Ultimately addicts were forced onto the street into a criminal subculture in order to deal with their addiction. Heroin was a much more efficient way to deal with an ongoing addiction: The amount of the drug needed was smaller, and it was easier to smuggle than were the other opiates. It offered more "bang for the buck," and as a result, recreational and nonmedical use of opium and morphine radically declined.

The criminal element, having grown efficient with the ongoing failed experiment of Prohibition (of alcohol in the United States, 1920–33), was up to the challenge of meeting demand with supply. Many early smugglers diverted supplies by legal subterfuge from legitimate European and American pharmaceutical houses. Other criminal importers in the 1920s were formerly legal merchants who simply maintained their suppliers in Asia, usually Shanghai, and shipped their opiates through seemingly legitimate front companies located in China or Manchuria. Later, Manchuria became an important shipping point for Japanese pharmaceutical companies smuggling opiates into China, where demand remained large, and sometimes into the United States. Other suppliers were Greek nationals located in France, protected by French officials who smuggled Turkish opium through the Balkans into Europe and the United States. In the early 1930s, using a pharmacy in Athens as a cover, Georges Bakladjoglou was able to sell heroin in Europe at prices lower than those in Turkey. Using ships' stewards on Italian liners who carried loads of no more than one kilo on a trip, he was able to smuggle large amounts of heroin into New York City. The couriers picked up the drugs on the ships' Mediterranean stops and delivered them to buyers on board ship in New York harbor. Buyers, who represented Jewish and Italian organized crime syndicates, were responsible for getting the drugs to shore. Undoubtedly bribery of customs officials in both Europe and the United States was employed to aid in this endeavor. Bakladjoglou preferred to deal in cash, although many of his contemporaries were using bank transfers and elaborate codes.

A more common source for addicts in the 1920s and 1930s was street peddlers who had secured their supplies through theft from legitimate U.S. pharmaceutical firms or from Mexican and Canadian drug companies, smuggling these drugs into the United States. The latter source dried up, however, when the Jones-Miller Act of 1922 prohibited drug firms from making questionable shipments to front companies in other countries. Again, organized crime figures in the United States were willing to meet market demands. Closely tied to the Tammany Hall political machine, Arnold Rothstein and Waxey Gordon had previously bootlegged many gallons of alcohol into the country from Canada and Mexico. In the case of heroin, however, they found Europe to be a better source of supply. Through the use of third parties and ocean liners, organized crime groups were able to smuggle in many shipments of opiates and cocaine in the 1920s. Rothstein used many different suppliers and couriers and became the kingpin of New York drug operations. He was murdered, probably at the behest of Legs Diamond, in 1928. The network that he developed continued to operate, however, and it was suggested that federal complicity was involved.

In 1930, the enforcement climate changed with the ascension of hardliner Harry Anslinger to the post of commissioner of the Federal Bureau of Narcotics (FBN). Experienced in diplomacy and with ties to the U.S. State Department, Anslinger created a secret international network of narcotics officers and operatives, referred to as Anslinger's "Briefcase Agents." Some were located in key locations like Shanghai, Prague, and Hong Kong and provided critical intelligence. Agents were able to break huge cases, such as intercepting 20,000 pounds of morphine on the SS *Alesia*, in 1930. Informants were paid large bounties for information leading to such shipments. Anslinger found that tips from insiders led to significant drug seizures, and he was willing to pay the price. The problem was that insiders were generally drug smugglers themselves. This practice of paying criminals to expose other criminals is highly problematic. Some criminals became "professional informants" who might use their clout to exact vengeance on a rival or extort money or drugs from other criminals. Some acted in continuously duplicitous ways, informing on one rival while protecting another. Also, many informants continued their own illegal activities notwithstanding their situational and episodic cooperation with the bureau.

Although the use of such informants was fraught with moral and practical implications, Anslinger was generally careful and successful in his hiring of agents. Both Europe and Asia ceased to be important transshipment points in the early 1930s as a result. In the celebrated *Île de France* case, FBN agents seized more than 600 pounds of morphine on a French ocean liner. The drugs had originated in Turkey and had been packed in Paris, but through carelessness, one of the drug-containing trunks ended up going awry. FBN agents were able to arrest three known large-scale drug traffickers. The smugglers lost $144,000 in drugs, and the chief instigator was sentenced to eight years. This served as an example to other would-be smugglers: smuggle smaller amounts, and avoid American courts. This led to an overall decline in drug shipments from Europe to the United States. Drug labs in the Balkans and France continued to operate, but on a smaller scale, and drug supplies from Asia began to increase.

Organized crime figure Yasha (Jack) Katzenberg shifted operations to Asia and smuggled 650 kilos of opiates into New York City in the late 1930s. His operatives bought heroin from Japanese suppliers, then sent the operatives and drugs to Marseilles, France. From this point they were rerouted to Cherbourg and eventually to New York City.

Customs officials were bribed to let both couriers and drugs enter the country. After reaching the United States, the drugs were sold to wholesalers. Katzenberg's New York contacts were problematic and linked to Lepke Buchalter, a notoriously brutal crime figure who interfered with Katzenberg's management of his network. Ironically, Buchalter's ties to this drug network were to lead to his eventual imprisonment. Katzenberg's ties to organized crime left him impoverished and imprisoned.

The 1940s Through the 1960s

Cuba was a smuggling center of some importance in the 1920s and later, although by the 1940s Mexico had become a production center. One drug cartel of the period was centered in Juarez and openly sold drugs of all kinds to drug tourists from the United States. The head of this operation, a woman, was indicted through the work of Anslinger and but never extradited for trial in the United States. Her apparent bribery of Mexican officials had proved very productive. She was sentenced to a token term in a Mexican prison in the early 1940s. However, Latin American states were not anxious to surrender their nationals to North American justice. This still remains the case.

Organized crime luminary Lucky Luciano was continually cited as a drug kingpin by Anslinger, though this is discounted by experts today. It is thought that Anslinger needed a "villain" to parade before Congress in order to obtain funding. The flow of opiates into the United States had shrunk to extremely low levels, but the official line was that organized crime, dominated by a few kingpins like Luciano, was part of a vast conspiracy. Opiates were in short supply well into the late 1940s, even in New York City. It was only in the 1960s that the heroin trade, boosted by the revolution in drug use, began to flourish. Today there are four main areas of production.

Today's Heroin Centers

Most heroin in the southwestern United States is black tar heroin from Mexico. Available evidence suggests that its quality has increased while acreage devoted to its cultivation has slightly decreased. Most producers are small farmers who have standing arrangements with larger organizations. The raw opium gum is carried by a middleman to a processing facility, usually a small warehouse in a isolated area or neighborhood, where it is transformed into heroin. This is centered in the Guadalajara area and controlled by one family, the Herreras. The finished product is smuggled into the United States by plane, truck, and private vehicle. It is sometimes transported on foot on the bodies of illegal aliens as they cross the border. From the crossing points, this particular drug is transported throughout California and the southwestern United States, but it is also found in urban areas with large Mexican populations such as Atlanta and Chicago.

Colombia is also a supplier of heroin to American markets. In fact, the Drug Enforcement Administration claims that 80 percent of heroin in the United States is grown in Colombia. Coming from fields high in the Andes Mountains and grown by small farmers, much of the opium is controlled by groups of right- or left-wing terrorists. Some of these groups receive most of their operating expenses from "taxes" that they levy on opium farmers. The heroin is refined locally, and much of it is smuggled by air by passengers on commercial lines. Sometimes Colombian heroin is transported through Mexico and brought to the United States through Mexican networks. Once in the United States, it is often transported and sold by Dominican nationals who operate large heroin networks in the northeastern cities. At this point it may be sold to urban gangs, who often deal in cocaine as well. It is usually of high quality.

The Golden Crescent of Pakistan, Afghanistan, Iran, and Turkey has been a region of opium cultivation since antiquity. It is thought that Afghanistan alone accounts for more than 90 percent of the world's supply of heroin. As in Colombia, it is a major source of income for terrorists and private armies. Although banned, in the absence of an effective state it is grown with impunity. Efforts by Afghan and American authorities to ban it or to get farmers to substitute other crops for opium have been ineffective because alternative crops do no yield the high return realized from opium. Most Golden Crescent opium is destined for Europe, where it is marketed by Russian and Italian organized crime groups. There is significant local addiction to crude products of opium in the urban areas of these opium-producing countries, as well.

The Golden Triangle of Southeast Asia is the other major heroin-producing center. During the era of the Vietnam War in the 1960s and early 1970s, heroin from Vietnam, Laos, Burma (Myanmar), and Laos was perceived as a major threat to U.S. servicemen. The drug was sometimes smuggled by service personnel into the United States, but more commonly it was sent by ship to the West Coast and Canada. Much of this heroin ended up in the cities of the Midwest and eastern United States. Most of the contemporary trafficking of this drug is conducted by Asian crime networks called triads or tongs. Some of these organizations have existed since the 1700s and have been in the United States since the 1840s. Infiltrating and dismantling them is extremely difficult.

Rationale for Heroin Production

Although heroin has a high potential for abuse, overdose, addiction, and the spreading of disease (through shared paraphernalia such as needles), many people throughout the world grow the opium poppy and process, transport, and market the finished product, heroin. There are three chief reasons for the continuing commerce in the drug. Primarily, the drug has a huge profit margin that is irresistible to poverty-stricken farmers throughout the world. The production of this drug far outstrips other crops in terms of profitability. That is why substitution efforts have failed and will continue to fail. Second, in the absence of an effective state, rebellious and terrorist groups will use drugs as a source of revenue. Third, in Asia, at least, these plants have been grown from antiquity and no opprobrium is attached to growing or selling them. Drug smugglers and marketers, of course, rely more on the first two rationales, but tradition plays a part there, as well, as some may come from organized crime families who have long been involved in the distribution of drugs.

Dealing With Profits

Money laundering—that is, dealing with the profits of illegal enterprises to make their origin invisible to authorities—involves two primary parties, the trafficker and the person who launders the money. Both expect to get something of value from the transaction. Illegal profits are often "cleaned" through the creation and activities of a "front" corporation. A front can be either a phony or a legitimate company or activity that functions, in this case, to launder profits. For instance, a small-time distributor might set up a pawnshop or restaurant in order to clean his money. Money could be deposited in the account of that business in order to be used. Money can be laundered through informal networks that are based on ethnicity or even religious affiliation. Buying and selling real estate is another means of moving illegal gains from point A to point B. Finally, drug traffickers frequently use banks in countries that allow questionable transactions to take place. So-called offshore banks in the Caribbean and Switzerland were once favorite laundering locales of drug traffickers' ill-gotten gains. More comprehensive banking legislation and airport security have made these laundering methods increasingly problematic, and American drug traffickers are increasingly forced to launder their loot closer to home. Federal and local agencies have also seized goods bought with illegal profits. Items such as boats, homes, cars, and stocks and bonds have fattened the coffers of law enforcement, giving them an added incentive to deal with drug-trafficking cases. Agencies have the obligation to prove that the assets seized derive from illicit sources.

Francis Frederick Hawley
Western Carolina University

See also Antiterrorist Financing; Criminal Forfeiture and Seizure; Money Laundering: History; Money Laundering: Methods; Money Laundering: Targeting Criminal Proceeds; Money Laundering: Vulnerable Commodities and Services; Southeast Asia

Further Readings

Goode, E. *Drugs in American Society.* Boston: McGraw-Hill, 2008.

Inciardi, J. *The War on Drugs IV.* Boston: Allyn & Bacon, 2008.

Levinthal, C. *Drugs, Society and Criminal Justice.* Boston: Pearson, 2008.

Mares, D. *Drug Wars and Coffeehouses: The Political Economy of the International Drug Trade.* Washington, DC: CQ Press, 2006.

Meyer, K. and T. Parssinen. *Webs of Smoke: Smugglers, Warlords, Spies and the History of the International Drug Trade.* Lanham, MD: Rowman & Littlefield, 1998.

Musto, D. *The American Disease: Origins of Narcotic Control,* 3rd ed. New York: Oxford University Press, 1999.

Nadelmann, Ethan Avram. *Cops Across Borders: The Internationalization of U.S. Criminal Law Enforcement.* University Park: Pennsylvania State University Press, 1993.

HUMAN SMUGGLING

Human smuggling refers to the illegal transport of people across national boundaries. It includes both bringing migrants into a nation in a manner that deliberately violates immigration laws and harboring persons already living in a country and doing so for financial or other material gain. Human smuggling is a pervasive criminal activity that occurs around the globe and undermines national, state, municipal, and community economic stability. It is a human rights issue, as many people die or are injured as a result of the transport process. Women and girls especially suffer because of their vulnerability at the hands of smugglers. While exact numbers cannot be obtained given the clandestine nature of the activity, some information can be obtained by analyzing the smuggling activity in the various nations in the world and the migration routes used.

The migration of people is an age-old phenomenon, but recent factors involving globalization have resulted in the "pushes" that drive people from economic instability and other crisis conditions and the "pulls" that offer the potential for a better life in more accommodating financial markets. Because of the increasing economic decline in many nations, the pushes are more pronounced, and because of improvements in media communication, the pulls make people in poorer nations more aware that migration through smuggling could mean an improved standard of living.

People cross borders from less developed areas, such as South America, Asia, Africa, and eastern Europe, into the more economically stable locales of North America, western Europe, and Australia with the assistance of entrepreneurs who reap the profits from helping the migrants gain safe passage to their destinations. These smugglers have been more in demand in recent years as a result of tighter restrictions on immigration. The conditions encountered by the migrants is often inhumane, as they are crowded into trucks or boats or other forms of transportation and are exposed to accidents on the trip—accidents that are not infrequent and that often involve fatalities or injuries. In addition, migrants often are exploited by the smugglers through forced labor or other means when they arrive at their destinations; the correct term for this is *trafficking* and often results from the smuggling process.

The relationship between human smuggling and trafficking in humans is often ambiguous, and an academic analysis of the definitional differences came about only in the scholarly literature in the late 1990s. The terms were often used interchangeably into the early part of the next decade, generating further confusion in quantitative and qualitative analyses and academic discourse. The United Nations Office on Drugs and Crime (UNODC) outlined the differences between the two in three separate categories—the source of profit, transnational issues, and victimization. The source of profit for human smuggling is produced from the migrants entering the host area; the profit for traffickers is generated through the activities for which trafficking victims are exploited—such as forced labor, prostitution, forced marriage, and pornography—after they have arrived at the new location. Human smuggling is always transnational in character, as there is an illegal passage from one country into another; human trafficking often involves crossing of a person illegally into another country, but this is not always the case. Whereas smuggling does not always involve victimization, as smuggled migrants normally consent to the transport and are at least generally aware of the reasons for the smuggling (victimization may occur during the transport but this is not a defining feature), human trafficking always involves victimization, which is evident in the fact that it always involves some degree of exploitation—including inhumane treatment involving force, coercion, and violence or the threat of violence—for profit. In addition, people trafficked are considered victims and therefore are able to obtain financial remedies and legal protections from governments, whereas those smuggled cannot.

Three theories have provided insight into a better understanding of human smuggling: the migration business theory, the security threat theory, and the network theory. Each of these offers explanations of the phenomenon of smuggling. First, smugglers often adopt a business approach to their activity and are often perceived as entrepreneurs in global migration; the migrants are seen as the product of the business. The "smuggling business" is certainly a form of organized transnational crime, and there are three stages to the migration business theory: the recruitment of those to be smuggled, the transport of these people to the host nation, and their integration into the labor markets of their destination.

The second theoretical perspective views human smuggling as a transnational criminal endeavor similar to other types of organized crime and has been termed the security threat theory. Smuggling is seen as a highly structured, stringently controlled and organized hierarchal network of actors with specific roles whose primary focus is the illegal transport of persons across borders. The actions in these syndicates include those who recruit the smuggled people, those who provide the transportation, those who network behind the scenes to maintain lines of communication for smuggling, those who actually specialize in the specific criminal actions such as money laundering, and those who provide financing for the enterprise. This perspective focuses on the security threat that evolves from the criminal venture, such as the drug cartel and criminal gang connections that often accompany the migrant smuggling activities along the U.S.-Mexican border.

In addition to the strictly commercial model of smuggling, the activity can also be seen as a family business as described by what is known as the network theory of human migration. In this perspective, the people who are smuggled are willing and actively engaged in the process and are making a conscious effort to better their lives through the illegal migration. The migrants use family connections to facilitate the process; therefore, family networks are the primary focus of this view. Though large criminal enterprises exist in the smuggling process, there are also smaller "mom-and-pop" operations that illustrate that the relationship between the smuggler and the smuggled is often based on social, rather than strictly financial, capital. Assistance from extended family and friends is often enlisted to find and integrate migrants into their host communities and labor markets.

In addition to these three theoretical models of human smuggling, three other models of smuggling have been suggested that examine the means utilized by smugglers to assist migrants in crossing borders illegally: ad hoc services, smuggling through the use of fraudulent documentation, and preorganized state-to-state activity. The ad hoc type, which is not preorganized, is often employed by those in eastern Europe; the migrants travel mostly on their own but use services provided by smugglers primarily to facilitate their crossing of borders, as is found in smuggling operations along the U.S.-Mexican border, the Iranian-Turkish border, and the Slovenian-Italian border. In smuggling by the use of fraudulent documents, which includes the misuse of appropriate travel visas as well as fraudulent visas, a key component is corruption—by the government officials who issue travel documents, by the clerical staff who prepare them, and by the passport officials who allow illegal entry into the host country. The third type involves an organized division of labor involving specific players who facilitate the process either from the target nation (such as migrants joining family members in another area) or from the sending nation (such as migrants leaving impoverished or otherwise crisis conditions in the sending nation); patterns in this third type can be found in migrant smuggling from Asia to western Europe.

In North America, the largest migration into the country flows from the Mexican border into the southern regions of the United States. Canada is somewhat shielded from mass immigration because of both geography and tightened border control measures. The migrants crossing the United States' southern border originate not only from Mexico but also Guatemala, El Salvador, Brazil, and Honduras. Attempts by border control agents to control the flow into the country increased significantly in the 1990s, especially since 1993, because of a number of border enforcement campaigns created when the numbers of immigrants began to increase remarkably. It is estimated that 80 percent of migrants began to enlist the services of professional smugglers. The 1990 Immigration Reform Act and the 1996 Immigrant Responsibility Act applied pressure to Mexico to better control the northern flow of illegal immigrants into the United States, which, despite some success, shows no sign of abating. It is likely that high enforcement at some points along the border simply creates increased flow along the less protected areas. Three different types of smugglers have been identified coming into Texas from parts farther south—the *pateras*, who simply transport migrants into the country with no further involvement after arrival, the *coyotes* who are Mexicans who provide smuggling services to groups in their communities, and the "border commercial smugglers," who operate in business enterprises and who constitute the largest group of the three. There is evidence that the Mexican smugglers are becoming less affiliated with the mom-and-pop smuggling operations and more closely aligned with criminal enterprises, particularly those involving drug cartels, smuggling rings, and U.S.-based gang activity. The use of technological advancements such as advanced weaponry, night vision equipment, and body armor also characterizes the criminal smuggling operations as well as the violence that accompanies these changes.

Although the largest amount of human smuggling in America occurs along the U.S.-Mexican border, migrants are smuggled from other destinations as well. There is an increasing flow of Chinese migrants smuggled into the country, approximately 30,000–40,000 annually, according to government data, although many experts believe the number to be 50,000–100,000. Large ships carry people from China to the West Coast of the United States, and although border control efforts have slowed the flow, these migrants are still being smuggled into the country. Most of the Chinese smuggling operations, called snakeheads, are usually loosely organized groups with familial rather than organized crime connections. Also, groups from the Caribbean are smuggled into the United States from the archipelagoes of the Bahamas, Haiti, Cuba, the Dominican Republic, and others.

Programs to combat human smuggling have been initiated by many international groups, such as UNODC, the International Organization of Migration, and numerous national and regional human rights groups. The International Criminal Police Organization (Interpol), the world's largest policing agency, is actively engaged in the investigation, prevention, and prosecution of human smuggling and illegal immigration. In the United States, Immigration and Customs Enforcement, or ICE, is the primary federal agency responsible for addressing illegal immigration. It often coordinates its resources with U.S. Customs and Border Protection to combat human smuggling.

Leonard A. Steverson
South Georgia College

See also Human Trafficking; Organ Trafficking; Sex Slavery

Further Readings

Bales, K. *Disposable People: New Slavery in the Global Economy*. Berkeley: University of California Press, 1999.

Kyle, David and Rey Koslowski. *Global Human Smuggling: Comparative Perspectives*. Baltimore, MD: Johns Hopkins University Press, 2001.

Mountz, Alison. *Seeking Asylum: Human Smuggling and Bureaucracy at the Border*. Minneapolis: University of Minnesota Press, 2010.

Thachuk, Kimberley L. *Transnational Threats: Smuggling and Trafficking in Arms, Drugs, and Human Life*. Westport, CT: Praeger Security International, 2007.

United Nations Office on Drugs and Crime. "Smuggling of Migrants: A Global Review and Annotated Bibliography of Recent Publications." 2010. http://www.unodc.org/documents/human-trafficking/ Marian/Smuggling_of_Migrants_A_Global_Review.pdf (Accessed October 2010).

Zhang, Sheldon. *Smuggling and Trafficking in Human Beings: All Roads Lead to America*. Westport, CT: Praeger, 2007.

HUMAN TRAFFICKING

Trafficking in persons, also called human trafficking, is defined in the UN Convention Against Transnational Organized Crime and its supporting document the Protocol to Prevent, Suppress, and Punish Trafficking in Persons, Especially Women and Children as the following:

> The recruitment, transportation, transfer, harboring or receipt of persons, by means of the threat or use of force or other forms of coercion, of abduction, of fraud, of deception, of the abuse of power or of a position of vulnerability or of the giving or receiving of payments or benefits to achieve the consent of a person having control over another person, for the purpose of exploitation. Exploitation shall include, at a minimum, the exploitation of the prostitution of others or other forms of sexual exploitation, forced labor or services, slavery or practices similar to slavery, servitude or the removal of organs.

By this definition, human trafficking refers to more than the transport of people to an area where they will be exploited in some manner; it also refers to an active process of recruitment and harboring them by using force or other types of coercion. The exploitation can include forced labor, slavery in its different forms, and the illegal trade in human body organs.

As many as 800,000 people are trafficked across national borders annually, and millions more are trafficked within national boundaries. It is likely that fewer people have been trafficked into the United States and some other countries after the

September 11, 2001, terrorist attacks, as a result of increased border security. Generally, however, people are trafficked from poorer nations to wealthier ones.

Trafficking has a very long history, but it was not until the 1990s that major international attention was given to it. Globalization has helped the practice flourish, but the burgeoning women's and human rights movements, increasing labor migration, the so-called feminization of poverty, and a focus on organized criminal activity in relation to human trafficking have put the spotlight on the activity. The recognition that the United States was a major destination of trafficked persons led the Clinton administration to create a program known as the "Three Ps": prosecution (of traffickers), prevention (of trafficking), and protection (of trafficking victims). The administration worked with the United Nations (UN) and the U.S. Congress to create more effective laws against trafficking in a national effort called the Trafficking Victims Protection Act of 2000.

Second only to the illicit drug trade as the world's largest illegal enterprise, the phenomenon of human trafficking is not new. Trafficking, especially for the purpose of enslaving people for various reasons, has a long history. In the transatlantic slave trade, for example, between 10 million and 28 million people were trafficked from Africa to Europe, North America, and South America from the 15th to the 18th centuries. Large numbers of people were also trafficked in routes from Africa and the Middle East around the same time period. Many people are smuggled as a part of the trafficking process; smuggling is different from trafficking, in that smuggling primarily refers to the illegal transport of people across borders, whereas trafficking involves different types of exploitation that occur after the smuggling has taken place.

To understand human trafficking, it is beneficial to analyze the types of trafficking that occur, how the process is conducted, and why it exists across the globe. People, including small children, are recruited into trafficking to fill a number of roles, including domestic laborers, factory workers, farmworkers and other outdoor laborers, fishers and shrimpers, quarry and mill workers, and restaurant employees. Some jobs are quite specialized or specific to certain geographical areas, such as charcoal makers in Brazil, sugar-mill workers in the Dominican Republic, fireworks makers in India, cocoa growers in the Ivory Coast, and child camel racers in many Arab nations (a practice that has been outlawed, though it probably still exists in underground networks). Many people are employed in sweatshops, working long hours in deplorable conditions. There is also a market for trafficking disabled people for work in factories, brothels (deaf girls are particularly valuable as they cannot adequately communicate their enslavement to authorities), or begging on the street; for example, children with deformities, including those deliberately inflicted by the traffickers (as depicted in the 2008 movie *Slumdog Millionaire*), are often used as street beggars, as it is believed that they will elicit sympathy and generous donations from passersby.

Traffickers often dupe the trafficked persons into thinking that there will be legitimate jobs available when they arrive at their destinations. The trafficked persons are then required to work for free or extremely low wages in order to repay their transportation costs. Often they are totally unaware that they will be working in areas other than those promised and that moreover are illegal or exploitative. Finding themselves in a foreign country without visas, they are forced to comply with the demands of the criminals involved in the trafficking enterprise.

One particularly lucrative and disconcerting form of slavery is sex slavery. In sex slavery, people, primarily women and girls, are trafficked and kept against their will for the commercial sex trade, forced to engage in prostitution and pornography.

Prostitutes in front of a Go-Go bar in Pattaya, Thailand. Between 500,000 and 2 million people are trafficked globally for the illicit sex trade and are forced into prostitution and pornography. (Kay Chernush for the U.S. State Department)

The traffickers and pimps in the sex slavery enterprise exploit the facts that women occupy a lower status globally and that there is a high demand for prostitutes. Many are forced to work in massage parlors, spas, and other "front" establishments that are actually brothels. They often acquire a debt to the traffickers that is difficult or impossible to repay and that forces them to remain in bondage until their usefulness as sex workers is over. This period of usefulness is sometimes short-lived, because the profits from their sex slavery begin to dissolve as the prostitutes age or become sick. Health-related problems, including both physical and mental illnesses, are common, brought about by trauma, sexually transmitted diseases, substance addictions, and limited access to adequate healthcare. Human immunodeficiency syndrome and acquired immune deficiency syndrome (HIV/AIDS) are major health risks for sex slaves. It is estimated that between 500,000 and 2 million people annually are trafficked globally for the illicit sex trade.

Another form of exploitation in human trafficking is the unlawful trade in human organs. People who are poor and living in desperate situations are often transported across national boundaries to sell their organs for money to traffickers, who then sell the organs—most often kidneys but also other organs and tissues—to needy recipients. In contrast to other forms of trafficking, such as the trafficking of illegal drugs, the trafficked material usually does not result in harm to the recipient but is actually necessary. The practice is so common in poorer nations that communities that contribute a large number of their organs for subsistence have been described as "kidney villages." The traffickers and others involved in the trade, often called the "body mafia," include brokers, organ transporters, medical personnel who carry out and oversee the transplantations, corrupt government officials who ignore the illegal activity, and organized crime figures who help conduct the transactions. The traffickers in human organs take advantage of the low supply of human organs for legitimate transplant and normally make very large profits from this form of exploitation.

In 2000, the UN fully outlined the issue in its Protocol to Prevent, Suppress, and Punish Trafficking in Persons, Especially Women and Children, which is part of the UN Convention Against Transnational Organized Crime. This document fully defined human trafficking for the first time, and sustained recommendations were made to eradicate or at least diminish the problem. The protocol requires nations to criminalize the offense, create efforts to deal with trafficking and related offenses, coordinate security and documentation measures, negotiate boundary and exchange issues, and provide for the protection and assistance of trafficking victims. The UN also created the Global Initiative to Fight Human Trafficking, which labeled the problem "the crime that shames us all" and which provides a framework that recommends a global effort to promote awareness, prevention measures, a reduction in demand, support and protection for trafficking victims, and improved policing measures. The Blue Heart Campaign Against Human Trafficking, sponsored by the UN Department on Drugs and Crime, exists to promote awareness. There have also been many national and regional campaigns to address the issue, including Free the Slaves, Anti-Slavery International, and a host of others.

Leonard A. Steverson
South Georgia College

See also Human Smuggling; Organ Trafficking; Sex Slavery

Further Readings

Bales, K. *Disposable People: New Slavery in the Global Economy.* Berkeley: University of California Press, 1999.

Bales, K. and B. Cornell. *Slavery Today.* Toronto, ON: Groundwork Books, 2008.

Chuang, J. A. "Rescuing Trafficking From Ideological Capture: Prostitution Reform and Anti-Trafficking Law and Policy." *University of Pennsylvania Law Review*, v.158 (2010).

United Nations Office on Drugs and Crime. "The Global Initiative to Fight Human Trafficking." http://www.unodc.org/pdf/gift%20brochure.pdf (Accessed October 2010).

United Nations Office on Drugs and Crime. "United Nations Convention Against Transnational Organized Crime and the Protocols Thereto." New York: Author, 2000. http://www.unodc.org/documents/treaties/UNTOC/Publications/TOC%20Convention/TOCebook-e.pdf (Accessed October 2010).

United Nations Office on Drugs and Crime. "What Is Human Trafficking?" http://www.unodc.org/unodc/en/human-trafficking/what-is-human-trafficking.html (Accessed October 2010).

I

IDENTITY THEFT

Identity theft is a form of fraud commonly (but not always) committed for financial gain. The following discussion argues that identity theft involves the illicit use of personally identifying information tied a person's legal identity: that is, the information used to establish his or her personhood in the eyes of the law, including the birth certificate. It is essential to recognize the nature of identity theft in the modern world, especially the key role played by information technology and the Internet in its execution. There has been rapid development in national legislation in the last two decades to tackle identity theft. However, the development of international legislation and cooperation to tackle identity theft at a transnational level is still in its infancy.

Identity thieves typically use a person's information to obtain money, loans, financing and credit, state benefits, pensions, and other entitlements. Generally victims of identity theft are not immediately aware that their identity has been stolen; indeed, it can take many months and even years before the theft comes to light. Identity theft is big business. It is estimated to cost the U.S. economy alone $54 billion a year and in 2009 affected more than 11 million individual U.S. citizens, according to the 2010 Javelin Strategy and Research Report. Identity theft is often committed by perpetrators pursuing personal financial gain, but it can also be used by organized crime syndicates to fund other illegal activities, such as drug trafficking, terrorist activity, and illegal immigration.

When examining identity theft, it is necessary first to explore the multifaceted nature of the concept that is identity. Traditionally within Western philosophy, the concept of identity has been taken to mean the sense of selfhood (and mortality) that comes from being aware of oneself as residing in the present while simultaneously possessing both a past and a future. This awareness of oneself moving through space and time from birth to death is arguably a unique experience, which sets human beings individually and collectively apart from other living creatures. Furthermore, identity can possess individual and social aspects that are tightly intertwined. As they go about their day-to-day business, individuals possess a sense of collective identity as members of a particular social group, local community, or nation-state, in addition their awareness of their individuality and unique personhood. The concept of legal identity must be added to this mixture of individual and social identity—not least because, while individual and social identity can certainly be affected by identity theft, it nevertheless is the legal aspects of an individual's identity that typically are targeted by identity thieves. This is because a legal identity is the means whereby an individual establishes his or her personhood and social identity and communicates it to others through confirmatory social-legal documentation (such as a birth certificate, a driver's license, or a social security number). Hence, this type of information possesses significant value for potential identity thieves.

Identity theft is not a new phenomenon. The history of human art and civilization, from the ancient Greeks onward, attests to the fact that human beings

Identity theft is often committed for personal financial gain but it is also popular with organized crime syndicates to fund other illegal activities, such as drug trafficking, terrorist activity, and illegal immigration. (Photos.com)

possess an uncanny ability to reinvent themselves and adopt new personas. However, the gradual emergence during the 19th and 20th centuries of population census-taking technology as an aid to social administration and welfare policy making—alongside the growth of increasingly complex financial, taxation, and social security systems—together laid the foundation for the growth of identity theft as a distinctively modern crime. Certainly the ability to obtain and use another individual's personal identity information to obtain a state benefit or a bank loan without that individual's knowledge requires the presence of a complex official documentary reality well beyond that which existed in Western nation-states until relatively recently.

For conceptual purposes, it is possible to put together a threefold categorization of identity theft involving duration, level of immersion, and motivation. Duration stretches from a single incident lasting a few moments to an individual effectively passing himself or herself off as someone else for a lifetime. Immersion relates to the depth of involvement an identity thief has with an individual's personal information. A name, address, and date of birth can, in the simplest of cases, be used to commit identity

theft, but to obtain greater financial reward, a thief may need to obtain an individual's full financial accounts and personal family history. Motivation pertains to the extent to which a theft of another's personal information is undertaken in order to commit further criminal activity. Indeed, although in the main identity theft is undertaken with the aim of committing further criminal activity, on occasion an individual can engage in identity theft for noncriminal reasons—for example, to escape a traumatic abusive marriage.

The emergence in the 1990s of computerized record systems and the Internet reinforces the modern nature of identity theft as well as the diffuse and spatially scattered nature of an individual's legal identity. The documentary reality associated with a legal identity—address, birth certificate, social security number, income tax history, pension plan, marriage (and divorce) papers, and so on—is no longer situated in a clearly defined office filing cabinet (if indeed it ever was). An individual's identity today resides in a mixture of cyberspace, corporate- and government-held electronic databases, and the global banking system. The growth of cyberspace and online banking and financial systems has arguably made it easier for fraudsters to access the information they need to commit identity theft across nation-states, making it an increasingly significant transnational crime.

Since the 1990s, national governments have recognized the need to introduce legislation specifically designed to tackle identity theft. For example, in the United States the Identity Theft Prevention Act of 2005 seeks to limit the distribution of an individual's personal information as a measure to stop identity theft. This legislation has led to the prosecution of cases such as that of Albert Gonzalez, a computer hacker sentenced in 2010 to 20 years' imprisonment for using online computer technology to obtain personal information in order to commit credit card theft. At an international level, the Council of Europe Convention on Cybercrime (2004) seeks to establish greater transnational cooperation between member states in regard to the identification and prosecution of identity theft as part of its response to tackling cybercrime. The United States, Japan, South Africa, and Canada have all signed this convention. Although Russia, India, and China have yet to sign, there is a general recognition by all members of the United Nations (UN) that identity theft and cybercrime are closely linked to terrorist activity and human trafficking and therefore international legislation needs to be developed to tackle it. However, at the moment moves toward greater transnational cooperation and legislative action to prosecute identity theft are very much in an early stage of development.

John Martyn Chamberlain
Loughborough University

See also Computer-Generated Scams; Human Trafficking

Further Readings

Caplan, J. and J. Torpey. *Documenting Individual Identity.* Princeton, NJ: Princeton University Press, 2001.

Javelin Strategy and Research Report. *Identity Fraud Survey Report.* Pleasanton, CA: Author, 2010. https://www.javelinstrategy.com (Accessed February 2011).

Marcus, R. and G. Hastings. *Identity Theft Inc.* London: Disinformation Company, 2008.

Newman, J. Q. *Identity Theft: The Cybercrime of the Millennium.* Port Townsend, WA: Loompanics, 1999.

IMPACT OF TRANSNATIONAL CRIME

The characteristic of transnational crime that defines its impact is its capacity to articulate the local with the global by making use of the comparative advantages that the blend of globalization and illegality offer. Taking stock of the exponential speed in the flow of people, goods, information, capital, and services in an increasingly interconnected and borderless world, transnational crime networks have come to act as powerful brokers that bridge local, impoverished areas of the globe and regions where there are lucrative global markets. This process of globalizing the illicit has the capacity to disrupt the state and civil society in unprecedented ways that impact local, national, and international spheres, albeit in different manners.

At the global level, transnational crime impacts the breadth and scope of international relations and foreign policy; the possibilities of success of international peace operations; the legitimacy of global financial markets and the global economy; and the possibilities for equitable development in the global South. Transnational crime generates highly flexible international networks of operators, fixers, and distributors who connect all sorts of nonstate armed actors to an illegal international circuitry, and it therefore poses a substantial threat to global stability and security. The impact of this new threat is twofold. On one hand, the increasingly blurred distinction between organized crime and terrorism calls for an overhaul of international relations and foreign policy as countries try to articulate more informed responses of prevention, containment, interdiction, and intervention. On the other hand, the articulation of transnational crime with other nonstate armed actors (religious, ethnic, or political armed movements) poses new challenges to the international peace architecture. Traditionally, international peace missions (whether peacemaking, peacekeeping, or peace-building missions) operate within strategic and operational paradigms based on the assumption that hostilities between rivals stem from political, religious, or ethnic conflicts over territories. When the actors in internal conflicts are associated with transnational crime networks, the international peace operations paradigm often falls short, failing to respond appropriately to the ways in which transnational crime networks operate in local contexts and failing to understand the peace-spoiling capabilities they might be able to mobilize.

As for its impact on the global financial architecture, transnational crime, while building its core business around illegal international networks, benefits from and uses financial market integration as a means to disperse illicit revenues and cover up illicit activities through money laundering, terrorist financing, tax evasion, embezzlement, and sale of fictitious financial instruments—all of which compromise the integrity, legitimacy, and stability of global financial circuits. This use of international financial systems points to the immense flows of cash from the shadow economies of transnational crime (such as human trafficking, drugs, weapons, illicit trades of natural resources, and counterfeiting). These shadow economies benefit from the exploitation of impoverished populations in the global South that offer cheap manual labor, from the extraction of immense amounts of wealth in countries where most of the population is under the poverty line, and from harvesting massive corruption and adding fuel to internal conflicts—all of which derail initiatives for sustainable and equitable development.

Notwithstanding the effects of these global factors at national levels, transnational crime's impact within a country is equally challenging. Perhaps one of the most destabilizing effects is the power of transnational crime to reshape state institutions, be that as result of its own capacity for intimidation, coercion, and cooptation or as a result of the ability of existing power structures to use transnational crime for their own benefit. In any case, the organic interaction between power and transnational crime affects the ability of democratic institutions and practices to flourish by compromising the rule of law (through intimidation, coercion, or cooptation of the justice system); the integrity and legitimacy of the security system (segments of the military, police, intelligence, penitentiary, and border police systems that offer protection and partake of the spoils); and the legitimacy of political systems (in particular when they become recipients of illicit finances and defenders of policies that benefit the interests of transnational crime networks). All these distortions add to a weakening of state institutions, a crisis in political representation, and systematic failures in public service delivery to such degrees that countries with democratic traditions and state institutions might find themselves sliding into state weakness and, in extreme cases, state failure.

Less studied is the impact of transnational crime over national economies and licit businesses. Transnational crime networks can insinuate themselves into national economies by creating legal businesses that use the informal sector (networks of small street entrepreneurs, for example) as a start-up structure. When rooted in a country, transnational crime networks accommodate to the formal economy by benefiting from established links with political and entrepreneurial elites. In this last case, complete sectors of the economy might find themselves compromised; this can happen, for example, in the construction and real estate sectors in countries with a high index of money laundering, in the energy and infrastructure sectors in countries where the collusion between crime and politics is at its peak, or in agro-industry, insurance and financial markets, or recycling and waste management industry via penetration of illicit investments. While these "captures" affect the transparency and functioning of national markets, distorting market prices and fair competition, they are often accompanied by even more destabilizing processes, such as counteragrarian reforms and disenfranchisement of poor segments of the population, which in turn exacerbates poverty gaps and undermines national integration and development.

Perhaps the least understood and most profound impact of transnational crime at a national level is its capacity to reshape social and cultural life. When entrenched in a territory, transnational crime networks bring deterioration in the quality of life through high rates of crime; a dramatic shift in societal values through the enthronement of violence and the illicit as means to gain social standing; a lack of public trust in state institutions and their capacity to deliver public services; a discontent toward political processes, which are seen as corrupted; and a disdain for political and economic elites, which are seen as compromised. Overall, the fluid interaction between transnational crime networks and power structures (whether political or economic), blended with these social and cultural effects, favors the promotion of authoritarian regimes that endorse totally deregulated forms of extreme capitalism that impair equitable development, social justice, and democratic institutions and practices.

Finally, transnational crime networks impact subnational (local) levels of society, where illicit production, extraction, and trading take place. The encroachment of transnational crime networks on local structures occurs when crime offers significant comparative advantages, whether at the extraction and trade levels or in the form of legal investment. In the first instance, transnational crime networks flourish in jurisdictions where government is either weak or nonexistent; criminal networks fill these gaps, turning themselves into employment and service providers for the local population and thus usurping the functions of the state by generating parallel structures of authority and governance. The overall impact in such cases is that the legitimate state loses territorial control. In cases where transnational crime networks coexist with local state institutions, a more complex impact unfolds: Transnational crime captures, through intimidation, coercion, or cooptation, local governance structures, appointing local bureaucracies and mobilizing local politicians and electorates. In more acute cases, where the weakness of state institutions in a territory is accompanied by the existence of nonstate armed actors such as religious, ethnic, or political armed groups, the impact of transnational crime networks is yet more detrimental. While forging functional alliances based on mutual opportunities for territorial control and access to illicit global markets, the symbiosis between transnational crime networks and local nonstate armed actors feeds internal violence, undermines comprehensive peace efforts, and affects national and regional stability, especially when such territories lie within volatile international borders.

The impact of transnational crime networks at the subnational level, when their interest is in reinvesting the cash flows of the illicit trades, is different. In these cases, transnational crime networks seek the lavish and extremely wealthy enclaves of the global North (for example, Costa del Sol in Spain) to use as their playgrounds. The encroachment of these networks is often accompanied by abnormal hikes in prices (such as real estate prices), a deterioration of local governance structures, and a decline in justice delivery.

Santiago Villaveces-Izquierdo
Independent Scholar

See also Child Exploitation; Electoral Manipulation; Failed States; Gender-Based Violence; Genocide; Globalization; Legal and Illegal Economies; Terrorism Versus Transnational Crime; Transnational Crime: Defined

Further Readings

Allum, F. and R. Siebert, eds. *Organized Crime and the Challenge to Democracy*. London: Routledge, 2003.

Glenny, M. *McMafia: A Journey Through the Global Criminal Underworld*. New York: Knopf, 2008.

Heine, J. and R. Thakur, eds. *The Dark Side of Globalization*. Tokyo: United Nations University Press, 2011.

Naim, M. *Illicit: How Smugglers, Traffickers, and Copycats Are Hijacking the Global Economy*. New York: Anchor, 2006.

Siegel, D. and H. Nelen, eds. *Organized Crime: Culture, Markets and Policies*. New York: Springer, 2008.

Solís, L. and F. Rojas, eds. *Organized Crime in Latin America and the Caribbean*. San José, Costa Rica: FLACSO, 2009.

INFLUENCE AND POSITION

As globalization and technological advances allow the nations of the world to become more interconnected, questions surrounding how the global community addresses transnational crime are becoming a pressing issue for policy makers. The influence of position and status within this international framework is perhaps one of the greatest challenges for the international community and victims of crimes that cross international borders. Power and influence can be seen in multiple areas of transnational justice, through the structure and agendas of international organizations, the drafting and implementation of international law, and the apprehension and prosecution of international criminals. Within the international framework, nations that hold economic, military, and political power hold hegemonic influence over the institutions of international justice, and influential members of these nations tend to enjoy protections not afforded to less powerful members of the global community.

Indeed, the issue of how to regulate conduct on a global scale is an important topic that should be addressed. Through globalization and technological advances, criminal acts regularly and easily cross international boundaries and impact individuals and societies alike. Beyond obvious problems such as the illegal drug trade and terrorism, other crimes—including corporate crime and misconduct, computer-related crime, trademark and copyright infringement, and environmental harm—are also important topics that fall under the umbrella of transnational crime and justice. However, this entry will use the crime of genocide to illustrate the challenges faced within the global community and the role of influence and position within the institutions of international justice.

At the center of the debate on efforts to address transnational crime and justice is the challenge of respecting international sovereignty and jurisdiction. Nations, especially the United States, typically have a political culture that resists the interference of international organizations regarding matters of crime. At present, there is no legally recognized mechanism whereby a nation can unilaterally enter another nation's sovereign boundaries in order to investigate a crime or apprehend a suspected criminal. Many crimes that cross national borders, including drug trafficking, sex tourism, human trafficking, computer crime, and counterfeiting, are extremely difficult to deal with, because the perpetrators are typically well outside the jurisdictional reach of authorities. To complicate this situation, many nations where transnational crimes originate do not possess the physical resources, financial resources, legal framework, or motivation to investigate crimes that cross national boundaries. These can be the result of internal strife, economic hardship, war, or political animosity toward the victim nation. Finally, it is unclear to what degree individuals can be held culpable for harmful acts committed by organizations, including governments and multinational corporations.

A similar debate exists over the rights retained by individuals within the global framework. The Universal Declaration of Human Rights addresses many issues of global crime and justice, including political crimes and environmental harm, for example. However, this declaration—being a political document—contains provisions that are essentially at odds with rights as dictated within the individual constitutions of nation-states. The U.S. Constitution is perhaps the most visible example of this contrast, particularly given its focus on individual rights, in comparison to the collective rights, of people in a society. This is a very important distinction, because it lays the foundation for the amount of power vested in the national government. In societies where rights are seen as in the collective interest of society, government has greater authority to control individual freedom in the name of the greater good of society. The U.S. Constitution, in its original interpretation, was strongly in favor of individual rights for the purpose of expanding individual freedom of choice, thus limiting the government's power over individuals. This distinction becomes significant in the global community because the political culture of the United States is unique in comparison to the values of most other nations. As a result, the United States has not officially adopted many international treaties regarding crime and justice. As the symbolic leader of democratic ideals within the global community, the United States has therefore taken a conspicuous position of noncompliance that effectively reduces the legitimacy of institutions such as the International Criminal Court.

When examining the history of international crime and justice, one can see glaring inconsistencies regarding how international law and policy are utilized and when they are ignored. There have been numerous circumstances of transnational crime committed by nations and corporations, including human rights violations, genocide, environmental degradation, and state-sponsored crime, but the determination of whether the international community will intervene is typically mired in political and economic interests of the nations involved, not just in the interests of international justice or individual human rights. To explain this process, it is important to examine the institutions that are given the responsibility to establish and enforce these global norms and values.

The responsibility for global policy making and enforcement is primarily the focus of individual nations that act through international political organizations, including the United Nations (UN), the International Court of Justice (ICJ), and the International Criminal Court (ICC). However, a variety of other groups influence policy on a global scale. These range from politically sanctioned economic bodies, such as the World Trade Organization (WTO) and the World Bank, to international nongovernmental organizations (NGOs), such as the International Red Cross and Amnesty International. Added to the mix are multiple regional cooperative groups, such as the Organization of Petroleum Exporting Countries (OPEC) and treaty groups such as the North Atlantic Treaty Organization (NATO). Within this complex network of actors, conflicts regularly arise between organizational goals and ideologies, on one hand, and the interests of individual actors within these organizations, on the other.

Some have described this very complicated landscape as an "anarchy of norms" where such a wide variety of perspectives is presented that the correct path to identifying and solving problems is extremely difficult to find. As a result, influence is gained through leverage applied by member nations and groups that have the military and/or economic resources needed to bring their ideas to the forefront. The policies implemented reflect the interests of these powerful nations, many times at the expense of those weaker nations that need assistance and protection the most or, more important, individual victims who lack any sufficient means to engage the global arena for assistance.

The most obvious example of this assertion can be seen through the UN. Although the UN was established to give all nations a voice in global policy through "sovereign equality," the organization is dominated by the five permanent Security Council nations: China, France, Russia, the United Kingdom, and the United States. Decisions on policy and use of military force to enforce UN resolutions generally reflect the overall stance of these five nations. It is not difficult to identify cases where UN policies and institutions (including the ICC and ICJ) have been selectively manipulated by powerful members of the organization. One example concerns the 1951 UN Genocide Convention. The purpose of the meeting was to outline a clear definition of what constitutes genocide on the part of nation-states. The final document prohibits a variety of acts that are aimed at destroying any "national, ethnical, racial, or religious group." Missing from this definition are political groups, which were included in the original document. The language was removed based on protests from the former Soviet Union, which had been engaged in genocidal activity toward political dissidents within that nation. Because of its position within the international community, the Soviet Union was able to influence international law in a way that insulated it from the symbolic leaders of democratic principles. The United States also has a troubling record of selectively promoting and ignoring international law as political expediency dictates. A recent example is the United States' rejection of the Rome Statute of the International Criminal Court, which gives the ICC permanent jurisdiction to prosecute cases of genocide, crimes against humanity, war crimes, and the crime of aggression by states. The United States is one of only seven nations to reject the treaty, which some in the global community have seen as hypocritical and damaging to the legitimacy and effectiveness of the ICC and similar international justice efforts.

One final area of concern is the prosecution of powerful individuals who are the perpetrators of criminal acts by powerful organizations, especially corporations or nations. Corporate or state actors are guided by leadership that enlists subordinates to implement the policies that result in harm. The legal framework is ill equipped in many cases to hold individual members culpable for the actions of the organization. Criminal laws are tailored to prosecuting individual actors for their roles in committing criminal acts, which requires the actor both to possess criminal intent (*mens rea*) and actually to have taken steps toward completing the crime (*actus reus*). Crimes committed by powerful groups typically involve multiple perpetrators who occupy all levels of the organization's hierarchy. Because of the division of labor within bureaucratic organizations, it is difficult to ascertain the true level of awareness

that any individual, including a leader, has over events, therefore making it very difficult to establish the required legal proof of criminal intent. This same specialization of job tasks within the organization can also fragment the overall criminal act to a degree that no individual actor has made a significant overall contribution toward completion of the crime. Corporate crime is further complicated by the legal status of corporations as abstract legal entities that cannot be held criminally liable as organizations.

The issues discussed here do only a superficial job of explaining the complex influence of power and status within global efforts to address transnational crime and justice. The challenge is primarily one of how the relatively weak members of the global community can influence the powerful actors to implement and submit themselves to the oversight and sanctions of the international organizations that they establish. This is clearly a difficult task given the multiple political, social, and economic interests represented within the global community. The task is made even more difficult by the fact that political cultures within individual nations can be very resistant to giving up some degree of national sovereignty on behalf of furthering democratic principles on a global scale. This conflict is unlikely to be resolved in the near future, but it is essential that nations continue to improve mechanisms of global justice and protect the weakest among us, who rely on these institutions the most.

Robert M. Keeton
University of Tennessee

See also Conventions, Agreements, and Regulations; Genocide; Globalization; Impact of Transnational Crime; International Criminal Court; International Monetary Fund; Internationalized Criminal Tribunals; Interpol; Networks; Policing: Transnational; Terrorism Versus Transnational Crime; Transnational Crime: Research Centers; UN Convention Against Transnational Organized Crime; United Nations; War Crimes Tribunals; World Court

Further Readings

Araujo, Robert. "Sovereignty, Human Rights, and Self-Determination: The Meaning of International Law." *Fordham International Law Journal*, v.24/5 (2000).
Gilbert, Michael J. and Steve Russell. "Globalization of Criminal Justice in the Corporate Context." *Crime, Law and Social Change*, v.38 (2002).

Hagan, John. "Crime Wars, War Crimes, and State Crimes." In *Who Are the Criminals? The Politics of Crime Policy From the Age of Roosevelt to the Age of Reagan.* Princeton, NJ: Princeton University Press, 2010.

Hagan, John and Wenona Rymond-Richmond. "The Crime of Crimes." In *Darfur and the Crime of Genocide.* New York: Cambridge University Press, 2009.

Halliday, Terence C. "Recursivity of Global Normmaking: A Sociolegal Agenda." *Annual Review of Law and Social Science,* v.5 (2009).

Savelsberg, Joachim J. *Crime and Human Rights: Criminology of Genocide and Atrocities.* Thousand Oaks, CA: Sage, 2010.

INFORMAL VALUE TRANSFER SYSTEMS

Informal value transfer systems or underground banking systems are often better known as hawala, a remittance system that developed during the Abbasid caliphate (c. 750–945 c.e., 133–334 Hijra), centuries before the invention of free-market capitalism. Designed to lower the risks of commerce along the old Silk Road, hawala enabled trade by freeing merchants from having to carry large quantities of cash along the way. The word *hawala* is Arabic, meaning "bill of exchange" or "promissory note." The Chinese used the term *fei ch'ien* to refer to informal value transfer systems; in Sanskrit, the term used is *hundi*, which means "truth" and "reference." Hawala in many ways resembles the Jewish banking system prominent in medieval Europe, though upgraded to incorporate cell phones, computers, e-mail, and faxes. Given that different jurisdictions use different words, the accepted term today is *informal value transfer systems*, or IVTS's.

IVTS's range from basic to highly complex. In its simplest form, the customer visits an operator, known in some jurisdictions as a hawaladar. The customer wants to send money to his home country and hands over dollars in cash. In some of these transactions, the customer will instruct that the family member receiving the money provide a password, which the customer shares with the operator. Usually within 24 hours (to allow for time zone differences), the operator instructs a fellow operator in the home country to make the money available to the customer's family member. The operator will charge a fee, often between 0.25 and 1.25 percent

of the total transaction, for the services. Thus, the family member in the home country receives approximately 98.75–99.75 percent of the money after the fee is paid for the safe transaction.

Transactions can become more expensive and complex, especially if the operator needs to rely on a third party to make money available in a city or country where a direct operator/partner does not exist. In this case, the third-party operator has the relationships needed to make the transaction. Fees may rise to as much as 5 percent (although no limit actually exists).

Cash actually leaves an operator only when the recipient customer comes to collect the amount that is "sent." In reality, IVTS's fit the description of "money transfer without money movement." The records kept by the operator are very few: mostly the passwords that are used for a transaction (which are usually discarded after use) and IOU papers recording how much one operator owes another. Customer identification records are not kept, and there is no customer account number to track the parties using these services. Moreover, commission fees are not necessarily evenly split between operators: One might owe another a significant sum as the result of a recent large transaction, so often one operator is gradually repaying the debt owed to another.

IVTS's are used for many reasons that are not criminal in nature. Hawala is extremely efficient, largely because of its minimal overhead costs; most transactions can be completed in hours, whereas in the commercial banking sector transactions may take a week. Operators do not observe bank holidays, usually making them available on a moment's notice. The fees charged by operators are almost always far less than those charged by banks. Additionally, many operators offer currency exchanges rates that are more favorable than official international exchange rates. IVTS's may also offer the ability to transfer money to very remote parts of the world, outside the reach of commercial banks, which may judge the location "overly risky" or just too isolated to support a formal banking system. Also attractive to criminals and noncriminals alike is the anonymity of the system: IVTS's do not require a social security number, fingerprint, proof of citizenship, or a government identity card. Money transfers along hawala networks are untaxed and unscrutinized.

Therefore, IVTS's are almost totally nontransparent and unregulated systems of remittance and can be used by criminal enterprises to help move and launder money between parties and across international borders unnoticed. Illicit funds from narcotics, fraud, alien smuggling, human trafficking, and terror financing regularly make their way into such networks. Some customers may request (and pay for) layering services, whereby the operator distributes portions of the money across several operators, complicating efforts to attempt to trace the money.

It should not be assumed that there are no records of hawala financial transactions. Frequently the records are very meticulous but focus on details of little value to financial regulators. Such details may include type of currency traded, deposit totals, and cash on hand—and may go back many years, even decades.

Informal value transfer systems are primarily located in the Middle East, North Africa, the Horn of Africa, and South Asia. IVTS's are regarded as legitimate in many countries; in the United States, they are supposed to be registered. IVTS's are one channel for currency entering the economy, and even though it is untaxed at the entry point, it will likely be spent or invested, a stimulus to the local economy. Some countries also overlook IVTS's for economic survival. Economic sanctions could cripple a country, making IVTS's an important means of success, even under economic sanctions.

Countries under sanctions have been known to allow unlicensed operator to work as long as they are conducting large transactions for the government. This way, the government can move money across international borders and purchase goods forbidden to them by economic sanctions. Commission fees may be low to nonexistent under these circumstances. According to one estimate, about $5 billion per year moves through Pakistani IVTS networks. In India, some believe that IVTS's are involved with as much as 40 percent of the gross domestic product. The hawala capital of the world is Dubai, an oil-rich emirate almost without any regulation of money transfers along its IVTS networks. Worldwide, about $100 billion is believed to move through IVTS channels annually.

IVTS's are often distributed among family groups. Operators on both sides of the transaction are very often related, if not by blood then through marriage.

There are numerous cases in which sons and daughters marry into a potentially business-strengthening relationship that benefits all parties involved. Besides marriage and family relations, IVTS's often maximize ethnic ties among hawaladars. Often, however, Saudi operators trust only fellow Saudis, with Sudanese, Pakistanis, and Bangladeshis similarly following suit. IVTS's might appear highly vulnerable to embezzling of funds by insiders, but remarkably, cooperation with fellow operators allows far more money to be made, which in turn lowers the risk of fraud.

Following the September 11, 2001 (9/11), terrorist attacks, the United States tightened laws governing IVTS's such as hawala. New regulations in 2002 required operators to report all transactions exceeding $10,000 and inform U.S. authorities of any "suspicious" incidents. The U.S. government classifies hawala as an IVTS, and hawala transactions therefore are regulated in the United States under Executive Order 13224. Hawala remains legal in the United States, unless it involves money laundering, criminal financing, or the financing of terrorist activities.

The use of IVTS's in terrorist financing is not a relic of pre-9/11 days. The disrupted terror plot against Times Square by Faisal Shahzad was financed by the Pakistani Taliban (Tehrik-i-Taliban Pakistan) through transactions in hawala networks. The Somali-based Al Qaeda affiliate terrorist organization Harakat al-Shabaab al-Mujahideen has also made extensive use of hawala financing of its terrorist operations to transfer funding from the United States back into Africa.

Krishna Mungur
Solution Concepts Consulting

See also Antiterrorist Financing; Money Laundering: History; Money Laundering: Methods; Money Laundering: Targeting Criminal Proceeds; Money Laundering: Vulnerable Commodities and Services

Further Readings

Berkowitz, Steven D., Lloyd H. Woodward, and Caitlin Woodward. "Use of Formal Methods to Map, Analyze, and Interpret Hawala and Terrorist-Related Alternative Remittance Systems." *Structure and Dynamics*, v.1/2 (2006).

El-Qorchi, Mohammed. "The Hawala System." *Finance and Development*, v.39/4 (December 2002).

Fifield, Anna. "How Iranians Are Avoiding Sanctions." *Financial Times* (April 14, 2008).

Ganguly, Meenakshi. "A Banking System Built for Terrorism." *Time* (October 5, 2001).

Hancock, Daniel A. "The Olive Branch and the Hammer: A Strategic Analysis of Hawala in the Financial War on Terrorism." *The Culture and Conflict Review*, v.2/3 (Summer 2008).

Money Laundering Threat Assessment Group. *U.S. Money Laundering Threat Assessment*. Washington, DC: U.S. Treasury Department, 2005.

Passas, Nikko. *Informal Value Transfer Systems, Terrorism and Money Laundering*. Washington, DC: National Institute of Justice, 2003.

Intelligence Agencies: Collaboration Within the United States

The term *intelligence* broadly refers to information assessments concerning potential security risks that are used in national security policy decisions and action. Intelligence agencies gather, archive, and analyze intelligence information to combat a variety of transnational security threats, including terrorism, the narcotics and arms trades, human trafficking, cybercrime, and weapons proliferation. The terrorist attacks of September 11, 2001, placed increased emphasis on national security threats that emanate from ubiquitous transnational sources and the need for increased coordination, collaboration, and communication between intelligence agencies at regional, national, and international levels. According to the former chief intelligence officer of the Federal Bureau of Investigation (FBI), Donald Van Duyn, combating transnational crime and terrorism threats to the United States increasingly requires coordination between law-enforcement and intelligence agencies throughout the world. The U.S. government participates in a variety of regional and multilateral collaborative efforts to combat activities of terrorism and transnational crime. Examples of intelligence-sharing efforts include the FBI's Intelligence and Operations 2 (IOC-2) fusion center and the Department of Justice's Overseas Prosecutorial Development Assistance and Training (OPDAT) and International Criminal Investigative Training Assistance Program (ICITAP) programs.

9/11: A Catalyst for Reform

The events of 9/11 placed increased emphasis on national security threats that emanate from ubiquitous transnational sources and the need for increased coordination across intelligence agencies at regional, national, and international levels. In the wake of 9/11, a joint inquiry was conducted by congressional intelligence committees and the National Commission on Terrorist Attacks Upon the United States (the 9/11 Commission) to investigate why intelligence agencies were unable to provide sufficient warnings of the 9/11 attacks. The joint inquiry highlighted the lack of coordination, communication, and collaboration between agencies within the intelligence community. In response to the joint inquiry's recommendations, the U.S. Congress passed the Intelligence Reform and Terrorism Prevention Act of 2004 (IRTPA, Public Law 108-458).

The IRTPA strengthened the collaborative capacity of the intelligence community by establishing a number of national fusion centers that facilitate the collaborative sharing, collection, and analysis of intelligence information among members of the intelligence community. In addition to the IRTPA, President George W. Bush established Executive Order 13356 in August 2004, which mandated U.S. federal agencies to share terrorism-related information and established guidelines and procedures to facilitate intelligence-sharing activities. Reforms that were established in the aftermath of 9/11 not only strengthened the capacity of the intelligence community to share intelligence information domestically but also strengthened the capacity of intelligence agencies to work multilaterally with foreign governments to address issues of terrorism and transnational crime.

Collaborative Intelligence-Sharing Activities

The U.S. Department of Homeland Security (DHS) participates in a variety of interagency task forces that share and integrate intelligence information to identify sources of transnational crime that threaten U.S. national security. For example, the DHS has partnered with the Federal Bureau of Investigation (FBI), National Security Branch, to provide an integrated approach to intelligence that better supports domestic law-enforcement activities. Today the National Security Branch integrates counterterrorism, counterintelligence, and weapons of mass destruction components of intelligence under one roof.

Housed within the Department of Homeland Security, the U.S. Immigration and Customs Enforcement (ICE) agency is mandated to combat terrorism and transnational crime. Although ICE's mission is to secure the U.S. borders, its responsibility is to prevent terrorists and criminals from entering U.S. ports of entry; therefore, the agency's mandate has been interpreted broadly to encompass investigative and enforcement activities throughout the world. ICE operates a threat analysis unit that engages in intelligence-led investigation activities, including data mining to detect suspected transnational criminals. ICE also participates in a variety of interagency and multilateral task forces aimed at preventing and enforcing transnational crime, which include the Joint Terrorism Task Force, the Extraterritorial Criminal Travel Strike Force, and the Human Smuggling and Trafficking Center.

The FBI provides investigative and intelligence support services to the Department of Justice (DOJ). The FBI's Office of International Operations and Legal Attaché offices, located in U.S. embassies, are responsible for coordinating law-enforcement and security operations with foreign governments to fight against transnational crime and terrorism. The FBI also hosts the National Joint Terrorism Task Force, contributes resources to the International Criminal Police Organization's (Interpol's) Fusion Task Force, and participates in the International Organized Crime Intelligence and Operations Center (IOC-2). The IOC-2 is an interagency crime intelligence operations center that serves as a fusion center or repository of crime intelligence information for a number of U.S. federal agencies.

The DOJ also leads the Office of Overseas Prosecutorial Development Assistance and Training (OPDAT) and the International Criminal Investigative Training and Assistance (ICITAP) programs. These programs seek to improve U.S. security and address issues of transnational crime by improving criminal justice processes and institutions abroad. The OPDAT and ICITAP are criminal justice institution development organizations that assist foreign governments in developing criminal justice

capacity in the areas of policing, courts, prosecution, and corrections. These programs also seek to facilitate international cooperation in intelligence sharing, information sharing, and strategic development.

The Bureau of International Narcotics and Law Enforcement Affairs and the Office of the Coordinator of Counterterrorism, housed within the U.S. Department of State, coordinate efforts to combat transnational crime and terrorism with foreign governments. These programs coordinate multilateral policy making with foreign governments, train foreign law-enforcement officials, and support programs to combat a variety of transnational crime issues. In coordination with the Department of Justice and the Department of Homeland Security, the Department of State leads the Human Smuggling and Trafficking Center (HSTC), which was established in 2004 under the IRTPA. The HSTC coordinates law enforcement, intelligence, and diplomatic efforts to combat human trafficking, migrant smuggling, and the illicit travel of transnational criminals. The HSTC maintains information-sharing agreements with foreign law enforcement and anti-trafficking organizations and has capability to link Department of Defense intelligence on foreign terrorist and criminal networks with human smuggling organizations.

The U.S. Department of Defense (DOD) is responsible for a number of counternarcotics and counterterrorism operations. As a result of the events of September 11, 2001, national security policy makers recognized the growing link between drug trafficking and terrorism-related activities, which are particularly evident in Colombia and Afghanistan. The DOD has been engaged in an ongoing campaign with the Colombian government to counter narcotics trade and terrorism-related activities of the Revolutionary Armed Forces of Colombia (FARC). In this collaborative effort, the DOD assists the Colombian government by providing it with military training, equipment, and other sources of military support. The U.S. DOD is also engaged in a collaborative task force with the British government to combat the illicit drug trade in Afghanistan. In 2009, the Senate Foreign Relations Committee reported the development of a new task force that comprises the U.S. and British militaries, the United Kingdom's Serious Organised Crime Agency (SOCA), and the U.S. Drug Enforcement

Administration, which is tasked with identifying and thwarting drug networks that are associated with the Taliban.

Blake M. Randol
Washington State University

See also Drug Trade: Source, Destination, and Transit Countries; Human Trafficking; Money Laundering: History; Money Laundering: Methods; Money Laundering: Targeting Criminal Proceeds; Money Laundering: Vulnerable Commodities and Services; Narco-Terrorism

Further Readings

Office of the Director of National Intelligence. *The National Intelligence Strategy of the United States of America*. Washington, DC: Author, 2009. http://www .dni.gov/reports/2009_NIS.pdf (Accessed February 2011).

Rollins, J. and L. S. Wyler. *International Terrorism and Transnational Crime: Security Threats, U.S. Policy, and Considerations for Congress*. Washington, DC: Congressional Research Service, 2010.

Rosenbach, E. and A. J. Peritz. *Confrontation and Collaboration: Congress and the Intelligence Community*. Cambridge, MA: Belief Center for Science and International Affairs, John F. Kennedy School of Government, 2009.

INTELLIGENCE AGENCIES: ILLEGAL ENGAGEMENTS

As a result of the purpose and structure of intelligence agencies—secretive organizations with large, undisclosed budgets organized to target and disrupt supposed "enemies"—they are perhaps particularly susceptible to illegal engagements. Some would suggest that criminality is inherent within these organizations and their actions, particularly where broader concerns of civil and human rights are taken into account. Close relations with arms manufacturers and other corporations also provide opportunities for state-corporate crime.

Illegal activities have been regular features of U.S. counterinsurgency efforts targeting leftist groups within and outside the United States, as well as legitimate and recognized nominally left-wing governments. The Kennedy administration, for example, initiated an expansive counterinsurgency program involving tens of millions of dollars and thousands of personnel. By the time of Kennedy's assassination in November 1963, counterinsurgency operations were active in a dozen countries. Notably, Operation Mongoose provided a $50 million annual budget to American and Cuban operatives to undermine the communist regime in Cuba. Operated by the Miami station of the Central Intelligence Agency (CIA), Operation Mongoose violated the Neutrality Act and legislation prohibiting the CIA from operating within the United States.

Between the late 1950s and early 1970s the Federal Bureau of Investigation (FBI) organized and operated the Counter Intelligence Program (COINTELPRO), which engaged in a range of illegal activities designed to disrupt and destroy left-wing groups in the United States, notably including the Black Panther Party, the Congress of Racial Equality (CORE), Students for a Democratic Society (SDS), and the Socialist Workers Party. COINTELPRO's actions against progressive groups included psychological warfare, wrongful imprisonment, illegal surveillance, violence, and assassinations. COINTELPRO was a covert operation only uncovered by a community group, the Citizens' Commission to Investigate the FBI. An investigation into COINTELPRO was launched in 1976 under the Select Committee to Study Governmental Operations with Respect to Intelligence Activities of the United States Senate, and the committee concluded that COINTELPRO was an illegal vigilante operation and ordered it disbanded.

U.S. counterinsurgency operations engaged various illegal activities in other countries, from Vietnam in the early 1960s to the present. An early success, initiated in Vietnam in 1961, was Operation Black Eagle. This operation involved the training of Vietnamese in death squads prepared for acts of terror and assassination with the Viet Cong as primary targets. Similar squads were organized in Central America, notably in El Salvador and Guatemala in the 1960s, and continued throughout the Cold War era. During the El Contra Terror in Guatemala during 1966–67, an estimated 8,000 people were killed. Covert and illegal schemes were also used to finance Contra death squads in Central America.

One of the greatest scandals involving U.S. intelligence services became public in 1986. During this episode, dubbed the Iran-Contra affair, the United States conducted a $417 million secret, and illegal, arms deal with Iran, brokered by Adnan Khashoggi, a Saudi arms dealer. The Contras were an illegal paramilitary group formed to oppose the leftist Sandinistas in Nicaragua. The Contras, who received aid from the CIA, were responsible for a range of atrocities, including mass killings in Nicaragua and El Salvador. Iran-Contra involved the illegal sale of arms to Iran. Profits from the sale were used to fund the Contras.

In the period of alternative globalization movements, in the late 20th and early 21st centuries, security services have been accused of violating a variety of laws regarding civil and human rights. There have been particular concerns about the surveillance of activists, infiltration of groups, and use of agents provocateurs.

During the period of the War on Terror, intelligence services have been involved in a range of activities against citizens in their own country of operation that have raised serious questions about their legality. These activities have included the extradition of supposed terror suspects to states that practice torture. In some cases, intelligence services in liberal democracies have collaborated to effect deportation to torture regimes. One infamous case involves the Canadian Security and Intelligence Service (CSIS), which made erroneous information about Canadian citizen Maher Arar available to the U.S. government. On the basis of this evidence, Arar, who had been arrested and detained in the United States, was deported to Syria, where he was subjected to months of torture. The transfer of information and the deportation to torture were violations of Canadian and international laws. Arar sued the Canadian government and was awarded a multi-million-dollar settlement.

Western governments have played key roles in the development of terrorism. They have been involved in the funding of terror groups, the establishment of terror networks, and the provision of resources to those networks. Often Western nations' intelligence services have been involved in sponsoring intelligence services in poorer countries with their own undemocratic polities.

Perhaps most notorious is the U.S. sponsorship of the war against the Soviet Union in Afghanistan. The Directorate of Inter-Services Intelligence (ISI) in Pakistan was charged with providing support for mujahideen forces attacking the Soviet military and their local allies in Afghanistan. The ISI became a massive structure, with more than 150,000 employees, and wielded significant power, operating as something of a parallel organization to the Pakistani state.

Under the administration of U.S. President Ronald Reagan, the war in Afghanistan would become the largest covert operation in the history of the United States. The CIA supplied arms through the ISI as a means of avoiding direct contact with the mujahideen. A covert network of couriers moved arms, ammunition, money, and people from Pakistan to Afghanistan through the "Afghan pipeline." Lorreta Napoleoni reports that the cost of the Afghan war to sponsors of the mujahideen was no less than $5 billion per year. The ISI spent about $1.5 million per month to ship and store goods.

Not only were shipments of arms, ammunition, supplies, and people illegal, but the ISI also directed bribes and war profiteering through the pipeline. Bribes were made at borders to border officials and within prisons to prison officials. U.S. funding came through the so-called black budget of the Pentagon, hidden funds used to finance covert operations. Napoleoni notes that this budget rose from around $9 billion in 1981 to about $36 billion by the mid-1990s. Napoleoni suggests that William Casey, CIA director under Reagan, used the black budget as the CIA's private fund.

The CIA also tried to replicate the success of its covert operations in Afghanistan in Yugoslavia. In 1991 a secret alliance was established with Islamist groups in Yugoslavia, and a Croatian pipeline was set up on the model of the Afghan pipeline. To provide arms, supplies, and finances through the pipeline, the U.S. intelligence authorities broke the United Nations (UN) embargo against Bosnia. The program, which was approved by President Bill Clinton, had been suggested by Anthony Lake, future leader of the CIA. In addition to arms and supplies, the Croatian pipeline also brought Iran's revolutionary guards and spies of its Ministry of Intelligence and National Security (VEVAK) into Bosnia, increasing the influence of Iran in the region. The Clinton administration even inspected Iranian missiles that went through the pipeline.

One of the illegal activities in which intelligence agencies regularly engage, because it is so lucrative, is the production and trade of drugs. The CIA networks in Asia had long been involved in drug smuggling. During the Vietnam War, the CIA ran heroin through Cambodia. In the 1980s and 1990s, the CIA was involved in the processing of opium and smuggling of heroin to Western markets. The CIA and ISI helped to develop Afghanistan from a small regional provider of opium to the largest production center for heroin in the world. Providing expertise and financing, ISI and the CIA transformed Afghanistan's traditional agrarian economy into a narcotics-based economy that would become the largest supplier of heroin to the United States, accounting for 60 percent of U.S. demand, with annual profits of around $200 billion. Despite the fact that these connections became known in the United States during the most active period of the War on Drugs, there was no investigation into the trade in heroin from Pakistan to the United States by U.S. narcotics officials or the Drug Enforcement Agency.

These operations are largely about business and serve to transfer billions through arms producers and brokers and politicians. Criminal activity carried out by intelligence services requires ad hoc infrastructures of international finance to transfer funds. One of the financial institutions employed most regularly by the CIA under Casey was the Bank of Credit and Commerce International (BCCI), located in Karachi, Pakistan. Founded in 1972, the BCCI would become the largest Muslim banking institution in the world. A leading shareholder in BCCI was Kamal Adham, a former head of the Saudi Intelligence Agency. His partner was Raymond Close, the former CIA station chief in Saudi Arabia. The CIA has routinely used BCCI for its covert operations. Israeli spy agencies have used BCCI for their own arms purchases. In addition to engaging in illegal arms deals, BCCI networks have been used to fund illegal paramilitaries, including the Contras in Nicaragua, the Union for the Total Independence of Angola (UNITA), and Manuel Noriega in Panama. The CIA has used the black networks of BCCI to bribe Pakistani officers, and the U.S. National Security Council used BCCI channels to transfer money in the Iran-Contra arms deal.

Jeffrey Shantz
Kwantlen Polytechnic University

See also Communication Technologies; Egmont Group of Financial Intelligence Units; European Union;

Europol; Extradition; Extraordinary Rendition; Intelligence Agencies: Collaboration Within the United States; Intelligence Agencies: Illegal Engagements; Intelligence Agencies: U.S.; Interpol; Joint Force Policing and Integrated Models; Policing: High Versus Low; Policing: National Security; Policing: Transnational; Rule of Law Versus Security; Securitization After Terror; Stings and Reverse Stings

Further Readings

Blackstock, Nelson. *COINTELPRO: The FBI's Secret War on Political Freedom.* New York: Pathfinder, 1988.

Michalowski, Raymond J. and Ronald C. Kramer. *State-Corporate Crime: Wrongdoing at the Intersection of Business and Government.* New Brunswick, NJ: Rutgers University Press, 2006.

Napoleoni, Loretta. *Terror Incorporated: Tracing the Dollars Behind the Terror Networks.* New York: Seven Stories, 2005.

Napoleoni, Loretta. *Terrorism and the Economy: How the War on Terror Is Bankrupting the World.* New York: Seven Stories, 2010.

Scott, Peter Dale. *American War Machine: Deep Politics, the CIA Global Drug Connection, and the Road to Afghanistan.* Lanham, MD: Rowman & Littlefield, 2010.

Simon, David R. *Elite Deviance.* New York: Allyn & Bacon, 2007.

INTELLIGENCE AGENCIES: U.S.

National security policy is driven by intelligence, which consists of information assessments concerning potential security risks. Raw information is contextualized and analyzed in order to produce intelligence from it. That intelligence is then used to inform the policy-making process and to augment the utility and information-richness of existing intelligence. Typically, intelligence analysis deals with information pertaining to threats such as terrorism, criminal extremism, and organized crime, assessing potential targets and their vulnerability. Intelligence agencies gather, archive, and analyze intelligence information to combat a variety of transnational security threats, including terrorism, narcotics and arms trade, human trafficking, cybercrime, and weapons proliferation. Intelligence-gathering activities often include evaluating public sources, technical and physical surveillance activities, liaison relationships, human source operations, and data searches.

Intelligence analysis converts intelligence into clear and comprehensible information, which is delivered to the U.S. president, policy makers, and military commanders and is used for strategic planning and policy. The United States employs a number of strategic programs that are designed to integrate intelligence and law-enforcement activities to address several issues of transnational crime. Examples include the Drug Enforcement Administration, Organized Crime Drug Enforcement Task Force, and the Department of State, Human Smuggling and Trafficking Center.

U.S. Intelligence Community

The U.S. intelligence community includes 17 federal agencies that are responsible for both foreign and domestic national security intelligence functions. These agencies collect and analyze intelligence information to protect the United States from a variety of transnational security threats, including terrorism, narcotics and arms trade, human trafficking, cybercrime, and weapons proliferation. The collected efforts of the intelligence community are supervised by the director of national intelligence. The Office of the Director of National Intelligence (ODNI) was established in 2004 with the passage of the Intelligence Reform and Terrorism Prevention Act of 2004 (IRTPA), which unified the efforts of the intelligence community. Prior to the establishment of the IRTPA, the intelligence community was overseen by the director of the Central Intelligence Agency (CIA), also known as the director of central intelligence.

U.S. Intelligence Agencies

Agency	Activities
Office of the Director of National Intelligence	Coordinates intelligence integration and collaboration within the intelligence community and is the principal adviser to the president, National Security Council, and Homeland Security Council.
Program Managers Central Intelligence Agency	Collects, analyzes, evaluates, and disseminates foreign intelligence. CIA intelligence aids policy makers in making national security decisions.
Department of Defense (DOD), Intelligence Agency	Produces and manages foreign military intelligence, assesses foreign military intentions and capabilities, and provides intelligence information to military commanders and policy makers.
DOD, National Geospatial-Intelligence Agency	Collects geospatial intelligence to aid in a variety of national security efforts, including navigation, military operations, and humanitarian aid efforts.
DOD, National Reconnaissance Office	Designs and operates the nation's signals and imagery reconnaissance satellites, which provide national security agencies with information relating to foreign military threats, environmental impacts, and the impact of natural and human-made disasters.
DOD, National Security Agency	Provides cryptologic services to protect the government's information systems and is the world's largest producer of foreign signals intelligence information.
Federal Bureau of Investigation (FBI), National Security Branch	Gathers intelligence pertaining to domestic and transnational criminal networks that are capable of threatening national security, including criminal enterprises, terrorist organizations, weapons proliferators, and foreign intelligence services.

(continued)

U.S. Intelligence Agencies (continued)

Agency	Activities
Departmental Intelligence Units	
Department of Energy, Office of Intelligence and Counterintelligence	Provides technical intelligence analysis relating to global energy issues, foreign nuclear weapons, and materials.
Department of Homeland Security, Office of Intelligence and Analysis	Responsible for integrating law enforcement and intelligence information relating to domestic terrorism threats. Participates in interagency counterterrorism efforts and collaborates with the FBI in sharing terrorism intelligence with state and local governments.
Department of State, Bureau of Intelligence and Research	Coordinates intelligence activities to support diplomatic efforts. Provides a wide range of intelligence services for the secretary of state, ambassadors, and policy makers.
Department of the Treasury, Office of Intelligence and Analysis	Provides focused intelligence support services to Treasury officials pertaining to a wide range of economic security issues.
Drug Enforcement Administration, Office of National Security Intelligence	Collects and shares drug-related intelligence with other members of the intelligence community.
Armed Forces Intelligence	
Air Force Intelligence	Conducts surveillance and reconnaissance and provides tactical information to the armed forces.
Army Intelligence	Supplies information to the armed forces relating to ground troop operations.
Coast Guard Intelligence	As part of the Department of Homeland Security, collects and manages intelligence information relating to port security, maritime safety, search and rescue, alien migration, and counter-narcotics activities.
Marine Corps Intelligence	Responsible for a variety of intelligence, counterintelligence, terrorism, and cryptologic activities.
Naval Intelligence	Provides intelligence services to support maritime operations worldwide.

Source: Office of the Director of National Intelligence, 2011.

The events of September 11, 2001 (9/11), and the findings of the National Commission on Terrorist Attacks Upon the United States (the 9/11 Commission) highlighted the shortcomings of the intelligence community's traditional operations, which had been organized under the 1947 National Security Act and continued to be conducted with a Cold War mentality. The IRTPA has strengthened the intelligence community by establishing central leadership, reorganizing the intelligence community, clarifying the community's collective goals, placing budgetary control in the hands of the director of national intelligence, and establishing a number of national fusion centers that facilitate the collaborative sharing, collection, and analysis of intelligence information among members of the intelligence community to address a variety of specialized issues.

The director of national intelligence oversees the federal agencies that make up the intelligence

Seventeen U.S. federal agencies are responsible for foreign and domestic national security intelligence functions, including the Central Intelligence Agency (CIA). The CIA is primarily involved in collecting information about foreign governments, corporations, and individuals, and in advising public policy makers. (CIA)

community; serves as the principal adviser to the president, the National Security Council, and the Homeland Security Council; and manages the implementation of the National Intelligence Program. The federal agencies of the intelligence community are divided into three functional groups: program managers, who advise and assist the ODNI in identifying objectives, managing finances, developing budgets, and evaluating performance; departmental intelligence units, which are responsible for managing the intelligence-based needs of their respective federal agencies; and services, the intelligence personnel employed by the armed forces.

Intelligence Community Oversight and Accountability

The intelligence community is subject to external oversight by executive and legislative branches of the U.S. government. Federal agencies within the intelligence community report national security issues to key policy makers in the executive and legislative branches, and they cooperate with intelligence oversight activities. A variety of executive entities oversee the operations of the intelligence community, including the president's Intelligence Oversight Board, the president's Foreign Intelligence Advisory

Board, and the Office of Management and Budget. Congressional oversight of the intelligence community principally resides in the House Permanent Select Committee on Intelligence and the Senate Select Committee on Intelligence.

Intelligence Gathering and Analysis

Intelligence agencies are devoted primarily to information gathering and intelligence analysis. The intelligence process begins with identifying intelligence gaps and areas of concern for policy makers. Once raw information is collected, analysts sort through and analyze the information and report their findings to national security policy makers. The information-gathering and intelligence analysis processes often identify additional intelligence gaps and areas of concern, which leads to additional questions that serve as inputs that fuel the intelligence cycle.

Information-gathering activities include evaluating public sources, technical and physical surveillance activities, liaison relationships, human source operations, and data searches. Sources of information include signals intelligence (SIGINT), imagery intelligence (IMINT), measurement and signature intelligence (MASINT), human source intelligence (HUMINT), open-source intelligence (OSINT), and geospatial intelligence (GEOINT). SIGINT is acquired through the interception of signals, whether they are between machines, people, or a combination of the two. The National Security Agency (NSA) is primarily responsible for collecting, analyzing, and reporting SIGINT, and the NSA's requirements system is managed by the director of national intelligence. According to Michael Hayden, the NSA is the world's largest collector of SIGINT.

IMINT consists of electronic images produced by film, photography, or other media, radar sensors, infrared sensors, or other optical devices. The National Geospatial Intelligence Agency manages all IMINT activities for the U.S. government.

MASINT consists of technical and scientific information that is used to identify distinctive characteristics of targets. Examples of MASINT include the identification of chemical compositions of air and water samples and the identification of radar signals produced by particular aircraft. The Central MASINT organization, housed within the Defense

Intelligence Agency, is responsible for all national MASINT activities.

HUMINT consists of intelligence derived from human sources. HUMINT is the oldest form of intelligence gathering and is often associated with covert espionage activities. Despite popular belief, most HUMINT is gathered through overt sources, such as embassy personnel, interviewing U.S. citizens and foreign nationals abroad, and official contacts with foreign governments. Open-source intelligence is gathered through publicly available information sources, such as newspapers, television, radio, and the Internet. According to Loch K. Johnson, historically about 80 percent of intelligence was gathered through open sources; however, that figure may have changed as a result of technological developments in the past few decades.

GEONIT is produced through the integration of imagery intelligence and geospatial information. Raw GEONIT imagery information is derived from reconnaissance aircraft, government satellites, and commercial satellites; other sources of GEONIT information include databases, U.S. census information, maps, and a variety of other sources.

Intelligence analysis begins with the organization of large amounts of raw, unfiltered data. Raw data are first filtered using a number of techniques, decoded if necessary, and entered into computers for processing. Once data are filtered, they are analyzed, evaluated, and integrated into deliverable intelligence products that can be utilized by managers and policy makers. Intelligence analysts who are specialized in particular areas often use the data to produce target and vulnerability assessments to understand the current state of affairs, forecast future trends and predict outcomes, warn against dangers that are posed by U.S. security threats, and produce defense intelligence assessments that are used to assist in national security operations.

The United States employs a variety of strategic programs that are designed to integrate intelligence and enforcement activities to address several areas of transnational crime, including narcotics and arms trade, human trafficking, terrorism, money laundering, financial crime, and cybercrime.

Department of Homeland Security

The U.S. Department of Homeland Security (DHS) participates in a variety of interagency task forces that share and integrate intelligence information to identify sources of transnational crime that threaten U.S. national security. For example, the DHS has partnered with the National Security Branch of the Federal Bureau of Investigation (FBI) to provide an integrated approach to intelligence that better supports domestic law-enforcement activities. Today the National Security Branch integrates counterterrorism, counterintelligence, and weapons-of-mass-destruction components of intelligence under one roof. The Suspicious Activity Report program is another collaborative program between DHS and the FBI that establishes a process to gather, analyze, and share terrorism-related intelligence, coordinating activities with state and local law-enforcement agencies to identify potential threats. Furthermore, the Homeland Security Information Network was developed to provide a secure Internet-based platform for federal, state, and local agencies, as well as private organizations, to share and analyze homeland-security-related information. The DHS 2008 Strategic Plan recognizes that technological developments and increasing global interconnectivity are opportunities for transnational crime, and that understanding threats emanating from transnational crime is integral to maintaining homeland security.

Federal Bureau of Investigation

The FBI provides investigative and intelligence support services to the Department of Justice. The FBI's Office of International Operations and Legal Attaché Offices, located in U.S. embassies, are responsible for coordinating law-enforcement and security operations with foreign governments to fight against transnational crime and terrorism. Combating transnational crime and terrorism threats to the United States increasingly requires coordination between law-enforcement and intelligence agencies throughout the world. The FBI also hosts the National Joint Terrorism Task Force, contributes resources to the Fusion Task Force (part of the International Criminal Police Organization, known as Interpol), and participates in the International Organized Crime Intelligence and Operations Center (IOC-2).

Drug Enforcement Administration

The U.S. Drug Enforcement Administration (DEA) is the federal agency that is primarily responsible for combating drug crime, both domestically and internationally. The DEA is engaged in a variety of operations to combat organizations involved in the international drug trade. The agency has placed key emphasis on using intelligence-led operations to combat drug-trafficking and bulk-currency money-laundering operations. The Organized Crime Drug Enforcement Task Force (OCDETF) coordinates efforts with a number of federal agencies to reduce the drug supply. The OCDETF Fusion Center (OFC) gathers and analyzes intelligence related to drug-trafficking and drug money-laundering operations, using the information in intra-agency and international efforts to thwart transnational drug crime activities. The DEA also coordinates intelligence-based drug enforcement efforts with the Treasury Department's Office of Foreign Assets Control to target movements of bulk currency smuggling that are intended for drug-trafficking operations.

Department of Defense

The U.S. Department of Defense (DOD) is responsible for a number of counternarcotics and counterterrorism operations. As a result of the events of September 11, 2001, national security policy makers recognized the growing link between drug-trafficking and terrorism-related activities, which are particularly evident in Colombia and Afghanistan. As a result, the DOD's counternarcotics and counterterrorism operations were placed under the leadership of the Office of the Assistant Secretary of Defense, Office for Special Operations and Low-Intensity Conflict (SO/LIC) to improve coordination activities. The DOD has been engaged in an ongoing campaign to provide military assistance to the Colombian government in efforts to counter the drug-trafficking activities of the Revolutionary Armed Forces of Colombia (FARC). In 2004, DOD-led interagency task forces were authorized by Congress to increase counternarcotics and counterterrorism activities. The DOD plays a key role in combating terrorism and drug-trafficking activities in Afghanistan. In conjunction with the Department of the Treasury, the DOD coleads the Afghan Threat Finance Cell, which gathers and analyzes financial intelligence to assist in combating antigovernment insurgency in Afghanistan.

Department of State

The Bureau of International Narcotics and Law Enforcement Affairs and the Office of the Coordinator of Counterterrorism, housed within the U.S. Department of State, coordinate efforts to combat transnational crime and terrorism with foreign governments. These programs coordinate multilateral policy making with foreign governments, train foreign law-enforcement officials, and support programs to combat a variety of transnational crime issues. In coordination with the Department of Justice and the Department of Homeland Security, the Department of State leads the Human Smuggling and Trafficking Center (HSTC), which was established in 2004 under the IRTPA. The HSTC coordinates law-enforcement, intelligence, and diplomatic efforts to combat human trafficking, migrant smuggling, and the illicit travel of transnational criminals. The HSTC maintains information-sharing agreements with foreign law-enforcement and antitrafficking organizations, and it has the capability to link DOD intelligence of foreign terrorist and criminal networks with human-smuggling organizations.

Department of the Treasury

The U.S. Treasury Department's Office of Terrorism and Financial Intelligence (TFI) uses financial intelligence to combat illicit finances used by terrorist and transnational crime organizations. Established in 2004, TFI combines operations of the Treasury's Office of Intelligence and Analysis, Office of Terrorism Financing and Financial Crimes, Financial Crimes Enforcement Network, and Office of Foreign Asset Control to link and coordinate Treasury's transnational crime efforts with the greater U.S. intelligence community.

Blake M. Randol
Washington State University

See also Drug Trade: Source, Destination, and Transit Countries; Human Trafficking; Intelligence Agencies: Collaboration Within the United States; Money Laundering: History; Money Laundering: Methods; Money Laundering: Targeting Criminal Proceeds; Money Laundering: Vulnerable Commodities and Services; Narco-Terrorism

Further Readings

Carter, D. L. *The Concept and Implementation of Intelligence-Led Policing (ILP).* East Lansing: School of Criminal Justice, Michigan State University, 2008.

Hayden, M. V. "Balancing Security and Liberty: The Challenge of Sharing Foreign Signals Intelligence." *Notre Dame Journal of Law, Ethics and Public Policy*, v.19 (2005).

Johnson, Lock K. *Secret Agencies: U.S. Intelligence in a Hostile World*. New Haven, CT: Yale University Press, 1996.

Office of the Director of National Intelligence. *The National Intelligence Strategy of the United States of America*. 2009. http://www.dni.gov/reports/2009_NIS .pdf (Accessed February 2011).

Rollins, J. and L. S. Wyler. *International Terrorism and Transnational Crime: Security Threats, U.S. Policy, and Considerations for Congress*. Washington, DC: Congressional Research Service, 2010.

Rosenbach, E. and A. J. Peritz. *Confrontation and Collaboration: Congress and the Intelligence Community*. Cambridge, MA: Belief Center for Science and International Affairs, John F. Kennedy School of Government, 2009.

U.S. Department of Homeland Security. *One Team, One Mission, Securing Our Homeland*. 2008. http://www .dhs.gov/xlibrary/assets/DHS_StratPlan_FINAL_spread .pdf (Accessed February 2011).

U.S. Drug Enforcement Administration. "Money Laundering." http://www.justice.gov/dea/programs/ money.htm (Accessed February 2011).

INTERNATIONAL ASSOCIATION OF CHIEFS OF POLICE

The International Association of Chiefs of Police (IACP) is a group of police administrative officers. The IACP was founded in 1893 in Chicago, Illinois. It currently has a membership of about 20,000 police chief executive officers, from about 100 countries. The primary goal of the IACP is the joining of forces in the police fight against crime. IACP has also adopted as its mandate the improvement of services and policing effectiveness globally. At its inception, the IACP adopted the name the National Chiefs of Police Union, with the declared goal of forging a platform for police executive officers to exchange information to enhance their crime-fighting capabilities in both the international and domestic arenas. The collaborative relationship was instrumental in the development of some of the innovative crime-fighting methods employed by the police in the world today. It is claimed that the IACP has been in the forefront in facilitating the apprehension of fugitives across the world.

The IACP is arguably the world's oldest and largest police executive organization. It is a non-profit organization with membership drawn from participating countries' federal, state, and local police agencies. Approximately 135 staff members work in the IACP Secretariat. As a law-enforcement body, the IACP has played key roles in the development and promotion of police services and science. Its contribution to police reform, especially in the first two decades of the 20th century, has been widely acknowledged. Many credit the IACP for making the police a civil service organization that is detached from the political tutelage and influence of politicians. The IACP is also known to have spearheaded the centralization and professionalization of police administration and services. The introduction of specialized units in law enforcement, such as juvenile delinquency departments and terrorism control squads, is the handiwork of the IACP.

The IACP has identified as its central mission the promotion and advancement of the science and art of police services. It has also set for itself the goal of developing and disseminating effective technical and operational practices in police work. The IACP has also identified the fostering of police cooperation and exchange of valuable information as essential to the role of policing in society. It has been involved in creating and sharing manuals and performance standards for its membership, including training bulletins used by federal, state, and local police academies. It is a major advocate of high standards of professional conduct and practice among all law-enforcement officers.

Over its history, the IACP has been involved in key events in the evolution of policing: In 1897, the IACP played key roles in the establishment of the National Bureau of Criminal Identification and in selling the idea and its operation to its membership. As early as 1904, the IACP was involved in the use of fingerprinting as a means of identifying criminals. In 1922, the IACP championed the introduction of a uniform crime recording and reporting system. In 1924, IACP criminal identification files were used to create the Identification Division of the Federal Bureau of Investigation (FBI). During the 1927 annual meeting of the IACP, the Committee on Uniform Crime Records received the directive to review national crime data; this committee created a manual for the preparation of standardized crime-reporting data for police agencies across the United States, and through its recommendations to Congress the FBI eventually adopted the IACP's uniform crime recording system in 1930. The establishment of the national, state, and local police academies in 1934 is also the result of initiatives by the IACP and the FBI.

To standardize police training and practice, the IACP started the publication of the *Police Chief Newsletter*. This publication was later retitled *Police Chief* and was published monthly. It is widely recognized as the "professional voice of law enforcement" and is circulated to most police departments worldwide. The IACP established its administrative headquarters in Washington, D.C., in 1940, where it could more effectively advance its organizational stability and its ability to provide needed services to its membership. The IACP has also developed manuals in which it outlines criteria for holding police accountable. In addition, the IACP and the Commission on Accreditation for Law Enforcement Agencies (CALEA) have established policies and standards to address the efficiency of methods for receiving and processing complaints of misconduct involving law-enforcement personnel. The IACP is a major source of ideas for containing social disorder, sabotage, and movement of troops during wartime.

During the 1960s, the IACP, in collaboration with the International Association of Police Professors (the forerunner of the present Academy of Criminal Justice Sciences, ACJS), started the campaign and promotion of higher education and professional training for law-enforcement personnel. The idea and practice quickly spread, and by the 1970s many countries had adopted the practice of requiring higher education for police officers. In recognition of the IACP's role in creating the framework for training police officers worldwide, the United Nations (UN) conferred a consultative status on the IACP.

To consolidate its leadership in police training and practice worldwide, the IACP opened its first World Regional Office in Europe during the 1980s. To maintain minimum policing standards across the world, the IACP regularly conducts policing seminars in both Europe and Asia. It also provides criteria for commissioning police agencies. In 1986, the IACP created the Private Sector Liaison Committee (PSLC) to develop and implement best practices in law enforcement.

During the 1990s, the IACP focused on strategies for eradicating international narcotics trafficking, human trafficking, and terrorism. In the United States, it has also focused its attention on curbing drunk driving, eliminating police abuse (including the excessive use of force), and the treatment of criminal aliens. The IACP also provides expertise and strategies to participating members interested in establishing community policing programs.

The IACP continues to be a major resource for law-enforcement agencies throughout the world. It conducts research and provides ideas and expertise to its members interested in adopting new policing programs and publishes manuals on a wide range of policing issues, from the prevention and control of school violence to policing approaches to individuals with mental disorders. It produces videos on such topics as policing of offenders who have served sentences and are reentering the community. The IACP is a major resource on policing functions and accountability, both to governments and to civil society.

Rochelle E. Cobbs
Mississippi Valley State University
O. Oko Elechi
Prairie View A&M University

See also Data Sources: Police Data; Joint Force Policing and Integrated Models; Police Cooperation; Policing: Domestic; Policing: High Versus Low; Policing: National Security; Policing: Privately Contracted; Policing: Transnational

Further Readings

Bennett, Wayne W. and Karen M. Hess. *Management and Supervision in Law Enforcement*, 5th ed. Belmont, CA: Thomson-Wadsworth, 2007.

Hess, Karen M. *Introduction to Law Enforcement and Criminal Justice*, 9th ed. Belmont, CA: Thomson-Wadsworth, 2009.

Inciardi, James A. *Criminal Justice*, 9th ed. New York: McGraw-Hill, 2010.

International Association of Chiefs of Police. "Global Leadership in Policing: Timeline." http://www.theiacp .org/About/History/Timeline/tabid/101/Default.aspx (Accessed June 2011).

International Association of Chiefs of Police. "IACP Overview: History and Background." http://www .theiacp.org (Accessed June 2011).

Siegel, Larry J. and Joseph J. Senna. *Introduction to Criminal Justice*, 11th ed. Belmont, CA: Thomson-Wadsworth, 2008.

Stojkovic, Stan, David Kalinich, and John Klofas. *Criminal Justice Organizations: Administration and Management*, 4th ed. Belmont, CA: Thomson-Wadsworth, 2008.

Wrobleski, Henry M. and Karen M. Hess. *Introduction to Law Enforcement and Criminal Justice*, 8th ed. Belmont, CA: Thomson-Wadsworth, 2006.

INTERNATIONAL CRIMES

International crimes are violations of international law that shock the consciences of all people throughout the international community. Just as state crimes victimize all members of the state, international crimes victimize all members of the international community. Crimes against the peace, war crimes, and crimes against humanity were first prosecuted at the international military tribunals at Nüremberg and Tokyo after World War II. Subsequently, these were affirmed as crimes under international law included in the Nüremberg Principles of 1950, which had previously been affirmed by the United Nations (UN) General Assembly in 1946. Also in 1946, the General Assembly affirmed genocide as a crime under international law. Therefore, international crimes, in the strictest sense, include the crime of genocide, crimes against humanity, war crimes, and the crime of aggression (formerly referred to as crimes against the peace).

Historically, the first international crime is claimed to have been piracy. Since piracy was and is committed on the high seas, shared by all members of the international community, it was understood that the territory in which a pirate landed had the authority to prosecute him on behalf of the international community.

The term *genocide* was coined by Raphael Lemkin in his 1944 publication *Axis Rule of Occupied Europe*. Lemkin formed the term by combining the Greek word *genos* (tribe, race) with the Latin word *cide* (killing). On December 11, 1946, the UN General Assembly passed Resolution 96(I), which affirmed genocide as a crime under international law. In the same resolution, the General Assembly asked the Economic and Social Council to undertake the necessary studies to draw up a convention on the crime of genocide. The council established the Ad Hoc Committee on Genocide for that purpose; the committee submitted its report on May 24, 1948. After further negotiations, the General Assembly, on December 9, 1948, adopted the Convention on the Prevention and Punishment of the Crime of Genocide. Article 2 of the convention defines genocide as

> any of the following acts committed with the intent to destroy, in whole or in part, a national, ethnical, racial, or religious group, as such: killing members of the group; causing serious bodily or mental harm to members of the group; deliberately inflicting on the group conditions of life calculated to bring about its physical destruction in whole or in part; imposing measures intended to prevent births within the group; forcibly transferring children of the group to another group.

Scholars from other disciplines have attempted to expand the definition of genocide to include cultural and political groups. However, Article 2 is the only definition of genocide that has been included verbatim in subsequent statutes and treaties. On January 12, 1951, the Genocide Convention entered into force, and the International Court of Justice ruled that genocide was a crime under customary international law, which meant that all states were legally obligated to observe the convention regardless of whether they had deposited their ratification.

Crimes against humanity have a longer history than genocide, however. In a case often described as the first prosecution by an international tribunal, Peter von Hagenbach was prosecuted in 1474 by the Holy Roman Empire for violating "the laws of God and man." This evidence demonstrates that some offenses considered to be violations of the laws of man could be prosecuted as crimes. In May 1915, the phrase *crimes against humanity* was officially used for the first time in a warning issued by the British Empire, France, and Russia to the Young Turks, who were governing the Ottoman Empire. They had implemented deportation laws to rid the Ottoman Empire of certain religious and ethnic minority groups, including Armenian Christians.

After World War I, the multinational Commission on the Responsibility of the Authors of the War and on Enforcement of Penalties was established to investigate which states had been responsible for initiating the war and to recommend an appropriate tribunal to prosecute and punish the individuals responsible. The commission included 15 members, most of whom pushed for the creation of an international criminal tribunal in order to prosecute the former German emperor, William II, for violating the laws of war and the laws of humanity. The United States and Japan disagreed with prosecuting violations of the laws of humanity, since there were no statutory laws of humanity and no legal precedent for the prosecution of such crimes. Although William II was arraigned for violating the law of treaties, he was not prosecuted; instead, he eluded capture by taking advantage of the Netherlands' offer of sanctuary.

After World War II, the Allied victors, including the United States, the United Kingdom, the Soviet Union, and France, established the International Military Tribunal to prosecute high-ranking Nazis for the atrocities they had committed both before and during the war. Article 6 of the Charter of the International Military Tribunal included crimes against humanity in its jurisdiction and defined them as follows: "namely, murder, extermination, enslavement, deportation, and other inhumane acts committed against any civilian population, before or during the war, or persecutions on political, racial or religious grounds." For the first time in history, government officials were prosecuted by another state for committing atrocities against their own civilians. Definitions of crimes against humanity have changed over the decades. The Statute for the International Criminal Tribunal for Rwanda redefined crimes against humanity so that they were connected not only to armed conflict. As a result, crimes against humanity could, by legal standards, be committed during times of peace as well as times of armed conflict.

The Rome Statute of the International Criminal Court expanded previous definitions of crimes against humanity by including and defining several examples. The Rome Statute defines crimes against humanity as "any of the following acts when committed as part of a widespread or systematic attack directed against any civilian population, with knowledge of the attack" and goes on to include murder, extermination, enslavement, torture, and rape as crimes that—if committed as part of a widespread or systematic attack on a civilian population with the participant's knowledge that the attack is part of a larger or systematic attack—qualify as a crime against humanity.

War crimes are serious violations of international humanitarian law during an armed conflict. Armed conflicts may be either international or internal (noninternational). International armed conflicts occur between two or more states, whereas internal armed conflicts (such as a civil war) occur within one state. International humanitarian law, also referred to as the law of war, developed over many centuries through international law established from customs rather than conventions and treaties. Two

forms of law govern international humanitarian law. The first is *jus ad bellum*, which governs the legality of initiating an armed conflict. The second is *jus in bello*, which governs the legality of acts during an armed conflict. While the two are related, they are definitely distinct laws. For example, if a state unlawfully attacks another state in violation of *jus ad bellum*, then *jus in bello* is still applicable to belligerents participating in the armed conflict. Contrarily, if a state lawfully attacks another state, *jus in bello* is still applicable to prevent and punish those individuals who may commit war crimes during the armed conflict.

The first codification of international humanitarian law occurred in the establishment of the Lieber Code in 1863, named for its codifier, Francis Lieber, who was authorized by the U.S. War Department under President Abraham Lincoln to develop a code of conduct for the army in response to reports of atrocities committed during the American Civil War. The Lieber Code consisted of 157 articles defining how military personnel were to conduct themselves in the field.

Since the Lieber Code, many international conventions drafting treaties have defined unlawful conduct and the use of weapons during armed conflict. Most notable are the 1899 and 1907 Hague Conventions on the laws and customs of war on land, which govern the legality of methods of warfare. In 1949, the four Geneva Conventions were adopted. Each of the four conventions protects a category of persons during armed conflicts. For example, the third convention protects prisoners of war and the fourth convention protects civilians during armed conflicts.

War crimes are a common charge included in prosecutions of international crimes. From the Nüremberg Tribunal after World War II to the International Criminal Court and the Iraqi High Tribunal that prosecuted Saddam Hussein, war crimes are the least controversial of international criminal offenses. The first international criminal tribunal to prosecute war crimes since the 1949 Geneva Conventions was the International Criminal Tribunal for the former Yugoslavia in 1993, which was established by the UN Security Council for the prosecution of genocide, crimes against humanity, and war crimes. In 1994, the UN Security Council established the International Criminal Tribunal for Rwanda for the prosecution of genocide, crimes against humanity, and war crimes by applying Common Article 3 (in the four Geneva Conventions of 1949), which applies to noninternational armed conflicts. The conflict in Rwanda was internal; therefore, Common Article 3 was necessary to prosecute certain violations of the Geneva Conventions of 1949.

The two basic elements that define a war crime are (1) a serious violation that (2) occurs during an armed conflict. The latter element requires that the violation has a connection to an armed conflict so that if there is no war, there can be no war crime. For example, if a murder is committed in a state that is at war with another state, but the murder has no connection to the war itself, then a war crime has not been committed. Thus, the result is a murder to be prosecuted by the state with jurisdiction over such crimes. Similarly, if a crime is committed in connection with a war but does not constitute a serious violation (as when a soldier takes a loaf of bread from a village that has much food), a war crime has not been committed, since the offense is not considered serious.

The fourth international crime is the crime of aggression. Aggression was first prosecuted at the International Military Tribunal at Nüremberg after World War II as a crime against the peace. Article 6 of the Charter of the International Military Tribunal defines crimes against the peace as "namely, planning, preparation, initiation or waging of a war of aggression, or a war in violation of international treaties, agreements or assurances, or participation in a common plan or conspiracy for the accomplishment of any of the foregoing" crimes, including war crimes and crimes against humanity. Article 5 of the Charter of the International Military Tribunal for the Far East had a similar definition of crimes against the peace.

In 1946, the UN General Assembly invited the International Law Commission to study the desirability and probability of creating an international criminal court to prosecute international crimes, but the effort to complete its task was interrupted when the General Assembly passed a resolution to postpone the task indefinitely until a definition of aggression could be adopted. In 1974, the General Assembly adopted a definition of aggression, and in 1989 it asked the International Law Commission to address the question of establishing an international criminal court. Although a definition of aggression had been adopted, it really gave the Security Council only the ability to determine acts of aggression,

which it now has the authority to do under Chapter 7 of the Charter of the UN. If the Security Council determines that an act of aggression has occurred, it can impose sanctions on the aggressive state. The UN definition of aggression did not need to be adopted by an international criminal court independent of the Security Council.

On July 17, 1998, after nine years of studies and negotiations, the Rome Statute of the International Criminal Court was adopted. Article 5 of the Rome Statute lists the crimes within the International Criminal Court's jurisdiction. These crimes include genocide, crimes against humanity, war crimes, and aggression. Starting with Article 6, genocide, crimes against humanity, and war crimes have their own articles that specifically define them. Aggression does not have its own article because delegates in Rome were unable to agree on a definition. Instead, they agreed to include aggression and adopt a definition at a later date. In May 2010, the Assembly of States Parties to the International Criminal Court adopted a criminal definition of aggression, which allows states to agree to be within the crime's jurisdiction. This option was necessary to gain enough votes to adopt the definition.

The Rome Statute of the International Criminal Court is the most authoritative international criminal code. It was adopted with 120 countries voting in favor, seven voting against, and 21 abstaining. The United States was one of the seven countries that voted against the adoption of the Rome Statute, since the International Criminal Court is independent of the UN Security Council, which is responsible for responding to breaches of the peace. On December 31, 2000, the United States signed the Rome Statute, but it has remained reluctant to ratify it. Currently, of the five permanent members on the Security Council, France and the United Kingdom have ratified the Rome Statute, and the United States, China, and Russia have not.

Harry M. Rhea
Richard Stockton College of New Jersey

See also Crimes Against Humanity; Genocide; International Criminal Court; War Crimes

Further Readings

Bassiouni, M. Cherif. *Crimes Against Humanity: Historical Evolution and Contemporary Application.* New York: Cambridge University Press, 2011.

Schabas, William A. *Genocide in International Law*, 2nd ed. New York: Cambridge University Press, 2009.

Schabas, William A. *An Introduction to the International Criminal Court*, 4th ed. New York: Cambridge University Press, 2011.

INTERNATIONAL CRIMINAL COURT

Throughout human history, there have been numerous acts of war crimes, crimes against humanity, and genocide. Prior to the 20th century, most of these crimes went unpunished. Between the late 19th century and the mid-20th century, through such treaties as the Geneva Conventions and the Hague Conventions, certain acts were defined as war crimes. It was not until World War II and the Holocaust inflicted by Nazi Germany against the Jews and various other racial and ethnic groups, however, that the crime of genocide was defined and recognized. At the end of World War II, the Nazi leaders were tried, judged, and punished by the Nüremberg Tribunal, which formally recognized such crimes. Shortly after World War II, the United Nations (UN) and the International Court of Justice were created and the Convention on the Prevention and Punishment of Genocide was enacted. However, the International Court of Justice lacked jurisdiction over individuals to try them for such crimes.

The purposes of the International Criminal Court are to prevent serious crimes against humanity and bring to justice those who commit them. The historical record of humanity reveals that, all too often, powerful leaders and dictators who have committed or caused or allowed to be committed horrific acts against people and specific groups of people have escaped prosecution and punishment. Although it is true that temporary tribunals have been created to address such crimes retroactively, such temporary tribunals have not proven effective. The International Criminal Court is an attempt to create a permanent institution that has the power and authority to address such situations.

The International Criminal Court was not created until 1998, even though there had been several attempts to create a permanent international institution to address war crimes, crimes against humanity, genocide, and wars of aggression. The International Criminal Court, unlike the International Court of Justice or the World Court, is not part of the United Nations. It is a separate entity that was created by a treaty known as the Rome Statute. It is located at The Hague but can sit anywhere. On July 17, 1998, 120 nations adopted it and it came into force on July 1, 2002.

It is interesting to note that the United States has not ratified the Rome Statute to become a member of the International Criminal Court. The refusal of the United States to become a member of the International Criminal Court has engendered much criticism both domestically and internationally. One of the most significant reasons for this criticism is that the United States makes much about supporting international law, preventing war crimes, protecting humanity, and doing justice but refuses to subject itself to the same law to which it would subject other nations. Indeed, after the International Criminal Court came into being and was ratified by so many nations of the world, the United States began a campaign approaching many nations of the world to make treaties such that those nations would never submit the United States or any of its officials or soldiers to the International Criminal Court in exchange for certain concessions, such as increased foreign aid. Many nations accepted the U.S. offers and entered into such treaties.

The International Criminal Court consists of four separate organs. These organs are the Presidency, the Judicial Divisions, the Office of the Prosecutor, and the Registry. The Presidency consists of three of the judges of the International Criminal Court and is responsible for the general administration of the International Criminal Court. There are three Judicial Divisions staffed by 18 judges. These divisions are the Pre-Trial Division, the Trial Division, and the Appeals Division. Each division handles the proceedings appropriate to that division. Judges are nominated and elected by the member states. There can be only one judge from each member state, and each judge must be a citizen of that member state. The Office of the Prosecutor is responsible for receiving referrals to the International Criminal Court. The Office of the Prosecutor will examine referrals, investigate them, and, if appropriate, prosecute such referrals before the International Criminal Court. The prosecutor, who heads the Office of the Prosecutor, is elected to the office by the member states for a term of nine years. The prosecutor and the deputy prosecutors cannot be from the same member state. The Registry handles the nonjudicial administration of the International Criminal Court and is headed by the registrar. There are several other semiautonomous offices in the International Criminal Court that address other aspects of a prosecution.

Jurisdiction has several parts. First, jurisdiction involves the power and authority to adjudicate particular crimes. The International Criminal Court has the power and authority to hear and decide cases based on the following crimes: genocide, crimes against humanity, war crimes, and the crimes of aggression. Genocide generally involves acts committed with intent to destroy, in whole or in part, a national, ethnic, racial, or religious group. Crimes against humanity include systematic attacks against a civilian population that include murder, enslavement, torture, rape, deportation, and imprisonment without due process of law. War crimes include grave breaches of the Geneva Conventions of 1949, intentionally attacking civilian populations, attacking military personnel who have surrendered, pillaging of civilian towns or cities, employing poison gas, attacking medical personnel or installations, subjecting people to medical experimentation, using bullets designed to expand upon contact with the human body, starving civilian populations, and using children as soldiers. The Rome Statute has a reservation that the crimes of aggression will fall within the International Criminal Court's jurisdiction only after the crime of aggression has been defined. Although the crime of aggression has been generally accepted to mean the initiation of a war by one nation against another without just cause, the crime of aggression has yet to be formally defined. It is interesting that the crimes of terrorism, drug trafficking, and mercenarism were excluded from the jurisdiction of the International Criminal Court because they were not deemed sufficiently serious crimes.

Second, jurisdiction involves the power to hear and adjudicate cases against particular persons. In contrast to the International Court of Justice, where only states may be parties, the International Criminal Court has jurisdiction over individual persons. Although it would seem that the International Criminal Court could exercise jurisdiction over any person anywhere in the world for the commission of the crimes previously listed (otherwise known as universal jurisdiction), such is not the case. The International Criminal Court can exercise jurisdiction only where at least the person who has committed the crime is a citizen of a member state or the crime was committed within the territory or on a vessel or airplane of a member state. This limitation on jurisdiction reflects the reservations of some nations, including the United States, which feared that their own personnel might be brought before the International Criminal Court for political purposes rather than for the commission of actual crimes.

Statutes of limitations are laws that prohibit the prosecution of a crime after a certain period of time has elapsed. Thus, a person who has committed a crime might escape prosecution if the prosecutor fails to initiate charges within the specified period of time. One important provision of the Rome Statute is that there are no statutes of limitations for any of the crimes for which the International Criminal Court can take cognizance. This provision highlights the fact that the world considers the crimes listed in the Rome Statute as sufficiently serious that criminals of this magnitude should not be allowed to escape prosecution by merely hiding for a period of time.

Despite the highly laudable purposes of the International Criminal Court, it has met with many doubts and criticisms. Like the UN, which has frequently been criticized as a toothless tiger, the International Criminal Court is unable to address its mandate adequately, since its ability to address the crimes of genocide, crimes against humanity, and war crimes has been challenged. These challenges have been highlighted by the actions of the United States in arranging for treaties with multiple nations to prevent U.S. officials and military personnel from being brought before it. Given the internationally and almost universally condemned actions of the United States at Abu Ghraib prison and Guantanamo Bay, it would seem that the challenges to the ability of the International Criminal Court to execute its mandate fairly and equally would depend on the military, economic, and political power of the nation (and its officials and military personnel) accused of criminal acts.

Wm. C. Plouffe Jr.
Independent Scholar

See also Adjudicating International Crimes; Crimes Against Humanity; Extraordinary Rendition; Genocide; Globalization; Internationalized Criminal Tribunals; Offenders or Offenses; Prosecution: International; Sex Slavery; War Crimes; War Crimes Tribunals

Further Readings

Guffey-Landers, Nancy. "Establishing an International Criminal Court: Will It Do Justice?" *Maryland Journal of International Law and Trade*, v.20/2 (Fall 1996).

International Criminal Court. http://www.icc-cpi.int (Accessed February 2011).

Jamison, Sandra. "A Permanent International Criminal Court: A Proposal That Overcomes Past Objections." *Denver Journal of International Law and Policy*, v.23/2 (Spring 1995).

Marquardt, Paul. "Law Without Borders: The Constitutionality of an International Criminal Court: Will It Meet Constitutional Standards of Civil Rights?" *Columbia Journal of Transnational Law*, v.33/73 (1995).

Sadat, L. N. and S. R. Carden. "The New International Criminal Court: An Uneasy Revolution." *Georgetown Law Journal*, v.88 (2000).

Schabas, William A. *The International Criminal Court: A Commentary on the Rome Statute*. New York: Oxford University Press, 2010.

INTERNATIONAL MONETARY FUND

At Bretton Woods, New Hampshire, a multinational conference with representatives from more than 40 nations met in July 1944 to focus on the creation of a bank that would help finance the rebuilding necessary after World War II, short-term financial problems, and ways to promote free trade. In the end, the Bretton Woods Agreement was created and established the International Monetary Fund (IMF) and the World Bank. According to the Bretton Woods Agreement, the nations created a new international monetary system based on the value of the U.S. dollar.

Originally, the new system was created to balance the flexibility that nations required in addressing short-term domestic monetary difficulties with the gold standard. Additionally, the Bretton Woods Agreement included fixed exchange rates by linking the value of the U.S. dollar directly to gold, as well as the value of other currencies to the value of the dollar. The par value of the U.S. dollar was fixed at $35 per ounce of gold. Other currencies were then given par values against the U.S. dollar instead of gold. Member nations were expected to keep their currencies from deviating by more than 1 percent above or below their par values. The Bretton Woods

Agreement also improved on the gold standard by extending the right to exchange gold for dollars only to national governments. As part of the agreement, the IMF was created to serve as the agency to regulate the fixed exchange rates and enforce the rules of the international monetary system. At the time of its formation, the IMF had just 29 members. For approximately 20 years, the system developed at Bretton Woods worked as envisioned. Additionally, this was a time of unprecedented stability in exchange rates. However, in the 1960s, the Bretton Woods system began to weaken.

During the 1960s, the United States faced a trade deficit; imports to the United States exceeded exports, and a budget deficit meant that expenses were surpassing revenues. Complicating matters, other nations that were holding dollars began to question whether the U.S. government had a sufficient amount of gold reserves to convert all its paper currency held outside the country. Thus, these governments, by demanding gold in exchange for dollars, caused a large sell-off of dollars on the world financial markets. Additionally, in the 1960s, the activities of the IMF required greater amounts of dollars and gold. However, the world financial reserves of dollars and gold were limited. Hence, the IMF created "special drawing rights" (SDRs), IMF assets whose value is based on a "basket" of its five largest members' currencies. The value of the IMF's SDRs is set daily and fluctuates with increases and decreases in the values of its underlying currencies. The significance of the SDRs is that they constitute the unit of account for the IMF. Moreover, when a nation enters the IMF, it is assigned a quota based on the size of its economy. As a result of each nation paying this quota, the IMF is able to allocate short-term loans to member nations.

The strength and stability of the Bretton Woods system depended on the U.S. dollar maintaining a solid reserve currency. However, several economic variables interfered with the United States' ability to maintain a strong reserve currency. These factors included both a persistent trade deficit that kept the dollar weak and high inflation. This highlighted a debilitating weakness in the system. More precisely, the weak U.S. dollar made it extremely difficult for central banks in most European countries and Japan to maintain exchange rates with the dollar. As the value of the dollar continued to tumble (because these nations' currencies were tied to the

U.S. dollar), these nations also experienced a decline in the value of their currencies. In 1972, Britain left the system and allowed the pound to float freely against the dollar. In January 1973, the dollar was again devalued, and many nations began attempting to cash in their reserves of the dollar. As a result, and in an attempt to stop the process, currency markets were temporarily closed. After the currency markets reopened, the values of most major currencies were floating against the U.S. dollar and the international monetary system was no longer based on fixed exchange rates.

In 1976, members of the IMF met and drafted the Jamaica Agreement, which officially proclaimed that the current system of floating exchange rates was the new basis for the International Monetary System. Additionally, the Jamaica Agreement explicitly authorized a managed float system of exchange rates. In the new system—unlike a free float system in which currencies floated freely against one another without governments' intervention—governments would intervene to stabilize their currencies at particular target exchange rates. The Jamaica Agreement also announced that gold was no longer the primary reserve asset of the IMF. Thus, member nations were able to retrieve their gold from the IMF. Finally, per the Jamaica Agreement, the IMF was transformed into a lender of last resort for countries with severe financial difficulties. Hence, contributions of member nations were increased to fund the IMF's new agenda.

By the early 1980s, once again, U.S. trade deficits were on the rise. The increase in the trade deficits was the result of the U.S. dollar's rising against other currencies. As a result, the price of U.S. exports increased. In September 1985, the world's five largest industrialized nations at the time—Britain, France, Germany, Japan, and the United States—entered into the Plaza Accord to act collectively in forcing down the value of the U.S. dollar. As a result of the Plaza Accord, traders sold the dollar and its value decreased, which resulted in a price decrease of U.S. exports. However, by early 1987, the parties to the Plaza Accord, as well as Italy and Canada, were worried that the value of the dollar was at risk of falling too low. Thus, in Paris, Italy, Canada, Britain, France, Germany, Japan, and the United States created the Louvre Accord, which declared that the U.S. dollar was appropriately valued and that collectively

these nations would intervene in currency markets to maintain its current market value. As a result, the dollar stabilized.

Today, some of the primary functions of the IMF include encouraging international monetary cooperation, coordinating expansion and reasonable growth of international trade, supporting exchange stability, maintaining orderly exchange arrangements, and avoiding competitive exchange devaluation. Additionally, the IMF works to make the resources of the fund temporarily available to members. Headquartered in Washington, D.C., the IMF has nearly 200 member nations.

Neil Guzy
University of Pittsburgh, Greensburg

See also Money Laundering: Countermeasures; South America; Terrorism: Financing; World Bank

Further Readings

Baker, Raymond W. *Capitalism's Achilles Heel: Dirty Money and How to Renew the Free-Market System.* New York: Wiley, 2005.
Copelovitch, Mark S. *The International Monetary Fund in the Global Economy: Banks, Bonds, and Bailouts.* New York: Cambridge University Press, 2010.
Vreeland, James Raymond. *The International Monetary Fund: Politics of Conditional Lending.* New York: Routledge, 2007.

INTERNATIONALIZED CRIMINAL TRIBUNALS

Internationalized criminal courts, otherwise known as "hybrid" or "mixed" criminal courts, are a recently developed method of prosecuting persons charged with international and national crimes. They are national criminal courts that include international components. Historically, states prosecuted persons charged with international or national crimes in their national courts. Multinational and international criminal courts evolved in the 20th century for the prosecution of international crimes. The first multinational criminal court to prosecute international crimes was the International Military Tribunal at Nüremberg, which was established on August 8, 1945, by the Allied victors of World

War II to prosecute major Nazi war criminals. This court joined military jurisdictions from four states: the United States, the United Kingdom, the Soviet Union, and France.

Three significant international criminal courts were established in the 1990s. In 1993 and 1994, the UN Security Council created the International Criminal Tribunal for the former Yugoslavia and the International Criminal Tribunal for Rwanda. The Rome Statute of the International Criminal Court was adopted on July 17, 1998, and entered into force on July 1, 2002. The international criminal tribunals for the former Yugoslavia and Rwanda were controversial shortly after they were created. They were established by the Security Council under Article 42 of the Charter of the United Nations (UN) and therefore had coercive powers over state parties to the UN. This coercive power of the tribunals was referred to as the principle of primacy, which means that their jurisdictions superseded the jurisdictions of national courts. For several reasons, it was argued that states should have more participation in the prosecution of their accused criminals. The problem, however, was that many states were unable to prosecute perpetrators within the standards of international law. As a result, internationalized criminal courts started to be established.

Internationalized criminal courts are national courts that acquire the assistance of key international players. For example, international prosecutors and defense counsels partner with national prosecutors and defense counsels. International judges also work alongside national judges. Therefore, national criminal courts become "internationalized." Competent national criminal courts are the best forum in which to prosecute international and national crimes. The problems emerge when national courts are willing but unable to competently prosecute certain crimes, which often are serious human rights violations and fall outside the jurisdiction of international criminal courts.

The result is usually a special tribunal established to prosecute certain crimes within a limited time period. These tribunals are established under national and international law. International components, such as prosecutors, advisers, defense attorneys, judges, and researchers, work with national prosecutors, defense attorneys, and judges. Two examples of internationalized criminal tribunals are the Special Court of Sierra Leone and the Special Tribunal for Lebanon.

On August 14, 2002, the UN Security Council requested the UN secretary-general to negotiate an agreement with the government of Sierra Leone to create a "special court." The Agreement Between the UN and the Government of Sierra Leone on the Establishment of a Special Court for Sierra Leone was adopted on January 16, 2002. It entered into force on April 12, 2002. The Special Court for Sierra Leone (SCSL) has jurisdiction over crimes against humanity, war crimes, and certain crimes under Sierra Leonean law. Three judges serve in the Trial Chamber, of which the UN secretary-general appoints two and the government of Sierra Leone appoints one. The secretary-general appoints the prosecutor, who is assisted by a Sierra Leonean deputy prosecutor. Most of the other dimensions of the SCSL are similarly constituted.

On May 30, 2007, the Special Tribunal for Lebanon was established pursuant to the Agreement Between the UN and the Lebanese Republic on the Establishment of a Special Tribunal for Lebanon. The Special Tribunal for Lebanon (STL) has jurisdiction over the provisions of the Lebanese Criminal Code relating to the prosecution and punishment of acts of terrorism. Three judges serve in the Trial Chamber, of which one is a Lebanese judge and two are international judges. The prosecutor is appointed by the UN secretary-general and is assisted by a Lebanese deputy prosecutor. The secretary-general also appoints an independent head of the defense office.

Harry M. Rhea
Richard Stockton College of New Jersey

See also International Criminal Court

Further Readings

Klip, André and Göran Sluiter. *Annotated Leading Cases of International Criminal Tribunals.* Antwerp, Belgium: Intersentia, 1999–2011.

Romano, Cesare P. R., André Nollkaemper, and Jann K. Kleffner, eds. *International Criminal Courts: Sierra Leone, East Timor, Kosovo, and Cambodia.* New York: Oxford University Press, 2004.

Schabas, William A. *The UN International Criminal Tribunals: The Former Yugoslavia, Rwanda and Sierra Leone.* New York: Cambridge University Press, 2006.

INTERNET CRIME

Criminal use of the Internet differs substantially from traditional computer crimes, where the technology is typically used as an instrument of financial gain (through such schemes and scams as online banking frauds), copyright infringements, or communication between members of illegal enterprises. Nowadays, a significant segment of many criminal activities is based on the Internet, which can be used at all stages of the crime commission process: planning, preparation, completion of an act, destroying or altering of evidence, preparing an alibi, or manipulating witnesses. The Internet becomes a powerful tool that is readily available, inexpensive, and easy to use. New generations of criminals consider it to be the obvious weapon to be employed in their endeavors, as it is a natural element of their environment. The categories of crime in which the Internet plays an important role, both national and transnational, are increasing such that the World Wide Web may be considered a new battlefield for criminals and law-enforcement agencies. Such a situation poses a major challenge in terms of investigation and prevention, as it often involves parties based in different jurisdictions. In addition, that challenge is magnified by a lack of police cooperation, issues of personal rights and freedoms, and technical obstacles.

The Internet is used during the planning stage of the crime for know-how and intelligence gathering, data mining, and selection of victims as targets. This is true in the case of international terrorism (Al Qaeda operatives have been using the Web in this way since the late 1990s) and in extreme instances of violent crime that have important transnational effects even though they are locally based. An example is the phenomenon of post-Columbine school shootings. The majority of perpetrators of mass homicide in schools and other academic environments after the Columbine shootings of 1999 have used the Internet to obtain instructions for the preparation of the crime. Sources of such information include not only online versions of amateur documents (such as *The Anarchist Cookbook*) but also military and police files (such as the *TM 31–210 Improvised Munitions Handbook*, the Department of the U.S. Army's technical manual describing

methods for the manufacture of improvised weapons and explosives). The Internet is also used to purchase weaponry and its components. Additionally, the perpetrators use the Web as a free broadcasting "tube," employed to publicize their homicidal plans, which are often telegraphed months in advance. In order to achieve the greatest notoriety and reach the widest audience, such killers use English, regardless of their ethnic origin and the geographic location of the planned crime.

Some Internet tools can be used not only to prepare the crime but also to perform the attack. In the case of Al Qaeda's attempted bombing of cargo flights from Yemen to United States in October 2010, plastic explosives secreted in a computer printer were to be detonated by cell-phone signals. The parcels were shipped through delivery firms, and the terrorists planned to trace them using online tracking systems provided by courier companies. These systems were to be used for synchronizing the location and timing of the explosions. Similar opportunities are available through Websites that provide users with live flight tracking (including geographic positioning), the ability to listen to live Air Traffic Control communication with pilots, and other Internet sites originally designed for aviation enthusiasts. All such sites may be used to orchestrate an attack such that it would cause maximum destruction. It should be noted that Internet technologies (such as voice-over Internet protocol

Sexual predators and stalkers can send malicious software to an intended victims' phone with data sent over the Internet. This malware can activate the global positioning system (GPS) in the victim's cell phone and give the predator access to his or her precise location. (Photos.com)

communications and global positioning system, or GPS, tracking) were used by the terrorists in the 2008 Mumbai attacks.

Another example of malevolent exploitation of the Internet (combined with GPS technologies) is its use by sexual predators and stalkers to select and monitor their victims. In some instances, such strategies were used by criminals operating from abroad. The perpetrators can "infect" their victims' phones with malicious software that is sent to them over the Internet. Such malware can enable the stalker to activate the GPS in the victim's cell phone and determine the precise location of that person. Using other online tools, such as satellite mapping (such as Google street views), one can virtually "follow" the victim, learning not only about the routes the victim takes but also about the physical characteristics of the victim's surroundings. Additionally, social networking sites begin to play a very important role in the process of victim selection and monitoring, providing criminals with an unprecedented wealth of open-source intelligence—knowledge about their victims' lifestyles, income, customs, character, and even physical fitness. All of this information is crucial for making a proper assessment regarding whether the selected person is a high- or low-risk victim.

Internet technologies and social networking sites may also be used for preparing alibis. Online profiles can be updated using smart phones while their users are present at a crime scene, giving the impression that they are elsewhere. Such information is not incontrovertible proof, because it can be overturned through billing analysis and phone positioning, but it gives criminals time to prepare better alibis or destroy evidence that links them to the crime scene.

Preventive and investigative measures that might be used against such threats involve automated cyberspace monitoring and multivariate risk assessment. However, such technology infringes on the rights and freedoms of the majority of citizens who have no involvement in illegal activities. In that case, basic rights protected by law—the right to privacy and the right to safety—are in competition. Thus, instead of using the "dragnet" approach to finding criminals, highly precise information-technology instruments must be used to pinpoint the perpetrators. International law harmonization and law-enforcement cooperation are crucial to the effective combat of Internet-based crimes.

Kacper T. Gradon
University College London

See also Al Qaeda; Computer-Generated Scams; Narco-Terrorism

Further Readings

Gradon, Kacper. *Multiple Homicide: Criminal Profiling.* Warsaw: Wolters Kluwer, 2010.

Haberfeld, M. R. and Agostino von Hassell, eds. *A New Understanding of Terrorism: Case Studies, Trajectories and Lessons Learned.* New York: Springer, 2009.

Johnson, Thomas A. *The War on Terrorism: A Collision of Values, Strategies and Societies.* Boca Raton, FL: CRC Press, 2009.

INTERPOL

Formally known as the International Criminal Police Organization, Interpol is a supranational information and intelligence clearinghouse that links law-enforcement agencies of member countries and facilitates their cooperation by providing secure global communication and database services and assistance. It also serves as an international police association to plan and coordinate conferences for police training and development opportunities, sharing knowledge, skills, methods, and best practices for establishing global standards in order to effectively tackle transnational crimes.

Interpol has a set of defined crime priorities, which include fugitive identification and apprehension, public safety and terrorism, drug and criminal organizations, financial and high-tech crime, human trafficking, and anticorruption. The work of Interpol revolves around crimes with a transnational dimension: terrorism; genocide and atrocities; smuggling of people including trafficking of women; crimes against children, such as child abuse and child pornography; crimes against the environment, such as poaching, endangered species trafficking, illegal dumping of hazardous wastes, and use of illegal pesticides; illicit narcotics production and trafficking; illegal diversion of rivers; trafficking of weapons, including nuclear materials; white-collar and organized crime, such as corruption, money laundering, and other financial crimes; piracy; crimes involving computers and intellectual property; and other transnational threats. Of the 192 member states of the United Nations (UN) in 2010, only four were not members of Interpol: Palau, Kiribati, Tuvalu, and Vanuatu. Four additional sovereign states—North Korea, the Federated States of Micronesia, Taiwan, and Greenland—were members of neither the UN nor Interpol.

The idea for an international police organization originated in 1914 in Monte Carlo, Monaco, when a group of police practitioners, lawyers, and magistrates from 14 countries gathered to discuss identification techniques, arrest procedures, and extradition proceedings for transnational offenders, which were growing in number in the early 1900s because of advances in transportation, communication, and technology. Delayed by World War I, the organization was officially founded in 1923, then known as the International Criminal Police Commission (ICPC) and headquartered in Vienna, Austria. The latter half of the 1920s saw the establishment of a number of national chapter bureaus (NCBs) in member countries across the world to serve as contact points for foreign police officials. The organization continued to develop in the 1930s, with specific divisions created to respond to certain crimes, such as currency counterfeiting and passport forgery, and an international radio network in 1935. A few years later, Nazis gained control of the ICPC from 1938 until 1946, and many countries therefore stopped participating and operations ceased. After the end of World War II, in 1946, Belgium led the rebuilding efforts for ICPC and helped establish the first headquarters in Paris. In the same year, the organization was officially named the International Criminal Police Organization, or more commonly, Interpol. The organization grew steadily over the following decades; however, it was unable to keep up with growing demands in response to the increasing internationalization of crime. In the 1970s and 1980s, Interpol was criticized for its antiquated technology and communication operations, making the organization ill equipped to respond effectively to crime; this, in turn, spurred the idea among European officials to establish a regional form of Interpol, presently known as Europol (the European Police Office). The 1990s saw an extensive modernization of Interpol's resources in these areas, with a move to their new headquarters in Lyon, France, in 1989 and

a range a new of computer databases introduced in the 1990s. In the 2000s, especially after the terrorist attacks of September 11, 2001, Interpol greatly improved and expanded operations by significantly increasing staff, overseas resources, and round-the-clock communications services called I-24/7, which allows staff in member countries to communicate time-sensitive information quickly and efficiently.

Beginning in the 1990s, a wide range of databases was created to store information and intelligence on a variety of crimes and offenders; they are the lifeblood of Interpol's communications and services. Collectively, these databases contain millions of records that are accessible by varying levels of restriction to Interpol staff, seconded officers, national bureaus, and even third parties under certain circumstances. The Stolen and Lost Travel Documents database contains more than 20 million records, and more than 300 million searches were conducted in 2009. The Stolen Motor Vehicles (SMV) database contains more than 6.2 million details of stolen vehicles, with more than 9 million searches conducted in 2009. The Stolen Works of Art database contains more than 34,000 registered objects and is accessible to more than 1,100 users, ranging from law-enforcement agencies to ministries of culture, museums, auction houses, and art galleries in more than 60 countries. The Child Abuse Image Database (ICAID), which was replaced by the International Child Sexual Exploitation database in 2009, has helped to identify and rescue more than 1,500 victims worldwide. Created in 2009, the Ballistic Information Network (IBIN) allows for large-scale international sharing and comparing of more than 71,000 records of ballistics data. The Interpol DNA Database resulted in 74 positive matches in 2009. Other databases include the Interpol Weapons Electronic Tracing System (IWETS) and the Terrorism Watch List. The development of Missing Persons and Unidentified Dead Bodies database is under way. Interpol also has agreements to use databases created by other governments, such as the Real-Time Analytical Intelligence Database (RAID) by the U.S. National Drug Intelligence Center. These databases and all Interpol's communication are linked through I-24/7, which allow staff from member countries to access one another's databases and information and to send encrypted messages. The only country not connected to I-24/7 is Somalia. Finally, Interpol headquarters operates the Automated Search Facility (ASF), a tool to search for information in international records of people (which include such vital statistics as names, birthdates, nationalities, and phonetic spellings), including those linked to crime and their aliases.

Interpol produces seven types of color-coded notices to help police in member countries to share time-sensitive crime-related information. A red notice seeks to arrest or detain a wanted person with a view to extradition; there are two types, one for a person wanted for prosecution and a second for a judicial decision for a person wanted to serve a sentence. A blue notice aims to gather further information on the identity of a person or activities in relation to crime. A green notice serves to provide warnings and intelligence on individuals who have committed offenses and are likely to perpetrate these crimes in other countries. A yellow notice helps to locate missing persons, especially children and minors, and to help identify persons who may be unable to identify themselves. A black notice seeks information on unidentified human remains. An orange notice aims to warn police, public agencies, and other international organizations about threats from disguised weapons, bombs, and other dangerous materials. Finally, the newly introduced UN Security Council special notices are specifically produced for individuals and entities associated with Al Qaeda and the Taliban and targets of UN sanctions. These notices also restrict the movements and operations of such people by imposing asset freezes, arms embargoes, and travel bans. In 2009, Interpol produced 5,020 red, 522 blue, 1,139 green, 462 yellow, 103 black, 17 orange, and 26 UN special notices.

The governance and operations of Interpol are conducted in different ways. The main governing body of Interpol is called the General Assembly, consisting of delegates appointed by their member states. By meeting annually, this group serves to make decisions on a number of key areas, such as operations, policy, resources, finances, and programs. This group also elects 13 members to form the Executive Committee, which comprises the president, three vice presidents, and nine members representing four regions: Africa, the Americas, Asia, and Europe. Under the presidency of Khoo Boon Hui of Singapore until 2012, this committee also appoints a number of advisory experts for certain areas. The General Secretariat is headquartered in Lyon, France, and operates 24 hours per day, 365 days per year, and houses hundreds of Interpol staff from more than 80 countries, working together in one of four official languages: Arabic, English, French, and Spanish. The Secretariat operates and maintains close links with seven regional offices around the globe, located in Argentina, Cameroon, Ivory Coast, El Salvador, Kenya, Thailand, and Zimbabwe. These offices help to support regional committees, such as the Southern African Regional Police Chiefs Cooperation Organization (SARPCCO), the Central Asian Regional Information and Coordination Center (CARICC), the Pacific Transnational Crime Control Center (PTCCC), and other international policing initiatives, such as Gulfpol and ASEANAPOL. Each member country of Interpol operates a National Central Bureau (NCB) to serve as the designated point of contact for the above-listed offices as well for NCBs of other member countries seeking investigative assistance. Finally, an independent body called the Commission for the Control of Interpol's Files (CCF) serves to ensure the compliance of Interpol with various regulations on matters of personal information.

Over the years, Interpol has faced a number of criticisms and challenges. While growing in the early half of the 20th century, Interpol was often viewed as an international police fraternity or policeman's club, because membership was and still is limited to certain police agencies (such as those agencies dealing with international crimes, unlike smaller municipalities). Even after the organization expanded in size over the following decades, until the 1960s Interpol was often criticized as too bureaucratic and hampered by red tape, and therefore unable to respond to transnational crime problems. Due to Interpol's combination of outdated technology and methods, a view emerged in Europe regarding the inefficiency of the organization in responding to the region's crime problems, and as a result, the idea was proposed by German Chancellor Helmut Kohl in 1991 to establish an international police agency modeled after Interpol, now in operation as Europol, which resulted in some early friction between these agencies. This was also the case with the spread of related police cooperation initiatives, such as ASEANAPOL. During the 1960s, when terrorist activity was on the rise throughout the world, Interpol was initially forbidden to interfere with these crimes, as Article 3 prevented the organization from involvement in political, military, religious, and racial matters. Because of this limitation, in 1985 Article 3 was amended to allow Interpol to handle terrorism. The introduction of the various computer databases in the 1990s, although an invaluable resource today, was initially met with reluctance by some countries, which were hesitant to make their information and database resources available to other states through Interpol. As a major international police agency operating with a relatively small budget, Interpol relies heavily on police seconded from their native agencies. Differences in language, culture, and politics, among other factors, pose additional challenges to police cooperation.

Each year, Interpol produces an annual report to highlight achievements and to summarize operations and activities for each of its priority areas. In 2009, Samoa became the 188th country added to Interpol's network of national chapter bureaus. Interpol also enhanced its regional presence by opening two additional offices: the Office of the Special Representative in the European Union, and a new regional bureau in Yaoundé, the capital city of Cameroon. A prototype for an Interpol passport was also unveiled in order to facilitate international travel by Interpol staff. As of 2009, Interpol consisted of 645 staff at the General Secretariat and regional bureaus around the globe, with 438 (68 percent) employed directly by Interpol while 207 (32 percent) are seconded law-enforcement personnel. Women make up 42 percent of Interpol staff. With 84 percent of Interpol's member countries contributing to their 2009 operating budget of 59 million euros, Interpol's efforts resulted in 1,246 arrests, including a Rwandan genocide fugitive, and allowed staff to provide more than 140 specialized training sessions to more than 4,500 law-enforcement officers. During 2009, Interpol officially launched its Global Learning Centre (GLC), which provides Web-based resources to authorized users on a number of learning opportunities in specific crime areas and investigative techniques. Increasingly, Interpol has begun to take an active stand in peacekeeping efforts around the world, in 2009 signing three cooperation agreements in these areas with the UN. Additionally for 2009, 5,020 red notices were issued for wanted persons, 77 million database searches were conducted,

and (based on Interpol's DNA database of more than 94,000 profiles) 74 positive matches were made.

Michael J. Puniskis
Middlesex University

See also Europol; Globalization; Nongovernmental Organizations

Further Readings

Cameron-Waller, Stuart. "Interpol: A Global Service Provider." In *Combating International Crime: The Longer Arm of the Law*, Steven David Brown, ed. London: Routledge-Cavendish, 2008.

Deflem, Mathieu. "'Wild Beasts Without Nationality': The Uncertain Origins of Interpol, 1898–1910." In *The Handbook of Transnational Crime and Justice*, Philip Reichel, ed. Thousand Oaks, CA: Sage, 2005.

Deflem, Mathieu and Lindsay Maybin. "Interpol and the Policing of International Terrorism: Developments and Dynamics Since September 11." In *Terrorism: Research, Readings, and Realities*, Lynne L. Snowden and Brad Whitsel, eds. Upper Saddle River, NJ: Pearson/Prentice Hall, 2005.

Imhoff, John and Stephen Cutlet. "INTERPOL: Expanding Law Enforcement's Reach Around the World." *FBI Law Enforcement Bulletin*, v.67/12 (1998).

Interpol. "Annual Report 2009." http://www.interpol.int (Accessed October 2010).

Martha, Rutsel Silvestre J. *The Legal Foundation of Interpol*. Portland, OR: Hart, 2010.

INVESTMENT CRIMES

The 21st-century financial crisis following the deregulation of the finance sector in the 1980s and 1990s not only led to the collapse of numerous banks but also turned large-scale investment criminals into household names. However, investment crimes can be traced back to the Great Depression and are a natural—if deviant—outgrowth of the modern financial system. The costs to individuals, corporations, and states can run into billions of dollars, and investment crime has become one of the most serious forms of nonviolent crime in the 21st century. Securities and investment fraud may be committed by a number of actors in the financial sector, including investors, brokers, financial advisers, and financial accountants.

Theoretical Concepts

The emergence of corporate crime in the 1920s and 1930s in the era of the Great Depression led criminologist Edwin H. Sutherland to coin the term *white-collar crime*, referring to a crime "committed by a person of respectability and high social status in the course of his occupation," including not only investment crimes but also bribery, embezzling, money laundering, and, more recently, computer crime. Sutherland viewed the violation of the public's trust and the corporate code of ethics as a serious one that deserved sanctions comparable with those imposed on "blue-collar" criminals of the working classes. This incorporation of white-collar crimes was important for criminological inquiry, as it challenged the prevailing understandings of crime as a primarily working-class phenomenon that could be associated with conditions of poverty. Sutherland would go on to oversee a study of 70 large corporations that had in some way broken the law. Sutherland also highlighted the discrepancy in arrest and conviction rates between white-collar and blue-collar criminals.

Sutherland articulated his understanding of the causes of white-collar crime, incorporating the associational element of his differential theory. He argued that behavior such as investment crime is learned behavior, passed on as a part of the corporate culture that prioritizes profit over ethical conduct. Travis Hirschi, Michael R. Gottfredson, Kenneth Polk, and others have established further understandings of crime that identify many top-level executives involved in investment crimes as having affluent white-collar backgrounds, which differs from the traditional understanding of the impulsiveness of criminal behavior. According to Hirschi and Gottfredson, white-collar criminals are less immediately dangerous to society but cause more overall harm because of the financial costs of investment crimes.

Types of Investment Crime

There are several common types of investment fraud, including manipulation of "insider knowledge" for financial gain, misrepresentation of finances (accounting fraud), making deals before certain stock issues are made public, or the invention of false corporate entities to disguise financial transactions.

Securities and investment frauds are forms of deceptive practices in the stock and commodities markets. Fraud of this nature may occur when individuals or corporations falsely inflate stock values to make profits from investors or post falsified returns. Fraud may also occur when people use professional knowledge unfairly to gain an advantage in stock market trading or other investment-related financial dealings, thereby obtaining profits for themselves or their company. There are many varieties of securities and investment fraud, as international financial deregulation leads to more opportunities for criminal activity on a global level.

"Pump and dump" schemes manipulate the market by creating artificial buying pressure on a targeted security, usually a low-trading volume issued in the over-the-counter securities market. This artificially increased trading volume has the effect of increasing the price of the targeted security (the pump), which is rapidly sold off into the inflated market for the security by the fraud perpetrators (the dump). Typically, the increased trading volume is generated by inducing unwitting investors to purchase shares of the targeted security through deceptive sales practices or public information releases. A modern variation on these schemes involves largely foreign-based computer criminals gaining unauthorized access and intruding into the online brokerage accounts of unsuspecting victims in the United States. These victim accounts are then used to coordinate online purchases of the targeted security in order to manipulate the value of the shares, and to cause the value of the shares to rise. The fraud perpetrators then sell their own preexisting holdings in the targeted security into the inflated market.

High-yield investment fraud schemes take many forms but are characterized by offers of low- or no-risk investments with high rates of return. The common pyramid scheme, for instance, requires customers to become intermediary vendors, recruiting more customers. The similar Ponzi scheme uses the money collected from the newest investors to pay existing investors; these payments are represented to be the profits from some underlying (but nonexistent) business venture or investment portfolio.

Various fraud schemes involve the deceptive or fraudulent sale of commodities instruments. In such instances, false or deceptive sales practices are used to solicit victims' funds for commodities transactions that either never occur or are inconsistent with the original sales pitches. Alternatively, commodities market participants may attempt to manipulate the market for a commodity illegally by such actions as fraudulently reporting price information or cornering the market to increase the price of the targeted commodity. A variant on the scheme is the prime bank scheme, in which the perpetrator claims to have access to a secret worldwide exchange open only to the world's largest financial institutions and sells the victim financial instruments he claims have a high rate of return.

Late-day trading schemes rely on market-moving information that is released after the close of regular trading and involve the illegal buying and selling of securities after the market has closed.

Investments and Corporate Fraud

The majority of corporate fraud cases involve accounting schemes designed to deceive investors, auditors, and analysts about the true financial condition of a corporation. Through the manipulation of financial data, the share price of a corporation remains artificially inflated based on fictitious performance indicators provided to the investing public. In addition to causing significant financial losses to investors, corporate fraud may cause immeasurable damage to the economy and investor confidence.

A subprime mortgage lender is a business that lends to borrowers who do not qualify for loans from mainstream lenders. Once the subprime loans have been issued, they are bundled and sold as securities—a process known as securitization. Fraud has been identified throughout the loan process, which commences with the borrower providing false information to the mortgage broker or lender. The next layer of potential fraud, the corporate fraud, occurs with the banks, brokerage houses, and other financial institutions that package loans through the securitization process. As the housing market declined in 2007–08, subprime lenders were forced to buy back a number of nonperforming loans. Many of these subprime lenders relied on a continuous increase in real estate values to allow the borrowers to refinance or sell their properties before going into default. However, based on the sales slowdown in the housing market, loan defaults increased, the secondary market for subprime securities dwindled, and the securities lost value. As a result, publicly traded stocks dramatically decreased in value as financial institutions realized large losses from the subprime securities they held or insured, resulting in financial difficulties and bankruptcies.

As publicly traded companies suffered financial difficulties with the fall of the subprime market, analyses of company financials identified instances of false accounting entries and fraudulently inflated assets and revenues. Investigations determined that several of these companies manipulated their reported loan portfolio risks and used various accounting schemes to inflate their financial reports. In addition, before these companies' stocks rapidly declined in value, executives with insider information sold their equity positions and profited illegally.

Investment Crime Sanctions

Investment crimes have been met with harsher sanctions in the aftermath of high-profile cases such as the 2001–02 Enron accounting scandal. The scale of such crimes has revealed their significant national and global financial impacts, dissolving the old perception of white-collar frauds as victimless crimes. Securities and investment violations in the United States are investigated by the Securities and Exchange Commission (SEC). The SEC can investigate individuals or corporations if it suspects a violation of laws and regulations. Violating securities laws can result in a range of civil or criminal charges and sanctions, and charges can be made after time has elapsed, as allowed within the statute of limitations.

The penalties for securities fraud vary, and they may be levied in different ways against individuals and corporations. A points system may be utilized to determine the magnitude of the crime under investigation, including its wider impact. Such points systems may take into account the number of victims, the amount of the financial losses incurred, and the aggregate disruption to the financial markets. Once these impacts of the crime are ascertained, punishment may include prison sentences, penalties, or fines with possible repayment of losses accrued by the investors. Sanctions that restrict an offender from involvement in future business actions may also be imposed. Individuals and corporations may receive separate punishments for their respective roles in securities fraud; executives of the corporation violating investment laws may receive a custodial sentence, whereas the corporation involved may be fined.

The Federal Bureau of Investigation works with the U.S. Department of Justice, the SEC, and other U.S. regulatory agencies to identify possible corporate fraud centered on violations of insider trading, securities fraud, and accounting fraud.

Liam Leonard
Paula Bridget Kenny
Institute of Technology, Sligo

See also Accounting Fraud; Charities and Financing; Charity Fraud; Financial Fraud; Nigerian Money Scams; Pyramid Schemes

Further Readings

Block, Alan A. and Sean Patrick Griffin. "Transnational Financial Crime: Crooked Lawyers, Tax Evasion, and Securities Fraud." *Journal of Contemporary Criminal Justice*, v.18/4 (2002).

Croall, Hazel. *Understanding White Collar Crime*. Philadelphia: Open University Press, 2001.

Fisher, Kenneth L. and Lara Hoffmans. *How to Smell a Rat: The Five Signs of Financial Fraud*. Hoboken, NJ: Wiley, 2009.

Pinto, Amanda and Martin Evans. *Corporate Criminal Liability*, 2nd ed. London: Sweet and Maxwell, 2008.

JIHAD

The literal translation of the Arabic word *jihad* is to "struggle in the way of Allah." However, jihad has become a controversial religious term, because its meaning has been altered to justify the use of violence against Muslims and non-Muslims. Jihad in mainstream Islam has two different interpretations, distinguished as lesser and greater jihad. Greater jihad is defined as fighting against inner forces that detract morally and spiritually from submitting to Allah. Lesser jihad is defined as the right to defend Muslims who are under attack from non-Muslims. The concept of jihad as it applies to extremists and terrorists elevates the concept of lesser jihad above greater jihad into a sixth pillar of Islam. Requiring jihad as a sixth pillar of Islam makes it equal to the other five pillars: prayer, pilgrimage, profession of monotheism, fasting, and almsgiving. Those who adhere to an elevated form of jihad are known as violent jihadis. Leading violent jihadis include Sayyid Qutb, Abdullah Azzam, Osama bin Laden, Ayman al-Zawahiri, and Muhammad Maqdisi. Al Qaeda, Hamas, Hezbollah, Al Shabaab, Egyptian Islamic Jihad, and the Al-Aqsa Martyrs Brigade are examples of groups that adhere to violent jihadism.

Violent jihadis assert that the Islamic world has entered a period of occupation and division. Propaganda is then used to prove that all Muslims are under attack economically, militarily, religiously, and culturally, and that it is the defensive obligation of every true Muslim to fight against attacking

Violent jihadis claim that Western non-Muslim forces are occupying and dividing Islam and believe that victory in battle is a sign of favor from Allah. Not all jihadis are violent: a lesser jihad is defined as a fight against inner forces that detract from submitting to Allah morally and spiritually. (Photos.com)

forces. Using propaganda, violent jihadis claim that non-Muslim forces are occupying and dividing Islam through covert and overt tactics. Covert tactics include materialism, secularism, liberal education, feminism, postmodernism, secular music, and movies. Overt tactics involve killing or wounding Muslims in Iraq, Afghanistan, Chechnya, Bosnia, the Philippines, and Palestine. Israel/Palestine is central to what violent jihadis list as one of the prominent "invasions" to repel. The Israeli invasion, according to a violent jihadi, represents an extension of non-Muslim imperialism to dominate the Islamic world. While non-Muslim invasion continues, violent jihadis rage in their propaganda that Muslims remain passive or indifferent.

Violent jihadis profess that their definition of jihad is the pure manifestation of the concept in Islam, defined by Sharia (Islamic sacred law) and the teachings of the Prophet Muhammad. Apostasies combined with Muslim religious ignorance have led Islam to become impure. Violent jihadi propaganda claims that "impure Islam" is what makes Muslim armies unable to remove Israel and repel non-Muslim invasions. Violent jihadis seek full submission to the Quran in order to regain the spiritual, economic, and political supremacy that Islam maintained in the past. Full submission to the Quran is implemented by establishing a sociocultural religious system that acts as a strong form of social control. Violent jihadis assault Muslims who value secularism, human laws, and lifestyles over what has been cited in the Quran. Their version of Islam dictates every facet of life; anything else is an invention and labeled blasphemous.

According to violent jihadis, victory in battle is a sign of favor from Allah, and jihadis cite their victory in Afghanistan against the Soviets as evidence of the power of their version of jihad. Violent jihadism seeks to remove from the Muslim world the influence of materialism and anti-Islamic "isms," which they claim constitute a covert invasion to uproot Islamic culture, undermining the moral fabric of society and family and encouraging passivity. Imperialism is used to describe how non-Muslim governments and companies are bent on extracting the wealth of the Middle East and taking it away from the majority of Muslims. The few Muslims who benefit from Western wealth are corrupt Muslim governmental officials who serve as local puppets for the West. Violent jihadis label these Muslims as apostates because they are living in a state of ignorance of what constitutes the "true" faith.

Violent jihadis' propagandist message is intended to reach Muslims who are discontented and are feeling either humiliated or frustrated in their current suppressed status. Violent jihadists' propaganda is constructed to bombard Muslims with "evidence" that the West perceives Muslims as "inferior" and powerless and that therefore the "crusaders" and "infidels" are killing Muslims. An unjust inferior status is shameful, because, violent jihadis assert, Muslims are Allah's standard-bearers and therefore they should be honored, yet they are treated with contempt by the "great and little Satan." In their propaganda, violent jihadis assault Muslims with shame for their ignorance, passivity, or indifference to the plight of fellow Muslims under siege by infidels and apostate Muslims. Passive Muslims are ignorant Muslims, according to this line, and are to blame for the current polluted state of Islam because they are not following the true faith and therefore are allowing non-Muslims to dominate them.

Travis Morris
Norwich University

See also Al Qaeda; Middle East; Narco-Terrorism

Further Readings

Gerges, F. *Journey of the Jihadist: Inside Muslim Militancy.* New York: Harcourt, 2006.

Habeck, M. *Knowing the Enemy: Jihadist Ideology and the War on Terror.* New Haven, CT: Yale University Press, 2006.

Kepel, G. *Jihad: The Trail of Political Islam.* New York: I. B. Tauris, 2004.

Wright, L. *The Looming Tower: Al-Qaeda and the Road to 9/11.* New York: Knopf, 2006.

JOB OFFER SCAMS

An international job offer scam is a type of fraud that involves individuals overseas pretending to be employers or agencies by offering fake "lucrative jobs," often requiring an advanced payment for processing of paperwork and travel expenses and usually occurring between two or more nations. Anyone in any region of the world can be victimized. The scam is often conducted through e-mail. A job scam is commonly referred to as a 419 fraud or an advance fee fraud. Given recent economic downturns, many have turned to the Internet in search of jobs, and many fall prey to such offers. The scams have become popularized with so-called offers to work in areas such as West Africa, Southeast Asia (namely, Malaysia), Europe, and the Middle East. The estimated losses from job offer scams differ, but figures are purported to be in the billions.

An international job offer scam may be done through numerous avenues, but typically the potential victim will receive an e-mail from an unknown person under the guise of a recruiter offering lucrative job opportunities despite the potential employee's limited experience. Normally, job offers from companies that are nonexistent use free e-mail providers including gmail, Yahoo!, and Hotmail accounts, among others. Also, many of the "jobs" are advertised on free Websites that change frequently to ensure the continuity of such scams. The recruiter seeks an advanced payment from the victim, under the pretext of travel expenses, processing of work visas, and additional expenses. The scammer will attempt to gain the trust of the victim in order to access personal information such as a bank account number and social security numbers. After the victim has provided the scammer with the necessary detailed information, the scammer will proceed to remove funds from the victim's account. On the other hand, the scammer may ask the victim to wire funds via Western Union or MoneyGram, which does not leave a paper trail. If the scammer suspects that the victim is becoming hesitant, then he or she may change tactics to appear more genuine. For example, sometimes the scammer may issue the victim a fake traveler's check, which requires that the check be deposited in the victim's account; the victim keeps a fraction, and a large share of the money is to be sent to someone overseas, a third party. The scammer notifies the victim that the check is a deposit of confirmation that he or she has received the job. For example, a victim may be "recruited" as a "babysitter" or an "au pair" and be given an advanced wage to purchase items for the (nonexistent) home or child in which he or she is about to work. Thereafter, the victim may be asked to submit résumés and references, requirements that appear consistent with a legitimate job offer. This is intended to distract the victim with the hope of obtaining his or her trust, which is essential for the scam to be completed. Generally, however, an individual does not have to apply for a job to receive such offers but may be contacted after posting résumés on legitimate Websites such as Monster.com, Hotjobs.com, and CareerBuilder.com. The latter from of an international job offer scam is a bit more sophisticated, as it appears legitimate because the scammers may refer to the résumés posted on those sites.

Unemployed, migrant, elderly, and poor persons are often targets of international job offer scams. The scam tends to work because the job offer opportunities seem to be attractive, especially to those in desperate need of employment. While such scams have become more sophisticated, there are ways of

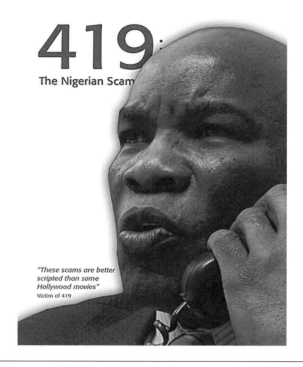

A poster of a docudrama film titled *419: The Nigerian Scam* reveals the workings of the *419 fraud or advance fee fraud*, the terms used to refer to job scams. The estimated losses from these scams are thought to be in the billions of dollars. (Wikimedia)

identifying whether a job offer is real or fake. Some indications of a scam are that the potential victim did not apply for the job, an advance payment to secure the job offer or for visa or other paperwork is required, and such payment is required to be made in cash, by money order, or through Western Union; in addition, personal information (such as a credit card number, social security number, or date of birth) is requested over the telephone or through e-mail in order to obtain a credit report as a qualification for the job. In addition, if correspondence is in poor English or the job offer is "too good to be true," applicants should be suspicious. Scammers may work in groups and usually operate from a country other than the one disclosed to the victim. Also, the victim may receive a check or other documents about the nonexistent job that contains fake information or logos.

The fundamental purpose of an international job offer scam is to enrich the scammer through fraudulent means by taking advantage of unsuspecting individuals. Once the victim responds to the scammer, then there is an indication of interest. The scammer never reveals his or her true identity to the victim and will disappear once the victim follows through with the requests. In the end, the victim loses a lot of money, his or her identity, and/or other possessions permanently.

Marika Dawkins
Prairie View A&M University

See also Financial Fraud; Nigerian Money Scams

Further Readings

Ahmad, Anwar. *Scammsters Use Malaysian "Job Offers" to Prey on Residents*. Washington, DC: McClatchy-Tribune Business News, 2009.

Buck, Claudia. *Better Business Bureau Warns of 10 Most Common Scams*. Washington, DC: McClatchy-Tribune Business News, 2011.

Mychasuk, Emiliya and Emiko Terazono. *Tullow Jobs Scam*. London: Financial Times, 2010.

U.S. Fed News Service. *Business Scam Thwarted in Mississippi: Consumers Warned of Reshipping Jobs*. Washington, DC: Author, 2010.

JOINT FORCE POLICING AND INTEGRATED MODELS

Policing has been common for centuries, with designated individuals acting to apply the police powers of the state. Police officers are empowered to protect property, reduce disorder, and enforce the law. Since the advent of modern police forces during the 18th and 19th centuries, great emphasis has been placed on the independence and autonomy of these agencies—at least in part to emphasize the self-sufficiency and integrity of police forces, which in earlier times were often accused of graft, corruption, and dishonesty. As crime has become more sophisticated, often crossing borders and using a variety of systems and procedures to produce ill-gotten gains, joint force policing and integrated models of fighting crime have grown in popularity. Combining the skills of various agencies and individuals permits law-enforcement officials to better combat the increasingly complicated and highly developed schemes that criminals have devised to break laws. Members of integrated models include police officers, lawyers, accountants, technological experts, forensic specialists, and others. As crime

continues to grow ever more refined and transnational, the use of joint force policing and integrated models to combat it seems likely.

Background

Policing has existed in some form since ancient times. In ancient Greece, for example, magistrates used publicly owned slaves for policing purposes. The Romans, in contrast, used their army, rather than a dedicated police force, to provide security, with local watchmen hired by individual municipalities to provide additional services. During the reign of Augustus, a system of *vigiles* was adopted; these individuals served as firefighters and watchmen and were responsible for the capture of runaway slaves and the apprehension of criminals. During the Middle Ages, this formal system of policing broke down, and a local constable was paid through a tithing system to keep the peace. In areas where a feudal lord was in power, he was responsible for maintaining order in the land he controlled, and often he did this through the appointment of a constable. After the Norman Conquest, the English developed a system of policing that centered on sheriffs, reeves, and juries. The sheriff represented the primary law-enforcement agent for a county, responsible for apprehending criminals and enforcing the peace. The reeve represented the Crown as the chief magistrate of a city or town and was also charged with investigating and preventing crimes. Juries, specifically grand juries, examined evidence presented to them by law-enforcement agents and issued indictments when they believed a sufficient threshold was met regarding the probability of a defendant's guilt. All three of these law-enforcement branches exist today, albeit in slightly altered forms. Beginning in 1800, modern police forces were established in cities such as Glasgow (1800), London (1829), and other locations. These forces, especially with regard to their structure and independence, became a model for police forces throughout the globe.

Policing in the United States in many ways followed the examples set by the British. To help protect public safety, police forces were formed in several cities, including Philadelphia (1751), Richmond (1807), Boston (1838), and New York (1845). The U.S. Department of Justice, an American cabinet-level agency, started the U.S. Marshals Service (USMS) in 1789, and this agency served as the enforcement arm of the federal courts.

The U.S. Secret Service, founded in 1865 as a division of the Treasury Department, was for many years the chief investigative group of the federal government. Although originally charged with the mission of suppressing counterfeiting of U.S. currency, the Secret Service soon was investigating a variety of crimes, including murders, bank robberies, and illegal gambling. For a while, the Secret Service was able to deal adequately with such investigations. As transportation became more convenient and rapid communication was possible, however, a more systematic means of dealing with crime in a coordinated manner became necessary.

In 1887, the U.S. Congress passed the Interstate Commerce Act, which gave the federal government responsibility for interstate law enforcement. It was not until 1908, however, that the Bureau of Investigation (BOI) was formed as an agency of the Department of Justice. The BOI operated until 1935, when it was renamed the Federal Bureau of Investigation (FBI), an independent service within the Department of Justice. Under its director, J. Edgar Hoover, the newly named FBI took a lead role in professionalizing investigations and incorporating scientific methods into the fight against crime. Hoover invested heavily in the development of the Scientific Crime Detection Laboratory, also known as the FBI Laboratory. The FBI Laboratory provides forensic analysis support services to FBI special agents and makes its services available to state and municipal law-enforcement agencies without charge. Hoover was also instrumental in establishing the FBI Academy in Quantico, Virginia. The FBI Academy provides training for FBI special agents and other law-enforcement personnel. Areas of specialty include field training, firearms instruction, investigative computer work, behavioral analysis (profiling), technology services, investigative guidance, communications support, and practical applications. The services of the FBI Academy, which have been replicated on a smaller scale by several state and local law-enforcement agencies, have led to increased communication between and familiarity with other law-enforcement agencies, leading to increased willingness by many to engage in joint force policing and integrated models to battle crime.

Joint Force Policing and Integrated Models

Most crimes are local in nature and are most effectively dealt with by local law-enforcement authorities. Certain types of crimes, however, tend to be organized in such a manner that their ambit crosses state and national borders. These organized and transnational crimes, involving illicit narcotics, weapons smuggling, computer fraud, child pornography, and the like, often require sophisticated analyses and cooperation from a variety of different experts and professionals to be addressed successfully. Joint force policing efforts and integrated model approaches often bring together individuals from multiple government agencies as well as interested third parties, including members of the media. Transnational efforts must consider a variety of issues that traditional law-enforcement practices seldom encounter, including sovereignty issues, drawn-out mutual legal assistance treaty processes, budgetary concerns, and evidentiary restrictions.

As the European Union (EU) evolved from the European Economic Community, founded in 1958, many changes occurred that made transnational crime more common and joint force policing and integrated models of fighting that crime more attractive. The creation of a single European market within the EU, as well as the end of the Cold War, has resulted in fewer barriers to trade. This shift has encouraged legitimate economic activity, to be sure, but it has also resulted in an increase of transnational criminal endeavors. As criminal organizations have seen the possibility of increased opportunities for higher profits, they have moved away from family-based and local models of operation to increasingly sophisticated approaches that utilize complicated and refined business techniques. Economic crimes, which are estimated to result in losses totaling more than $500 billion per year globally, are especially serious, since crimes such as money laundering have the potential to create economic instability and threaten national governments. Changes in many eastern European nations' governments since the end of the Cold War have left them ill equipped to deal with criminal activity that involves arms trafficking, illegal drugs, smuggling, and economic fraud. The traditional separation between intelligence agencies, law-enforcement departments, and the military has proven inadequate now that criminal activity blurs the established distinctions between criminal and security offenses.

Some of the reaction to this rise in transnational crime has been handled through long-established organizations, such as the United Nations (UN) and the International Criminal Police Organization

(Interpol). Based in Lyon, France, Interpol is an organization that comprises 188 member states that have agreed to facilitate international cooperation between law-enforcement agencies. Although its constitution forbids its participation in investigating crimes that have a military, political, racial, or religious nature, Interpol actively focuses on working to secure public safety in Europe and globally. As such, Interpol is actively involved in preventing and investigating organized crime, environmental misdeeds, illicit drug manufacture and transporting, money laundering, pornography, corruption, counterfeiting, and a variety of other crimes. Interpol serves as a liaison between law-enforcement agencies of member nations, facilitating communication and providing database support. Interpol thus permits joint force policing on a case-by-case basis and encourages longer cooperative initiatives between members. Interpol's analysts also review its extensive databases, looking for trends and patterns that might be helpful in fighting crime. European nations have also developed a number of regional organizations to fight crime, including the Stability Pact Initiative Against Organized Crime (SPOC) in southeastern Europe and the Southeastern Europe Cooperation Initiative (SECI). Individual nations have also developed agencies to facilitate joint force policing and integrated models, such as the United Kingdom's National Criminal Intelligence Service (NCIS) and Italy's Anti-Mafia Investigative Directorate (DIA).

In North America, long-standing collaborations between law-enforcement agencies in the United States, Canada, and Mexico have evolved over time to deal with crime. Historically, these efforts have been coordinated through organizations and agencies such as Interpol and the FBI. However, as certain criminal activities, especially those related to illegal drug production and trafficking, have increased, new approaches have been developed to confront them. These approaches include such operations as the Western Hemisphere Institute for Security Cooperation (WHISC), formerly the School for the Americas (SOA). The WHISC is a U.S. Department of Defense facility, currently located at Fort Benning, Georgia, that trains Latin American soldiers and police officers. WHISC training is conducted primarily in Spanish and focuses upon providing

professional education related to law-enforcement and military operations. WHISC training focuses on leadership development, the use of infantry weapons, antidrug operations, technical support, and resource management. The WHISC experience also encourages cooperation among law-enforcement personnel from various nations and provides networking opportunities that facilitate international cooperation in the War on Drugs. Some observers have criticized the WHISC for alleged human rights violations committed by a number of its graduates, and its facility has been the site of numerous protests. As efforts to combat transnational drug trafficking have proven disappointing, new initiatives have been developed. These include the Mérida Initiative, begun in 2008, which represents a cooperative effort between Belize, Costa Rica, the Dominican Republic, El Salvador, Guatemala, Haiti, Honduras, Mexico, Nicaragua, Panama, and the United States. The Mérida Initiative seeks to battle drug trafficking, transnational crime, and money laundering by means of joint training, equipment sharing, and pooled intelligence between law-enforcement agencies of the various nations involved. If it is successful, similar operations might be expected to be initiated in other parts of the globe.

Stephen T. Schroth
Jason A. Helfer
Kiara A. Booth
Knox College

See also Anticorruption Legislation; Centralization; North America; Policing: Transnational; Racketeer Influenced and Corrupt Organizations Act; Western Europe

Further Readings

Deflem, M. *Policing World Society: Historical Foundations of International Police Cooperation.* Oxford, UK: Clarendon, 2004.

Goldsmith, A. and J. Sheptycki. *Crafting Transnational Policing: State-Building and Global Policing Reform.* Oxford, UK: Hart Law Publishers, 2007.

Nadelmann, E. A. *Cops Across Borders: The Internationalization of U.S. Law Enforcement.* University Park: Pennsylvania State University Press, 1993.

L

LEGAL AND ILLEGAL ECONOMIES

The linkages between legal and illegal economies are often not acknowledged in scholarly and policy discourse. One possible explanation for this oversight is that the label *illegal* presents unregulated economic activities as immoral, parasitic, and alien to legitimate society. However, legal and illegal economies all conform to free-market economic dictates and are therefore driven by the forces of supply and demand. Although illegal economic activities may be difficult to detect and control, illegal economies are thought to constitute a significant portion of the national economies of most countries, ranging from about 8 to 30 percent of the economies of developed countries and about 13 to 76 percent of the economies of developing countries; in the transition countries, the proportion of illegal economies is about 7 to 43 percent. The commodities that are produced through the illegal economic activities can be said to be demand-driven. In this respect, therefore, a case can be made for public complicity in the fostering and expansion of illegal economic activities, as societal support is essential for illegal economies to thrive. Furthermore, an unintended consequence of the artificial regulation of economic activities is the enablement of illegal as well as legal economic activities. This entry briefly seeks to give some insight into the understanding and causes of illegal economies and their linkages to legal economies.

The term *illegal economy* is generally used to describe economic activities that are not detected and taxed by the authorized agents of a country.

The term is also used to describe otherwise legal economic activities that are hidden from the tax authorities of a country—that is, legal economic activities whose beneficiaries fail to pay the requisite taxes to their governments. Illegal economies therefore describe trade, goods, and services that fall outside the purview of the taxing authorities and are not recognized as part of the official economy of a country. Other terms used to describe illegal economies include *underground economy*, *black market economy*, *parallel economy*, *shadow economy*, *unreported economy*, and *informal economy*.

The known examples of illegal economic activity range from babysitting and hairdressing to the sale of stolen goods, human trafficking, illegal drug manufacturing and distribution, arms trafficking, prostitution, gambling, smuggling, and fraud. Some activities stemming from legal economic activity that link to the illegal economy include failure to report income from legal self-employment, failure to report wages and salaries (in part or in full), failure to report employee discounts and fringe benefits, and failure to report income or profit from bartering of legal services and commodities.

To understand the concept and emergence of illegal economies, one must understand why some behaviors and enterprises are criminalized. It is trite to note that not all behaviors that are prohibited reflect the beliefs and values of the majority of society. Many, therefore, perceive some of the laws as serving parochial interests, often those of the group that dominates the economic and political sphere of society. A good example would be the criminalization of opium in Canada as an attempt to control and stifle the economic activities of Chinese immigrants. The prohibition of alcohol in the United States and the criminalization of marijuana are also seen in this light, as attempts to control the economic activities of minority groups. The understanding is that behaviors and enterprises associated with minority groups are likely to be outlawed. Illegal economies are also likely to develop in societies where many are politically and economically marginalized. Colonial and postcolonial African and some Asian societies are good examples, where some of the cultures and economic activities of the indigenous people are outlawed. Other schools of thought view the emergence of illegal economies as a form of protest by marginalized groups. In Africa and Asia, significant members of the working class earn wages that are so meager that without bribery and corruption and participation in other illegal business activities, they would not be able to survive. Racism and the mass incarceration of African Americans have cut many people out of the mainstream economy, forcing them to engage in the underground economy for survival. The inequality in the international economic system has made it difficult for developing countries to compete, forcing them into the production of prohibited goods.

Illegal economies are also known to flourish in countries where corruption is endemic and where the regulation and legal monopolies stifle and undermine free trade. For example, the estimated size of the illegal economies of Nigeria and Egypt is about 68 to 76 percent of those nations' total economies. On the other hand, the illegal economies of Japan, the United States, and Switzerland constitute between 8 and 10 percent. One known major cause of the underground economy is excessive taxation. When the taxing of proceeds of certain commodities is too high, businesses are forced underground in an attempt to keep most of their profits. Price-fixing is typical of socialist societies and other societies whose governments play dominant roles in economic production and distribution. In such cases, monopolies on popular consumer products can lead to the development of illegal economies as individuals seek to produce such goods at a competitive price for profit. Some countries, especially in the developing world, may politically manipulate their exchange rates. In such situations, parallel markets that are more realistic in regard to the prevailing exchange rate can develop.

The prohibition of goods, especially ones that are in high demand, can give rise to illegal economic distribution and sale of such products. A good example is the prohibition of alcohol in the United States in the 1920s. Organized crime syndicates arose to brew and distribute alcoholic beverages for big profits. Similarly, countries engaged in warfare tend to restrict the consumption of certain goods and services essential for the prosecution of the war. Such policies can lead to scarcity and sometimes rationing, if the restricted commodities are essential, such as food and gasoline. The high demand for such scarce and necessary products can give rise to underground economic activities as sharp business people seek to take advantage of the spike in demand.

Arguments against the illegal economic activity are legion. Many believe that illegal economic activities have negative effects on economic development. According to these critics, illegal economic activities are capable of damaging the financial institutions that are essential for economic growth. Illegal economic activities are also said to undermine productivity in the economy's legal or "real" sector, because resources that should have accrued to the real sector of the economy are diverted to other sectors, such as private individuals engaging in illegal activity and even foreign interests that cannot be held accountable. Illegal economic activity is therefore seen as detrimental to the long-term interests of the overall economy and also as capable of spreading crime and corruption. Unchecked illegal activities are capable of weakening government's power and undermining its ability to meet its responsibilities. The drug cartels of Colombia, Mexico, and Afghanistan offer good examples of the problems that underground economies under the control of clandestine groups can cause. When enormous economic resources flow to private individuals and groups at the expense of governments, such individuals can become too powerful and become laws unto themselves. This can be dangerous, for such groups lack the people's political and legal mandate and therefore are not accountable to the society. Democratic institutions can be weakened as a result, leading to dictatorship and erosion of human rights. Moreover, illegal economies can create opportunities for the corruption of government officials and lead to monopolies of the production and distribution of essential goods and services.

Some view illegal economies as beneficial to society, seeing some illegal activity as empowering otherwise marginalized members of the society. Poor inner-city neighborhoods, for example, have accommodated illegal enterprises because they create jobs and contribute to local tax revenues. There are other schools of thought that view illegal economies as open and flexible economic systems that provide alternative commodities and services to consumers. In this respect, agorists posit that illegal economies meet the criteria of true free-market economy, as the commodities' value and exchange are solely determined by demand and supply—unlike the regulated economy, which suffers from the interference of governments and other economic institutions.

To conclude, there is a strong linkage between legal and illegal economies of many countries. Many eke out a living through the illegal activity. Illegal economic activities flourish more in authoritarian societies. In addition to providing a living for the marginalized classes, illegal economies provide them leverage for negotiating with the dominant class. The existence of illegal economies highlights the undemocratic processes through which laws are created. Furthermore, excessive taxation and regulation of enterprises can force many otherwise popular economic activities underground. Making lawmaking more democratic and transparent and the economic system more inclusive will go a long way toward merging legal and illegal economies. Allowing market forces to determine what is legal and illegal is instrumental to the understanding of the concepts and their linkages.

Rochelle E. Cobbs
Mississippi Valley State University
O. Oko Elechi
Prairie View A&M University

See also Black Market Peso Exchange; Cigarette Smuggling; Cocaine; Copyright Infringement; Counterfeit Goods; Drug Trade: Source, Destination, and Transit Countries; Globalization; Heroin; Human Smuggling; Human Trafficking; Informal Value Transfer Systems; Internet Crime; Measuring Transnational Crime; Networks; Nigerian Money Scams; Organ Trafficking; Organized Crime: Defined; Organized Crime: Ethnic- Versus Market-Based; Price-Fixing; Sex Slavery; Tax Evasion; Terrorism: Financing; Tobacco Smuggling; Underground Banking Regulations; Value-Added Tax Fraud

Further Readings

Andreas, Peter. "Illicit International Political Economy: The Clandestine Side of Globalization." *Review of International Political Economy*, v.11/3 (2004).

Bartlett, Brent L. (2002). "The Negative Effects of Money Laundering on Economic Development." http://www .adb.org/documents/others/ogc-toolkits/anti-money -laundering/documents/money_laundering_neg_effects .pdf (Accessed February 2011).

Beare, Margaret E. and R. T. Naylor. "Major Issues Relating to Organized Crime: Within the Context of Economic Relationships." http://www.ncjrs.gov/ nathanson/organized.html (Accessed February 2011).

Buchanan, Bonnie. "Money Laundering: A Global Obstacle." *Research in International Business and Finance*, v.18 (2004).

Katsios, Stavros. "The Shadow Economy and Corruption in Greece." *South-Eastern Europe of Economics*, v.1 (2006).

Schneider, Friedrich and Dominik H. Enste. "Shadow Economies: Size, Causes, and Consequences." *Journal of Economic Literature*, v.38/1 (2000).

Thale, Christopher. "Underground Economy." In *Encyclopedia of Chicago*. http://encyclopedia .chicagohistory.org/pages/1280.html (Accessed February 2011).

LEGISLATING MORALITY

The state legislation of morality is perhaps most closely associated with theocratic states or governments in which morals derived from religious beliefs coincide with and are expressed in state policies, legislation, and punishment regimes. Under such regimes, there is no separation of church and state and, indeed, the head of state is often the head of the dominant religious organization.

During the medieval period in Europe, monarchs asserted their right to rule and establish laws on the basis of divine right in which their power was construed to derive from their nearness to God. The nobility placed themselves at the top of the "great chain of being," with the serfs over whom they ruled being closer to base animals and therefore unfit to rule. Only the nobility were created in the image of God; indeed, they proclaimed that they had been touched by God. This ideology was used to justify the absolute authority of the monarch, whose power was believed to have been conferred directly by God as an act of His will and therefore could not be challenged by the people. The dictates of the monarch, an unconditional authority, legislated morality as an expression of God's will on earth. Only God could judge a monarch's behavior; thus, any rebellion or disobedience against the monarch would be construed as an act of sacrilege.

In China, rulers referred to the Mandate of Heaven to justify their rule. In a manner similar to divine right in Europe, the mandate legitimized rulership through reference to divine will. From this perspective, ruling morality was legislated as divine will on earth. Unlike divine right in Europe, the mandate could transfer away from unfit or unjust rulers and did not grant unconditional authority. In addition, it did not dictate that rulers be restricted to members of the nobility.

In the current period, theocratic governments continue to unify state and religious authority. Modern theocratic states operate in several countries, including Iran, Oman, Saudi Arabia, and Yemen. In Egypt, legislation is vetted for its agreement with religious teachings. Vatican City represents another form of theocratic government. Some suggest that the Israeli state is yet another form of theocracy. Others have warned that the United States, particularly insofar as it has been influenced by fundamentalist Protestantism, has drifted precariously close to becoming a theocracy.

With the emergence of liberal democratic governments and the assertion of separation between church and state as a principle of democratic government, ruling authorities have used different approaches to legislate morality beyond direct appeals to religious teachings. Practices within liberal democratic capitalist systems are sometimes identified as bourgeois morality. In diverse societies there is always a subjective, contested element in the definition of social issues. Definitions of social problems depend on the moral and social stances of those who are able to do the defining. Definitions are constructed through a range of processes involving relations of power. Definitions of actions as deviant, criminal, or wrong may be based on morals and values that are not widely shared. The notion of deviance itself implies disagreement over norms.

The state legislation of morality involves practices of what is often described as "moral regulation"—the establishment by governments, by means of laws

and regulations, of right and wrong, good and bad. Moral regulation encourages certain forms of conduct and expression while discouraging others. To do so, states establish disciplinary regimes, including systems of reward and punishment. Moral regulation can be carried out through state practices with respect to finance, taxation, social policy, and citizenship itself. Moral regulation is carried out in nearly every aspect of state practice.

Commentators note that the modern state has grown through increasing involvement in all areas of social life, from work to consumption practices to sexuality, childrearing, and education. Among the most familiar examples are legislation against drinking and driving, growing penalties against smoking, and long-standing prohibitions against recreational drug use. In these cases, where there is much social debate and conflict over the question of legislation, the contested character of moral perspectives in diverse, democratic societies is clear. Instances such as the failed attempt to enforce prohibition against alcohol in the United States during the 1920s experiment known as Prohibition show how tenuous the state legislation of morality can be and how steadfastly it might be opposed. State legislation has made use of new intellectual practices and disciplines, from medicine to psychology to social work.

One of the areas where moral regulation and the legislation of morality have been exhibited throughout the course of capitalist modernity involves the regulation of poverty and the development of the corporate work ethic. In the early stages of capitalist development and industrialization, liberal democratic states developed punishments targeting poor and homeless people simply for being poor and homeless. Various "poor laws" were used to arrest and detain poor people, who were then made to labor in state work camps. Such laws persist in the 20th century in legislation such as the Safe Streets Acts in Ontario and British Columbia, whereby Canada has given police officers the power to arrest people for street survival acts such as panhandling. Robert Miles argues that the model for contemporary practices of class inferiorization began in 16th-century Europe as discrimination against the poor, especially beggars. This came under the guise of "civilizing projects" designed to establish and legitimize a social system of emerging power differentials. Feudal rulers changed their behaviors initially by making their bodily functions more private.

This behavioral shift allowed them to contrast their "refined" activities with those of the "inferior" people whom they ruled. People in the business and industrial classes imitated this "civilized" behavior, eventually presenting their prudent values as inherited rather than socially constructed. Miles suggests that this civilizing project encompassed forms of domestic racism in Europe, in which privileged Europeans portrayed themselves as superior to the people they ruled; the result was a foundation for colonial racism. These practices are reflected in contemporary policies of citizenship and immigration controls. Within capitalist culture, the identifying characteristics of a good person become constructed as rejecting idleness and unproductive pleasures and attending to one's business with thrift and industriousness. Poverty is constructed as evidence of moral weakness or lack of character, which the state is expected to discourage.

Critical theorists suggest that in stratified societies the norms of elite groups are typically constructed as legitimate, common, or shared. Elite needs are presented as "the common good," and dominant morality reflects the interests and concerns of elites. Critics, however, question whose values are viewed as normal and whose are viewed as pathological. Alongside this question, they consider who is regulated and who does the regulating.

Jeffrey Shantz
Kwantlen Polytechnic University

See also Anticorruption Legislation; Drug Trade: Legislative Debates; Gambling: Illegal; Gambling: Legal; Marijuana or Cannabis; Legislation as a Source of Crime; Public Perceptions of Crime; Responsibilization

Further Readings

Agamben, Giorgio. *Means Without End: Notes on Politics.* Minneapolis: University of Minnesota Press, 2000.

Elias, Norbert. *The Civilizing Process.* Oxford, UK: Blackwell, 1978.

Foucault, Michel. *Discipline and Punish: The Birth of the Prison.* New York: Random House, 1975.

Foucault, Michel. *The History of Sexuality.* Vol. 1, *The Will to Knowledge.* London: Penguin, 1976.

Miles, Robert. *Racism After "Race Relations."* London: Routledge, 1993.

Weber, Max. *The Protestant Ethic and the Spirit of Capitalism.* London: Penguin, 2002.

LEGISLATION AS A SOURCE OF CRIME

Largely ignored in discussions of the criminal justice system are the lawmakers—the city, county, state, and federal officials—who enact the laws intended to govern daily life and promote conformity within society. The work of most is driven by the best of intentions. However, even the noblest legislators lack the ability to see into the future—to predict the unintended and often deleterious consequences that surface once a proposal becomes law. Of added concern are the elected officials who, unknown to many, are blatantly self-serving. Unscrupulous, yet both persuasive and charismatic, these individuals all too often successfully lobby for laws that prove to be self-benefiting in nature while exploiting the already disadvantaged in society.

Technological advances, cultural change, and historical events have forever altered life not just in the United States but globally as well. Hence, U.S. lawmakers find themselves at a crossroads, needing collaborative efforts aimed at crime control both within and beyond the national borders. No stronger evidence of this exists than the events and aftermath of September 11, 2001, when international terrorists infiltrated our borders and, using our own commercial aircraft as weapons, forever changed life as we knew it. Those in the highest echelons of government moved quickly to pass legislation aimed at protecting the United States from further attack. Largely reactionary in nature, the federal government passed the U.S.A. Patriot Act a mere six days later. Still controversial in its own right, the Patriot Act is hailed by some as paramount in having prevented further such attacks. Others, less willing to accept the wording of the Patriot Act, express concern regarding its ambiguous language, which may well open the door for government intervention into the lives of the general citizenry.

Legislative Reform as a Source of Increased Criminality

Perhaps the most notable failure in America's attempts to regulate behavior via legislative reform is the introduction of Prohibition in 1920. Intended to control the manufacture, transport, import, export, sale, and consumption of alcohol, Prohibition did not, as many think, have its roots firmly planted only in the work of America's religious zealots. As early as 1907, alcohol was banned in the territories of Prince Edward Island, Russia, Iceland, Norway, Hungary, and Finland. Under pressure from groups such as the Woman's Christian Temperance Union, the United States joined hands with those countries that had already banned alcohol. In 1919, both the Volstead Act and the 18th Amendment to the U.S. Constitution were passed, resulting in Prohibition. Both were dismal failures. As moral entrepreneurs reveled in their accomplishments, little time passed before Prohibition became a mechanism by which unscrupulous individuals profited. Crime flourished as bootlegging, individual brewing, speakeasies, and the Mafia assumed control of the alcohol trade. By 1933, Prohibition was repealed as lawmakers were compelled to admit their efforts had merely served to escalate crime and corruption. Both national and global history is rife with similar examples. For instance, a vast literature has argued that the legislation that makes up the current U.S. War on Drugs has contributed enormously to crime—both in that criminals sell drugs and in the corruption of officials supposedly controlling the industry.

Of more contemporary concern to politicians and citizens alike is the ongoing battle against illegal immigration, portrayed by the media as entry under the cloak of darkness and enduring the perils of the desert, in flagrant violation of the law. Purported to serve as yet another layer of protection from external attack, the Immigration and Naturalization Service (INS) was officially dissolved in 2002 by then President George W. Bush and placed under the auspices of the newly formed Homeland Security Agency. Following the 2001 terrorist attacks, both the general public and elected officials remained reactionary. Hence, Congress lost no time in approving the change of leadership and authorizing the expansion of the Border Patrol by adding 10,000 new agents over a five-year span to further protect national security. While these increased efforts have proved successful in the minds of some, few laypersons are fully aware of the real cost to the American economy, which have been deleterious to the labor market as well as the families and children of undocumented workers. As is often the case when

debating the passage of new laws, many tend to forget their actions affect people rather than statistics. Regardless of one's position on illegal immigration, it must be noted that current efforts to seal the U.S. borders have largely proved futile.

The Effects of Nonlegislation

In October 2004, the devastation wrought by the Indian Ocean tsunami secured its place in history. Releasing the energy of 23,000 Hiroshima bombs, the tsunami had its origins in Sumatra, and its ripple effects were felt as far away as Africa. Entire villages were destroyed and little was left in its aftermath. The human toll was far greater. As the media provided daily casualty updates, little attention was given to the children who survived. Almost immediately, and with the best intentions in mind, relief agencies acted swiftly to reunite families separated by the deadly tsunami and its aftermath. Unfortunately, several weeks passed before it became apparent that those working long hours to reunite families were, instead, helping to perpetuate international human trafficking. In the absence of verifiable documentation, children—many as young as four—were placed not in the hands of loving family members but under the control of profiteers. As quickly as the tsunami wreaked its havoc, these children were sold for sex to those willing to pay the price.

Estimates, although flawed, indicate that approximately 820,000 individuals are bought and sold annually via a global underground market. Some are used as slave labor. Most, however, are purchased by those intent on fulfilling their most deviant fantasies. Largely unknown—or perhaps ignored—by those with the authority to end human sex trafficking, this trade continues to flourish. Although it is a global industry, the United States has set itself apart as one of the largest purchasers of the youngest for sale. Though lawmakers are becoming aware of the extent of, and damage done by, human sex trafficking little has been done to educate the general public. Even less has been done to promote global legislation aimed at ending the sale and trade of humans by unscrupulous profiteers. In the face of nonlegislation, the industry flourishes at the expense of those least able to protect themselves.

Conclusion

Legislation and the work of lawmakers provide the foundation for the peacekeepers of society in their efforts to keep the general citizenry safe from crime and corruption. Unfortunately, the same individuals and the decisions they make or issues they fail to address often serve as the source of global crime and corruption.

Unintended consequences emanating from legislative decision making often spur the imagination of the criminal, thus resulting in new types of crime rather than inhibiting criminality. Other legislative decisions aimed at dictating morality provide fertile ground for the emergence of crime where it was once absent. Finally, nonenforcement via the lack of needed legislation allows for the perpetuation and growth of crime affecting the most innocent. Hence, just as the work of law-enforcement officers, corrections officials, and the courts is scrutinized as a component of the criminal justice system, so, too, should the lawmakers and their decisions be equally examined if we are to halt crime and corruption in a global society.

Martha L. Shockey-Eckles
Saint Louis University

See also Human Smuggling; Securitization After Terror; Violence: Protection

Further Readings

Behr, Edward. *Thirteen Years That Changed America.* New York: Arcade Publishing, 2011.

Farr, Kathryn. *Sex Trafficking: The Global Market in Women and Children.* New York: Worth Publishers, 2004.

Garibaldi, Mario. "Illegal Immigration: Pros and Cons." *Credit Secrets* (May 8, 2006).

Garrison, Carl A. et al. *The Legal Process: An Introduction to Decision-Making by Judicial, Legislative, Executive, and Administrative Agencies.* San Francisco: Chandler, 1961.

Kingdon, John W. *Congressmen's Voting Decisions.* Ann Arbor: University of Michigan Press, 1989.

Lewis, Jack. "The Birth of the EPA." *EPA Journal* (November 1985).

Marx, Gary. "Ironies of Social Control: Authorities as Contributors to Deviance Through Escalation, Nonenforcement, and Covert Facilitation." *Social Problems*, v.28/3 (1981).

National Geographic. "The Deadliest Tsunami in History?" *National Geographic* (January 7, 2005).

Okrent, Daniel. *Last Call: The Rise and Fall of Prohibition.* New York: Scribner, 2010.

MAFIA MYTHS AND MYTHOLOGIES

The Mafia is a secret criminal organization that originated in Sicily. Mafia myths and mythologies were fostered by the mysterious and surreptitious nature of the group as well as by dramatic media accounts; both created a fictionalized aura that encompassed the group and its legendary exploits, which later became accepted as truths. In some cases, life in the Mafia imitated the dramatized newspaper or other media characterizations of the organization. The myths and mythologies surrounding the Mafia apply largely to organized crime (OC) groups in the United States, not to the real Mafia in Sicily. The criminal influence and activities of the Mafia and other organized crime groups, with few exceptions, are concentrated in their home countries.

The etymology of the word *mafia* is unknown. Some language scholars suggest that it might be an Arabic word meaning "boldness." Others note that the term *mafioso* connotes a "man of respect." The history of the Mafia is inextricably linked to the turbulent history of Sicily itself, which was repeatedly overrun by foreign invaders: Spaniards, Saracens, Arabs, and Normans. Subjected to numerous military incursions over the course of centuries, the people of Sicily became highly suspicious of outsiders and hostile toward occupying governments. The Mafia arose in response to political oppression and became a protective and clandestine force that served as a shadow government in fierce opposition to tyrannical regimes.

Over many decades, the Mafia evolved into a vast underground band of criminals that consolidated its power to exploit, rather than protect, Sicily's population. The Mafia gained its reputation through a ruthless campaign of unremitting intimidation, violence, and terror. Mafiosi robbed, extorted, and misappropriated land and property in order to amass wealth and power over the local residents, who fell under the control of the Mafia bosses.

Myth 1: The Mafia Operates in America and Around the World

The most pervasive and enduring myth about the Mafia is that the organization simply transplanted itself en bloc into American society at the height of Italian immigration, between 1880 and 1924. Proponents of the alien conspiracy theory argue that the Mafia arrived in the United States fully intact and ready to unleash its reign of terror in the New World. In Italy, the dictator Benito Mussolini engaged in systematic attempts to destroy the Mafia through imprisonment and deportation of its members. Hundreds of mafiosi fled to the United States, including Carlo Gambino and Joseph Bonnano, who became the bosses of powerful crime families in New York City. However, only scanty evidence, at best, supports the notion that the Sicilian Mafia became entrenched in American life or in the societies of other countries; this belief was encouraged by sensationalistic newspaper accounts.

The first media account that created the myth of the Mafia in the United States arose from the murder of Police Chief David Hennessey in New Orleans in 1890. Responsibility for his assassination was ascribed to the "Mafia" and was based on the unreliable confession of a possibly deranged suspect/witness. The media frenzy that developed shortly after the murder led to the use of the term *Mafia* in the New Orleans press; stories about the Mafia quickly spread throughout the country. The trial of nine suspects ended in not-guilty verdicts for three of the defendants and mistrials for the other six. Claiming that the jurors had been bribed, an enraged mob led by prominent attorneys and a newspaper editor stormed the jail and killed 11 of the 19 suspects implicated in the chief's murder, including four men of Sicilian origin who were not even involved in the case. None of the vigilantes was arrested.

In profound indignation over this horrific event, the Italian government severed diplomatic relations with the United States. The accusations of jury tampering were never proved, and the murder of Chief Hennessey was never solved. However, the damage was done. The Mafia became implanted in the American consciousness. Unless proven otherwise, the media dubbed all murders involving Italians, especially Sicilians—as suspected assailants or victims—as "Mafia killings," fueling hatred and mistrust of Italians and lending credence to the alien conspiracy theory.

The founders of traditional Italian American organized crime (TIAOC) shared with their Mafia counterparts some elements (for example, Old World values and organizational structure) but never attempted to replicate the Mafia in all its aspects. Many of the leaders of TIAOC either had been born in the United States or came to America as children and readily assimilated into American culture. Their experiences growing up in urban ghettos (Little Italys) laid the foundation for a distinctly Americanized version of organized crime. Unlike mafiosi, members of organized crime in the United States created or took advantage of the decidedly urban opportunities for criminal gain, which were absent from Sicily—a largely rural, undeveloped, and agrarian region.

TIAOC had its roots in the corrupt political machines of rapidly growing cities in the United States, such as New York, Chicago, Boston, and New Orleans; these machines controlled jobs, businesses, and labor unions as well as gambling, prostitution, and other illegal activities. Through political corruption, organized crime insinuated itself into all aspects of 20th-century urban life. In this sense, the term Mafia is a misleading description of TIAOC in the United States. The organized crime families in New York City and New Jersey are known as La Costa Nostra; in Chicago, as the Crime Syndicate or Mob; and in New England, as the Office.

The Mafia is indigenous to Sicily. Except for isolated situations (such as the drug trade), TIAOC has also been quite insular in its criminal activities. Among New York City's Five Crime Families, crime is confined mostly to the city or to criminal opportunities that originate there. These crime families rarely collaborate with one another. Even the street crews that constitute a crime family tend to commit their crimes mostly within their own ranks and on their own territory. Hence, since their inception, the Mafia and TIAOC, overall, have been parochial in their criminal endeavors and influence.

Myth 2: TIAOC Consists Only of Italians

The myth of Italian-American exclusivity in organized crime is only partially true. Often recruiting members from neighborhood streets in urban enclaves, TIAOC groups insisted that aspiring members had to be full-blooded Italians with family origins that were traceable to Italy or Sicily. Indeed, TIAOC groups are referred to as "families." Selecting recruits because of their ethnic backgrounds helped create closer ties and camaraderie among the members of organized crime families and prevented infiltration by undercover law-enforcement agents. However, much evidence suggests that organized crime associates were frequently of other ethnic origins than the core members of the organization.

Early organized crime groups in New York aligned closely with Jewish gangsters, who grew up in the same hardscrabble environments as the Italian gangsters. These allegiances were critical to the development of TIAOC. For example, Meyer Lansky (Jewish), a childhood friend of Charles "Lucky" Luciano, was instrumental in constructing a cooperative business model of organized crime and promoting the formation of what the press called the National Crime Syndicate, both of which were crucial to the early growth and success of TIAOC. The notorious group of organized crime assassins known as Murder Incorporated had both a Jewish faction, led by Jacob "Gurrah" Shapiro, and an Italian faction, led by Albert "the Mad Hatter"

Anastasia. Among New York's organized crime families, there are many instances of other ethnic groups (such as the Irish organized crime group known as the Westies) that participated in crimes at the behest of Italian bosses.

The Outfit is perhaps the most inclusive TIAOC family in the United States. In Chicago, many high-ranking but supposedly not indoctrinated or "made" members of organized crime had ethnic origins other than Italian. The leader of Chicago's organized crime family in the 1920s, Al Capone, forged many alliances with other ethnic groups before he gained hegemony over the market for illicit alcohol and eventually over all other major criminal enterprises in the city following the 1929 St. Valentine's Day Massacre. Influential members of the Outfit included Jake "Greasy Thumb" Guzik (Jewish), Gus Alex (Greek), Ed Vogel (Bohemian), Murray "the Camel" Humphreys (Welsh), Lenny Patrick (Jewish), David Yaras (Jewish), Sam "Golf Bag" Hunt (English), Ralph Pierce (English), and Frank Schweihs (German). Despite the inclusion of members of non-Italian descent, the deliberate and systematic cooperation of organized crime families with criminal groups outside the United States has been limited.

Myth 3: All Members of TIAOC Must Take an Oath

The ubiquity of the induction ceremony or ritual is another partial truth about organized crime. The Federal Bureau of Investigation (FBI) recorded a member of the Patriarca crime family of New England being indoctrinated into the ranks of organized crime. The inductee was required to prick his finger to draw blood and then burn a holy picture in the palm of his hand while reciting a pledge of lifelong loyalty to the crime family and faithfulness to the code of secrecy, or Omertà, also known as the code of silence. References to the organized crime induction ceremony can also be found in the testimonies of former members of organized crime who later became FBI informants, such as Jimmy "the Weasel" Fratianno. Joe Valachi was the first organized crime apostate to share the particulars of the secret ceremony during his testimony in 1963 before the Senate's Permanent Subcommittee on Investigations. Hence, the induction ceremony has a firm basis in the culture of TIAOC. However, it is unclear whether

this ceremony is required for inductees to all of the (approximately) 25 organized crime families identified in the United States in the 1950s. For example, in Chicago, decades-long crime boss Joey "the Clown" Lombardo stated in a classified advertisement in a local newspaper that he "never took a secret oath, with guns and daggers, pricked my finger, drew blood or burned paper to join a criminal organization."

Mob experts agree that the swearing-in oath in Chicago might have occurred only sporadically and at the special request of the capo (leader) of a street crew (a smaller group in the larger organizational structure of the crime family). Therefore, membership in Chicago's Mob requires sponsorship by a member and a track record of productive earnings but no oath of allegiance. In general, the oath taken by organized crime members applies only to their own family and never to any transcendent criminal organizations or conspiracies.

Myth 4: Nobody Testifies in Organized Crime Families

As noted above, the oath of secrecy is an integral component of the induction ceremony into TIAOC. New members' pledge to uphold the code of silence is threefold. First, it is a pledge to keep the existence of the organization itself a secret from outsiders. Hiding the existence of TIAOC became impossible after the testimony of Joe Valachi and the discovery by state police officers of the National Commission Member Summit in Apalachin, New York, which was held on November 14, 1957. Second, it is a promise to keep one's own membership a secret. Third, it is a commitment to refrain from testifying against other organized crime members. Organized crime associates who never take an oath of Omertà are also expected to uphold the secrecy of the organization and to steadfastly withhold information about criminal activities even if doing so would increase the likelihood that they would suffer legal consequences. The cost of violating the code was death. Many paid the ultimate price simply for being suspected of cooperating with authorities.

In the 1980s, federal prosecutors adopted legal tools that sorely tested the code of Omertà and shattered the wall of secrecy at the highest levels of TIAOC. These tools included the Racketeer Influenced and Corrupt Organizations (RICO) Act, which allowed federal prosecutors to charge the leaders of organized crime with a long list of predicate offenses committed by any members of the organization. A conviction under the RICO statute guarantees a lengthy (typically life) prison sentence and indicts the organization as an entity rather than simply charging individual members of the organized crime family. In addition, the widespread use of electronic surveillance and undercover agents helped create insurmountable cases against organized crime members and encouraged them to plead guilty or participate in the Witness Protection Program, which promises relocation, a new identity, and insulation of the witnesses and their family members against retaliation by organized crime.

Since these tools have been used against TIAOC, thousands of members have become government informants, testifying against "the family." Members at the highest ranks of TIAOC families betrayed the organization in order to broker a lesser sentence for themselves. Such informants include Sammy "the Bull" Gravano (underboss of the Gambino family), Anthony "Gaspipe" Casso (underboss of the Lucchese family), Phillip "Crazy Phil" Leonetti (underboss of the Philadelphia crime family), and "Big Joey" Massino (boss of the Bonnano family). The defection of organized crime members has seriously weakened the ranks of TIAOC groups throughout the United States and has greatly reduced their power and control over all their criminal enterprises. The diminishment of traditional organized crime families has created possibilities for newly arrived criminal groups from Russia, Yugoslavia, and Jamaica to encroach on their territories and enterprises.

Myth 5: Drug Sales in TIAOC Are Prohibited

A common myth about organized crime is that its members are forbidden to sell illegal drugs. In his autobiography *Man of Honor*, Joe Bonanno (boss of New York's Bonanno crime family) called drug sales a "dirty business." In reality, the Bonanno crime family was the hub of heroin trafficking in the United States, participating in an elaborate scheme in the 1970s to smuggle heroin from Sicily, sell it in pizza parlors throughout the city, and launder the profits as legitimate business earnings. John Gotti, boss of the Gambino crime family from 1985 to 1991, rose to prominence as a capo in part because of the drug-related earnings of his crew. At one time or another, all the TIAOC families were major drug traffickers,

distributors, and sellers, as documented in several government reports about the illicit drug trade in the United States dating back to the 1930s. In this arena, TIAOC has engaged in transnational crime, forging worldwide connections in the drug trade.

Conclusion

The ranks of organized crime families in the United States have been decimated by the unrelenting attention and efforts of the FBI, which has employed three effective tools against the Crime Syndicate. The first is the use of electronic surveillance and wiretapping devices, which are authorized by federal electronic surveillance statutes. Surveillance activities have provided the FBI with invaluable intelligence and useful evidence in the pursuit of successful convictions against organized crime members at all levels. The second, as mentioned above, is the Racketeer Influenced and Corrupt Organizations (RICO) Act, which allows the government to indict an organized crime member for the commission of any two of 35 predicate crimes committed in the furtherance of the organization within a 10-year period, a practice known as racketeering. A RICO conviction leads to lengthy prison sentences—a minimum of 20 years for each offense. Under RICO, the leaders of an organized crime family can be convicted for the crimes committed by any member of the organization. In a civil action, RICO also permits the seizure of illegal income as well as possessions and property purchased with illegal income. The third is the Witness Protection Program, which has encouraged thousands of organized crime members and associates to testify against crime families in exchange for a new identity and safety as well as lesser charges and shorter sentences. Organized crime members at the highest ranks have become government witnesses. The defection and conviction of organized crime members have seriously weakened the ranks of organized crime groups throughout the United States and have greatly reduced their power and control over their criminal empires. The diminishment of traditional organized crime families has created opportunities for other criminal groups in the United States and abroad—from Russia, China, Yugoslavia, and Jamaica—to encroach on their traditional organized crime territories and enterprises.

Arthur J. Lurigio
Loyola University, Chicago

See also Alien Conspiracies and Protection Systems; Criminal Associations; Drug Trade: Source, Destination, and Transit Countries; Heroin; Organized Crime: Defined; Racketeer Influenced and Corrupt Organizations Act

Further Readings

Bonanno, J. and S. Lalli. *A Man of Honor*. New York: St. Martin's Press, 2001.

Kenny, D. and J. Finckenauer. *Organized Crime in America*. Belmont, CA: Wadsworth, 1995.

Lupo, S. *History of the Mafia*. New York: Columbia University Press, 2009.

Lyman, M. D. and G. W. Potter. *Organized Crime*. Upper Saddle River, NJ: Prentice Hall, 2000.

MARIJUANA OR CANNABIS

Cannabis (the preferred usage), or marijuana, is one of the oldest drugs known to humankind. Its use in antiquity is well documented; it was cultivated in China as early as 4000 B.C.E. and in Turkestan in 3000 B.C.E. Experts believe that its use as a cultigen predates those dates by at least four millennia. Although known to Eastern medicine as a mild intoxicant with medicinal uses, it was scarcely used in the West until Napoleon's troops brought hashish back from Egypt in the 1790s. Hashish is a potent, and usually solid, cannabis preparation. Its use as an intoxicant was popularized by French Romantic writers such as Charles Baudelaire and Alexandre Dumas in the 1830s and 1840s. However, in that era it never was particularly popular or well known in the United States. It was used in patent medicines and in medical practice, but its intoxicant properties were not generally appreciated. In the 1920s, its use by Mexican immigrants and black musicians in New Orleans set up a wave of inaccurate and highly prejudicial yellow press articles on the drug as an "assassin of youth." In fact, the value-laden usage of the term *marijuana* comes from successful federal efforts to link leaf cannabis to illegal immigrants from Mexico in the 1920s. Its use is uniquely American and is not common elsewhere. Shortly thereafter, in the late 1920s and early 1930s, ridiculously distorted presentations of cannabis users such as the film *Reefer Madness* (1936) mobilized biases and created a climate in which harsh regulation was

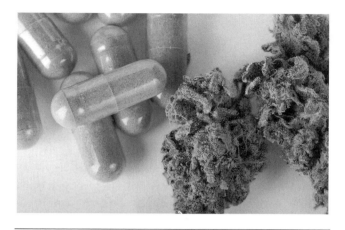

The amount of the active ingredient in cannabis (delta-9-tetrahydrocannabinol or THC) has increased from an average of 1 or 2 percent in the 1960s and 1970s to 6 to 8 percent in 2011. (Photos.com)

received with some enthusiasm. Harsh state and federal laws were passed in the 1930s. The use of cannabis was equated with opioid abuse, and even casual and recreational users were harshly suppressed.

Some Recent History

Despite the bizarre stereotypes of marijuana-using youth and the gross distortion of drug reactions presented by the media, the press, and educators in the 1950s, large numbers of young people began to experiment with the drug beginning in the 1960s. In this exploration they had been preceded by the Beats, a group of urban bohemians who were immortalized by Jack Kerouac in the 1950s in his epic book *On the Road*. Allen Ginsberg's then shocking poem, "Howl," articulated young people's questioning the verities of the white-bread, white-shirt-and-tie treadmill that life in mid-century America seemed to offer. This sense of dissatisfaction with the status quo led to the hippie movement, in which Ginsberg was a transitional figure.

Timothy Leary, a psychology professor and the self-appointed "high priest of LSD," a man of considerable charisma and charm, spoke to thousands, spreading a gospel of "Turn on, tune in, drop out"—that is, try drugs, get the message that you can live an alternative lifestyle, and leave your old self and your old world behind. The notion was that something better was in the offing. Cannabis, not LSD, was the major drug of the alternative youth culture in this era. LSD's effects were too unpredictable and often too stark and self-confrontational for frequent, much less everyday, use. The hippies were much less literary, and some might say much less literate, than the Beats, preferring experience over acquired knowledge and academe. The hippie movement reached its climax in the Summer of Love in San Francisco in 1967. Thereafter, hard drugs and harder people intruded on their idyll, and many, in fact, dropped out even further, moving to communes and rural communities to get back to the earth. These individuals took the opportunity to start growing cannabis for their own use and then became small-scale commercial growers in rural California. The area around Humboldt County became the epicenter of commercial cannabis cultivation in the western United States and is known to produce a bountiful harvest of the potent leaf. Federal and state efforts to control the drug monoculture in the area have proven unpopular and unsuccessful.

However strong and prevalent Humboldt County cannabis is today, it must be emphasized that most cannabis used in the United States between the 1960s and the 1990s came from Mexico. Much cannabis grown in other Latin American countries, such as Panama and Colombia, also slipped across the Mexican border into the United States by plane, by car, or on individuals. Some particularly potent strains of Latin American products came into major U.S. ports by ship, and much was smuggled into the dark bayous of Louisiana and along the lengthy coast of Florida. San Francisco was also a major port for offloading of Colombian cannabis. In the Southwest, Austin, Texas, was and remains a major transshipment point for Mexican marijuana, as does Tucson, Arizona.

Although the large cities of the southeastern United States are still major centers of Latin American cannabis, considerable amounts of the product are also shipped in from Jamaica. These shipments come in on a variety of boats and pleasure craft, carefully hidden in areas too small and tedious to search thoroughly. Typically, ports such as Miami, Jacksonville, Savannah, and Charleston are the destinations, but frequently the swampy Sea Islands off the coast of Georgia and South Carolina receive their own cannabis from points farther south. Almost all of this cannabis is distributed along the East Coast, where it brings high prices.

A major development in the marijuana industry is the tremendous growth and increase in potency of domestic cannabis. Although cannabis can and does grow in any state, its commercial concentrations are found in California, the Pacific Northwest, and the hollows and hills of Appalachia. Many growers are poor whites who, because of high unemployment and a cultural history of resistance to law enforcement, grow and distribute a high-quality product. They also are extremely reluctant to expose friends and relations to prosecution and generally do not cooperate with law-enforcement agencies. Other growers, particularly in the western United States, may be Mexican nationals employed by Mexican syndicates who grow marijuana in remote locations in national and state forests. Living in tents and temporary shacks, they tend their carefully camouflaged plots and hope to avoid aerial detection. Using large amounts of highly toxic chemicals and sometimes setting up intrusive irrigation systems, they often create hazardous situations and traps for thieves and law enforcement and have wreaked havoc on fragile ecosystems. The harvested product is then sold throughout the western United States by Mexican syndicates. Finally, many growers in California have no criminal connections or history but, seeking a way to survive the economic downturn, have turned to cannabis cultivation.

Medical Marijuana

Cannabis is a relatively mild drug with some proven medical applications. Glaucoma patients, those with chronic pain, and people dealing with nausea resulting from chemotherapy for cancer have benefited from treatment with cannabis. Testimonials from such individuals supported the revolutionary medical marijuana movement throughout the United States, notably in California. Under this regime, those with a doctor's prescription can get cannabis products at designated dispensaries. Although this has afforded some people significant analgesia and relief from a variety of symptoms, some experts believe that the dispensaries are mainly servicing dysfunctional drug users and burned-out hippies. Most experts also agree that medical marijuana is a "foot in the door" that has proved effective for the general movement for state-by-state cannabis legalization. In any event, the medical marijuana movement has increased enthusiasm for fine-tuning cannabis effects in order to treat specific syndromes more precisely, thus creating demands for new strains of the drug. It has also increased both licit and illicit demand.

The Netherlands and Canada

One of the primary sources of new strains of cannabis to be introduced to the American gene pool is western Canada, where the laws against the drug have not been actively enforced, and, more important, from seed banks in the Netherlands, where the drug enjoys a quasi-legal status and cannabis-oriented businesses flourish. "Drug tourists" from all over the world flock to Amsterdam and other Dutch cities. Although so-called coffee shops are few and far between in the provinces of the Netherlands, in Amsterdam one can buy and smoke small amounts of cannabis and consume other cannabis products, such as hashish or "space cake" in these establishments. Coffee shops obtain much of their supply from Dutch horticulturists. The varieties and potency of cannabis products to be found there are mind-boggling in several respects. However, some of these shops' wares are obviously not homegrown. Thai and African strains are for sale, as are hashish and leaf cannabis from Latin America and the Indian subcontinent. These more exotic varieties are brought into the Netherlands from their native countries through cargo ships docked in Rotterdam, Europe's largest and busiest port. Because many natives of cannabis-exporting countries reside in the Netherlands, these communities provide the personnel for trans-European trafficking networks. Hashish from Morocco is often trafficked by Moroccans, that from Turkey by Turks, and so on. The types and amounts of the cannabis products available in the Netherlands are so large that they can only have entered the country in large, regular, and frequent shipments. German law-enforcement officials complain about their native drug tourists bringing drugs home through open borders. Especially vociferous in their objections to Dutch drug policies have been the French, who are known to subject bus and air passengers arriving from Amsterdam to rigorous customs examinations. The French also maintain that the permissive attitude in the Netherlands extends to hard drugs and that Rotterdam is a chief center for heroin smuggling. Another consideration for law-enforcement officials is that drug tourists, on the way to the airport, can buy a few seeds of very potent cannabis at a head shop or seed shop and, upon arriving at home, can start growing superior cannabis in a closet. Thus, the genetic contributions of Dutch cannabis have had a major impact on the potency of cannabis worldwide.

Canadian seeds have also made their way into the cannabis gene pool. Although the precise legal status of cannabis is in dispute in Canada, in some locales the laws are ignored in the name of "harm reduction." Cannabis possession and cultivation are illegal, but the enforcement of these laws is variable. In Vancouver, for example, a few Dutch-like coffee shops and seed shops conduct business in certain neighborhoods and are treated with indulgence by municipal police. The magazine *Cannabis Culture* is published in Canada, and its owner is deeply involved in selling seeds to American drug tourists and by mail, thus triggering the ire of U.S. law-enforcement agencies. Large indoor growing facilities and small outdoor plots exist throughout British Columbia, often owned by Asian syndicates. Other "grow ops" in the province are operated by native Canadian criminal organizations, the Hells Angels, and former hippies. The Royal Canadian Mounted Police estimates that there are 20,000 such residential facilities in the province. These operations smuggle large amounts of potent Canadian "bud" into the northwestern United States.

Cannabis Potency

The active ingredients in cannabis are called cannabinoids. The most notable is delta-9-tetrahydrocannabinol, hereafter referred to as THC. During the 1960s and 1970s, the average THC content of cannabis found in the United States was 1 or 2 percent. Today, the average THC content is commonly 6 to 8 percent, and some potent forms of leaf cannabis called sinsemilla may have as much as 8 to 15 percent THC content. THC content of 20 percent has been reported in some samples, but such a high percentage is unusual. Much of this growth in potency is the result of serious botanical efforts by committed amateurs in the Netherlands, Canada, and the United States.

Hashish, a more potent cannabis preparation, not commonly found in the United States since the 1970s, averages about 20 percent THC content. Most hashish in Europe comes from Morocco, although Dutch coffee houses have samples purportedly from other

North African sites, as well as Lebanon, Nepal, and Holland itself ("Nederhash"). The reasons for the American decline in hashish are puzzling, as its use is very common in Europe and it is much easier to smuggle than leaf cannabis. It has been suggested that the end of the war in Vietnam and the curtailing of a U.S. presence in that region and in Turkey negatively impacted the supply line. The implication is that previously a large portion of the drug entered the United States through the agency of individual members of the armed forces stationed in drug-exporting locales. Therefore, the strengthening of antidrug efforts in the armed forces may also have played a part in discouraging experimentation and subsequent smuggling from recent military adventures in southwest Asia. In any case, in the United States today "hash" is seldom seen outside the big cities of the East Coast, and there only rarely.

Some maintain that the increased potency of cannabis makes the drug inherently more dangerous than the "pot" enjoyed by the Woodstock Generation of the 1960s. Many experts discount this commonsense notion and continue to promulgate the belief of that generation that the drug is basically harmless and that legal penalties against the drug are draconian, disproportionate to any possible damage that might be inflicted, and therefore counterproductive.

Francis Frederick Hawley
Western Carolina University

See also Drug Trade: Source, Destination, and Transit Countries

Further Readings

Goode, E. *Drugs in American Society*. Boston: McGraw-Hill, 2008.

Inciardi, J. *The War on Drugs IV*. Boston: Allyn & Bacon, 2008.

Levinthal, C. *Drugs, Society and Criminal Justice*. Boston: Pearson, 2008.

Mares, D. *Drug Wars and Coffeehouses: The Political Economy of the International Drug Trade*. Washington, DC: CQ Press, 2006.

Meyer, K. and T. Parssinen. *Webs of Smoke: Smugglers, Warlords, Spies, and the History of the International Drug Trade*. Lanham, MD: Rowman & Littlefield, 1998.

Musto, D. *The American Disease: Origins of Narcotic Control*, 3rd ed. New York: Oxford University Press, 1999.

MEASURING TRANSNATIONAL CRIME

To understand the nature and dimensions of transnational crime, one needs to know many facts about crime. The answer to most questions about transnational crime requires aggregated data on specific related crime variables. However, there are clearly complexities and pitfalls inherent in these efforts.

The measurement of crime, which is difficult enough on the national level, is far more challenging in a transnational context. Among the host of obstacles to measuring transnational crime are the lack of crime-reporting consistency and the variability present within definitions of what constitutes crime, as well as what specific criteria are used to define particular crimes, which are neither self-evident nor universal. The measuring of murder on a transnational scale, for instance, is rife with complex difficulties. These include culture-specific ideas on the taking of a life of a human being that are bound by myriad issues, such as honor killing, euthanasia, execution, abortion, warfare, witchcraft, possession, and ethnic cleansing.

Historical Background

Developments in the measurement of crime have a considerable history. Two statisticians, André Guerry and Adolphe Quetelet, made significant contributions to the area of crime measurement in the early 19th century. Guerry computed crime rates for different parts of France in the late 1820s; he mapped these out and developed the idea of moral statistics to describe criminal behavior. He noted, for instance, that unequal distribution of wealth helped explain the distribution of property crimes, with considerable differences between urban and rural settings. Quetelet, a Belgian working at about the same time, developed the notion of social statistics; by measuring what people had in common, he could correlate crime with social conditions. In the middle of the 19th century, Henry Mayhew, a British cartographer, analyzed the distribution of crimes and found relationships with living conditions. By the late 19th century, most European countries were collecting crime statistics. In the early 20th century, American sociologists like Clifford Shaw and Henry McKay concluded that variations in criminal activity and delinquency declined with respect to distance from the centers of cities. Uniform crime reports began to be collected in the United States in 1929–30, and the Federal Bureau of Investigation (FBI) took responsibility for national crime statistics beginning in 1931. The National Incident-Based Reporting System of the United States grew out of those efforts.

Drug Sales

The illicit drug trade is estimated to be worth many hundreds of billions of dollars annually. Unfortunately, the relationship between transnational crime and drug sales is an old problem. During the 13 years of Prohibition in the United States, for example, there was a brisk transnational trafficking in alcohol, particularly from Canada and the Caribbean; other drugs were traded through the same illicit networks created for smuggling alcohol.

Drug trafficking is recognized to fund terrorist activities around the globe. The U.S. Drug Enforcement Agency reported that 17 of the 41 foreign terrorist organizations designated by the U.S. Department of State engaged in narco-terrorism. The State Department's Bureau of International Narcotics and Law Enforcement Affairs coordinates with other agencies, such as the Justice Department and Homeland Security, to combat narco-terrorism. Measuring terroristic activities, let alone narco-terrorism, is notoriously difficult.

Many different methods have been used in attempts to measure criminal drug sales. Self-report surveys of drug use have frequently been used to estimate prevalence of use and thereby, indirectly, of drug sales as well. The volume of drugs confiscated has also been used to measure drug sales, but this may reflect more the level of law enforcement's focus than actual drug use or sales. Other data sources used to extrapolate drug estimates include arrestee reports, records on hospital emergency room visits, and ethnographic studies.

Any accurate estimation of drug sales is a pervasive research problem that typically results from many factors, including incomplete sampling frames, respondents' underreporting of use, and nonresponses. Studies focused on alcohol and other drugs have generally revealed that estimates of at least alcohol consumption extrapolated from survey data are usually substantially below levels indicated from tax records. Unfortunately, of course, there are no tax records available for illicit drug sales, but the lack of significant correlation with respect to alcohol lends caution to formulating estimates for other drugs, particularly those for which there is greater social stigma.

Despite the limitations, general estimates of the annual value of drug sales can be made. Although it must be recognized that the credibility of such estimates is somewhat suspect, they can at least be used to indicate relative, if not absolute, values. The market value of the illicit trade for cannabis products is estimated to be about $142 billion each year, whereas the market value for cocaine is estimated to be about $70 billion each year and the market value for heroin and other opiates is estimated to be about $65 billion each year. The distribution of prescription drugs in the black market is estimated to have a market value of about $73 billion each year, and that of counterfeit pharmaceutical drugs is estimated to be about $75 billion each year. Global drug sales are estimated, in a broad sense, to generate approximately $450 billion each year.

Underground Economies

The underground economy, also known as the shadow economy or the black market, consists of an exchange of goods and services that is hidden from the official economy of a country. It is, by definition, difficult, if not impossible, to measure the underground economy accurately; nevertheless, it is generally estimated that the total value of the underground economy is more than $1 trillion. It consists of those transactions that occur outside the readily observable and taxable realm of the official economy as measured by the gross domestic product (GDP); this includes both illegal activities and otherwise legal ones that are evading being taxed. More individuals globally appear to be resorting to informal transactions in the official and underground economies, at least in part, to avoid the burden of taxation.

Varied approaches have been used to attempt to measure underground economies. Macroeconomists, for instance, have used displacements in time series for currency demand to measure the underground economy using a two-sector dynamic equilibrium model. Microeconomists have compiled data collected from assorted data sets, including studies of street knowledge, medical records, and financial reports. Prostitution, for example, has long been a part of underground economies; one way of measuring the export of prostitution services is by estimating the number of individuals providing such services abroad. These sorts of approaches have yielded large variations in the size of underground economies, typically reported as a percentage of GDP. For example, for the United Kingdom it may be between 1 and 15 percent, 2 and 11 percent for Germany, 4 and 12 percent for Australia, 4 and 15 percent for Japan, 4 and 33 percent for the United States, and 10 and 33 percent for Italy. However, as systematic and random errors are inherent in all attempts to measure underground economies, it must be acknowledge that, at best, efforts can indicate only the scale of such economies, not the actual monetary levels.

Many approaches have, nevertheless, been used in efforts to measure underground economies. The latent variable approach estimates the size of the underground economy as a function of observed variables assumed to influence it, such as the unemployment rate, the burden of taxation, and governmental regulation. A major advantage of the latent variable approach is that it simultaneously considers multiple causes and effects. Another popular approach to measuring the underground economy is based on currency demand, on the assumption that the demand for cash increases in relation to the size of the underground economy. Another technique utilizes national accounting statistics by aggregating the discrepancies between expenditures and reported income. The growth of the underground economy has been measured by subtracting the growth rate of the official GDP from the growth rate of total electricity consumption, assuming it is the best single indicator of overall economic activity. Declines in labor force statistics have also been employed to estimate the growth of the underground economy. The amount of overall monetary transactions has also been used to calculate a total nominal GDP that incorporates both official and unofficial activities; then the official GDP is subtracted from the nominal GDP to measure the volume of the underground economy. Audit measurements of undeclared taxable income have also been used to measure the underground economy. Survey data have also been collected in attempts to measure segments of the underground economy.

Efforts to combat the underground economy have focused mainly on deterrence, typically imposing higher fines and, at times, prison sentences. Another tactic has been to enhance the benefits of being in the official economy—for example, by reducing tax burdens and improving public services, such as social security and other pension benefits, as has been used in the United Kingdom. The omission of certain types of economic activity, such as prostitution or gambling, from the calculation of GDP (or the official economy) in some countries, but not others, makes the comparability of data on the underground economy problematic across countries.

Money Laundering

Money laundering is the act of hiding and transforming the proceeds of criminal activity in order to conceal their illicit origin, as well as hide who owns such proceeds. Money laundering is conservatively estimated to account for about 2 to 5 percent of global GDP. Although estimates vary widely, it is thought that somewhere between $590 billion and $1.5 trillion worth of transnational criminal assets are laundered each year. The profits from illicit drug sales certainly constitute a substantial proportion of the annual total for money laundering, but profits from myriad other criminal activities contribute their share as well, including such activities as human trafficking and arms sales.

Money laundering generally takes place in jurisdictions with loose financial regulations and limited law-enforcement resources. Nevertheless, it is thought that the United States, which is not such a country, is probably the largest single country in terms of source and ultimate destination of laundered money. The U.S. Treasury Department, along with the Department of Justice and Homeland Security, leads U.S. efforts to combat money laundering. The Treasury's Office of Terrorism and Financial Intelligence and its subsidiary bureaus guard domestic and foreign financial systems by means of financial regulation, supervision, private-sector outreach, and other methods. The Financial Crimes Enforcement Network of the Treasury's Office of Terrorism and Financial Intelligence also supports U.S. law-enforcement agencies in the investigation of international financial crimes. It also provides U.S. policy makers with analyses of global money laundering. The Financial Crimes Enforcement Network cooperates with 32 foreign governments to improve international money-laundering standards through the Financial Action Task Force. In December 2005, the United States became a signatory to the United Nations (UN) Convention Against Transnational Organized Crime. Article 6 of this convention recognized that money laundering can involve the conversion or transfer of property obtained as proceeds of crime. Conversion of such proceeds into marketable commodities or acceptable currencies facilitates transnational transmission.

As with other areas of transnational crime, myriad methodological approaches have been employed to measure money laundering. The gravity model is one approach that has been used to measure money laundering; it allows estimation of how much global illegal money flows to respective countries. Other methods include the use of proxy variables and case studies. Estimation of the scale of money laundering enables analysis of its macroeconomic effects; conversely, it permits measurement of the effectiveness of anti-money-laundering efforts.

Arms Trafficking

The trafficking of arms supplies the demands for the array of weapons that are not legally obtainable in the jurisdiction of purchase. This includes criminal operations established to evade laws, permits, fees, and taxes. Among the three protocols of the UN Convention Against Transnational Organized Crime is the Protocol Against the Illicit Manufacturing of and Trafficking in Firearms, Their Parts and Components and Ammunition, which entered into force on May 31, 2001.

Various methods have been used in efforts to measure arms trafficking. For example, investor knowledge indirectly embedded in financial markets has been used to loosely measure the trade in illegal arms. Accordingly, analysis of stock prices of companies in countries under a UN arms embargo is used with this technique to detect illegal arms trading under the assumption that such knowledge gives detectable financial advantages to those involved compared to those who are not. Estimates for profits from arms dealing for a median company in an embargoed country are assumed to be between $1 million and $3 million each year. This implies annual profits for illegal arms trading to be on the order of hundreds of millions of dollars per

conflict. A more sophisticated approach is based on econometric modeling: specifically, an infinite-period model for companies manufacturing arms to sell in a market with stochastic demand. This model incorporates several other measures developed for aspects of the arms trade, including the Small Arms Trade Transparency Barometer, which is based on exports from arms-manufacturing countries, as well as international customs data, to formulate an index measuring the extent to which a country provides transparent information on small arms exports. Another is the Bribe Payers Index, which is based on the opinions of business executives regarding the likelihood that arms-exporting countries might bribe corrupt officials in importing countries. At any rate, the total value of illicit arms trading is estimated to be in the billions of dollars each year, although very little is known about how many arms are actually produced, let alone available at specific conflict locales around the globe.

Prostitution and Sex Trafficking

Globalization, including the rise of less expensive international travel opportunities, has led to a significant increase in prostitution overall. Escalating poverty has fueled the increased numbers of individuals, male and female (and the young), from developing countries—especially those in Southeast Asia and the Caribbean, as well as those from eastern European countries—trafficked into prostitution, particularly in Europe, Australia, and North America. The international sex trafficking of women and girls is estimated to amount to $7 billion annually, making it the third most profitable arena of transnational crime.

In 2000, the U.S. Congress passed the Trafficking Victims Protection Act not only to punish sex traffickers but also to improve law-enforcement efforts and to advance victims' services. The UN Office on Drugs and Crime estimates that there are between 200,000 and 500,000 illegal sex workers in the European Union alone, 66 percent of whom were trafficked from eastern Europe. Globally, it is estimated that between 700,000 and 2 million women and children are sex-trafficked each year. Among the three protocols of the UN Convention Against Transnational Organized Crime is the Protocol to Prevent, Suppress, and Punish Trafficking in Persons, Especially Women and Children, which entered into force on December 25, 2003.

The responses of respective countries to prostitution and sex trafficking is used as an indirect indicator of the underlying nature of the problem. Analysis of crime justice data is used to better understand the nature of both the victims and the perpetrators involved in these activities. Women, for example, are the most common perpetrators of sex trafficking convicted around the globe; women also comprise 66 percent of the victims, and girls constitute 13 percent. The current state of data available on this issue permits only the monitoring of trends and patterns, not a reliable direct measure of the full magnitude of the problem. The global market value of prostitution is roughly estimated to be about $108 billion each year.

Technology Factors

Technology factors have altered some of the approaches used to measure aspects of transnational crime. The overwhelming volume of data generated and more readily available today than in the past have radically altered how we think about measuring transnational crime. Furthermore, technology itself has become a component of many transnational crime operations. Black market distribution of technological goods comprises a substantial proportion of contemporary transnational crime. This includes the selling of counterfeit technology products, which is estimated to have an annual market value of around $100 billion. Web video piracy is estimated to have a market value of about $60 billion each year, while software piracy is estimated to have an annual market value of $53 billion.

Summary

Measuring the amount of transnational crime is highly challenging, if not actually impossible, as it is both illegal and mostly hidden. Several methods have been developed in attempts to measure aspects of transnational crime, but there are limitations to each approach. When feasible, it is recommended that several different methods be employed in order to allow for cross-validation of what are, at best, approximations.

Some of the major components of transnational crime, such as drug sales, underground economies, money laundering, arms trafficking, and prostitution and sex trafficking, have been tackled by an array of measurement approaches. Strategies to address transnational crime must, of necessity, be concerned

with its measurement. Clearly, the measurement of transnational crime is one of the most important ways to focus attention on the overall issue. As measurement requires conceptual clarity, it forces the creation of operational definitions of transnational crime, which, in turn, helps policy makers direct their efforts more specifically. We certainly have a significant lack of very specific measures of most dimensions of transnational crime, but such methods by their very nature are likely to remain elusive. In fact, although data and information on transnational crime have been compiled in reports for some time, the soundness of such estimates and their in-depth analysis have generally been lacking, and we are essentially unable to make meaningful and reliable statements about the true threat of such transnational criminality. Therefore, those estimates that are made must be understood to serve, at best, as general gauges of the actual phenomena, useful more as relative assessments than as certain calculations.

Victor B. Stolberg
Essex County College

See also Drug Trade: Source, Destination, and Transit Countries; Informal Value Transfer Systems; Legal and Illegal Economies; Money Laundering: Methods; Transnational Crime: Defined; Transnational Crime: Research Centers

Further Readings

Busatos, Francesco and Bruno Chiarini. "Market and Underground Activities in a Two-Sector Dynamic Equilibrium Model." *Economic Theory*, v.23 (1993).

Lippert, Owen and Michael Walker, eds. *The Underground Economy: Global Evidence of Its Size and Impact.* Vancouver, BC: The Fraser Institute, 1997.

Reuter, Peter and Victoria Greenfield. "Measuring Global Drug Markets: How Good Are the Numbers and Why Should We Care About Them?" *World Economics*, v.2/4 (2001).

Schneider, Friedrich and Dominik H. Enste. "Shadow Economies: Size, Causes, and Consequences." *Journal of Economic Literature*, v.38 (2000).

Tanzi, Vito. "Uses and Abuses of Estimates of the Underground Economy." *The Economic Journal*, v.109/456 (1999).

Tyldum, Guri and Anette Brunovskis. "Describing the Unobserved: Methodological Challenges in Empirical Studies on Human Trafficking." *International Migration*, v.43/1–2 (2005).

Vander Beken, Tom. "Risky Business: A Risk-Based Methodology to Measure Organized Crime." *Crime, Law and Social Change*, v.41 (2004).

Walker, John. "How Big Is Global Money Laundering?" *Journal of Money Laundering Control*, v.3 (1999).

Walker, John and Brigitte Unger. "Measuring Global Money Laundering: A Gravity Model." *Review of Law and Economics*, v.5 (1998).

MEGA-TRIALS

The term *mega-trial* emerged in relation to domestic criminal trials in the late 1980s and early 1990s. More recently, the term has also been applied to large cases before the various international courts and tribunals. Several important distinctions need to be drawn when talking about mega-trials, including the distinction between international and domestic mega-trials and the distinction between procedural and substantive mega-trials. Of course, these distinctions often overlap and one sees international mega-trials that are substantive in nature and domestic mega-trials that are procedural in nature. For example, whereas international mega-trials might include the International Criminal Tribunal for the former Yugoslavia (ICTY), the International Criminal Court (ICC), or the International Criminal Tribunal for Rwanda (ICTR), domestic cases are dealt with solely by the local courts of a particular state.

However, there is no precise definition of what constitutes a mega-trial; there is no magic minimum number of days of trial or number of accused persons or victims that would convert a trial from regular to "mega." Rather, the identification of a trial as a mega-trial seems to be an arbitrary decision made by those involved in the justice process. There have been several calls for reform, as mega-trials can be very problematic with regard to the effective distribution of justice and a defendant's right to a fair trial.

A discussion of mega-trials is relevant in relation to transnational crime because, by definition, transnational crime involves, at a minimum, offenses in at least two jurisdictions spanning multiple crime bases (places where the offense actually took place). Examples of transnational crimes that may lead to a mega-trial include drug trafficking, arms smuggling, corruption, terrorism, war crimes, crimes against humanity, organized crime, human trafficking, and piracy. Transnational crimes can also involve hugely complicated issues of procedural law, contributing to the length of proceedings.

A mega-trial can arise out of a number of substantive fact instances. First, a trial may involve multiple accused persons; for example, in January 2011 Bangladesh instituted a domestic mega-trial with more than 800 defendants arising out of the 2009 revolt by the Bangladesh Rifles (BDR), a paramilitary group charged with guarding Bangladesh's borders, which resulted in the deaths of many military officers and civilians. Second, a trial may concern multiple crime bases; for example, Radovan Karadži was charged before the ICTY with genocide, crimes against humanity, and violations of the laws or customs of war for conduct carried out in multiple locations throughout Bosnian-Serb-claimed territory between 1992 and 1995. Finally, a trial may deal with the occurrence of a continuing crime through multiple jurisdictions—for example, the trafficking of drugs across state borders.

Another contributing factor to the phenomenon of the mega-trial is the increasing complexity of rules of criminal procedure and evidence, both internationally and domestically. Standards of proof may require the submission of vast quantities of evidence from both prosecution and defense to prove or disprove a case. For example, the Vujadin Popovi case before the ICTY had six defendants accused of crimes against humanity and genocide arising out of the killing of more than 7000 Muslim men and boys at Srebrenica during the summer of 1995. The trial began with opening arguments on July 14, 2006, and closed on September 15, 2009, encompassing 425 trial days, 182 prosecution witnesses, 132 defense witnesses, and 5,383 exhibits. Another problem can arise as a result of decisions made by the justice system itself: Decisions to join trials and defendants together can have extremely detrimental effects on the criminal justice process, particularly when multiple defendants are not charged with crimes closely related to one another. Poor case management systems can also delay trials; for example, if strict deadlines are not imposed for filing motions and no workable time line put in place for the progression of the trial, then procedural issues can hold up what may otherwise be a relatively simple case.

Related to domestic mega-trials is the legislative focus on criminal organizations and criminal associations, which tends to mean that three or more people are involved—but this number can reach 100, given the role of "facilitators." Outlaw biker cases, street-gang cases, and any other "group" that is targeted by law enforcement with the object of "taking down" the organization can lead to mega-trials.

Mega-trials have direct implications for a defendant's right to a fair trial. Attorneys may be reluctant to commit such a large amount of time to a case, and so the defendant may lose his or her right to counsel of his or her own choosing. Similarly, in domestic cases, it can be difficult to find a panel of jurors able to commit such a large amount of time to a case, and it may also be difficult for the jurors to remember the vast quantities of evidence and witnesses called when the time comes for deliberations, so the accused may not have all the evidence considered. Moreover, a judge may realize, months into a trial, that there is a conflict of interest.

Several possible reforms to deal with the issue of mega-trials have been suggested. A strengthened system of case management would go a long way to avoiding mega-trials that arise because of procedural deficits. Providing a system for alternate judges or jurors would avoid the problems of mistrials if the judge recuses himself or herself or the number of jurors falls below the statutory minimum required for a fair trial. The relevant authorities should also consider severing cases in situations in which there are different fact scenarios, in order to facilitate the effective administration of justice.

Jessica Peake
University of Pennsylvania

See also Adjudicating International Crimes; Crimes Against Humanity; Genocide; Globalization; Human Smuggling; Human Trafficking; International Criminal Court; Internationalized Criminal Tribunals; War Crimes; War Crimes Tribunals

Further Readings

Code, Michael. "Law Reform Initiative Relating to the Mega-Trial Phenomenon." 22nd International Conference of the International Society for the Reform of Criminal Law, Dublin, Ireland, July 2008. http://www.isrcl.org/Conference_Papers.htm (Accessed February 2011).

Judge, Brendan. "No Easy Solution to the Problem of Criminal Mega-Trials." *Notre Dame Law Review*, v.66 (1990).

Middle East

Transnational crime occurs through all regions of the world, and globalization has made the commission of these crimes easier than ever. The study of transnational crime is particularly important in the region known as the Middle East, which extends from the Mediterranean Sea to Afghanistan and includes

U.S. Army mortarmen push against Al Qaeda remnants by launching a 120mm round in the desert west of Iskandariyah, Iraq. Al Qaeda also operates in North Africa and in the Arabian Peninsula (Saudi Arabia, Yemen, and Oman). (U.S. Army/Ben Brody)

parts of northern Africa. Groups that commit transnational crimes in the Middle East and North Africa are often indistinguishable from terrorist organizations. At the core, the operations committed by terrorist organizations are criminal, regardless of their political, economic, or religious motives. The major transnational crimes committed by these groups are kidnapping, arms smuggling, drug trafficking, and financial crimes. There is a close relationship among drug trafficking, financial crimes, and terrorism. Different transnational groups in the Middle East and other parts of the world work closely together, making it difficult to combat these crimes.

Al Qaeda in the Islamic Maghreb

Several regions within the Middle East are significant with regard to transnational crimes. These include, first, North Africa, mainly the Maghreb region, which comprises Morocco, Algeria, Tunisia, and Libya, and second, the Sahel region, the area south of the Maghreb, which consists of southern Algeria, Mauritania, and other Saharan countries. These regions are important in the study of transnational crime in the Middle East because of the characteristics of the terrorist groups that operate in the regions as well as the crimes they commit. Specifically, a large and powerful segment of Al Qaeda known as Al Qaeda in Islamic Maghreb (AQIM) operates in North Africa throughout the Maghreb and Sahel regions. Typically, this group has focused its efforts primarily on kidnappings, notably of American and European citizens. The kidnappings performed by the AQIM are distinguishable by the rates at which they are performed as well as the heinousness of the crimes.

AQIM was previously known as the Groupe Salafiste Pour la Prédication et le Combat (GSPC) and operated mostly in the once French-occupied territory that now forms Algeria and Tunisia. After the conclusion of the Algerian Civil War, the GSPC was the strongest and greatest armed militant group in Algeria. As GSPC's influence spread and its strength grew, it made a request to be admitted to Al Qaeda, and in 2003 GSPC was accepted into the terrorist organization. As a result, the GSPC adopted a new name: Al Qaeda in Islamic Maghreb (AQIM). The incorporation of the term *Al Qaeda* into its newly adopted name was intended to establish legitimacy among the organization's associates. With the support and coalition of Al Qaeda, the newly established AQIM began to increase its presence in North Africa and soon progressed in the commission of transnational crimes throughout the Maghreb and Sahel regions of Africa. Beyond North Africa, AQIM has expanded into other parts of the Middle East, and it now has cells throughout Europe as well as operatives in Iraq that assist in the fight against U.S. forces. AQIM funding continues to accelerate at an alarming rate, giving the terrorist group the opportunity to increase its operations and commit transnational crimes throughout the Middle East and North Africa.

A large collateral suppression by law enforcement forced AQIM to move south into the Sahel region, infiltrating Mali, Mauritania, and Chad. AQIM has since taken full advantage of the lack in security forces throughout both Mali and Mauritania. Both of these countries have since experienced increased rates of kidnapping and hostage taking of both American and French citizens. While the group was in Algeria, AQIM was strong, but it was under the watchful eye of Algerian security forces. This prevented the group from operating at full strength and later caused its migration into the Sahel region. This expansion became beneficial to AQIM, which subsequently increased its attacks in Mali and Mauritania.

The criminal activity most widespread throughout the Maghreb and the Sahel regions is kidnapping, which is defined as the unlawful detainment of a person or persons for economic, political, or monetary gain. Kidnapping is a common transnational crime throughout North Africa, particularly in Tunisia. Tunisia has the fifth highest rate of kidnapping in the world, as well as the highest rate of kidnapping within the Middle East and North Africa. The prevalence of kidnapping in Tunisia is due to the predominance of a number of terrorist organizations throughout Tunisia. AQIM has become more involved in kidnapping because of the benefits and profits the group has received from the commission of this crime. Victims include tourists and other foreign nationals, based on AQIM's political and religious motives. AQIM has declared the United States, France, and Spain as its enemies and therefore has increased its violence against citizens of these countries. Since the expansion of AQIM into the Sahel, this region has experienced kidnappings of individuals the group believes to be of Western descent. The majority of AQIM's profits are from payments gained through kidnappings, which remain the largest source of funding for AQIM terrorist operations within the Maghreb and the Sahel.

In addition to kidnappings, AQIM gains a smaller amount of revenue through the commission of weapons and drug trafficking, as well as funding from small AQIM cells throughout Europe. The fight against terrorism therefore includes combating transnational crimes that supply the monies needed for terrorist operations. Cutting off the resources for AQIM will make it difficult for the group to perpetuate its terrorist agenda.

Al Qaeda in the Arabian Peninsula

Transnational crime is also evident throughout the Arabian Peninsula. This area consists of Saudi Arabia, Yemen, and Oman. Within this region, the most well-recognized and active terrorist group is the Al Qaeda affiliate known as Al Qaeda in the Arabian Peninsula (AQAP), formed by a merger of Saudi and Yemeni Al Qaeda groups. AQAP is responsible for many transnational crimes throughout the Arabian Peninsula, as well as crimes that have been committed throughout the world. AQAP located its headquarters in Yemen and has concentrated its recruitment efforts within that country. As the strength of AQAP began to increase within the region, the influence and strength of the Yemeni government began to weaken. The weakness of the Yemeni government has allowed AQAP to flourish, and its membership has increased. Despite antiterrorism efforts by both the U.S. and Yemeni governments, AQAP has proliferated throughout Yemen, in mostly rural areas. Throughout late 2008 and 2009, AQAP became more active within Yemen and began operations in southern Saudi Arabia. International counterterrorism organizations witnessed the attacks by AQAP within Yemen and Saudi Arabia but questioned whether the group possessed the ability to conduct a large-scale international attack.

The doubts concerning the capabilities of AQAP were answered when the group orchestrated attacks involving affiliates in the United States. These include the 2009 Christmas Day attempted bombings of Flight 253 by Umar Farouk Abdulmutallab. Although Abdulmutallab was a Nigerian citizen, he maintained strong ties to AQAP, particularly within Yemen. The interactions of Abdulmutallab and AQAP were largely ignored by the U.S. intelligence community, giving AQAP a prime opportunity to commit transnational crimes throughout the United States, as well as the world. Despite the surge of involvement in transnational crime by AQAP, the group was still able to organize and conduct another attack on U.S. soil. Shortly after the thwarted Christmas bombings, in 2010 AQAP attempted to ship explosives through U.S. cargo planes. The packages, containing printer cartridges packed with the explosives, were shipped from Yemen and were destined for Chicago. The AQAP attacks were performed by direct members of the terrorist group, who managed to enter the United States undetected.

The main target of AQAP is the United States. One of AQAP's leaders is Anwar al-Awlaki, a Yemeni American cleric involved with AQAP who publicly denounces both the United States and its policies. The influential teachings of this prominent AQAP cleric have been studied by the American terrorist Major Nidal Hasan. Hassan began to follow the teachings of al-Awlaki, which became quite influential in Hasan's plan to attack the U.S. Army base at Fort Hood, Texas. That attack, perpetrated solely by Hasan, resulted in the killing of 13 and wounding of 29 others at the Soldier Readiness Center on November 5, 2009.

AQAP was also involved with the 2010 attempted bombings of New York City's Times Square by Faisal Shahzad. Shahzad also followed the teachings of al-Awlaki. Although Shahzad's plan was unsuccessful, that failure was a technical one (due to the explosives' faulty wiring) and not the result of detection.

In 2009, American Abdulhakim Mujahid Muhammad fired on a U.S. armed forces recruitment center in Arkansas. Upon his arrest, Abdulhakim admitted that he had studied Islam and Arabic in Yemen with al-Awlaki, from whom he received manuals on explosives.

Hezbollah

Weapons trafficking is another criminal activity that is expanding and escalating throughout the Middle East, driven by conflict throughout the region. Weapons trafficking consists of the illegal sale of arms to a prohibited group or country, mainly occurring in areas of political instability and strife. It has been estimated that nearly 500 million weapons are bought and sold in illegal black markets throughout the world. Weapons are trafficked for the purpose of supporting military groups in areas of conflict and civil war. For example, weapons are smuggled across the Egyptian border into the Gaza Strip, and seaports in the United Arab Emirates (UAE) are the gateway for contraband that is later distributed through the Middle East.

The most well-recognized and well-documented supplier of illegal weapons throughout the Middle East is the Islamic Republic of Iran. Iran experienced an Islamic Revolution in 1979. The revolution established the Ayatollah Khomeini as the supreme ruler and Shiite Islam as the state religion. Since then, Iran has been an influential supporter of Shiite governments throughout the Middle East by providing arms and monetary support for Hezbollah, a Lebanese Shiite militant group dedicated to the destruction of Israel. Iran has provided Hezbollah with an estimated $20 million to $30 million in aid. Iran does not control or run Hezbollah, but it maintains a dominant presence in the militant group. For example, Iran provides a large portion of Hezbollah's military personnel and supplies, one report claiming that an estimated 500 to 600 Iranian Revolutionary Guards have been sent to fight with the Lebanese militant group. When these Iranian volunteers enter Lebanon, they bring with them banned weaponry. Iran has also provided Hezbollah with short-range missiles that have been used against their common enemy, Israel. Even more notably, Iran has given Hezbollah long-range missiles, which have been used to fire into Israel's major Mediterranean port city of Haifa. The Iranian government has also provided defensive weaponry, such as antitank missiles.

It is not particularly clear how the short- and long-range missiles infiltrated into Lebanon and into the hands of Hezbollah. It has been suggested that the illegal arms are smuggled into sanctioned areas through otherwise legitimate means. For example, smuggled weaponry can be masked under shipments of humanitarian aid or some type of legitimate equipment that is being provided to an otherwise sanctioned area. The smuggled arms then make their way to the intended recipient, likely a terrorist group. The smuggling is detected only when the arms have reached the hands of their intended recipients and are used to commit crimes. Therefore, the tracking and dismantlement of illegal arms—beginning in the country of origin with the objective of discovery before the weapons reach their intended recipients—are crucial in the fight of transnational crime in the Middle East.

The Taliban

Another very profitable transnational crime is drug smuggling. The Middle East is home to what is known as the Golden Crescent, consisting of Afghanistan, Iran, and Pakistan, where most of the world's opium supply originates. Afghanistan produces the world's largest supply of opium. The Taliban is a militant group that took over Afghanistan in 1996 and turned the country into an Islamic extremist state. Since the Taliban takeover, the presence of Afghan opium on the world drug market has increased dramatically, reaching almost 30 percent in the late 1990s. In 1998, Afghanistan produced 62 percent of the world's opium supply. Overall, Afghanistan currently produces 93 percent of the opium on the world market. In 2000, the Taliban banned cultivation of opium poppies, but it has done little to enforce this restriction, and in fact the Taliban benefits from the profits reaped by the production and sale of opium on the world's illegal drug market. Monies obtained from the drug sales were used by the Taliban to stay in power.

In 2001, the American invasion of Afghanistan brought about the Taliban's increased involvement in the opium trade to fund its fight against U.S. forces. It is estimated that the Taliban receives more than $40 million annually in profits from the production and sale of opium. These profits from opium sales, combined with contributions from supporters, have enabled the Taliban to combat American forces. To suppress the Taliban, a concentrated effort to halt the production and sale of Afghan-produced opium must be made. Although such an effort would not halt the Taliban entirely, it would hinder the Taliban's operations.

Financial Crimes

Finally, financial crimes have become quite lucrative for criminals throughout the world, but in recent years, terrorists have been gravitating toward financial crimes as a means to support their organizations. Financial fraud is the fastest growing type of crime in the world for many reasons. First, financial fraud can go virtually undetected by law-enforcement agencies, which are too focused on violent terrorist crimes. Second, financial fraud generates millions of dollars in profits annually. All one needs to commit a financial crime is a computer with Internet capabilities. Compare this with the cost of a terrorist attack: It is estimated that the September 11, 2001, attacks on the United States cost roughly $500,000 to orchestrate and execute, for example. Although this may be an elaborate example, the cost of terrorism is relatively high; financial fraud makes it relatively easily to generate revenues for such expensive attacks quickly and inexpensively. Third, because of our society's growth in dependency on the Internet, the opportunity for financial fraud has grown as well. It is reported that more than 1 percent of people in the world who use credit cards have been the victims of financial fraud. Because of the accessibility of personal and financial information through the Internet, the relative simplicity of mounting financial crimes, and their low cost, these crimes have become a new frontier for terrorists to make quick and easy profits to fund their operations.

Both transnational crime and terrorism occur together, in the same time and space. As a result, the suppression of transnational crime throughout the Middle East is closely related to the suppression of terrorism. Law-enforcement agencies need to have a dual focus. First, law-enforcement agencies must concentrate on the terrorist organizations themselves, notably AQIM, Hezbollah, and the

Taliban. Their correspondence, proliferation into other regions, associates, and interactions with other terrorist organizations must be carefully monitored and analyzed for potential threats. Equally important, the transnational crimes committed by terrorists need to be carefully watched and assessed. The primary motive for terrorist groups to commit transnational crimes is their need for funds and profits. Transnational crimes committed by terrorists might not be acts of terrorism per se, but the commission of transnational crimes by terrorist organizations generates revenue for violent acts of terrorism.

Marisha D. Ziajor
Janine Kremlin
California State University, San Bernardino

See also Al Qaeda; Art and Antiquities: Plunder; Drug Trade: Source, Destination, and Transit Countries; East Asia; Eastern Europe and Russia; Executive Order 13581; Extraordinary Rendition; Failed States; Informal Value Transfer Systems; Jihad; Military Forces: Private or Contracted; Military Industries; Networks; Policing: National Security; Policing: Transnational; Public Perceptions of Crime; Sanctions and Blacklisting; South Asia; Southeast Asia; Terrorism: Financing; Terrorism: Nondomestic; Weapons Smuggling; West Asia

Further Readings

Addis, Casey L. et al. *The Middle East: Selected Key Issues and Options for the 112th Congress.* Washington, DC: Congressional Research Service, 2011.

Almoq, Doron. "Tunnel-Vision in Gaza." *The Middle East Quarterly Review,* v.11 (2004).

Detzi, Daniel. *Denying Al Qaeda Safe Haven in a Weak State: An Analysis of U.S. Strategy in Yemen.* Monterey, CA: Naval Postgraduate School, 2010. http://www.hsdl .org/?view&did=11152 (Accessed February 2011).

Grey, David H. and Erik Stockham. "Al-Qaeda in the Islamic Maghreb: The Evolution From Algerian Islamism to Transnational Terror." *African Journal of Political Science and International Relations,* v.2/4 (December 2008).

Khalil, Lydia. *The Next Base? Concerns About Somalia and Yemen.* Barton, ACT: Australian Strategic Policy Institute, 2011. http://www.aspi.org.au/publications/ publication_details.aspx?ContentID=283 (Accessed August 2011).

Migdalovitz, Carol. *Algeria: Current Issues.* Washington, DC: Congressional Research Service, 2010. http://assets .opencrs.com/rpts/RS21532_20100121.pdf (Accessed February 2011).

Migdalovitz, Carol. *Tunisia: Current Issues.* Washington, DC: Congressional Research Service, 2009. http://assets .opencrs.com/rpts/RS21666_20091119.pdf (Accessed February 2011).

National Commission on Terrorist Attacks Upon the United States. *The 9/11 Commission Report.* New York: Norton, 2004. http://www.9-11commission.gov/ report/911Report.pdf (Accessed February 2011).

Rollins, John. *Al-Qaeda and Affiliates: Historical Perspective, Global Presence and Implications for U.S. Policy.* Washington, DC: Congressional Research Service, 2010.

Sharp, Jeremy M. *Yemen: Background and U.S. Relations.* Washington, DC: Congressional Research Service, 2010.

Steinberg, Guido and Isabelle Werefels. "Between the 'Near' and the 'Far' Enemy: Al-Qaeda in the Islamic Magreb." *Mediterranean Politics,* v.12 (2007).

United Nations Office on Drugs and Crime, Centre for International Crime Prevention. "8th United Nations Survey on Crime Trends and the Operations of Criminal Systems (2001–2002)." New York City, 2005. http:// www.unodc.org/unodc/en/data-and-analysis/Eighth -United-Nations-Survey-on-Crime-Trends-and-the -Operations-of-Criminal-Justice-Systems.html (Accessed February 2011).

U.S. Senate. "Attempted Terrorist Attack on Northwest Airlines Flight 253: Report of the Select Committee on Intelligence." Washington, DC: U.S. Government Printing Office, 2010.

Van Dijk, Jan. *The World of Crime: Breaking the Silence on Problems of Security, Justice and Development Across the World.* Thousand Oaks, CA: Sage, 2008.

Walther, Oliver and Dennis Retaille. "Sahara or Sahel? The Fuzzy Geography of Terrorism in West Africa." *CEPS/ Instead Working Papers,* v.35 (2010). http://www.ceps .lu/pdf/3/art1577.pdf (Accessed February 2011).

White, Jonathan R. *Terrorism and Homeland Security.* Belmont, CA: Wadsworth, Cengage Learning, 2012.

Zoubir, Yania H. "The United States and Maghreb-Sahel." *International Affairs,* 85 (2009).

Military Forces: Private or Contracted

The private, contracted military industry has played an increased global role in the post–Cold War world in terms of both size and scope. This presence is likely to keep expanding because of its cost-effectiveness and the proliferation of global conflicts, as well as criminal and terrorist activities and the increase in military spending they have engendered. Private, contracted military forces participate in international military conflicts, peacekeeping and nation-building efforts, and security activities across the globe. Critics view the growing role of private, contracted military forces as a threat to national sovereignty and global security, whereas advocates note their cost-effectiveness and their work in ending global conflicts and instability along with the transnational crimes that accompany these phenomena.

Involvement in Conflicts and Peacekeeping Missions

The presence of private, contracted military forces on the world stage has been increasing. The private military industry is a loosely defined group of organizations and mercenary soldiers providing a wide range of both standard and specialized services to a wide range of contractors across the globe, making annual profits in the billions of dollars. Many U.S. private military companies have offshore registrations for tax purposes at the same time that they receive taxpayer-funded government contracts. Well-known private military companies include ArmorGroup, DynCorp, Kroll, Control Risks Group (CRG), Military Professional Resources, Inc. (MPRI), Group 4 Securicor, Vinnell, and Blackwater Worldwide (now known as Academi).

Many private military companies are part of larger military contracting conglomerates that have acquired them through mergers and acquisitions. The industry also features trade groups such as the International Peace Operations Association. Key corporation and industry leaders are often former national military officers and intelligence personnel from countries such as the United States, Great Britain, and Israel. Soldiers employed by private military companies are not always recruited from the companies' nations of origin. Many come from the country in which the private military force is operating or are young people from economically disadvantaged countries seeking opportunities abroad.

National governments, international nongovernmental organizations (NGOs), and government bodies such as the United Nations (UN), media organizations, government diplomats, and private corporations contract private military forces to aid national military forces in international conflicts and peacekeeping missions or for protection in such areas. Although the contracting of private military companies is a global phenomenon, the United

A Blackwater Security Company MD-530F helicopter aids in securing the site of a car bomb explosion in Baghdad, Iraq, during Operation Iraqi Freedom in 2004. Blackwater was one of the private contractors employed during the Iraq War to guard officials and installations. (U.S. Air Force)

States and Great Britain dominate the global market. Prominent examples include U.S. government contracts to private military companies in Iraq and North Atlantic Treaty Organization (NATO) contracts to private military companies in the Balkans.

Services provided by private contracted military include risk advising, defense planning, the sale of weapons and other military supplies; weapons management; logistics support; training of foreign forces; the use of mercenary soldiers in fighting, peacekeeping, democracy transition, and nation-building missions; prisoner interrogation; espionage and intelligence work; psychological warfare; maritime security; counterterrorism and the guarding of media, diplomats, embassies, and overseas businesses operating in theaters of conflict. Some companies provide a variety of these services, while others specialize in key areas such as intelligence or counterterrorism. Older companies have expanded or adapted their services to meet changing global needs; newer companies have formed in response to global demand.

Private, contracted military are commonly regulated at the national level but lack the clear regulations required of national military forces, and problems can still arise when such entities engage in transnational activities. For example, U.S. government regulations such as the International Traffic in Arms Regulations (ITAR) law and the Defense Department's Foreign Military Sales (FMS) program allow private military companies to contract themselves out to foreign governments. These private military companies, however, face fewer restrictions when operating internationally than do the regular U.S. armed forces, despite government contracting regulations. Lax regulations open the door for links between private, contracted military forces and transnational crimes such as trafficking, war crimes, and human rights violations.

Regulation and Accountability

Some private, contracted military forces have illicit ties to international criminal enterprises, such as various types of trafficking operations, whereas others aid in the battle against such enterprises. The private military's international recruitment of soldiers and employees has led to criticism of the lack of clear jurisdiction and the exploitation of foreign citizens who assume the risks of operating in conflict areas. Other criticisms include loss of government control and oversight, lack of clearly defined national and international laws governing their usage, and a reduction in the quality of national armed forces as soldiers leave for better-paid opportunities in the private military sector.

The use of private, contracted military forces in international conflicts, peacekeeping, and nation-building missions has also given rise to concerns over their accountability, particularly in the commission of war crimes and human rights violations. Private military companies, like government military forces, are required to follow the Geneva Convention, which defines international laws of armed conflict. National military personnel, however, are much more likely to face prosecution for war crimes than are private, contracted military personnel, given the problems of unclear jurisdiction regarding criminal violations by nationally contracted private forces. The international recruitment of private soldiers compounds these problems.

Autocratic regimes utilize private military forces and mercenary soldiers in the formation of death squads, which terrorize civilian populations in order to maintain the current regime and crush rebellions. Tactics include kidnappings, torture, and murder. Private military companies not directly involved in war crimes or human rights violations may provide training to national military forces that are. The Clinton administration contracted MPRI in 1994 in part to train the Croatian army during conflicts in the former Yugoslavia. The Croatian army was later accused of ethnic cleansing in its campaign against the Serbs. Private military forces have also been directly and indirectly implicated in the overthrow of governments, sometimes the very governments that originally contracted for their services.

Other highly publicized examples of private military companies and links to international criminal activities have centered on the involvement of U.S.-government-contracted forces operating in Iraq and Afghanistan. For example, operatives of Blackwater Worldwide, one of the private firms contracted by the U.S. government to operate in Iraq, were involved in gunfights that resulted in questionable civilian deaths. Other private companies contracted by the United States, such as CACI and the Titan Corporation, were involved in prisoner abuse scandals in the 2004 Abu Ghraib scandal in Iraq.

Ties to other transnational crimes have also emerged. Private military forces, like their national counterparts, have been implicated in the plundering and smuggling of art and antiquities and other valuables from the personal homes and museums of areas in which they were operating. Allegations were made claiming that DynCorp, a private military company operating in the Balkans, was tied to an international child pornography ring. Likewise, claims were made that Executive Outcomes, a private military company founded in South Africa and operating in Sierra Leone, was tied to illicit conflict-diamond mining and facilitating the overthrow of the government that had contracted its services.

Globalization has increased the threat of international terrorism while decreasing border security. International terrorist organizations such as Al Qaeda target failed states, developing nations, and areas of political instability to establish bases. Their activities, such as the attacks on the World Trade Center, Pentagon, and United Airlines Flight 93 on September 11, 2001, have created an increased market for the private military companies involved in security and intelligence. Private military companies have also been contracted in the fight against other sources of international crime, such as drug trafficking and maritime piracy.

Marcella Bush Trevino
Barry University

See also Extraordinary Rendition; Military Industries; Military-Political-Industrial Nexus; War Crimes

Further Readings

Avant, Deborah D. *The Market for Force: The Consequences of Privatizing Security*. New York: Cambridge University Press, 2005.

Chesterman, Simon and Chia Lehnardt. *From Mercenaries to Market: The Rise and Regulation of Private Military Companies*. New York: Oxford University Press, 2007.

Krahmann, Elke. *States, Citizens and the Privatization of Security*. New York: Cambridge University Press, 2010.

May, Larry. *War Crimes and Just War*. New York: Cambridge University Press, 2007.

Ortiz, Carlos. *Private Armed Forces and Global Security: A Guide to the Issues*. Santa Barbara, CA: Praeger, 2010.

MILITARY INDUSTRIES

The parts played directly by military initiatives and their impacts on the development of terrorism and crime are numerous and varied. Military activities influence terrorism through impacts that are economic, political, and social. Military initiatives also impact terrorism in ways that are both direct and indirect.

Wars, violence, and military initiatives have their most direct effect in mobilizing affected communities to engage in acts of terrorism and resistance, either to halt military endeavors or to exact revenge for harms inflicted by military forces. Terrorism can occur as a means to halt aggression after it has begun or as a means to deter aggression prior to military attack. Commentators have noted the role that Western dominance of economies and politics in developing nations, not exclusively in Muslim countries, has played a role in the development of terrorist networks. Western dominance has included support and assistance to undemocratic, corrupt, repressive, and violent regimes. In addition to thwarting the political aspirations of millions of people, the military policies of Western powers have impoverished much of the populations in developing countries while imposing durable barriers to their economic improvement.

Militarization, including the military defense of global corporatization, foments anger and resentment in poorer countries. Militarization not only contributes to increased poverty in the short term but also serves to undermine local producers and local markets in the long term, as control is centralized to serve international companies and local resources are diverted to serve global markets and export production. Western corporate interests abroad are secured and defended through military initiatives. In addition, Western military products are used by brutal domestic regimes within developing countries and become instruments in the suppression of popular dissent, the quelling of local uprisings, and the subversion of political processes. Western military products, personnel, and training are deployed by governments seeking to deny appeals for democratic practices and maintain totalitarian rule. The result can be a combination of popular resentment and desperation that makes people receptive and agreeable to appeals to resist through methods of terrorism.

Since September 11, 2001 (9/11), the deaths attributed to terrorism in the Muslim world have increased notably. Attacks in the Middle East and Persian Gulf region increased from 50 just prior to 9/11 to around 4,800 in 2006. Over the same period, the number of deaths in the region attributed to terrorism leapt from fewer than 100 to almost 9,800. The primary victims of terrorism have been people in the Muslim world. Much of this harm can be linked to military initiatives taken by Western powers.

The invasion of Iraq has had the effect of ramping up terrorist activity in the region rather than reducing it. In the period between the start of the war in 2003 and 2006, the number of terrorist attacks had increased by 607 and the average level of resultant deaths had increased by 237 on a global scale. In the first two years of the war, more than 100,000 people died. Incredibly, this number represented more than the combined total of victims of terrorism globally over the entire course of the 20th century.

Many commentators have noted the growing connections among mercenaries, arms traders and gunrunners, drug cartels, and legitimized members of Western military, industrial, and political networks. Loretta Napoleoni suggests that this illicit underground economy, sponsored by aboveground Western elites, accounts for approximately $1.5 trillion in trade each year. Almost 40 percent of this illicit trade is funneled through the U.S. economy. Not surprisingly, the corruption, fraud, and shadow governance that mark the military-industrial complex in the United States are also expressed in the "democracies" of Afghanistan and Iraq. Terrorism has not been put down, and military presence in one form or another will be extended, perhaps under the guise of training and policing. At the same time, the military interventions have impacts on the underground economies. A thriving trade in heroin has sustained the Taliban. Production of heroin has risen 400-fold since the U.S. invasion in 2001. The growth of the trade has impacted local communities and resources, simultaneously helping to foil the most powerful military apparatus on the planet.

Military actions increasingly bear the character of actions against civilians—in other words, terrorist acts. Significantly, they are viewed as such by people on the ground and observers, including actual organizers of terrorist groups who reference military initiatives in their appeals to recruits. Civilians make up the largest number of casualties in armed conflicts. The war economy is more and more based on materials for the killing of noncombatants. It is, in this sense, truly a terror economy—though not in the sense implied by Washington, London, and Ottawa. Terrorist acts are justified, in this context, as acts of war. President Bush's treatment of terrorism as a threat to national security, to be dealt with militarily, gave terrorists the status of combatants.

At the same time, legitimized military industries have also been identified as participants in terrorism. Most obviously, weapons produced by arms manufacturers are used by terrorist groups. Beyond this, however, there is the issue of arms use by legitimized forces against civilian populations, which some designate as acts of terror. Critics have suggested that Israel Military Industries has played a significant part in global terrorism, not only because of the use of its Uzi submachine guns by terrorists but also because the company has supplied armaments for the Israel Defense Forces (IDF) and its weapons have been used to kill civilians in Gaza. Others have been critical of Canadian company SNC-Lavalin, which produced most of the bullets used during the invasion and occupation of Iraq since 2003. SNC-Lavalin has also been involved in contracting with totalitarian and terror regimes, such as the government of Lybian dictator Muammar al-Qaddafi. Like other weapons and armaments producers, SNC-Lavalin is involved in a range of industrial efforts, including the construction of rail infrastructure.

The impacts of militarization are also deeply felt in economic terms. Military intervention in Iraq and Afghanistan is at the heart of the credit crunch and the accumulation of historically massive debt in the United States. The credit crunch and debt are externalities of the military-industrial complex, offloading the costs of profit making onto the public. The financial bailout and refusal by Washington to regulate banking and finance are really about the wars in Iraq and Afghanistan. The War on Terrorism is not about defeating Al Qaeda; rather, it is the rationale, the legitimation, for expanding military endeavors. At the same time, the War on Terrorism has played a central part in the global recession and the credit squeeze. The wars in Iraq and Afghanistan have drained U.S. finances, turning a small surplus built up under the Clinton administration into a national debt of $10 trillion after two terms of George W. Bush. The War on Terrorism has impoverished the working class and poor, made their financial horizons bleak, and placed a burden on their children. The monthly Pentagon budget for Iraq has run around $8 billion. With Afghanistan included, the numbers run to $12 billion.

Beyond the direct role of military development in instigating terrorism, the indirect effects of militarization give rise to terrorist activities as well. Many commentators, including C. Wright Mills and President Dwight D. Eisenhower as far back as the 1950s, have noted that expenditures on military industries involve more than issues of financing and cost. They are fundamentally social policy choices and societal initiatives, impacting society as a whole. Military spending expresses a social planning commitment that prioritizes military development over social development. Money spent on military projects is money not spent on housing, healthcare, education, social welfare, or foreign aid. Reducing or withdrawing resources from any of these areas in favor of military expenditures can breed resentment and conflict that can feed into violent oppositional groups or movements.

Jeffrey Shantz
Kwantlen Polytechnic University

See also Military Forces: Private or Contracted; Military-Political-Industrial Nexus; Political Influence Peddling

Further Readings

Bryant, Clifton D. *Khaki-Collar Crime: Deviant Behavior in the Military Context.* Glencoe, IL: Free Press, 1979.

Dal Lago, Alessandro and Salvatore Palidda, eds. *Conflict, Security, and the Reshaping of Society: The Civilization of War.* London: Routledge, 2010.

Napoleoni, Loretta. *Rogue Economics: Capitalism's New Reality.* New York: Seven Stories, 2008.

Napoleoni, Loretta. *Terror Incorporated: Tracing the Dollars Behind the Terror Networks.* New York: Seven Stories, 2005.

Napoleoni, Loretta. *Terrorism and the Economy: How the War on Terror Is Bankrupting the World.* New York: Seven Stories, 2010.

Scott, Peter Dale. *Drugs, Oil, and War: The United States in Afghanistan, Colombia, and Indonesia.* Lanham, MD: Rowman and Littlefield, 2003.

Wolin, Sheldon S. *Democracy Incorporated: Managed Democracy and the Specter of Inverted Totalitarianism.* Princeton, NJ: Princeton University Press, 2010.

MILITARY-POLITICAL-INDUSTRIAL NEXUS

The often hidden connections between state, corporate, and military actors, and their roles in determining social development, have long been concerns within modern industrial societies. These alliances involve circuits of contracts, finances, resources, and personnel between institutions, including those of state representatives, defense contractors, arms manufacturers, and military leadership. These networks are typically informal and operate behind the scenes through personal relationships, lobbying efforts, campaign work, and professional associations. Thus, they raise important questions about the real nature of decision making, and the distribution and structure of power within contemporary liberal democracies. This nexus of power holders has been called the military-industrial complex.

Contemporary military machinery, highly mechanized and integrated with computerized information technology systems, has required new regimes of production and capital accumulation. Militarization extends beyond weapons to establish systems of research, development, production, and deployment that rely upon extensive integrated state-corporate networks. These systems are based on complex divisions of labor, specialized knowledge, and advanced technological apparatuses. In order to maintain advanced military production, ongoing mass infrastructures are required, rather than ad hoc facilities that might emerge to meet specific war needs. Countries with major military forces have been compelled to establish permanent war economies, ongoing structures responsible for the regular production of war equipment. This requirement has provided the context for durable state-corporate-military alliances as growing sections of national economies are given over to military development. State-corporate-military alliances shape priorities of research and development, scientific investigations, and university teaching through funding, research grants, and endowed university chairs. There are concerns that military research comes at the expense of other research.

The 20th century saw a massive and broad transformation in the size and scope of military operations and expenditures in countries such as the United States. Beginning with World War I, the United States shifted from a peacetime military, which was relatively small and relied upon militia and reserves in times of war, to a constantly growing standing army. The United States never fully demobilized after World War I, and the total mobilization that accompanied the U.S. involvement in World War II, along with the decimation of European and Japanese forces, left the United States with the largest, most advanced military on the planet by war's end. In the postwar period, the competition and distrust between the remaining global powers, the United States and the Soviet Union, encouraged the growth and development of military equipment and infrastructures in the United States. Military buildup during the Cold War cost taxpayers an average of about 6 percent of gross domestic product (GDP) annually. At the height of the Vietnam War, the military apparatus impacted the public treasury to the tune of 9.3 percent of GDP annually. That war also exhausted U.S. gold reserves, leading eventually to the end of the gold standard, which has resulted in monetary crises (and associated food crises) related to financial speculation. This, in turn, has deeply and negatively impacted poor people around the globe.

It is estimated that current military expenditures in the United States make up almost half of the value of arms purchases each year, according to the Stockholm International Peace Research Institute (SIPRI). U.S. defense spending is twice as much as the combined total of the 15 nations with the next highest military expenditures. By the middle of 2007, U.S. public debt represented around 40 percent of GDP, largely because of military expenditures. Between 2004 and 2008, the annual budget of the Pentagon grew from US$420 billion to $700 billion.

SIPRI suggests that world expenditures on military sources reached $1.531 trillion in 2009. Of this amount, almost $712 billion was paid by the United States. Other sources suggest that the total U.S. spending on military sources is close to $1 trillion when all materials and sources, including those outside Defense Department budgets, are taken into account. Economic consequences of the war economy include public debt, inflation, and recession. There is concern that military-driven policies, along with associated cuts to corporate taxes, could lead the United States to bankruptcy.

The term *military-industrial complex* gained popular notice following its use during President Dwight D. Eisenhower's farewell address in 1960. In his speech, Eisenhower warned citizens to be vigilant against the accumulation of power, whether sought or unsought, by the military-industrial complex. Noting the rise of a mechanized standing army, which was different in size and character from a citizens' army or yeomen's militia, Eisenhower raised concerns about the influence that a permanent army and its military infrastructures, as a significant portion of the national economy, could have on democratic practice and social matters. As Eisenhower noted, the decision to build tanks, bombs, or fighter jets is not simply a matter of military, or even economic, policy regarding state expenditures. More important, the decision to build and purchase armaments is a social policy decision. It is simultaneously a decision not to fund housing, healthcare, education, or agriculture. Policies that benefit the military and industrial contractors change the character of society as a whole. They define the type of society that will develop over the course of generations. A society that prioritizes the needs of state-corporate-military networks will not be able to meet other, more pressing, social needs. The result will be a society driven by undemocratic structures that fails to meet the needs of its citizenry. It will become an oligarchy of economic and political power holders rather than a democracy, and social needs of the many will be made secondary to the financial interests of the few. Eisenhower's address was a profound warning, generally considered to be the most significant presidential speech on economic matters of the last 50 years.

An early analysis of the mutually reinforcing networks among corporations, the state, and the military was provided by the anarchist Daniel Guérin in his book *Fascism and Big Business* in 1936. One of the first and most significant early analyses of political cal economic structures of fascism, Guérin's work details the role of fascist governments in rapid industrialization and the central place played by arms manufacturers in the modernization of industry and new forms of capital accumulation through state partnerships with private capital. Guérin defines the state-corporate-military associations under fascism as informal coalitions made up of groups from each sector that act behind the scenes to establish and maintain policies and practices beneficial to the network. These practices and policies are centered on the development and wielding of high concentrations of weaponry, the maintenance of colonial markets, and conceptions of domestic affairs dominated by strategic military perspectives rather than social policy perspectives. Thus, social problems, such as unemployment, poverty, and dissent, are viewed as strategic issues to be addressed through military responses. Notably, Guérin identifies the members of the network as sharing more than material interests. They also share psychological and moral views of society. Significantly, these networks wield power in a manner that is beyond public view.

Perhaps the most significant and influential analysis of the emergent state-corporate-military alliance in the United States came from critical sociologist C. Wright Mills. In his work *The Power Elite* (1956), still relevant more than half a century after its publication, Mills argued that a new stratum of political, corporate, and military leaders has become the real social and political power holder in society, not elected government representatives. This nexus of elites holds mutually reinforcing economic and political interests based on the growth of arms manufacturing and military infrastructures. Notably, Mills suggested that these elites function as an unseen government, one that operates beyond popular view or democratic control. The power elite are not associated with any one political party, whether Republican or Democrat, and they cannot be voted out of office. In any event, even those members who are officeholders will simply take up positions within another organization, typically corporate, within the network. It was Mills's work that most influenced Eisenhower's discussion of the military-industrial complex.

For Mills, the power elite shared not only economic interests but also a common view of society.

Their perspective is based on four characteristics. First, they hold to a "military metaphysic" in which social and cultural issues are viewed militaristically. Thus, poverty might be addressed through a "war on poverty" rather than other, more socially oriented, means. Second, they possess a shared class identity and view themselves as privileged actors who are beyond the law. Third, they enjoy interchangeability within the network. They hold overlapping positions and readily move between institutional structures when necessary. An example would be a politician who moves between corporate boards and directorships and public office or government administration and back again, as in the case of Vice President Dick Cheney and Halliburton. Fourth, elite members socialize recruits to be part of the network and advance them as they show their willingness and capacity to promote the elite worldview. For Mills, the significant lesson is the way in which such alliances can arise within democratic societies and subvert those democracies. According to Mills, this threat was as real in postwar U.S. society, with its rapid militarization and advanced mechanical weaponry, as it had been in Nazi Germany. Mills's work influenced the discussions of state-corporate-military alliances for decades.

More recently, critical criminologists have examined the ongoing interplay between government agencies and private capital that owns and operates means of production as part of the regular, if illegitimate, functioning of capitalist economies. Harmful activities that emerge as part of this interplay are referred to as state-corporate crime by criminologists such as Ronald Kramer and Raymond Michalowski. Kramer and Michalowski define state-corporate crime as "illegal or socially injurious actions that occur when one or more institutions of political governance pursue a goal in direct cooperation with one or more institutions of economic production and distribution." The work of Kramer and Michalowski has helped to shift criminological study of elite deviance away from studies of the state, capital, and military as atomized institutions, moving the emphasis toward networked practices and ongoing alliances within and between institutions. In more recent analyses, Kramer and Michalowski (2005) have examined military events such as the Iraq War and occupation after September 11, 2001, as an example of state-corporate crime. They provide an analysis of these events, which they define

as criminal, that situates the war and occupation as part of broader organizational deviance. Their work offers an integrated model that looks at historical as well as contemporary state-corporate-military structures.

Jeffrey Shantz
Kwantlen Polytechnic University

See also Military Forces: Private or Contracted; Military Industries; Political Influence Peddling

Further Readings

Guérin, Daniel. *Fascism and Big Business.* 1936. Reprint, New York: Pathfinder Press, 1994.
Kramer, Ronald. "War, Aggression and State Crime: A Criminological Analysis of the Invasion and Occupation of Iraq." *The British Journal of Criminology*, v.45/4 (2005).
Kramer, Ronald and Raymond Michalowski. "State-Corporate Crime." Annual Meeting of the American Society of Criminology, November 7–12, 1990.
Michalowski, Raymond and Ronald Kramer, eds. *State-Corporate Crime: Wrongdoing at the Intersection of Business and Government.* Piscataway, NJ: Rutgers University Press, 2006.
Mills, C. Wright. *The Power Elite.* Oxford, UK: Oxford University Press, 1956.
Napoleoni, Loretta. *Terrorism and the World Economy: How the War on Terror Is Bankrupting the World.* New York: Seven Stories, 2010.
O'Grady, William. *Crime in Canadian Context: Debates and Controversies.* New York: Oxford University Press, 2007.
Stockholm International Peace Research Institute. *SIPRI Yearbook 2010: Armaments, Disarmaments and International Security.* Stockholm: Author, 2010.

Money Laundering: Countermeasures

As noted by the Law Enforcement, Organized Crime and Anti-Money-Laundering Unit (the Unit) of the UN Office on Drugs and Crime (UNODC), money is the prime reason for engaging in almost any type of criminal activity. The Unit defines money laundering as the method whereby criminals disguise the illegal origins of their wealth and protect their asset bases, so as to avoid the suspicion of law-enforcement agencies and prevent leaving a trail of incriminating evidence.

The Financial Action Task Force (FATF) is the main international antilaundering body. The FATF was established by the G7 Summit held in Paris in 1989. In October 2001, terrorist financing was added to the FATF mandate, the FATF was given the responsibility of examining money-laundering techniques and trends, reviewing the action that had already been taken at a national or international level, and setting out the measures that still needed to be taken to combat money laundering.

Through the Global Program, FATF encourages states to develop policies to counter money laundering and the financing of terrorism, monitors and analyzes related problems and responses, raises public awareness about money laundering and the financing of terrorism, and acts as a coordinator of initiatives carried out jointly by the United Nations (UN) and other international organizations. FATF also has the power to "blacklist" countries that fail to meet the standards and recommendations set forth by FATF.

UN General Assembly Resolution 60/288 encouraged states to implement the comprehensive international standards embodied in the FATF's 40 Recommendations on Money Laundering and nine Special Recommendations on Terrorist Financing. Initially developed in 1990, the 40 recommendations were revised in 1996 to take into account changes in money-laundering trends and to anticipate potential future threats. In 2003, they were again revised and updated. In addition, various interpretative notes were adopted. The interpretative notes are designed to clarify the application of specific recommendations and to provide additional guidance.

The Unit's mandate was set forth in 1998 by the Political Declaration and the Measures for Countering Money Laundering adopted by the General Assembly at its 20th special session. The declaration broadened the scope of the Unit's mandate to cover all serious crime, not just drug-related offenses. The principal instrument in combating money laundering is the UN Convention Against Transnational Organized Crime, which was adopted by General Assembly Resolution 55/25 of November 15, 2000.

The Unit is assigned the responsibility for carrying out the UN's Global Program against Money Laundering, Proceeds of Crime, and the Financing of Terrorism. The Unit was established in 1997 in response to the mandate given to UNODC through the UN Convention against Illicit Traffic in Narcotic Drugs and Psychotropic Substances of 1988. The broad objective of the Global Program is to strengthen the ability of nations to implement measures against money laundering and the financing of terrorism and to assist them in detecting, seizing, and confiscating illicit proceeds, as required pursuant to UN instruments and other globally accepted standards, by providing relevant and appropriate technical assistance upon request.

The 40 recommendations are considered a complete set of countermeasures against money laundering covering the criminal justice system and law enforcement, the financial system and its regulation, and international cooperation. These recommendations have been adopted by many international bodies and countries. The recommendations are designed to ensure that they are not complex or difficult to implement and do not compromise the freedom to engage in legitimate transactions or threaten economic development. The recommendations contain principles for action and allow countries a measure of flexibility in implementing them. While the recommendations are not a binding international convention, many countries have made a political commitment to combat money laundering by implementing them.

According to the FATF, terrorists and terrorist organizations rely on money to sustain themselves and to carry out terrorist acts. Money for terrorists is derived from a wide variety of sources. While terrorists are not concerned with disguising the origin of money, they are concerned with concealing its destination and the purpose for which it is being used. Accordingly, terrorists and terrorist organizations employ techniques similar to those used by money launderers to hide their money. A key factor in combating money laundering, according to UNOCD, is the ability to detect and prevent money-laundering operations. The office contends that the application of intelligence and investigative techniques is an effective way of detecting and disrupting the activities of terrorists and terrorist organizations.

According to UNODC, money laundering fuels corruption and organized crime. The office also notes that corrupt public officials need to be able to launder bribes, kickbacks, public funds, and, on occasion, even development loans from international financial institutions. In addition, organized criminal groups need to be able to launder the proceeds of drug trafficking and commodity smuggling. As noted by UNODC, terrorist groups use money-laundering channels to get cash to buy arms. Criminals are taking advantage of the current globalization of the world economy by transferring funds quickly across international borders. The social consequences of allowing these groups to launder money can be disastrous. The Unit contends that taking the proceeds of crimes from corrupt public officials, traffickers, and organized crime groups is one way to deter this type of criminal activity.

Objectives of the Global Program Against Money-Laundering, Proceeds of Crime and the Financing of Terrorism (GPML) include the following: to assist in the ability of all states to adopt legislation that furthers the universal legal instruments against money laundering and countering the financing of terrorism; to provide the states with the necessary knowledge, means, and expertise to implement national legislation and the provisions contained in the measures for countering money laundering; to assist beneficiary states in all regions to increase the specialized expertise and skills of criminal justice officials in the investigation and prosecution of complex financial crimes, particularly with regard to the financing of terrorism; to enhance international and regional cooperation in combating the financing of terrorism through information exchange and mutual legal assistance; and to strengthen the legal, financial, and operational capacities of beneficiary states to deal effectively with money laundering and the financing of terrorism.

UNODC provides assistance to governments that confront criminals involved in the laundering of the proceeds of crime through the international financial system. The office also provides law-enforcement authorities and financial intelligence units with recommended strategies to counter money laundering, advises on improved banking and financial policies, and assists national financial investigation services. The assistance includes granting technical assistance to authorities from developing countries, organizing training workshops, providing training materials, and transferring expertise between jurisdictions.

UNODC's Legal Advisory Section and the International Monetary Fund (IMF) have drafted model laws for both common law and civil law legal systems, to assist countries in setting up their programs against money laundering and terrorist financing. Currently, there are three model laws that countries may use: the 2005 UNODC Model Legislation on Money Laundering and Financing of Terrorism, the 2009 Model Provisions for Common Law Legal Systems on Money Laundering, and the Terrorist Financing, Preventive Measures and the Proceeds of Crime. The model laws serve as guidelines for states that are in the process of upgrading their laws to meet the new international standards. The model laws may be adjusted or modified to meet the particularities of each nation's legal system and administrative culture.

Cliff Roberson
Kaplan University
Elena Azaola
Centro de Investigaciones y Estudios Superiores en Antropologia Social

See also Money Laundering: History; Money Laundering: Methods; Money Laundering: Targeting Criminal Proceeds; Money Laundering: Vulnerable Commodities and Services

Further Readings

Financial Action Task Force. *FATA: 40 Recommendations.* Geneva: United Nations, 2003. http://www.fatf-gafi.org (Accessed February 2011).

Gilmore, William C. *Dirty Money: The Evolution of Money Laundering Countermeasures.* Strasbourg, Austria: Council of Europe, 1999.

International Money Laundering Information Network. *Model Provisions for Common Law Legal Systems on Money Laundering, Terrorist Financing, Preventive Measures and Proceeds of Crime Finalised.* Geneva: United Nations, 2009. http://www.unodc.org/documents/money-laundering/Model_Provisions_2009_Final.pdf (Accessed February 2011).

Money Laundering: History

To the layperson, the concept of money laundering is generally used to refer to efforts to obscure the origins of illegal wealth and to provide a veil of legitimacy—or, put simply, to turn "dirty money" into "clean money." The technical understanding of money laundering adds to that concept the violation or evasion of pertinent laws and regulations. The first definition typically relates to the (often assumed and sometimes demonstrable) complex efforts of organized and professional criminals to thwart the identification or recovery of illegal assets by victims or law enforcement. The second definition typically relates to the acquisition, possession, use, or any disposition of the proceeds of crime that may involve a wide range of individuals, including organized and professional criminals. Although these definitions can be separated for analytical purposes, the two understandings are often implicitly or explicitly drawn together and confused.

One might assume that money laundering is a thoroughly modern problem. Indeed, in early or simple forms of human social organization (in the past or today), there may be little demonstrable wealth to attain and limited or nonexistent methods to hide such wealth from others. Moreover, in such circumstances all possible wealth may be considered as the property of a ruler or deity rather than belonging to individuals.

Money laundering becomes a possible activity alongside the accumulation of capital and wealth in societies as well as the efforts of authorities to monitor or control its distribution through taxation or other means. The problem of money laundering may not have been properly defined as such (see the two definitions above) until the modern period, beginning from around the 1960s; however, evidence of its underlying conditions and its existence can be found in early human history. The reader may wish to refer to Keith Hopwood's book *Organised Crime in Antiquity* for a collection of essays on organized crime in ancient civilizations and several insightful references to financial and economic crime in such contexts.

The modern drive to identify and target money laundering began, in earnest, with the advent of international efforts to curb the illicit drug trade, the associated accumulation of illicit wealth, and the potential influence of such wealth upon "legitimate" society. Although there were domestic and international efforts to address the illicit drug trade at the outset of the 20th century, the touchstone of modern efforts to target illicit drugs began in the 1960s. The 1961 Single Convention on Narcotic Drugs, established by the United Nations (UN), recognized narcotic drugs as a "social and economic danger to mankind" and set the international standard for criminalizing virtually any interaction with narcotic drugs and, in Section 36(2,a,ii), added:

Intentional participation in, conspiracy to commit and attempts to commit, any of such offences, and preparatory acts and financial operations in connexion with the offences referred to in this article, shall be punishable offences.

With the growth of the illicit drug trade during the 1960s and 1970s, it was becoming clear that the Single Convention was inadequate to tackle this problem or the associated money laundering. The 1988 UN Convention Against Illicit Traffic in Narcotic Drugs and Psychotropic Substances expressed that the demand and supply for narcotic and psychotropic substances posed a "serious threat to the health and welfare of human beings and adversely affects the economic, cultural and political foundations of society." It also recognized the enormous profits and wealth attached to such trafficking, as well as the dangers of such wealth, in that transnational criminal organizations were able to penetrate and corrupt government, business, and society. The convention went further in that it expressed its intention to deprive such criminals of the proceeds of crime in order to eliminate their underlying reason for involvement in the illegal trade in narcotic and psychotropic substances. Adding to the previous criminalization of financial operations, the 1988 convention included "the organization, management or financing of any" designated offense and the conversion, transfer, or concealment of the proceeds of crime. It further added to and bridged enforcement and preventive measures to counteract money laundering via Articles 5(2) and 5(3):

Each Party shall also adopt such measures as may be necessary to enable its competent authorities to identify, trace, and freeze or seize proceeds, property, instrumentalities or any other things referred to in paragraph 1 of this article, for the purpose of eventual confiscation. In order to carry out the measures referred to in this article, each Party shall empower its courts or other competent authorities to order that bank, financial or commercial records be made available or be seized. A Party shall not decline to act under the provisions of this paragraph on the ground of bank secrecy.

The 1988 convention was a substantial expansion and intensification of the international fight against the illicit drug trade, organized crime, and money laundering. It expanded the scope of related activities that may be subject to regulatory and criminal controls. It also recognized that such offenders may be involved in a range of "other illegal activities" or designated offenses connected to the primary focus of the convention prohibitions.

The development of the 1988 convention appears to have been inspired by two 1970 pieces of pioneering legislation in the United States, the Bank Secrecy Act (BSA) and the Racketeer Influenced and Corrupt Organizations (RICO) Act. The BSA compelled financial institutions to report to the U.S. Treasury cash transactions of $10,000 or more, and RICO provided enhanced controls (restraining orders against proceeds of crime) and penalties (up to 20 years in prison for each count and fines and forfeiture or confiscation of the proceeds of crime) against those involved in criminal enterprise. Individuals convicted under the criminal and civil provisions of RICO were also liable for paying damages of up to three times the amount of damages linked to their racketeering activities. The convention was also inspired by the Money Laundering Control Act of 1986, which consolidated the previous controls and represents the core of prevention and control efforts by the United States under Section 18 U.S.C., Sections 1956 and 1957. The inspiration for these three pieces of legislation appeared to be efforts to control, respectively, tax evasion, organized crime, and money laundering—notwithstanding that these provisions have increasingly been used to target a broad range of actors who may not correspond to the stereotypical images that inspired the controls.

In 1989, the group of seven (G7) leading industrial nations formed the Financial Action Task Force (FATF). It provides the benchmark international standards through its 1990 publication of the 40 Recommendations (as amended) to tackle money laundering and its 2001 publication of the nine Special Recommendations (as amended) to tackle terrorist finance. The FATF recommendations provide practical guidance for nation-states in implementing the relevant international conventions. This guidance ranges from steps to criminalize money laundering to guidelines on how financial institutions should maintain records, submit suspicious and large-cash transaction reports to a national financial intelligence unit (FIU), and support international cooperation. The recommendations also pay attention to informal value transfer systems, such as hawala, that may be used within various communities to send and receive monies across borders without using mainstream financial services.

As a complement to its mandate to develop and promote the implementation of international standards, the FATF is also empowered to conduct periodic mutual evaluations of national compliance with the recommendations. Such assessments have offered the opportunity for the naming and shaming of poor practices and have also included potential blacklisting via the list of Non-Cooperative Countries and Territories (NCCT). Compliance failures may result in sanctions, such as additional scrutiny of transactions by other states and potential exclusion from access to international financial networks. The diffusion of standards and sharing of information are also supported by the Egmont Group of Financial Intelligence Units, which was established in 1995 for member and would-be member FIUs.

The 2000 UN Convention Against Transnational Organized Crime is the touchstone of contemporary efforts at definition and control. It is also, arguably, the last step in the convergence and confusion of the commonsense and technical understanding of money laundering. The fusion is evident in the encouragement for states to include the "widest range of predicate [underlying] offences" and to include virtually any interaction with or disposition of the proceeds of crime committed within or outside a given jurisdiction, including converting or concealing, acquisition, possession, use, and association or conspiracy to aid, abet, facilitate, or counsel the commission of such offenses. Under article 7(1), the convention compels that each state party:

a. Shall institute a comprehensive domestic regulatory and supervisory regime for banks and nonbank financial institutions and, where appropriate, other bodies particularly susceptible to money-laundering, within its competence, in order to deter and detect all forms of money-laundering, which regime shall emphasize requirements for customer identification, record-keeping and the reporting of suspicious transactions.

b. Shall, without prejudice to articles 18 and 27 of this Convention, ensure that administrative, regulatory, law enforcement and other authorities dedicated to combating money-laundering (including, where appropriate under domestic law, judicial authorities) have the ability to cooperate and exchange information at the national and international levels within the conditions prescribed by its domestic law and, to that end, shall consider the establishment of a financial intelligence unit to serve as a national centre for the collection, analysis and dissemination of information regarding potential money laundering.

Thus, the 2000 convention establishes the current scope of the national and international framework through which to formalize and institutionalize the fight against money laundering. In most jurisdictions, this has led, at a minimum, to a regime of reporting by financial institutions on potentially suspicious activities and transactions. In many Western countries it has led to comprehensive regimes that include suspicious and large-volume transaction reporting by financial and many other institutions that may handle any significant monies or assets. The objective reporting threshold is typically US$10,000 or the equivalent in local currency, whereas the subjective reporting threshold can occur at any monetary valuation. These reporting requirements generally apply to all in-country transactions as well as to the physical and electronic movement of cash across borders. The convention also encourages parties to employ the guidelines issued by relevant international and regional bodies and to promote global and subregional cooperation among judicial, law-enforcement, and financial regulatory authorities in tackling the problem of money laundering.

The underlying or predicate offenses associated with money laundering have dramatically expanded from the 1960s focus on illicit drugs to the expansion into connected and designated offenses in the 1980s, and they currently include almost any offense one could imagine. The technical understanding of money laundering has similarly expanded from financial operations linked to the drug trade to designated offenses that include virtually any interaction with or disposition of the proceeds of crime. The history of money laundering is an example of an ever-expanding definition combined with a generalized absence of scientific evidence on the phenomenon that would justify growth in the prevention and control apparatus.

David C. Hicks
Independent Scholar

See also Antiterrorist Financing; Civil Forfeiture: The Experience of the United States; Conventions, Agreements, and Regulations; Criminal Forfeiture and Seizure; Egmont Group of Financial Intelligence Units; Financial Action Task Force; Financial Fraud; Globalization; Informal Value Transfer Systems; Intelligence Agencies: Collaboration Within the United States; Money Laundering: Countermeasures; Money Laundering: History; Money Laundering: Methods; Money Laundering: Targeting Criminal Proceeds; Money Laundering: Vulnerable Commodities and Services; Mutual Legal Assistance Treaties; Racketeer Influenced and Corrupt Organizations Act; Sanctions and Blacklisting; Tax Evasion; UN Convention Against Transnational Organized Crime

Further Readings

Hicks, David C. "Money Laundering." In *Handbook of Crime*, Fiona Brookman et al., eds. Devon, UK: Willan, 2010.

Hopwood, Keith, ed. *Organised Crime in Antiquity*. London: Duckworth, 1999.

Levi, Michael and Peter Reuter. "Money Laundering." *Crime and Justice: A Review of Research*, v.34 (2006).

MONEY LAUNDERING: METHODS

Money laundering is the practice of concealing information about financial transactions in order to convert the ill-gotten gains of criminal activities into "clean" or "laundered" assets. At least $500 billion is laundered every year. Typically associated with organized crime, the sale of illegal goods (such as in the arms trade or the fencing of stolen property), and the narcotics trade, money can also be laundered to conceal the gains of tax evasion, embezzlement, bribery, accounting fraud, and other white-collar crimes. Various methods are employed, and money may be cleaned multiple times through multiple streams, but all involve three steps, described by financial intelligence experts as placement, layering, and integration. Criminal organizations that need to launder money

Money laundering involves three steps: placement, layering, and integration. Whether it is cleaned once or multiple times through multiple streams, this practice is always used to convert the illegally obtained gains. (Photos.com)

on a regular or ongoing basis and criminals who have a large amount of money to launder may outsource the task to an accountant or other expert, who not only has specialized skills for the purpose but also may have contacts in financial institutions, businesses, and even law enforcement to assist in the process.

Placement is the distribution of dirty money to legitimate financial institutions, such as through bank deposits. Layering, the second step, is the creation of financial transactions that camouflage the source of the cash. Frequently, layering involves moving money between different countries—for example, in the form of transfers from one account to another (typically under different names). Assets may also be purchased and subsequently sold in order to further conceal the source of the money and cloud its history. Integration is the acquisition of the money generated by layering—the folding back in of the now laundered cash into the economy, and the criminal's possession, in a seemingly legitimate form. Very few arrests are made at the integration stage; even when law-enforcement authorities are confident that clean-looking money began as dirty money, without evidence from the placement or layering stages, there is no basis for a case.

Methods vary greatly, and different methods are suited to different quantities of money and types of

criminals. Money can be laundered through a legitimate business owned by the criminal, for instance. Large-scale criminal operations such as those connected with the Mafia typically own and operate legitimate businesses for multiple purposes, including money laundering; a retail store can include a portion of illegitimate cash along with its cash deposits each week, exaggerating its profits in order to camouflage the revenue streams from illegal activities. This is one reason that, in many countries, cash transactions in excess of a certain ceiling ($10,000 in the United States) must be reported in order to highlight suspicious patterns.

A retail store sells physical products, and if an investigation were to occur, discrepancies between the store's purchases and inventory, on one hand, and its deposits, on the other, could be uncovered to point at potential money laundering. Covering this up would require further tampering with the bookkeeping. The laundering of money through a service business can be harder to prove. Fictitious clients may be invented for businesses such as dental practices and law firms; in the case of businesses that take anonymous walk-ins, such as tattoo parlors and nail salons, fictitious appointments can simply be written into the books. Car washes, strip clubs, check-cashing stores, and bars are all cash-intensive businesses popular with money launderers. Businesses used to launder money may not always have an obvious or provable connection to the launderers; particularly when the task of money laundering is outsourced to an expert, that expert may maintain a business relationship with various real and fictitious businesses used to launder money for multiple clients. This can also make it more difficult to prove money laundering on the part of any one of those clients, as unrelated revenue streams are muddled together by the criminal accountant. An expert money launderer may also use shell companies: companies that exist only to launder money. Unlike the businesses mentioned earlier, these shells do no legitimate business; they exist only on paper, in the form of fictitious transactions and business activity. As risky as it sounds—since an investigation would fairly easily reveal that the business exists only on paper—a shell company can be especially useful when placed in a foreign country, which complicates the investigation for any local or national authorities whose attention the launderer is trying to escape.

Money may also be laundered through smurfing or structuring: the division of a large amount of money into smaller lots, each of which is below the cash transaction reporting threshold of $10,000. These smaller lots are then deposited into multiple bank accounts over a period of time. If multiple individuals are used to make the deposits, the depositors are known as smurfs. The money can then be transferred or withdrawn, preferably at a later date. Wide-scale laundering efforts can involve dozens, even hundreds, of different banks for the same laundering operation. Smurfing is itself a crime—on top of any other criminal activities that its conduct is part of or necessary to—under the U.S. Bank Secrecy Act, if it can be shown that the multiple deposits are being made specifically to evade banks' reporting requirements.

Money laundering frequently depends on various special (legitimate) banks. Internet services such as PayPal have actually not been greatly implicated in money laundering, because they are not very useful for the purpose: The $500 per month withdrawal limit on normal PayPal accounts makes laundering complicated, and the fact that PayPal is not a bank gives that entity powers that make it undesirable for launderers. (PayPal has been known to freeze accounts with little provocation, for instance, and the appeals process may involve greater exposure than a launderer is willing to accept.)

Much more useful to launderers are overseas banks. Bank secrecy laws in Switzerland and the major "offshore banking" centers of Singapore, the Bahamas, Bahrain, the Cayman Islands, Hong Kong, the Antilles, and Panama create the potential for a nearly anonymous banking environment. Furthermore, many legitimate banking institutions in Asia descend from ancient trust-based banking systems that create no paper trail and are lightly regulated or entirely unregulated, permitting undocumented, unrecorded withdrawals, transfers, and deposits. In other countries, inexpensive bribery may be enough to falsify or eliminate records in order to facilitate laundering—though one needs to know whom to bribe. Since 2002, the euro has made major gains on the dollar as the most popular currency in money laundering; because it is the legal tender of more than a dozen countries, it passes borders without notice, in tremendous quantities, and presents no complication in transfers between banks in different countries.

Bill Kte'pi
Independent Scholar

See also Accounting Fraud; Money Laundering: Countermeasures; Money Laundering: History; Money Laundering: Targeting Criminal Proceeds; Money Laundering: Vulnerable Commodities and Services; Narco-Terrorism

Further Readings

Beare, Margaret and Stephen Schneider. *Money Laundering in Canada: Chasing Dirty and Dangerous Dollars.* Toronto, ON: University of Toronto Press, 2007.

Madinger, John. *Money Laundering: A Guide for Criminal Investigators.* New York: CRC Press, 2006.

Mathers, Chris. *Crime School: Money Laundering.* Richmond Hill, ON: Firefly Books, 2004.

Richards, James. *Transnational Criminal Organizations, Cybercrime, and Money Laundering.* New York: CRC Press, 1998.

MONEY LAUNDERING: TARGETING CRIMINAL PROCEEDS

Targeting the proceeds of crime is a key element in law enforcement, both because it disincentivizes crime and because it can be the only way to cripple a criminal organization such as a multinational drug-trafficking cartel, which can easily withstand the loss of personnel to arrests or drug shipments to seizures. Furthermore, tying an organization to a financial transaction involving drug money can be the best or sometimes the only way of linking an organization to the drugs themselves and providing sufficient evidence for prosecution. Without a bank or other institution providing a lead by reporting suspicious activity, it can be difficult to uncover money laundering. Even then, many of the leads reported by banks will prove to be innocent.

Various agencies have adopted different strategies for attempting to target the proceeds of criminal activity. Efforts have been especially vigorous since the September 11, 2001, terrorist attacks because of the connections between money laundering and terrorism and the necessity of the global underground economy—which includes laundered money, fenced and stolen goods, illegal arms and narcotics, and unregulated banks—to the financing of terrorism and rogue states. The Financial Action Task Force (FATF), founded in 1989 by the G7 countries, is an intergovernmental body developing an international response to money laundering and the financing of terrorism.

In 2011, its membership included 34 jurisdictions and two regional organizations, working together to form anti-money-laundering (AML) policies.

Whereas the United States stipulates a specific ceiling on cash transactions, $10,000, over which activity must be reported, in other countries the burden of interpreting what is "suspicious" and thus reportable behavior is left to the institution. However, this is not to say that in such jurisdictions money launderers need worry only about triggering a teller's "gut instincts." Banks are actually very scientific and rigorous in their study of potentially suspicious activity. Various AML software packages have been developed for use by financial institutions in order to analyze customer data and detect suspicious transactions, and these are used in conjunction with data-sifting programs that look for transcription errors, signs of possible identity theft or fraud, and other problems that need to be brought to the bank's attention. Among the anomalies for which these systems monitor are sudden shifts in funds (withdrawals or deposits), as well as multiple deposits less than $10,000 made in a short period of time. Transactions involving watch-listed names, organizations, or countries are flagged, as in some cases are accounts involving a high proportion of cash transactions (as opposed to checks, direct deposits, and other transfers).

Much of the burden of looking out for money laundering that falls on the financial institutions is referred to in shorthand as "know your customer," or KYC. KYC policy in the United States includes the bank's customer identification program, as mandated under both the Bank Secrecy Act and the U.S.A. Patriot Act; most countries have similar requirements. Those countries that do permit anonymous banking quickly become havens for laundered funds.

For cash transactions in excess of $10,000, a bank must file a currency transaction report (CTR). Making multiple small transactions in order to avoid reporting requirements, a practice called smurfing or structuring, is a crime. CTRs and other reports of suspicious activity, including those generated by AML software, are examined in the United States by the Financial Crimes Enforcement Network (FinCEN), a bureau of the Treasury Department. Analysis is conducted by both agents and software and includes statistical analysis and profiling, time sequence matching, and risk scoring based on the known data about a given transaction or series of transactions.

Sometimes discoveries of money laundering are made in the course of investigating other crimes, and information sharing among agencies and governments has become increasingly useful. For instance, the 1990s talks between the Colombian government and the U.S. Treasury Department led to the discovery of what the Drug Enforcement Administration (DEA) subsequently identified as the West's largest money-laundering system for narcotics proceeds: Colombia's Black Market Peso Exchange. Colombia was concerned about the number of American goods being illegally imported (avoiding tariffs), and over time discussions uncovered the fact that the goods were being used to launder drug money. Colombian importers avoid the tariff on imported goods and the Colombian tax on converting pesos to dollars by working with "peso brokers" operating on the black market. The same peso brokers take the U.S. dollars generated by drug traffickers' sales to American distributors and use them to buy the American goods they sell to the Colombian importers, while the importers' pesos are exchanged to the drug traffickers as clean domestic currency.

Bill Kte'pi
Independent Scholar

See also Accounting Fraud; Black Market Peso Exchange; Money Laundering: Countermeasures; Money Laundering: History; Money Laundering: Methods; Money Laundering: Vulnerable Commodities and Services; Narco-Terrorism

Further Readings

Madinger, John. *Money Laundering: A Guide for Criminal Investigators.* New York: CRC Press, 2006.
Mathers, Chris. *Crime School: Money Laundering.* Richmond Hill, ON: Firefly Books, 2004.
Richards, James. *Transnational Criminal Organizations, Cybercrime, and Money Laundering.* New York: CRC Press, 1998.

MONEY LAUNDERING: VULNERABLE COMMODITIES AND SERVICES

The term *commodity* typically refers to tangible goods that are demanded by the market. Commodities may range from coffee to silicon computer chips. *Services* refers to intangible goods consisting of the time and skills of individuals, and these may range from retail sales to accounting and legal advice. The concept of money laundering is generally used to refer to efforts to obscure the origins of illegal wealth and to provide a veil of legitimacy—or, put simply, to turn "dirty money" into "clean money." The technical definition adds violating or evading pertinent laws and regulations. The two conceptualizations are often drawn together and confused.

The first definition is used to refer implicitly or explicitly to the activities of organized and professional criminals, and the second definition is used to refer to the widest range of individuals and virtually any interaction with the proceeds of crime. Under the 2000 United Nations (UN) Convention Against Transnational Organized Crime and parallel national legislation implemented by signatory states, money laundering is defined in the widest possible sense to include all serious predicate or underlying offenses (with four or more years' imprisonment as the maximum penalty) and virtually every imaginable interaction with the proceeds of crime.

Our knowledge of which commodities and services may be vulnerable to money laundering is clearly a function of the nature of the prevention and control systems in place as well as examples that may arise from happenstance or luck. Michael Levi and Peter Reuter (2006) offer a generic anti-money-laundering (AML) structure of prevention and enforcement components that highlights the core sources of data on the phenomenon of money laundering. Their prevention components include customer due diligence (knowing your clients), reporting of suspicious and prescribed (large) transactions, regulation and supervision, and administrative or regulatory sanctions for noncompliance. Enforcement components include a list of underlying or predicate offenses, investigation, prosecution and punishment, and civil and criminal confiscation and forfeiture. These core components exist in most jurisdictions, as they seek to be in compliance with the relevant international standards. Such standards include relevant UN conventions as well as guidelines issued by international bodies such as the Financial Action Task Force (FATF), which specifies the benchmark international standards for the prevention and control of money laundering and terrorist finance.

In order to present an overview of commodities and services that are vulnerable to money laundering from a transnational rather than a national perspective, the author will draw upon the findings of Peter Reuter and Edwin M. Truman (2004) and John Stamp and John Walker (2007).

Reuter and Truman reviewed 580 cases drawn from FATF typology reports between 1998 and 2004, as well as a 2000 report from the Egmont Group of Financial Intelligence Units. The Egmont Group is an international network for the national financial intelligence units (FIUs), which receive financial reports and disclose relevant intelligence for investigation and prosecution. It is important to note that the authors were not drawing on a scientific sample but rather on examples submitted by member states. The data revealed that the three largest categories of underlying or predicate offending were drug trafficking (32 percent), fraud (22 percent), and nondrug smuggling (16 percent). The remaining modest categories of underlying or predicate offending were related to terrorism, unknown crimes, prostitution and illegal gambling, bribery/corruption, and tax evasion.

From their sample of predicate offenses, Reuter and Truman found that eight money-laundering methods were most prevalent across all categories. The use of wire transfers (23 percent) was the most popular method across the categories. A wire transfer refers to the conversion of cash or checks into electronic form and then the movement of this electronic currency between financial institutions, often crossing national borders to complicate regulatory and enforcement efforts to trace or investigate. This finding illustrates the vulnerability of financial institutions and other institutions that may handle large sums of money and have facilities to transfer value electronically within and across national borders.

The use of a front company or organization (13 percent) was the next most popular method across all the categories of predicate offenses. This method exploits an otherwise legitimate business to conduct illegal activities and laundering of the proceeds of crime or the direct ownership of such a business by those substantively involved in ongoing criminal activity. In the case of illicit drug activity, a front company or organization can be useful for a variety of activities, such as inserting the proceeds of crime into the accounts and profits of legitimate sales activities. The company may also be an otherwise legitimate supplier of related services; for instance, a hydroponic retailer can offer equipment and advice to assist in growing illegal drugs as well as a facility to launder the proceeds of crime.

The following six examples each accounted for 6 percent or less of the money-laundering methods present in the sample reviewed by Reuter and Truman. These included the use of accountants and financial officers, the purchase of high-value goods, shell corporations, money orders and cashier's checks, real estate, and offshore accounts. The laundering methods of wire transfer and the use of a front company or organization were consistent and dominant themes across the three offense categories of illicit drugs, fraud, and nondrug smuggling.

It should be expected that the laundering methods would vary with respect to the underlying or predicate offense that generates the proceeds of crime. For instance, the cash-intensive nature of the illicit drug trade necessitates a greater emphasis on the placement of such monies within convertible assets. This will often involve the purchase of high-value goods, such as luxury cars, jewelry, precious stones, and real estate; all of these illustrate the need to dispose of "dirty money" and to exchange it for assets that can hold value that can be moved or easily sold to further obscure the underlying proceeds of crime. Once the dirty money is placed into assets, money laundering associated with illicit drugs may involve greater emphasis on financial instruments and the services of lawyers and accountants to further undermine potential linkages that law enforcement may draw between the assets and the underlying or predicate offending.

By contrast, fraud will typically have a less cash-intensive focus (compared with illicit drugs), as the proceeds of crime are often generated within transactions that are already placed within the financial system. For instance, investors in a nonexistent or dubious stock of a given company or market commodity will generally conduct the transaction via check or electronic transfer rather than physically transporting large amounts of cash. Thus, fraud has a built-in tendency toward the layering and integration of the proceeds of crime via the use of shell corporations, employing the professional services of lawyers and accountants, and the purchase and sale of securities.

Stamp and Walker (2007) highlight the findings of a survey that involved 21 overseas FIUs, 14 Australian law-enforcement agencies, and four researchers and criminologists. It found a marked contrast to earlier findings, in that the survey revealed that fraud accounted for 82 percent and illicit drugs 11 percent of the underlying or predicate offenses generated within Australia and laundered within or outside the country. The authors estimated that the proceeds of crime in Australia each year were most often laundered through real estate investments (23 percent), further crime activities (21 percent), gambling (16 percent), luxury goods (15 percent), legitimate business (12 percent), and professional services such as accountants and lawyers (7 percent). They additionally found that fraud and tax/customs evasion occurred four times more often than drug trafficking in the suspicious activity or transaction reports that overseas FIUs reported in the survey.

The reader should not be surprised to see similarities and differences between jurisdictions in the proportions of various predicate or underlying offenses or the relative emphasis on different money-laundering methods. Nevertheless, it is clear that there is a need to construct and implement a more systematic and scientific evidence base to better understand the vulnerability of particular commodities and services to money laundering within and between jurisdictions over time.

David C. Hicks
Independent Scholar

See also Accounting Fraud; Antiterrorist Financing; Australia; Civil Forfeiture: The Experience of the United States; Conventions, Agreements, and Regulations; Criminal Forfeiture and Seizure; Egmont Group of Financial Intelligence Units; Financial Action Task Force; Financial Fraud; Globalization; Informal Value Transfer Systems; Intelligence Agencies: Collaboration Within the United States; Investment Crimes; Legal and Illegal Economies; Money Laundering: Countermeasures; Money Laundering: Methods; Money Laundering: Targeting Criminal Proceeds; Mutual Legal Assistance Treaties; Racketeer Influenced and Corrupt Organizations Act; Sanctions and Blacklisting; Tax Evasion; Telemarketing Fraud; UN Convention Against Transnational Organized Crime

Further Readings

Beare, Margaret and Stephen Schneider. *Money Laundering in Canada: Chasing Dirty and Dangerous Dollars.* Toronto, ON: University of Toronto Press, 2007.

Hicks, David C., and Adam Graycar. "Money
    Laundering." In *International Crime and Justice*,
    Mangai Natarajan, ed. New York: Cambridge
    University Press, 2011.

Levi, Michael and Peter Reuter. "Money Laundering."
    Crime and Justice: A Review of Research, v.34 (2006).

Reuter, Peter and Edwin M. Truman. *Chasing Dirty
    Money: The Fight Against Money Laundering.*
    Washington, DC: Institute for International Economics,
    2004.

Stamp, John and John Walker. "Money Laundering in and
    Through Australia, 2004." *Trends and Issues in Crime
    and Criminal Justice*, v.342 (2007).

Vander Beken, Tom. *Organised Crime and Vulnerability of
    Economic Sectors: The European Transport and Music
    Sector.* Antwerp, Belgium: Maklu, 2005.

MUTUAL LEGAL ASSISTANCE TREATIES

A mutual legal assistance treaty (MLAT) is an agreement between countries to share information and provide assistance to one another in the enforcement of criminal laws. These treaties, which are generally bilateral in scope, aim to increase the effectiveness of transnational law-enforcement efforts by improving cooperation and offering more efficient allocation of investigative and prosecutorial resources. Such treaties often contain extradition agreements that require the country in which a criminal suspect is located to deliver that suspect to the prosecuting authority of the country seeking to prosecute him or her, subject to certain conditions. MLATs can confer on a requesting country the power to compel the production of documentary evidence such as tax information or financial records, the power to summon witnesses, the power to issue search warrants, and so forth.

Each party to an MLAT will designate a central authority (such as the U.S. Department of Justice) with which to communicate directly. Investigators and prosecutors share information and convey requirements and enforcement strategies through these channels. It is generally believed that using these channels of communication to employ the prosecutorial resources of both countries can yield significant benefits in terms of both making the enforcement of domestic criminal statutes against transnational criminal targets more effective and efficient, and providing stable procedures for the

Secretary of State Hillary Clinton participates in the 2009 signing ceremony of Protocols of Exchange of Instruments of Ratification for the U.S.-Slovenia Mutual Legal Assistance Protocol and the U.S.-Slovenia Extradition Treaty, with His Excellency Samuel Žbogar. (U.S. Department of State)

resolution of issues such as asset forfeiture and sharing.

Most MLATs contain right-of-refusal provisions that reserve signatory nations' rights to refuse requested assistance if, for example, the state being requested believes that granting the request would impair its sovereignty, national security, or other fundamental public interests. Model agreements have provisions for refusal of assistance when a requested nation believes that the crime at issue is of a political nature; when there are substantial grounds for believing that the target of prosecution is being discriminated against on the basis of race, religion, gender, or political beliefs; when the prosecution would violate the requested country's laws against double jeopardy; or when the method of investigation or prosecution entails measures that are inconsistent with the laws of the host country.

On February 1, 2010, 56 new MLAT agreements entered into force between the United States, the European Union, and each of the EU member states. These treaties had been under negotiation since the September 11, 2001, terrorist attacks, and are expected to make it substantially easier for U.S. and EU law-enforcement agencies to investigate and prosecute acts of terrorism, violations of antibribery and antifraud statutes (such as the United States' Foreign Corrupt Practices Act), and other transnational crimes.

In addition to using modern technological tools to facilitate increased sharing of the information needed to investigate and prosecute crime, the 2010 MLATs are aimed at making it easier for criminals to be extradited from one country to another. Under the prior MLAT regime between the United States and the EU, for an offense to be deemed extraditable it had to have been explicitly set forth as such in the treaty. If the offense was made criminal by statute in a country *after* the effective date of the treaty, individuals charged with crimes could defeat attempts at extradition for such crimes. The new treaties address this issue by adopting a "dual criminality" standard. This standard provides that if the charged offense is a crime in both the country in which the suspect is located and the country requesting extradition, then the suspect can be extradited regardless of whether the charged offense is actually listed in the MLAT between the two countries.

The new U.S.-EU MLATs are considered in many ways to be models for future efforts at international cooperation in law enforcement. They allow for speedier identification of financial account information, authorize signatory nations to acquire evidence (including, for example, deposition testimony) using video conferencing and other cost-saving tools, and authorize the participation of foreign investigators and prosecutorial officials in joint investigative teams in partner countries. The treaties do away with the former requirement that host countries designate a local prosecutor to act on behalf of the prosecutorial team in the requesting country when resource constraints prevent them from being present in the host country.

MLATs are binding on ratifying countries. They are thus distinguishable from, although similar in objectives to, executive agreements or memoranda of understanding (MOUs) that provide for cooperation in criminal matters. One example of a widely utilized cooperative framework that does not take the form of an MLAT is found in the various MOUs and exchanges of letters in place between the U.S. Treasury Department's Financial Crimes Enforcement Network (FinCEN) and the financial intelligence units (FIUs) of other countries. Financial information exchange agreements (FIEAs) between the U.S. Treasury Department and other nations' finance ministries, which provide for the exchange of currency transaction information between countries, aim at similar objectives.

Robert D. Williams
United States Court of Appeals, Fifth Circuit

See also Adjudicating International Crimes; Antiterrorist Financing; Conventions, Agreements, and Regulations; Criminal Forfeiture and Seizure; Extradition; Money Laundering: Countermeasures; Police Cooperation; Prosecution: International; United Nations

Further Readings

Terwilliger, George J., III et al. *New Extradition and Mutual Legal Assistance Treaties Take Effect Throughout Europe and the United States.* Washington, DC: White and Case, 2010.

United Nations. *Model Treaty on Mutual Assistance in Criminal Matters.* UN General Assembly Resolution 45/117, amended by Resolution 53/112 (1990).

U.S. Department of State. *International Narcotics Control Strategy Report.* Washington, DC: Author, 2006.

NARCO-TERRORISM

Modern society is increasingly complex, with large and growing populations, massive world poverty, decreasing natural resources, environmental pollution, increased technology, religious fundamentalism, lack of equal opportunity for all people, and an ever-widening gap between rich and poor all contributing to today's political and societal problems. Two of the major problems facing the world are illegal narcotics and terrorism. Unfortunately, since the 1990s these two activities have combined in ways that greatly enhance their individual destructive potential. This phenomenon has been called narco-terrorism.

All of the major developed nations have a serious illegal narcotics problem, albeit to different degrees, depending upon each nation's approach to the problem as one of treatment and education or as one of criminal activity. The more common narcotics that are listed as illegal in most nations are heroin, opium, morphine, codeine, cocaine, and marijuana, although it is questionable if marijuana is, in fact, a narcotic. Narcotic drugs are defined as drugs that are used for relieving pain and inducing sleep and are considered addictive. Opium, heroin, morphine, and codeine are made from the poppy plant, which is grown across the Asian continent. Cocaine originates in South America. The location and source of narcotics are important in the relationship with certain terrorist groups.

Laws concerning illegal narcotic drugs usually prohibit the possession, the use, the sale, and the manufacture of such drugs. The punishments for violations of these laws usually increase in severity depending upon the nature of the crime (possession to use to sale to manufacture) and the amount of drugs involved (for example, whether a single joint or several tons of marijuana). The difference between a drug trafficker and a drug dealer is that drug dealers usually deal with their customers on an individual basis. Drug traffickers are those people who transport massive amounts of illegal narcotics for distribution by drug dealers.

The trafficking in these illegal narcotic drugs yields an incredible amount of profit for those people willing to take the risk. The profits are so huge that many drug traffickers have become highly organized into cartels. These international drug cartels are so large and so well organized that they have become international organizations. What is remarkable about these international drug cartels is their internal discipline. Law-enforcement agencies have, for all practical purposes, found it impossible to stop them. What is also remarkable and also very frightening is the willingness of the international drug cartels to employ extreme violence without regard for innocent victims.

By its very nature, terrorism is fundamentally different from illegal drug violations. Whereas illegal drug violations are essentially crimes, terrorism is more akin to political activity and crimes. Indeed, terrorism can be defined as the use of violence or threat of violence to compel a person or entity to act or not to act in a particular way, usually for a social, religious, or political purpose or goal. Thus, violence is an essential element of the crime of terrorism, whereas the use of violence is not an element of the use, sale, or manufacture of illegal narcotic drugs. This does not, of course, mean that violence is not employed by those who deal in illegal narcotic drugs. Indeed, as the level of profit increases, the amount of violence that the drug dealers are willing to employ also increases.

As previously stated, terrorism can involve several purposes or goals. These can include social, political, or religious goals, and these goals frequently overlap. An example of a social goal and terrorism is demonstrated by the Environmental Liberation Front (ELF). The goal of this American terrorist group is the protection of the environment. ELF's activities are reported to include arson of buildings that ELF considers to be environmentally damaging and the spiking of trees with nails so that when lumberjacks try to cut those trees down, their chain saws are broken. By these activities, ELF hopes to advance the social cause of environmentalism. ELF tries to avoid harming people but allows property destruction as a means to achieving the group's mission. Another example of the use of terrorism to achieve social goals concerns the "pro-life" movement in America. The past few decades have seen a number of abortion clinics bombed and even the murder of doctors who are willing to perform abortions. The social goal is to stop abortions, and the use of terrorism and other crimes has been rationalized by some radical groups in the pro-life movement as acceptable to meet that goal.

An obvious example of a religious goal involving terrorism involves Al Qaeda. Al Qaeda is an extremely well-organized, international terrorist organization. A radical Islamic group, Al Qaeda has advanced as one of its goals the protection and expansion of the Islamic religion, although many if not most mainstream Muslims would take issue with that assertion. Al Qaeda is infamous for its use of violence to accomplish its goals and does not hesitate to injure or kill innocent human beings in its quest to eliminate the Western forces and institutions it sees as its enemies, as the September 11, 2001, attacks on the Pentagon, the World Trade Center, and United Airlines Flight 93 over Pennsylvania attest.

An example of a political goal involving terrorism can be illustrated by reference to the Irish Republican Army, otherwise known as the IRA, although in recent years the IRA has significantly lessened and even ceased its violent activities. The primary goal of the IRA was the liberation of Ireland and Northern Ireland from the British Empire. As history shows, the IRA was highly skilled at the use of explosives, causing injury and death to thousands of people.

The previous examples provide a brief overview of the two components of narco-terrorism: illegal narcotics and terrorism. Unfortunately, for much of the world, these two phenomena have combined in their activities for several different purposes. The resulting synergies for both narcotics trafficking and terrorism have greatly increased the danger to civilized society.

There are two perspectives with which to view and analyze narco-terrorism. The first view is that the international drug cartels have increased their use of force to such an extent that their activities can be considered terroristic. The drug traffickers are using violence not only to accomplish a specific immediate goal, such as the transfer of a shipment of illegal narcotic drugs across an international border, but also preemptively to terrorize individuals, groups, municipalities, and even governments into not even attempting to interfere with or prevent their drug trade. In this sense, the aspects of terrorism are subordinate to the ultimate goal of profiting from the trade in illegal narcotic drugs. The terrorism is merely the drug traffickers' tool for advancing their illegal enterprise.

Such activity is occurring in Mexico. The border between Mexico and the United States has erupted with significant acts of violence involving international drug cartels. These cartels have been assassinating government and police officials in Mexico to such an extent that many local police simply have refused to try and stop the illegal drug activities in their jurisdictions, recognizing that to attempt to do so may result in death for them and their families. At one point in 2005, when the Mexican federal police attempted to enter the municipality of Nuevo Laredo, they were fired upon by the local police. Thus, the police have been literally terrorized into acquiescing to the activities of the drug cartels. The violence has also been directed at rival drug cartels. With the fall of the Colombian Cali and Medellín drug cartels in the 1990s, a number of rival groups have vied for preeminence in the international drug trade. The intercartel violence has been even greater than the violence directed at the various criminal justice organizations and innocent civilians. The corruption was so widespread that in June

2007, the Mexican government purged 284 federal police commanders. The Mexican police have been reported to work as enforcers for the international drug cartels and have even been involved in kidnappings for ransom. As of December 2010, 30,000 deaths were reported to be the result of Mexico's drug war, and the number was growing. The corruption and terrorism in Mexico over illegal narcotics is so widespread that the U.S. government has tried to address the matter with the Mexican government by providing significant aid. Between 2004 and 2007, American aid for the control of the illegal narcotic drug trade was almost $40 million per year.

The use of terror tactics by the international drug cartels does not technically meet the definition of terrorism. However, it employs the same methods, uses the same level of violence, and results in the same types of destruction, injury, and death. Thus, as a practical matter, this is almost a distinction without a difference, although the difference takes on greater importance when trying to deal with the source of the violence, which will be discussed later.

The second perspective on narco-terrorism sees the international narcotic drug trade as the means terrorists employ to finance their terrorist activities. From this perspective, unlike the first, the profits of the drug trade are secondary; the drug trade is subordinated to the terrorist activities and is merely a tool for the accomplishment of the terrorists' primary purpose, whether social, political, or religious.

The Taliban in Afghanistan is an excellent example of the intersection of illegal narcotic drug trafficking and this sort of terrorism. The Taliban indisputably has both a religious and a political agenda in Afghanistan, which is to seize power and install an Islamic fundamentalist regime by the use of threats and force. The Taliban came into existence and then took control of Afghanistan after the Soviet Union was forced out of the country. Afghanistan is a major grower of poppies and a supplier of narcotic drugs. Because of its sponsorship of terroristic activities and continued involvement in the international narcotic drug trade, Afghanistan was invaded by a multinational force and the Taliban was removed from power. Since its removal from power, the Taliban has been conducting a terror campaign to regain power. It has had some success in the more rural areas of Afghanistan. However, conducting a terrorist campaign requires a great deal of money. The source of much of this money for the Taliban

has been the international narcotic drug trade, as poppies are a major crop in Afghanistan.

Another example of the intersection of international illegal narcotic drug trafficking and terrorism has occurred in Colombia with the Revolutionary Armed Forces of Colombia (FARC). The FARC is a communist guerrilla group that has existed in South America, with a recent concentration in Colombia, for decades. It opposes U.S. domination in Colombia and has engaged in extensive violence and kidnapping in its resistance activities. Colombia is a major source of cocaine, which is derived from the coca plant. The FARC is reported to finance much of its activity through the illegal narcotic drug trade. The purposes of the FARC are political and social. Its primary purposes are not focused on profits from international narcotic drug trafficking; these profits are secondary to the political mission and help support it. Thus, the FARC is an example of the use of international narcotic drug trafficking to support the broader social terrorist goals of the group.

The examples of the Taliban and the FARC illustrate how terrorism intersects with international illegal narcotic drug trafficking. The location and source of drugs are very important when determining the nexus between illegal drug trafficking and terrorism. With the Taliban, the poppies are located in the very country where the terrorist activities are occurring. Likewise, with the FARC, the coca plants are located in the country where the terrorist activities are occurring. This does not mean that terrorist groups that are not located in narcotic-drug-producing countries cannot or do not use illegal narcotic drug trafficking to support their terrorist activities. In fact, just the opposite is true. Many terrorist groups have and do employ trafficking to support their activities. However, those terrorist groups located in narcotic-drug-producing nations usually have greater access to the product and enjoy a greater share of the profits.

As a practical matter, the results of narco-terrorism from the perspective of an international narcotic drug-trafficking cartel and from the perspective of an international terrorist group are quite similar: violence, death, destruction, and the undermining of legal and governmental institutions. However, the two types of narco-terrorism are employed to meet very different ends: one being sheer criminal profit and the other driven by social, political, and religious goals. Likewise, the ways of addressing these two forms of narco-terrorism and preventing future acts of violence will diverge according to the goals of the narco-terrorism involved.

Wm. C. Plouffe Jr.
Independent Scholar

See also Al Qaeda; Cocaine; Drug Trade: Source, Destination, and Transit Countries; Heroin; Marijuana or Cannabis; Terrorism Versus Transnational Crime; Violence: Intimidation; Violence: Uses

Further Readings

British Broadcasting Corporation. "Mexico's Drug War: Number of Dead Passes 30,000." December 16, 2010. http://www.bbc.co.uk/news/world-latin-america-12012425 (Accessed February 2011).

Cook, Colleen W. *CRS Report for Congress: Mexico's Drug Cartels.* Washington, DC: Congressional Research Service, 2007.

Davids, Douglas. *Narco-Terrorism: A Unified Strategy to Fight a Growing Terrorist Menace.* Ardsley, NY: Transnational, 2002.

Fleming, Gary. *Drug Wars: Narco Warfare in the 21st Century.* Charleston, SC: BookSurge, 2008.

Gould, Jens Erik. "Mexico's Drug War Turns Into Terrorism After Grenades." October 20, 2008. http://www.bloomberg.com/apps/newsarchive&sid=akDCw.fUKYOc (Accessed February 2011).

Hollis, André. "Narcoterrorism: A Definitional and Operational Transnational Challenge." In *Transnational Threats: Smuggling and Trafficking in Arms, Drugs, and Human Life*, Kimberley L. Thachuk, ed. Westport, CT: Praeger Security International, 2007.

Livingstone, Grace. *Inside Colombia: Drugs, Democracy and War.* New Brunswick, NJ: Rutgers University Press, 2004.

McMahon, Betty. "Mideast Terrorists Team Up With Drug Cartels." GroundReport July 14, 2008. http://www.groundreport.com/World/Mideast-Terrorists-Team-Up-With-Drug-Cartels/2865040 (Accessed February 2011).

Tarazona-Sevillano, Gabriela and John Reuter. *Sendero Luminoso and the Threat of Narco-Terrorism.* New York: Praeger, 1990.

Walsh, Frank. "Synchronizing Colombian Narco-Terrorism Policy With the War on Terror: The Legality of Military Deployment by the United States and the Organization of American States." *Georgetown Journal of Law and Public Policy*, v.4 (2006).

NETWORKS

Since the 1990s, transnational criminal groups have been engaged in redefining the scope of criminal activity. They operate through networks made up of extremely flexible memberships that often draw on lessons learned from traditional organized crime groups while taking their activities to unprecedented levels of global involvement. Unlike hierarchical organized crime groups, these decentralized criminal networks not only add fluidity to operations but also provide flexibility and adaptability. Operating in all sections of the world, transnational criminal networks have infiltrated virtually every nation, affecting the lives of millions of people who are unaware of their very existence. While their activities are often accompanied by violence, transnational crime groups have become expert at accomplishing their goals in ways that seek to avoid detection. This is often accomplished by their involvement in legitimate business ventures and through their ability to wield political power. Criminal activities range from human and narcotics trafficking to the smuggling of weapons, human body parts, endangered species, and nuclear material. Transnational criminals have become expert at providing an unsuspecting public with fake medicines, clothes, CDs, DVDs, automobiles, and artwork. Such activity is responsible for the loss of billions of dollars, and it may be life-threatening at times, as was the case with a counterfeit cough medicine that killed almost a hundred children in Haiti in the mid-1990s because it contained contaminated liquid acetaminophen.

While many of the activities conducted by transnational criminals take place in countries of the former Soviet Union and in countries, such as Italy, with long histories of organized crime, globalization, the Internet, liberal trade policies, and porous borders have made it much easier to expand activities to nations that have traditionally been considered safe from such activities. For instance, eastern European crime families are successful at laundering money from criminal activities through financial institutions in Cyprus and Liechtenstein. Heroin originating in Afghanistan is channeled through the Balkans to destinations in Germany and Scandinavia. Albanians traffic women from the countries of the former Soviet Union to Western Europe. Terrorist groups headquartered in Pakistan carry out attacks in India. Traditional organized crime groups, including the Italian-based Sicilian Mafia, the Neapolitan Camorra, the Calabrian 'Ndrangheta, and Puglian Sacra Corona, have increasingly become transnational in the ways in which their operations are conducted. The ease with which criminals can hack into computers around the world has enabled cyber-criminals to engage in a host of transnational crimes, particularly cyberterrorism and money laundering. Despite the fact that many countries have enacted laws against cybercrime, the Computer Security Institute and the Computer Intrusion Squad, the latter overseen by the U.S. Federal Bureau of Investigation (FBI), have estimated that the incidence of cybercrime rose from 42 percent to 70 percent between 1996 and 2000.

Scholars, journalists, and government officials who study transnational crime have identified a number of characteristics that make it easy to identify countries that are likely to be hospitable to transnational crime, thus promoting the fluidity and flexibility of criminal networks. Government corruption is generally widespread. Legislation regulating criminal activity is often ineffective, and law enforcement is poor. Financial institutions exhibit a lack of transparency. Borders are likely to be porous. A lack of economic opportunity facilitates recruitment, as does a general lack of respect for the rule of law. On the other hand, many countries that do not mirror these characteristics have unwittingly become bases for transnational crime networks. Countries with long histories of organized crime are also extremely susceptible to transnational criminal activity. In both Chechnya and the tri-border area of Paraguay, some overlapping of membership occurs. The notorious Colombian drug cartel is partially funded by eastern European arms suppliers.

Although drug trafficking and smuggling have long been recognized as the major problem in the field of transnational crime, transnational criminal networks are increasingly engaging in human trafficking and smuggling. Between 800,000 and 900,000 women and children are trafficked each year. Traditionally, women were trafficked from Asian countries to be sexually exploited in other parts of the world. Following the dissolution of the Soviet Union in the early 1990s, women of eastern Europe, Latin America, and the Middle East also began to be trafficked into the United States and to Central and Western Europe. The problem of eastern European gangs forcibly restraining women whom they had enslaved in Belgium and the Netherlands became so severe that the European Union intervened. All trafficking is not conducted for the purpose of sexual exploitation. It also occurs as a means of remedying labor shortages. China,

for instance, is involved in widespread smuggling of males from the Fujian province.

Network Membership

Governments and international monitoring groups are well aware of the activities of transnational criminal groups, such as the triads of Hong Kong, the Cali cartel of Colombia, the Vory v Zakonye of Russia, and the Yakuza of Japan. The triads have historically raked in more money than any of these groups, netting some $210.2 billion in the mid-1990s, with 70 percent of that profit deriving from drug trafficking. The political and religious orientation of criminal groups often dictates the kind of criminal activity in which they engage. For instance, jihadists are more likely to use explosives, firearms, aircraft, and motor vehicles in the commission of crimes than are right-wingers, who resort to such crimes as mail fraud, racketeering, and robbery. While transnational crime groups are generally separate from traditional organized crime groups, they do recruit specialists from that field to perform required activities. The membership of terrorist groups may be either international or domestic. Such groups are often small, but they have become expert at making themselves appear both larger and stronger than they actually are. Terrorist networks often engage in traditional crimes to finance terrorist operations. Striking examples of such activity include the Baader-Meinhof gang of West Germany, which held up banks in the late 1960s, and the Chilean Movement of the Revolutionary Left, which worked with French criminals in 1992 to carry out the biggest bank robbery that ever occurred in France. While alliances between organized crime groups and transnational crime groups are fairly common, most alliances tend to be short-lived once a particular goal is accomplished.

The dissolution of the Soviet Union in 1991 was hailed as a victory for democracy, but an unexpected result of the breakup has been the ease with which transnational criminal networks have been able to operate in former Soviet countries that are characterized by instability and that have ready access to abandoned Soviet weapons and arms. Many of the wars occurring in the politically unstable nations of Africa are the result of transnational crime networks exporting illegal weapons from former communist countries and eastern Europe into Africa. Since the terrorist attacks on the United States on September

11, 2001, Al Qaeda has become the most notorious transnational criminal network in the world. The group has successfully expanded its activities to countries that include Armenia, Azerbaijan, and Tajikistan. Al Qaeda has also used access to Soviet weaponry to carry out such crimes as the unsuccessful bombing of an Israeli airliner over Kenya in 2002. Groups that have formerly been labeled as domestic criminals have now entered the world of transnational crime by spreading their reach to other countries.

Elizabeth Rholetter Purdy
Independent Scholar

See also Al Qaeda; Computer-Generated Scams; Government Reports

Further Readings

Curtis, Glenn et al. *Nations Hospitable to Organized Crime and Terrorism.* Washington, DC: Library of Congress, Federal Research Division, 2003.

Emerson, Steven. *American Jihad: The Terrorists Living Among Us.* New York: Free Press, 2002.

Gerspacher, Nadia and Benoît Dupont. "The Nodal Structure of International Police Cooperation: An Exploration of Transnational Security Networks." *Global Governance* v.13 (2007).

Hamm, Mark S. and Cécile Van de Voorde. "Crimes Committed by Terrorist Groups: Theory, Research, and Prevention." *Trends in Organized Crime*, v.9/2 (Winter 2005).

Lilley, Peter. *Dirty Dealing: The Untold Truth About Global Money Laundering.* London: Kogan Page, 2000.

Naím, Moisés. *Illicit: How Smugglers, Traffickers, and Copycats Are Hijacking the Global Economy.* New York: Doubleday, 2005.

Ricchiardi, Sherry. "Playing Defense." *American Journalism Review*, v.32/2 (Summer 2010).

Shelley, Louise I. and John T. Picarelli. "Methods and Motives: Exploring Links Between Transnational Organized Crime and International Terrorism." *Trends in Organized Crime*, v.9/2 (Winter 2005).

Stroeker, Sally and Louise Shelley, eds. *Human Traffic and Transnational Crime.* Lanham, MD: Littlefield, 2004.

NIGERIAN MONEY SCAMS

Nigerian scammers have bilked millions of dollars from a range of worldwide targets. Old confidence, or "con," games, such as the 419 fraud (419 is Nigeria's criminal code for the offense), continue to be used, but Nigerians have more recently pitched scams to the lonely and lovelorn and have posed as legitimate business owners trying to do business with people outside Nigeria. These seemingly legitimate operations are almost completely fraudulent. In addition, West African gangs are now well organized and have evolved far beyond 419-type cons, perpetrating more sophisticated criminal enterprises such as bank and investment fraud, identity theft, money laundering, drug dealing, human trafficking, and terrorism.

The 419 fraud begins with Nigerian nationals purporting to be officials of their government or banking institutions. These criminals fax, mail, or e-mail letters to prospective victims promising a quick and generous return (as high as 40 percent) if the potential victim will provide the scammer with a bank account number. Supposedly, a high-status company or individual outside Nigeria is needed for the deposit of an overpayment on a procurement contract, because the Nigerian government paid far too much—up to $60 million on the contract. Then, the individual is asked to provide funds to cover various fees. Scammers ask for social security and bank account numbers as well as other kinds of sensitive personal identifiers. When the scammer has the victim's account number, he or she uses a bank draft to clear all the money from the account.

A variant of 419 fraud is called advance-fee fraud. This scheme usually begins with an unsolicited letter, e-mail, or fax, supposedly from a West African official (usually but not always in Nigeria) seeking the recipient's cooperation in transferring a very large sum of money out of the sender's country. This money may be from a dormant bank account belonging to a deceased businessman with no next of kin or may be the product of some "overinvoiced contract." The correspondence is shrouded in secrecy and promises that the transaction is risk-free. However, some unforeseen problem always arises, and the payment of a fee becomes necessary. This may be presented as an insurance fee, a legal fee, a delivery charge, a transfer tax, a local tax, a levy, or a bribe, to mention but a few of numerous advance fees used in this scam. Payment of the fee does not end the scam. More complications arise, which require still more advance payments, until the victim either quits or runs out of money. Even then, the scam continues, as perpetrators may use the checks and personal information they have already received to impersonate the victim, thereby draining credit card balances and bank accounts.

Educators around the world have been subjected to a variety of fraudulent schemes believed to originate in Nigeria. One such scheme involved a company that purportedly registered Internet addresses, or universal resource locators (URLs). An educational institution in the United States received authentic-looking correspondence from a registration company informing it that somewhere in the world an institution was interested in purchasing a URL similar to that of the American institution. The only way for the American school to keep the other school from purchasing the URL—and thus creating market confusion—was to buy the URL directly from the scamming company. The fake registration company backed off if challenged or ignored. In another very realistic scam, a consortium of fraudulent academic journals operating out of Germany promised quick reviews of scholarly manuscripts after submission to a series of online journals such as *Journal of Applied Science* and *Journal of Renewable Energy*. Each journal had all the trappings of legitimate peer review, such as an international advisory board and a cadre of experts the founding editor claims are peer reviewers of manuscripts. However, the journal collects publication fees from authors in core countries but does not publish their manuscripts. To finish off the ruse with a touch of legitimacy, the editor sends "thank you" correspondence at the end of the year to all who participated in the scheme, including the international experts duped into serving on the advisory board or as peer reviewers.

Lovelorn adults in America and elsewhere have been sought out by Nigerian suitors posing as Americans or as citizens of the targeted country. In these "romance scams," a romance develops online and the couple's relationship blossoms until a problem develops. The "American" says he is doing business in Nigeria and needs his sweetheart to cash some money orders in the United States and then wire the money back to Nigeria. American authorities then discover that the money orders were purchased for a nominal amount (such as $20) but were later "cleaned" so as to show a worth of $900 dollars or more.

The money raised by Nigerian fraud supports a corrupt government and is now thought to be diverted to other kinds of illicit enterprises. Nigeria is a notable transit point for heroin and cocaine intended for East Asian, North American, and European markets. For Nigerian narco-traffickers operating worldwide, the country provides a safe haven and is a well-known center for international money laundering.

Stan C. Weeber
McNeese State University

See also Financial Fraud

Further Readings

DuBoff, Leonard and Christy King. "Educators Beware: Avoiding the Scams." *TechTrends*, v.53 (2009).

Durkin, Keith and Richard Brinkman. "419 Fraud: A Crime Without Borders in a Post-Modern World." *International Review of Modern Sociology*, v.35 (2009).

U.S. Secret Service. "Public Awareness Advisory Regarding '4-1-9' or 'Advance Fee Fraud' Schemes." http://www.secretservice.gov (Accessed February 2011).

NONGOVERNMENTAL ORGANIZATIONS

In a world increasingly defined by global communication, cross-cultural and transnational cooperation, and governmental restructuring often at the behest of its own people, the role of the international nongovernmental organization (NGO) has never been more important. Although there is no single standard or delineated form given to such groups, an international NGO is a private organization that serves as a mechanism for cooperation among individuals and other national groups in international affairs. Also called "transnational associations," NGOs are distinct from many other bodies in the international arena because of their origins and membership. Although not officially part of the governing body within a state, these transnational associations often bring together interests from both private and governmental spheres and, in doing so, are uniquely situated to support, implement, and refocus transnational criminal law initiatives in creative and important ways.

Despite the influence of private, transnational associations within international affairs over the last century, the term *nongovernmental organization* was brought into popular international usage only since the UN Economic and Social Council (ECOSOC) codified the consultative status of NGOs in Resolution 288 X (B) of February 27, 1950. Since that time, the UN has revised this statute, once through Resolution 1296 (XLIV) of 1968 and again in 1996 through Resolution 1996/31. The 1996 revision removed the presumption of international activity from the term NGO, identifying many state-level NGOs whose focus and reach do not extend beyond a nation's geopolitical boundaries.

Because the term NGO suggests a dissociation from government structure and activity, it is easily misunderstood as wholly distinct from, or even contrary to, the purposes and practices of a state's government. Moreover, while these organizations do not often involve public or state elements, NGOs may, at times, incorporate government actors, ministries, agencies, and objectives and, in doing so, gain some legitimacy as operatives endowed by the state. However, to maintain the necessary separation from state authority and enjoy the freedom that NGOs so often require to fulfill their objectives, they are traditionally not endowed with governmental tasks, even if their goals and those of the state or states in which they are working happen to coincide.

NGOs that do not include public or state elements derive their legitimacy and authority, then, from several sources. First, one may look to Article 71 of the UN Charter, which gives to ECOSOC the power to "make suitable arrangements for consultation with NGOs which are concerned with matters within its competence." Currently, there are more than 3,336 NGOs in consultative status with ECOSOC and more than 18,300 identified by the UN worldwide. By tasking a policy-making body with consultation with NGOs, UN member states indirectly accord power to what many see as the backbone of "civil society" at the national and international levels.

Although treaties and international law do not create or establish NGOs, treaties and international arrangements may recognize the legal status of NGOs. In some instances, such arrangements may also delegate functions to NGOs that represent shared governmental interests in tackling particular challenges. An example of this is evident in the Geneva Conventions of 1949 and their Additional Protocols, which give to the International Committee of the Red Cross (ICRC) the right to offer its services to the parties of the conflict.

Whatever their official source of authority may be, NGOs most commonly derive their credibility as supporting and innovating organizations from the justness of their cause and methods of promotion, as reflected in their membership and funding. Because an NGO relies on private donations, endowments, and government grants, the legitimacy and authority an NGO wields are often a function of the degree to which donors, supporters, volunteers, staff, and directors participate in the realization of that organization's goals.

While NGOs may have a broad focus in their policy and practice, they more commonly have a narrower field of interest within academic, economic, development, technical, social, cultural, humanitarian, gender, rule of law enforcement, or government-related fields. Of particular note in addressing aspects common to all NGOs is that unlike governmental and intergovernmental bodies (such as the UN), NGOs may not bring legal actions in international tribunals, conclude treaties, or create peace forces or mission objectives. Besides sharing a broad topical field in which one NGO may find its focus, individual NGOs often have very little else in common. From Amnesty International to the International Chamber of Commerce, from the Association of the Indigenous People of the North Republic of Buryatia (Okinsk, Russia) to the Roman Catholic Church, NGOs may vary as widely in focus as do individual ideals and concerns.

As states globally demonstrate an increased concern for ensuring human rights and substantial protections to their people through revised legislation, NGOs are playing an increasingly important role in the political arena to make the voice of unrepresented and underrepresented minorities heard and considered. Because they are removed from government regulation and direction, NGOs are also uniquely suited to bring together individuals of similar interests to advocate for and work toward treaties, conventions, and international instruments that are ultimately adopted by a nation or nations. Several examples of international conventions whose adoption is owed in large part to NGOs would include the Ottawa Mine Ban Treaty of 1997 (Geneva Call) and the Convention on the Rights of the Child of 1989 (Child Rights Information Network).

NGOs at both the national and international levels have been effective in collaborating with government officials to bring substantive policy changes that both define and deter transnational crime. Although human trafficking is typically thought of as a crime that involves movement across national borders, it is equally a crime that may happen entirely domestically, under recently enacted statutory models. NGOs like the Polaris Project, Shared Hope International, and Girls Educational and Mentoring Services (GEMS) routinely provide experts to advise the U.S. Congress on the current status of criminal penalties and convictions related to human trafficking cases within the United States, which often involve victims and implicate perpetrators who have crossed international borders.

NGOs like the International Organization for Migration (IOM) or Migrant Forum in Asia provide governments with important facts and figures about those moving in and across their borders that legislative bodies often have neither the time nor the resources to collect themselves. By informing ministers and other special representatives within the relevant country what trends are evident in immigration and migration studies, NGOs are able to help governments institute policy initiatives that lead to more consistent training of law enforcement, less corruption in immigration, and greater respect for the rule of law.

As governments look for more effective and creative ways to implement the rule of law once established, transnational associations provide varied and often well-tailored methods of assisting with that implementation. Because they may be topic-specific (such as Doctors Without Borders) or homogeneous in their origin (such as the American Bar Association's Rule of Law Initiative), NGOs may be better situated to help victims of poverty and injustice overcome a particular challenge than are local law enforcement and relevant government officials. Some NGOs, such as the Rule of Law Initiative and International Justice Mission, operate exclusively through partnerships with local police, prosecutors, judges, and government ministers to effect the reforms to criminal justice guiding their organizational mandate.

NGOs can reduce the burden on government officials trying to combat transnational crime by bringing prohibited working standards to the attention of responsible authorities (as does the Migrant Workers Protection Society in Bahrain) or by taking over the reintegration of refugees whose return to their home country may subject them to further persecution (as does Mediators Beyond Borders with returning female child-soldiers in Liberia).

An important criticism of NGOs recognizes that when individuals come together under a common purpose that may or may not be aligned with the interests of their state, the exclusive control function of a state can become marginalized. In the United States alone, NGOs such as Amnesty International and Greenpeace have demonstrated that the interests of these organizations may contradict those of the state and, in rare instances, may directly challenge the state on issues related to human rights. A conceptual example would be the many privately funded, immigrant legal aid NGOs in the United States that are exempt from the ban on providing legal assistance to aliens with funds appropriated to the Legal Services Corporation.

Those NGOs that are free from restrictive funding policies are able to define their goals, as well as actions, based on self-given mandates that make them important and often underrepresented voices in international civil society. Whereas the state once was the exclusive manager of international relations, we are now seeing a movement toward denationalization with the rise in influence and prestige of many international NGOs. In an era of unprecedented development, delivery of resources, and public outcry in the face of oppression, NGOs make possible international institutionalized cooperation and dialogue that state agendas could not foster to the same degree.

NGOs can no longer be disregarded by those who shape, approve, and implement transnational criminal codes and sanctions. The perspective, expertise, vision, and ability NGOs bring to the implementation of criminal justice reforms is unparalleled in the global arena and suggests, if anything, an increasingly significant role for NGOs in the coming decades. Rules now must be negotiated between state and nonstate actors alike, making international law no longer based on the solitary ideals of the state but instead on a transnational framework based on cooperation and increased dialogue between the various actors. States and NGOs alike are forming customary international law through their practice, as well as *opinio juris*. The effective regulation of global problems moving forward, then, must be based on these legal cooperative partnerships that give a voice to NGOs, while bringing them into meaningful dialogue and cooperation with their complementary state actors and governing officials.

John V. Rafferty
Villanova University

See also Charities and Financing; Policing: Transnational; Prosecution: International; United Nations

Further Readings

Bledsoe, Robert L. et al. *The International Law Dictionary.* Santa Barbara, CA: ABC-CLIO, 1987.

Likosky, Michael, ed. *Transnational Legal Processes.* Oxford, UK: Butterworths, 2002.

Parry, John P. et al. *Encyclopedic Dictionary of International Law.* New York: Oceana, 2004.

Van Dervort, Thomas R. *International Law and Organization: An Introduction.* Thousand Oaks, CA: Sage, 1998.

NORTH AMERICA

The continent of North America covers the American landmass north of the Isthmus of Panama and includes Canada, the United States, Mexico, and the countries and dependent territories of Central America and the Caribbean. Because of their separate cultural and economic development, Central America and the Caribbean are typically treated separately; the North American Free Trade Agreement, for instance, includes as signatories only the three largest countries, Canada, the United States, and Mexico. Modern advances, the growth of the middle class and its mobility, and trade agreements have increased the sense of connectedness among North American countries. Technological advances and the increasing globalization of trade have made transactions between those living in other nations easier, including interactions that would not have been considered a generation before. While these advances have had tremendous benefits and repercussions for banking, finance, and commerce, they have also affected those involved in investigating criminal activities. Transnational crime has increased greatly in frequency and scope, involving areas that previously never experienced such activity. This surge in transnational crime has caused law-enforcement agencies in North America to explore new ways to combat this crime.

Increase in Transnational Crime

Technological advances and changed attitudes regarding mobility make it much easier for individuals, groups, or businesses from one nation to communicate and interact with those from another country on a daily basis. Customers can purchase items from a company overseas by means of a Website or other online service. Business owners often order supplies from a supplier in Country A to deliver merchandise to a customer in Country B, all while residing in Country C. While these advancements are productive in terms of socialization and business efficiency, they also prove efficient and productive for those with malicious intentions. Activities that draw the attention of law-enforcement agencies range from verbal assaults online to transnational crimes.

Many traditional law-enforcement agencies find themselves unprepared to deal with transnational crimes. Transnational crimes may occur in one country or a variety of nations, but even those that occur within a single set of borders can greatly impact residents of other countries. Some examples of transnational crimes include human trafficking, smuggling of weapons, manufacturing and trafficking of narcotics, and many financial crimes. In North America, the most common transnational crimes committed are the transportation of illegal immigrants and the movement of weapons and drugs. Organized crime groups, such as Mexican drug cartels and the Mafia, are often involved in these transactions. Mexican drug cartels are notorious for their ability to find new and unique ways to transport illicit drugs into the United States across the U.S.-Mexican border. Such trafficking has been done using underground tunnels, people who smuggle drugs within their bodies, and vehicles with hidden compartments. Many transnational crimes committed within North America are focused on the market that exists for products or actions within the United States. Although these crimes occur most often within a single nation, they negatively impact other countries involved as well. These crimes often are difficult for governments

Frank Costello, American mobster and gambling kingpin, testifying before the Kefauver Committee investigating organized crime in 1951. Costello was very well known and was the main attraction at the hearings. He agreed to testify without taking the Fifth Amendment, unlike previous mob figures taking the stand. (Library of Congress)

and law enforcement to address and are a growing global threat.

Transnational crimes are especially difficult because governments and law-enforcement agencies have had little experience investigating and prosecuting crimes that cross national borders. Additionally, the individuals and organized groups that commit these crimes are quick to adapt and use new technology and advancements that befuddle investigators. Most transnational crime is structured, organized, and sophisticated. This results in law-enforcement agencies and their governments having to think of alternative ways to combat these crimes. Organized crime groups such as the American Mafia, also known as La Cosa Nostra, have become aware of many of the methods used by law-enforcement agents and have adopted their practices to stay ahead of the authorities. Some organized crimes use legitimate businesses as fronts and well-known buildings to hide their illegal activities. These groups also have the luxury of being able to commit crimes across the globe.

Many law-enforcement agencies and national governments in North America have determined that traditional policing practices have left them ill prepared to deal with transnational crimes. A reason for this is that the government and law-enforcement agencies have historically focused on problems and crimes committed within their respective boundaries. Local police forces were developed to enforce the peace and investigate crimes facing local residents, whereas national organizations, such as the Federal Bureau of Investigation (FBI), were created to deal chiefly with national problems and to provide intelligence and forensic support to local law-enforcement agencies. Dealing with transnational crimes is relatively new to law enforcement, and efforts are being made to adopt current practices and develop new ones to meet this challenge.

Efforts to Combat Transnational Crime

U.S. law enforcement has found successful ways of prosecuting organized crime groups and other large-scale criminal activities, but these efforts have focused chiefly on combating criminal activity that occurs within the United States. Prosecuting transnational crimes has proven difficult, because potential defendants often are located in foreign countries that follow different laws and protocols. Techniques and methods that law-enforcement agencies traditionally use in the United States to obtain evidence, gain the assistance of witnesses, and prosecute organized crime groups and individuals are much less effective when used with individuals who reside outside the United States. American authorities, for example, may not use electronic surveillance obtained from another nation, provide protection to witnesses living abroad who testify on the United States' behalf, or have ready access to informants. To address these issues, governments and law-enforcement agencies throughout North America have worked to devise new ways to combat transnational crimes in North America.

A first concern to address transnational crime has been to develop alternative ways of obtaining evidence. Many transnational crimes take place within multiple countries and from great distances. Both the United States and Mexico face persistent problems relating to human trafficking and the smuggling of drugs and weapons. Although these drugs, weapons, and illegal immigrants end up in the United States, they often enter that nation from other countries, including Mexico and other Central American and Caribbean nations. Historically, law-enforcement efforts have focused on impounding the goods sought to be brought to the United States. While this prevents narcotics and contraband from reaching U.S. markets, it also prevents crime only for a limited time. Because the source of the smuggling and trafficking is not curtailed, criminals are able to continue to make future shipments of illegal goods into the United States. Because the demand for drugs in the United States has not been curtailed, the lucrative market continues. Law-enforcement agents in North America have explored ways to disrupt and eliminate the process by which such transactions occur. Noting the rapid increase in the use of technology that permits customers to purchase goods from abroad using technology, Canada, Mexico, and the United States have focused on ways of disrupting transnational crimes, including means of collaborating in addition to traditional means of national policing.

National Policing Efforts

Each North American nation attempts to keep the peace, but each also has its own method of running police operations. Differences exist with regard to the scope and scale of law-enforcement operations within nations. Smaller North American nations, for example, do not have the same resources and experience with sophisticated transnational crime that law-enforcement agencies within the United States have. The qualifications needed and training given to law enforcement and government officials may vary across countries. The resulting discrepancies among national law-enforcement systems and officials can increase the gap in the effectiveness of each country in prosecuting transnational crimes. If the officials are poorly trained, they will do little to identify those responsible for the crimes and will always lag behind the criminals. It also is much more difficult to obtain a conviction if investigations are done incorrectly or even sloppily, leading to lack of reliable evidence to prosecute. Each government and law-enforcement agency has its own rules and regulations, and those must be followed within their respective countries and jurisdictions.

The United States has several government and law-enforcement agencies that work to contain certain crimes. The FBI, established in 1908, handles federal investigations in cases where federal laws are believed to have been violated. Although the FBI often investigates crimes on its own, it also cooperates with state and local law-enforcement agencies on matters that are too sophisticated for smaller agencies to handle, including incidents involving transnational crime. The FBI maintains a sophisticated and comprehensive crime laboratory, known as the FBI Laboratory, that provides forensic analyses, logistical support, and profiling services to those investigating transnational crimes. The FBI also publishes regular reports on certain high-profile transnational crimes, such as drug trafficking, cybercrime, fraud, and arms smuggling. These reports assist the FBI's foreign partners and local U.S. law-enforcement agencies to prepare to respond to certain types of crimes. In addition to the FBI, the U.S. Immigration and Customs Enforcement (ICE) agency deals with the defense of U.S. borders. ICE agents are responsible for reducing incidents of human trafficking and smuggling of weapons and drugs. The Drug Enforcement Administration (DEA) and the Bureau of Alcohol, Tobacco, Firearms and Explosives (ATF) are among several other federal agencies that have investigative responsibility for certain criminal actions that at times are of transnational scope. These smaller federal agencies also have responsibility for the investigation, prevention, and prosecution of certain crimes.

Mexico has two primary national police agencies, the Federal Police (Policía Federal) and the Ministerial Federal Police (Policía Federal Ministerial, or PFM). The Federal Police, which are uniformed, and the PFM, who work under the guidance of the Secretariat of Public Security, are collectively known as the *federales* and work in conjunction to investigate and prevent crimes. The Federal Police function as a traditional police force, investigating crime primarily after it happens. While the PFM also may investigate crime after the fact, they serve primarily to prevent crimes. As such, the PFM often initiate programs designed to combat major crime rings, which often commit transnational crimes such as drug trafficking, illegal weapons transfers, cyberattacks, and financial fraud. Both the Federal Police and the PFM have worked extensively with American law-enforcement agencies in an effort to address transnational crimes that involve both nations, but charges of corruption among Mexican forces have frequently damaged these efforts and indeed had led to the formation of the PFM to replace the Federal Investigations Agency (Agencia Federal de Investigación), which was earlier implicated in numerous scandals.

Canada, organized into provinces and territories, has law-enforcement agencies that are organized at the local, provincial/territorial, and national levels. In addition to federal policing, the Royal Canadian Mounted Police (RCMP) operates under contract as the provincial police force in all provinces and territories except Ontario, Quebec, and Newfoundland-Labrador. The RCMP is one of the best-trained and best-known law-enforcement agencies globally. The RCMP's primary responsibility is enforcing federal laws, which include transnational matters such as financial and commercial wrongdoing, organized crime, drug trafficking, counterfeiting, smuggling, and illegal weapons trading, although the agency also is charged with mundane policing duties uncommon for most major national law-enforcement agencies. Providing forensic services and intelligence to local law-enforcement agencies, the RMPC also coordinates Canadian efforts to fight transnational crime with other nations.

Although all of the smaller North American nations have law-enforcement agencies, these are often underfunded and ill prepared to deal with sophisticated transnational crimes. In an effort to provide more resources to these nations, the United States established the School for the Americas (SOA), which has since been renamed the Western Hemisphere Institute for Security Cooperation (WHISC). The WHISC is a facility of the Department of Defense and is designed to help train police and military agents from smaller North American nations, in part to assist the United States with its War on Drugs. Located at Fort Benning, Georgia, WHISC conducts training primarily in Spanish. WHISC training focuses on a variety of skills that assist in dealing with transnational crime, including antidrug operations, technical support, and resource management. Networking opportunities that facilitate international cooperation and stem from the intermingling of police officers from a variety of nations offer one of the major benefits of WHISC training, although the process has been criticized for encouraging human rights violations.

Complications Facing International Joint Force Efforts

Because many other North American countries do not have the money to provide certain investigative, forensic, and support services to address transnational crimes, U.S. agencies often provide assistance, especially when these crimes affect the United States and its citizens. Cooperation to prevent transnational crimes sometimes causes conflicts regarding the due process and constitutional rights accorded defendants. In the United States, for example, constitutional safeguards provide defendants certain rights that restrict what law enforcement and government can do. U.S. law requires a lengthy process when either electronic surveillance or phone taps are used as a means to obtain evidence against criminals. Likewise in Canada the Charter of Rights and Freedoms dictates certain rules and protections that must be observed. Other countries may be more lenient or stricter regarding what steps law-enforcement agents may take to obtain incriminating information or evidence. What law-enforcement agents are allowed to do in one country may be illegal in another. An investigation or action must consequently be careful to adhere to the laws in the nation where evidence is gathered *and* in the nation where the defendants will be prosecuted.

Even when countries are not actively engaged in a joint effort, when they are in proximity they may hold to certain expectations of one another related to law-enforcement efforts. For instance, for years American law-enforcement officials in states near the Canadian border have complained that the border is too porous, allowing criminals to cross easily in either direction and illegal drugs to enter the United States. Canadian drug policy has generally been more liberal than American drug policy and lacks many of the provisions that U.S. federal law adopted as part of its War on Drugs—which, law-enforcement officials argue, makes Canada a more attractive venue for large-scale marijuana operations, for instance. Given this complaint, Canada's drug policy has become stricter over the years, a shift widely criticized within the country.

At the same time, the scale of the American efforts against the sale and proliferation of illegal drugs has had numerous adverse effects on both Canada and Mexico, incentivizing government corruption, creating an atmosphere conducive to organized crime and gang violence, and jailing large numbers of criminals guilty of minor drug offenses, who are then introduced to and recruited by more serious criminal networks in prison. Many of the important criminal groups in Mexico and Central America, for instance, have origins in the American prison system.

Stephen T. Schroth
Jason A. Helfer
Alejandro Varela
Knox College

See also Anticorruption Legislation; Centralization; Joint Force Policing and Integrated Models; Policing: Transnational; Racketeer Influenced and Corrupt Organizations Act; Western Europe

Further Readings

Andreas, P. *Border Games: Policing the U.S.-Mexico Divide*, 2nd ed. Ithaca, NY: Cornell University Press, 2009.

Hodgson, J. F. and C. Orban, eds. *Public Policing in the 21st Century: Dilemmas in the U.S. and Canada.* Monsey, NY: Criminal Justice Press, 2005.

Kessler, R. *The Bureau: The Secret History of the FBI.* New York: St. Martin's Press, 2002.

OFFENDERS OR OFFENSES

Transnational crime rates rose dramatically in the late 20th and early 21st centuries. Market-based activities such as trafficking dominate transnational criminal activity, providing illegal or illegally obtained goods and services to meet market demands. Drug trafficking is among the largest and most prosecuted of these crimes. Many transnational crimes are interrelated, with criminal organizations participating in a variety of criminal enterprises. The common flow of such crimes is from the developing to the developed world and often involves intermediary nations. Estimated annual profits from transnational criminal enterprise range in the billions of dollars. Transnational criminal organizations and terrorists utilize government corruption, lack of coordinated international prosecution, public complicity based on the demand for illicit goods and services, and the lack of economic opportunity in many failed states and developing nations.

Common Types of Offenses

Trafficking is one of the most common forms of transnational criminal activity. Types of illicit trafficking include drugs, arms and nuclear materials, automobiles, luxury and counterfeit goods, body organs, art and antiquities, natural and animal resources, hazardous and nuclear waste, and persons. Common natural and animal resources include elephant ivory illegally obtained from African countries. Human trafficking includes women and children sex slaves and illegal laborers and immigrants. Human trafficking is aided by limited economic opportunities in poor and developing nations, national restrictions on the global flow of immigrants and labor, and the growth of the tourism sex industry. The flow of illicit goods is generally from developing to developed countries with the exception of certain markets such as luxury automobiles and arms.

Illegal drug trafficking and sales is the most well-known and documented transnational offense. The most widely smuggled drugs include heroin and cocaine; others include methamphetamines and illegal prescription drugs. Other key transnational criminal offenses include intellectual property theft, kidnapping and extortion, terrorism, and maritime piracy. Various types of international frauds and scams have also increased in popularity, including charity frauds, stock frauds, telemarketing scams, and Internet-based frauds such as the infamous Nigerian lottery scam. The Internet has facilitated such frauds, as well as other transnational crimes such as child pornography, identity theft, illegal online banking and money laundering activities, terrorism, hacking, and other cyber crimes. The victims are usually located in wealthy, developed nations, while the perpetrators are usually located in developing nations or failed states that lack the resources and/or desire to police or prosecute.

Many types of transnational crimes are interrelated, with individual criminal organizations involved in a variety of illicit markets. Transnational criminal organizations involved in human trafficking or immigrant smuggling support other criminal activities such as document forging, while also using immigrant smuggling to extend their network's reach into other countries. Many transnational criminal organizations rely on the bribery and corruption of government and other officials to carry on illicit activities, which must sustain some degree of visibility in order to attract customers. Illicit and legal markets are also often interrelated, as illicit goods and services are sold in legal markets and vice versa. These organizations then rely on money laundering to cover the illicit nature of their profits. Terrorists utilize trafficking, fraud, and money laundering to finance their activities, sometimes working alongside criminal organizations in crimes such as narco-terrorism.

Well-Known Transnational Criminal Organizations

Globalization has extended the size and scope of transnational criminal and terrorist organizations, while also altering traditional organizational patterns. Some transnational criminals still operate within the older model of stable hierarchical organized criminal enterprises, while others operate within increasingly prevalent, newer, more loosely organized and fluid networks that follow the dictates of the global market. Transnational criminals and criminal organizations most often operate in failed states or developing countries to take advantage of lax government oversight. Common areas of origin include Africa, the countries of the former Soviet Union, Latin America, and the Caribbean.

Organized and loose criminal networks are generally characterized as market- and profit-oriented, while terrorists are generally characterized as politically or religiously oriented, and their motives are often difficult to pinpoint and their activities sometimes overlap. Transnational crimes associated with criminal organizations include racketeering, fraud, tax evasion, gambling, drug trafficking, arson, robbery, murder, torture and violence, bombings, loan-sharking, health insurance fraud, political and judicial corruption, human trafficking, prostitution, undermining licit businesses, smuggling, and money laundering and other financial crimes.

Well-known criminal organizations include the Russian Mafiya, the Italian-American La Cosa Nostra and other Italian mafia, the Japanese Yakuza and Boryokudan, the Chinese Fuk Ching, Tongs, and Snakeheads, the Hong Kong Triads, the Taiwanese Heijin, the Thai Jao Pho and Red Wa, American ethnic mafias, and street and motorcycle gangs in various countries. Well-known terrorists and terrorist organizations include Osama bin Laden and Al Qaeda. Well-known drug cartels include the Barranquilla, Medellin, Bogotá, and Cali cartels of Colombia and the Caro-Quintero, Sonora-Guadalajara, Gulf, Juarez (Amado Carrillo Fuentes), and Tijuana (Arellano Felix) cartels of Mexico. The street criminals that form the lower levels of many criminal organizations are often recruited from young urban poor and other disadvantaged groups. Some groups, such as the Chinese Snakeheads, use human smuggling to extend their international reach.

Marcella Bush Trevino
Barry University

See also Criminal Associations; Globalization; International Crimes; Narco-Terrorism; Transnational Crime: Defined

Further Readings

Brittain-Catlin, William. *Offshore: The Dark Side of the Global Economy*. New York: Farrar, Straus and Giroux, 2005.

Liddick, Don. *The Global Underworld: Transnational Crime and the United States*. Westport, CT: Praeger, 2004.

Mittelman, James H. and Robert Johnston. "Global Organized Crime." In *The Globalization Syndrome: Transformation and Resistance*, by James H. Mittelman. Princeton, NJ: Princeton University Press, 2000.

United Nations Office on Drugs and Crime. *The Globalization of Crime: A Transnational Organized Crime Threat Assessment*. New York: United Nations Publications, 2010.

ORGAN TRAFFICKING

In the UN Convention Against Transnational Organized Crime and its supporting document, the Protocol to Prevent, Suppress, and Punish Trafficking in Persons, Especially Women and Children (often shortened to the Trafficking in Persons Protocol), the concept of organ trafficking is included in the definition of the broader term *human trafficking*, which refers to the recruitment, transportation, transfer, harboring or receipt of persons, by means of the threat or use of force or other forms of coercion, of abduction, of fraud, of deception, of the abuse of power or of a position of vulnerability or of the giving or receiving of payments or benefits to achieve the consent of a person having control over another person, for the purpose of exploitation. Exploitation shall include, at a minimum, the exploitation of the prostitution of others or other forms of sexual exploitation, forced labor or services, slavery or practices similar to slavery, servitude or the removal of organs.

The last section of this definition provides the specific requirement for organ trafficking—that human organs (including cells and tissues) from living persons are removed and sold on the black market to people needing the organs in transplant procedures. Although in some instances the organs are removed from cadavers, organs are primarily obtained from living persons, since the organs are of better quality. Another variant of this process includes the use of the organs for witchcraft or other supernatural rituals. Organ trafficking requires the body parts to be transported across national boundaries, making the practice a transnational crime under the Trafficking in Persons Protocol.

The term *exploitation*, in the context of the definition above, is important in understanding the trafficking in human organs. A salient characteristic of organ trafficking involves exploitation that occurs when poor people agree to be organ donors for people who are desperate enough to pay a high price for the organs because of major deficits in legitimate avenues to secure organs for transplantation. The situation in which there exists a "money for body parts" exchange system is evidence of this exploitation. The areas that produce the largest numbers of donors are economically vulnerable; these are often developing countries. Therefore, three factors are involved in this black market activity: impoverished economic conditions for donors, a need for organ transplantation by recipients, and medical advancements that make transplantation easier.

The commonly held, media-promoted idea of organ trafficking as "organ snatching"—the forced removal of organs from unwilling victims—has found its way into many urban legends. While the forced snatching of organs, although infrequent, does occur, the actual trafficking in human organs

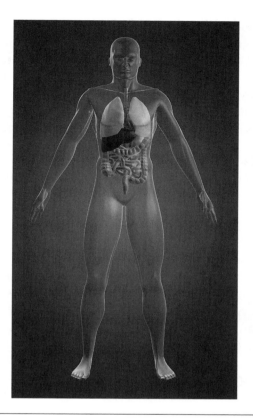

Organs are primarily trafficked from living persons because the organs are of better quality than organs removed from cadavers and will garner more on the black market. Kidneys and livers are the most common organs obtained illegally. (Photos.com)

normally involves a different process. Normally a person is agreeable, though often reluctant, to the sale of an organ for financial gain to a recipient who is in need of the organ to sustain life. In some cases prisoners waiting to be executed and the severely mentally challenged are the unwilling donors of their body parts. Because the process of licit organ donation is a lengthy one and there is a very high demand for organs and organ transplantation, the illicit route is amenable to many people around the world. The discrepancy between the donated organs and the need for transplanted organs can be extreme, as illustrated by the fact that in the United States, between 1990 and 2003, kidney donations increased by 33 percent while the recipient waiting list increased by 236 percent. Donors are often from poverty-stricken parts of the globe and desperately need the money; they decide that donating an organ, often a kidney but sometimes another key organ, is necessary for survival. The consequences to the donors can be pronounced: It is not uncommon for the donors to suffer ill health (both physical and psychological) as a result of the procedure to remove the organ; as a result, they are often unable to maintain employment, further increasing their financial problems; and, finally, they often suffer from the social stigma, from both families and communities, from being organ donors (in some villages, the practice of selling organs is considered to be similar to prostitution, for example). In addition, donors often are paid less than the agreed-upon amount or are not paid at all, exacerbating their financial problems. Patients who are awaiting legal organ transplants usually have a very long wait and are desperate for an organ. Criminal entrepreneurs often intervene to take advantage of the two desperate situations and can make a handsome profit; donors are often paid a paltry $1,000 to $5,000 for an organ, and recipients are charged much more; the brokers frequently reap a profit of between $100,000 and $200,000.

A term related to organ trafficking is *transplant tourism*, which refers to the transport of organs from a donor in one country to a national of another country, when the patient's country cannot supply its own demand for organ transplantation. Another concept is *transplant commercialism*, which refers to the notion that human organs should be treated as commodities subject to sale and purchase, like other commodities. A third term is *travel for transplantation*, which refers to the situation in which the transfer of organs occurs across national borders.

Trafficking in organs is indeed a transnational trafficking problem. One aspect that separates organ trafficking from other forms of trafficking, such as trafficking in drugs, is that the trafficked material does not result in harm to the receiver but is actually beneficial to the receiver. People who are involved with the illegal sale and purchase of human organs have been collectively dubbed the "body mafia." The players involved in organ trafficking include the donor, the recipient, the medical personnel who carry out and oversee the transplant operation, the transporters who drive one of the players (normally the recipient) to the correct destination, the brokers and other organized crime figures who carry out the transaction, and the corrupt government officials with whom the brokers have personal contact and who allow the process to remain covert. The key business organizers often use money laundering to hide the profits from the illegal activity. Several economically unstable countries produce many of the donated human organs, such as Peru, Bolivia, Brazil, and Turkey. The recipient countries include the United States, Canada, Italy, Australia, Saudi Arabia, Israel, and Japan. Donors are both male and female, although recipients are normally men.

It is difficult to know the true extent of organ trafficking throughout the world. Although the activity is often known to authorities, the brokers, donors, recipients, medical personnel, and others involved in the activity avoid exposure and for the most part succeed in remaining underground. Various initiatives to stop the practice have been proposed. In the United States, a task force was formed in 1997 by Columbia University to address the problem of organ trafficking, including the sale of organs from soon-to-be-executed prisoners. In 2004, the World Health Assembly (the decision-making body of the World Health Organization, or WHO) called on WHO's member nations of to address the problem of organ trafficking and recommended measures to protect citizens of the poorest and most vulnerable nations who are most prone to becoming illicit donors. The assembly passed a resolution at an international conference in 2008 in Turkey that involved 152 participants from 78 countries and culminated in the Declaration of Istanbul. This important document, which elaborates the principles of the Declaration of Human Rights, provided definitions of the terms *organ trafficking, transplant tourism,* and others, and provided principles for countries to control illegal organ trafficking. In 2008, the Vienna Forum to Fight Human Trafficking was convened by the United Nations (UN) Global Initiative to Fight Human Trafficking with the intention of raising awareness of the problem of human trafficking, specifically organ trafficking. Other initiatives include the Organs Watch program at the University of California (a result of 1995's Bellagio Task Force on the international traffic in organs), the Coalition for Organ-Failure Solutions (COFS), and the Initiative on Global Organ Trafficking (IGOT), which supports not only awareness of but also research on the problem. Other initiatives have been produced by a number of programs created and maintained by medical organizations and human rights organizations.

Leonard A. Steverson
South Georgia College

See also Human Smuggling; Human Trafficking

Further Readings

Budianai-Saberi, D. A. and F. L. Delmonico. "Organ Trafficking and Transplant Tourism: A Commentary on the Global Realities." *American Journal of Transplantation*, v.8 (2008).

"Declaration of Istanbul on Organ Trafficking and Transplant Tourism." *Indian Journal of Nephrology*, v.18/3 (2008).

Meyer, Silke. "Trafficking in Human Organs in Europe: A Myth or Actual Threat?" *European Journal of Crime, Criminal Law, and Criminal Justice*, v.14/2 (2006).

Scheper-Hughes, N. "The Global Traffic in Human Organs." *Current Anthropology*, v.41/2 (2000). http://pascalfroissart.free.fr/3-cache/2000-scheperhughes.pdf (Accessed October 2010).

United Nations Convention Against Transnational Organized Crime and the Protocols Thereto, 2000. http://www.unodc.org/documents/treaties/UNTOC/Publications/TOC%20Convention/TOCebook-e.pdf (Accessed October 2010).

ORGANIZED CRIME: DEFINED

Transnational crime and organized crime are concepts that have gained and continue to gain an international and domestic profile. However, there is no one definition of organized crime. The difficulty is that the concept of organized crime relates more closely to the method by which crime is committed than to a specific type of criminal activity. In a sense, it is the *process* by which a group of individuals commits crimes. Michael Woodiwiss provides us with an historical map to the widely accepted understanding of organized crime that has spread throughout the international community. He documents what he argues is the bias in what became labeled as organized crime. The view was largely driven by the U.S. preoccupation with the main Mafia crime families in the largest U.S. cities. The 1967 U.S. Task Force on Organized Crime (President's Commission on Law Enforcement and Administration of Justice) solidified a vision or version of what constituted organized crime in North America. Ever since, organized crime experts have engaged in an aggressive debate regarding the contribution made by Donald Cressey in the 1967 report. The Cressey report, titled *The Functions and Structure of Criminal Syndicates*, was further elaborated upon in his 1969 book titled *Theft of the Nation*. Cressey's most debated characteristics of organized crime (the Mafia or La Cosa Nostra) include his belief in a nationwide alliance of at least 24 tightly knit Mafia families who controlled organized crime in the United States and the idea of a rigid, ethnic-based hierarchy. Dwight Smith, along with Joseph Albini, Daniel Bell, and Alan Block, expressed skepticism about the existence of this tightly organized, alien, and conspiratorial group.

Leaving aside the more controversial findings, some core ideas from the task force and Cressey's work helped enunciate the need for distinct law-enforcement strategies against organized crime, methods that have continued to the present, and a concern regarding the potential for extensive involvement of organized crime in legitimate business. The latter became a strong justification for passing the Racketeer Influenced and Corrupt Organizations (RICO) statute. The accumulation of money—regardless of how it is acquired—makes organized crime particularly threatening in that these resources can be used to purchase corrupt officials and to further criminal activities.

Even researchers uninvolved in the organized crime debate per se have furthered the evolution of the concept. Robert Merton's sociological analysis of the political structure and function of political bosses and ward politics, Daniel Bell's analysis of "Racket Ridden Longshoremen," and William Chambliss's early work on corruption and the function of power brokers laid the groundwork for seeing links between crimes and corruption and the wider political and economic structure. As Daniel Bell stated with reference to why the rackets dominated the docks and the lives of the longshoremen: "The answer broadly, involves an understanding of the economics of the industry. . . . In our fascination these days with power and manipulation, we often ignore the economic fulcrum underneath" (1965, pp. 175–176).

In Italy, even the Mafia literature has undergone significant changes that reflect perceived modifications in the relationship between the Mafia and its role in the Italian economy. Traditionally, mafiosi were viewed as mediators of disputes in a society where the Italian state had little presence and less authority and/or acted as a predator extorting wealth from sectors of the Sicilian economy. The mafiosi's objective, it was claimed, was not the accumulation of wealth per se but of status or "honor." Pino Arlacchi argues that after the mid-1970s the money, first from cigarette smuggling and later from the drug trade, transformed the Mafia into a new "entrepreneurial" group whose capacity to corrupt and intimidate could drive down wages, cheat suppliers, defraud customers, and tap into underground sources of capital with impunity, and it began to spread throughout Italy, interfacing with corrupt elements of the major political parties and the right-wing underground terrorist network. Italy's famed 1982 Pio La Torre law created a new crime known as "Mafia conspiracy" and opened up Italy's hitherto closed banking system to police probes. In many ways this law, even more than the American RICO statute, was the precursor of the "proceeds of crime" approach to law enforcement.

However, there were dissenters to Arlacchi's views. Diego Gambetta sees the mafiosi not as entrepreneurs but as sellers of *protection*, some of which represents extortion but some of which is genuine given the weakness of the legal enforcement mechanism. He argues that it is therefore essential to differentiate between the Mafia and certain illegal enterprises in which members of the Mafia might engage. According to Gambetta, we can define the Mafia as a set of firms that

- is active in the protection industry under a common trademark with recognizable features;
- acknowledges one another as legitimate suppliers of authentic Mafia protection; and
- succeeds in preventing the unauthorized use of trademarks by private firms.

According to Gambetta, Arlacchi's fundamental error was to conflate the industry or market being protected with the firm doing the protection. In support of this view, Peter Reuter points out that much of the power of traditional organized crime in its heyday within the United States came from acting as enforcers—collecting illegal debts, union racketeering, and ensuring cartel arrangements among firms in legitimate industries.

Each country has had to come to some agreement as to how to define organized crime. The U.S. RICO model and the Italian model greatly influenced other countries. In Germany, state and federal police agencies established a commission in 1973 tasked with developing a definition of organized crime in order to revise law-enforcement strategies to counter it. The commission's work was influenced by the nature of organized crime in Germany, but it also struggled with whether it should conceptualize organized crime according to the American RICO-type paradigm or according to the German criminal law concept of the "gang." After a couple of failed versions, Germany defined organized crime as follows:

> [Organized crime] is not only to be understood in terms of a Mafia-like parallel society . . . but also as a conscious and willing, continuous cooperation in a division of labour between several persons for the purpose of committing criminal acts—frequently with the exploitation of modern infrastructure—with the aim of achieving high financial gain as quickly as possible. (Mitsilegas, 2003, quoting von Lampe)

Our understanding of organized crime is now much broader than a restricted Mafia focus. Vincenzo Ruggiero presents case materials that illustrate the essential role of professionals in facilitating many transnational crimes. He argues that white-collar crime and organized crime are increasingly blurred within the international cross-jurisdictional criminal environment. Ruggiero emphasizes the close links between legitimate business and illegitimate operations and argues that forms of social control help determine the forms crime will take. Globalization is seen to have changed social control mechanisms, in turn causing changes in criminal activity—with one result being an increasingly blurred relationship between white-collar crime and organized crime. Carlo Morselli offers scholars a social network analysis of criminal operations and, together with other academics, continues questioning and critiquing the previous stereotypes regarding the structures and operations of organized crime groups.

Specific to organized *transnational crime*, countries are bringing into force legislation that authorizes extra police investigative powers and longer sentences. A focus on money laundering and seizing the proceeds of crime, both criminally and civilly, has become a main enforcement strategy. Countries with forfeiture powers want more facilitating proceeds from crime legislation. Countries without these powers look covetously upon the much publicized, seized criminal "wealth" of their neighbors. In addition, countries without sufficiently robust seizure powers can be deemed to be in violation of various international agreements and bodies such as the Financial Action Task Force and the 2000

United Nations Convention Against Transnational Organized Crime and thereby risk various negative sanctions for being out of step with the thinking of the current international community.

Countries are under pressure to respond in a uniform manner to the numerous international agreements, conventions, and guidelines. The United Nations Convention Against Transnational Organized Crime (2000) outlines what countries agreed to bring into force in terms of the "criminalization of participation in an organized criminal group." Under the UN convention, countries agreed to criminalize the conduct of "organized criminal groups," and the convention uses terminology that describes the acts of *participation in* (or facilitating), *counseling,* and/or actual *commission* of a crime involving an organized criminal group. In essence, this UN definition has become the international view of what organized crime is as well as dictates how it ought to be controlled. Defining organized crime, however, appears to be a non-static enterprise for both researchers and policy makers.

Margaret E. Beare
York University

See also Disorganized Crime: Reuter's Thesis; Mafia Myths and Mythologies; Money Laundering: Targeting Criminal Proceeds; Profit-Driven Crime: Naylor's Typology; Racketeer Influenced and Corrupt Organizations Act; UN Convention Against Transnational Organized Crime; United Nations: Typologies of Criminal Structures

Further Readings

Albini, Joseph. *The American Mafia: Genesis of a Legend.* New York: Appleton-Century, 1971.

Albini, Joseph. "Donald Cressey's Contribution to the Study of Organized Crime: An Evaluation." *Crime and Delinquency,* v.34/3 (1988).

Albini, Joseph. "The Mafia and the Devil: What They Have in Common." *Journal of Contemporary Criminal Justice,* v.9/3 (1993).

Arlacchi, Pino. "Effects of the New Anti-Mafia Law on the Proceeds of Crime and on the Italian Economy." *Bulletin on Narcotics,* v.36/4 (1984).

Arlacchi, Pino. *Men of Dishonour.* New York: William Morrow, 1992.

Beare, Margaret E. and Tom Naylor. *Major Issues Relating to Organized Crime: Within the Context of Economic Relationships.* Law Commission of Canada, Ottawa,

Ontario. April 14, 1999. http://www.ncjrs.gov/nathanson/organized.html (Accessed January 2012).

Bell, Daniel. *The End of Ideology.* New York: Free Press, 1960.

Block, Alan. *East Side—West Side: Organized Crime in New York, 1930–1950.* Cardiff, UK: University College Cardiff Press, 1980.

Chambliss, William. 1978. *On the Take: From Petty Crooks to Presidents.* Bloomington: Indiana University Press, 1978.

Cressey, D. R. *Theft of the Nation.* New York: Harper & Row, 1969.

Gambetta, Diego. *The Sicilian Mafia: The Business of Private Protection.* Cambridge, MA: Harvard University Press, 1993.

Merton, Robert K. *On Theoretical Sociology.* New York: Free Press, 1967.

Mitsilegas, Valsamis. "From National to Global, From Empirical to Legal: The Ambivalent Concept of Transnational Organized Crime." In *Critical Reflections on Transnational Organized Crime, Money Laundering and Corruption,* Margaret E. Beare, ed. Toronto, ON: University of Toronto Press, 2003.

Morselli, Carlo. *Contacts, Opportunities, and Criminal Enterprise.* Toronto, ON: University of Toronto Press, 2005.

Naylor, R. T. "From Underworld to Underground: Enterprise Crime. 'Informal Sector' Business and the Public Policy Response." *Crime, Law and Social Change,* v.24 (1996).

Reuter, Peter. *Disorganized Crime: The Economics of the Visible Hand.* Cambridge, MA: MIT Press, 1983.

Reuter, Peter. "Racketeers as Cartel Organizers." In *The Economics and Politics of Organized Crime,* Herbert Alexander and Gerald Caiden, eds. Lexington, MA: Lexington Books, 1985.

Reuter, Peter and Diego Gambetta. "Conspiracy Among the Many: The Mafia in Legitimate Industries." In *The Economics Of Organized Crime,* Gianluca Fiorentini and Sam Peltzman, eds. Cambridge, NY: Cambridge University Press, 1995.

Ruggiero, Vincenzo. "Global Markets and Crime." In *Critical Reflections on Transnational Organized Crime, Money Laundering and Corruption,* Margaret E. Beare, ed. Toronto, ON: University of Toronto Press, 2003.

Ruggiero, Vincenzo. "Organized Crime in Italy: Testing Alternative Definitions." *Social and Legal Studies,* v.2 (1993).

Smith, Dwight. *The Mafia Mystique.* New York: Basic Books, 1975.

Task Force on Organized Crime, President's Commission on Law Enforcement and Administration of Justice. *The*

Functions and Structure of Criminal Syndicates. Washington, DC: U.S. Government Printing Office, 1967.

United Nations Convention Against Transnational Organized Crime. 2000. http://www.unodc.org/unodc/en/treaties/CTOC (Accessed January 2012).

United States Committee on the Judiciary, House of Representatives. *The Growing Threat of International Organized Crime: Hearing Before the Subcommittee on Crime*, 2d sess., January 25, 1996. Washington, DC: U.S. Government Printing Office.

Von Lampe, Klaus. *The Concept of Organized Crime in Historical Perspective.* http://www.organized-crime.de/lauhtm01.htm (Accessed January 2012).

Woodiwiss, Michael. *Gangster Capitalism: The United States and the Global Rise of Organized Crime.* New York: Carroll & Graf Publishers, 2005.

Woodiwiss, Michael. *Organized Crime and American Power.* Toronto, ON: University of Toronto Press, 2001.

ORGANIZED CRIME: ETHNIC-VERSUS MARKET-BASED

Research and police documents that have attempted to cast light on the operation of organized crime groups have looked at their criminal operations in two ways: either as ethnic-based criminal operations or as market-based criminal operations. The first tends to see organized crime groups as fairly rigid in terms of structure and limited in membership to criminals from the same ethnicity (Italian organized crime, Jamaican organized crime, and so on). Market-based organized crime operations, by contrast, are seen to be loosely "structured" with networks of different members who fulfill different tasks within that specific illegal market. The individuals within the market-structured operations are designated based on their skills, their contacts, the services that they can provide to the operation. There may be no strict separation between these two views, because (depending on the market), one or more ethnic-based criminal groups may have more access to illicit goods or services, and perhaps the ethnic communities they represent may place more of a demand on securing those illegal goods.

A market is an organized relational system made up of infrastructures that allow individuals or businesses to sell their goods, services, and labor to others in exchange for currency, others' goods, or information. Markets can relate to the environment and context in which the relationships are formed and can differ in size, scope, and types of goods and services. Most markets are based on consumers' demand; hence, markets can be illegal or legal. In both legal and illegal markets, supply and demand are based on what is significant to the people living in the environment, including ethnic groups living in the market area. Some call this ethnic marketing, which is built on the understanding of what factors are significant to ethnic groups contextually; the market depends on establishing a product base related to this knowledge. Ethnicity is therefore at times a key factor in operations related to many areas of criminal activity.

In most developed nations, markets are classified as mixed economies where the market is driven by supply and demand; the government is involved only to provide order, through regulation, tariffs, tax incentives and subsidies, and other means. The market generates revenue and allows the distribution and provision of resources in a society. In some circumstances, laws and rules for markets are created so that the environment as a whole is protected and a status quo is maintained—for example, monitoring the border to ensure that some fruits and vegetables do not cross state or international territory lines, in order to prevent the spread of disease or pests that they could carry.

Illegal or black markets constitute the exchange of goods, services, labor, or information that is prohibited but for which there is a high demand because of their scarcity or unavailability in that society's traditional markets. It is probable that taxes are not paid on these items. Examples include classified information, illegal drugs, firearms, and prostitution, to name a few. Usually, as in traditional markets, the items in demand can be common to the environment or region but scarce as a result of government regulations. Most societies, since they are built on an entrepreneurial structure that is regulated by government, develop black markets to meet these needs by circumventing regulations imposed on restricted goods and services. Black markets tend to develop more readily between environments with very different levels of regulation. For example, most illegal drugs originate in areas with lesser restrictions or where the product is in greater abundance and then is smuggled into areas with higher restrictions. Even though a good or service becomes outlawed or heavily regulated, the market may continue to meet the demand. As a result, the black market springs up to meet consumers' demands.

Often, illegal markets emerge because ethnic minorities in the area lack the skills or education needed to be a part of the society's traditional markets. The lure of huge profits and quick access to the outward trappings of the wealthy minorities draw many to illegal activities. Illegal markets are seen as a tool for economic empowerment, to seek opportunities not otherwise open and to create economic equality. Moreover, illegal markets also create a society that has a centralized structure that allocates leadership and authority pertaining to the goods and services of that particular ethnic trade group. For example, during Prohibition, Italian immigrants were overseeing alcohol-related illegal activities that created jobs for many of the U.S. Italian immigrant population during the 1920s and early 1930s. These jobs boosted the economy of the traditional economic system and created revenue for this ethnic group to gain skills or support the group. Most consumers of black market products are willing to overlook the illegality of the transaction if they feel that the good or service is "harmless"; however, the money generated is often used to continue or expand illegal activity. The Italian Mafia in the United States thrived during Prohibition, resulting in bloody battles over turf and profits. Governments combating black markets spend vast fortunes fighting organized crime and racketeering and lose millions in tax revenues from the prohibited good.

Just as the divisions between countries' economic markets have become blurred and diminished, the lines between different ethnic black markets have done the same. New borderlines between lawful and unlawful conduct have emerged. The divisions between ethnic groups are no longer as rigid as they were because of economic pressure to maintain a share of the illegal market. A fluid network of associations links these ethnic markets based on supply and demand. An illegal market based on ethnicity alone can no longer depend on its regular consumers to support it because, as in the legal market, price drives the consumer's decisions. This fluid network allows illegal markets to communicate and do business with one another, providing the best price for the consumer and keeping previously ethnic-based markets alive.

Debra Warner
Maria Pasqualetti
The Chicago School of Professional Psychology

See also Alien Conspiracies and Protection Systems; Centralization; Criminal Associations; Organized Crime: Defined

Further Readings

Bovenkerk, F., D. Siegel, and D. Zaitch. "Organized Crime and Ethnic Reputation Manipulation." *Crime, Law and Social Change*, v.39/1 (2003).

Chua, A. L. "Markets, Democracy, and Ethnicity: Toward a New Paradigm for Law and Development." *Yale Law Journal*, v.10 (1998).

Chua, A. L. "The Privatization-Nationalization Cycle: The Link Between Markets and Ethnicity in Developing Countries." *The Columbia Law Review*, v.95/2 (1995).

Weber, M. *Economy and Society*. 1922. Reprint, Guenther Roth et al., trans. Berkeley: University of California Press, 1978.

PHARMACEUTICALS

Transnational Internet-facilitated commerce in pharmaceuticals, legal or illicit, presents interesting issues and problems. Contributing to the difficulty in defining these issues is the quasi-legal status that some international Internet-based sales, such as ethical Canadian pharmacies, present for bargain-hunting consumers. Although a few online pharmacies are legitimate and require a doctor's prescription before they will supply and send the drug to the consumer, most do not. These may require filling out an online questionnaire that is supposedly examined by a "cyberdoctor"; the pharmacy may be based in a country where a prescription is not required for the drug in question (or, for that matter, for any drug). If these sites are shut down by government edict or by the Internet service provider, they can start up again in matter of hours under a different address and with another Internet service provider.

Some 300 overtly bogus Internet pharmacies were uncovered by one researcher; this figure is thought to be very conservative. Most advertise easy and cheap availability of various controlled substances such as benzodiazepines (sedatives), opioids (analgesics), and stimulants (such as Adderal and Ritalin). Many of these are located in Third World countries that impose few or no regulations on Internet commerce or pharmaceutical sales.

Problems With Internet Pharmacies

Of course the most pressing problem with bogus Internet pharmacies is that they are selling therapeutically active and potentially dangerous agents without requiring a proper physical examination performed by a qualified physician. This is especially problematic as not all drugs sought by Internet-using "patients" are psychoactive stimulants or sedatives. Some with legitimate medical problems may be trying to self-diagnose and self-medicate in order avoid expensive visits to a doctor and the associated tests and revisits. Self-diagnosis is a questionable behavior in itself; as the proverb goes, only a fool acts as his own physician. For example, taking antibiotics for a sore throat is often the wrong approach; the problem may not be an infection but an allergy, acid reflux disease, or a more serious condition. A doctor who has ordered and analyzed the appropriate tests should be the one to make that diagnosis and prescribe treatment, not someone poking his or her computer keys at midnight. Although some online pharmacies offer cyberdoctors, it is doubtful that they can give the patient the level of care that he or she would receive from a physician conducting a physical examination and tests. Even if well intentioned, such online doctors can have no detailed knowledge of the patient's medical history or what other drugs that he or she might be taking, and they cannot order or analyze critical tests. Some customers have ordered drugs for erectile dysfunction without determining if there might be a serious medical condition at the base of their particular problem. Such drugs are widely marketed at these pharmacies and are sometimes linked to pornographic Websites. Fraudulent Internet pharmacies are motivated to sell products to make a profit, not to issue correct diagnoses, and they do not subscribe to a code of ethical practice. In general, online pharmacy Websites typically do not warn consumers about drug risks or contraindications and, when based in foreign countries (as is typical) do not generally declare their shipped contents to customs as drugs.

Another issue with Internet pharmacies is that they sometimes package drug A as drug B. That is, a patient ordering lorazepam, a benzodiazepine, might receive what is purportedly a "generic" version that actually contains a weakened dosage of a major tranquilizer, a totally inappropriate and potentially hazardous treatment. Drugs may also be of inferior quality or contain buffers and other ingredients that are not approved for use in the country of the purchaser. Sometimes the fillers used to bulk up and slow release of the active ingredients may actually be dangerous and toxic. Cases in which pharmacies have knowingly dispensed expired drugs have frequently been reported. Online pharmacies have also been known to dispense pills that are fake look-alikes; some of these are simply ineffective and may be placebos, and others may again contain dangerous substances. In Europe, 62 percent of drugs purchased online are substandard or fakes. Patients counting on that drug to their lower blood pressure or to control their asthma may find themselves getting much worse. A sad fact is that many who order therapeutic drugs online are poor or elderly on fixed incomes who are simply trying to economize. Some 22 percent of the elderly skip doses or cannot fill prescriptions as written and are not ordering drugs for recreational use or to get high; such persons are often unaware of the health dangers and legal issues that may result from ordering from such sources. That being said, some seniors, having come of age in the 1960s, are, in fact, ordering drugs such as Viagra and other "lifestyle" drugs for recreational purposes.

Whether people are ordering drugs online to address legitimate health issues or for recreational or illegitimate reasons, law-enforcement agencies are particularly concerned with minors and young adults gaining illegal access to controlled substances,

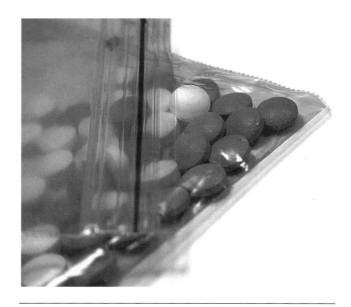

A small number of online pharmacies are legitimate and require a doctor's prescription to fill an order, but most Internet pharmacies are operating illegally. Many are located in less developed countries that impose few or no regulations on Internet commerce or pharmaceutical sales. (Photos.com)

such as benzodiazepines and opioids, for recreational use. Moreover, these drugs may be sold to users other than the original patient and become a genuine hazard. Major concerns are that addiction might develop and overdoses might occur. Moreover, increased emergency room visits are often attributable to Internet-ordered pharmaceuticals.

Another problem with fraudulent Internet pharmacies is that they can be used as vehicles for terrorist attacks. Although this seems rather far-fetched at first blush, it is entirely plausible to envision cases in which both illegal and legal pharmacies could be used to send out contaminated cosmetics or pharmaceuticals; such preparations might contain poisons, chemical wastes, bacteria (such as anthrax), or various viruses. Such packages would not excite official interest if they did not contain controlled substances and could pass through customs undetected. In the process, thousands could be infected. Terrorists could then shut down their operation and vanish before public health officials could determine where the problem originated. To combat this eventuality, experts suggest the creation of a strong regulatory system that would have to exist on a global scale. The political and logistical obstacles to such a system, however, are legion.

Individuals can protect themselves from the problems associated with online pharmaceuticals by using only local brick-and-mortar pharmacies or approved mail-order pharmacies (whose use is sometimes mandated by medical insurance companies). The savings can be considerable in the latter instance, and reputable mail-order Canadian pharmacies can offer substantial discounts. Customers should never order from a company that is not licensed to dispense drugs in the state where the patient resides. Furthermore, patients should be wary of a site that dispenses drugs without a prescription. Sites without a U.S. address or telephone number are suspect, as are sites that offer no information or inserts on the drug (its use, dosage, potential side effects, and so on). Moreover, one should never take an Internet pharmacy's claims to be accredited and located in the United States at face value.

Club Drugs

In the early to mid-1970s, various "club drugs"—drugs used in concert with attendance at discotheques and often favored in the gay community—became fashionable. In that era, Quaaludes (methaqualone), a strong sedative and reputed "love drug," was available by prescription. When it was banned from manufacture in the United States, it was smuggled from Europe and, more frequently, from Mexico. Ultimately it became almost unobtainable by the early 1980s. By the 1990s, MDMA, or Ecstasy, became a popular club drug, both in the United States and abroad. It is an amphetamine with psychedelic properties often used where young people congregate: in discotheques and other clubs and at "house parties" and raves. The drug is reputed to increase empathy and produce a sense of intimacy. It is legitimately used in therapy to help couples break down communication barriers. The drug's reputed harmfulness is widely disputed. For example, in the Netherlands it has been widely tolerated by law enforcement and viewed as a mild recreational drug. The drug is not so regarded in the United States by most criminal justice personnel. In the first decade of the 2000s, the use of Ecstasy doubled among high school seniors and was widely available nationwide. It is widely thought that the drug is manufactured in the Netherlands or Belgium and marketed by many crime syndicates. One such group, operating in Arizona, was run by mafiosi (specifically by a former hired killer who had been relocated there by the Federal Witness Protection Program) in concert with Israeli mobsters. Russian organized crime groups have also been named as traders in this drug. One Israeli, Oded Tuito, trafficked millions of MDMA doses into the United State; the drug was imported from Frankfurt, Paris, and Brussels.

Typically the drug is brought into the United States, then broken into smaller units and shipped by carriers to dealers in other cities. The Tuito organization used dozens of topless dancers as couriers. These women brought in 30,000 to 60,000 units at a time and returned to Europe with thousands of dollars on their persons. One would have thought that such unusual "mules" (those who smuggle drugs secreted on their persons) would have attracted the interest of customs officials early in the scheme. In 2001, the seizure of one shipment on an Air France flight from Paris netted 210,100 hits of this drug. The general levels of seizures went from 400,000 in 1997 to 9.3 million in 2000. Today the drug enjoys worldwide popularity and is frequently manufactured and used in Asia and well as in North America and Europe.

Francis Frederick Hawley
Western Carolina University

See also Biopiracy; Cocaine; Drug Trade: Legislative Debates; Drug Trade: Source, Destination, and Transit Countries; Heroin

Further Readings

Cohen, J. "Pushing the Borders: The Moral Dilemma of International Internet Pharmacies." *Hasting Center Report*, v.34/2 (2004).

Letkeiwicz, S. and A. Gorksi. "The Potential Dual Use of Online Pharmaceuticals." *Science and Engineering Ethics*, v.16 (2010).

Maxwell, R. and D. Webb. "Internet Pharmacy: A Web of Mistrust?" *British Journal of Clinical Pharmacology*, v.66/2 (2008).

Piracy: Failed States

Piracy has increased dramatically off the coast of Somalia over the last 10 years. In 2007, 16 percent of all reported piracy took place in Somali waters. By 2010, piracy attacks in Somalia's waters accounted for 50 percent of reported attacks. It is suspected that Somali pirates are particularly successful because when they are arrested, officials settle by taking a share of the goods or money that the pirates have accumulated. Additionally, those arrested for piracy typically are released quickly and resume their trade. The complicit nature of officials exacerbates piracy. The systemic collusion between offenders and officials is a characteristic of a weak state. However, Somalia is more than a weak state; it is a failed state.

The recent rapid explosion of piracy cases off the coastal waters of Somalia is an indicator of the endemic violence that has plagued the country since its centralized government collapsed in 1991. Armed groups fight for dominance over scant resources in a nation lacking supplies. Continued and pervasive internal conflict creates even higher demand for food sources when there are limits to available food due to the impaired infrastructure and land. Engaging in piracy and ransom collection are reliable methods for garnering needed funds. As a result, Somali waters are the most dangerous shipping lanes in the world.

Piracy began in Somalia when local fishermen were unable to sustain themselves due to depleted fish stocks. For hundreds of years Somalis relied upon fishing for income as well as a primary food source. In the 1990s, most of the world's fish stocks were depleted by the large fishing vessels of the wealthiest nations. The Somali fishermen found foreign-flagged trawlers draining their coastal fish stocks. With little recourse and no other source of income or food, the desperate fishermen created de facto navies that harassed foreign fishing fleets. Eventually, enterprising criminal warlords understood that these unofficial maritime crews could be recruited into piracy.

Piracy succeeds in Somalia because government officials are so corrupt that they submit to the demands and practices of the organized groups that engage in the pursuit of ransom, the taking of hostages, and the seizure of cargos. The coastline of Somalia, like the interior of the country, is beholden to the warlords who control the transfer of commodities and currency. The Transitional Federal Government, the 14th attempt since 1991 to create a permanent government authority, has been unable to establish stability or democracy in the beleaguered nation. All efforts to suppress the tribalism that dominates life in Somalia have failed. In 2009, the Council of Foreign Affairs ranked Somalia as the most unstable, dangerous, and failed state in the world.

Indicators of failed states include continuous and significant human flight from the area, a collapsed economy with little potential for recovery in the short term or without significant long-term aid from other nations, lack of infrastructure and social services, sustained high demand for food with a decreased sustainability rate of agricultural products or secure water sources, large-scale disputes over land or territories, consistent exclusion of local groups from political processes, emergence of militias that are supported or act on behalf of government agencies or offices, widespread corruption of political power structures, and a high crime rate that cannot be addressed effectively by the local criminal justice system. The United Nations agreed with the U.S. government's position that an international cooperative patrol was needed to ensure safe passage off the Somali coast. The ongoing collaboration by various nations' navies demonstrates the universal acknowledgment of Somalia's lawless shores.

Although piracy takes place in many areas of the world, contemporary focus has been largely on Somalia. While the inadequacies of the government in Somalia can lead to the conclusion that piracy is the result of failed states, data from the previous 20 years indicate otherwise. For most of the 20th century, maritime piracy was concentrated in Southeast Asia. The waters of the Malacca Straits, the Straits of Singapore, and the South China Sea represent areas that have been plagued in modern times by hundreds of piratical attacks. The bordering nations of Singapore, Indonesia, and Malaysia are not considered failed states, yet piracy flourished in this region for decades. The reason had more to do with transnational shipping patterns, natural chokepoints in the waterways, and the role of state-supported piracy.

Portrayals of piracy vary greatly in the media, stimulating dramatically different responses. The success of pirates in Asian waters and the western Pacific did not create a stir in the American press, whereas a few notable incidents in the Gulf of Aden, off the African coast, did. Extensive coverage by the media of the *Maersk Alabama* incident, involving a U.S.-registered vessel that was taken over by Somali pirates in April 2009, helped to stimulate an intense response by the U.S. federal government. The government not only sent a U.S. naval vessel, the U.S.S. *Bainbridge*, but also a number of Federal Bureau of Investigation agents who negotiated with the four Somali pirates involved in the piracy. A military response by the world's preeminent superpower to a civilian, commercial crime has furthered the notion that Somalia cannot control its own waterways. The response by the U.S. Navy sent the message that regional government officials cannot be relied upon to assert their authority in domestic waterways.

Karen K. Clark
Western Oregon University

See also Failed States; Piracy: History; Transnational Crime: Defined

Further Readings

Abruzzese, Leo. "The Worst Country on Earth." *The Economist*. World in 2010 Supplement (2009).

Arman, Abukar. "Piracy, Geopolitics and Private Security." *The Huffington Post* (April 24, 2009).

Gettleman, Jeffrey. "The Most Dangerous Place in the World." *Foreign Policy* (March/April 2009).

Hastings, James V. "Geographies of State Failure and Sophistication of Maritime Piracy Hijackings." *Political Geography*, v.28/4 (2009).

Kraska, James, and Brian Wilson. "Somali Piracy: A Nasty Problem, a Web of Responses." *Current History*, v.108 (2009).

Piracy: History

Since the 1980s, piracy has emerged as an international problem, raising the concern of national governments as well as ship owners and transportation companies. However, piracy is an old phenomenon, dating back to the beginning of seafaring, and the analysis of its history and causes can facilitate the understanding of its modern manifestations. For a complete narration of its history throughout the centuries, enumerating all the forms in which it manifested itself, the definition of piracy proposed by the International Maritime Bureau of the International Chamber of Commerce (the ICC-IMB) is preferred to narrower definitions. The ICC-IMB defines maritime or sea piracy as any act of boarding or attempting to board a ship, regardless of the location of the incident. Both piratical attacks on the high seas and cases of armed robbery against ships in territorial waters or in port are hence included in the definition. The ICC-IMB definition also specifies that the aim of the attack must be the commission of a theft or another crime and that pirates must use or be willing to use force in the furtherance of the act.

Modern piracy is a transnational phenomenon, since it involves the ship owners, crew members, ports, and territorial waters of different states. However, it is a local problem as well, particularly concentrated in a few areas: Southeast Asia, Somali waters, the West African coast, and parts of South America. Indeed, piracy arises in geographically favorable areas, namely along the main trading routes. Pirates also favor territories with coves and coastal outlets of creeks, where they can easily hide, as well as narrow seas that foster the concentration of transport ships—and thus the concentration of targets.

In addition to geographical factors, certain political and socioeconomic conditions are more likely to encourage piracy than others. In past centuries, governments have at times tolerated and even supported piracy. Although the explicit support of piratical activities has ended, political instability or state failure is still a favorable condition for piracy. On the one hand, weak governments are unable to enforce effective piracy countermeasures; on the other, in these states pirates can often benefit from the presence of corrupt government and police officials and thus act undisturbed.

The history of piracy confirms the importance of the above-mentioned factors in the birth and development of the phenomenon. The first piracy-prone area was the Mediterranean Sea, characterized by the presence of coves and bays where pirates could easily hide. Moreover, since it is an enclosed sea with many islands, ships often sailed close to the shore, becoming more vulnerable to attacks.

The first recorded piratical attack dates back to the 14th century B.C.E., when the Lukkans, based in Asia Minor, raided Cyprus. Besides being one of the first groups of sea raiders, the Lukkans first benefited from the protection of a foreign power—in this case the Hittites—in exchange for their pledge not to attack Hittite ships.

The lack of a nation with a powerful navy capable of and invested in patrolling the Mediterranean is another reason for the proliferation of piracy in the ancient world. The Greeks were organized in independent city-states, often at war with one another and in some cases encouraging piracy. Even when Athens achieved naval and political power, its navy never succeeded in completely eliminating the pirates that infested their own arm of the Mediterranean, the Aegean Sea.

At the beginning of their history, most of the Romans were employed in agriculture, and maritime trade constituted only a small part of their economy. The control over the Mediterranean then devolved upon Rhodes and Carthage; as a result, when the Romans defeated these two powers in 166 B.C.E. and 146 B.C.E., respectively, piracy soared. In the 1st century B.C.E., Rome had become a trading nation and finally decided to limit the phenomenon. In 74 B.C.E., Pompey was entrusted with a large fleet, and in less than three months piracy was mostly eliminated. Even though some pirates resisted in the frontier areas, especially in the Black Sea, piracy ceased to be a serious threat to maritime trade for the following four centuries.

With the collapse of the Western Roman Empire in 476 C.E., the Byzantine Empire took charge of maintaining control over the Mediterranean. After the sacking of Constantinople by Crusaders in 1204, piracy revived, and several Aegean islands and mainland ports became safe havens for pirates. In the Adriatic Sea, piracy revived as well, and the Dalmatians restarted the piratical activities they had partially abandoned when the Byzantines controlled the region.

The situation changed again in the 16th century. From that moment and for more than four centuries thereafter, the Mediterranean was infested by Barbary corsairs, who had their bases in the principalities of the northern African coast. Piracy in those times was sponsored by states and involved primarily acts of depredation, with pirates plundering villages and towns and capturing their inhabitants, who were subsequently either enslaved or released after the payment of a ransom. Their success also depended upon the attitude of European nations, which tolerated Barbary pirates for a long time and never combined their efforts to eradicate the phenomenon. The end of the Barbary corsairs came only after the French conquest of North Africa in 1830.

During the Middle Ages, the Vikings also started to plunder villages along the northwestern European coast. While Mediterranean pirates also attacked vessels, both under way and anchored at ports, coastal villages and towns constituted the Vikings' sole targets, and they used ships only to reach them. In some cases, instead of preying on villages, they preferred to extort payment in return for protection. Their first attack was in 789, and from that time on, regular expeditions were undertaken. They also started to extend their influence and to conquer and

settle in those territories they were infesting—especially the British islands and Normandy. In 1241, the Hanseatic League was formed to limit their power; the Vikings were finally defeated, but their defeaters soon replaced them with their own piratical activities.

About three centuries later, in the early 16th century, English pirates started to attack Spanish vessels coming back from the West Indies laden with gold, silver, and New World commodities and products. After its early exploration of the Americas, Spain had claimed the sole right to establish colonies there and to trade with indigenous Americans. At the beginning of their activities, British and later French and Dutch pirates had their bases in Europe, from where they sailed to intercept Spanish fleets in the eastern Atlantic Ocean. By the early 17th century, however, French and English pirates had moved closer to their targets and established bases in the Caribbean, where a large number of small islands with coves and bays along their shorelines allowed them to hide from Spanish fleets, which could not effectively patrol such a vast area. These pirates were dubbed privateers and were legitimated by their governments through "letters of marque" (which conferred permission to attack and prey on vessels of any nationality listed in the letter). Piracy was then legalized—although Spain still considered privateers to be criminals—and in the meantime the British, French, and Dutch governments benefited from piratical activities that resulted in Spain's financial decline. This situation lasted until the 1670s, when Spain was so economically weakened by the continual attacks that it was no longer necessary to perpetrate them. Britain first, followed by France, offered pardons to their privateers; some of them, however, preferred to go on practicing piracy, shifting their attacks to ships of any nationality. Several expeditions against piracy followed, until the British navy finally curbed it at the beginning of the 18th century.

In the first decade of the 19th century, Spain's colonial possessions in the West Indies sought independence, causing political turmoil. Again, privateers received permission to attack Spanish vessels. Spain issued several letters of marque as well, authorizing other privateers to prey on ships of the emerging nations. Again the British, in this case with the support of the Americans, brought piracy to an end in the Caribbean in the early 19th century.

Piracy in Asia has a long history as well. The first record of piracy dates back to the Hammurabi code, which provided for norms against piracy in response to repeated attacks on Sumerians by pirates. However, piracy became a serious menace in the Persian Gulf only in the late 18th century, when Arab corsairs began to threaten British ships sailing to and from the East Indies. The Persian Gulf was a fundamental passage for European trading ships. These pirates had their bases on the western coast of the Arabian Peninsula and usually attacked vessels under way, while they were passing through the Persian Gulf or sailing the Indian Ocean. In the first decades of the 19th century three expeditions against Arab pirates were organized by the East India Company, with the support of the British navy, and the third one in 1819 resulted in a substantial and lasting decline of piratical activities in that area.

Since the 16th century, pirates have also threatened vessels coming from the East Indies by sailing around the Cape of Good Hope. Trading ships sailing to Europe were attacked while under way, and crew members were often killed. These attacks took place along both the western coast of Africa and the eastern African coast, especially off the island of Madagascar, famous as a safe haven for pirates.

Pirates also attacked European ships in the Malay Archipelago, characterized by thousands of small islands with many bays and creeks, where pirates could hide, and a number of straits through which vessels were forced to pass, becoming more vulnerable to attacks. These pirates were particularly hard to combat because they could count upon the protection of many of the sultans who governed the islands. In the 1840s, however, the British navy, with several expeditions, defeated pirates operating in the Malay Archipelago, especially those along the northern coast of Borneo and in the Strait of Malacca.

In the 19th century, piracy also developed along the coasts of China, especially close to the main ports of Hong Kong and Macao. Chinese pirates usually attacked vessels of their own nationality, and killings of passengers and crew members were frequent. When pirates started to organize themselves in large groups and attack foreign vessels, the British and the Americans intervened, and by the second half of the century they had suppressed Chinese piracy.

Since the 1980s, piracy has reemerged and attacks have gradually increased. The enabling factors do not differ from the ones that have favored the development of piracy throughout history. However, the types of attacks have changed, and they differ from one area to another. Acts of depredation and plundering of coastal villages and towns, frequently carried out in the ancient world and during the Middle Ages, have ended; the boarding of vessels in port areas and attacks of ships under way have increased, with pirates traveling farther away from shore. Moreover, piracy attacks in Southeast Asia usually take place in territorial waters against ships, which are often hijacked and robbed of their entire cargo. Somali pirates, on the other hand, frequently act in international waters, kidnapping the crew members or passengers and demanding ransom. Finally, attacks along the West African coast and in South America are characterized by the frequent use of violence against persons; the targets of these attacks are usually berthed or anchored ships from which the crew's personal effects, as well as the ship's equipment and often the entire cargo, are stolen.

Giulia Berlusconi
Università Cattolica/Transcrime

See also Failed States; Piracy: Failed States; Transnational Crime: Defined

Further Readings

Gosse, Philip. *The History of Piracy*. London: Longmans, Green, 1934.

ICC International Maritime Bureau. "Annual Piracy Reports." http://www.icc-ccs.org/piracy-reporting-centre/piracynewsafigures (Accessed February 2011).

Konstam, Angus. *Piracy: The Complete History*. Oxford, UK: Osprey, 2008.

Wombwell, James A. *The Long War Against Piracy: Historical Trends*. Fort Leavenworth, KS: Combat Studies Institute Press, U.S. Army Combined Arms Center, 2010.

Police Cooperation

Police cooperation across national and international borders is increasingly important, given the greater interaction between national police services in the course of dealing with transnational crime and their role in international peacekeeping and in relation to natural disasters. A number of trends signal a greater movement toward global systems of law enforcement: the negotiation of bilateral and multilateral law-enforcement agreements, the inclusion of foreign police agents in training programs, the stationing of liaison officers in foreign countries, and further development of transnational police organizations at both regional and wider international levels.

The local, regional, and global dimensions of transnational crime pose a number of challenges for effective policing. Such crimes may be difficult to detect (as in the case of some forms of toxic pollution that are not detectable by human senses, such as radioactive emissions from nuclear plants after disasters). They may demand intensive cross-jurisdictional negotiation and intervention, and even disagreement between nation-states, in regard to specific events or crime patterns. Some crimes, such as illegal drug trading or the illegal arms trade, may be highly organized and involve criminal syndicates. Others may include a wide range of criminal actors, ranging from the killing of endangered species by individual collectors to the systematic disposal of toxic waste via third parties. These various dimensions of criminality and harm pose particular challenges for law enforcement, especially from the point of view of police interagency collaboration, the nature of investigative techniques and approaches, and the different types of knowledge required for dealing with specific kinds of crime. Moreover, many of the operational matters pertaining to transnational crime are inherently international in scope and substance.

Criminal justice responses take varied forms, and police are required to orient their tasks in relation to different agencies and institutions. The International Criminal Court (ICC), for instance, deals with cases of gross violations of human rights, war crimes, and crimes against humanity. The police role here is basically to investigate and prosecute in the context of international law, and in relation to international legal institutions whose jurisdiction is agreed to by participating countries. Some countries, such as the United States, have decided not to acknowledge the legitimacy and powers of the ICC. In this instance, therefore, specific participation in particular kinds of policing is bounded by whether or not a particular nation-state is a signatory country.

International police cooperation takes other forms as well. Countries may have bilateral relationships with other countries, involving specific police agencies. For instance, U.S. federal law-enforcement agencies such as the Drug Enforcement Administration, the Federal Bureau of Investigation, and U.S. Customs all have offices in foreign countries (including Canada, Mexico, Panama, Uruguay, Italy, and the United Kingdom). Likewise, the Australian Federal Police have active police contingents in places such as the Solomon Islands and regional offices in Indonesia and other parts of Southeast Asia and the Pacific. Under a United Nations (UN) mandate, police have also been intrinsically involved in peacekeeping missions associated with transitional policing situations in places such as Timor-Leste (East Timor), the Democratic Republic of the Congo, Kosovo, Burundi, and Sudan.

From the point of view of international law enforcement, agencies such as the International Criminal Police Organization (Interpol) provide an organizational platform to address major crimes such as terrorism; illegal trade in arms, drugs, and wildlife; and human trafficking. The role of personnel working within and in collaboration with Interpol tends to be advisory rather than substantive. That is, Interpol acts as a conduit for the exchange of information, training, intelligence, and operational knowledge but does not necessarily carry out direct investigations per se. It provides an active forum in which criminal investigators from around the globe meet to discuss issues such as determining the role of organized crime in specific types of criminal enterprises (such as people smuggling) and developing training and enforcement actions to combat

A U.S. Customs and Border Patrol agent monitors the Canada–United States border near Sweet Grass, Montana. National and international police cooperation is crucial given the transborder nature of illegal criminal operations—across state as well as international boundaries. (U.S. Department of Homeland Security)

particular sorts of criminal activity (such as illegal oil pollution of oceans, seas, and inland waterways).

At a regional level, and particularly in light of the further development of the European Union as a political and economic body, agencies such as Europol (the European Police Office) have emerged. Europol was initially established to deal with illicit drug issues in a way that involves active collaboration among national police services throughout Europe, including (among others) those of the Netherlands, Belgium, Germany, and France. It performs a coordinating function similar to that provided by Interpol.

The transborder nature of illegal criminal operations—across state as well as international boundaries—means that often a local police service (such as the Toronto Metropolitan Police) or state/provincial police service (such as the Ontario Provincial Police) will necessarily have to work collaboratively with national agencies (such as the Royal Canadian Mounted Police). These national agencies, in turn, will have relationships with regional partner organizations (such as Interpol). In some instances, as with the Task Force on Organized Crime in the Baltic Sea Region (which includes representatives from Denmark, Estonia, the European Commission, Finland, Germany, Latvia, Lithuania, Poland, Russia, and Sweden), specific organizational structures are established in order to share intelligence, in this instance on environmental crime, and to develop cooperative enforcement structures to deal with offenders.

Dealing with transnational crime demands new ways of thinking about the world, the development of a global perspective on analysis of issues and trends, the formation of formal and informal networks, and a commitment to particular crimes (such as drug trafficking) or thematic areas (such as cybercrime) as priority areas on which to focus concerted police intervention. The challenges faced by police in affluent countries of the West will be different from those faced by counterparts in Third World countries, in countries undergoing rapid social and economic changes, and in countries where coercion and corruption are generally unfettered by stable institutional controls. Law-enforcement practices and institutions in countries such as Brazil, Mexico, Indonesia, and the Philippines are beset by problems like poor interagency cooperation, inadequate budgetary resources, and technical deficiencies in laws,

agency policies, and procedures. These challenges are not unique to these countries: More investment in enforcement policy, enforcement capacity, and performance management is essential, regardless of jurisdiction.

The adoption of particular kinds of policing models across jurisdictions is an ongoing and contentious issue, especially in areas such as public order policing. The assumptions about the policed, the techniques and style of intervention, and the operational strategies employed to deal with events such as riots all have an impact on the course and consequences of these events. The policing of demonstrations in recent years has been accompanied by critical examination of policing practices, including police violence and overreaction, whether in Melbourne, Seattle, or Genoa. Years of experience with demonstrations, across many different national contexts, have been consolidated into forward planning and preventative work that draw upon a mix of coercive, persuasive, and information strategies. Issues surrounding public order policing relate to matters such as the influence of the wider political environment on specific event policing, the tensions between paramilitary styles and peacekeeping modes of operation, and the precipitation and amplification of violence that may result from the policing approach adopted.

Specific forms of criminal law enforcement will require collaboration between different nation-states and different police services. The development of capabilities in the specific area of transnational law enforcement is necessary—and inevitable, given world trends. This includes the "soft skills" of interpersonal communication that enhance cooperation between groups. An important part of this process is the development of a shared consciousness of issues and a sense of what represents justice among enforcement personnel. Understanding the complexities of global issues is an important step in forging a transnational value system protective of collective social interests and human rights.

Rob White
University of Tasmania

See also Europol; Globalization; Policing: Transnational

Further Readings

Andreas, P. and E. Nadelmann. *Policing the Globe: Criminalization and Crime Control in International Relations.* Oxford, UK: Oxford University Press, 2006.

Haberfeld, M. and I. Cerrah, eds. *Comparative Policing: The Struggle for Democratization.* Thousand Oaks, CA: Sage, 2008.

Sheptycki, J. *In Search of Transnational Policing.* Burlington, VT: Ashgate, 2002.

Walker, N. "The pattern of transnational policing." In *Handbook of Policing,* 2nd ed., T. Newburn, ed. Devon, UK: Willan, 2008.

POLICING: DOMESTIC

Contemporary policing involves different tiers of government (from local to international) and different specialist agencies (from wildlife to drug enforcement). Domestic police services include and engage with a wide range of organizations, with distinct responsibilities, spheres of expertise, and missions. The complexity of transnational crime and the proliferation of agencies mean that issues of interagency cooperation loom large, as do questions of resources, collaboration, and capacity.

Specific problems demand specific kinds of responses, and a one-size-fits-all policy is rarely adequate to the task. This applies as much to the policing of transnational crime as to policing of other types of crime. One of the initial questions to be asked is who is actually going to do the policing in relation to which specific crimes? In many cases, this determination is made by the configuration of police agencies within a particular jurisdiction.

Many jurisdictions have specialist agencies to tackle particular sorts of crime. Environmental protection agencies, for example, may be given the mandate to investigate and prosecute environmental crimes. The police may only play an auxiliary role in relation to the work of these agencies. In other circumstances and for other purposes, members of the police service may be especially trained as law-enforcement officers in defined areas of work. In China, for example, in addition to generalist public security police, there are railway police, civil aviation police, transportation police, forest police, and anti-smuggling police. In Brazil, the main police forces are composed of federal police, military police, highway police, civil police, and municipal guards.

When it comes to crimes that cross borders, such as drug smuggling, the illegal arms trade, human trafficking, and terrorism, generalist and specialist agencies, as well as local, regional, and national agencies, may overlap in their areas of responsibility. For example, the U.S. Drug Enforcement Agency (DEA) may share an interest with the Federal Bureau of Investigation (FBI) and U.S. Customs in investigating certain criminal groups and the movement of people and substances across borders. In some instances, joint operations may involve not only law-enforcement agencies such as these but also the military, as in the case of antidrug operations along the Mexican border. In Canada, the Royal Canadian Mounted Police (RCMP) undertake a wide range of ordinary policing tasks, but they are also meant to collaborate with a civilian security service, the Canadian Security Intelligence Service, on issues pertaining to the prevention and suppression of terrorism. Specific domestic police services thus may have to liaise and work with a wide range and number of bodies, depending on the nature of the transnational crime in question.

Many different agencies, at many different levels, deal with transnational crimes. This can be illustrated by looking at environmental law enforcement. For some, the central mandate of the agency is driven by the specific type of crime. For example, environmental protection agencies (or their equivalent) often focus on "brown" issues pertaining to pollution and waste. Forestry commissions or national park authorities tend to concentrate on "green" issues and so deal with matters of conservation, animal welfare, and land use. Bodies such as the Royal Society for the Prevention of Cruelty

Federal Bureau of Investigation (FBI) police officers provide protective security at and around FBI facilities in Washington, D.C. Local, regional, and national agencies like the local Washington police, U.S. Drug Enforcement Agency (DEA), the FBI, and U.S. Customs may overlap in their areas of responsibility. (Wikimedia)

to Animals are charged with the responsibility to intervene in cases of harsh treatment of particular domesticated animals (such as companion animals or those destined to be food). Customs services typically are on the lookout for trade in illegal fauna and flora, as well as international shipments of toxic wastes and banned substances. Police services may have a general duty to protect animals and monitor the environment, while in some cases being vested with the lead role in wildlife offenses. The regulation and policing of fisheries may involve specific fisheries management authorities and specially trained fisheries officers. Health departments may be the key authorities when it comes to disposal of radioactive and clinical waste. Park rangers could be tasked with the job of preventing the poaching of animals from national parks and private reserves. And so the list of agencies that have some role in environmental law enforcement goes on.

Who is doing what at the domestic level is further complicated by the geographical proximity of countries, as in the case in the European Union (EU), which facilitates the transference and extension of crime problems across national borders. This can be compounded by political arrangements, such as a common European passport and currency that make it easier to move within the boundaries of the EU as a whole. From a domestic policing perspective, this means that there is a need for both vertical connections within a particular national context (around particular crime issues that involve local, regional, and national interests) and horizontal connections with relevant agencies outside that specific country (given the relative ease of crossover into other jurisdictions).

Domestic policing thus is carried out in the light of both considerable variations in policing functions and agencies and different levels of government. To put it differently, those who do "policing" work may not be *the* police, and the police are not necessarily involved directly in all types of law-enforcement work. Again taking environmental law enforcement as an example, the accompanying table demonstrates the complexity of the law-enforcement picture, one that includes nonpolice services as well as traditional law-enforcement agencies. Who precisely is going to deal with which type of crime is partly a function of the alleged offense, since this will often dictate the agency deemed to be responsible for a particular area—whether this is drug enforcement, counterterrorism, or money laundering.

Australian Environmental Law Enforcement Agencies

Geopolitical Scale	Examples at the Operational Level
Local councils	• Urban and metropolitan councils • Regional or rural (shires)
State	• Environmental protection agencies • Local government associations • State police services • Royal Society for the Prevention of Cruelty to Animals (RSPCA) • Parks and wildlife
National	• Australian Fisheries Management Authority • Australian Federal Police • Australian Customs Service • Office of Consumer Affairs • Department of Sustainability, Environment, Water, Population and Communities
National/state bodies	• Australian Crime Commission • National Pollution Inventory • Australasian Environmental Law Enforcement and Regulators Network (AELERT)
International	• Interpol • International Network of Environmental Enforcement and Compliance (INECE)

The composition of domestic police and the orientation of policing may differ from country to country. In some countries, local specialists or specially trained police can also wear more than one hat. For example, in the United States, "conservation police" (a term that broadly refers to fish and wildlife officers, wildlife management officers, game wardens, park rangers, and natural resources police) have authority to deal with both conventional crime and environmental crime. This means that in addition to investigation and enforcement of laws relating specifically to fish and wildlife issues, their activities can incorporate more general policing concerns, including those involving things such as drug law enforcement and human trafficking. Environmental crime, of course, includes transnational crimes such as the illegal transborder movement of wildlife species.

Within a particular national context, then, there may be considerable diversity in law-enforcement agencies and personnel, and there are often myriad bodies that in some way or another are charged with policing functions. For example, in the United Kingdom there are specialist policing and investigatory bodies that include state security services such as MI5 and MI6, regulatory authorities such as the Environment Agency, and municipal police such as Royal Parks Police, as well as the usual Home Office police—all of whom may be called upon to play a role in combating transnational crime.

Police will have quite different roles in transnational law enforcement depending upon the city, state/province, or region within which they work and the agency within which they are employed. In federal systems of governance, for example—such as those of the United States, Canada, and Australia—there will be great variation in enforcement practices depending upon whether the police operate at the local municipal level (such as the Toronto Police Service) or the federal level (RCMP). In dealing with specific crimes and particular sorts of criminality, lines of authority will be dictated by interjurisdictional protocols (such as federal laws that override local laws and national security legislation that supersedes state and territory or provincial laws) and in some instances by specific court decisions (that establish the limits of legal encroachment by diverse authorities).

The plethora of players and laws demands an approach to law enforcement and compliance that necessarily must be collaborative in nature and that acknowledges that the skill set of domestic police is expanding. Dealing with transnational crime will demand extraordinary efforts to relate to one another across distance, language, and cultural borders; to understand specific issues; to coordinate actions; to enforce national and international laws and conventions; and to gather and share information and intelligence. This occurs within a domestic context as well as internationally. Knowing with whom to speak and under which circumstances requires a sophisticated understanding of the mission and capacities of multiple allied law-enforcement agencies. It also demands close attention to interagency protocols, such as those relating to the sharing of information and intelligence.

Among the many issues pertaining to the proliferation of agencies dealing with transnational crime is that each may be driven by different aims and objectives and different methods of intervention, with different powers and exhibiting different levels of expertise and collaboration with others. Differences in work practices and workplace cultures can affect how law-enforcement officers work together on the ground.

Another issue relates to the need to distinguish between organizational affiliation (which may be formal and policy oriented) and interagency collaboration (which refers to actual operational practices and linkages). In some cases, there is a clear need for capacity building in order for collaboration and, especially, for rapid response to be successfully institutionalized as part of the agency's normal practice. There can also be agency differences in defining and interpreting just what the crime is or how serious it is (for example, illegal fishing versus drug running) and how to respond to it.

Powers of investigation, particularly in relation to the gathering of suitable evidence for the specific crime, are inevitably shaped by state/provincial, federal, and international conventions and protocols, as well as by availability of local expertise, staff, and resources. One perennial problem is insufficient sharing of information by agencies and at times a poor track record of successful collaboration across jurisdictions. This can occur through lack of formal agreements between agencies, including the development of protocols to enable the sharing of information that does not breach privacy provisions (subject to some degree of agreement on the purpose of sharing the information and what the expected benefits are to all parties). It can also reflect differing priorities among agencies that can affect the success of joint operations, as well as the willingness of agencies to collaborate with information and resource commitments.

As previously indicated, the role of nonpolicing agencies in law-enforcement activities is also of note. Whether it is U.S. Customs or the Australian Quarantine Inspection Service, surveillance and use of coercive powers are not the sole preserve of the formal police services. However, it is important that the latter collaborate with the former if certain types and classes of transnational crime are to be adequately addressed.

The role of nongovernmental organizations (NGOs) in dealing cooperatively with police and other law-enforcement officials to bring criminals to justice should also not be underestimated. For example, convictions for illegal logging and for illegal trade in wildlife in places such as Brazil or Russia have been produced through the direct engagement of formal police services with NGO environmental activist organizations. This has involved collection of evidence by NGO personnel that has then been forwarded to relevant authorities in the respective jurisdictions. While the NGOs (such as Greenpeace) may at one level be transnational organizations, it is relationships forged with domestic police that make the difference when it comes to prosecution and sentencing.

Fighting transnational crime will frequently demand a worldwide response. The role and capacity of domestic law-enforcement agencies play an essential role in how responses to harms of a global nature will be framed and implemented. Most intervention occurs locally, even where national and international law-enforcement agencies are called in and directly involved. In the end, to be effective, agencies need to be able to harness the cooperation and expertise of many different contributors and to liaise with relevant partners from the local to the international level.

Rob White
University of Tasmania

See also Joint Force Policing and Integrated Models; Police Cooperation

Further Readings

Crawford, A. "Plural Policing in the UK: Policing Beyond the Police." In *Handbook of Policing*, 2nd ed., T. Newburn, ed. Devon, UK: Willan, 2008.

Haberfeld, M. and I. Cerrah, eds. *Comparative Policing: The Struggle for Democratization*. Thousand Oaks, CA: Sage, 2008.

POLICING: HIGH VERSUS LOW

Jean-Paul Brodeur coined the term *high policing* in 1983 as a way to differentiate between the use of the police to maintain political order in the face of political activities and the use of the police to maintain public order in the face of everyday crime. He originally used the term to illustrate the use of the police as an instrument of political control in the 1960s and 1970s in United States and Canada. In response to the use of the police by the state for political purposes, beginning in the 1970s both the United States and Canada moved to separate those organizations engaging in high policing and those focused on low policing. Since Brodeur's original article, the term high policing has expanded to incorporate the use of the police to protect the state in the face of a broad range of transnational crimes, especially terrorism, where the gathering of intelligence is a key component of the police's activities. In the 21st century, the trend now appears to be toward a closer relationship among organizations engaging in high and low policing.

Definition and Origins

High policing refers to the use of police by the state to monitor (and potentially to manage) the political actions of politically motivated organizations that disagree with the state's current practices or policies. In a democratic society, high policing focuses on preserving government institutions in the face of potentially disruptive (and potentially violent) political activities. In authoritarian regimes, high policing seeks not only to preserve government institutions but also to maintain the power of a particular regime; that is, it is used to preserve the power of those already in power.

Brodeur conceived of the idea of high policing as a result of the use of policing for political purposes in the United States and in Canada in the 1960s and 1970s. In particular, he examined the case of the Federal Bureau of Investigation's (FBI's) Counter Intelligence Program (COINTELPRO) and that of the Royal Canadian Mounted Police's (RCMP's) Disruptive Tactics program. In each case, the police gathered intelligence on, and in some cases infiltrated, political organizations whose political activities were directed in opposition to the prevailing government's policies. As a result of journalistic and governmental inquiries into these events, both the United States and Canada sought to separate internal security functions from law-enforcement functions. In the United States, this was achieved by limiting the authority of the FBI (and the Central Intelligence Agency) to gather and share intelligence within the domestic United States. In Canada, the separation was originally achieved by splitting the enforcement functions of national security and criminal code policing but keeping them both within the RCMP. In 1984, the national security functions were removed from the RCMP with the creation of the Canadian Security Intelligence Service (CSIS).

Characteristics of High Policing

Brodeur characterized high policing in four ways. First, he noted that high policing is "highly absorbent" because of its use of an all-encompassing approach to gathering and storing intelligence (that is, it "absorbs" all the information it can about those targeted individuals or groups) as a way to maintain order. Second, high policing is not bound by any strict interpretation of the law. The police organizations in the historical cases Brodeur examined not only carried out the law but also interpreted it to give them greater authority. Third, high policing is willing to use crime itself as a tool to enforce order or to gain intelligence and is not primarily focused on crime control. Fourth, high policing is characterized as open about its use of informants and surveillance. Unlike low policing, which minimizes the public's awareness of its use of informants and intelligence, high policing acknowledges its use of these tactics, possibly in order to create fear in the populations as a means of control.

9/11 and High Policing

From the end of the Cold War onward to the terrorist attacks of September 11, 2001 (9/11), and beyond, high policing has taken on a broader application than its original focus. High policing now means policing that seeks to protect the institutions of government in the face of "national security" threats, both those that may emanate from domestic sources and those with overseas origins. The key characteristics that distinguish high policing from low policing remain the same, but the role of "intelligence gathering" is elevated to a defining aspect of high policing.

In reevaluating his original thesis at the beginning of the 21st century, Brodeur argues that policing today, unlike policing in the late 20th century, when governments sought to separate law enforcement from national security, tends toward greater blending of high and low policing. This is taking place both generally, in response to transnational crime (as in the case of drug trafficking being redefined as a "threat to national security"), and in relation to an array of offenses (such as money laundering) that are now being linked to terrorism. Looking again at the United States and Canada, Brodeur concludes that in both countries the movement is toward stronger relationships between the police and security intelligence services. In the United States, this is in reaction to the perceived role the "wall of separation" between law-enforcement and national intelligence organizations played in the events of 9/11.

In Canada, the move toward a stronger relationship between its security service and its police service came as a result of the terrorist attacks on two Air India flights departing Canada in 1983 (which left 331 dead) and the failure to investigate the event successfully after the fact. In this instance, a commission (initiated in 2006 and releasing its final report in 2010) implicated the strained relationship between internal security and law-enforcement organizations as responsible for the failure of the investigation. Getting enforcement agencies to share their intelligence—both among traditional policing agencies and between national security and policing bodies—is a well-recognized problem in policing. The demands for an increased security capability following the terrorist attacks within the United States also had an impact on Canada. Pressures on Canada to respond resulted in funding being given to the RCMP, which in many ways brought that "policing" organization back into national security policing.

In his final book in 2010, Brodeur revisited his earlier thesis on high and low policing, concluding that his thesis continued to illuminate policing in the age of mass terrorism. In addition to reviewing and expanding his thesis, Brodeur singles out two aspects of high policing for additional discussion. First, he discusses in great detail the extensive use of infiltration and police informants on a regular basis by police agencies and raises a question of whether the police in the future will attempt to infiltrate, or use informants in, government departments and private corporations. Second, Brodeur highlights the way in which high policing contributes to the conflation of executive, legislative, and judicial powers, leading to the concentration of power in the executive. He mentions, by way of example, the renditions the administration of George W. Bush authorized that were administered by the Central Intelligence Agency (CIA), which he refers to as a high policing agency, with the support of sympathetic legal advisers. Brodeur refers to these high policing agencies as secret police, secret jailors, secret judges, and secret lawmakers taking on all the powers of the government and administering them on the basis of executive fiat.

Criticism

Some authors criticized Brodeur's original thesis because it did not acknowledge the growing role of the private security industry (policing provided by private security firms). They contend that private security can also be high policing, because it skews the role of the police toward protecting a client (such as a corporation or individual) versus protecting the public. Brodeur's final book takes on this criticism, and he devotes an entire chapter to examining the increasing role of private security.

Justin Lewis Abold
Oxford University

See also Policing: Domestic; Policing: National Security; Policing: Transnational

Further Readings

Brodeur, Jean-Paul. "High and Low Policing: Remarks About the Policing of Political Activities." *Social Problems*, v.30/5 (1983).

Brodeur, Jean-Paul. "High and Low Policing in Post-9/11 Times." *Policing*, v.1/1 (2007).

Brodeur, Jean-Paul. *The Policing Web*. New York: Oxford University Press, 2010.

Commission of Inquiry Into the Investigation of the Bombing of Air India Flight 182. *Air India Flight 182: A Canadian Tragedy*. http://epe.lac-bac.gc.ca/100/206/301/pco-bcp/commissions/air_india/2010-07-23/www.majorcomm.ca/en/reports/finalreport/default.htm (Accessed February 2011).

O'Reilly, Conor and Graham Ellison. "'Eye Spy Private High' Re-conceptualizing High Policing Theory." *British Journal of Criminology*, v.46 (2006).

POLICING: NATIONAL SECURITY

National security policing is a term that brings together two elements of the modern security state. First, it designates a "type of policing." As a result, it draws upon the traditional founts of police analysis as well as the various organizational and institutional strategies and problems of such a field. For example, it deals with issues of proper training and recruitment as well as the most effective hierarchy. Policing of the traditional sort, however, is a purposely visible and dramatized social institution. In contrast, national security policing largely seeks to be invisible and out of the public eye. This does not mean, however, that national security policing agencies do not dramatize and engage with public opinion. It simply means that they approach the whole issue in a differently ordered manner.

Definitions

The main task of national security policing bodies is to offer security through surveillance and information gathering. This facet ties national security policing to traditional forms of law enforcement. Although one cannot draw a straight line of correlation between traditional and national security policing, they both actively seek information. Information is a resource essential to any form of policing. In order to fight crime, the traditional police draw on various sources of information, usually gained through bartering and/or bargaining. Likewise, national security policing relies on the ability of agents to gather information from numerous sources. The ability to gather and analyze information leads to the idea of intelligence. That is, an agency may have information in the simplest and most cumulative sense, but what is done with and understood through this information is what is known as intelligence. In traditional policing, this information-gathering process and its analysis are reflected in various attempts at "crime mapping." In national security policing, information gathering and the development of viable intelligence can lead to foreign policy decisions at the highest levels. The national security establishment in the United States, for example, entails a wide circuit of intelligence-gathering agencies housed in numerous locales, from the Department of State to the Department of Defense and the Central Intelligence Agency (CIA). All of these agencies deliver information and intelligence to the office of the president and his or her National Security Council as well as the appropriate committees in the Senate and House of Representatives.

National security policing is strongly tied to the concept of national security, which is an organizational concept designed to motivate and give direction to a variety of government agencies. *National security* entails the defense of the nation against outside forces, or national enemies. Within the conceptual framework of this idea, such enemies seek the overthrow of the national government. The immediate expression of national security is to be found in military preparedness and vigilance at borders. A strong idea of national security often entails, for many both inside and outside the government, a strong military capability. At the same time, national security threats can often surpass the demarcations of borders and direct military force. When this is the case, the government must turn its attention to a possible "fifth column" or underground network of spies and agitators within its own borders. In essence, this means that national security policing is actively involved in observing its own citizenry. Threats may arise from outside, but often they are home-grown.

Communication Challenges

Globalization has made it more likely that terrorist groups can operate within the borders of a target state. Furthermore, it is quite possible that citizens themselves can become involved as potential threats or terrorists. The Oklahoma City bombing of 1995 offers a good example. This explosion—which killed 168 persons (including 19 children), injured many others, destroyed the multistory Murrah Federal Building, and damaged hundreds of structures in the surrounding area—was perpetrated by two Americans, Timothy McVeigh, a militia movement sympathizer motivated by what he saw as the federal government's mishandling of the Ruby Ridge and Waco incidents, and Terry Nichols, who assisted McVeigh in preparing the bomb. National security threats can also surpass the limits of the

nation itself. In the case of the September 11, 2001 (9/11), attacks, for example, the threat originated within the confines of an unfriendly regime abroad. Therefore, a coherent national security policy must also draw on the extraborder capacities of agents working within foreign contexts. National security agents engage established diplomatic resources such as embassies and embassy workers in gathering information. They also look to induce "enemy agents" into provide them with useful information. The forms of inducement may include cash as well as protection and asylum.

National security policing, therefore, brings together a wide array of government agencies working, in most cases, for the same goal. However, the problem is approached from multiple vantage points. The Federal Bureau of Investigation (FBI) and the Department of Homeland Security are assigned to cover the domestic side of national security while the CIA, the National Security Agency (NSA), and various military intelligence networks are given the rest of the world. However, without established means for sharing, collating, and analyzing data from these agencies, important information can be overlooked and key connections missed. After 9/11, for example, many commentators, including the National Commission on Terrorist Attacks Upon the United States (the 9/11 Commission), identified this problem as one of the main reasons, if not the main reason, that the catastrophe was not detected and averted. The problem, the commission noted, was exacerbated by competition and mistrust between agencies within the government.

Another problem involves the ability of the hierarchy to respond in a flexible and adaptive manner to threats that emerge and to channel information on these threats up the appropriate chain of command. In the American case, for example, the way news about major threats reaches the desk of the president and the timing of such communications are critical. Furthermore, effective national security policing requires the coordination of numerous federal, state, and municipal bodies. The byzantine intricacies of the bureaucracy can hinder communication both up and down the chain of command, and information can take a while to reach the intended targets. In contrast, terrorist cells are composed of small and flexible bodies of individuals who can respond quickly to changing circumstances. National security policing must therefore adapt to the practices of its enemies. "Field agents" with the capacity to move quickly and comprehend the mind-set of the enemy are most effective in these types of cases. Once again, the problem is moving this information quickly and efficiently from the local context to the level of geopolitics and state-level decision-making.

History

National security policing has its source in military intelligence. In the late 19th century, the spy became a literary as well as a real figure. The Germans, in their endeavor to compete with the established British Empire, focused on sending spies into the smallest of English villages with the intent of preparing for a future war and invasion. At this time, all states relied on the military as the source of intelligence. Local constabularies were not trained or prepared to deal with sophisticated spy networks that took them beyond their jurisdictions. However, militaries in all countries were concerned primarily with knowledge about troop movements, enemy technology, and concentrations of power. As a result, they spent little time seeking out the fifth column of spies and conspirators within their own borders.

Furthermore, the military must be understood as a traditionally conspicuous institution—especially in old Europe—that was not used to "sneaking around." Intelligence before the 20th century often passed through diplomatic channels and the personal relationships that were often forged between those who interacted at this level. Yet the importance of intelligence was never denied. One state's knowledge of the plans of another has always been decisive in war; discovery of troop concentrations, movements, and plans for attack obviously offer an advantage. Further, new technologies, strategies, and codes could be stolen and used to great advantage on the day of battle. Despite these distinct advantages, states did not effectively move toward national security policing until the eve of World War I.

One possible exception to this general historical trend may have been the use of a national security policing model in Napoleon's France. Napoleon, as well as earlier revolutionary leaders, was very concerned about the possibility of foreign encroachment and invasion. As a result, an intricate network of spies and *agents provocateurs* was created to watch the population and, if possible, ferret out dangerous individuals. In England such a police force was a real

obstacle to the formation of any nationally coordinated policing—even if it was not like the French model. The "in-born sense of English liberty" was always suspicious of any national police force.

By the 20th century, many high-ranking members of the government, such as Winston Churchill, argued for a new approach to national security. The British had numerous interests scattered across the globe. The British Empire covered a huge expanse and exerted great power, but it was also one with many weak points and vulnerabilities. Britain's enemies sought to strike at these weak points and, by doing so, redraw the map of imperial power. The Russians, for example, were interested in expanding southward in order to find a warm-water port. This meant that they were interested in destabilizing the British position in India—the jewel of the empire. The Russians had organized a very sophisticated and well-funded secret service that watched Russian citizens intently; this secret service could be turned against British interests. The British government eventually responded by creating Military Intelligence, Section 5, popularly known as MI5. The task of this body was to watch for enemy agitation at home and to seek out information abroad. Only two agencies were involved, one in charge at home and one in charge abroad. Eventually these two aspects were split into MI5 at home and MI6 in the world at large. Before and during World War I these agencies were active in pursuing German agents. After the war, these agencies, as well as governments across North America and western Europe, turned their attention to a possible communist fifth column. The heightened fear of communism that ensued became known as the Red Scare.

The American national security establishment did not come into its own until the end of World War II. During the war, the Americans tended to rely on British expertise in this area. The Allied effort was able to break the German Enigma code, which may have been a decisive factor in winning the war. Intelligence was becoming ever more important to successful warfare. In the United States, the direct ancestor of the CIA was the Office of Strategic Services (OSS). This agency worked in and through the American military establishment. After the war, the global situation dramatically changed the nature of national security. The new threat was the Soviet Union, and the United States had limited knowledge and information about this new power.

George Kennan, an embassy worker with experience in the Soviet Union, argued that the Russian state was totalitarian and would inevitably become a direct threat to the United States and its interests. Furthermore, communist threats appeared to exist across the globe, and there was some intelligence claiming that these threats were being funded by the Soviet Union through its own clandestine agency, known as the Committee for State Security (KGB). Eventually President Harry Truman and Congress were convinced of the urgency of creating a national security establishment to deal with the communist threat. The National Security Act of 1947 established the CIA as well as the National Security Council. The National Security Council and the national security advisor were to counsel the president about foreign policy concerns. The CIA, on the other hand, had control over the coordination of intelligence.

By the early 1950s, these agencies became much more actively involved in covert action. Initially they did such things as drop leaflets into enemy territory. They next tried to organize anticommunist dissidents and have them enter the Soviet Union, China, and North Korea. This tactic usually failed, and many of these dissidents were captured and executed. Eventually, the CIA turned its efforts toward controlling and manipulating Third World countries. This was considered an appropriate avenue for clandestine activity because money and supplies could have a large impact in supposedly undeveloped countries.

A classic example of this type of national security policing on a global scale was the overthrow of Mohammed Mossadeq in Iran and his replacement with the young Mohammad Reza Shah Pahlavi. The British had long-standing interests in Iran, and the Anglo-Persian or Anglo-Iranian oil consortium was very concerned about Mossadeq's overtures to the Soviets. Like many Third World leaders of the Cold War era, Mossadeq believed that he could play the superpowers off against each other. The British were deeply worried about their interests but were involved in a large-scale dismantling of many of their military positions across the globe and claimed that they could not afford to intervene. The CIA took over the mantle of British hegemonic management and sought to overthrow this troublesome yet democratically elected leader. National security police officers bribed, cajoled, and manipulated domestic Iranian actors—especially the military and the young and inexperienced shah—into removing Mossadeq from power. In his place, the CIA and its allies installed a stalwartly pro-Western government. CIA operatives took great pride in this coup d'état. It showed how covert action could allow for the United States to succeed but set a dangerous and malevolent precedent. Buoyed by this success, the CIA and the United States went ahead and intervened with great impunity in many nations across the globe. This was a crass display of American power. However, it also disengaged the United States from a global concern with the spread of democracy and liberal values. In fact, it seemed to many in the Third World that the United States preferred to deal with autocratic and repressive regimes that would unhesitatingly do what the United States wanted.

For much of the 20th century, national security policing was based, at least in the West, on the containment of communism. This meant that national policing involved keeping a watchful eye on one's citizenry as well as taking an aggressive stance in the rest of the world. When the Soviet Union invaded Afghanistan at the end of December 1979 to prop up a communist government, the United States funded anti-Soviet forces. Many of these anti-Soviet forces would eventually become the bedrock of a new threat—namely, Islamic terrorism. Especially since 9/11, Islamic terrorists have become the main concern of national security policing. This has had a deep impact on the legal and political landscape. It has resulted in the creation of the Department of Homeland Security and the passage of the Patriot Act in October 2001. As governments try to fit into this new agenda, questions of jurisdictional control have become important. To what extent can American agents operate in places like the Pakistani frontier—a crucial area of concern in the War on Terror? Can American national security policing rely on the aid of its allies? Finally, how porous and penetrable have borders become?

In the present age of terror, a threat does not come in the form of a column of coordinated tanks or even guerrilla groups. The threat can and does come from a limited number of actors taking full advantage of the freedom of movement characteristic of the West. Because of this, governments have emphasized the global nature of the War on Terror. There is definitely a strong link between multiple sites of action. That is, what happens in Afghanistan may have a direct impact on the future possibility of terrorist attack in the West. A networked world born of multiple linkages is the very source of potential danger. It is important to remember that the CIA and the U.S. intelligence community in general were actively involved in promoting Islamic-style militias in the war against the Soviets in Afghanistan. In conjunction with the Pakistani secret service (the ISI), the American intelligence community was able to run weapons and money from western Pakistan into the southeastern areas of Afghanistan. Many of the groups sponsored by the CIA, known broadly as the mujahideen, later became the bedrock of the new terrorist threat.

When the Soviets eventually pulled out of Afghanistan in 1991, American interest in the country declined. As a result, the religious groupings that received ample aid during the war were in a good position to challenge for power. The Taliban was one of these fortunate groups. It benefited from a power vacuum left by the retreating Soviet forces, patronage on the part of the Pakistani ISI, and a decline in American interest. This "failure of American intelligence" was grounded in a repetitive pattern of distance and engagement. This pattern is based on the very logic of national security policing, which relies on a clearly identified enemy as a way to rally money and support for its covert activities. Afghanistan and the war were seen simply as an efficient and effective way of harming the Soviet Union. No long-term goals and strategies of stability were implemented or even discussed within the intelligence community. As a result, this form of national security policing is often a source of potential danger and instability. American national security actions in Afghanistan clearly show this.

Events in the Arab world during 2011 (particularly in Tunisia and Egypt) have raised the question of long-term national security practices in the West. For many years, the repressive regimes of the Middle East—from the shah in Iran to Hosni Mubarak's Egypt—have gained material and financial support from the West. The reason given was national security or national interest. Quite simply, these regimes were able to guarantee compliance with Western interests in and through their repressive practices. Democracy, in contrast, was considered a "national security risk" that could not be experimented with. The public in these nations might not be as amenable to "American interests." Therefore, American

support for these regimes became the grounding for a foreign policy that associated the United States and the West with political and social repression. Yet is support for these regimes really an appropriate way to ensure national security? Do these regimes not open the possibility of long-term instability and civilian dissatisfaction? If so, is it in the West's interest to support and prop up such regimes?

Paul Brienza
York University

See also Joint Force Policing and Integrated Models; Narco-Terrorism; Policing: Domestic; Policing: High Versus Low

Further Readings

Christopher, Andrew. *The Defence of the Realm: The Authorized History of MI5.* New York: Penguin, 2010.

Coll, Steve. *Ghost Wars: The Secret History of the CIA, Afghanistan, and Bin Laden, From the Soviet Invasion to September 10, 2001.* New York: Penguin, 2004.

Lowenthal, Mark M. *Intelligence: From Secrets to Policy,* 4th ed. London: Sage, 2009.

Manning, Peter. *Police Work: The Social Organization of Policing.* Prospect Heights, IL: Waveland Press, 1997.

Rhodri, Jeffrey-Jones. *Cloak and Dollar: A History of American Secret Intelligence.* New Haven, CT: Yale University Press, 2003.

Weiner, Tim. *Legacy of Ashes: The History of the CIA.* New York: Anchor Books, 2008.

POLICING: PRIVATELY CONTRACTED

Policing in the United States and in much of the world has been undergoing a transformation for approximately the past 30 years in which it is no longer the exclusive realm of the state. A larger share of policing is being done by nongovernmental agencies and persons. For much of the 20th century, the public police were thought to have a monopoly on the provision of police services and protection of person and property, but by the end of the century privately employed police outnumbered public police officers by a margin of almost three to one.

Public Versus Private Policing

The public police can be defined generally as those authorized by the state to use force, to enforce the law, and to maintain order. They are also said to be public servants whose purpose is for the common good and welfare of society. Common to all definitions of public police is some mention of state authorization to use force for social control purposes. The public police are funded through public dollars, their service is to be available to all members of the community, and they patrol public areas of the community.

Private policing, also called private security, is a policing activity that includes crime prevention, detection, and apprehension. It is not publicly funded but instead is conducted by private organizations or persons for commercial purposes. Private police, therefore, are nongovernmental agents of crime control who operate on a profit motive. They may have duties to protect life and property and to maintain order. While the public police serve all members of a community, private police have a client-driven focus; that is, they serve their clients' interests and needs.

There are other differences between public and private police, most of which are found in the manner of policing or in what they do. Public police must provide a full range of services to the community. Private police have a much more limited area of expertise, in that they serve only the interests of their clients and not those of the community as a whole. The public police attempt to deter crime through the use of force, the threat of arrest, detention of suspects, and the use of searches. Private police crime prevention efforts focus on attempts to regulate behavior and circumstances to reduce the possibility of the occurrence of crime. They use risk identification and risk reduction techniques and rely heavily on the use of surveillance. Whereas the public police focus on punishment of offenders, private police look for compliance of persons. Finally, whereas public police move offenders into the criminal justice system for prosecution, private police instead use a private justice system that favors banning or firing as alternatives to prosecution.

In spite of the differences between private and public police, there is increasingly a blur between the two, as their services often overlap. Many functions and responsibilities of the public police are often now assumed by private police. The role of private police has increased to the point that they now perform many of the duties formerly handled by public police. It is felt that the distinction between the two is progressively decreasing. Private police protect almost every kind of space, including both commercial and residential properties. It is likely that people see private police more often than public ones. In addition, government at all levels has contracted out some form of policing and security. Further obscuring the difference is the tendency of public police to hire themselves out for private purposes to private employers while still portrayed as public police. Some police departments now charge for services that they once provided for free. In addition, many times private police will seek to have themselves commissioned in some fashion to give them the powers of public police officers.

History

Prior to the Industrial Revolution, the state had very little role in law enforcement and crime prevention. Matters of crime were handled by private individuals themselves; there were no governmental agencies to which to turn for assistance. Often, those with the means hired others to protect them. Some, such as merchants, would hire private parties to retrieve stolen property.

Social changes brought by the Industrial Revolution caused the development of public policing services, first in England, then in the United States, and eventually in other nations. The growth of public policing was slow, and private policing continued to exist. In the early part of the 20th century, it was believed that formal social control and the provision of policing services should be the exclusive domain of the state. By the late 20th century, private policing remained, with a diminished role. It was looked upon as less than respectable by many, including the public police. However, this changed in the later part of the century, and private policing began to grow at a much faster rate than public policing.

Some of the factors that revivified private policing include rising crime, fear of crime, and the realization that the public police were overburdened and unable to handle their increased workload effectively. This brought public dissatisfaction with the effectiveness of the police and an acknowledgment that crime could not be satisfactorily handled by the public police alone. That situation was exacerbated by economic difficulties leading to cutbacks in public spending, including the amount of funds that could be allocated to policing. The American Society for Industrial Security has predicted increases in certain crimes such as retail crime, bank robberies, fraud, workplace violence, and acts of terrorism, which will have an impact on private businesses.

The idea of mass private property has also driven the increase in private policing. This is property in which traditional ideas regarding private ownership and privacy change. Mass private property is property that, although privately owned, is considered a public place. This is so because the general public is routinely invited to it and there are economic reasons for them to be invited. Examples of such properties include shopping malls, sports stadiums, airports, hotels, and train and bus stations. Other types of communal properties, such as public areas of gated communities, public housing projects, and condominiums, hire private police to patrol their properties. In addition, it is estimated that approximately 40 percent of the security work performed by government at all levels is contracted out to private security. This includes such duties as guarding of courthouses and other public buildings and, in some communities, handling routine public police tasks, such as minor automobile accidents.

Other factors have contributed to the growth of private policing. First, as society moves from an industrially based to an information-based economy, the nature of policing is changing to meet associated new needs. Investigating and gathering evidence about cybercrimes and identity theft, for example, requires expertise that is sometimes beyond that of traditional policing. Next, as certain corporate and industrial crimes become more sophisticated, there is a growing need for specially trained personnel to investigate, usually coming from the private sector. Finally, as more government-run enterprises become privatized, the new owners must consider their own security needs, creating further demand for private policing.

These changes are transnational in scope and are not limited to any one nation; these developments are occurring in the United States, Canada, Australia, India, China, and the nations of the European Union. Private security firms have become multinational companies as they market their services globally. For example, one firm reports that it has approximately 340,000 employees operating in 108 countries. The marketization, or commodification, of policing has allowed for the growth of transnational private policing firms, and the trend is likely to continue.

There are some issues regarding private policing, with equity being one of the first. Private policing could become the province of those who can afford it, for example, with the less privileged population being left to fend for themselves. Moreover, public police are accountable for their actions to the public through various means; often the private police are not, or their commercial interests may conflict with public priorities. Not subject to the same rules of conduct, private police may raise more concerns regarding possible infringements of civil and human rights surrounding the use of force, profiling, equal treatment, and equal protection. It has been said that private policing is more security-conscious than rights-conscious. As private policing grows and assumes an increased market share of policing, interactions of all kinds will increase, potentially leading to abuse in the absence of public and legal oversight. Such concerns will need to be addressed by governments moving forward.

Marcel F. Beausoleil
Fitchburg State University

See also Globalization; Policing: Domestic; Policing: Transnational

Further Readings

Bayley, David H. and Clifford D. Shearing. "The Future of Policing." *Law and Society Review*, v.30/3 (1996).

Bayley, David H. and Clifford D. Shearing. *The New Structure of Policing*. Washington, DC: National Institute of Justice, 2001.

Forst, Brian. "The Privatization and Civilianization of Policing." *Criminal Justice 2000*. Vol. 2, *Boundary Changes in Criminal Justice Organizations*. Washington, DC: U.S. Department of Justice, 2000.

Jones, Trevor and Tim Newburn. "The Transformation of Policing? Understanding Current Trends in Policing Systems." *British Journal of Criminology*, v.42 (2002).

POLICING: TRANSNATIONAL

Transnational policing is a complex and multifaceted approach to crime control that can reach across national borders, often requiring collaboration among multiple organizations and their agents. Although this type of law-enforcement activity is not new, it has become more extensive—and, some might say, more necessary—with the rise of international terrorism and the globalization of crime.

The types of crimes that naturally extend beyond state boundaries often include immigration and border-related offenses. Transnational crimes also can occur within the borders of one specific state if the consequences of those crimes significantly affect another state or all of humanity. Human smuggling, money laundering, piracy, narcotics trafficking, and international terrorism are examples of transnational crimes.

In response to the surge in crimes of this nature, transnational policing has increased in recent years. To better understand this approach to crime fighting, one must become familiar with the basics of transnational policing and its connection to modern transnational crimes, as well as the various policing methods used in response to these crimes.

Transnational policing can be undertaken through national, regional, or international law-enforcement efforts. At a national level, for example, law-enforcement efforts can be pursued in a particular state when the offenders perpetrated their crimes in other states, when the victims are within the borders of the investigating state, through intelligence sharing with other states, and by working in other states with or without operational authority to act unilaterally or to make arrests. At the regional level, states that border each other work together to combat crimes that frequently occur at the border or where the border is used to facilitate the crimes in one way or another. At the international level, police investigators appointed by the United Nations (UN) address serious crimes against humanity such as rape, torture, murder, and extermination.

The police response to these types of crimes can come in a number of ways, including direct national police operations, regional police efforts, bilateral and multilateral treaties, liaison officers, and criminal intelligence. Regardless of the specific method of transnational policing, there are successes, challenges, and areas for improvement and reform.

Transnational policing has been going on for years, long before international terrorism and global crime reached their current levels. At the beginning of the 20th century, for example, organized crime tied to the group known as the Black Hand was on the rise in the United States. In response, New York City police detective Lieutenant Joseph Petrosino formed a new criminal investigations squad to combat Italian organized crime in New York.

To investigate these Mafia crimes and capture the criminal perpetrators, Petrosino traveled to Italy, where he gathered evidence that was extremely useful in many criminal prosecutions in the United States. In 1909, the Mafia assassinated Petrosino while he was in Italy. He was the first New York City Police Department (NYPD) officer to be killed in the line of duty while on foreign soil.

Another early example of transnational policing was the International Police Commission, established in 1923. The agency later became known as the International Criminal Police Organization, or Interpol. Information sharing among various national police agencies led to some initial success with criminal investigations, but World War II interrupted many of Interpol's activities.

Nevertheless, the agency is still active today. In spite of the image of "international" police officers pursuing and capturing criminals across the globe, Interpol remains an intelligence-led and information-sharing organization. Headquartered in Lyon, France, it currently has more than 180 member states successfully and collaboratively working together and sharing intelligence, with the organization serving as an administrative liaison between the member states. Interpol databases hold fingerprints, photographs, and DNA information, which are used strictly for criminal investigative purposes. Although political crimes are specifically excluded from its mandate, acts of political violence directed toward civilians by terrorists and war criminals do not escape its mandate. Interpol has come a long way through the years, and in 2009 the agency issued its own passport, allowing its officials to travel more easily across borders on transnational policing missions and operations.

Transnational Policing at the National Level

The fight against transnational crime often begins at the state level, and many national police agencies take the lead in solving relevant crimes. The Australian Federal Police (AFP) International Liaison Officer Network and its Law Enforcement Cooperation Program are excellent examples of national police agencies engaged in the fight against international terrorism, child exploitation, and human smuggling. The AFP does this through intelligence gathering, capacity building, and collaboration with police agencies throughout the world.

The Royal Canadian Mounted Police (RCMP) also has a long history of undertaking international policing missions. Some of the RCMP's operations include capacity building and establishing the rule of law in Afghanistan and the UN operations in Côte d'Ivoire (UNOCI) and the Democratic Republic of the Congo. RCMP members have also contributed significantly to investigations of torture, murder, and political assassinations by serving with the Special Tribunal for Lebanon, the International Criminal Tribunal for the former Yugoslavia, and the International Criminal Tribunal for Rwanda. The RCMP also has members stationed as liaison officers at embassies throughout the world, as well as at Canada's Permanent Mission to the UN in New York, where they work on many initiatives, including transnational crime.

In the United States, local law-enforcement officers have become increasingly involved in international policing efforts. For example, the NYPD has an International Liaison Program with police officers stationed in Europe, the Middle East, Latin America, and elsewhere around the world. These officers actively work with their counterparts in host countries to collect relevant criminal intelligence for the purpose of protecting the citizens of New York and visitors to that city. The Los Angeles Police Department (LAPD) is another example of a major local U.S. police department that has the resources to pursue special cases of interest anywhere in the world.

On the federal level in the United States, the Drug Enforcement Administration (DEA) and its predecessor agencies are well known for pursuing leads on all continents and for working with their host-nation counterparts in areas of mutual concern, such as drug trafficking and money laundering. Since 1941, because of threats against the United States by agents of the Axis Powers, the Federal Bureau of Investigation has had special agents assigned as legal attachés, or "legats," at U.S. embassies. As a result of increasing international terrorism and transnational crime, the number of legats and their roles expanded greatly in the 1990s. These special agents have proven to be excellent liaisons on transnational crime issues; in some states they have, like agents of the DEA, taken on a more operational role, actually making arrests while working with police from other states. Through these legats, the FBI provides investigative assistance around the world, lending expertise in cases that include the 2002 nightclub bombing in Bali, Indonesia, and the 2004 train bombings in Spain.

Transnational policing no longer lies solely within the realm of traditional police agencies. Diplomatic officers are stationed at embassies and consulates around the world, and they have become more concerned with transnational crime as it affects their states. Accordingly, these foreign service officers frequently work with the law-enforcement officials attached to the embassies and with local law-enforcement officials in areas of mutual concern. Similarly, national security and intelligence agencies, such as the Central Intelligence Agency (CIA) and the British security services MI5 and MI6, are actively involved not only in counterterrorism operations and investigations but also in combating more traditional transnational crimes, such as narcotics trafficking and human smuggling.

The U.S. military, which is principally prohibited from undertaking domestic law-enforcement operations related to civilians inside the territory of the United States, is permitted to assist or to act unilaterally in law-enforcement activities outside the country. Consequently, members of the U.S. armed forces are involved in a wide range of transnational law-enforcement activities, including counterterrorism and counternarcotics efforts. In fact, military special operations teams have helped to capture international war criminals, in addition to locating Colombian drug lord Pablo Escobar.

U.S. military criminal investigative organizations (MCIOs), such as the Naval Criminal Investigative Service (NCIS), the Air Force's Office of Special Investigations (OSI), and the Army's Criminal Investigations Command (CID), also operate internationally. These law-enforcement agencies have worldwide jurisdiction over members of the armed forces and authority to investigate threats against U.S. interests regardless of the source. Special agents of the MCIOs frequently are involved in investigating many forms of transnational crimes, including human smuggling, narcotics trafficking, and international terrorism.

The notion of extraterritorial jurisdiction also gives state authorities the legal right to investigate and prosecute transnational crimes. This means that the state, through appropriate legislation, has given itself jurisdiction over specified criminal acts that occur outside its boundaries or borders. For example, many states, including the United States, exercise criminal jurisdiction over members of their armed services for crimes that occur anywhere in the world, regardless of whether the offense is a so-called military crime. In many instances, this jurisdiction extends to family members who accompany the service member abroad, and it also applies to the service member once he or she has been discharged. A solider who becomes involved in the black market or an international drug-trafficking ring can be prosecuted in the United States, for example, even though the crime occurred outside the United States and the defendant is no longer in the military.

The same principle has been used to protect children and other victims from sexual exploitation in what often has been referred to as "sex tourism." Many states around the world have enacted legislation that provides extraterritorial jurisdiction to prosecute in their home states any individual who has traveled abroad for the purpose of having sex with children. Thailand, Cambodia, and Brazil are frequent destinations for this purpose. Partially in response to the increase in three types of acts, the U.S. Congress enacted the "Prosecutorial Remedies and Other Tools to End the Exploitation of Children Today" (PROTECT) Act in 2003. Under the PROTECT Act, the U.S. government retains jurisdiction to prosecute U.S. citizens accused of committing such acts, regardless of whether the acts are criminal under the laws of the state where they occurred.

Regional Efforts

Regional transnational policing efforts often are undertaken in areas along national borders. Along the U.S.-Canadian and U.S.-Mexican borders, for example, law-enforcement activities address immigration and customs violations, as well as theft, narcotics violations, and human smuggling. Another notable example of regional cooperation can be found in the Republic of Ireland and in Northern Ireland, where the Garda Síochána and the Police Service of Northern Ireland have worked together to fight transnational crime. Transnational enforcement efforts against terrorism are of particular note for these two police agencies, but they also cooperate on many other initiatives, including those designed to address drug trafficking and organized crime.

Another regional initiative is the Schengen Agreement, which was adopted in 1985 to eliminate border controls for more than 20 European states. This agreement also facilitates cross-border police and judicial cooperation, including intelligence sharing, locating stolen cars, interdicting narcotics shipments, locating fugitives from justice, and providing the right of the police to cross borders while in hot pursuit of criminals.

Founded in 1992, the European Union (EU) law-enforcement agency known as Europol (the European Police Office) is yet another example of transnational policing efforts. Headquartered at The Hague in the Netherlands, it facilitates the exchange of information between liaison officers of member states, as well as operational analysis and support, expertise, and technical support for work with serious crimes, which often transcend national borders. However, Europol has no power of arrest, which is viewed as a sovereign function reserved for the individual member states.

International Efforts

Transnational policing efforts go beyond the activities undertaken by either national or regional law-enforcement agencies. Several international law-enforcement agencies operate under the auspices of the UN or by way of treaty.

In 1995, for example, the International Criminal Tribunal for the former Yugoslavia (ICTY) was established by the UN. The Office of the Prosecutor within the ICTY has an Investigations Division staffed by police officers who were either seconded to the ICTY or appointed by the UN. These officers had worldwide jurisdiction to investigate war crimes and crimes against humanity (such as rape, murder, extermination, and torture) that were committed in the territory of the former Yugoslavia. While the international investigators rely on national jurisdictions or on North Atlantic Treaty Organization (NATO) and other military forces to make the physical arrests, the Investigations Division carries out the investigations from inception to indictment. The International Criminal Tribunal for Rwanda was similarly tasked.

Although its jurisdictional matters are not as straightforward as they are with the ICTY, the International Criminal Court (ICC) also has jurisdiction to investigate serious crimes such as murder, rape, torture, and persecution. The ICC also has an Investigations Division, but its investigators come from different backgrounds and are not strictly police investigators. The ICC's investigative activities on the ground are not as operational as the ICTY's, as they rely more heavily on national police cooperation for investigative services.

The UN is involved in capacity building, in that it assists states—often developing countries or those having been involved in internal or international armed conflict—with activities such as establishing the rule of law, training police, establishing security, protecting borders, and ensuring oversight of human rights investigations. One example is the International Police Task Force (IPTF), which was established by the UN Security Council as part of the UN Mission in Bosnia and Herzegovina (UNMIBH). The IPTF was composed of police officers from all over the world; its specific mission was to monitor local law-enforcement activities, training, and assessment.

The IPTF was succeeded by the EU Police Mission in 2003. Its mission was to ensure sustainable policing, including the transformation of the State Investigation and Protection Agency (SIPA) into a successful law-enforcement agency poised to combat organized crime and corruption. The EU Police Mission also was tasked with ensuring more comprehensive and quality investigative efforts against organized crime in cross-border scenarios by the police in Bosnia and Herzegovina.

Other UN missions have had a more operational focus, such as the UN Mission in Kosovo (UNMIK). It was created by a Security Council resolution in 1999 that established an armed police agency with priorities including (1) providing a temporary police presence; (2) establishing the Kosovo Police Service; and (3) fighting human trafficking, prostitution, and other serious forms of organized crime.

The UN Civilian Police, or UNCIVPOL, has participated in many peacekeeping and law-enforcement missions around the world. Each mission is headed by an appointed police commissioner who directs an international police force composed of many national contingents. Typically, UNCIVPOL accompanies a UN military mission in country, and it often provides technical assistance in relation to the suppression and investigation of transnational crimes. For example, the UN Civilian Police Mission to Haiti, which completed its mandate in 2000, was tasked with providing training and assistance to the Haitian police. This differed from other missions in that UNCIVPOL did not accompany a military peacekeeping force. Other UNCIVPOL missions have sent law-enforcement officers to Darfur, Bosnia, Liberia, the Democratic Republic of the Congo, Western Sahara, and Ivory Coast.

Specialized international training programs also are part of transnational policing. For instance, the International Criminal Investigative Training Assistance Program (ICITAP), hosted by the U.S. Department of Justice, provides training that is specifically designed to assist other states in the area of transnational crime. There are also five international law enforcement academies (ILEAs) around the world; one of their stated missions is to enhance the suppression of transnational crime. Administered by the U.S. Department of State, the ILEAs are located in Hungary, Thailand, Botswana, El Salvador, and the U.S. state of New Mexico.

Challenges for Transnational Policing

The globalization of crime has led to transnational and international policing models whose efforts have been increasingly successful in the fight against international terrorism, human smuggling, and the emerging, contemporary form of piracy on the high seas. However, these efforts also bring challenges—not just in preventing, investigating, and eradicating crime but also in the areas of sovereignty, legislation, privacy, and human rights protections. These are public policy areas that should be addressed with a view to improvement or reform. For example, questions are often raised concerning the retention of intelligence or personal information about a national of one state by a law-enforcement agency of another. Indeed, privacy laws vary greatly from nation to nation. Perhaps more critical than mere invasion of privacy is the potential for human rights abuses to occur in some states when information is misused or handled inappropriately.

Contemporary challenges include the incorporation into bilateral or multilateral treaties of provisions for full or partial immunity for members of one state who are operating in another state. UN staff members, for example, often have similar immunity, which provides protection from civil action and unwarranted criminal prosecution. In some instances, however, immunity serves to protect agents of a state who commit crimes such as espionage or sex offenses.

As the notion of transnational policing expands, practitioners and academics are studying the practices from a number of perspectives, with public policy, sovereignty, and the protection of human rights in the forefront. Indeed, research and relevant literature on the subject of transnational policing are limited. Consequently, transnational policing is a field ripe for more rigorous study, with the aim of improving policies and procedures and preventing and eradicating crimes while respecting privacy, human rights, and national sovereignty.

John R. Cencich
California University of Pennsylvania

See also Europol; Interpol; Police Cooperation; Transnational Crime: Defined; War Crimes Tribunals

Further Readings

Aden, Hartmut. "Convergence of Policing Policies and Transnational Policing in Europe." *European Journal of Crime, Criminal Law and Criminal Justice*, v.9 (2001).

Casey, John. *Policing the World: The Practice of International and Transnational Policing*. Durham, NC: Carolina Academic Press, 2009.

Goldsmith, Andrew and James Sheptycki, eds. *Crafting Transnational Policing: Police Capacity-Building and Global Policing Reform*. Portland, OR: International Specialized Book Services, 2007.

Loader, Ian and Neil Walker. "Locating the Public Interest in Transnational Policing." EUI-Law Working Papers, European University Institute. http://papers.ssrn.com/sol3/papers.cfm?abstract_id=1022882 (Accessed February 2011).

Scheptycki, James, ed. *Issues in Transnational Policing*. New York: Routledge, 2000.

POLITICAL INFLUENCE PEDDLING

Influence peddling is often viewed as synonymous with bribery, the practice of using money, wealth, personal undertaking, or gifts to purchase a favorable outcome or decision from an official, government officeholder, or public authority. Typically, bribery involves direct provision of financial inducements by a private interest to a public official in exchange for a decision beneficial to the purchaser. Common examples involve corporate bribery of government representatives in exchange for a policy favorable to the corporation or for a government contract with the company.

Some make a distinction between bribery and influence peddling and focus on the role of third-party entities in the latter. In this definition, influence peddling involves payment to a third party, which is then responsible for influencing the decision-making entity. It is the expectation of the buyer that the third party receiving payment has a close enough connection to ensure a favorable outcome for the purchaser. In this sense, much of the concern with influence peddling focuses on lobbying and the activities, legal or illegal, of formal or informal lobbyists. In cases of influence peddling, personal gain is placed above the proper fulfillment of public service.

Within criminology, influence peddling, along with other forms of elite deviance or white-collar crime, was once largely overlooked, as the disciplinary focus was overwhelmingly placed on so-called street crimes, or crimes of the poor. Influence peddling is identified as a central concern for criminology by Edwin Sutherland in his groundbreaking work on corporate crime, *White Collar Crime* (1949). Sutherland identifies bribery and influence peddling among his seven dominant forms of white-collar crime. For critics, there is some concern that much of everyday lobbying practice amounts to, or is based on, influence peddling. Indeed, lobbying is largely about the use of direct meetings and relations with government representatives or officials to shape and frame policy or purchasing decisions. Because lobbying meetings are not subject to public observance, there is concern that it can operate within gray areas or cross the line from legitimate to illegitimate with little real oversight. Influencing private individuals by providing them with money, gifts, or services is not illegal. Thus, there is often some debate over whether a public official was approached in his or her capacity as a public figure or simply as a private individual. This is typically the case where former members of government or of a political party engage in new and different capacities with their former colleagues, with whom they may well have maintained close friendships, associations, or even family ties.

Indeed, some suggest that gray areas emerge in the everyday work of government officials in representative democracies. Representatives of government, such as members of the U.S. Congress, are tasked with representing the interests of their constituents and playing active parts in the formation and implementation of public policy and budgetary policies and allocations. Representing the interests of constituents is obviously not viewed as a crime, but ambiguities can arise in the determination of those interests and how they might be served. Which constituents are really being represented and how, for example, become relevant questions. A crime is said to occur when decisions of the governmental representative are determined to have been arrived at in exchange for personal gain.

In the context of corporate globalization and transnational trade, influence peddling has become a major concern. Some have noted that influence peddling is likely to be prevalent where host countries lack resources relative to corporations that are looking to invest or locate in those countries. In such cases, particularly where the government in question is not an established democracy subject to external or independent oversight, opportunities for influence peddling are coupled with financial pressures to engage in such practices. It is particularly common for tax breaks and incentives to be traded through influence peddling in cases in which governments seek foreign direct investments. In terms of lobbying by foreign entities in the United States, the only requirement is that the lobbyist in question register with the government, as required under the Foreign Agents Registration Act of 1938.

Much concern over influence peddling involves relations between governments and representatives of corporations associated with the manufacture of arms or armaments. Military production firms maintain some of the most intensive and regular interactions with government officials and have among the most extensive lobbying networks, often involving former military officers and politicians with prior or ongoing connections to defense departments. Concerns about influence peddling with regard to the military-industrial complex have given rise to some of the most public and troubling cases. In Canada, a scandal emerged in the last decade involving former Prime Minister Brian Mulroney and accusations of influence peddling involving the purchase of Airbus jets. A public inquiry into the so-called Airbus scandal focused on the relationship between Mulroney and international arms industry lobbyist Karlheinz Schreiber. The findings of the Oliphant Inquiry concluded that Mulroney had acted inappropriately, but no penalties resulted.

In Canada the Criminal Code prohibits influence peddling but includes anyone who claims to have influence with the government or with a minister, whether the influence is real or fabricated. This applies to anyone who makes such a claim, not strictly government officials, provided they are deemed to have a connection with government that might reasonably be expected to contribute to affecting a government decision. In Canada, conviction for influence peddling is punishable by a term of imprisonment of up to five years. In the United States, punishment can include imprisonment for not more than one year or a fine of not more than $1000. In addition, there can be a range of administrative penalties, including prohibition against future contracting with the government, a ban against holding any public office, removal from the official lobbying registry, and a ban against future lobbying.

Jeffrey Shantz
Kwantlen Polytechnic University

See also Anticorruption Legislation; Bribery and Graft; Corporate Influence Peddling; Corruption; Influence and Position

Further Readings

Baroud, Aline and Andrew Gibbs. *Improper Use of Public Office*. Ottawa, ON: Department of Justice Canada, 2009. http://www.justice.gc.ca/eng/pi/icg-gci/po-cp/index.html (Accessed February 2011).
Edmiston, Kelly D., Shannon Mudd, and Neven T. Valev. "Incentive Targeting, Influence Peddling, and Foreign Direct Investment." *International Tax and Public Finance*, v.11 (2004).
Geis, Gilbert. *White Collar Crime*. Upper Saddle River, NJ: Prentice Hall, 2006.
Rosoff, Stephen, Henry Pontell, and Robert Tillman. *Profit Without Honor: White-Collar Crime and the Looting of America*. Upper Saddle River, NJ: Prentice Hall, 2009.
Simon, David R. *Elite Deviance*. Boston: Pearson, 2007.
Sutherland, Edwin Hardin. *White Collar Crime*. New York: Dryden Press, 1949.

POLITICALLY EXPOSED PERSONS

Politically exposed persons (PEPs), sometimes referred to as senior foreign political figures, are considered to be past or present high-ranking or senior-level individuals in the executive, legislative, administrative, military, and judicial branches of a foreign government who are currently or formerly entrusted with high-level public duties and responsibilities.

Such persons may be heads of state, senior politicians, heads of political parties, high-level government officials, senior judicial officials, military officials, senior executives of state-owned or state-affiliated enterprises and corporations, and members of their family and close business associates. Politically exposed persons, by virtue of their official title, the position of their office, prominence, sphere of influence, and access to funds and finances, may be considered high-risk to themselves, their affiliate organizations, their government, and the financial institutions with which they conduct business; this is particularly applicable to those individuals who come from high-risk countries.

The designation "politically exposed persons" was influenced in particular by high-profile cases such as those involving Ferdinand and Imelda Marcos of the Philippines and General Sani Abacha of Nigeria. During their 20-year reign (1965–86), the Marcoses allegedly looted millions from the government of the Philippines, much of which was hidden in Swiss banks. Similarly, General Abacha, the former dictator of Nigeria (1993–98), allegedly embezzled an estimated $3 billion from the Nigerian government, from which an undisclosed amount was transferred to banks within Switzerland and the United Kingdom. In both cases, Switzerland's Office of Justice ruled that $458 million and $450 million be returned to the countries of Nigeria and the Philippines, respectively. These cases in particular underscored the importance for banking and financial institutions' obligation for employing due diligence and heightened scrutiny in vetting clients and the source of their monies, which has been deemed even more important given the growing threats and increased incidence of global terrorism. Some key organizations, documents, and legislation that address the term, designation, and significance of PEPs are the U.S.A. Patriot Act (officially, the Uniting and Strengthening America by Providing Appropriate Tools Required to Intercept and Obstruct Terrorism Act of 2001); the 2003 United Nations Convention Against Corruption (UNCAC); the Financial Action Task Force on Money Laundering (FATF); the Basel Committee on Banking Supervision; the Foreign Corrupt Practices Act of 1977 (FCPA); the U.S. Department of the Treasury, Financial Crimes Enforcement Network (FinCEN); the Association of Certified Anti-Money-Laundering Specialists (ACAMS); the European Union Money Laundering Directive; the Swiss Federal Banking Commission; the American Bankers Association; and the Office of Foreign Assets Control (OFAC).

Although relationships with such high-profile individuals may yield innumerable positive and productive benefits, and the majority of PEPs do not engage in criminal or corrupt activities, given the nature and importance of their office and relationships, they are susceptible to engaging in, or falling victim to, any number of transnational crimes. Specific challenges involving PEPs occur in the contexts of their real estate purchases; their acquisition and movement of precious metals, jewels, and artwork; their transport of currency, commodities, and negotiable instruments; and the manner in which they use banking and financial institutions. The criminal activities in which PEPs may be involved include (and are not necessarily limited to) misappropriation and diversion of funds, embezzlement, extortion, bribery, corruption, asset theft, money laundering, and terrorism. Notwithstanding the seriousness of these crimes, money laundering, along with grand corruption and bribery, has been particularly cited as a significant concern to worldwide banking and financial institutions; according to some estimates, it can reach costs in excess of $1 trillion annually.

Despite the relatively small number of PEPs who engage in illicit or criminal activities, those who do can have a severe and adverse financial impact on their affiliate organizations and the financial institutions with which they conduct business. Their actions can have a disproportionate and adverse impact domestically, regionally, and internationally across a wide range of venues and may undermine public trust and confidence, disrupt social services, compromise government revenue streams, and weaken the climate for private investments. The potential risks associated with such prominent individuals, particularly within banking and financial institution venues, call for heightened due caution, diligence, and monitoring in conducting business with PEPs. Exposure to such risks may vary, depending on the products and services used, the relationship with foreign entities or individuals, and other factors, such as the nature of the official's position, duties, responsibilities, sphere of influence, level and nature of authority or influence over government activities and officials, and access to governmental assets or funds.

In response to this need, entrusted third-party financial organizations provide enhanced background investigations of PEPs in order to mitigate the risk, liability, and reputation of a banking client and the banking institution at large. Organizations such as the World Bank, World-Check, WorldCompliance, Dow Jones Watchlist, Tracesmart Corporate, SourceMedia, and RDC are among these groups. Relying on up-to-date integrated and analytical intelligence databases, many such service providers ensure risk and compliance protection. Not only do they take into consideration the individual and his or her position; they also consider any number of factors germane to the country's social and political environment. Such databases identify heads of state, cabinet members, members of parliament, high members of the judiciary, national bank governors, political and religious leaders, military officials, senior executives of state-owned companies, ambassadors, former PEPs, and their families and close associates. The goal of practicing due diligence is to prevent, thwart, and mitigate the risk and liability to banks and financial institutions and, in doing so, provide an environment that discourages illicit, criminal, and corrupt practices, thus encouraging the integrity and trustworthiness common to most PEPs.

Robert F. Vodde
Fairleigh Dickinson University

See also Electoral Manipulation; Recovery of Stolen Assets

Further Readings

Australian Institute of Criminology. *Challenges in Dealing With Politically Exposed Persons.* Canberra, Australia: Author, 2010.

Gray, Larissa et al. *Politically Exposed Persons: Preventive Measures for the Banking Sector.* Washington, DC: World Bank, 2010.

Serio, Mario. "Politically Exposed Persons: AML, Taking the Profit Out of Corruption and Problems for the Banks." *Journal of Money Laundering Control*, v.11/3 (2008).

POLLUTION: AIR AND WATER

Crimes connected to air and water pollution are considered transnational environmental crimes. These criminal offenses either cause or permit this particular kind of pollution, and they are inherently transnational because most toxins and pollutants travel freely on the wind and in surface and ground-water, moving from one country to another. In fact, once they are introduced in an ecosystem, the travel of pollutants is not stopped by borders: ecosystems are open systems, governed not by political boundaries and rules but by the biological, chemical, and geographical laws of nature.

Air and water pollution is caused mainly by the illegal disposal of toxic industrial waste, which is currently one of the main illegal services offered by many organized criminal groups. Paradoxically, this illegal service has become more relevant and appealing for many toxic industrial waste producers since governments have started to implement environmental legislation and spread environmental awareness. New rules have increased the costs and complexity of toxic industrial waste disposal procedures, whereas the low costs and relative simplicity of services proposed by criminal groups, even if unlawful, are becoming more and more affordable.

Pollution is the introduction into the environment, as a result of human activity, of substances (or energy) liable to cause hazard or harm to human beings, other living organisms, and ecological systems; damage to structures and material property; or interference with legitimate environment use. The different types of pollution can be classified according to the affected environment: soil, water (the hydrosphere, including underground water and water from lakes, rivers, and seas), or air (the atmosphere). In some cases, different kinds of pollution can be connected. For example, soil pollution can be linked to risk of air pollution if the pollutant is volatile.

Air pollution is caused by the discharge into the atmosphere of harmful substances such as carbon monoxide, sulfur dioxide, and lead. This pollution is caused by airborne particulates (in dust, mist, fumes, gas, vapor, and smoke) from a variety of sources, such as fuel combustion and waste incineration. Water pollution can be chemical or bacterial. Chemical pollution is caused by the introduction of substances, such as sewage, domestic waste, industrial waste, and lead and other heavy metals, into streams, groundwater and other water resources. Bacterial pollution is usually connected to fecal pollution caused by bacterial organisms from the coliform group, largely *Escherichia coli*.

Crimes involving air and water pollution are considered transnational environmental crimes. New regulations have increased the cost of industrial toxic waste disposal and lawbreakers turn to the low cost and ease of disposal services offered by criminal groups. (Photos.com)

National and international laws and regulations address air and water pollution by prescribing preventive measures to avoid discharge of pollutants; specific actions and procedures to limit damages caused by their accidental spread; and penalties and sanctions for the perpetrators of violations to the prescribed rules. However, air and water pollution is increasingly systematic, and it is one of the fastest-growing areas of illegal activity in the field of environmental crimes.

Human activities connected to air and water pollution are mainly the illegal emission, transport, management, and dumping of hazardous, toxic, radioactive, and other dangerous wastes. Hazardous waste is associated with a wide range of industrial processes whose wastes include solvents, acids, asbestos, electrical components, computer monitors, televisions, fluorescent tubes, and end-of-life vehicles. Heavy metals such as copper, lead, zinc, cadmium, nickel, and mercury, which cause damage to one or more physiological functions, are considered toxic waste. Heavy metal pollution of the air is caused by the burning of fossil fuels, burning of toxic waste, and industrial processes that release into the atmosphere high levels of these metals in smoke, smog, dust, and fumes. Heavy metal pollution of water is caused by elevated levels of arsenic, copper, nickel, mercury, lead, chromium, cadmium, and zinc ions that accumulate in sediments and are gradually released into the water. These metals, ingested or absorbed through the skin, become more

concentrated as they progress from smaller to larger organisms in the food chain. They are therefore among the main persistent organic pollutants. They persist in the environment, resisting degradation in air, water, and soil for long periods; they bioaccumulate; and they have the potential for long-range transport, traveling long distances from the source of origin mainly through air and water. The main types of radioactive waste are hospital waste (produced by nuclear medicine departments and radio-analytical laboratories) and nuclear waste (produced by military and energy applications of radioactivity). Finally, it is necessary to add that intensive farming and agriculture are major sources of water pollution and significant sources of air pollution, because organic manures and inorganic fertilizers release large amounts of nitrates and phosphates into the air and water environments.

Pollution can be local (when it occurs in the vicinity of the source) or transboundary, in which case it has transnational relevance. Considering that borders do not stop air and water, in most cases air and water pollution has great transnational relevance. Moreover, illegal dumping of dangerous, toxic, and nuclear waste connected to criminal activity occurs mainly in developing countries, where waste from industrial countries is often buried, dumped at sea, or incinerated. In fact, the illegal movement and dumping of hazardous and other wastes, as well as the smuggling of illegal pollutants directly connected with air and water pollution, are becoming increasingly transnational, according to the United Nations (UN). These crimes are committed in more than one state; committed in one state but with a substantial part of their preparation, planning, direction, or control taking place in another state; committed in one state involving one or more organized criminal groups that engage in criminal activities in more than one state; or committed in one state but have substantial effects in another state. These crimes are most often committed to avoid taxes, fees, and other costs of disposal, and they are characterized by high returns and low risk. They rely heavily on both corruption and the involvement of organized criminal groups.

Even though air and water pollution is often caused by negligent, malicious, or fraudulent individuals (through occupational crimes, committed by individuals or small groups), usually the worst pollution crimes are the responsibility of companies (such as the one resulting from organizational negligence at the Union Carbide India Limited company in Bhopal, India, in December 1984) and in many cases they are deliberately carried out by commercial bodies (and thus are organizational crimes committed by corporations). These malicious organizational crimes are committed mainly to avoid high disposal costs but also to avoid high internal security costs and, in some cases, to hide unlawful hazardous industrial processes or irregularities in the use of raw materials and resulting wastes.

These corporations (as well as many individuals) practically create a demand for illegal services aimed at affordable and discrete waste disposal. This demand is promptly satisfied by organized criminal groups, and criminal organizations are deeply involved in these activities. Some of them, like the Italian Camorra, actually adopted real holding structures, managing toxic, hazardous, and radioactive wastes coming from different countries. International criminal organizations collect these wastes from producers in developed countries, taking no particular care or precautions and charging low fees. They then transport these substances to specific areas in developing countries, often in Africa and Asia. There the wastes are buried, burned, or dumped at sea: in some cases, they are simply abandoned in deserts or other unpopulated areas. The resulting air and water pollution can be immediate or only slightly delayed. Along the Somali coast during the 2004 tsunami, for example, many containers of hazardous toxic waste, which had been produced in Europe and dumped more than a decade before only a short distance offshore, broke open. Pollutants such as radioactive and hospital wastes, lead, cadmium, mercury, and other highly toxic substances spread into the water and air. The exact number of casualties resulting from people breathing in toxic fumes and dust is difficult to determine and remains unknown. In the following years, however, cancer clusters in the area increased dramatically. In some cases, criminal organizations that illegally dispose of toxic waste adopt other methods: instead of dumping the pollutant containers at sea, they simply sink old cargo ships with their holds full of waste. The *Marco Polo*, for example, was sunk in May 1993 near Sicily, with the hold full of radioactive waste. This system allows criminal groups to obtain insurance compensation as extra income.

In most cases, illegal dumping is possible thanks to high levels of corruption and bribery in the receiving countries and false documents and certificates produced by corrupted public officials in the producing countries. It is not easy to prove the relationships between members of criminal groups and their activities, and other actors from commerce and politics. Actually, the demarcation between corporate and organized crime is increasingly blurred, most of all in the area of air and water pollution, where relationships and cooperation are getting stronger day by day. In these cases, it is very difficult to get behind the crime to the principal offender. In most cases, countries' sentencing systems are not adequate to punish corporate bodies or managers within those organizations. Moreover, corporate and white-collar crimes are made up of many acts and omissions that, though unethical, are not always illegal and, as such, might not merit prosecution.

From a criminological viewpoint, transnational air or water pollution requires three elements: local pollution (and therefore a source), transnational transfer of this local pollution (and therefore a transfer vector), and a receiver (victim). According to this analysis, usually so-called global pollution (such as the depletion of the ozone layer or the greenhouse effect) is not considered a kind of transnational pollution. In fact, even though it is transboundary in nature, this kind of pollution does not have clearly established relationships between source and receiver, especially from a legal viewpoint. Demonstrating such a relationship is absolutely fundamental in order to prosecute air and water pollution crimes. Considering that most of these crimes are transnational and that the receiver (victim) is always very far from the original source of the pollutants, it is obviously very difficult to collect evidence in these cases, both at a national and an international level.

It is also important to consider the differences in national legislation regarding air and water pollution. Pollution control standards and rules vary among countries, and these differences can seriously affect operating costs and profits. Therefore, in many cases commercial bodies decide to relocate industries to countries with less stringent laws. This variability in environmental law is very relevant and is exploited not only by corporations (more or less legally) but most of all by international criminal groups (always illegally). Less stringent national environmental laws also mean milder criminal, civil, and administrative punishments, producing higher returns and lowering risk.

State sovereignty issues make it very difficult to establish an international law for transnational air and water pollution. Difficulty in obtaining evidence, enforcing international law, and the choice of forums are the main obstacles. As a result of these difficulties, investigations and trials against corporations and international criminal groups are not possible. Perpetrators are therefore encouraged to continue in their criminal activities.

From a transnational viewpoint, air and water pollution crimes are addressed by bilateral, multilateral, or global treaties (conventional law). Bilateral treaties (involving two neighboring countries) address mainly the pollution of shared waters (such as rivers) and the reduction of immediate air pollution. Multilateral treaties, such as the 1995 Convention for the Protection of the Marine Environment and the Coastal Region of the Mediterranean, are signed by a group of states in order to mitigate shared air and water pollution problems. Bilateral and multilateral treaties are very specific and are based on a common interest in protecting clearly defined shared resources. Global treaties, such as the 1982 UN Convention on the Law of the Sea, are agreements that have a broader scope and address global issues affecting many nations. They are very difficult to negotiate and implement, largely because they address not only environmental and pollution issues but also industrial and economic issues. The Kyoto Protocol of the UN Framework Convention on Climate Change, for example, imposed limits on emissions of four greenhouse gases and thus has had a direct impact on the economic activities of signatory nations. However, there is a growing international awareness that only global agreements to which nations can and do adhere will adequately address transnational crimes such as air and water pollution.

Silvia Ciotti
EuroCrime—Research, Training and Consultancy

See also Adjudicating International Crimes; Pollution: Corporate; Pollution: Shipping-Related; Toxic Dumping

Further Readings

Andreas, Peter. "Transnational Crime and Economic Globalization." In *Transnational Organized Crime and International Security*, Mats Berdal and Monica Serrano, eds. Boulder, CO: Lynne Rienner, 2002.

Hamelin, Raymond, Jean Laporte, and André Picot. *Environnement et Nuisances*. Paris: Axxio-Édition Clartés, 2000.

Hayman, Gavin and Duncan Brack. *International Environmental Crime: The Nature and Control of Environmental Black Markets*. London: Royal Institute of International Affairs, 2002.

Kubasek, Nancy and Gary Silverman. *Environmental Law*. Upper Saddle River, NJ: Pearson/Prentice Hall, 2008.

Michalowski, Raymond and Kevin Bitten. "Transnational Environmental Crime." In *Handbook of Transnational Crime and Justice*, Philip Reichel, ed. Thousand Oaks, CA: Sage, 2005.

White, Rob. *Crimes Against Nature: Environmental Criminology and Ecological Justice*. Devon, UK: Willan, 2008.

White, Rob, ed. *Environmental Crime: A Reader*. Devon, UK: Willan, 2009.

POLLUTION: CORPORATE

Considered an autonomous legal entity separate from its shareholders, a corporation possesses most of the legal rights and responsibilities that individuals possess. For example, a corporation has the right to enter into contracts, own assets, and borrow money. Additionally, a corporation may both initiate a lawsuit and be forced to defend itself against a lawsuit. Although corporate profits are taxed both when received by the corporation and when distributed to the shareholders, the major benefit of a corporation is that it provides limited liability for shareholders through the existence of the corporate veil. This mechanism protects corporate shareholders from corporate liability by limiting the extent of a shareholder's liability to the amount he or she invested in the corporation. However, if the corporate veil is pierced, shareholders can be held personally liable for the acts of the corporation. Thus, a properly functioning corporation allows shareholders the right to participate in the profits and escape personal liability for the company's debts.

Corporations are included within the definition of individuals to be prosecuted for violating environmental laws and/or statutes. In the United States, some of the major federal legislation impacting corporate liability and at the center of litigation involving claims of corporate polluting include the Clean Air Act of 1970; the National Environmental Policy Act of 1970; the Clean Water Act of 1972; the Endangered Species Act of 1973; the Safe Drinking Water Act of 1974; the Toxic Substances Control Act of 1976; the Surface Mining Control and Reclamation Act of 1977; the Comprehensive Environmental Response, Compensation, and Liability Act of 1980 (CERCLA); and the Emergency Planning and Community Right-to-Know Act of 1986. Some of the federal agencies that are especially germane to environmental crimes associated with pollution include the U.S. Environmental Protection Agency, the Agency for Toxic Substances and Disease Registry, and the Council on Environmental Quality.

CERCLA was at the center of one major court case that had a significant impact on corporate liability in regard to pollution within the United States. CERCLA strives to ensure that the polluting corporation pays for cleanup. In *United States v. Bestfoods* (524 U.S. 51, 1998), the Supreme Court reconciled conflicting positions among the various federal circuits in regard to the liability of parent corporations over corporate subsidiaries accused of polluting. Prior to the Court's decision, the lower courts, depending on the circuit, had taken three different approaches to determining a parent corporation's liability as an operator of a facility owned or operated by its subsidiary. Per *United States v. Bestfoods*, the Court held that a parent corporation may be found liable only for illegal acts of its subsidiaries when there is sufficient evidence to pierce the protection of the corporate veil or if the parent corporation is directly liable for the violation. More specifically, the protection of the corporate veil is destroyed when a corporation has directly managed and/or exercised control over the operation of a subsidiary responsible for pollution. The Court's holding was not based on the level of the corporation's activities in controlling the subsidiary as a whole. Rather, the Court found that the germane inquiry concerned the corporation's level of control over the subsidiary, specifically in regard to the waste disposal activities involved in the alleged pollution. In other words, the "actual control" test articulated by the Court in *United States v. Bestfoods* demands active participation on the part of the corporation in the waste disposal activities of the subsidiary. Thus, the Court established that under CERCLA parent corporations are not indirectly liable as owners for the acts of a subsidiary. Additionally, the Court offered examples to illustrate situations in which direct liability would apply to a parent corporation. In sum, the Court's opinion in *United States v. Bestfoods*, clarified that for corporate liability, in cases involving pollution under CERCLA, an actual participation threshold is the appropriate standard, versus previous standards that imposed liability upon a corporation if it merely had the authority to control the subsidiary. The Supreme Court has not addressed the question of whether a corporation can be held criminally liable for criminal acts of its subsidiaries. Another important case involving pollution within the United States was *Massachusetts v. Environmental Protection Agency* (549 U.S. 497, 2007). In this case, several states sued the Environmental Protection Agency (EPA). Specifically, the plaintiffs argued that the EPA had an obligation to regulate certain greenhouse gases, such as carbon dioxide, as pollutants. The Court held that greenhouse gases are pollutants, and that because of this, the EPA may regulate them. The EPA, however, argued that it had discretion in regulating greenhouse gas emissions such as carbon dioxide. In response, the Court found that the EPA's rationale for not regulating at the time of the decision was inadequate. Thus, the Court remanded the case to the agency and demanded the EPA articulate a more reasonable basis for choosing not to regulate greenhouse gas emissions.

Over the past few decades, several cases have been brought in U.S. courts against multinational corporations for environmental torts involving pollution committed abroad. Originally enacted by Congress in 1789, the Alien Torts Claims Act (ATCA), also known as the Alien Tort Statute, establishes the foundation for these cases. Specifically, the ATCA states that U.S. district courts shall have original jurisdiction over any civil action brought by an alien for a tort committed in violation of the law of nations or a treaty of the United States. Thus, the plaintiff initiating the suit against a multinational corporation for pollution must be an alien, must be suing in tort only, and must demonstrate that the tort violates the law of nations or a treaty of the United States. In *Filartiga v. Pena-Iral* (630 F.2d 876, 2d Cir., 1980), the Court first used the ATCA to allow U.S. courts to address human rights abuses that occurred abroad. Starting with *Amlon Metals, Inc. v. FMC Corp* (775 F. Supp. 668, S.D.N.Y.,

1991), courts have addressed a number of claims of pollution by a multinational corporation under the ATCA. These cases include *Beanal v. Freeport-McMoran, Inc.* (969 F. Supp. 362, E.D. La. 1997), *Jota v. Texaco Inc.* (157 F. 3d 153, 155, 159, 2d Cir., 1998), and *Flores v. S. Peru Copper, Corp.* (253 F.Supp. 2d 510, 514, S.D.N.Y., 2002). Generally, in these cases an alien plaintiff claimed to have suffered harm through pollution allegedly caused by a multinational corporation conducting business in their developing country. However, none of these cases have been successful. In 2004, the Supreme Court explored the modern-day scope of the ATCA. In *Sosa v. Alvarez-Machain* (542 U.S. 692, 2004), the Court stated that district courts may permit ATCA suits based on present-day customary international law rules. However, the Court required those rules to be comparable to the international law rules recognized at the time the ATCA was enacted. Thus, currently, the standard for bringing pollution claims under the ATCA is that the allegedly violated norm must be as definite and universally accepted as the norms constituting the law of nations when the ATCA was enacted. Since *Sosa v. Alvarez-Machain*, the only case to address environmental ATCA claims has been *Sarei v. Rio Tinto PLC and Rio Tinto Ltd* (650 F.Supp. 2d 1004, C.D. Cal. 2009).

Neil Guzy
University of Pittsburgh, Greensburg

See also Corporate Liability; Pollution: Air and Water; Toxic Dumping; Wildlife Crime

Further Readings

Amlon Metals, Inc. v. FMC Corp, 775 F.Supp. 668 (S.D.N.Y. 1991).
Bates, G. M. and Zada Lipman. *Corporate Liability for Pollution.* Pyrmont, Australia: LBC Information Services, 1998.
Beanal v. Freeport-McMoran, Inc., 969 F.Supp. 362 (E.D. La. 1997).
Brookman, Fiona et al. *Handbook on Crime.* Portland, OR: Willan, 2010.
Case, Phil. *Environmental Risk Management and Corporate Lending: A Global Perspective.* Boca Raton, FL: CRC Press, 1999.
Croall, Hazel. *Understanding White Collar Crime.* Philadelphia: Open University Press, 2001.
Filartiga v. Pena-Iral, 630 F.2d 876 (2d Cir.1980).
Flores v. S. Peru Copper, Corp., 253 F.Supp. 2d 510, 514 (S.D.N.Y. 2002). 28 U.S.C., Section 1350.
Gunningham, Neil. *Corporate Environmental Responsibility.* Burlington, VT: Ashgate, 2009.
Jota v. Texaco Inc., 157 F. 3d 153, 155, 159 (2d Cir. 1998).
Mallin, Chris A. *Corporate Social Responsibility: A Case Study Approach.* Northampton, MA: Edward Elgar, 2009.
Massachusetts v. Environmental Protection Agency, 549 U.S. 497 (2007).
Raman, K. Ravi and Ronnie D. Lipschutz. *Corporate Social Responsibility: Comparative Critiques.* New York: Palgrave Macmillan, 2010.
Sarei v. Rio Tinto PLC and Rio Tinto Ltd, 650 F.Supp. 2d 1004 (C.D. Cal. 2009).
Sosa v. Alvarez-Machain, 542 U.S. 692 (2004).
United States v. Bestfoods, 524 U.S. 51 (1998).

POLLUTION: SHIPPING-RELATED

Marine pollution and climate change are recognized as two of the four primary threats to the world's oceans, along with overfishing and habitat destruction. Shipping stands with fishing as the most intensive human uses of the planet's oceans. Shipping is a major contributor to marine pollution as well as to climate change and is a major source of water and air pollution. Among the pollution and waste resulting from shipping are emissions of air contaminants, including sulfur dioxide, carbon dioxide, carbon monoxide, and hydrocarbons; chemical wastes released as part of regular operational processes, including industrial cleaning agents used in the upkeep of ships' mechanical operations as well as household chemicals used in cleaning human quarters; releases of solid waste materials, including onboard garbage; the intentional dumping of hazardous wastes; release of untreated or improperly treated sewage; and accidental spills of harmful materials, including chemical and oil spills. In addition to marine spills and pollution related to shipping, shipping has contributed to the spread of invasive species through the discharge of ballast water containing living organisms.

In the 21st century, shipping is a massive and fully global enterprise. With corporate globalization and the expansion of multinational trading regimes, the use of oceangoing vessels to transport freight has increased and continues to grow. Ocean-based shipping is now the means of transport for approximately 90 percent of world trade. It is clear that without the use of oceangoing transport, corporate globalization could not have developed in the broad manner that it has and would not have secured the economic rationality from which it currently profits.

Estimates suggest that there are approximately 85,000 commercial ships registered within flag states. These vessels transport approximately 5.4 billion metric ton of cargo across the world's oceans each year. Today's shipping employs a wide range of ships of various types and sizes, ranging from car ferries to container ships and supertankers. Shipping is categorized as domestic, international, or transit (shipping moves directly from one nation to another, passing through other regions without calling at any port).

Most ocean freighters are driven by diesel-powered engines. Pollution from diesel fuel represents one of the most dangerous sources of air contamination. Residual fuel used in powering shipping vessels contains sulfur levels almost 2,000 times greater than U.S. law allows for other diesel engines. It is estimated that emissions related to shipping contribute to almost 60,000 deaths globally each year and a range of respiratory ailments. Effects are pronounced along the coastal regions on major trade routes.

The massive and global shipping industry creates pollution and waste in the forms of air contaminants, chemical waste, releases of solid waste materials, the release of untreated or improperly treated sewage, and intentional or unintentional hazardous waste and chemical spills. (Photos.com)

It is also suggested that oceangoing vessels account for around 3 percent of worldwide emissions contributing to global climatic change. Shipping is responsible for an estimated 1.12 billion metric tons of carbon dioxide, representing almost 4.5 percent of all global emissions of carbon dioxide, the primary greenhouse gas. The shipping industry globally is responsible for more greenhouse gas emissions annually than all countries on the planet except for China, India, Japan, Russia, and the United States. One container shipping vessel is estimated to produce the greenhouse gas emissions of 50,000 cars.

Garbage has proven as harmful to marine life as chemical and oil spills. The material that makes up most of marine garbage—and the one that is the most harmful and poses the most lasting impact—is plastic. Some plastics can take nearly 500 years to dissolve in the oceans. It is estimated that about eight million items of marine litter enter the oceans each day, with about 60 percent from shipping activities, whether intentional or unintentional. The impact of plastic waste is severe. Plastics can contribute to habitat loss and the fouling of ecosystems and can pose a fatal threat to animals, which can ingest, become entrapped in, or otherwise become injured by the waste matter. Each year, approximately one million seabirds, 100,000 sea mammals, and untold numbers of fish are killed by plastic waste.

Marine debris can also pose navigational hazards to seagoing vessels. Some of these hazards have resulted in the capsizing of boats and ships, accompanied by the loss of human life.

Another growing problem is the issue of invasive species released from the ballast water of oceangoing shipping vessels. The development of larger ships and the expansion of the shipping trade have accelerated the spread of invasive species transported in ballast water. These invasive species have caused significant environmental damage to a variety of ecosystems, as in cases of the introduction of North Pacific starfish to Australian waters and zebra mussels and green crabs in Canada. In some cases, ecosystems have been dramatically transformed through the introduction of invasive plant species from ballast water into new environments, as has occurred with purple loosestrife in Canada.

Significant social repercussions are associated with shipping waste. The impacts of environmental waste are directly connected with issues of poverty in human communities. Poor people and communities are most negatively affected by damage to food sources caused by the impact of invasive species. They are also most negatively impacted economically by harm done to natural resources, particularly within subsistence economies. Poor people also have fewer resources available to deal with the effects of exposure to waste and toxic substances emitted by shipping activities. People whose diets consist of regular consumption of aquatic species can be threatened. Health impacts can be particularly severe for women and children. Fat-soluble toxins accumulate in all human bodies, but particularly women's bodies, because even fit women naturally have a higher percentage of fat than do men. The resulting health risks can be passed to infants through breast milk. Children are particularly vulnerable to contaminants such as lead or mercury.

Unfortunately, few steps have been taken to address shipping-related waste and pollution. Some global measures include the Convention on the Prevention of Marine Pollution by Dumping of Wastes and Other Matter (1972), the Basel Convention on the Control of Transboundary Movements of Hazardous Wastes and Their Disposal (1989), the International Convention for the Prevention of Pollution from Ships (1973) and its amended protocol of 1978, and the Rotterdam Convention on the Prior Informed Consent Procedure for Certain Hazardous Chemicals and Pesticides in International Trade (1998). With the centrality of shipping transport to the global economy, it is clear that community and workplace organizing, rather than industry initiatives, will be required to improve the situation.

Jeffrey Shantz
Kwantlen Polytechnic University

See also Corporate Liability; Pollution: Air and Water; Pollution: Corporate; Toxic Dumping; Wildlife Crime

Further Readings

Corbett, J. and J. Winebrake. "The Role of International Policy in Mitigating Global Shipping Emissions." *Brown Journal of World Affairs*, v.16/2 (2010).

Corbett, J. and J. Winebrake. "Ship Pollution Death Toll 60,000." *Portwatch*, v.1–2 (2007).

Corbett, J. and J. Winebrake. "Sustainable Movement of Goods: Energy and Environmental Implications of Trucks, Trains, Ships, and Planes." *Environmental Management* (November 2007).

Gerdes, L. I., ed. *Endangered Oceans*. San Diego, CA: Greenhaven Press, 2004.

Khee-Jin Tan, A. *Vessel-Source Marine Pollution: The Law and Politics of International Regulation*. Cambridge, UK: Cambridge University Press, 2006.

Talouli, Anthony. "Addressing Shipping Related Marine Pollution in the Pacific Islands Region." http://www.sprep .org/solid_waste/marine.htm (Accessed February 2011).

United Nations Environment Programme. *Ecosystems and Biodiversity in Deepwaters and High Seas*. UNEP Regional Seas Report and Studies 178. New York: Author, 2006.

Vidal, John. "Health Risks of Shipping Pollution Have Been 'Underestimated.'" *The Guardian* (April 2009).

POPULAR SUPPORT MECHANISMS: "ENABLERS" OF CRIMINAL ACTIVITY

Experts on transnational crime generally agree that rapid globalization and increasingly sophisticated technology have been at the root of increased transnational criminal activities since the 1990s. That increase has been fueled by popular support mechanisms that have allowed transnational criminals to operate almost unchecked in countries hospitable to such crimes and to flourish even in countries, such as the United States and the United Kingdom, that are engaged in well-organized efforts to block such activities. Corruption and government inaction are key requirements for attracting transnational crime networks to a given country.

Members of transnational crime groups often depend on intermediaries that provide support for their activities. Support may be provided by corrupt politicians, judges, lawyers, law-enforcement personnel, or insiders at various financial institutions. It may also be provided by other criminal and terrorist groups. In many countries, support is provided by members of the general population who are able to move freely across national borders. Not all of these people are corrupt; many, such as those who live in sub-Saharan Africa, are simply struggling to survive by any means offered. Although support by governments may be the result of corruption, it may also occur through ignorance or inaction.

By the 21st century, transnational crime networks were being identified as "disorganized" crime to differentiate them from traditional organized crime groups. There are a number of differences between older well-established criminal groups that were originally domestic in their operations and newer crime groups that have always operated transnationally. Louise Shelley, the director of the

Terrorism, Transnational Crime and Corruption Center, a research center within the School of Public Policy at George Mason University in Virginia, contends that organized crime groups outside Colombia rarely form links with terrorist groups. Newer transnational crime groups, however, often use members of terrorist organizations to perform specialized functions. Older criminal groups have traditionally forged links with the states in which they operate, choosing to operate in stable environments that help to mask their illegal activities. Working through support mechanisms provided by established financial institutions, such groups have long been able to launder money without fear of detection. Links with corrupt political, judicial, military, and legal officials have allowed them to avoid the radar of detection and prosecution. On the other hand, newer transnational criminal groups serve as nonstate actors, bypassing traditional support groups to instigate instability and chaos. Their support groups are often those with which they have common goals. This type of alliance is most common among jihadist groups and in areas of pronounced regional conflict. Thus, the Sendero Luminoso (Shining Path) was able to spread chaos in Peru, as were Maoist insurgents in Nepal. Afghani drug operatives worked hand in hand with the Taliban for the same purpose, underwriting conflicts in Chechnya and Kosovo.

In many cases, such as in North Korea, transnational crime is both funded and sanctioned by the government, which benefits both financially and politically from criminal activity. Experts on transnational crime maintain that despite chronic food shortages, producing drug crops is more important to the government than producing food crops. It is widely accepted that the North Korean government has expanded its nuclear capability with funds generated through transnational and organized crime. The involvement of the North Korean government in drug trafficking has been extremely well documented, and North Korean diplomats have been arrested in drug busts in a number of countries. The fact that Colombia, Bolivia, and Peru serve as virtually the sole producers of the world's supply of cocaine suggests a measure of official support for those activities. However, a joint effort by the United States and the Andean community has led to a mass eradication of drug crops in that area.

Even though traditional wisdom suggests that official support for transnational crime occurs only in unstable countries with high levels of corruption, support may occur in other areas through failure to monitor such activities rather than through acceptance of criminal activity. In such cases, support mechanisms are provided by officials who allow those activities to occur under the detection radar. In June 2006, the British Broadcasting Corporation reported that trafficking networks had publicly auctioned eastern European women at London-area airports, including facilities at Stansted and Gatwick. According to the Crown Prosecution Service, those women were sold for £8,000 (approximately US$15,000) each. Not a single official intervened, because human trafficking was not considered a high priority. The exploitation of children has also become a worldwide problem, which is often facilitated by a lack of official recognition. In India, children are intentionally maimed before being used by criminals as beggars, on the assumption that handicapped children generate more income than do healthy children. Governments sometimes support transnational crime by ignoring the exploitation of children transported to areas of conflict to serve as soldiers.

Transnational crimes identified as white-collar crimes are heavily dependent on liberal trade policies that allow them to operate in what has been identified as a "borderless world." Illegal gains from their activities are transferred to countries such as Afghanistan, Pakistan, and Yemen, where government inaction and corruption enable criminals to profit from their crimes without interference. Recruitment of insiders is another tool widely employed by white-collar criminal groups to gain support for their activities, and Internet access has allowed that tool to be employed on a global basis. In 2000, a loose network of Mafia-connected individuals plotted with an insider at the Bank of Sicily to clone the bank's online component, targeting $400 million that the European Union had deposited to pay for regional projects. The intention was to transfer the funds to global financial institutions in the Vatican, Switzerland, and Portugal. The crime was foiled when a member of the group notified authorities of the planned heist.

Elizabeth Rholetter Purdy
Independent Scholar

See also Networks; Police Cooperation

Further Readings

Barton, Lee V., ed. *Illegal Drugs and Government Policies.* New York: Nova Science, 2007.

Elges, Rafael and Emma Sutcliffe. "An Overview of Transnational Organized Cyber Crime." *Information Security Journal*, v.17/2 (March 2008).

Gerspacher, Nadia and Benoît Dupont. "The Nodal Structure of International Police Cooperation: An Exploration of Transnational Security Networks." *Global Governance*, v.13 (2007).

Shelley, Louise. *Human Trafficking: A Global Perspective*. New York: Cambridge University Press, 2010.

Shelley, Louise. "The Unholy Trinity: Trans-Crime, Corruption, and Terrorism." *Brown Journal of World Affairs*, v.11/2 (Winter/Spring 2005).

Williams, Phil. "Organized Crime and Cybercrime: Synergies, Trends, and Responses." http://www.crime-research.org/library/Cybercrime.htm (Accessed February 2011).

Zagaris, Bruce. *International White Collar Crime: Causes and Materials*. New York: Cambridge University Press, 2010.

Pornography

While it has been claimed that the pornography industry has three centers—the United States, Brazil, and Hungary—given the increasing use of the Internet, such a clear distinction may no longer be valid. Although American companies centered in southern California produce a huge amount of pornography (11,000 films in 2001 alone), other countries have entered the industry. Japan, for example, probably produces more films (14,000 per year), but they are generally of poor quality and are intended for niche markets. China has seized more than 5 million pirated films being smuggled into that country.

The Growth of Pornography

In Europe, France, though off to a fast start with adult films in the 1970s, faltered and has a very limited output today. Britain and most continental countries have robust adult entertainment industries. An indicator of the omnipresence of pornography is that one can buy explicit hard-core materials in some in Benelux countries as well as in the red light district of Amsterdam. Thus, the industry's reach is pervasive in Common Market countries. In fact, the growth in hardcore pornography has been fueled by the draining of stock of the soft-core variety. Films of the latter genre are simply not being replenished because of the perception that only a very small market for less explicit material exists. Almost all cable companies in Europe now feature hard-core films; some state film networks present hard-core films at all hours. Hotels worldwide feature hard-core films, a fact well known to conventioneers. In addition, many American cable companies now feature both hard-core and soft-core films by subscription, some of European origin. American tastes, however, generally run to a more "robust" female type than one might see in films of European origin, and thus adult films of American origin are generally more popular with domestic audiences.

The primary variable in market domination of the pornography field is distribution, not production, and the United States leads in both areas. Adult film industry fairs in major European cities focus on both, but it is clear that the leading continental companies are those that achieved early market domination. Germany and Spain are the leading European consumers of pornography. Restrictive laws and uneven enforcement put many sex shops in Great Britain out of business. Although Britain has almost no adult film industry of its own, it does have a modest presence in adult-oriented Internet Websites, some of them soft-core.

Hungary is the pornography capital of Europe, and its output dominates that market. Following the fall of its communist government, the nascent capitalist economy was in desperate need of hard currency. Accordingly, it gave the adult entertainment industry free rein starting in 1990. As unsophisticated but beautiful village girls flocked to the city,

Hungary is the pornography capital of Europe, dominating the European pornography production market and dotted with sex shops and small pornography companies. (Photos.com)

the supply of performers outstripped demand and foreign producers, performers, and directors came in force to the country. Technical experts, unemployed after the closure of state-supported film companies, were available to handle production details. The public, weary of communist Puritanism and restrictions, was receptive, as were politicians and officials. Sexually explicit glossy magazines were among the first products of the new industry and gained widespread popularity at home and in European sex shops. Films were to follow in 1993, when former state film production facilities were rented to pornographic filmmakers. Today sex shops and small pornography companies dot the Budapest cityscape. By the mid-1990s Hungary dominated the European pornography market. Although taxation on the industry is high (25 percent), those in the industry accept it as the price of doing business freely. Thus, the state reaps tax revenues from the activity and, far from being an obstacle or a threat to the industry, has a substantial interest in maintaining this area of highly profitable business.

Hungarian female performers are touted as having "the Magyar look," that is, a sensuous gaze, slim figure, good posture, and uninhibited sexual adventurousness. The focus in these films is on natural-looking women who are striking and interesting in appearance rather than on those who have the stereotypical American *Playboy*-type, artificially enhanced look. This media affirmation of Hungarian-looking women is a source of pride in that country's industry, and to some in the country as well. However, the fact that adult films often showcase Budapest's cultural scenery, such as monasteries and churches, understandably appalls many Hungarians. The films almost invariably feature sex acts that progress from the jejune and mundane to the extreme and daring during the course of the "plot." The large number of participants and fast pace of action have led some to compare Hungarian films to track meets rather than orgies. Plots are generally minimal, as is typical of the genre in general. In Hungary the industry grinds out about 300 films a year, of which almost all are restricted to European audiences. Some have made it into the American pornography market but are generally appreciated by limited audiences.

Fortunately, Hungary has been more successful than has Russia in keeping organized crime involvement in the industry at a minimal level. Historically, Russian pornography was literary or revolved around making illegal copies of films from other countries, but that has changed. Russian criminal involvement in making original pornography is mainly Internet-based and is more recent. Low wages, lack of employment opportunities, and grim socioeconomic conditions in the Ukraine and Russia make involvement in the pornography industry a viable, if not altogether attractive, option for young women, however, so the industry is expected to grow in these areas. From Internet sites originating in the former Soviet Union, both hard-core and soft-core sites featuring attractive Slavic women exist in profusion. Such women are also shown in natural settings, sometimes even echoing the Soviet past, sitting on haystacks or in kolkhoz fields looking like "heroines of the People's Agriculture," albeit au natural, but sometimes in rural tableaux in authentic peasant garb (at least when the film starts). As one might expect of those who are strictly secondary to the main attraction, male participants, when present, are generally nondescript or thuggish. It should be noted that in much of eastern Europe, outside Hungary, the hard-core pornography industry is linked to prostitution, the sex trade in general, and organized crime in particular. In Hungary, however, adult film figures are likened to actors rather than to prostitutes and the stigma of crime does not necessarily apply.

Child Pornography

Of greater concern than adult-oriented pornography is the related industry involving the sexual exploitation of minors. From the perspective of transnational crime, this has been a gray area, since different countries define the age of majority differently. In northern Europe, where sexuality has been liberated from years of Protestant legal and social domination, there is very real resistance to strengthening laws against the free expression of sexuality. Uncertainty over these issues hampered the clarification of laws against child pornography in the 1970s. In general, the concept of sexual exploitation of minors was poorly understood, and the Swedes, Danes, and Dutch were loath to hinder childish sexual experimentation. In all three countries, throughout the 1970s, frankly sexual material depicting minors was available at commercial sexual outlets. It was only in the 1980s that a consensus to end this came into being. The Dutch, for example, allowed teenage girls to be depicted nude, in sexualized poses in magazines, until the legislature in 1984 raised the age of consent to 16, which was more consistent with Common Market practice and world sensibilities. U.S. law maintains that models must be at least 18, and records must be kept verifying that fact. Artistic displays—photos, for example—are generally excluded from coverage by such laws, though such depictions are extremely popular with pedophiles. Additionally, a substantial number of Internet sites that claim to show 18-year-olds actually show only young women who look much younger.

In 2006, more than 100 overtly illegal child pornography Websites were shut down in the Netherlands. There is a large market for the "barely legal" or "teen" genre, in any event, be the subjects authentically teenagers or merely very youthful young women of legal age. The same issue has cropped up in Sweden, where the age of consent is 13, and Denmark, which has a large pornography industry. Although all three countries mentioned above cracked down on child pornography sold from sex shops and adult book stores in the 1980s, sexual content claiming to be from Swedish and Dutch "nudist" sites remains widely available on the Internet. Following links from these largely innocuous sites could lead one into ambiguous territory. It is thought that these Websites are actually based in eastern Europe, but in truth, they could be based anywhere. This fact obviously creates jurisdictional problems and facilitates the trafficking in this sort of material.

The U.S. Congress banned production of child pornography in 1986 and in 1988 it made the use of computers illegal for facilitating the transfer or storage of such material. The Protection of Children From Sexual Predators Act of 1999 expanded the scope of protections. An atmosphere of moral panic in the 1990s led some to be reported by photo labs for taking innocent nude photos of their children at the beach or in the bath; bookstores had artistic depictions of children seized, and libraries put similar photo essays in locked or closed sections, some removing them altogether. A general self-imposed restriction on any commercial form of child nudity evolved. Ads featuring naked children gamboling in the sand, while common elsewhere in the world, are unknown in the United States and shocking to Americans when viewed abroad. Postal and customs inspectors have intercepted large numbers of materials at the borders and in the mail, and sting operations became a regular feature of American media coverage. A related development was the airing of *To Catch a Predator*, an MSNBC offering in which Internet vigilantes lure would-be exploiters of minors to a prearranged sting rather than the expected assignation. The predator is then confronted by a television personality and upon leaving the scene is roughly handled by police, arrested, booked, and interviewed, all on camera for the benefit of middle America and the presumed edification of other would-be predators. Issues of entrapment abound, but the sting format remains highly popular to audiences.

Internet bulletin boards are frequently used by those who trade or sell sexual material featuring minors. Well before the Internet was widely understood or used by the public, child pornographers comprehended its potential and were using it in their activities. The very difficulty of using the incipient technology allowed motivated traffickers to flourish. Thus they were able to establish Internet bulletin boards throughout the 1980s with little fear of detection by authorities. They began to swap pornography and lists of victims and potential targets for exploitation. These online bulletin boards were also used for solicitation. Eventually major Internet service providers (ISPs), such America Online, MSN, and Yahoo!, were found to have user-initiated chat rooms devoted to this and other questionable sexual practices. One researcher ran a search of MSN in 2000 and found more than 100 groups by using the term "preteen." Twenty of these were explicitly sexual in nature. This same phenomenon was noted on other ISPs. Some ISPs in the former Soviet Union and in Asia have proven to be major resources or havens for Internet child pornographers and informal networks of enthusiasts. They are generally nonresponsive to requests from the public or law enforcement to close down offending bulletin boards. Although most Western providers work hard at finding and eliminating this sort of material, it is exceedingly difficult to police such online access. Bulletin boards continue to be a problem in the United States, Israel, the United Kingdom, and the former Soviet Union. They work on the same principle that allows the Internet itself to be impervious to external threat: that is, one offensive bulletin board can easily be shut down, but that in no way impacts the viability of the system itself. Thus, a very active subculture had been strengthened through the medium of computer-based networks.

In the 1990s an international moral panic developed when several spectacular cases were tied to child pornography "rings." In England in 1990, Robert Black, a violent sex offender, was arrested. Evidence revealed that he was involved in the murder of little girls and was a child pornography enthusiast. It was further suggested that he might have been a serial murderer of children across Europe, where he had traveled in search of child pornography. In 1997, the Marc Detroux case in Belgium revealed that a group of men kidnapped young girls, kept them in dungeons, used them in pornography, and ultimately murdered them. It is thought that he may have sold children into international sex slavery. This created a huge, angry public response in the usually quiet country. In 2000, a major pedophile ring in Latvia was purported to have prominent government officials as members.

Nations have moved to deal with the general problem of sexual exploitation of children. One solution is laws against sexual tourism; that is, nationals from Norway, Finland, Germany, France, Australia, Belgium, or Sweden who are apprehended in Thailand, for example, sexually abusing children, can be prosecuted in courts of their own nation. Major dragnets have occurred in all Common Market nations and in the United States as well.

Francis Frederick Hawley
Western Carolina University

See also Child Exploitation; Eastern Europe and Russia; Europol; Gender-Based Violence; Human Smuggling; Human Trafficking; Sex Slavery; Southeast Asia; Violence: Protection; Western Europe

Further Readings

Jenkins, P. *Beyond Tolerance: Child Pornography on the Internet*. New York: New York University Press, 2001.

Sigel, Lisa. *International Exposure: Perspectives on Modern European Pornography, 1800–2000*. New Brunswick, NJ: Rutgers University Press, 2005.

Wall, D. *Cybercrime*. Cambridge, UK: Polity Press, 2007.

PRICE-FIXING

Price-fixing is an illegal act whereby two or more companies in presumed competition with one another conspire to set or fix prices for a good or service in an attempt to maximize profits. Competitors agree to manipulate prices, thereby forcing consumers to pay artificially inflated costs. This results in a loss to taxpayers, consumers, and the economy. The illegal act of price-fixing is estimated to cost consumers $60 billion each year. Price-fixing is criminalized in the United States under the Sherman Antitrust Act of 1890. Unfortunately, violations of antitrust laws are common among a wide array of industries. Price-fixing has been found in the steel, glass, pipe, lead, oil-drilling, gasoline, industrial chemical, natural gas, fertilizer, disability insurance, auto repair, diamond, airline ticket, real estate, accounting, sports equipment, athletic-shoe-manufacturing, vitamin, infant formula, baking, dairy, toy, music, video game, and many other industries.

In a truly competitive market, businesses compete to entice consumers by keeping their prices low and the quality of their products high. When companies agree to fix prices, consumers pay more for inferior products. In essence, it is more profitable for companies to collude than to compete. For example, the Great Electrical Conspiracy is an infamous price-fixing case involving electrical equipment manufacturers. From the mid-1940s through the 1950s, nearly all companies in the electrical equipment industry in the United States were actively engaged in covert activities to maximize prices. Twenty-nine companies, including Westinghouse and General Electric, were convicted of price-fixing and bid rigging. Bid rigging is a form of price-fixing whereby the government (and therefore the tax-paying public), instead of individual consumers, is most often the victim. Rather than submitting competitive bids for lucrative government contracts, company executives hold secret meetings in which they agree on prices in advance and then divide the contracts. The winning bid has, therefore, essentially been predetermined, not by the government (the buyer) but by the companies themselves (the suppliers). In the Great Electrical Conspiracy, the electrical manufacturing companies cheated taxpayers out of nearly $1 billion. The 29 companies were ultimately issued fines totaling $2 million—an amount that seems rather insignificant compared to the total value of the crime. (As noted by criminologist Gilbert Geis, a $400,000 fine issued to General Electric is equivalent to a $3 fine for an individual who earns $175,000 a year.)

Companies also engage in a form of market manipulation related to price-fixing known as parallel pricing or price leadership. This occurs when industry leaders establish inflated prices and expect their competitors to follow suit. The practice is made possible by the fact that industry leaders have a strong market share, or brand-loyal consumers, who will continue to purchase their products. As a result of these price increases, competitors can take advantage of the inflated pricing by increasing their prices for similar products. Parallel pricing is essentially beyond the reach of the law and has been estimated to cost consumers more than $100 million annually. Both price-fixing and parallel pricing result in exaggerated costs to consumers, negating any benefit of free-market competition. Again, when companies agree to fix prices, consumers are deprived of the advantages of competition.

Unfortunately, criminal prosecution of antitrust law violations is relatively rare compared to the actual amount of price-fixing and parallel pricing that occurs among U.S. corporations. The potential profits generated for companies that conspire to fix and set prices are high and the chances of apprehension are slim. The chance of corporate executives getting caught for price-fixing activities is low for several reasons. First, most price-fixing and parallel pricing agreements are made in secret meetings behind closed doors. For example, the executives involved in the Great Electrical Conspiracy referred to their covert meetings as "choir practice" and their list of executives in attendance as the "Christmas card list." Second, the government's budget for investigating and prosecuting such violations is small. Finally, even though such conspiracies financially harm consumers, price-fixing remained a misdemeanor in the United States until 1974.

In cases where the government does charge corporations with antitrust law violations, the punishments are minor. Most price-fixing cases are typically punished through corporate fines and often are negotiated out of court. The criminal justice system has been reluctant to impose criminal sanctions on corporations, including jail and prison time for the individuals directly responsible for the violations. For example, nearly three-quarters of antitrust law violation cases in the United States result in companies pleading *nolo contendere*. These cases do not go to trial; rather, those corporations accused of price-fixing refuse to acknowledge guilt, accept a punishment (usually a small corporate fine), and subsequently avoid being labeled criminal by the justice system. Of the cases that do go to trial, 55 percent are tried as civil matters. Similar examples

of leniency for price-fixing cases are evident in other countries as well. Additionally, governments in other capitalistic countries often have little concern over price-fixing, mainly because their laissez-faire market is largely unregulated.

In recent years, the U.S. government has begun to develop more rigorous enforcement of antitrust laws and impose harsher penalties for their violation in an attempt to combat the harmful effects of price-fixing and parallel pricing on consumers. For example, in June 2004, the Antitrust Criminal Penalty Enhancement and Reform Act was passed. This law greatly increased monetary penalties and jail time for corporations and individuals involved in price-fixing, bid rigging, and other antitrust law violations. Maximum monetary fines were increased from $350,000 to $1 million for individuals and from $10 million to $100 million for corporations. The maximum prison sentence for individuals convicted of antitrust law violations increased from three to 10 years. Although in practice few individuals convicted of price-fixing are sentenced to prison, the Justice Department has successfully prosecuted some regional, national, and international price-fixing schemes. Following the United States, governments in Asia and Europe are also beginning to prosecute and punish more severely those companies involved in price-fixing.

Price-fixing and similar market manipulation constitute a form of economic exploitation. These crimes negatively impact the general public, consumers, taxpayers, employees, competitors, shareholders, and the economy as a whole. Several patterns have emerged from an examination of price-fixing cases. Price-fixing is more likely to transpire and persist when the product is homogeneous, when few companies are involved in the scheme, and when fewer than five companies dominate at least half of the market. Unfortunately, the extent of price-fixing and parallel pricing that occurs is much greater than the prosecution levels for such illegal behaviors.

Alicia H. Sitren
University of North Florida

See also Financial Fraud; Globalization; Legal and Illegal Economies

Further Readings

Rosoff, Stephen et al. *Profit Without Honor: White-Collar Crime and the Looting of America,* 5th ed. Boston: Prentice Hall, 2010.

Simon, David. *Elite Deviance*, 9th ed. Boston: Pearson Education, 2008.

Whinston, Michael. *Lectures on Antitrust Economics*. Cambridge: MIT Press, 2006.

PROFIT-DRIVEN CRIME: NAYLOR'S TYPOLOGY

Professor R. T. Naylor, an economist, criminologist, and historian at McGill University in Montreal, Canada, gives a typology of profit-driven crimes that is based on economic terms and is centered on activities or groups of activities that make an action criminal (not the perpetrators of that criminal action). He considers that every criminal action represents a certain chain of special activities and suggests that there are certain patterns of activities that can be categorized. Each of the categories suggested by him can be defined by a series of actions, the willingness or unwillingness of actors, the actors themselves, the effects on GNP, secondary criminal actions connected to the crimes, and things that the criminal justice system should address in relation to the crime category. According to him, there are three main categories of profit-driven crimes: (1) predatory offenses, (2) market-based offenses, and (3) commercial offenses.

Predatory offenses, according to Naylor, involve the redistribution of legally earned fortune against a person's will, including violence. Victims of this type of criminal activity are citizens, business institutions, and the public sector. Naylor claims that the key characteristic of this category is involuntary transfer of ownership of existing goods. This category does not have any influence on GNP. Considering unwillingness, this category raises the level of violence as a secondary criminal action. The criminal justice system should first of all deal with problems of restitution. Actors in this category are primarily individuals or organized gangs. An example of this type of criminal act is armed robbery. According to Naylor, this involves an unwilling redistribution of money with use of force where it is easy to define a loss, actors, and victims, and there is no dilemma in defining morality of action.

Market-based offenses are the production and/or distribution of goods and services that are illegal. They appeared as a consequence of the decision to criminalize personal vices (e.g., alcohol, drugs, and gambling). This category represents a set of willing activities of all interested parties that is regulated by demand and, unlike the previous category, it is very difficult to determine who the victim is. It includes a great number of interested parties, from producers to final users as creators of needs. Furthermore, Naylor divides this category into subcategories that include avoiding regulations (e.g., terms of sale, to whom the product or service is available, and quotas), taxes (e.g., for alcohol and cigarettes) and prohibitions (e.g., absolute ones, such as child pornography) and it shows that each of these types includes one price of a product or service (an increase, decrease, or arbitrary formation) in a parallel or black market. Since this category involves production of new goods and services, it affects the rise of GNP, so every state has to decide independently how to deal with this type of criminal. Secondary criminal actions that are connected to this category include money laundering and tax evasion, while corruption and violence are rare. The criminal justice system should primarily deal with taxation of goods or with defining and compensating losses. This category is connected to organized crime. One example for this category would be drug production and distribution.

Commercial crime offenses, according to Naylor, represent a set of activities of legal entrepreneurs, investors, and corporations that are voluntary and represent an illegal way of producing legal goods and services. Victims of these activities can be clearly defined (workers, consumers, suppliers, or even society as a whole). This category is further divided by Naylor into the following subcategories: fraud of suppliers by inputs, fraud of final users, and transfer of expenses to the wider community. This category is the most complicated for classification of actions because very often it is not clear where the border between sharp market competition and the fraud exists. This category represents unclearly defined fair market values, which vary from pure ideological to pure operational definitions. Frauds of suppliers of inputs do not affect GNP, but they represent a simple redistribution of goods; frauds of final users decrease GNP because they generate additional expenses to final users to compensate loss. Transfer of expenses to the final community (e.g., disposal of toxic material) decreases expenses, decreases the price of a product or service, or it makes it available to a wider market for the same price, so it raises GNP. Secondary criminal actions that characterize this category are corruption, while violence, tax evasion, and money laundering are rare. This category requires the criminal justice system to deal with both compensation and taxation or with state losses. Actors from this category are corporations.

As with all categorizations, this one is not perfect, and there is the possibility that certain sets of criminal actions do not belong exclusively to one category, but can be put into two or even into all three. However, the Naylor typology clearly defines concepts that tend to be poorly elaborated. To quote Naylor, "Given the fact that diagnosis and prescription have historically focussed on the who rather than the what, on actors rather than on actions, the result has also been to gloss over very real differences in the nature of economically motivated crimes in terms of their *social harm*. Since all are seen to fall under the concept of organized crime, they are presumed to have much more in common than they really do when judged as economic acts."

Mladen Pecujlija
University of Novi Sad, Serbia

See also Corruption; Financial Fraud; United Nations: Typologies of Criminal Structures/Operations

Further Readings

Beare, Margaret E. and R. T. Naylor. *Major Issues Relating to Organized Crime Within the Context of Economic Relationships*. Law Commission of Canada. 1999. https://www.ncjrs.gov/nathanson/organized.html (Accessed January 2012).

Naylor, R. T. *Hot Money and Politics of Debt*. London: Allen and Unwin, 1987.

Naylor, R. T. "Towards a General Theory of Profit-Driven Crimes." *British Journal of Criminology*, v.43 (2003).

PROSECUTION: INTERNATIONAL

A state's ability to prosecute and punish those who commit crimes outside the borders of the prosecuting state is limited. Typically, international law addresses the regulation of actions that transcend international boundaries. While it is often noted that international crimes are not required to be transnational crimes per se, often there is a strong relationship between the two. Crimes against humanity, slavery, and apartheid are so egregious that they may be included in both areas. In other words, it could be argued that the widespread economic, political, and sociological implications and effects blur the distinctions between international crime and transnational criminality.

Consequently, issues related to terrorism and international security present challenges necessitating the application of similar foundational elements.

The United Nations (UN) was formed in 1945, more fully realizing much of the work that had been set out for its predecessor, the League of Nations, with a mission of peacekeeping activities, humanitarian efforts, and economic, social, and cultural development. Questions about the jurisdiction of international bodies that had been raised under the League of Nations had never been resolved and so needed to be addressed anew by the UN judicial bodies, the International Court of Justice (ICJ) and the International Criminal Court (ICC). Under the UN's supremacy clause, Article 10(3), the UN Charter would prevail in any conflict between the UN and another international agreement; however, there was a stipulation in the Charter preventing it from interfering with the domestic jurisdiction of any state.

The Nüremberg Trials

In 1944, following the victory of the Allies in World War II, indictments were presented against the leaders of the Nazi Party at Nüremberg, Germany. The trial judges included representatives from the United States, Great Britain, France, and the Soviet Union. The charges included the following crimes:

- *Crimes against the peace:* Emerging from the Kellogg-Briand Pact, these crimes included the "planning, preparation, initiation or waging of war of aggression, or a war in violation of international treaties, agreements or assurances, or participation in a common plan or conspiracy."
- *Crimes against humanity:* These crimes consisted of inhumane acts against civilians: murder, extermination, enslavement, deportation, and other inhumane acts committed against any civilian population, before or during the war; or persecutions on political, racial or religious grounds in execution of or in connection with any crime within the jurisdiction of the tribunal.
- *War crimes:* These crimes constituted violations of the customs or laws of war, typically as articulated in the Fourth Hague Convention (1907) and the Geneva Convention (1929).

Included in the defenses were the arguments that defendants' actions were acts of state (conducted in an official capacity) and were therefore immune to prosecution under international law. This contention was not accepted by the International Military Tribunal (IMT). The IMT argued that the occupancy of official positions would not excuse the defendants from responsibility. Ultimately, the court determined that a subordinate had a legal duty to refuse compliance with an order considered unlawful.

The strongest defense concerned the ex post facto nature of the law. It was argued that, prior to 1939, neither through treaties nor under customary international law could the crimes referenced have been committed. This defense, however, was rejected. The IMT contended that the German defendants had been sufficiently notified of the punishment for aggressive war. The IMT's verdict was delivered on September 30 and October 1, 1946.

The Nüremberg Trials, combined with those conducted by the International Military Tribunal for the Far East (the Tokyo war crimes tribunal), established a precedent for the acceptance of individual responsibility in the violation of international law. Ultimately, the 1948 Genocide Convention ruled that the targeting and destruction of populations (based on ethnicity or religion) were in violation of the norms established by international law. These international norms were considered part of a progression that included the treaty-based Kellogg-Briand Pact, the Fourth Hague Convention (1907), and the Geneva Convention (1929) as well.

A view of the defendants in the dock at the International Military Tribunal trial of war criminals at Nüremberg. Indictments were presented against the S.S. Gestapo and the leadership corps of the Nazi Party at Nüremberg, Germany, following the 1944 victory of the Allies. (National Archives and Records)

Universal Jurisdiction and Extradition

Universal jurisdictional authority of a nation has as a foundation the ability to enforce international law, regardless of the locale of the offense or the nationality of the offender or victim. This jurisdiction can be established either through customary international law or through an international agreement. Under the universality principle, the international community in its entirety is obligated to refrain from engaging in activities that are considered globally reprehensible. On this basis, the traditional rules of jurisdiction are waived. Significantly, those states apprehending the perpetrator of certain activities not only are considered competent to exercise jurisdiction but also are considered to have an obligation to the international community. These obligations can be triggered by specified core activities, which include such universal crimes as piracy, slave trafficking, genocide, torture, crimes against humanity, and war crimes.

Extradition is the process involving the reciprocal arrangements involving the handing over of an alleged offender to another state. Typically, this process is dependent on the obligations specified in either a bilateral or a multilateral treaty. However, it is also possible under the treaty for there to be an allowance for the extradition of a state's own nationals. Notably, the refusal of the extradition of a national imposes on the state refusing extradition the obligation to conduct a trial.

The Case of John Demjanjuk

In 1952, John Demjanjuk, a native of Ukraine, was admitted to the United States under the 1948 Displaced Persons Act. In 1958, Demjanjuk became a naturalized U.S. citizen. However, in 1981 the U.S. District Court for the Northern District of Ohio found that his naturalization certificate and the order granting him citizenship had been illegally obtained. His certificate of naturalization was revoked.

In late 1942, Demjanjuk had become a guard at the Treblinka concentration camp. Not only did Demjanjuk misstate his places of residency during the 1937–48 time period; he also failed to reveal his work for the Schutzstaffel (SS) at Treblinka or his service in a German military unit. Even though during his trial Demjanjuk admitted the falsity of his statements regarding residency, he denied his service as a guard at Treblinka. Following the government's denaturalization order, deportation orders were begun. Concurrently, Israel filed an extradition request with the U.S. Department of State. This action was followed by the filing of a complaint in the district court seeking Demjanjuk's arrest by the U.S. Attorney. Basing its extradition order on a treaty between the United States and Israel, the district court emphasized Article II, which included persons convicted of murder, manslaughter, or malicious wounding. Under Article III of the treaty, it was noted that extradition "need not" be granted with offenses committed outside the territorial jurisdiction of the requesting party, unless that party's laws provide for punishment of offenses committed under similar circumstances.

Demjanjuk was charged with the murder of "tens of thousands of Jews and non Jews" during the operation of gas chambers provided to exterminate prisoners at Treblinka. It was charged that the offenses were committed "with intention of destroying the Jewish people and to commit crimes against humanity." These charges were equated with the treaty's provision against crimes of "murder and malicious wounding and inflicting grievous bodily harm." Included in the charge of "crimes against the Jewish people" were the following crimes in whole or part: killing Jews; causing serious bodily harm or mental harm to Jews; placing Jews in living conditions designed to cause physical destruction; the imposition of measures intended to prevent births among Jews; the destruction or desecration of Jewish religious or cultural assets or values; forcible transferring of Jewish children to another nationality or religious group; inciting hatred of Jews; and crimes against humanity. (Inclusive in the latter were murder, extermination, enslavement, starvation, deportation, and any other acts committed against a civilian population, including persecution on national, racial, religious, or political grounds.)

War crimes were defined to include murder; ill treatment or deportation; forced labor of a civilian population of or in occupied territory; murder or ill treatment of prisoners of war or persons on the high seas; killing of hostages; plunder of public or private property; wanton destruction of cities, towns, or villages; and devastation not necessarily caused by military necessity.

Emphasizing the distinction between international law and criminal law, the court noted the lack of a clear embodiment of the criminal law concept of retroactivity in the context of international law. Acknowledging the possible existence of this distinction in state constitutions, the court, while recognizing the possibility of the correlation to the moral value in this position, nevertheless emphasized the lack of this position's universality. Consequently, even though the court acknowledged a compatibility with British law, it also noted the distinction between morality and universality in the application of international law. Additionally, it was emphasized that the law should be applied "as it is and not as it ought to be from the moral point of view."

The court addressed the appellant's focal jurisdictional argument on the commission of criminal acts by foreign nationals abroad. Acknowledging the contention that these laws conflict with the principle of territorial sovereignty, the court also noted that this rule did not exist in customary international law and had not "obtained international agreement." As a result, the universal character of the crimes gave every state the authority for trial and punishment.

By recognizing the "general principle of law acknowledged by civilized nations," the court provided an explanation of the practical applications of the law. Underlying this application was an emphasis on the acts damaging "vital" international interests. Included in this consideration was the violation of both the moral norms and humanitarian principles incorporated "in the criminal law systems adopted by civilized nations."

It was emphasized that since there was neither an International Criminal Court nor an "international penal machinery," it was the responsibility of the "authorizing countries" to provide for those violations of customary international law specifically referenced in the UN Convention for the Prevention and Punishment of Genocide and the affirmation of the May 1951 Advisory Opinion of the International Court of Justice. Ultimately, the court interpreted this foundation for inclusion as "crimes against humanity."

The International Court of Justice

Today the global community is host to a number of international courts. They include the Court of Justice of the European Community, the European Court of Human Rights, the African Court of Human and People's Rights, the International Tribunal for the Law of the Sea, the International Criminal

Court, and the International Criminal Tribunals for Rwanda and for the former Yugoslavia.

Perhaps the most prominent of these courts is the International Court of Justice (ICJ), commonly called the World Court. A successor to the Permanent Court of Justice for the League of Nations, the ICJ was established under the UN Charter. Member states of the UN are automatically parties to the ICJ statute. Consequently, the sources and applications of these statutes can be found under the Articles of the ICJ.

Statutory association does not constitute automatic submission to the court's jurisdiction. ICJ Article 34, Section 1, states must consent to jurisdiction. The two types of jurisdiction exercised by the ICJ are contentious jurisdiction and advisory jurisdiction. Under contentious jurisdiction, there must be either express or implied consent of the parties. Only those states that have been parties to the ICJ statute can be parties to contentious jurisdiction. The decisions in these cases are binding.

On the other hand, advisory opinions are nonbinding. Rendered upon the request of those bodies authorized by the UN Charter, these decisions are implemented under Article 36 of the charter. This article provides for consent by state referral of disputes on an ad hoc basis, by a treaty provision for settlement by the ICJ, or by way of the optional clause under Article 36, Section 2 of the charter.

The International Criminal Court

Established in The Hague, Netherlands, in July 2002, the International Criminal Court (ICC) is an organ of the UN and is the first permanent criminal tribunal. Consisting of more than 100 nations, the ICC was established under the Rome Statute, which was the result of the June 1998 General Assembly Conference in Rome. Several principles form the foundation for jurisdictions. Importantly, these principles may be used collectively or in concert with one another.

The most common basis for jurisdiction, the territorial principle is based on the premise that the crime is committed within the territory of the state. Inclusive in this concept are actions occurring on vessels or aircraft registered in that state. The included actions may have begun in the state but completed in another state abroad.

Under the objective principle, acts begun abroad but having either substantial effects or the intention of producing substantial effects within a state's territory are to be given to the jurisdiction of the prosecuting state.

The nationality principle comprises two categories: the active nationality principle and the passive nationality principle. The former is the basis for jurisdiction under the ICC. Under the active nationality principle, the state of the perpetrator may assert jurisdiction over the actions wherever they occur. Consequently, the state regulates the activities of its citizens outside its territory.

Article 17 of the Rome Statute limits jurisdiction to those cases in which there has been a failure of operational justice in the domestic courts of states. More directly, the court's authority is triggered under Article 13(b) and under Chapter 7 of the UN Charter. This article is triggered by a referral to the prosecutor by the Security Council. Accordingly, this provision eliminates the need for the UN to establish ad hoc tribunals for the prosecution of crimes against humanity.

However, since this action is dependent on a Security Council referral, there are complications. If the questionable conduct has occurred on the territory of a state that is a party to the Rome Statute, an impasse could be created. Additionally, if the nation-state is both a party in the prosecution and a member of the Security Council, the nation-state can veto the action.

Transnational Implications

Even though the boundaries between international law, humanitarian law, and international criminal law are blurred, there have been efforts to provide a global consensus on the necessary core elements for legal analysis and applications. As a result, there has been a review of jurisdictional guidelines and prosecutorial standards. However, while there may be disagreements on specific case facts, the reality is that substantive issues and procedural rights must be considered through the prism of a jurisdictional lens. Decisions on these questions are now at the apex of the prosecution triangle.

In concert with this understanding of the jurisdictional and procedural rules and applications of international law, international criminal law, and transnational criminality, there is the necessity for a progressive and contextual understanding of the development of substantive law. The combined progression provides an opportunity for understanding the impact of the globalization process and the contemporary nexus between national and international concerns. Consequently, the convergence of both national and international issues and concerns is unsurprising and expected.

Carol J. Pretlow
Norfolk State University

See also Adjudicating International Crimes; Conventions, Agreements, and Regulations; Crime Commissions; Crimes Against Humanity; Data Sources: Prosecution and Courts; Intelligence Agencies: Collaboration Within the United States; International Criminal Court; Internationalized Criminal Tribunals; Mega-Trials; Transitional Justice; War Crimes Tribunals; World Court

Further Readings

Akehurst, Michael. *A Modern Introduction to International Law*, 6th ed. London: Unwin Hyman, 1987.

Bederman, David J. *International Law Frameworks*. New York: Foundation Press, 2001.

Blakesley, Christopher, Edwin B. Firmage, Richard F. Scott, and Sharon A. Williams. *The International Legal System: Cases and Materials*, 5th ed. New York: Foundation Press, 2001.

Brownlie, Ian. *Principles of Public International Law*, 3rd ed. Oxford, UK: Clarendon Press, 1985.

Buergenthal, Thomas and Daniel Stewart. *International Human Rights in a Nutshell*, 4th ed. St. Paul, MN: West, 2002.

Epps, Valerie. *International Law*, 4th ed. Durham, NC: Carolina Academic Press, 2009.

Maris, Gary L. *International Law: An Introduction*. Boston: University Press of America, 1984.

McCaffrey, Stephen C. *Understanding International Law*. Newark, NJ: LexisNexis, 2006.

Parry, Clive, John Grant, Anthony Parry, and Arthur Watts. *Parry and Grant Encyclopedic Dictionary of International Law*. New York: Oceana, 1988.

Paust, Jordan J. et al. *International Criminal Law Cases and Materials*, 2nd ed. Durham, NC: Carolina Academic Press, 2000.

Sweeney, Joseph et al. *Documentary Supplement to Cases and Materials on the International Legal System*, 3rd ed. Westbury, NY: The Foundation Press, 1988.

PUBLIC EXPENDITURE TRACKING SYSTEMS (PETS)

Public expenditure tracking is used as a means to determine whether or not allocated government or public funds are utilized specifically for their intended or dictated purposes. Many times government or public funds earmarked for a specific purpose are diverted and used for a different purpose altogether. The inappropriate diversion of these funds may be unintended, deliberate, or both. Funding may be unintentionally diverted because unqualified workers are confused about the specifications or requirements of the funding policies or because of simple distribution or accounting errors. The deliberate misappropriation of funds may be the result of fraud, embezzlement, or the funding of criminal organizations; it may occur to enrich the officials whose job it is to disperse the funds in accordance with the specific government or public policies. By tracking the fund expenditures at each level of dispersal, government leaders and public policy makers can determine how funds are being distributed and which persons are in charge of the distributions. Tracking such information allows policy makers to take specific actions to ensure that future funding will be dispersed as intended and to prosecute any individuals or groups seeking profits from the deliberate misappropriation of allocated public funds.

In 2005, Hurricane Katrina made landfall in the United States, causing devastation from Florida to Texas. The effects of Katrina resulted in the loss of 1,836 lives and more than $81 billion in property damage. The area hardest hit by Katrina was New Orleans, Louisiana, where levies failed and massive flooding ensued throughout the city. The U.S. Federal Emergency Management Agency (FEMA) was sent in to rescue and aid those adversely affected by the hurricane. FEMA was charged with providing both physical and financial aid to the victims. All told, FEMA spent more than $19 billion in aid to the victim of Katrina. The U.S. Department of Justice (DOJ) was charged with tracking these massive public expenditures to ensure that the monies allotted were spent in accordance with FEMA's mandate to provide aid to Katrina victims. To this end, the U.S. DOJ created a large task force, which comprised representatives of the DOJ Criminal Division, the U.S. Attorney's Office, the Federal Bureau of Investigation (FBI), the Postal Inspection Service, the U.S. Secret Service, the Federal Trade Commission, the Securities and Exchange Commission, federal inspectors general, and various state and local law-enforcement agencies. Throughout 2010, members of the U.S. DOJ's task force referred more than 11,000 potential fraud cases to the U.S. Department of Homeland Security for prosecution and estimated that more than $2 billion of the overall $19 billion in public expenditures had been lost to fraud and waste (also termed leakage).

In April 2010, the United States suffered another catastrophic loss, this time an ecological disaster in the form of a massive oil spill caused by the explosion of the Deepwater Horizon oil rig, run by BP. The explosion resulted in a seafloor oil gusher lasting 3 months and releasing 4.9 million barrels of oil into the Gulf of Mexico, affecting the environment for 180,000 square kilometers. BP allocated $20 billion in aid for victims suffering property damage and financial losses as a result of the oil spill. BP established the Gulf Coast Claim Facility as its distribution center for dispersal of the $20 billion. The U.S. DOJ, taking preventive measures in the wake of what it had learned from its tracking of the Katrina funds, planned again to utilize many different U.S. agencies in an attempt to minimize fraud and other forms of leakage while tracking the massive BP reimbursement funds.

Utilizing a variety of federal agencies may be necessary in detecting and prosecuting fraud and leakage surrounding massive expenditures following a natural or environmental disaster. However, simpler yet equally effective methods have been used by many nations to track large service expenditures, such as funds allocated for education. Surveys have been very successful in not only detecting but also substantially decreasing fraud and leakage. Public expenditure tracking surveys (PETS) track how funds originally allocated for a specifically designated service are distributed at each level of government through to the final recipients. These surveys are capable of capturing at what level and by whom funds have been diverted and whether or not those diverted funds were utilized for legitimate or illegitimate purposes. PETS are most often performed by independent researchers, who not only report their findings to the government issuing the funds but also report their findings at every dispersal level, including the final recipients. PETS make the reports public by giving the results to various news outlets.

In 1996, Uganda was the first country to utilize PETS after it provided a substantial increase in public educational spending, yet school reports showed no increase in enrollment and testing revealed no increase in scoring. Ugandan officials feared that much of the funding was misappropriated by local politicians and public officials and did not reach the

schools and facilities as intended. A PETS was conducted to determine whether the funds were appropriately allocated at each descending government level down to the schools themselves. The PETS found that only 13 percent of the annual funding had reached the schools in the previous five years. The majority of missing funds were diverted to corrupt or inefficient practices of numerous public officials (including school accountants and auditors). Furthermore, in the schools themselves there were numerous instances of ghost teachers (teachers who did not exist) appearing on school payrolls, as well as full pay for teachers with extreme absenteeism. After the public release of the PETS findings, the Ugandan government took measures to prevent further leakage of its school funds, publishing intergovernmental transfers of public funds in newspapers and through radio broadcasts and requiring the schools to post their incoming funds, including how those funds were to be used, publicly. Through the use of PETS, the leakage of Uganda's public education funding was reduced from 87 percent to 18 percent. Since Uganda's successful use of PETS to track public education expenditures, Ghana, Madagascar, Peru, Tanzania, and Zambia have begun using PETS to track their public expenditures.

Timothy J. O'Boyle
Kutztown University

See also Anticorruption Legislation; Government Reports; Political Influence Peddling

Further Readings

Albo, Emmanuel and Ritva Reinikka. "Do Budgets Really Matter? Evidence From Public Spending on Education and Health in Uganda." World Bank Policy Research Working Paper 1926 (June 1998).

Reinikka, Ritva and Nathanael Smith. *Public Expenditure Tracking Surveys in Education.* Paris: UNESCO, International Institute for Educational Planning, 2004. http://www.unesco.org/iiep/PDF/pubs/Reinikka.pdf (Accessed February 2011).

Sundet, Geir. *Following the Money: Do Public Expenditure Tracking Surveys Matter?* Bergen, Norway: Chr. Michelsen Institute, 2008.

PUBLIC PERCEPTIONS OF CRIME

It is well recognized by scholars and practitioners alike that public perceptions of crime affect how citizens go about their daily lives, the trust they place in law enforcement, and the overall quality of life for those in the United States and abroad. As the latter half of the 20th century unfolded, stark differences regarding the reality of crime and the fear of victimization created a divide between governmental policy makers, law-enforcement agencies, and the general citizenry. In stark contrast to Franklin Delano Roosevelt's claim that the only thing we have to fear is fear itself, the 21st century brought with it a far different message from those at the helm of national government. Following the World Trade Center terrorist attacks on September 11, 2011 (9/11), government officials actively used fear as a key mechanism in their attempts to unite Americans, strengthen ties with international allies, and gain support for U.S. policies and actions.

Public Perceptions of National Threats

The 9/11 attacks were unprecedented for most Americans, with the exception of those who recalled the December 7, 1941, Japanese attack on Pearl Harbor, which precipitated U.S. entry into World War II. Even so, many of today's Americans were not alive during the Pearl Harbor attack, and at the time Pearl Harbor was located in the continental United States, but in a distant island territory. Hence, on 9/11, most Americans faced the heretofore unthinkable: warlike threats emanating from both internal and external sources. A generation of young adults watched in stunned silence as dramatic changes in domestic and international policy were ushered in. Concomitantly, subjective fears and objective data collided with full force.

Without diminishing the very real atrocities exacted on the American public as the events of 9/11 and its aftermath unfolded, the political use of fear as a uniting factor among the general citizenry had far-reaching effects. For perhaps the first time in U.S. history the general public now faced a heretofore unknown and unseen enemy. It has been said that a generalized sense of fear affected most, if not all, Americans as they attempted to restore a sense of normality to daily life in America in the days and months following 9/11. This fear was exacerbated by new official policies as the federal government worked to demonstrate that it was taking action. Such action took the form of color-coded levels of alert, a new cabinet-level Department of Homeland Security, precedent-setting legislation in the form of the USA Patriot Act, and preparations for overseas wars that had a questionable relation to the terrorist attacks. All these policies were in large part enabled by the public's perception of imminent threat and hence a tacit approval of what some would judge extreme measures (including the notion of "preemptive war" in response to what later were found to be nonexistent weapons of mass destruction). Hence, public perceptions of national threats, particularly under the fear such threats engender, can give legislators and other government officials license to respond in ways that may or may not be appropriate or in alignment with the citizenry's long-term interests.

Public Perceptions of Domestic Crime

As citizens' subjective perceptions of an increased likelihood of victimization have escalated nationwide, so, too, did the scholarly research aimed at measuring both the perceptions and the reality of crime in the United States. With the increased use of methodological instruments such as the National Crime Victimization Survey (NCVS) and Self-Reported Criminal Activity Survey, however, a more objective picture of crime and victimization in America has emerged. As a result, those in law enforcement have been compelled to admit that numeric data (such as those from Uniform Crime Reports), in and of themselves, fall short of providing an accurate picture of crime in America.

Unfortunately, even the most sophisticated research efforts cannot outweigh the role of the media in shaping public perceptions of crime. A review of the most recent literature indicates myriad factors affect public perceptions of crime and the likelihood of victimization. Due, in large part, to the technological advances available to the general public (such as the ubiquitous Internet, smart phones, television, and radio) and the ability of the media to put an immediate face on community crime, many now fear the very neighborhoods they once found safe. "If it bleeds, it leads" has long been the mantra of the media, and that principle remains the guiding force among most reporters.

It has been said by many in law enforcement the media can and do portray those in uniform as villains one day and heroes the next, especially in the case of a line-of-duty death caused by a police officer. If an officer's actions are called into question, he or she makes front-page news even before the facts of a given situation have been fully investigated.

Unknown to the layperson is the fact that some police actions—even those most warranted on the part of the officer (as in officer-involved shootings)—compel the employing department to place such officers on administrative leave while the incident is under investigation. This is routine procedure, yet few in the media report it as such, although the routine nature of such measures should be common knowledge among competent journalists.

The 2007 criminal victimization data provided by the U.S. Department of Justice indicated 21.5 individuals per one thousand experienced criminal victimization at the hands of another. Furthermore, the media sensationalize stranger-precipitated crime, which is the least likely to occur. Instead, the most egregious victimization often occurs at the hands of a personal acquaintance or cohabiting partner. While any crime against another is one too many, public reporting of actual crime is not the only mechanism by which fear becomes a contagion. The media, politicians, and corporate entities create and use public fear as a means to a specific end, whether profit or votes. In so doing, they exploit the general public by undermining the individual's sense of well-being and replacing it with a distrust of others in society.

All who watch television are familiar with advertisements hawking the latest technology in home protection. With Father out of town, the children sit quietly on the couch in their upper-middle-class homes awaiting Mom's appearance with popcorn in hand. This idyllic scene is brutally interrupted with the sounds of breaking glass, the ensuing whine of the home alarm system, and the inevitable call from the home security company whose job it is (for a monthly fee) to respond to the fear of invasion and, in so doing, restore family safety. Engaged in little more than fearmongering, corporate America thus reaps untold profits by playing on a society already fearful of crime. Advertisements such as these are intended to evoke fear. Implicit in these portrayals is the guilt-inducing message that good parenting includes protecting children from harm in whatever way possible.

United in Fear: The Fear of Transnational Victimization

Rhetorically and politically manufactured fear of victimization has existed for centuries, well before the attacks of 9/11. For example, the World War II

generation witnessed during the postwar years how Senator Joseph McCarthy's ideology and fearmongering swept the nation, heightening fears of communism and the "domino theory," which posited that Soviet-style, totalitarian governments might eventually rule the world by encouraging communism among developing nations, which at the time included China as well as several east European and many Southeast Asian and African nations. In his zeal to exterminate the political forces that supposedly threatened the American way of life, McCarthy targeted U.S. citizens suspected of sympathizing with communists and, in so doing, sought to demonstrate their lack of patriotism through public exposure. Although McCarthy's mission finally imploded, ruining his reputation and his career, the witch hunt he initiated did not end before ruining the lives of many prominent and innocent American citizens. Individual patriotism was once again challenged when those who actively worked to bring about the end of the Vietnam War, as well as many who survived service in that war, were criticized.

The Cold War era that began with postwar fear of communism finally ended with the destruction of the Berlin Wall in 1989 and the dissolution of the Soviet Union in 1991. Most Americans believed that the United States was free from the most insidious external threat it had faced: the Soviet Union and its brand of communism. Little did they realize that internally and externally based crime would grow in its wake and invoke a level of fear heretofore never experienced. As the Soviet Union collapsed economically and divided into a series of poor nations, some of which easily became havens for corruption and transnational crime, it became apparent that nuclear arsenals no longer were subject to the jurisdiction and control of the former superpower; this, added to the governmental vacuum left in several states, exacerbated both organized crime and terrorism. The ongoing tensions in the Middle East, where both superpowers had strategic interests involving oil, were exacerbated by the growing poverty of generations of Muslim people under the yoke of foreign-dominated dictatorships and economic influence. These circumstances made the world ripe for the sort of radical fundamentalism and jihad advocated by a variety of anti-American and anti-Israel terror organizations, culminating in Al Qaeda.

From the 1993 attempt to level the World Trade Center to the successful destruction of the Twin Towers in 2001 and ultimately the death of Osama bin Laden in 2011, the United States and its allies came to realize they were trapped in a synergistic relationship defined and perpetuated by international and transnational crime. Such events were exacerbated by home-grown acts of terror and mass murder, from the 1995 Oklahoma City bombing spearheaded by Timothy McVeigh to the 1999 Columbine High School killings. The Cold War world appeared, by comparison, if not preferable at least more controlled.

Today, although Americans continue to fear terrorism and its far-reaching capabilities, the reality for most has been a return to the concerns that consumed their lives prior to September 11, 2011. Once again, the general public has turned its attention to the crimes affecting their individual safety, the neighborhoods in which they live, and the larger communities in which they reside. For many these concerns are genuine, as indicated by the plethora of studies that annually identify the most crime-ridden cities in the United States. For others the fear of crime—exacerbated by an overzealous media, a corporate America interested in taking advantage of fear to generate profits, and political platforms that prey on the most vulnerable—does little more than imprison law-abiding citizens who perceive themselves to be at risk.

When considering the fear of crime among the American public, a paradox appears. Fostered by many factors, this fear is often more real and debilitating than crime itself. Media sensationalism, corporate profit making, inaccurate or incomplete data, and the self-serving nature of many politicians often perpetuate and exacerbate the fears of the most vulnerable in society. While these perceptions are often ossified in the minds of those most subject to victimization, international policy along with the words of politicians sustains the residual belief that the events of 9/11 could revisit the American people. Hence, those most fearful of victimization live daily with the threat of crime from two sources: internal and external. As such, they become prisoners of their own fears. Especially for those who allow fear to rule their lives, perhaps Roosevelt provided the best advice possible in his admonition that the greatest thing we have to fear is fear itself.

Martha L. Shockey-Eckles
Saint Louis University

See also Securitization After Terror

Further Readings

Duffy, Bobby, Rhonda Wake, Tamara Burrows, and Pamela Bremner. "Closing the Gaps: Crime and Public Perception." *International Review of Law Computers and Technology*, v.22/1–2 (July 2008).

Faucher, Chantal. "Fear and Loathing in the News: A Qualitative Analysis of Canadian Print News Coverage of Youthful Offending in the 20th Century." *Journal of Youth Studies*, v.12/4 (August 2009).

Pfaff, William. "When Fear Rules: Why the United States Won't Leave Iraq." *Commonwealth* (June 1, 2007).

Romer, Daniel, Kathleen Hall Jamieson, and Sean Aday. "Television News and the Cultivation of Fear of Crime." *Violence and Abuse Abstracts*, v.9/4 (2003).

Smolej, Mirka, and Janne Kivivuori. "The Relation Between Crime News and Fear of Violence." *Journal of Scandinavian Studies in Criminology and Crime Prevention*, v.7/2 (2006).

Weiter, Ronald and Charis E. Kubrin. "Breaking News: How Local TV News and Real-World Conditions Affect Fear of Crime." *Justice Quarterly*, v.21/3 (2004).

PYRAMID SCHEMES

Fraud schemes known as pyramid schemes are also called chain referral, multilevel marketing, and matrix marketing schemes. They may be local, national, or international cross-country scams. These schemes lure people into getting involved with product distributorships or franchises in order to make a quick fortune. The schemes use advertisements on the Internet and newspapers, e-mails, telephone calls, postal mail, mass meetings, seminars, and in-person meetings to present fraudulent solicitations. Victims are often those with limited money or poor credit who need to raise cash quickly.

Pyramid schemes are illegal moneymaking scams designed to earn profits by the sale of new distributorships or franchises for a product. Pyramid schemes should not be confused with *legitimate* multilevel marketing schemes, and it is important to know the distinction. In a pyramid scheme, the emphasis is on recruitment of more distributors rather than the sale of the product. Even if there is a product, it is sold within the distributorship rather than to the general public. The products are generally overpriced or no real market exists for them.

These schemes appear to be genuine when advertised, and people invest in them with the best hope of making a fortune. The promoter is usually a master of psychology who can persuade people into believing that they are "getting in early" and thus can make a lot of money from future recruits. The participants may or may not understand anything about distributorships or franchise business or investment plans and may have never have established their own business. Participants in these schemes are offered a large monetary benefit in a short time, such as 30 days, if they recruit more distributors as the next level of members. When the scheme fails, the participants may blame themselves for their poor recruiting skills. They may never earn anything and generally lose their investment.

This form of fraud has been called a pyramid scheme because it is structured as a pyramid in its distributorship, with one master mind on top who recruits others and encourages each one to recruit more "down line"; thus, the structure spreads out like a pyramid. In a basic pyramid scheme, the confidence (con) artist who is at the top of the pyramid recruits two investors, who pay a certain amount to the promoter/con artist (for example, $250) for a new venture or an investment scheme. The investors are asked to recruit three other investors, each of whom pays $250 to the promoter. In return, the first two investors are promised a percentage as commission from their directly recruited investors' investment and a lower percentage of commission from the money of every investor recruited by the lower-layer members. Every investor is thus supposed to pay $250 to the promoter in return for a certain percentage from the directly recruited investor and a lower percentage from every subsequent investor. To the potential investor it looks like a promising scheme of making thousands in return of the basic $250 investment.

The promoter may pay a few top investors some percentage to make the scheme look genuine and attract additional membership, but the lower investors may get very little or no return on their investment before the scheme falls apart. In such a scheme, the victims themselves become perpetrators. Usually, by the time the lowest-level participants realize that they have been tricked, the con artist and the top allies may be long gone.

Sometimes in such schemes there are thousands and even millions of participants who have been recruited, and it becomes unmanageable. For example, if every recruit gets six friends to join, very quickly the participants will grow to more than 10 million. The people at the lower levels and bottom will find it difficult to recruit participants who are willing to invest; recruitment becomes more and more difficult with the increase in participants already involved. For example, in a small town, if almost everyone who would be willing to be an investor is already on board, further investors will not be found, and thus the pyramid's base will cease to grow and will therefore collapse, with investors losing their money. Pyramid fraud schemes are similar to Ponzi schemes, except in a Ponzi operation the fraudster interacts with each of the "clients" directly. A Ponzi scheme can continue as long as the existing investors agree to reinvest. Bernard Madoff's fraudulent operation in 2009 is a classic example of a Ponzi scheme.

Pyramid schemes are banned as illegal and are regarded as a criminal offense in several countries around the world, including Albania, Australia, Brazil, Canada, China, Colombia, Denmark, Estonia, France, Germany, Hungry, Iceland, Iran, Italy, Japan, Malaysia, Nepal, the Netherlands, New Zealand, Norway, the Philippines, Poland, Portugal, Romania, South Africa, Spain, Sri Lanka, Switzerland, Taiwan, Thailand, Turkey, the United Kingdom, and the United States. In this age of the Internet, when victims can be solicited from around the world, there is a need for international laws and treaties among all countries, with possible help from the International Criminal Police Organization (Interpol) and the United Nations (UN) to extradite and prosecute these criminals.

In the United States, the Federal Trade Commission (FTC) is responsible for protecting its citizens from pyramid fraud schemes. The FTC has a Website devoted to consumer and business education to warn against pyramid fraud schemes and educate the public at http://www.ftc.gov. The commission brings cases against pyramid schemes under the FTC Act. The act allows the FTC to file suit in a federal court and prohibits "unfair or deceptive acts or practices in or affecting commerce." It provides several relief measures for the victims of this crime, including an injunctive relief, a freeze on the defendants' assets, a receivership over the defendants' business, and redress or restitution for consumers.

Rupendra Simlot
Richard Stockton College of New Jersey
Alka Simlot
South Jersey Legal Services

See also Accounting Fraud; Charities and Financing; Charity Fraud; Financial Fraud; Investment Crimes; Job Offer Scams; Nigerian Money Scams; Telemarketing Fraud

Further Readings

British Broadcasting Corporation. "Colombia Scam: 'I Lost My Money.'" 2008. http://news.bbc.co.uk/2/hi/7736124.stm (Accessed February 2011).

Conde, Carlos H. "Investors in Philippine Pyramid Scheme Lose Over $2 Billion." *The New York Times* (March 30, 2003).

ConsumerFraudReporting.org. "Multi-Level Marketing (MLM) Scams: Why It *Is* a Scam, 99.9999% of the Time!" http://www.consumerfraudreporting.org/MLM.php. (Accessed February 2011).

Crimes-of-Persuasion.com. "Internet-Based Pyramid Schemes Fraud Web Scams by E-Mail." http://www.crimes-of-persuasion.com (Accessed February 2011).

Federal Bureau of Investigation. "Common Fraud Schemes." http://www.fbi.gov (Accessed February 2011).

Federal Trade Commission. "Pyramid Schemes, Modified." June 25, 2007. http://www.ftc.gov (Accessed February 2011).

Heakal, Reem. "What Is a Pyramid Scheme?" http://www.investopedia.com (Accessed February 2011).

RACKETEER INFLUENCED AND CORRUPT ORGANIZATIONS ACT

The Racketeer Influenced and Corrupt Organizations (RICO) Act was passed in 1970 as part of U.S. president Richard Nixon's Organized Crime Control Act. It was Title IX of the Organized Crime Control Act and is considered by many to be the single most important piece of organized crime legislation enacted (Jacobs, 2001). RICO has become one of the dominant tools used in organized crime prosecutions within the United States. The arrests of Mafia figures are reputed to be accomplished in large part due to wiretaps and informants, and the lengthy sentences that can be received under a RICO conviction are claimed to have weakened the legendary vow of *omertà* or code of silence.

The bill was originally drafted by Robert Blakey, and Blakey remains the scholar and expert on issues pertaining to this statute. The key feature of RICO is that it gives greater legal flexibility and scope to prosecutors in their actions against what are considered to be organized crime activities. In legal terms, it is something of a watershed because of its refocusing of criminal culpability away from the exclusive concern with individual actions and toward an examination of one's criminal associations. It is also designed to combat the movement of money from illegitimate to legitimate business. It thus attacks organized crime's ability to profit, in terms of both financial gain and respectability, from its illicit business. In a sense, the RICO Act seeks to draw legal boundaries around the practice of organized crime and to expose its links with "legitimate society."

History

The act was passed in an atmosphere of conservative reaction, political expediency, and prosecutorial frustration. The late 1960s was a time of growing social unrest; civil disobedience was common. The nation saw the rise of organized social movements able to challenge American policy both at home and abroad. At the same time, urban riots, anti-Vietnam war protests, and the role of the police were being questioned by the more vocal and boisterous liberal streams of American society. Simultaneously, crime was on the rise, although no direct link need be drawn between this rise and growing radical politicization. In this historical context, Nixon was able to coordinate and manage a conservative reaction that drew from the support of the "silent majority" for tougher laws against criminality. In many ways, this inaugurated the modern "law and order" agenda. This powerful political tool of rhetoric gave new impetus and local fervor to the conservative movement. RICO was born, therefore, in an environment of political reaction. It was advertised as a centerpiece to this new "get tough on crime" approach. Finally, this new approach to law and order was able to tie into a long tradition of prosecutorial frustration at the inability to get long-standing organized criminals such as those of La Cosa Nostra behind bars.

Prosecutors had been trying for years to go after these intricate and sophisticated networks of criminal activity; however, they kept running up against problems of conspiracy and collusion, that is, how to argue for criminal culpability when the criminal enterprise itself was unacknowledged. Some authors have maintained that, as head of the Federal Bureau of Investigation (FBI), J. Edgar Hoover held the view that there was no such thing as La Cosa Nostra. However, a careful examination of Hoover's various speeches refutes this contention. The issue appears to be that Hoover felt that neither the federal executive nor Congress was ready to consider the federalization of law enforcement. Hoover's position was that local and state officials should "vigorously and relentlessly" enforce their laws (see Woodiwiss, 2001, p. 242). He believed that, at that time, most organized crimes were locally organized and too often involved the corruption of local law enforcement and criminal justice officials. However, driven in part by a series of commissions—including the Kefauver Committee during the 1950s; the Senator McClellan Congressional Committee hearing, which included the testimony by Joseph Valachi; and perhaps culminating in the 1967 President's Commission on Law Enforcement and the Administration of Justice, the Challenge of Crime in a Free Society—a "new" perception prevailed. Hoover's views that focused on "honest and effective" local enforcement were replaced by views that insisted on national coordinated action.

Legal Aspects

Since its inception in the 1970s, prosecutors have been able to apply the act—as Blakey intended—beyond the traditional arena of the battle against the Mafia to include a broader array of "racketeers." Blakey has always maintained that, although the Mafia was one of the targets of RICO, corporate crime and corruption and white-collar criminals are also appropriate targets if they are operating like racketeers. For example, Rudolph Giuliani turned the vague language of RICO against some prominent Wall Street financial barons such as Michael Milken. The argument for RICO's applicability in these cases, according to William L. Anderson and Candice E. Jackson, is that "regulatory violation that involves a business enterprise" is akin to traditional forms of racketeering and influence peddling.

In the case of insider trading, for example, prosecutors argued that collusion and criminal knowledge allowed Milken and others to profit. In this way, RICO has enabled new law to be written because it has criminalized certain actions that may not have been understood previously as necessarily illegal. RICO created four new offenses aimed at organized crime's activities (Moon, 1998–1999, p. 474). It is an offense

1. for any person to use or invest any income derived from a pattern of racketeering activity;

2. to acquire or maintain an interest in, or control of, any enterprise through a pattern of racketeering activity;

3. for any person to be employed by, or associated with, any enterprise in or affecting interstate commerce through a pattern of racketeering or collection of unlawful debt; or

4. to participate in any conspiracies to violate any or all of the above.

As a statute that comes within the jurisdiction of U.S. federal law, critics have argued that RICO has undermined the legal and prosecutorial independence of American states. This is the case because RICO statutes allow the federal government to prosecute the activities of an ongoing criminal organization that operates across state lines. Second, prior to some of the successful high-profile RICO prosecutions, critics questioned the concept of "criminal association" as being a direct challenge to the notion of each individual being innocent until proven guilty in court. The supporters of RICO would point out that it avoids the guilt by association charge because it "implicitly defined organized crime by what it did, rather than by what it was"; it lists a variety of crimes to which the prohibitions of the act apply (Lynch, 1987).

Under U.S. Code Title 18, 1961, subsection 1, the bill attempts to define the main source of its power of prosecution through an understanding of "racketeering." The law draws much from the U.S. "criminal-specific" code and other statutes in order to define fully what is meant by *racketeering*. These are termed "predicate acts," meaning that they define a broad range of criminal activity encompassed by other laws. What is therefore created through RICO is an "umbrella law" under which stands a collection of indictable offenses. The novelty of RICO is in its ability to shelter these diverse laws relating to racketeering activity under the canopy of large-scale organizational criminal enterprise. For example, the act refers to section 659 of the U.S. Code when it discusses theft based on interstate shipment.

An important element of the RICO Act has to do with criminal penalties. In section 1963, the law lays out the conditions of punishment, which include prison terms as well as criminal forfeiture. Anyone who violates the law is subject to governmental seizure of his or her interests, which may include "property or contractual right of any kind affording a source of influence." Furthermore, any property derived from the profits of these illegal enterprises may also suffer government forfeiture. Finally, the law, under section 1964, allows for civil remedies. In subsection c, the law argues that any "person injured in his business or property by reason of a violation . . . may sue therefore in any appropriate United States district court and shall recover three-fold the damages he sustains and the cost of the suit." Therefore, private citizens who feel aggrieved and damaged by racketeering activity may seek appropriate redress. Once again, a concern is that this type of clause may lead to legal expansion and greater levels of litigation in an already overly litigious society.

Transnational Impact

Although it was seldom used until the early 1980s, by the end of that decade RICO was serving as the model for legislation on fighting organized crime internationally, including the 2000 United Nations Convention against Transnational Organized Crime and country legislation such as the criminal association laws in Canada. The U.S. successes in going after its major Mafia crime families and the wide publicity given to the amount of money that countries could gain from the criminal and civil seizure and forfeiture of illicit proceeds likely served as an incentive for other jurisdictions. The idea of a terrorist act being perpetrated by a criminal conspiracy has contributed to more RICO-like measures. The Patriot Act in the United States and Canadian antiterrorism laws have increased the profile of group-level criminal activity. It seems to be inevitable that, as nation-states become more integrated in terms of labor, capital, communication, and information exchange, they will see the need to harmonize their approaches to the control of transnational criminality.

Paul Brienza
York University

See also Bikers and Motorcycle Gangs; Criminal Forfeiture and Seizure; Joint Force Policing and Integrated Models; Mafia Myths and Mythologies; Money Laundering: History; Money Laundering: Vulnerable Commodities and Services; North America; Organized Crime: Defined; Western Europe

Further Readings

Abadinsky, Howard. *Organized Crime*. Belmont, CA: Thomson-Wadsworth, 2010.

Anderson, William L. and Candice E. Jackson. "Law as a Weapon: How RICO Subverts Liberty and the True Purpose of Law." *The Independent Review*, v.9/1 (June 22, 2004).

Beare, Margaret E. *Criminal Conspiracies*. Toronto, ON: Nelson, 1996.

Finklea, Kristin M. *Organized Crime in the United States: Trends and Issues for Congress*. December 22, 2010. http://www.fas.org/sgp/crs/misc/R40525.pdf (Accessed February 2012).

Henderson, A. G. and Jill McIntyre. *The Business of Crime: An Evaluation of the American RICO Statute From a Canadian Perspective*. Victoria, BC: Province of British Columbia, 1980.

Jacobs, James. *Gotham Unbound: How New York City Was Liberated From the Grip of Organized Crime*. New York: New York University Press, 2001.

Lynch Gerald. "RICO: The Crime of Being a Criminal." *Columbia Law Review*, v.661 (1987).

Moon Michael A. "Outlawing the Outlaws: Importing RICO's Notion of 'Criminal Enterprise' Into Canada to Combat Organized Crime." *Queen's Law Journal*, v.24 (1998–1999).

Morselli, Carlo and Lila Kazemian. *Scrutinizing RICO*. Dordrecht, Netherlands: Kluwer, 2004.

United Nations Convention Against Transnational Organized Crime, 2000. http://www.unodc.org/unodc/en/treaties/CTOC/index.html (Accessed February 2012).

President's Commission on Law Enforcement and the Administration of Justice. *The Challenge of Crime in a Free Society*. Washington, DC: Government Printing Office, 1967.

Woodiwiss, Michael. *Organized Crime and American Power*. Toronto, ON: University of Toronto Press, 2001.

RECOVERY OF STOLEN ASSETS

Recovery of stolen assets is a term used by law enforcement, international development, and human rights organizations to describe efforts by governments and individuals to identify, recover, and repatriate the proceeds of corruption by politically exposed persons (PEPs). PEPs are typically senior government officials usually hidden in foreign jurisdictions. Such proceeds may include monies in bank accounts, real estate, vehicles, artworks, jewelry, and precious metals. As defined under the UN Convention Against Corruption (UNCAC), *asset recovery* (often used as shorthand for recovery of stolen assets) refers to recovering the proceeds of corruption, as opposed to broader terms such as *asset confiscation* or *asset forfeiture*, which refer to recovering the proceeds or instrumentalities of crime in general, but all these terms are often used in the same context.

Asset recovery emphasizes both the high-level public position of the individuals typically targeted and the "multijurisdictional" or "cross-border" aspect of associated investigations. Recovering such illicit assets as stolen funds in a bank account is a complex endeavor and often a sequential process that typically includes four steps. First, the government of the former PEP, often referred to as the "victim" or "requesting" country, begins tracing the asset abroad. Tracing assets may include following domestic leads and consulting publicly available information, but it also typically involves asking for protected information, such as bank account records, via mutual legal assistance (MLA) requests. Upon finding an active bank account or physical property, the victim country requests a freezing order from the state or jurisdiction where the assets are being held, known as the "requested country." Third, the victim country and the requested country may work to obtain a judicial order for confiscation. Finally, if the process is successful, the assets are repatriated to the victim country.

Improvements in finance, transportation, and communications technologies have made it much easier for corrupt leaders and other PEPs to conceal massive amounts of stolen wealth in offshore financial centers. As a result, there are many jurisdictions where high levels of banking secrecy, uncooperative officials, and the use of corporate shells facilitate the safekeeping of illicit assets. Nevertheless, persistent efforts have brought several asset recovery cases

against high-level officials, such as Sani Abacha of Nigeria, Ferdinand Marcos of the Philippines, Jean-Claude "Baby Doc" Duvalier of Haiti, and ministerial-level officials such as Vladimiro Montesinos, the former head of the Peruvian intelligence service.

Tracing and freezing assets is the first step, but legally confiscating those assets and repatriating such assets to a victim country can be a particularly difficult and lengthy process. Generally, there are three methods of confiscating such illicit assets: (1) enforcement of a victim country's domestic criminal conviction; (2) in common-law countries, filing a lawsuit in civil courts to freeze and forfeit assets; and (3) nonconviction-based forfeiture (NCBF), which allows for confiscation of assets without a corresponding criminal conviction. Popularized by the U.S. *in rem* forfeiture actions against drug smugglers, NCBF remains controversial but is finding some acceptance in both civil- and common-law jurisdictions.

Prior to the enactment of UNCAC, the ability to request official assistance in recovering assets was often determined by individual mutual legal assistance treaties (MLATs) negotiated between states. However, UNCAC treaty now serves an acceptable legal basis for assistance between UNCAC state parties with regard to corruption offenses. Entered into force in 2005, UNCAC specifically cites asset recovery as a "fundamental principle" of the convention, and requires state parties to "afford one another the widest measure of cooperation and assistance in this regard." In order to further asset recovery cases, UNCAC requires state parties to provide mutual legal assistance, participate in information sharing with international counterparts, and recognize the judgments of other state-party courts.

Although many asset recovery cases are conducted on an ad hoc basis, the link between stolen asset recovery and global development has led to increased international attention to the issue. Asset recovery operations are currently supported by a variety of national governments and organizations, including the International Criminal Police Organization (Interpol), Camden Asset Recovery Inter-Agency Network (CARIN), the French nongovernmental organization SHERPA, the International Centre for Asset Recovery, and the World Bank–United Nations (UN) Stolen Asset Recovery (StAR) initiative. A high-level initiative launched by World Bank president Robert Zoellick and UN secretary-general

Ban Ki-moon, STAR focuses on increasing global knowledge and advocacy, providing assistance in the recovery of stolen assets, and building national capacity.

Despite the recent enhancement of international cooperation, many technical, legal, political, and material challenges to asset recovery cases still exist. These challenges include slow response times from requested countries, lack of technical capacity and funding, lack of remedial procedures, and lack of political will to initiate and continue cases. Additionally, there is strong disagreement concerning the purpose and monitoring of assets repatriated to victim countries.

Mark V. Vlasic
Georgetown University
Gregory Cooper
University of Texas

See also Corruption; Recovery of Stolen Assets

Further Readings

Smith, Jack, Mark Pieth, and Guillermo Jorge. *The Recovery of Stolen Assets: A Fundamental Principle of the UN Convention Against Corruption.* 2007. http://www.u4.no (Accessed February 2011).

Stolen Asset Recovery Initiative. http://www1.worldbank.org/finance/star_site (Accessed February 2011).

Vlasic, Mark and Greg Cooper. "Fast Cash: Recovering Stolen Assets." *Americas Quarterly* (Fall 2010). http://www.americasquarterly.org/node/1901 (Accessed February 2011).

Vlasic, Mark and Jenae Noell. "Fighting Corruption to Improve Global Security: An Analysis of International Asset Recovery Systems." *Yale Journal of International Affairs*, v.5/2 (Summer 2010).

Vlasic, Mark and Jenae Noell. "Fighting Impunity: Recent International Asset Recovery Efforts to Combat Corruption." *Cayman Financial Review* (January 5, 2010). http://www.assetrecovery.org/kc/node/7606d7d4-3752-11df-b10d-f33d33a7f7e7.0;jsessionid=A0639CCE037AE3149BD6F5040D59BCA5 (Accessed February 2011).

RESPONSIBILIZATION

Responsibilization concerns a shift of primary responsibility for crime prevention and public security away from the state and toward businesses, organizations, individuals, families, and communities. It is a strategy that involves a way of thinking and a variety of techniques designed to change the manner in which governments act upon crime. Instead of addressing crime in a direct fashion by means of the police, the courts, and the prisons, this approach promotes a new kind of indirect action, in which state agencies activate or generate action by nonstate organizations and actors. State agencies now adopt a strategic relation to other forces of social control. They seek to build broader alliances, enlisting the powers of private actors and shaping them to the ends of crime control. Nation-states adopting such a strategy are said to adopt a "steering" rather than "rowing" function when it comes to crime control.

One of the first to focus on this process was Nikolas Rose in his analysis of "advanced liberal" modes of governance. David Garland develops the notion in the context of crime control and refers to a community responsibilization strategy, involving central government seeking to act upon crime by directly involving nonstate agencies and organizations.

Such a strategy has been adopted by governments in the United States and especially the United Kingdom since the 1990s. The key terminology attached to the strategy includes *partnership, public/private alliance, interagency cooperation*, the *multiagency approach, activating communities*, and *help for self-help*. The primary purpose is to spread responsibility for crime control onto agencies, organizations, and individuals that operate outside the criminal justice state. The aim is to encourage the private sector and communities to take a more active role in reducing criminal opportunities. Redistributing the task of crime control, rendering others responsible, and forming alliances are seen as the new goals of government. The criminal justice state is required to shed its sovereign style of government by top-down command and develop a form of rule close to that described by Michel Foucault as "governmentality"—a modality that involves the enlistment of others, the shaping of incentives, and the creation of new forms of cooperative action.

A number of steps have been identified by Garland in bringing about this transition of ideas and ways of action. The first step is to identify people or organizations that have the competence to reduce criminal opportunities effectively. A number of targets and techniques of persuasion are then identified in order to engage these groups and organizations in crime prevention. The simplest and the most wide-ranging is the publicity campaign, targeted at the public as a whole. These campaigns, conducted through television advertising and the mass leafleting of households and businesses, aim to raise public consciousness, convince citizens that they are potential victims, create a sense of duty, connect the population to crime control agencies, and help change the way of thinking and practices of those involved. Similar goals are pursued by the police, who offer expert support and encouragement to residents and citizen self-help groups, assisting them in forming crime prevention projects such as "neighborhood watch" schemes and raising their awareness of crime, thus linking them more closely to the public authorities.

In order to coordinate such a strategy, the U.K. and U.S. governments have established a whole series of quasi-governmental organizations, such as the National Crime Prevention Council, Crime Concern UK, and the Safer Cities Program. These agencies work to form crime prevention and community safety projects and to establish local structures that will help govern crime problems by means of interagency cooperation and the activation of private initiatives.

The overall and recurring message of this approach is that the state is not alone responsible for preventing and controlling crime. The state's new strategy is not to command and control, as was the case historically, but rather to persuade and align, to organize, and to ensure that other actors play their part. These actors must be persuaded to exert their informal powers of social control and if necessary to modify their usual practices in order to help reduce criminal opportunities and enhance crime control. Sometimes the desired effects are achieved simply by exhortation—for example, when automobile manufacturers are persuaded to build greater security features into their cars or when insurance companies are encouraged to give discounts wherever neighborhood watch schemes operate. Some persuasion can take the form of an analysis of interests—for instance, where retailers and firms in city centers and downtown areas are presented with data on fear of crime and how this affects their trade in order to encourage them to adopt improved security practices and cooperate in joint initiatives.

Sometimes more forceful methods are proposed. It has been repeatedly suggested, for example, that governments should apply the "polluter pays" principle to criminogenic activities. Thus, retail firms may be made to do more to reduce shoplifting and retail crime by threatening to shift the costs of theft prosecutions to the retailers themselves. These tougher schemes, which aim to spread the costs as well as the responsibility for crime control, mesh neatly with neoliberal policies of privatization and public expenditure reduction. For example, legislation makes it a requirement that frontline tellers in banks, casinos, and other points of cash transactions file suspicious activity forms into a centralized financial intelligence unit, which may then send the file to law-enforcement agencies; hence, bank tellers and similar civilians are effectively tasked with law-enforcement duties.

The concept of responsibilization has helped open a series of debates about the relationship between the public and the private spheres; about the extent to which states are prepared to "govern at a distance"; about what constitutes "acceptable" and "responsible" citizenship; and how communities and families can be "empowered" in their self-governance. Significantly, the concept has developed alongside governmental critiques of state dependency and the withdrawal from universal measures of state protection and welfare support. It coalesces with a number of related developments whereby aspects of criminal justice have come to reflect marketlike conditions and processes, the welfarist core has been eroded, elements of the system have become privatized, and access to resources has been made dependent on acting "responsibly."

Guy Richard Kempster
Sheffield Hallam University

See also Gambling: Illegal; Gambling: Legal; Legislating Morality

Further Readings

Garland, David. "The Limits of the Sovereign State: Strategies of Crime Control in Contemporary Society." *British Journal of Criminology*, v.36 (1996).

Rose, Nikolas. "Governing Advanced Liberal Democracies." In *Foucault and Political Reason*, A. Barry et al., eds. London: UCL Press, 1996.

Scoular, Jane and Maggie O'Neill. *Regulating Prostitution: Social Inclusion, Responsibilization and the Politics of Prostitution Reform*. New York: Oxford University Press, 2007.

Silverstein, Martin. *What's Race Got to Do With Justice? Responsibilization Strategies at Parole Hearings*. New York: Oxford University Press, 2005.

RISK ASSESSMENTS

Risk assessment is a statistically based assessment tool that can be employed in the measurement of offender classification and prediction of offender behavior within the criminal justice system and other captive subpopulations. Risk assessment and implementation mark the midpoint between research and practice. It is widely believed that when risk-assessment tools are properly developed and implemented, they can enhance decision making in the criminal justice system. Risk assessment also has the potential of saving resources and improving public safety. Many countries, including the United States and Canada, have developed risk-assessment tools to determine if criminal acts are associated with organized crime groups. Organized crime groups can be transnational, national, or local. The majority of the transnational organized crime groups are motivated by economic benefits and/or political interests.

There are three major goals of risk assessment, namely (1) to meet the correctional goal of public safety; (2) to minimize the discretionary decision-making power of correctional professionals, such as decision making based on subjective and ideologically influenced grounds, in order to ensure equity and fairness in the process; and (3) to enhance behavior prediction and effective social control in the criminal justice system.

Some agents of the criminal justice system base their recommendations and decisions relating to parole, probation, bail, and diversion on risk-assessment instruments. These instruments also have been used to determine inmate placement in correctional programs, such as those encompassing competency enhancement and insanity treatment. Offender treatment, probation intensity, and sentencing decisions are also regularly based on risk-assessment tools. The value of risk assessment in the determination of the intensity of supervision and treatment of parolees and probationers in the community cannot be overemphasized. Furthermore, risk-assessment tools are very valuable in the prediction of offender compliance and offender potential in completing recommended programs.

Jay S. Albanese has also suggested that a risk-assessment tool can also be effective in the prediction and control of organized crime, both transnational and local. This instrument can greatly contribute to the improvements in data collection and the identification of common elements prevalent in organized crime. Albanese has proposed five ways of effectively predicting and controlling organized crime. This instrument will help in the determination of whether a criminal act was perpetrated by an individual or if the act was part of an organized crime group. Information about organized crime, according to the organized crime risk-assessment tool, is mostly discovered through the accounts of offenders, victims, law-enforcement agencies, and to some extent the accounts of eyewitnesses. The prevailing socioeconomic conditions of the society and the demand for and availability of prohibited products are fertile ground for organized crime that are measurable. The U.S. Department of Homeland Security, in collaboration with the Royal Canadian Mounted Police (RCMP), has also released a risk-assessment tool for identifying and mitigating transnational organized crime along the U.S.-Canadian border.

Risk-assessment tools can contribute to the efficient administration of the criminal justice system. Correctional agencies are better able to direct scarce resources efficiently with the classification of offenders according to their needs. The prediction of offenders who are more likely to recidivate is also enhanced with the proper application of risk-assessment tools. There are four notable justifications for classifying offenders according to their risks, including the expedient allocation of resources, the appropriate determination of a program or type of supervision for effective intervention, the adherence to procedures that reflect the needs of other offenders, and the potential of reducing risk of recidivism or incidents.

Risk-assessment tools are arguably one among the most important correctional innovations in recent times. This accounts for why they are widely used in the classification of inmates in the correctional systems. Success in the prediction of offender risk and treatment needs has been made possible because of risk-assessment tools. The role of risk assessment in the control of prison populations also cannot be overemphasized. It is now possible to assign inmates to programs that meet their needs, such as drug treatment and rehabilitation programs. Risk assessment has also made it possible to segregate high-risk from low-risk offenders and assign them to programs that are appropriate for their needs.

Risk-assessment instruments can be categorized into two types: those based on clinical assessments and those targeting actuarial experience. James Bonta has identified four generations of risk assessment. The first generation of risk assessment was used to predict offending behavior in an unstructured manner. The system has, however, been modified and is known to provide structured clinical assessment; hence, many refer to it as "structured clinical judgment." The second generation of risk assessment, as described by Bruce Hoffman, employs empirical factors in predicting future offending. It is said to be not based on any known theoretical framework and uses statistical items such as the Salient Factor Score (SFS). The third generation of risk assessment, as described by D. A. Andrews and Bonta, is also empirically based, although employing broader factors in its assessment. The risk items it assesses include criminogenic needs. It differs from the second-generation assessment in that it is theoretically informed. It is known by its professional label as Level of Service Inventory–Revised (LSI–R).

The fourth generation of assessment tools is more comprehensive. Assessment starts from when the offender is taken into custody and ends when the case is closed. These tools measure offender recidivism risk, strengths, needs, and responsiveness to treatment. Following reassessment, service plans and delivery are measured. These instruments can differentiate between criminogenic and noncriminogenic factors. In addition to assessing recidivism risks, they also measure elements of well-being, as well as service and treatment systems and management systems. The strength of the fourth-generation assessment instruments lies in their ability to measure the effectiveness of treatment programs while facilitating clinical supervision. Andrews, Bonta, and Stephen J. Wormith identified the Wisconsin system (known formally as the Correctional Assessment and Intervention System, or CAIS) and the Level of Service/Case Management Inventory (LS/CMI) as the most popular fourth-generation assessment instruments.

The application of risk-assessment tools in the corrections industry is not a recent innovation. Sociologist Ernest Burgess in 1928 applied an unweighted linear additive model in attempting to predict for the Illinois Board of Parole recidivism rates for prisoners. This instrument was further modified by the Sheldon and Eleanor Glueck in their classic work *Unraveling Juvenile*

Delinquency, published in 1950. Between 1960 and 1970, three risk-assessment scales were developed, which were widely accepted by agents of the criminal justice system: the Base Expectancy Score (BES), the Salient Factor Score (SFS), and the United States Statistical Index on Recidivism. The latter instrument is currently known as the General Statistical Information on Recidivism (GSIR) in Canada. The fourth-generation assessment tools have been hailed as contributing to a significant methodological improvement over other clinical assessment tools and have been credited with influencing the use of assessment tools in predicting recidivism rates in criminal justice policies. Other well-known risk-assessment instruments include Level of Service Inventory-Revised (LSI-R) and the Self-Appraisal Questionnaire (SAQ).

It is important to note that these risk-assessment instruments measure what they have been validated to assess. Caution should be used in generalizing results of risk assessment, as several factors do mediate assessment outcomes. It is therefore advisable for each agency periodically to generate its own risk-assessment tools to use in measuring risk with regard to its own clientele. Nonetheless, the following factors have been recognized as contributors to criminal behavior and reoffending: criminal history, education and employment history, the significant company that the individual keeps (people with whom he or she associates), alcohol and drug use and abuse, and mental health issues. Other risk factors for reoffending include the individual's attitudes and orientation. To assist with accurate risk assessment, Bonta has provided guidelines for selecting effective risk-assessment instruments and recommends that the assessment of offender risk should be based on actuarial measures of risk. Again, accurate assessment should be based on a relevant theoretical framework, and multiple domains should be explored. It is also important to assess criminogenic need factors, and it is recommended that general personality and cognitive tests be restricted to the measurement of responsivity. Albanese proposed risk-assessment instruments for organized crime and identified four parameters for the measurement of organized crime, both transnational and local, including location-specificity, activity-specificity, time-specificity, and that these factors must be comparable with similar conditions in other jurisdictions. Finally, it is appropriate to employ multiple assessment tools to measure risk and needs while exercising professional responsibility.

Rochelle E. Cobbs
Mississippi Valley State University
O. Oko Elechi
Prairie View A&M University

See also Bribery and Graft; Data Sources: Empirical Data; Data Sources: Media Coverage; Data Sources: Police Data; Data Sources: Prosecution and Courts; Internet Crime; Rule of Law Versus Security

Further Readings

Albanese, Jay S. "The Prediction and Control of Organized Crime: A Risk Assessment Instrument for Targeting Law Enforcements Efforts." 2004. https://www.ncjrs.gov/pdffiles1/pr/204370.pdf (Accessed August 2011).

Andrews, D. A. and James Bonta. *The Level of Supervision Inventory–Revised (LSI–R)*. New York: Multi-Health Systems, 1995.

Andrews, D. A. and James Bonta. *The Psychology of Criminal Conduct*. Cincinnati, OH: Anderson, 1994.

Andrews, D. A., James Bonta, and Stephen J. Wormith. *The Level of Service/Case Management Inventory (LS/CMI)*. Toronto, ON: Multi-Health Systems, 2004.

Andrews, D. A., James Bonta, and Stephen J. Wormith. "The Recent Past and Near Future of Risk and/or Need Assessment." *Crime and Delinquency*, v.52 (2006).

Bonta, J. "Risk-Needs Assessment and Treatment." In *Choosing Correctional Options That Work: Defining the Demand and Evaluating the Supply*, A. T. Harland, ed. Thousand Oaks, CA: Sage, 1996.

Brown, Shelley L. "The Dynamic Prediction of Criminal Recidivism. A Three-Wave Prospective Study." *Forum on Corrections Research*, v.14/1 (2002).

Gottfredson, Stephen D. and Laura J. Moriarty. "Statistical Risk Assessment: Old Problems and New Applications." *Crime and Delinquency*, v.52 (2006).

Henderson, Howard M. *The Predictive Utility of the Wisconsin Risk Needs Assessment in a Sample of Texas Probationers*. Unpublished doctoral dissertation. Sam Houston State University, Huntsville, Texas, 2006.

Schneider, Anne L., Laurie Ervin, and Zoann Snyder-Joy. "Further Exploration of the Flight From Discretion: The Role of Risk/Need Instruments in Probation Supervision Decisions." *Journal of Criminal Justice*, v.24/2 (1996).

U.S. Department of Homeland Security. "U.S. and Canada: Release Joint Border Threat and Risk Assessment." http://www.thegovmonitor.com/world_news/united_ states/u-s-and-canada-release-joint-border-threat-and-risk-assessment–47628.html (Accessed February 2011).

Van Voorhis, Patricia, Michael C. Braswell, and David Lester. *Correctional Counseling and Rehabilitation*, 7th ed. Cincinnati, OH: Anderson, 2009.

Zimmermann, Sherwood E., Randy Martin, and Thomas Rogosky. "Developing a Risk Assessment Instrument: Lessons About Validity Relearned." *Journal of Criminal Justice*, v.29 (2001).

RULE OF LAW VERSUS SECURITY

Democratic societies constantly struggle with maintaining the balance between preserving the legal rights of citizens and providing for the security of the state. The increase of international terrorism and the illicit drug trade have brought this debate to the forefront. As the move toward globalization created a new political and economic landscape, nations were forced to reevaluate policies and consider alternatives to already existing security measures and law-enforcement practices to address the rapidly changing threats. Advances in computer-based technologies have created a virtual world in which information and financial resources can be shared across the globe instantaneously. This access further complicates matters of international relations and security. As a result, many nations have proposed or adopted tactics for addressing these new conditions, but these policies often have met with legal and ethical challenges related to concerns over civil liberties and contradictions with established laws. The legal ramifications of these new policies are of particular concern for nations, including the United States, that have long subscribed to the legal concept of rule of law.

"Rule of law" has been a cornerstone of Western legal systems since the days of Plato and Aristotle, when legal scholars and political philosophers began to understand the importance of law in maintaining legitimacy and stability within democratic states. Rule of law is intended to ensure that all individuals are afforded equal protection under the law while placing social and political institutions under the specified restrictions contained within the law. This concept is embodied within the U.S. Constitution, a document that lays out the powers of government while specifically protecting the rights of the people. Many of these rights, especially those contained in the Fourth, Fifth, Sixth, and Eighth Amendments, are essential due process rights that act as safeguards restraining the ability of government to infringe on the individual's right to life, liberty, and property without following established legal processes. These rights are central to the American way of life and the American political system. The United States, as the preeminent representative of Western-style democracy, has also ratified several international treaties, including the Geneva Conventions, that establish the rules for international conflict and treatment of foreign citizens who fall under their jurisdiction. Many of these rules are fashioned after the due process rights outlined in the American system of justice and possess nearly universal support throughout the world.

Since the early 1980s, the United States has embarked on two major "wars" that have called into question the nation's dedication to democratic ideals of justice and the legal standard of rule of law: the War on Drugs, which was expanded by the Reagan administration in 1986, and the more recent War on Terror, which began in the days following the September 11, 2001, terrorist attacks on the United States. These two wars have posed significant challenges to the U.S. government's ability to tackle international threats while adhering to established laws and maintaining protection of civil liberties. By their very nature, reaction to these threats involves clandestine operations that may compromise the freedoms that democratic societies uphold. The difficulties associated with detecting, apprehending, and prosecuting individuals engaged in these activities have resulted in a variety of legal opinions and policy decisions that are questionable in comparison to established laws and treaties. Scholars and policy analysts have examined these legal issues in depth and have identified several areas of concern.

The Posse Comitatus Act is one such source of contention for civil libertarians with regard to the use of military resources to combat the drug trade and terrorist activities. The act, passed in 1878, limits the use of federal military forces in civilian police activities. The act was passed in response to historical abuses carried out by standing armies, but it still has value in contemporary society. Modern concern stems from the unique mission of the military, which is to engage in armed combat limited only by the established rules of war. This is in contrast to the role of civilian police agencies that are tasked with maintaining peace and order while giving utmost consideration to individual civil liberties. Ambiguity surrounding the Posse Comitatus Act stems from the law's wording and various legal interpretations that have attempted to clarify its scope. The law states that the military cannot be used "to execute the laws" of the state, which the courts have defined as traditional police actions including searches, arrests, and coercing citizens. It does not prohibit the military from training local law-enforcement officers or providing weapons or equipment to police agencies. The courts have also found that the use of the military for police actions is acceptable if it serves a "military purpose." Some argue that this exception is potentially problematic because of uncertainties on whether Al Qaeda qualifies as a military threat or a criminal threat. Although the group is not a traditional state-sponsored military force, the group has been engaged in military-style operations. As a result, federal policies have tended to treat the War on Terror as a military operation, which frees the government from restrictions under the act. There has also been a greater emphasis placed on cooperation between the military and local law enforcement in order to detect and apprehend potential terrorists, including those who legally reside in the United States and are subject to the protections of the Constitution. Combined with the reality that terrorist organizations commonly utilize conventional types of crime to fund their activities, it is unclear what role the military may play in these civilian police investigations.

The passage of the Patriot Act in 2001 is perhaps the most obvious example of the conflict between the need to secure the nation and the need to adhere to the rule of law. The act, in response to the unique nature of the terror threat and its reliance on Internet technology to carry out attacks, broadened the federal government's ability to gain access to information that was previously strictly protected by law. These new measures included "roving" wiretaps that followed individuals rather than being tied to a specific communication device, "sneak and peek" warrants that allowed investigators to search private property without notifying the property owner, and the ability to access personal records such as library borrowing history, private e-mails, and cellular phone records. Supporters insist that these measures are essential to tracking suspected terrorists who utilize electronic and mobile forms of communication in planning and conducting their criminal acts. Civil libertarians argue that these expanded federal powers have legalized domestic spying and place normal citizens at risk for guilt by association because of the relaxed standards for proving criminal involvement. Other critics point out that many aspects of the Patriot Act are also being utilized in the fight against illegal drug trafficking and border security, which are not necessarily part of the War on Terror.

Actions undertaken by the United States toward suspected terrorists have also garnered criticism from the international community. The United States is bound by the Geneva Conventions, which dictate the rights and protections that must be afforded to individuals captured during wartime. Many of the key provisions of the Geneva Conventions relate to humane treatment, due process, and prohibition of torture. These restrictions and guidelines were drafted in response to traditional military conflicts between warring nations using organized military forces. The unconventional nature of the terror threat has created a situation in which the lines between military combatant, nonmilitary combatant, and international criminal are blurred or totally nonexistent. The difficulties of clearly identifying an individual as fitting into a specific category for the purposes of law and custom have left suspected terrorists in a legal limbo with little protection from the law. Hundreds of individuals have been detained by the U.S. government and denied habeas corpus challenges to the legitimacy of their detentions. Detainees have also been denied other fundamental due process rights that are central to the American criminal justice system, including the right to be present at trials, the right to hear evidence against them, and the right to face their accusers. The United States has also been criticized for abandoning the use of military AR 190-8 hearings, intended to prevent erroneous detentions, and for allowing individuals to be detained solely for their "intelligence value," even if they have not been directly involved in terror-related activity. Perhaps most controversial, detainees have been subjected to "enhanced interrogation" techniques, which include methods such

as waterboarding. Members of the U.S. military and government officials have criticized these measures as violating the Geneva Conventions and placing the United States in a precarious position in the global community.

There is little disagreement that the threats posed by international terrorism and related criminal activity must be addressed by the free nations of the world. However, the extent to which nations such as the United States should go in pursuit of security is unclear. Unfortunately, the challenges presented by these threats are ever changing, and policy makers cannot prepare for all potential threats without severely restricting individual liberty and undermining the legitimacy of democratic institutions. As democratic nations construct and revise policies in response to the new and evolving threat, it is essential for policy makers to be mindful of the role that rule of law plays in protecting the stability of society and preservation of the way of life that democracy represents.

Robert M. Keeton
University of Tennessee

See also Al Qaeda; Narco-Terrorism; Securitization After Terror

Further Readings

American Civil Liberties Union. "Surveillance Under the USA PATRIOT Act." December 10, 2010. http://www.aclu.org/national-security/surveillance-under-usa-patriot-act (Accessed February 2011).

Etzioni, Amitai. *How Patriotic Is the Patriot Act? Freedom Versus Security in the Age of Terrorism*. New York: Routledge, 2004.

Hafetz, Jonathan. *Habeas Corpus After 9/11: Confronting America's New Global Detention System*. New York: New York University Press, 2011.

Healy, Gene. "Deployed in the U.S.A.: The Creeping Militarization of the Home Front." *Policy Analysis*, v.503 (December 17, 2003).

Macleod-Ball, Michael W. "Violent Extremism: How Are People Moved From Constitutionally-Protected Thought to Acts of Terrorism." Testimony Before the Subcommittee on Intelligence, Information Sharing, and Terrorism Risk Assessment, December 15, 2009. http://www.aclu.org/free-speech-national-security/aclu-testimony-violent-extremism-house-homeland-security-subcommittee (Accessed February 2011).

S

SALES TAX

Sales tax is often manipulated in several financial crimes, but principally in undercharging and in the smuggling of goods. Local and state sales taxes go unpaid, robbing the government of millions of dollars in potential revenue. As a result of unpaid taxes, local governments may choose to impose higher property taxes, whereas county and state governments might increase income taxes, to help pay for education or public safety.

Undercharging schemes are rampant in the Unites States. The classic example involves a storefront failing to give receipts to customers making cash purchases. The business might make change, bag the product, and provide excellent customer service. However, many cash registers can be opened without keying in a sale. In these cases, the sales clerk may open the register and handle the purchase normally but fail to provide a receipt. At the end of the day, cash purchases not keyed into the cash register are simply never reported as revenue. The lack of a receipt means there is no record of the sale, even in the event of a tax audit. In Washington State, undercharging costs the state an estimated $8 million in lost revenues annually. In New York, the loss is an estimated $1 billion each year. Modern innovations in computerized point-of-sale software have made it easier for criminals to defraud the government of sales tax revenue by simply deleting transactions from the records altogether and pocketing the cash. Some sources estimate that as many as 80 percent

of all small businesses commit sales tax fraud at some level.

Smuggling of goods involves the purchase of merchandise in one state and its resale in a different state, without proper authorization. Sales taxes are calculated according to local and state regulations; there is no uniform sales tax that applies across the United States. Therefore, the overall sales tax can vary widely from state to state. Five U.S. states lack any sales tax at all: Alaska, Delaware, Montana, New Hampshire, and Oregon. Since local government may add its own sales tax to purchases, even within a state, the overall sales tax paid at the time of purchase may vary widely as well. Eleven states have uniform sales tax laws throughout the state, making them the minority.

Sales tax fraud is committed when an individual or group purchases an item—for instance, a tobacco product—in a city and state with minimal sales tax. Typically the product is driven to another city and state, where the overall sales taxes are higher. The product is then sold directly to the general public. Alternatively, the product may be sold wholesale, in greater volume, and with lowered profits. The criminal enterprise may opt for the wholesale model because it makes it possible to unload large quantities of product much more quickly and then leave town.

Sales tax fraud cases have been reported involving organized crime groups, including the Mafia. In some instances, the crime is the work of lone operators, sometimes called "one-hit wonders." In other scenarios, both the original buyer and the wholesale

A cash payment provides an opportunity for a retailer to avoid paying sales tax on items sold. If a receipt is not issued for a cash purchase, it may not have been entered into the cash register, thus allowing the retailer to avoid reporting the revenue. (Photos.com)

customer in the other state are foreign-born, from the same home country, which increases their degree of trust and confidence in each other, especially if at least one party is in the country illegally.

Sales tax fraud has also been used in the United States to fund violent jihadist terror operations overseas. Between 1995 and 2000, the terrorist group Hezbollah had a fund-raising cell in North Carolina whose members purchased very large quantities of cigarettes from a tobacco wholesaler in Statesville. Frequently the purchases were made with cash carried in grocery bags holding as much as $20,000 to $30,000. Hezbollah operatives bought 299 cases of cigarettes at a time, just under the minimum allowed, without having to file for a license. The sales tax on the merchandise was only five cents per carton in North Carolina, but it was 75 cents in Michigan. The price differential was sufficiently high that the cell would drive 680 miles to Dearborn, Michigan, to sell the cigarettes, making 70 cents per carton through sales tax fraud alone. A single trip could make more than $10,000 in profit for Hezbollah. In five years, the cell made an estimated $8 million, most of it illegally. Cell members were charged with copyright violations, cigarette tax violations, counterfeit violations, bank scams, bribery, credit card fraud, immigration fraud, identity theft, tax evasion, and money laundering. Similar cases were discovered in Asheville, North Carolina, and Louisville, Kentucky.

The example of Hezbollah's fund-raising in the United States through avoiding sales tax involved the purchase, transportation, and resale of legally produced products. An entire genre of sales tax fraud also exists involving the transportation and sale of counterfeit goods. Many of these, manufactured in China, are sold on street corners and flea markets. The violations may include piracy and trademark or copyright infringement, as well as sales tax fraud. The sales might not be declared at all, or they may be drastically understated.

Some states, such as Texas, allow a sales tax rebate on products that are going to leave the country. The shopper is allowed to present sales receipts to a licensed customs broker. A statement needs to be signed in which the shopper promises that the products will be taken out of the Unites States. Then, the shopper is legally entitled to receive a sales tax refund from the store where the products were purchased. Violators face 180 days in jail and fines as high as $2,000. State tax officials say Mexican citizens living in the United States routinely misrepresent their residency status to avoid paying sales taxes, costing the state millions of dollars in lost revenue.

Krishna Mungur
Solution Concepts Consulting

See also Cigarette Smuggling; Financial Fraud; Sales Tax; Tax Evasion; Tobacco Smuggling

Further Readings

Conrad, Robert J., Jr., U.S. Attorney, Western District of North Carolina. "An Assessment of the Tools Needed to Fight the Financing of Terrorism." Testimony Before Senate Committee on the Judiciary, November 20, 2002.

Crudele, John. "Scam Dodges $400M in Sales Tax." *New York Daily News* (January 24, 2011).

Havrelly, Wayne. "Sales Tax Fraud Could Cost State Millions." KIROTV.com, February 6, 2006. http://www.kirotv.com/money/6791171/detail.html (Accessed February 2011).

Kaplan, David E. "Homegrown Terrorists: How a Hezbollah Cell Made Millions in Sleepy Charlotte, NC." *U.S. News and World Report* (March 2, 2003).

SANCTIONS AND BLACKLISTING

Sanction is a generic term encompassing the non-forcible coercive measures adopted by a state or collective of states for the purpose of altering the policies or practices of a targeted entity. There is an emerging trend among international authorities to apply the term *countermeasures* to coercive measures imposed by a single state and reserve the term sanctions for measures implemented collectively through a regional or international organization. The expression *sanction regime* is today widely used when discussing both unilateral and collective coercive measures.

Sanction regimes have been maintained by "senders" (or "sanctioners") to achieve a range of goals, including the suppression of terrorism, the protection of human rights, the restoration of democratically elected governments, and the promotion of compliance with treaties and the precepts of international law. The motives underlying the resort to sanctions and countermeasures are as varied as the means by which these instruments may be implemented. Sanction regimes have traditionally taken the form of comprehensive economic embargoes, but in recent decades they have also entailed the application of travel bans, asset freezes, strategic embargoes on specific goods or services, and other targeted measures designed to impact individual "blacklisted" entities.

Countermeasures (Unilateral Coercive Measures)

Comprehensive trade embargoes (nonforcible measures) that sever all economic ties between countries are among the oldest coercive tools used by states and were traditionally used to weaken a rival only in conjunction with armed attacks (forcible measures) in the course of waging "total war." The adoption of the UN Charter, which prohibits the "threat or use of force" by member states in Article 2(4), broke the long-established link between forcible and nonforcible measures and has forced states to rely exclusively on the latter. The International Court of Justice in *Gabcikovo-Nagymoros*, the International Law Commission (ILC) in its 2001 Articles on State Responsibility, and various arbitral tribunals have used the term *countermeasures* to describe the range of lawful nonforcible actions available to states seeking to vindicate their rights, and have clarified the international legal requirements associated with the implementation and termination of these actions.

Ultimately it is up to individual states to determine which breaches of obligations warrant the application of countermeasures. In many states, the responsibility for making this determination is shared between various legislative, executive, and administrative authorities. When the U.S. Congress, for example, has perceived that U.S. interests were

threatened by executive inaction, it has not hesitated to enact sanction regimes over the objection of the president. The president, however, retains independent authority to impose export controls on goods and financial assets entering or leaving the United States, under the International Emergency Economic Powers Act and the Export Administration Act. Meanwhile, Congress and the president have each authorized the U.S. Department of the Treasury to prepare secondary legal instruments outlining the scope of various sanction regimes and update the registers of individual or corporate entities subject to countermeasures.

Consistent with the generally accepted principles of international law relating to state sovereignty, most sanction regimes imposed by a single state prohibit only entities within the personal or territorial jurisdiction of that state from transacting business with a target. Upon occasion, however, a sender will design a countermeasure that inhibits interaction between third countries, their individual or corporate citizens, and a target. One example of such an "extraterritorial" countermeasure is the Iran and Libya Sanctions Act of 1996, which obliges the U.S. president to blacklist foreign entities that have invested in the Iranian or Libyan energy sector.

Sanctions (Collective Coercive Measures)

The 1919 Treaty of Versailles, which brought an end to World War I, was the first international legal instrument to bestow sanctioning powers on an international organization. Article 16 of the Covenant of the League of Nations authorized the League to apply comprehensive sanctions against member states acting in violation of their international obligations, a power it used or threatened to use seven times over the course of its 26-year existence. Between 1945 and 1990, the successor to the League, the United Nations (UN), took advantage of its power under Chapter 7 of the UN Charter to institute sanctions only twice during the Cold War, first against Rhodesia in 1968 and later against South Africa in 1977. The development of sanctions practice proceeded at a similarly glacial pace at the regional level. With the exception of the sanction regimes maintained by the Organization of American States against Cuba and the Dominican Republic in the 1960s and a sporadically implemented boycott of Israeli products adopted by the Arab League in 1948, between 1945 and 1990 the sanctioning powers of regional organizations remained dormant.

Multilateral sanction regimes became regular features of the global legal order only in the early 1990s, as the decline of the Soviet Union precipitated a redistribution of power to states formerly relegated to the periphery of global politics. Between 1990 and 1995, the UN Security Council (UNSC) authorized 10 new sanction regimes, and regional organizations, including the Economic Community of West African States (ECOWAS) and the European Union (EU), began to experiment with sanctions within their respective spheres of influence.

The vast majority of the sanctions implemented during this period, including those against Iraq, Haiti, and the former Socialist Republic of Yugoslavia, were economic in nature and comprehensive in scope. Regional and international organizations quickly discovered, however, that determined political elites in the targeted states could turn comprehensive sanctions to their advantage by providing their citizens with the services and goods denied by the international community and inducing a rally-around-the-flag effect that ultimately tightened their grip on power. Reluctant to continue imposing measures that consolidated the positions of truculent politicians and contributed to widespread humanitarian suffering, individual states and international organizations began to look for alternatives to traditional sanctions.

"Smart" Coercive Measures and Blacklists

The search for a comprehensive economic sanctions substitute prompted the development of "targeted" or "smart" sanctions and countermeasures, which were designed specifically to deny targets access to goods or services while avoiding harm to entities not responsible for the impugned policies or acts. Today, comprehensive sanctions have been almost entirely phased out, whereas smart sanction regimes have evolved to encompass a variety of measures, including those designed to isolate the target psychologically and physically (through, for example, travel and communication bans), disrupt a target's ability to fund its operation or generally transact business (via asset freezes and restrictions on the sale, purchase, or transport of specific commodities associated with the target's operations), and deny the target access to specific resources (by means of embargoes). Under various international

and domestic sanction regimes, entities subject to smart sanctions and countermeasures may be individual persons (citizens or government officials), business entities that provide support to the targeted individuals, nongovernmental organizations, or revolutionary groups.

Targeted sanction regimes that restrict the movement or freeze the assets of targets necessitate the creation and maintenance of modifiable registers of individual, corporate, and organizational entities to be denied access to a financial service or geographic area. These registers are commonly referred to as "blacklists," although this label does not appear in a single piece of contemporary national or international legislation authorizing the application of smart sanctions or countermeasures.

The word *blacklist* entered the lexicon of international relations during World War I, when the British government, pursuant to the Trading with the Enemy Act of 1915, issued a "black list" of persons and firms in neutral countries known to be aiding, or suspected of lending aid to, Great Britain's enemies. Under the authority of the 1915 act the British government prohibited its subjects from trading with (and forbade neutral countries from re-exporting British goods to) the proscribed entities. Blacklisted firms and individuals were also denied access to British vessels, banks, insurers, creditors, coal, and public facilities (including cable and mail services), as well as passage through British blockades. The British blacklist was so successful in isolating the economies of the Central Powers and impairing their capacity to wage war that by 1918 each of the principal belligerents, including France, Japan, Italy, Germany, Austria, and the United States, had adopted similar legislation targeting their respective enemies. Thereafter, the concept of an alterable register of targets was inexorably associated with the idea of sanctions in the minds of the European and American polity.

Since the close of World War I, blacklists have evolved from subordinate components of "total war" efforts to become the very *essentia* of contemporary sanctions regimes. As a case in point, one might consider that, of the 28 EU sanction regimes in force as of December 2010, 20 involved the application of travel bans or asset freezes requiring the issuance of a list of targeted entities. More tellingly, since the mid-1990s the rhetoric associated with the imposition of sanctions and countermeasures has changed, with incumbent politicians seldom pressing for the imposition of comprehensive measures.

The Efficacy of Sanctions and Countermeasures

The effectiveness of any particular sanction regime ultimately depends on characteristics unique to that regime, including the expectations of the relevant policy makers, the complex interaction between the sanctions or countermeasures and other coercive and noncoercive policy instruments that may have been relied upon, and the contextual political, legal, and economic factors that may reinforce or dampen the effects of the regime. With this in mind, a macro-level examination of the historical record does confirm that sanctions and countermeasures are likely to bring about the desired result only when a specific set of criteria associated with the targets, senders, third states, and coercive measures themselves are fulfilled.

A target's vulnerability to the measures imposed, its relationship with the sanctioning body, and the vehemence with which it opposes the proposed changes to its behavior are critical factors in determining whether sanctions and countermeasures will be effective. Sanction regimes have the greatest impact when the target is dependent on the benefits that have been removed or are threatened to be removed; has a preexisting relationship with the sender that raises the political, economic, or personal cost of noncompliance; and is open to modifying the impugned behavior. For example, in 1976 the Republic of Korea (ROK) was dissuaded from purchasing a French nuclear reprocessing plant and pursuing a nuclear weapons program when the United States threatened to withdraw from a U.S.-ROK security pact and block the export of U.S. technology to the Republic. Conversely, a decade's worth of sanctions and countermeasures have not succeeded in persuading Iran to fulfill its declaration obligations under the Treaty on the Non-Proliferation of Nuclear Weapons and have not deterred North Korea from developing nuclear weapons, largely because the tactical benefits of noncompliance are perceived by the targeted regimes as outweighing the economic, political, and legal costs.

A second set of criteria relates to the sanctioners and third states. Sanction regimes that impose a small economic cost on the sender are more likely to be enforced, and therefore felt, by the target. The blithe attitude with which certain states approached the implementation of UN Security Council sanctions on the National Union for the Total Independence of Angola (UNITA) illustrates this point. In June 1998, the Security Council passed Resolution 1173, which required that all states prohibit the direct or indirect import of UNITA-mined diamonds. Two years later, a UN Panel of Experts issued a lengthy report chastising the states with the largest diamond markets, Belgium and the United Kingdom, for failing to punish persons known to deal in UNITA diamonds or take other steps to curtail illegal diamond trading in their territories. Additionally, there must be a low probability that the targeted entities will receive offsetting assistance from a rival of the sender, as even a single sanctions-busting state can compromise an otherwise potentially successful sanction regime. Liberia, for example, for years openly violated UNSC and ECOWAS targeted sanctions imposed on the Sierra Leone military junta and Revolutionary United Front rebel force, a pretermission that fatally undermined the multilateral efforts to bring an end to the decade-long Sierra Leone Civil War.

Finally, a sanction regime must be designed in such a manner that it is actually capable of accomplishing its raison d'être. An underdeveloped or weak sanction regime will neither impact the target nor bring about the desired change in behavior. It is generally acknowledged that the first UNSC sanctions intended to stop the flow of foreign weapons into Rwanda proved ineffective, in part because they were too narrow in scope (insofar as they prohibited only the sale or supply of "arms or related matériel" to targeted entities within Rwanda) and could be ignored by third states with impunity. Today, it is standard practice to include in the legislation establishing a sanctions regime a provision authorizing the creation of a compliance-monitoring mechanism, an indication of the sanctioning entity's readiness to punish third states that violate the law, and a well-reasoned description of the prohibited behavior.

The Legal Limits of Sanction Regimes

Although international organizations have been vested with far-reaching sanctioning powers, their discretion in choosing when and how sanctions may be employed is not unlimited. At a minimum, the power of international organizations to implement coercive measures is constrained by their foundational instruments. Thus, the Security Council is bound by Article 24(2) of the UN Charter to act in a manner consistent with the Purposes and Principles of the UN (as laid down in Articles 1 and 2 of the UN Charter) and impose sanctions only after "the existence of any threat to the peace, breach of the peace, or act of aggression" has been confirmed (Articles 39–41 of the UN Charter), and the European Council, under the provisions of the Treaty of Rome, was empowered to implement only sanctions linked to the operation of the European common market. There is also an emerging consensus that international organizations are obliged to respect fundamental human rights and may not implement sanctions that contravene *jus cogens* norms of international law. Although the scope and precise content of this prohibition remain hotly debated, the core of this precept has been embraced by the UN Committee on Economic, Social and Cultural Rights, the Grand Chamber of the European Court of Justice, and various national courts. A third limitation is that international organizations are bound by general principles of international law, including the principle of proportionality. As a consequence, sanctions leveled by an international organization must correspond in magnitude and degree to the harm suffered and the ends sought to be achieved.

States resorting to countermeasures are bound by similar limitations. According to the ILC's Articles on State Responsibility, countermeasures may be leveled against only a state responsible for an internationally wrongful act, and only after the sanctioner has attempted to resolve the dispute diplomatically. Furthermore, under the Articles, countermeasures must be proportionate to the injury suffered, corrective or reparative (as opposed to punitive) in nature, reversible with respect to their application and consequences, and consistent with the peremptory norms of international law as well as the rights of third states. With respect to these last two requirements, a contentious debate has erupted over the legality of unilateral sanctions regimes with extraterritorial effects. Although the United States has embraced extraterritorial sanction regimes, other states have claimed that these measures are an affront to their sovereignty, violative of the United States' treaty obligations, and incompatible with

the bases of jurisdiction accepted in public international law. As of 2010, Canada, Belgium, Denmark, France, Germany, the United Kingdom, Sweden, and the EU each maintained "blocking statutes" neutralizing the effects of an extraterritorial sanction regime on entities within their jurisdictions. Finally, a sanctioner implementing a targeted countermeasure that has within its ambit one of the sender's individual or corporate citizens must take care that the measure does not run afoul of the constitutionally protected rights of the target, lest it be overturned by a domestic court.

Benjamin E. Brockman-Hawe
Independent Scholar

See also Antiterrorist Financing; European Union; United Nations; Weapons Smuggling

Further Readings

Cassese, A. *International Law*, 2nd ed. Oxford, UK: Oxford University Press, 2005.

Crawford, James. *The International Law Commission's Articles on State Responsibility*. Cambridge, UK: Cambridge University Press, 2002.

Gowlland-Debbas, Vera et al. *United Nations Sanctions and International Law*. The Hague: Kluwer, 2001.

White, Nigel and Ademola Abass. "Countermeasures and Sanctions." In *International Law*, Malcolm Evans, ed., 2nd ed. Oxford: Oxford University Press, 2006.

SECURITIZATION AFTER TERROR

In the initial aftermath of a terrorist attack, there is a common shock and outrage shared by the government and the citizenry. A direct result of this, coupled with fear and not knowing if more immediate attacks are pending, the government will always err on the side of caution and deploy additional personnel. This rapid increase in the overall level of security seeks to prevent any possible second wave of attack. At the same time, it serves to provide the frightened public with a measure of comfort. During the early stages of an event, such a response is a demanded and welcome sight, but that is relatively short-lived. As time passes—unless the attack is sustained on home soil—general fear and angst diminish, along with the perceived need for a greater security presence. For governments, these contrasting and quickly changing reactions represent a fine line that must be negotiated.

While the modern world has been no stranger to terrorism, terror has taken on new meaning since the horrific events of September 11, 2001. Since that tragic day, thousands more innocent victims have fallen to the violence of Islamic fundamentalism. Following each attack, there has been the inevitable finger-pointing as politicians seek answers regarding warning signs that were missed and "dots" that were not "connected." Laws are enacted to give the government more power to investigate and preempt future hostile activity. The "protective pendulum" will inevitably swing away from freedoms and ever closer to totalitarianism in an effort to prevent future attacks. In such a climate, citizens' freedoms can easily be encroached upon.

Terrorists, regardless of their political ideologies, have several factors that will always be in their favor. Principally, they have the benefit of selecting the type of attack to be conducted, including the target and the timing. Conversely, the government is generally ignorant of all of this information (at least to the point of having a clear picture of what is being planned) while still having the burden of protecting the citizenry. This fact has not gone unnoticed by terrorists and was perhaps best explained by a member of the Irish Republican Army (IRA). In October 1984, an unknown member of the IRA carried out the bombing of the Grand Hotel in Brighton, in southern England. The attack narrowly missed then prime minister Margaret Thatcher, but several others were killed and many more were wounded. During the claim of responsibility, the following prophetic statement was made: "Today we were unlucky, but remember, we only have to be lucky once; you will have to be lucky always."

The major change in security operations and responses to such attacks since September 2001 is that preparedness is no longer restricted to the territory of the victim country but now must extend well beyond that country's borders. Every nation realizes that it may be next and that it must learn from each event. Such preparedness has been made necessary primarily by attacks stemming from violent, extremist Islam, as opposed to domestic groups. The level of securitization, however, can differ immensely depending upon the government agency involved. It can range from a chief ordering subordinates to be more alert for suspicious activity to the redeployment of personnel to specific areas at risk. The level of securitization is largely dependent upon an educated decision with regard to all facts available, case by case.

Immediately following the attacks of September 11, 2001, the United States was hit again, this time by an anthrax attack as envelopes containing a white powder that harbored anthrax bacteria made their way, by post, to senate offices and other high-profile recipients. The immediate effects of these attacks extended rapidly across the country. First, airlines security was called into question, and then the entire U.S. Postal Service was shut down. Combined, these attacks led to a massive increase in security operations at all levels of government. Airports were staffed with extra police officers and National Guard members, often armed with combat rifles. The Department of Homeland Security was founded, which began funding domestic operations and training for all levels of law enforcement, fire protection, and emergency medical services on unprecedented levels. These same entities began to acquire the equipment necessary to respond to terrorist attacks, including potential incidents involving weapons of mass destruction.

The Federal Bureau of Investigation (FBI) rapidly expanded its Joint Terrorism Task Forces, establishing them in most major cities. Terrorist watch lists were expanded, and local law enforcement was given access in order to prevent the next attack. Local domestic intelligence organizations were established in order to improve the flow of intelligence and information between the various levels of government. Finally, on October 26, 2001, President George Bush signed into law the U.S.A. Patriot Act, which authorized the expanded use of investigative tools, such as wiretaps, search warrants, and national security letters. At the time, the law was welcomed with few effective exceptions, although civil libertarians raised concerns over abrogation of rights guaranteed by the U.S. Constitution.

The next major attack would occur 3,600 miles away from New York. On May 16, 2003, in Casablanca, Morocco, 10 men carried out coordinated suicide bombings at five separate locations within a 30-minute period. These attacks killed 45 individuals and wounded more than 100. With the exception of the Belgian consulate, all were soft targets consisting of a Jewish community center, the Safir Hotel, a social club, and the Casa de España restaurant. The attackers were wearing suicide devices in addition to being armed with grenades and edged weapons. The attack at the Spanish restaurant, which accounted for the greatest loss of life during the incident (with 15 killed), is perhaps the most enlightening part of the attack. Only moments before the attack on the Casa de España, closed-circuit television cameras caught the bombers attempting to enter the Positano Italian restaurant but being prevented from entering by an employee. The suspects then went into the unguarded Casa de España and detonated. This part of the attack offers a perfect example of how easily terrorists can complete their plans even when those plans are interrupted; these terrorists merely adjusted their target after encountering security and still accomplished their objective.

In response to the Casablanca bombings, the Moroccan government arrested some 3,000 individuals, ultimately charging 87 for their involvement in the attacks. These included three suicide bombers who failed to carry out their assigned attacks. Within 10 days, the Parliament of Morocco passed antiterrorism legislation. Interestingly, this legislation had originally been introduced in 2002 but had languished due to bureaucracy. The new laws authorized law enforcement to take action against political activities, including those deemed peaceful. The new legislation allowed for members of the media to be held criminally liable for publishing material deemed supportive of terrorist activities. The laws also increased to 12 the number of days a person could be detained without being charged, as well as reduced the requirements for use of the death penalty. In a final step, the "post of imam" was regulated by the government and required a promise to eliminate fundamentalism.

The country of Indonesia next found itself in the crosshairs of Islamic extremists. The island of Bali suffered first, when on Saturday, October 12, 2002, a vehicle-borne improvised explosive device (VBIED) was detonated outside the Sari Club at Kuta Beach. The resulting blast killed 187 people and wounded another 300. This was followed shortly afterward by a second device, near an adjacent disco club, as well as a third detonation, outside the U.S. consulate.

On August 5, 2003, in Jakarta, Islamic suicide terrorists struck again, killing 12 and injuring another 100 or more individuals. The target location for the attack, the Marriott Hotel, was considered to be one of the most secure in the region at the

time. Being set back a considerable distance from the main roadway was believed to make it more difficult to be targeted by a VBIED. This confidence resulted in the hotel's having recently held functions involving the U.S. and Australian diplomatic corps. Unfortunately, as in every successful terrorist attack, a weak link was identified by a hostile organization, in this case the Jemaah Islamiyah. The terrorists disguised their device to look like a taxi, which at the time of detonation was waiting within the taxi queue near the hotel entrance.

Ironically, this attack occurred while security in Jakarta was elevated in view of Parliament being in session as well as the ongoing trial of terrorists involved in the Bali bombing the year before. Even with the added security measures, the target location still fell within the classification of "soft target." Finally, on October 1, 2005, in Bali, three suicide bombers detonated themselves. Two hit at the Jimbaran Beach resort and one at Raja's Restaurant in Kuta Square. In this attack, 26 were killed and more than 100 injured. These attacks, all of which targeted tourist locations, led to local businesses establishing the Bali Hotel Association. The group's purpose was to develop common security measures and to share ideas and intelligence among individual businesses.

The European Union was soon reminded that Europe was not immune to the modern version of Islamic extremism. On March 11, 2004, 10 improvised explosive devices were detonated on trains in four locations around Madrid. The destruction resulted in a staggering 191 killed and 1,460 injured. The devices were positioned on various trains and triggered by cell phones. More than 20 individuals were later arrested following the attacks. Just over a year later, on July 7, 2005, four suicide bombers detonated themselves aboard London's Underground rail system. More than 50 people were killed and more than 100 wounded. These two attacks served as a severe global wake-up call, reminding authorities and citizens alike of the vulnerability of mass-transit systems. In England, all government facilities were cordoned off and assigned additional security. Most tourist attractions in and around London were closed. A massive increase in the reporting of suspicious people and activity ensued. The largest of these occurred on July 9, when 20,000 people were evacuated out of Birmingham, England. Police conducted four controlled explosions of suspicious packages that were later deemed not threatening. In Spain, the bombings, which had occurred shortly before a national election, resulted in a new party being voted into power.

In the United States, the Department of Homeland Security established the "See It, Say It" policy, which encouraged passengers using public transport to report immediately any suspicious activity to the authorities. While there has been public demand for more security on mass ground transport, that is virtually impossible without severely impeding commuters. What is of note in the Madrid and London attacks is that the two governments were no strangers to domestic terrorists carrying out bombing campaigns. Yet even with their vast experience and, in the case of London, an unrivaled close-circuit television system, they failed to prevent the carnage.

On November 26, 2008, 10 Islamic terrorists carried out a coordinated siege of Mumbai, which resulted in 183 people being killed and hundreds more injured. If anything, this attack served as a harsh reminder that terrorists will carry out their operations using whatever method best serves their purpose. However, while the method of operation was unique, the targets, or victimology, remained the same: soft. These 10 extremists armed with explosives and automatic weapons did not raid government offices, military installations, financial centers, or foreign embassies. They targeted two hotels, a railway station, a Jewish cultural center, a local café, a movie theater, and two hospitals.

Such locations epitomize the definition of *soft target*. Innocent civilians enjoying a meal or a movie, receiving care at a hospital, or checking into a hotel for business or pleasure are undertaking normal activities and generally not alert to possible danger; they certainly are not prepared to face an armed and determined adversary. India has the second largest military in the world, yet even that force could not provide protection at the level needed to have deterred the Mumbai attack. Even if it had, the terrorists would simply have shifted their targets to less protected ones. However, in the aftermath of the tragic Mumbai attack, the Indian government responded with an increase in the number of armed guards positioned at hotels and railway stations. Security at locations such as shopping malls, corporate offices, and other public areas has been increased, primarily consisting of uniformed personnel, the checking of bags, and the use of metal detectors. In June 2009, the newly appointed police commissioner

for Mumbai deployed 4,800 closed-circuit television cameras around the city. He also purchased armored vehicles, 2,000 machine guns, sniper rifles, and other weapons. Finally, he instigated the creation of quick response teams with a total force of 1,000 men in an effort to prevent a future event.

The attacks have continued in Russia. On January 24, 2011, a suicide bombing was perpetrated at the luggage pickup area at Moscow's Domodedovo Airport. This attack will no doubt cause a worldwide reexamination of safety and security procedures at such locations. Largely prevented from boarding aircraft, the terrorists adjusted their aim and targeted a less secure location, with lethal results. The incident provides further proof of the difficulty of preventing terrorist attacks.

If history is any teacher, it is clear that terrorists overwhelmingly strike soft targets. Since 2001, Islamic extremists have carried out successful operations in Israel, Jordan, Saudi Arabia, Egypt, Spain, England, Sweden, Indonesia, and the United States. Each country has represented a different form of government, a different form of security, and yet each has suffered. Each attack, however, provides important lessons with regard to how future attacks can be dissuaded while preserving the freedoms that society has come to enjoy. It is a delicate balance.

The sheer number of potential soft targets is overwhelming: restaurants, hotels, buses, trolleys, rail systems, ferries—the list goes on. It just is not possible to protect everything all the time. The San Francisco Police Department, for example, has a total force of approximately 2,300 sworn officers, from the chief to the newest recruit. They police a city that is 47 square miles in area and home to around 800,000 citizens. More than 220 million people ride the "Muni" system of buses, trolleys, and rail each year. More than 15 million people visit the city annually, staying in one of the more than 33,000 hotel rooms and/or visiting one of the more than 3,400 restaurants. Large cities around the world offer similarly rich targets. When terrorists strike, it is only after a considerable amount of time has been spent in surveillance and reconnaissance. They have identified the potential weaknesses in our armor and have planned their attack to kill efficiently.

At the end of the day, for terrorists, time is perhaps their greatest ally. With the passage of time comes the public's loss of fear, shock, outrage, and hypervigilance that are present immediately after an attack. With this loss of "memory" comes the political rhetoric and economic reality of security costs. Finally, there is the most dangerous factor of all: complacency. Terrorists know this and they are waiting. It is only a matter of time before they strike again.

Glenn P. McGovern
Santa Clara County District Attorney's Office

See also Violence: Protection

Further Readings

Friesen, Katie. "The Effects of the Madrid and London Subway Bombings on Europe's View of Terrorism." *Review Digest: Human Rights and the War on Terror*, 2007 Supplement. http://www.du.edu/korbel/hrhw/researchdigest/terror/europe_2007.pdf (Accessed August 2011).

Frost, Martin. "Response to the 2005 London Bombings." http://www.martinfrost.ws/htmlfiles/bombing_response1.html (Accessed August 2011).

Global Jihad. "Casablanca Bombings." August 2007. http://www.globaljihad.net, accessed 1/21/2011 (Accessed February 2011).

Maghraoui, Abdeslam. "Morocco's Reforms After the Casablanca Bombings." *Arab Reform Bulletin* (July 26, 2003). http://www.carnegieendowment.org/arb/?fa=show&article=21592 (Accessed February 2011).

STRATFOR. "Hotel Bombing: New Questions About Indonesian Security." August 5, 2003. http://www.stratfor.com/hotel_bombing_new_questions_about_indonesian_security (Accessed January 2011).

Separatists

Separatists are members of a distinct cultural, ethnic, political, or religious group who advocate various degrees of autonomy for their group or detachment of their group from the dominant population within a country. Many such movements advocate complete separation from the parent country and the establishment of full political sovereignty for the group in the territorial area it occupies. The concept of a separatist movement is often regarded as synonymous with an independence or secessionist movement. This is the type of separatist movement with which the general public is likely probably familiar, given the attention such groups have received in the popular media.

However, not all separatists advocate complete autonomy for their group. In the broadest of contexts, many regard separatism as synonymous with devolution, in that it entails advocacy of a group or region within a country to gain some degree of self-governance. As is the case with many devolutionary movements, some separatist groups do seek sovereign status as independent states, but others advocate limited internal control rather than a complete break with the existing state. Examples of movements that advocate limited internal control rather than complete sovereignty include those in Scotland and Wales, which have succeeded in gaining more autonomy in their local educational and court systems and more local legislative power at the expense of direct British authority. It should be noted that small minorities in both Scotland and Wales do in fact advocate secession from Britain.

As of 2011, approximately 70 to 80 separatist movements existed globally, of which around two dozen were active and viable. A multitude of small, ineffectual separatist groups exist that do not reflect the views of the majorities of the groups they purport to represent (and in fact may be regarded as fringe elements and extremists by most members of their own ethnic or cultural groups). Such separatist groups (which in the United States include small white separatist groups and Native American separatist groups) are unlikely to emerge as viable. Although separatist movements can be found in most world regions, the majority are concentrated in Asia and Europe, the latter being a thriving area for separatist activism in recent decades.

The formal analysis of separatist movements and the academic body of literature related to the subject are relatively modern developments, but separatism as a phenomenon is not new and has existed since the emergence of states in antiquity. Since the 20th century, there has been an upsurge in separatist and devolutionary movements. The latter trend largely reflects several historical events, including the decline of colonial powers and a corresponding spread of independence movements and concomitant creation of new states. As of 2011, the United Nations (UN) had 192 sovereign member states, a significant increase from the 51 members at the time the UN was created, in 1945.

In addition to colonial decline, the collapse of communism and communist states is closely linked to separatist and devolutionist trends and the relatively recent emergence of many new states. Most of the 26 new countries that have emerged since 1990 split from formerly communist states. The collapse of the Soviet Union in 1991 gave rise to 15 new countries, including the Russian Federation. To date, seven countries have emerged from the former Yugoslavia and two from the former Czechoslovakia. In both the former Soviet Union and the former Yugoslavia, multiple separatist movements remain active, and several areas, including Chechnya and Tatarstan (both located within the Russian Federation), contain significant populations that support independence as a goal for their people. The separatist trend that accelerated in the 20th century shows indications of continuing and even accelerating.

The desire for increased autonomy can stem from a range of sources: real or perceived inequities of treatment, a strong sense of cultural or other uniqueness of identity apart from the dominant group or groups within a country, or economic considerations. In both Scotland and Wales, the majority was concerned about perpetuating their own distinct languages and cultural traditions and was convinced that stronger provincial and local governments could achieve such goals more effectively than the national government in London, which had been perceived as historically ignoring Scottish and Welsh interests. Also, the perception existed that they were not receiving appropriate national government funding and services relative to the taxes collected by the British government. Accordingly, the desire existed to have more provincial control of tax revenues and governmental funding and projects.

Many separatist movements originate or are given significant impetus via the outright abuse or persecution of a distinct minority at the hands of the larger, dominant group. The majority group of Kosovo is Albanian in terms of ethnicity and Muslim in terms of religion, in sharp contrast to the majority of Serbians, who are Serb or Slavic ethnically and Orthodox Christians in terms of religious faith. Kosovar Albanians had long alleged mistreatment at the hands of the Serb-dominated national government and initiated armed resistance and independence efforts in the 1990s. Violence escalated between Serbian/Yugoslav security forces and Kosovar separatists, leading to Serbian efforts to drive ethnic Albanians out of the region, extending to instances of ethnic cleansing that captured world attention and ultimately led the North Atlantic Treaty Organization (NATO) to intervene militarily and the UN to deploy peacekeeping forces.

Josef Friedrich Matthes (head of the short-lived Rheinish Republic) photographed with separatists in 1923 in Koblenz, Germany. The separatists were part of a liberation struggle movement that began after Germany's defeat in World War I. (Library of Congress)

It should be stressed that the majority of separatist movements globally are not characterized by violence or armed insurrection. In most instances, separatist groups are focused on political and social activism, discourse, and democratic means rather than armed uprising or terrorist activity in furtherance of their agendas. While political tensions and public demonstrations may result from separatist political activism, in most areas where such movements exist, separatist activity is usually peaceful. Examples of such peaceful political movements include the sovereignty movements of Quebec to secede or obtain increased internal control from Canada, of the French-speaking Walloons to create their own state in what is now southern Belgium, and of many Aboriginal peoples to secede or obtain limited home rule from Australia.

Six of the world's active separatist movements involve violence (either generated by or directed toward separatists, usually a combination of the two), those of: the Basques, Palestine/Israel, Kurdistan, East Turkistan (western China), Tibet, and the Philippines. In several other instances, violence has abated at least temporarily, but the potential for conflict to be rekindled remains a possibility; such areas include Sri Lanka and Chechnya. The possibility of conflict also exists between the former parent country and several recently declared states, such as Kosovo-Serbia and South Ossetia/Abkhazia-Georgia, or de facto states that function separately from a larger country, such as Taiwan-China, Somaliland-Somalia, or North Cyprus-Cyprus. Just as other international developments can be fluid and changing, nearly each year separatist movements emerge, decline, or dissolve, change their goals or nature, devolve from political movements into violence, or are resolved through either diplomatic discourse or the military victory of one side—an example of the latter being the victory of government forces over Tamil separatists in the long-standing Sri Lankan civil war in 2009.

In most cases, violent separatist conflicts are marked by conflict between ethnic groups in which a racial or cultural minority is locked in struggle with a larger, more dominant group within a country. The type and the intensity of violence vary widely. Many separatist struggles and antiseparatist efforts are characterized by low-level conflict and violence, such as disorderly demonstrations, rioting, looting, vandalism, intimidation, and economic crimes that can include the destruction of government and private property. Even low-intensity conflict can cause death and injury, displace large numbers of people from their homes, inflict significant infrastructure damage, scare away tourist revenue and foreign investment, and otherwise generate significant turmoil. Such low-level conflict can also serve as an initial stage in an escalating vicious cycle of violence.

It is not entirely uncommon for separatist conflicts to lead to armed uprising or civil war. Of the seven countries that have emerged from the former Yugoslavia, three fought ultimately successful military campaigns against both internal and external forces. Croatia, Bosnia, and Kosovo fought both a civil war against local Serbs and others internally who sought to prevent secession, simultaneously fighting external military forces sent from Serbia/Yugoslavia to prevent their achieving independence and to keep the country's territory intact. The casualties and suffering that resulted were far out of proportion to the small territorial dimensions and relatively brief time spans of the Balkan Wars. In Bosnia alone, more than 100,000 people were killed and nearly 2 million displaced.

Ethnic clashes can be among the most violent and inhumane types of conflicts. Internal conflicts between ethnic groups can on occasion be characterized by the perpetration of war crimes and other severe human rights violations by one group against its perceived enemy. Separatist uprisings in Hussein-era Iraq led to the widespread use of poison gas by the government against the ethnic Kurdish minority in the north and against Shiite Muslims in the south. Following successful drives for independence in parts of the former Yugoslavia, many ethnic Serbs claim they were persecuted and without cause driven out of their homes and communities. Separatist efforts on the part of Bosnian Muslims and Croats led to incidents of ethnic cleansing perpetrated by some Serbian military units, in which Bosnian Muslim or Croat men of military age were often either imprisoned by Serb troops in concentration camps or killed outright, and many women were victimized by raping campaigns in which the goal was both to terrorize and to dilute the enemy bloodline.

Groups that allege that they have been victimized by war crimes or other inhumane acts can in many cases have at least some recourse for seeking justice internationally. The International Criminal Court (ICC) was established in 2002 and counts 114 countries as signatories. The ICC is designed to hear cases involving war crimes, crimes against humanity, and genocide. Prior to the ICC, special international bodies have been convened for similar purposes, usually in response to specific conflicts. For example, when it became apparent that the separatist wars of the former Yugoslavia were giving rise to war crimes and genocidal acts, the UN Security Council created a legal body in 1993 specifically to investigate and hear cases related to crimes perpetrated during that conflict: the International Criminal Tribunal for the former Yugoslavia.

Organized military operations are not the only sources of conflict, casualties, and disorder that occur within violent separatist conflicts. Civil wars and other armed conflicts are commonly accompanied by criminal acts in addition to military actions. For instance, in order to finance the purchase of armaments and other needed items, elements of separatist groups may engage in criminal activities such as smuggling, robbery, extortion, production or trafficking of narcotics, involvement in or partnership with the activities of organized crime figures, or kidnapping and ransoming persons whose families are perceived to have financial resources. One of many examples of separatist groups that have engaged in at least certain criminal activity, such as kidnapping and extortion, was the Zapatista movement of the Chiapas region of southern Mexico. It is worth noting many separatists allege criminal activity on the part of government forces as well. Separatists may assert that extralegal means were used against them or that they have been victimized by robbery, extortion, or other offenses committed by government forces, often using the broader conflict as an opportunity to engage in economic or other crimes.

Although not characteristic of all separatist movements, even those involving violence, many examples exist of terrorist acts perpetrated either by or against separatists. Examples of terrorist acts related to separatist struggles include assassinations, bombings, hijackings, and hostage taking. Those engaging in such acts may regard their actions as justifiable acts of war, and smaller, less militarily powerful groups may regard such actions as among the few means at their disposal to strike at their perceived enemy or gain international attention for their cause. Terrorism is closely linked in the minds of the general public to certain separatist groups, including those of the Basques and in the Philippines. Elements of some white separatist groups in Western nations, including the United States, have perpetrated or planned terrorist acts targeting either government institutions or groups they regard as their enemies.

A lack of clarity exists with regard to separatist movements in the standing of international law and the degree of legitimacy and legal rights such movements may or may not be entitled to claim. The UN recognizes the right of self-determination but international law and the laws and foreign policies of most countries have not been consistent with regard to separatist movements and independence/secession efforts. Most members of the international community have demonstrated reluctance to support separatist causes openly, even when the cause is clearly justifiable, such as in the case of oppression. In contrast to recognition of the right to self-determination is the simultaneous and paradoxical recognition by the UN and member states of the international community of the sovereign nature of countries and their right to maintain and defend their territorial integrity and prevent groups or regions from seceding.

The often contradictory foreign policies of many nations in supporting certain separatist groups or de facto states while ignoring or denouncing others usually reflects their individual vested national interests. For example, the United States does not support the efforts of the Sahrawi people to establish independence for Western Sahara (as the Sahrawi Arab Republic); the Moroccan government that currently controls the region is a close U.S. ally. Conversely, U.S. foreign policy supported secession efforts in Bosnia and Kosovo both out of sympathy for violence and human rights violations perpetrated against pro-independence elements and also because independent Bosnian and Kosovar states can serve as a hedge against the regional power and influence of Russian-allied Serbia within the Balkan Peninsula. The international community, including the United States, stopped short of supporting Chechen independence efforts because of the serious foreign-policy ramifications such an endorsement would have with the Russian government and partly because of the apparent ties of some Chechen separatists to international terrorist groups such as Al Qaeda.

Barry D. Mowell
Broward College

See also Jihad; South Asia; Southeast Asia; Terrorism: Defined; Terrorism: Domestic; Terrorism: Nondomestic; Terrorism Versus Transnational Crime

Further Readings

Beary, B. *Separatist Movements: A Global Reference.* Washington, DC: CQ Press, 2011.

Doyle, D. *Secession as an International Phenomenon: From America's Civil War to Contemporary Separatist Movements.* Athens: University of Georgia Press, 2010.

Hanzich, J. "Dying for Independence: World Separatist Movements and Terrorism." *Harvard International Review*, v.25/2 (June 22, 2003).

Hewitt, C. and T. Cheetham. *Encyclopedia of Modern Separatist Movements.* Santa Barbara, CA: ABC-CLIO, 2001.

Jenne, E., S. Saidemann, and W. Lowe. "Separatism as a Bargaining Posture: The Role of Leverage in Minority Radicalization." *Journal of Peace Research*, v.44/5 (September 2007).

SEX SLAVERY

Sex slavery involves the enslavement of people who are required to perform sex acts as part of their servitude for the slaveholder or others. There are many forms and varieties of sex slavery. Although both males and females are victims of sex slavery, a disproportionate number are women and girls. Victims of sex slavery are forced into prostitution, marriage, bonded labor, and traditional forms of enslavement and in some cases ritual slavery, carried out in the context of regional religious beliefs or other cultural practices. Human trafficking is often a component of sex slavery, as the slaves are commonly transported across national boundaries. The enslaved person is viewed as a commodity, and the services performed by that person result in financial gain for others. Sex slavery today is a major international concern with major consequences for its victims.

Slavery has existed throughout the world in many different forms. Most people are familiar with the enslavement of the Hebrews as described in the Bible and with the enslavement of Africans in the United States prior to emancipation. Slavery was a key social institution in the early civilizations of Mesopotamia, ancient Egypt, Greece, Rome, and China. Slave trades existed with other types of international trade, and a strong system of institutional slavery developed in the Middle East. Slavery was practiced throughout the world, however, and despite attempts by abolitionists in different areas at different times, the practice remains. The term *white slavery* has been used to refer primarily to sexual enslavement and forced prostitution, although it can involve persons of all ethnicities. Some people have been forced into sex slavery because of religious and other cultural rituals, such as the early West African and Indian practices of handing over young girls to priests; these officials used the girls as sex slaves or prostituted them to others for the atonement of sin.

White slavery became a cause for special concern, considered by some a moral panic, in the late 19th and early 20th centuries. In 1910, fears in the United States over white slavery led to the Mann Act, which prohibited transport of women or children for the sex trade. It became customary in Japan during World War II to enlist through slavery so-called comfort women, whose role was to provide sexual favors to the Japanese soldiers in government-supported brothels; these women were subjected to serial rape, murder, and torture. When the Cold War ended in 1989 and international borders were loosened for travel, the modern slave trade was born. In addition, women and girls have throughout history been used as pawns during periods of war conflict by actual and threatened rape and enslavement of the women and children of the enemy.

It is estimated that between 500,000 and 2 million people are trafficked for the commercial sex trade. The victims come from many countries, such as Thailand, China, Moldavia, and Ukraine, and are transported to destinations such as Japan, Israel, Thailand, many European nations, and the Americas. Although all types of people are enslaved, it is primarily women and girls who are forced into sex slavery. The types of servitude include forced prostitution and pornography. The women and girls often allow themselves to be transported across national boundaries in the hope of achieving a better livelihood and are often misled about the type of work to be performed. They are forced to work in massage parlors in the United States (which offer a cover for prostitution establishments), cantinas in Mexico, or brothels and apartments. In a system called debt peonage, many incur a debt to the pimps that cannot be repaid, forcing them to remain enslaved as long as they are useful as sex slaves; this period is sometimes short, in that profits for the traffickers begin to lessen as the prostitutes age or become ill. The women are expendable; there is usually a ready supply of others to fill these roles.

Alcohol and other drugs are often used by the pimps to control the slaves. These substances can introduce addictions, in addition to the serious health-related problems, ranging from sexually transmitted diseases to mental illness, brought about by the trauma of sex slavery and limited access to or denial of healthcare. The incidence of human immunodeficiency syndrome and acquired immune deficiency syndrome (HIV/AIDS) is a major problem for people in the sex trade. Psychological services are rarely provided for or sought by these women even when they have the freedom to seek help, since cultural prohibitions often stigmatize counseling.

Traffickers and pimps count on the fact that women (particularly women from developing and non-Western nations) occupy a lower status globally, coupled with a high demand for sexual services, to ensure the success of their sex-slave enterprises. Their business profits from society's large-scale objectification of women's and girls' bodies and sexuality, which ensures that they will have a continuing market for the illicit activity. Moreover, many government officials are corrupt and wink at sex slavery, allowing traffickers and pimps to perform their actions with impunity.

However, increased attention to this problem, particularly since the 1990s, has created some hope for the lessening, if not the eradication, of the problem. A number of international initiatives have been introduced that address sex slavery, including the United Nations' (UN's) highly influential Protocol to Prevent, Suppress, and Punish Trafficking in Persons, Especially Women and Children, which supplemented the Convention Against Transnational Organized Crime in 2000. There have also been national and regional human rights–based, women's rights–based, and health-related campaigns and initiatives to combat the problem. The UN sponsors an annual International Day of Remembrance of the Victims of Slavery and the Transatlantic Slave Trade; it is observed to bring attention to the plight of these victims of modern-day slavery.

Leonard A. Steverson
South Georgia College

See also Human Smuggling; Human Trafficking

Further Readings

Bales, K. *Disposable People: New Slavery in the Global Economy*. Berkeley: University of California Press, 1999.

Bales, K. and B. Cornell. *Slavery Today*. Toronto, ON: Groundwork Books, 2008.

Phinney, A. "Trafficking of Women and Children for Sexual Exploitation in the Americas: Women, Health and Development Program, Pan American Health Organization." http://www.paho.org/english/hdp/hdw/traffickingPaper.pdf (Accessed October 2010).

United Nations Convention Against Transnational Organized Crime and the Protocols Thereto. 2000. http://www.unodc.org/documents/treaties/UNTOC/Publications/TOC%20Convention/TOCebook-e.pdf (Accessed October 2010).

South America

Crime in South America cannot be dealt with as a simple case of domestic policy. This is so for a number of reasons. First, crime in South America is intractably linked to the ability of criminal networks to "market their goods" on an international scale. In traditional economic terms, supply and demand are linked in and through multiple networks of smuggling, drug trafficking, money laundering, and corruption. Second, crime in South America is a strong impediment to regional growth and political stability. Criminal networks, from the famous Medellín drug cartel in Colombia to narco-terrorist organizations such as Shining Path in Peru, are often able to undermine legitimate forms of governance and state control. Like any business that is able to deliver secure and constant profit margins, established and vested interests have a strong presence within the government. Huge profits from the drug trade in Colombia, for example, have allowed famous figures such as Pablo Escobar to put real pressure on government and to compete within an already corrupted political system.

The main issues in terms of combating transnational crime in South America are twofold. First, how are governments and law-enforcement agencies to coordinate the often competing issues of supply and demand? Surely, policies of eradication, such as those practiced by the U.S. government, are not capable of solving the problem. Eliminating a particular field of drug production, in an agricultural sense, does not necessarily translate into decreased production. In classical criminological discourse, this could be described as a case of *crime displacement*. As certain areas are focused upon for eradication, producers simply pick up and move to another location. Also, eradication policies often have deleterious effects on the local agrarian population. In other words, these policies often affect the poorest who farm the product and leave the criminal syndicates untouched. Second, despite the long American War on Drugs, narcotics consumption, in the First World, has not declined. In fact, consumption has increased. Furthermore, the purity and potency of drugs such as cocaine have also increased. The demand side of the equation has been the excessive focus of governments such as that of the United States. This has resulted in underdeveloped policies of demand control. In fact, many would argue that the American focus on supply networks has resulted in an unfair labeling of South American citizens.

The inability of the First World governments to control the narcotic excesses of their citizens has meant continuing instability for South American states. This is so because drug trafficking and selling continue to be very profitable enterprises, attracting criminal organizations. Furthermore, the capital held in drug profits can be "reinvested" in ways that stabilize the continuing movement of narcotics. These profits can be used, for example, to "buy off" border officials in both the supplying nation and the receiving nation. One of the issues that is often left underevaluated involves the *cross-border corruption* that stretches across sovereign states. In order to move billions of dollars of narcotics into the United States, for example, a wide circuit of corruption needs to be in place. Once again, First World governments are often more concerned about turning their resources of law enforcement against clearly designated foreign and domestic targets and less concerned with critically analyzing the networks of transnational crime that affect and infiltrate their own bureaucratic structures.

History

Most South American nations were founded in a general movement against Spanish and Portuguese colonial governance. The great figure of Simón Bolívar was able to overthrow Spanish rule in the 1820s. In its place emerged the present-day states of Peru, Bolivia, Colombia, Panama, Venezuela, and Ecuador. Although these nations declared their independence, the colonial mold continued to strongly influence the way these states are governed and the way they fit into the world economy. One characteristic feature of these states in economic terms has been their reliance on a staple model of production. In colonial times, these states were organized in terms of explicit "economies of scale." That is, the colonial powers often turned these states into one-product economies.

Sugar and coffee production for export, in Brazil for example, dominated the entire economy. As a result, weather that adversely affected coffee or sugar crops would lead to high levels of immediate poverty, unemployment, and the loss of capital. For much of the period from independence to the mid-20th century, this staple model of economic development continued to dominate South America. The power of commodities such as coffee and sugar are still strongly felt in many South American countries. At the same time, many of these countries faced competition from other postcolonial states around the world, which undercut their ability to dominate these commodity markets. Furthermore, these societies experienced population growth, particularly in urban areas, that made staple production insufficient as a path to economic development.

In many ways, these nations are still operating within a staple economy model. However, for some states the new staple economy has moved toward the production, transportation, and sale of narcotics. The inability of global organizations such as the International Monetary Fund (IMF) and the World Bank to help these countries develop a diverse economy has contributed to the overall reach and staying power of the criminal organizations that operate the production and sale of illicit staples. Simply put, there is little or nothing to replace the drug trade.

Furthermore, the destruction of the drug trade could threaten to lead to economic hardships, particularly in nations that do not have diverse economies. The issue of crime in South America and the broader issue of the wide-ranging global networks of organized crime are beyond the scope and power of a law-enforcement model. In order to overcome the power and the influence of these criminal networks, it is imperative to understand the social, economic, and historical context for their existence. A fight against crime in South America must, first and foremost, involve a commitment to producing viable noncriminal alternatives. This can be accomplished only by looking at crime as an issue that is intimately connected with wider social and economic development. The criminological perspective known as strain theory could be applied to describe the lack of legitimate opportunities as a source of lawbreaking. At the same time, agencies such as the Inter-American Bank and the World Bank argue that crime in South America contributes to income inequality and social inequality. In sum, crime leads to inequality, and inequality leads to crime. This vicious circle has dominated South American attempts to deal with crime.

Structural Features

Crime in South America has a structural edifice that is supported by some important features. First, criminal organizations have become strong and supported interest groups. This is especially the case within countries such as Colombia and Brazil, where criminal gangs have taken on something of a leadership role within low-income neighborhoods such as Rio de Janeiro's favelas or the town of Medellín.

Second, political instability and violence feed the high crime rates. This factor can be expressed in a variety of ways. In some locations, armed political groups become active criminal actors. They become involved in the drug trade as well as in activities such as kidnapping, extortion, money laundering, and protection rackets. In Colombia, for example, both rightists and leftists use the drug trade and other criminal activities to fund their explicit political goals. In July 2010, BBC News reported that the government in Colombia had been able to "demobilize more than 30,000 right-wing paramilitaries" and had attacked many drug-trading cartels. Although this appeared, on the surface, as a positive and progressive move toward the dismantling of these groups, they simply reformed themselves into smaller cells. Moreover, by dismantling the smaller groupings the government has actually encouraged greater violence. This has occurred because the status quo between the gangs has been upset and a new struggle for power has emerged. Medellín has a monthly drug trade worth US$20 million that was controlled by Diego Murillo. Murillo was Escobar's heir but was extradited to the United States in 2008. The control of Medellín's underworld was coordinated through what is called the Office of Envigado. The power vacuum created by Murillo's departure spawned a battle between Maximiliano Bonilla and Erick Vargas. Political violence has become intertwined with the desire to control some of the biggest economic rewards of criminality.

This issue relates to the next structural feature: the economy. South America has suffered from high levels of unemployment and low rates of economic growth. When high economic growth does occur, as it has in Brazil, it is uneven and usually focused on the upper classes.

Fourth, South America has experienced a massive urban growth. As a life of poverty becomes more difficult in rural areas, more individuals and families flock toward urban centers. On the one hand, this is a migration pattern that is about the seeking of economic opportunities. At the same time, these movements could be described in terms of economic dislocation. Once these individuals and families move into the large cities, the receiving urban centers are unable to accommodate the new arrivals. These arrivals become sedentary "squatters" on the outskirts of these large metropolises. These communal agglomerations become locations that are prone to dislocation, family decline, low health standards, and lack of youth supervision. Gangs and criminal enterprises take on multiple roles. They become surrogate families for wayward youth, they provide makeshift healthcare, and they deal with those in distress. These roles take the gang beyond the simple and immediate role of criminality and firmly ensconce it within the life of the community. Once again, the lack of government power and control feeds the power of these criminal units. If the government were able to provide the basic elements of a decent urban life, these gangs would lose some of their legitimacy in the eyes of the people. However, in some of Brazil's most notorious shantytowns or favelas, such as Rocinha, it is the criminal element that is able to deliver running water and healthcare. When this is the case, what chance does the government have in fighting crime and undermining these criminal enterprises? Therefore, another important factor is the lack of basic urban infrastructure.

Fifth, there is a growing availability of weapons. When this is so, the criminal violence becomes much more dangerous and deadly.

Sixth, there is a low level of police and government effectiveness in dealing with these criminal organizations. At the level of logistics, many police forces are unable to match the power of these criminal enterprises. They are often out-gunned by the criminals. When this occurs, governments have to rely on the military. However, in nations where the military itself has a history of taking direct power, there is a strong fear of giving the army enough of a legal mandate to deal effectively with these criminal groups. Such a scenario has surfaced in Colombia. As the police have been unable to deal with gangs armed with semiautomatic assault rifles and rocket-propelled grenades, the army has stepped in. However, in order to control the military, the government has made it difficult for the army to be involved in direct law-enforcement activities. In July 2010, for example, BBC News reported that a commander of Colombian troops involved in such law enforcement claimed that they had to wait for two months to get a search warrant. Thus hobbled, the police and army have proven largely ineffective. As a result, the government capacity to respond to criminal activity is uncoordinated, chaotic, and often unplanned.

Seventh, according to agencies such as the U.S. State Department, low levels of basic or primary education are a powerful contributing factor to gang violence. Low education levels often translate into low levels of legitimate opportunity. When this problem combines with a large population of homeless youth residing in shantytowns, criminal gangs become an outlet for opportunity and familial connection.

Finally, South America has a political and media culture that is grounded in violence. The colonial past, combined with an abusive and aggressive military as well as years of political division and war, has created a culture that sees violence as a viable option for solving problems and countering enemies. Political discourse has also been harmed by a weak civil society that is not accustomed to open and frank discussions of social and economic problems. Politics itself is often radicalized and prone to extremism. All these factors show that crime in South America is rooted in larger social, cultural, political, and economic factors.

South American Crime in a Global Environment

An important factor to emphasize in explaining crime in South America is its general global context; that is, South America's postcolonial status needs to be examined. Crime in South America is truly transnational in the sense that it is fed and nurtured by a global network of illicit trading. The drug market, for example, can continue to exist only if it is able to tie into the bad habits of the First World. Therefore, at a very direct level, crime in South America is caused and perpetuated by its position within an international political economy. No doubt, drug traffickers, as well as drug users in the First World, rely on weak governments as a way to perpetuate their trade. It is very difficult to imagine First World drug needs being met by domestic sources. At a more fundamental level, South America is part of a global economic and political system that has had a hand in keeping the continent poor and disempowered. The First World has been able, both directly and indirectly, to use South America as a source of primary material and cheap labor. Insufficient loan schemes and structuralized underdevelopment have also contributed to the rise and virtual institutionalization of crime as a viable economic alternative. Therefore, a long-term solution would require

significant global reorientations of South America's economic role.

Solutions

What can be done to solve the crime problem in South America? It is clear that pure enforcement policies, such as the War on Drugs, are unproductive. What is needed is a commitment to building strong governments with clear social agendas based on improving opportunity through education and economic growth. Furthermore, a concerted attack on political corruption at all levels is required. This attack would require the support of outside forces such as the United States, Europe, and agencies of the United Nations.

Paul Brienza
York University

See also Black Market Peso Exchange; Central America; Cigarette Smuggling; Cocaine; Criminal Associations; Drug Trade: Legislative Debates; Drug Trade: Source, Destination, and Transit Countries; East Asia; Eastern Europe and Russia; Failed States; Globalization; Heroin; Human Smuggling; Joint Force Policing and Integrated Models; Legal and Illegal Economies; Marijuana or Cannabis; Narco-Terrorism; Networks; North America; Policing: Transnational; Violence: Intimidation

Further Readings

Balakar, James B. and Lester Grinspoon. *Drugs in a Free Society*. Cambridge, UK: Cambridge University Press, 1984.
Farer, Tom, ed. *Transnational Crime in the Americas*. London: Routledge, 1999.
Merton, Robert K. *Anomie and Social Structure*. Cambridge, MA: Harvard University Press, 1955.
Thoumi, Francisco E. "Some Implications of the Growth of the Underground Economy in Colombia." *Journal of Interamerican Studies and World Affairs*, v.29/2 (Summer 1987).

SOUTH ASIA

Although legal scholars and policy analysts pointed out the link between transnational crime and security threats well before the terrorist attacks of September 11, 2001, the 9/11 attacks had a profound impact on the international mind-set regarding South Asian transnational crime. A consensus grew around the idea that transnational terrorism originated from Pakistani Islamic extremists, and the very events of 9/11 acted as a catalyst for those who had earlier argued that a military response should be prepared not only against traditional military attacks but also against transnational crime, especially transnational organized crime, insurgency, and terrorism.

It was concluded that cross-border terrorism in India as well as sectarian conflicts and to some degree also leftist insurgencies might all be linked to top leaders residing in Pakistan and that collaboration might exist among the Pakistani Directorate of Inter-Services Intelligence (ISI), Kashmiri groups, and Maoists in Nepal and in India. Nexuses were also alleged between Indian Maoists and the Liberation Tigers of Tamil Eelam (LTTE), the separatist socialist Tamil group based in Sri Lanka. The overlap between terrorism and transnational crime was made evident by the ways insurgents in South Asia, usually in the border areas, have engaged in crimes such as extortion, money laundering, contract killing, kidnapping, and trafficking in drugs, weapons, and persons in order to finance their own activities.

In fact, one of the causes hampering the peace talks between Pakistan and India is the widespread belief that most terrorist events in India have been masterminded in Pakistan or at least ideologically inspired by Al Qaeda, a militant Islamist group founded in the late 1980s and calling for global jihad. After 2008, when Mumbai, the largest city in India, was invaded with 10 coordinated shooting attacks and bombings in proximity to Pakistani seawaters, relations between India and Pakistan were frozen on the allegation that militants based in Pakistan were directing all terrorist action in India. However, in February 2011 it was agreed that talks would resume between India and Pakistan revolving around counterterrorism and border-related issues.

Inconclusive evidence, together with the fact that many recent acts of terrorism in India had Muslim targets, has identified the need for a more sophisticated analysis. Inquiries in the field have furthermore disclosed that insurgents in India as well as in Pakistan and in Bangladesh may take advantage of the high degree of polarization between the unprivileged strata of society and an unresponsive state. This situation, exacerbated by sectarian and ethnic conflicts in certain border areas, has led to perceptions of insurgency as a form of alternative governance that is appealing at the local level, either for being able to impose itself by force or because it ensures some degree of accountability by providing basic welfare, law and order, and justice settlement.

Modern insurgency is furthermore transnational in its modus operandi, but the leaders of the major insurgency in Northeast India, instead of being based just across the border, may reside in Europe, Thailand, and Burma. Hence, insurgent activities are characterized by extreme mobility, and even when bilateral cooperation among border countries is reached, insurgent groups swiftly relocate and reorganize themselves. At the request of India, Burma and Bhutan cooperated in the fight against insurgents by raiding Naga camps and evicting Bodo groups through military intervention that involved the deaths of hundreds civilians.

The conflict between the Sri Lankan government and the LTTE, which is often suggested as the most successful example of military intervention against transnational terrorism, shows that military intervention most often involves a heavy humanitarian toll. LTTE, not different from some Islamic insurgent groups linked to terrorism for deliberately targeting civilians, appeared to have global financial operations with profits that were equivalent to and might also have exceeded those of multinational corporations. These organizations usually thrive on money laundering, human trafficking, and illegal trade of weapons, but it is not unusual for them also to act through charitable front organizations that raise funds from expatriate communities, which are then invested to the benefit of the local population. LTTE, allegedly initiated in the 1970s by the Indian intelligence service, was blamed for the assassination of Rajiv Gandhi, the Indian prime minister, in 1991. LTTE's operations relied on cross-border illegal activities for the storage and provisioning of weapons and other supplies. The Indian government appears to have acted ruthlessly by sending the Indian Peace Keeping Force and the army to Sri Lanka in 1987 and 1990 in an offensive that was meant to disarm LTTE but caused humanitarian disasters—deaths of civilians—and did not end the conflict between Tamil separatists and the Sri Lanka government. In 2007, India also helped the Maldives to sink an LTTE ship bearing an Indian flag, which was later found to be transporting explosives. On May 16, 2009, LTTE was declared defeated after 26 years of conflict, which had been exacerbated since the massive attacks on LTTE strongholds by the Sri Lankan Army, apparently backed by the Indian Army. LTTE's defeat should have terminated one of the most onerous conflicts in South Asia. However, observers have registered attempts by LTTE to reorganize since 2010.

The Nepali Maoist Movement is a remarkable example of the subtle dynamics between governance and insurgency, because despite its being outlawed since 1996, it transformed into a parliamentary body in 2006 and took part in the interim government in 2007. In 2008, the first president of the Federal Democratic Republic of Nepal was sworn in. However, democracy seems to have done little to address communal and religious conflicts. The Terai region is well known for supporting a number of armed groups that have been labeled as pro-royalists and advancing requests against the Maoist leadership for effective proportional representation and adequate federalism. They constitute 40 percent of the Nepalese population and are said to entertain relations with the Nepal Defense Army, a Hindu extremist group allegedly receiving support from Hindu extremists across the Indian border in order to fight Christian zealots, communists, and Islamic fundamentalists.

After September 11, 2001, the insurgency in Bangladesh multiplied and emerged in Maldives and Bhutan. Maoists as well as Islamic extremist groups are active in Bangladesh. Maoists target landowners and rich contractors in order to extort levies to finance their struggle for power. Their main area of operation is at the border with West Bengal in India. Islamic Bangladeshi groups have been blamed for participating in terrorist activities in India: among them, the 2007 attack on the Samjhauta Express (a train connecting Delhi and Lahore), which killed 68 travelers, mostly Pakistani civilians; the Makkah Masjiid bombing in Hyderabad, allegedly also supported by Hindu extremist linked with the Hindu nationalist and militant organization RSS; and the Lumbini Amusement Park bombing, also in Hyderabad. Even if cross-border collaboration in terrorist activities is likely, it is not easily detectable and, most important, very difficult to fight in the long run because of its high mobility extending over more than two bordering countries. On top of all that, Bhutan expelled Indian insurgents conducting kidnapping missions, but abductions are recorded regularly in the border areas, where

insurgents continue their operations. There have been cases of South Asians kidnapped abroad and ransom demanded of their relatives in Pakistan and Bangladesh. Maldives is a dazzling example of the fact that counterterrorism can be instrumental for political opponents. The bomb blast that injured 12 tourists in Malé in 2007 was immediately defined as a conspiracy by President Maumoon Abdul Gayoom, who started to use counterterrorism laws to fight political opposition. This seems to have generated an increased radicalization of Muslim groups, especially among younger people whose networks extend beyond political borders. Hence, recent trends of transnational terrorist activity are registered with Britons and northern European citizens traveling to Pakistan and Bangladesh for training.

Nevertheless a considerable amount of transnational illegal trade is not necessarily directly linked to terrorism, even if terrorist groups might resort to it in order to finance their operations: the most common forms of illegal trade are in weapons and narcotics, as well as human trafficking, illegal migration, corruption networks, and currency transfers. A tripartite commission (Pakistan, Afghanistan, and the United States) was established in 2003 to fight the illicit trade of small arms and light weapons (SALW). However, again it seems that the high mobility of these illegal trade networks makes implementation very difficult when illegal arms are stored in a third country that is not part of the agreement. Cross-border armed activity is also important to the transit and trade of narcotics from Pakistan, Jammu, and Kashmir to Afghanistan and the European market, as well as between Burma and India. Although Khyber Pakhtunkhwa (formerly the North-West Frontier Province in Pakistan) has adopted very strict regulations regarding poppy cultivation, Pakistan remains the transit point for opium export from Afghanistan. Poppy production being highly profitable in comparison with conventional cultivation, it is not only hard to discourage with prohibition but also is often controlled or even occasionally seized by terrorist groups operating in the border area between Pakistan and Afghanistan. Disputes and riots between insurgents and local populations revolving around illicit opium trade are not unheard of on the Burma-India border as well, Burma being the second largest world producer of illicit opium.

Human trafficking and illegal migration are thriving from India to the Middle East, from

Burma to East and Southeast Asia, from Pakistan and Bangladesh to India and most developed countries in Europe and North America, and from Bangladesh to Pakistan and West Asia. The reasons for illegal migration and trafficking range from sexual exploitation to slavery and include domestic help and forced labor. The most frequent victims are women and children but also men, who are most easily trafficked for working on construction sites and desperate for work. These men find themselves living in inhuman conditions, are underpaid, and are subject to the constant threat of being deported. Trafficking in children is often accomplished by offering a better future to children who are without a principal caretaker in their home country; these children are sent to Europe or North America as an act of charity—usually by their family members.

Financial corruption and illegal transfers have been linked to terrorism with the discovery that most terrorist action in India has been financed through legitimate international money transfers. Hence, stricter banking regulations have been adopted to prevent illegal transfers through illicit channels. The most frequent form of currency transfer for financing illicit operations is the so-called hawala network. Originating from Islamic jurisprudence as early as the 8th century, it was later adopted by French and Italian law under the names *aval* and *avallo*, respectively. The term refers to the transfer of debt via a network of brokers who can settle the debt for their customers in a variety of ways that do not necessarily include cash transactions. Because of the fact that the hawala system does not require a physical transfer of money, it can extend over a large span of time, and being based on an honor system, it involves a very basic system of records, so it has been favored for illegal transfers.

The spread of the liberal economy and peacekeeping interventions that are often advanced as remedies for transnational crime not only have proved unsuccessful in the long run but also have at times generated fertile conditions for transnational crime and insurgency. It seems, in fact, that the prolonged stay of peacekeeping forces is very often linked with an increase in the trafficking of women for their entertainment. Human rights abuses, widespread poverty, forced relocation, and illegal trade have also been observed concomitantly with foreign investment, including the establishment of major infrastructures such as dams and pipelines. In summary, the relationship between security threats and transnational crime in South Asia cannot be denied. However, the conventional approach to transnational crime from a law-and-order perspective seems doomed to failure in that it is unable to address the social and economic factors in which local unrest is rooted.

Livia Holden
Lahore University of Management Sciences

See also Al Qaeda; Antiterrorist Financing; Child Exploitation; Drug Trade: Source, Destination, and Transit Countries; Financial Action Task Force; Globalization; Human Smuggling; Jihad; Money Laundering: History; Money Laundering: Methods; Money Laundering: Targeting Criminal Proceeds; Money Laundering: Vulnerable Commodities and Services; Organized Crime: Defined; Sex Slavery; Terrorism Versus Transnational Crime

Further Readings

Aromaa, Kauko and Terhi Viljanen. *Enhancing International Law Enforcement Co-Operation, Including Extradition Measures: Proceedings of the Workshop Held at the Eleventh United Nations Congress on Crime Prevention and Criminal Justice, Bangkok, Thailand, 18–25 April 2005.* Helsinki: European Institute for Crime Prevention and Control, 2005.

Lee, Maggy. *Human Trafficking.* Devon, UK: Willan, 2007.

Wilson, John and Parashar Swati. *Terrorism in Southeast Asia: Implications for South Asia.* Delhi, India: Pearson Education, 2005.

Southeast Asia

Southeast Asia (or southeastern Asia) is a subregion of 500 million people located south of China, east of India, and north of Australia. It is usually divided into two main geographic regions: (1) mainland Southeast Asia, including Cambodia, Laos, Burma (the Republic of the Union of Myanmar), Thailand, Vietnam, and Peninsular Malaysia, and (2) maritime Southeast Asia, including Brunei, East Malaysia, Timor-Leste (East Timor), Indonesia, the Philippines, and Singapore.

In 1967, Indonesia, Malaysia, the Philippines, Singapore, and Thailand created the Association of Southeast Asian Nations (ASEAN), with the aims of implementing economic growth, social progress, and cultural development and protecting the peace and stability of the region. Today, ASEAN also includes Brunei, Burma, Cambodia, Laos, and Vietnam. The ASEAN states grew rapidly, from both a military and an economic viewpoint, until the Asian crisis of 1997. Even though the region is recovering, especially from an economic standpoint, regional security is today threatened by instability because of terrorism, piracy, organized crime activities, drug trafficking, ethnonationalism, and religious fundamentalism.

Even though some organized criminal groups in Southeast Asia have long histories, it was about 50 years ago that organized crime became a serious problem in this region. In fact, unstable or weak governments, corruption, and the lack of adequate funds for criminal justice systems created the perfect background for the development of increasingly sophisticated and up-to-date criminal activities. That is why—in addition to an increase of traditional criminal activities such as theft, assault, and robbery—it is possible to detect a strong presence of organized illicit activities such as drug trafficking, human smuggling and trafficking (predominantly connected to the sexual exploitation of women and children), weapons trafficking, trafficking in stolen or plundered antiquities, and environmental crimes in the area. Drug trafficking is one of the main criminal activities in this region, with drugs ranging from poppy (for heroin) and mescaline to synthetic drugs such as methamphetamines, flunitrazepam (Rohypnol), and ketamine. Since about the 1920s, the area comprising Burma, Laos, and Thailand has been known as the Golden Triangle because it has been the main world producer and supplier of heroin and opium. Currently, political and judicial efforts to counter poppy production in the region, together with a significant change in the global drug market, have led to a decline in poppy cultivation. However, since 1998 this decline has been accompanied by a sharp increase in the production and export of methamphetamines, most of all in crystalline form (known as "ice"). Some synthetic drug laboratories in this region are capable of producing several hundred million methamphetamine tablets annually. These tablets are mostly consumed in regional markets but, given the large production capacity, a big part of production is also trafficked toward Europe and, mostly, the United States.

While Burma (Myanmar) remains the second largest opium poppy grower in the world, its share of world opium cultivation fell from 55 percent in 1998 to just 5 percent in 2006. Poppy is cultivated mainly in the Sha, Wa, and Kokang regions, near the border with China. In this area there are also opium-refining laboratories. These labs are mobile, in order to avoid police controls and seizures, and can be dismantled in a few minutes and reassembled in a safer place. A large part of Burmese opium and heroin is trafficked to China, to the capital city of the Yunnan district, Kunming, and then exported and managed by Chinese criminal organizations. Despite the decrease in poppy cultivation, Burma is a significant player in the production and regional trafficking of synthetic drugs such as amphetamine-type stimulants (ATS), methamphetamine, and ketamine.

The major transnational criminal activities in Cambodia are connected to drug production and trafficking. Cambodia is one of the main source countries for the cultivation of marijuana (most of all in the regions of Kandal, Kampong Cham, Koh Kong, and Kampot) and a transit country for the distribution of heroin. Southeast Asian heroin is moved from Laos and Thailand through the cities of Phnom Penh and Siem Riep to the rest of Asia and to Europe, relying as well on a high level of corruption. In many cases, drugs are trafficked using maritime routes, and the drug is escorted by criminal groups also involved in piracy activities.

Thailand has ceased to be a major source country for opium poppy or heroin. However, it is now a net importer of drugs and also serves as a transit country. The primary drugs of concern today in Thailand are ATS and social drugs such as MDMA (Ecstasy) and cocaine. Heroin and methamphetamine continue to move from Burma across Thailand's northern border for domestic consumption and export to regional and international markets. Amphetamines are currently the most lucrative drugs smuggled for the internal market in Thailand. Known as ya ma (crazy horse) or ya ba (drug of madness), these tablets are quite cheap and can be bought by the majority of the Thailand's numerous drug addicts.

Laos has made huge progress in reducing opium cultivation since 1989. However, even though poppy cultivation has declined 96 percent, from a high of 42,000 hectares to just 1,700 hectares in 2006, serious trafficking in illegal drugs and controlled chemicals continues unabated. While not a primary production country, because of its central location and new highways Laos is a transit route for Southeast Asian drugs to other nations in the region, most of all to Vietnam, China, Cambodia, and Thailand. The main criminal groups in this country are from China, Vietnam, and Thailand, and they manage all the local drug markets, including the cannabis and amphetamine markets. They use the Mekong River to connect the drug labs in Laos and supply them with chemical substances for refining opium.

Singapore has a strong central government that imposes stringent fines, extended prison sentences, and capital punishment to maintain public security. Despite these severe penalties, many relevant criminal syndicates are present in the Singapore territory, and in 2000 almost half of the 56 major operations conducted by the national Central Narcotic Bureau were against big criminal groups.

Increasingly since the 1980s, the smuggling and trafficking in human beings have become major sources of income for organized crime in this area, most of all because usually these activities are directed toward child pornography and the sexual exploitation of women and children. According to the international nongovernmental organization (NGO) Coalition Against Trafficking in Women, prostitution in Southeast Asia has developed into a lucrative business that influences employment and national income and contributes significantly to the region's economic growth. The International Labour Organization (ILO) estimates that in Indonesia, Malaysia, the Philippines, and Thailand, between 0.25 percent and 1.5 percent of the total female population of the four countries is engaged in prostitution and that the sex industry accounts for between 2 and 14 percent of the countries' gross domestic product (GDP). Considering as well the owners, managers, pimps, and other employees of sex establishments, the related entertainment industry, and some segments of the tourism industry, the number of workers earning a living directly or indirectly from prostitution is in the several millions.

Burma (Myanmar) is a major source of the women and children trafficked to Pakistan and Thailand. Many of them are under the age of 18. The sex industry in Thailand is one of the best known in the world and one of the most lucrative. It is estimated that organized crime groups have imported to Thailand more than one million women from China, Laos, and Vietnam and that, as of 1998, more than 400,000 children under the age of 16 worked in brothels, bars, and nightclubs. Cambodia rivals Thailand as one of the main havens for prostitution, often connected to gambling and money-laundering activities.

In the Philippines, as well, sexual exploitation of women and children is widespread. Organized criminal groups control every aspect of the trafficking, smuggling, and exploitation of women and children, both within the country and in export activities, sending them to Japan, Thailand, and other countries. Criminal groups from the Philippines are the main suppliers of young children to pedophiles all over the world.

All the above-mentioned criminal activities are facilitated and supported by high levels of governmental, judicial, and police corruption. According to the ILO, in areas where prostitution thrives government authorities collect substantial revenues, illegally from bribes and corruption and legally from licensing fees and taxes on the many hotels, bars, restaurants, and game rooms that flourish in prostitution's wake.

Corruption is endemic within Burma (Myanmar). According to the U.S. Department of State, between 2000 and 2002, 32 police officers were punished for drug-related corruption, 17 received jail sentences, four were terminated, and six were forced to retire. Corruption is a serious legal and social problem in Cambodia as well, rendering law-enforcement efforts against criminal groups largely ineffectual.

Even though most of the organized crime groups operating in Vietnam are from other countries, an increasing number of organized criminal groups, such as the Nam Cam gang and the Hmong group in the Nghe An region, have formed. The increased relevance of these local groups has exacerbated and increased the corruption of public officials and police officers.

In the Philippines, the endemic level of corruption makes it possible for international criminal groups (such as the Italian Cosa Nostra) to own and manage restaurants, nightclubs, bars, hotels, and other concerns connected not only to money-laundering activities but also to gambling and, most of all, prostitution and the sexual exploitation of children.

Southeast Asia is characterized also by an uncommon kind of organized crime activity: piracy. The geography of Southeast Asia provides an ideal haven for pirates, and it is possible to say that the pirate tradition in this region can be traced back, uninterrupted, for centuries. In modern times, with the exception of the particular situation of Somalia and the Horn of Africa, more incidents are reported in this region than anywhere else, starting in the 1990s and with a relevant increase since 2002. Considering the relevance of the phenomenon in this area, the Piracy Reporting Center of the International Maritime Bureau, a specialized bureau of the International Chamber of Commerce Commercial Crime Services and one of the main authorities in the fight against piracy together with the United Nations (UN) International Maritime Organization, is located in Kuala Lumpur, Malaysia.

The phenomenon of piracy in Southeast Asia is connected not only to the many havens that pirates can find among the islands, reefs, sandbars, creeks, and mangrove swamps of this region but also to a widespread cultural acceptance of piracy. Particularly in Indonesia and the Philippines, pirates mix with the local population without fear of betrayal. In many cases, besides big organized groups, it is also possible to find small groups, composed of people from different villages, that supplement their earnings from fishing with small piracy activities. However, piracy in this area is usually well organized and has a regional dimension: Pirates can easily cross maritime borders, and they may hijack a ship in one state's national waters and dispose of its cargo in the waters of another, while the pirates controlling and managing operations are based in a third state.

The Malacca and Singapore Straits are probably the areas most prone to piracy. Moreover, considering that a large proportion of the world's trade passes through these straits, pirate attacks tend to be subject to great political and media attention. Three types of pirates operate in these straits. The first is composed of small gangs of robbers committing ad hoc petty theft, with small earnings; the second is composed of pirates who go after tugboats to hijack and then sell them; and the third is armed and highly organized, targeting larger ships, especially tankers with foreign flags.

In some cases, piracy is connected to maritime terrorist activities. Incidents of terrorism have increased in Southeast Asia since 1997 and include serious attacks such as the 2002 bombings in Bali and the 2003 bombing in the Marriott Hotel in Jakarta (Indonesia). Jemaah Islamiyah (JI), an organization affiliated with Al Qaeda, is alleged to have carried out the latter.

Southeast Asia has had episodes of political violence that have been linked to terrorism. These have included activities by communist groups (for example, in Malaysia, Thailand, and the Philippines) and activities directed against local regimes (such as the bomb attacks in Laos in 2000–01). Terrorism has also been considered state sponsored, as in the cases of Christian antiseparatist groups in the southern Philippines opposing Muslim secessionists, and militias in East Timor and Indonesia. Currently, a relevant role is played in this region by Al Qaeda and connected groups such as JI, Laskar Jihad (LJ), the Front Pembela Islam (Islamic Defenders Front, FPI), Abu Sayyaf (Bearer of the Sword), and the Moro Islamic Liberation Front (MILF). All these groups have been authors of terrorist attacks and bombings in Southeast Asia as well as in the Middle East and other countries.

Silvia Ciotti
EuroCrime—Research, Training and Consultancy

See also Al Qaeda; Drug Trade: Source, Destination, and Transit Countries; Human Smuggling; Piracy: Failed States; Piracy: History; Terrorism: Nondomestic

Further Readings

Bator, Paul M. *The International Trade in Art*. Chicago: University of Chicago Press, 1983.

Elliott, Lorraine. "Transnational Environmental Crime in the Asia-Pacific: An 'Un(der)securitized' Security Problem?" In *Environmental Crime: A Reader*, Rob White, ed. Devon, UK: Willan, 2009.

Murphy, Martin N. *Contemporary Piracy and Maritime Terrorism*, Adelphi Paper 388. Oxford, UK: Routledge, 2007.

Rohan, Gunaratna. "Terrorist Trends and Patterns in the Asia-Pacific Region." In *The New Terrorism: Anatomy, Trends and Counter-Strategies*, Tan Andrew and Ramakrishna Kumar, eds. Singapore: Eastern University Press, 2002.

Ward, Richard H. and Daniel J. Mabrey. "Organized Crime in Asia." In *Handbook of Transnational Crime and Justice*, Philip Reichel, ed. Thousand Oaks, CA: Sage, 2005.

Whittaker, David J., ed. *The Terrorism Reader*. Oxford, UK: Routledge, 2007.

Stings and Reverse Stings

A sting operation is an operation by law enforcement designed to catch a person committing a crime by having a law-enforcement officer or cooperating civilian act as a criminal partner, potential victim, or transactional counterparty in order to induce an individual to commit a crime. Sting operations are used to prosecute a wide variety of crimes, including auto theft, hacking, drug dealing, prostitution, child molestation, and even terrorism. The most basic type of sting operation involves an undercover agent posing as a drug buyer in order to induce a drug dealer to consummate a transaction. A reverse sting operation is a variant on the sting operation whereby the government agent poses as a seller rather than as a buyer.

A Naval Criminal Investigative Service (NCIS) agent reviews a safety briefing while other NCIS agents prepare for an Ecstasy drug sting. The sting in Twentynine Palms, California, resulted in the arrest of several service members for drug trafficking and Ecstasy use. (U.S. Navy/Jim Watson)

Sting operations are very effective because, by definition, law enforcement (or its agents) is present when the crime is committed or attempted. Compelling evidence in the form of video or audio recordings, eyewitness testimony by agents, and physical evidence yielded in a search incident to arrest can be gathered. Government informants, particularly those who have been caught committing a crime and are cooperating in order to obtain a reduction in their sentence, are frequently asked to "wear a wire." This refers to the informant being fitted with concealed recording equipment for a meeting with a suspect. Because of this technique, it is common, particularly among organized crime members, to search a new associate for recording equipment before conducting a meeting.

One major disadvantage of sting operations is that, during ensuing litigation, a defense attorney will frequently attempt to assert an "entrapment" defense. Even if the defense is unsuccessful, law enforcement will be subject to unfavorable publicity if the operation is seen as overly aggressive or coercive. An entrapment defense essentially asserts that law enforcement induced a person to commit an offense that he or she would otherwise have been unlikely to commit. Factors relevant to an entrapment defense include whether (1) the idea for committing the crime originated with the government or with the person accused of committing the crime, (2) the degree of persuasion in which the government agents engaged, and (3) whether the suspect

was ready and willing to commit the crime before the intervention of the government agents. Persistent attempts by a government agent or informant to persuade a suspect to participate in a criminal activity are likely to result in a successful entrapment defense.

The act of pretending to be a law-enforcement officer does not, in and of itself, create entrapment, nor does the suspect's asking whether his purported counterpart is a member of law enforcement. Some suspects believe they can immunize themselves against a sting operation by asking, "Are you a cop?" This myth has been popularized by movies and television but has no basis in law. If this tactic worked, it would render sting operations obsolete. A person who asks the question will, if anything, impair his criminal defense, because the question shows a consciousness of guilt.

One method of obtaining incriminating evidence (and heading off an entrapment defense) is by offering the suspect the opportunity to withdraw from or reconsider the criminal act before it is consummated. A suspect who is warned of the possible effects of the crime on others or who is told that he or she need not follow through with the plan, yet chooses to continue, is more likely to appear guilty and have more difficulty asserting an entrapment defense. In one particularly compelling example, an undercover officer posing as a hit man was discussing his services with a woman hiring him to kill her husband so that she could collect on the husband's life insurance policy. The undercover officer, who purportedly would kill the husband using a sniper rifle, told the wife that his aim was good but he sometimes did not hit the intended part of the target's body, which would result in a slow and painful death. The wife was recorded stating that she did not care and just wanted the insurance money. This evidence was extremely compelling in the case against the wife.

Another major disadvantage of using sting operations is that they involve law enforcement in deception and unsavory activities. In fact, a particularly aggressive sting operation—one in which a government agent provides a suspect with ingredients to make drugs, for example—can result in a defense attorney asserting an "outrageous government conduct" defense. This defense, similar but distinct from the entrapment defense, asserts not that the suspect was not predisposed to commit the crime but that the government's participation was so egregious that it should not be allowed to result in successful prosecution of the defendant. This defense, however, is rarely successful. One example of a situation in which the defense was successful was the prosecution of the gang known as the Latin Kings, in Tampa, Florida. A former member of the Latin Kings was caught on unrelated charges and agreed to cooperate with law enforcement. Law enforcement was investigating the gang, which had been dormant for years. The informant was told to organize a meeting of the gang, and members were threatened with beatings if they did not attend. The informant carried out beatings and induced the members to attend the meetings. Eventually, one of the meetings was raided by law enforcement and the suspects were apprehended. The judge dismissed the case, noting that the government had manufactured a crime by compelling members to attend the meetings and engaged in outrageous conduct by actually carrying out threats against members who did not attend.

At least two television shows depicting sting operations have gained popularity in recent years. One is called *Bait Car* and targets prospective auto thieves. An expensive car rigged with hidden cameras, a tracking device, and a remote door-locking and engine-disabling device is left in an area where it is likely to be found. Sometimes the doors are left open and unlocked or the keys are left in the ignition. When a prospective thief takes the car, he is tracked until officers shut the car down and lock the perpetrators inside. The thieves are then arrested,

usually after they make statements incriminating themselves, either to a companion or, via cell phone, to a friend or relative.

Another, more controversial television show depicting a sting operation was the series *To Catch a Predator*, aired as part of the television news-magazine *Dateline NBC*. Adults posing as teenagers online eventually invite a suspect to their home. Prior to the meeting, the suspect is told online that the decoy is underage and willing to engage in sexual activity. When the suspect arrives at the home, the decoy makes a brief appearance but leaves and is replaced by the host of the show, who questions the suspect about his intentions in coming to the home. Eventually the suspect is allowed to leave and is immediately apprehended outside the home. Many of the apprehensions are conducted in a seemingly excessively violent manner, and the officers frequently approach the suspect with firearms drawn or may use tasers. In one incident, a suspect did not appear for the rendezvous with the decoy as planned. When law enforcement went to apprehend the suspect at his home instead, the suspect committed suicide. The incident resulted in a lawsuit, which was resolved by a settlement. The show was eventually canceled in 2008, not because its tactics were ethically or legally in question but because it had become so well known that it was difficult to entice new suspects to participate in the scheme. Frequently a sting operation becomes a victim of its own success when the technique becomes so well known that potential criminals take precautions or fail to be deceived by the scheme.

One type of sting operation that has become increasingly common in the past decade is the "fake bomb" operation. In that operation, a suspected would-be terrorist is recruited to help build, plant, and detonate an explosive device or other weapon of mass destruction. On the day of the supposed attack, the suspect is given a detonator, but when the suspect attempts to activate the explosive device he is arrested instead. One study concluded that the majority of terrorism prosecutions involved a sting operation. As of 2011, there were no cases of a successful entrapment defense in the terrorism context.

ABSCAM (a contraction of "Abdul scam") is perhaps the best known and most controversial sting operation in U.S. law-enforcement history. During the operation in the late 1970s and early 1980s, an agent of the Federal Bureau of Investigation (FBI) posed as a Middle Eastern sheikh offering money for asylum in the United States and assistance with a business scheme. The investigation led to the conviction of many elected officials, including a U.S. senator and five congressmen. Many other congressmen were embarrassed and had their reputations tarnished. Among these was John Murtha, who famously stated, "I'm not interested, I'm sorry. At this point . . . ," in direct response to an offer of $50,000 in cash. The ABSCAM operation was highly controversial, particularly given the issue of separation of powers; one branch of government had targeted an operation against another branch. Since the ABSCAM case, law enforcement has largely forgone the use of sting operations against members of Congress. An exception, however, occurred when Senator Larry Craig was caught in a sex sting operation at the Minneapolis airport in 2007. There was no evidence, however, that the sting operation in question was intended to target Senator Craig specifically or other politicians as well.

Related to sting operations are "Mr. Big operations," which involve a government employee or informant who gains the trust of the target of the investigation. The purpose of creating the relationship of trust and confidence is to induce the target to confess to a crime that the government is investigating. Although this type of operation is not as coercive as a sting operation, because the government's operation does not lead to the commission of a crime, it is still controversial. Critics of this technique assert that a Mr. Big operation may lead to a false confession and result in a wrongful conviction. Frequently, the investigators will pose as members of a criminal gang and involve the suspect in the planning or execution of simulated crimes. A suspect attempting to establish credibility or criminal fortitude with his new colleagues may exaggerate past criminal exploits or take credit for a crime in which he or she is only rumored to have participated, even if the suspect was not involved. Alternatively, a suspect may be pressured to reveal any past crimes to his or her new colleagues on the basis that gang leaders need to know about matters that could draw law-enforcement attention to them. The gang leader (the Mr. Big) usually promises to "take care" of the problem for the new member. The confessional-like promise of absolution in exchange for confession has a substantial psychological impact in inducing a suspect to divulge misdeeds.

The Mr. Big operation is favored by law-enforcement agencies in commonwealth countries, particularly Canada and Australia. The name Mr. Big comes from a 2007 documentary exposing the methods used by the Royal Canadian Mounted Police. Law-enforcement agencies have tried, without apparent success, to keep these methods out of the public eye. It remains to be seen whether the exposure of this technique will result in diminished effectiveness in the future.

Michael Paul Beltran
United States District Court

See also Counterfeit Goods; Drug Trade: Legislative Debates; Intelligence Agencies: Illegal Engagements; Pornography

Further Readings

Faull, Andrew and Thoko Mtsolongo. "From Stings to Wings: Integrity Management and the Directorate for Priority Crime Investigations." *SA Crime Quarterly*, v.1 (September 2009).

Greene, Robert W. *The Sting Man: Inside Abscam*. New York: Dutton, 1981.

Langworthy, Robert. "Do Stings Control Crime? An Evaluation of a Police Fencing Operation." *Justice Quarterly*, v.6/1 (1989).

Webster, D. W. "Effects of Undercover Police Stings of Gun Dealers on the Supply of New Guns to Criminals." *Injury Prevention: Journal of the International Society for Child and Adolescent Injury Prevention*, v.12/4 (August 2006).

T

Tariff Crimes

Tariff crimes are those that pertain to taxes collected on goods being imported or exported, especially the avoidance of such taxes, and involve customs fraud and smuggling. The purpose of such taxes, apart from simple revenue generation, is to impose some controls on trade in order to benefit domestic industries. When a good can be produced more cheaply (or with greater value) in another country, imposing a tariff on it increases the price so that domestic goods are better able to compete with it. Some tariffs, called protective tariffs, exist primarily for this purpose, to protect domestic business interests; others, particularly when the imported good has no domestic competitor, simply provide a revenue stream for the government. For much of American history, the bulk of the federal budget was funded by tariffs.

Neoclassical economics views tariffs as distorting free markets, and developing countries oppose tariffs imposed by developed countries because they hamper developing nations' ability to grow their export-based industries and take full advantage of the principal economic advantage of developing countries: cheap labor. When the 1948 General Agreement on Tariffs and Trade was succeeded in 1995 by the World Trade Organization, the WTO set out to liberalize global trade, to reduce tariffs, and to end the practice of varying tariffs according to country of origin. The WTO believes that the elimination of these trade barriers and discriminatory practices will facilitate overall prosperity of the global economy.

The high tariffs enacted by the United States in the 1930s, such as the Smoot-Hawley Tariff Act (1930), helped export the economic crisis to the rest of the world and provided economic incentives for smuggling and tariff avoidance. With incomes rapidly declining, however, the market for both legal and illegal goods during the 1930s Great Depression contracted. Originally, Smoot-Hawley was intended to protect the American economy and American business by raising the tariffs on more than 20,000 goods to record levels. American trading partners responded with retaliatory tariffs on American imports, and American exports and imports were reduced to less than half of their pretariff levels as a result. The legislation has been criticized as one of the factors that turned the Great Depression into a global phenomenon.

More recently, in the same global climate as that which saw the creation of the WTO, the United States, Canada, and Mexico created a trilateral trade bloc when the North American Free Trade Agreement (NAFTA) came into force in 1994. In combined gross domestic product, it is the largest trade bloc in the world, with no trade barriers or tariffs among its members. There is considerable disagreement over the long-term effects of NAFTA. There have been numerous disputes on Canada's part, the largest of which remains unresolved. For instance, because of the provision in Canadian law that once something has been sold as a commodity, the government cannot in the future intervene to stop its sale, Canada refused to export bulk water by marine tanker to California-based Sun Belt Water, Inc. Canada's refusal was motivated by the desire

President Bill Clinton signed the North American Free Trade Agreement into law. The 1994 agreement created a trade bloc between United States, Canada, and Mexico. (U.S. White House)

to protect Canadian ecosystems from private-sector exploitation. Sun Belt Water responded by filing a NAFTA arbitration claim, which as of 2010 had not been resolved. Canada has also been forced to end its ban of the gasoline additive methylcyclopentadienyl manganese tricarbonyl (MMT) because it has presented an obstacle to American trade. At the same time, the United States has imposed a stiff (27 percent) tariff on Canadian softwood lumber imports, which Canada has protested as an unfair protective tariff that hurts the Canadian lumber industry; because of domestic opposition, the compromise reached by Prime Minister Stephen Harper in 2006 was never ratified.

In the United States, NAFTA has been criticized as detrimental to American employment, by making it easier for American firms to relocate significant portions of their operations to Mexico, where labor is cheaper. Net manufacturing employment has declined considerably in the United States since NAFTA went into force. At the same time, while Mexican industry has benefited from NAFTA, the Mexican agricultural sector suffers from the subsidies the American government pays to American farmers, which keep some American crops—most important, corn—artificially cheap, a topic that has drawn ongoing international criticism for its impact on agricultural trade.

No regulation of commerce can increase the quantity of industry in any society beyond what its capital can maintain. It can divert only a part of it in a direction in which it might not otherwise have gone.

If an industry is set up and needs a protective tariff to survive, the price the consumer has to pay is but an index of the social loss involved in this particular employment of its energy. By putting difficulties in the way of foreign trade—and especially by discouraging the investment of capital in other foreign countries and taxing the imports of foodstuffs and manufacturers' tariffs—reform would undoubtedly decrease real wages by increasing the cost of materials used. The very fact that protection is necessary for an industry means that its goods cannot be produced at home as cheaply as abroad. It means that the consumer pays more than he or she would if he or she were allowed to buy the foreign article and, therefore, that there is a waste of national labor that would be better employed in some other way where the nation has an advantage.

It is argued that granting low tariffs to most favored nations will result in future prosperity, based on intellectual skills and managerial know-how more than on routine hand labor. Free trade means lower prices for consumers. However, it has also been argued that this system means lower wages, as well as fewer jobs for workers who cannot compete against lower wages.

In one of the largest customs fraud cases, directors of a California company were sentenced to jail and forced to pay $393 million in back taxes after it was discovered that it imported tens of millions of dollars in foods using false reports to evade duties and taxes. Other types of customs fraud include illegal transshipments, the pirating of American products for foreign importers, the undervaluation of goods to pay less, the illegal discounting of products (dumping), transfer pricing (whereby companies undervalue imported parts), and violations of regulations pertaining to nations of origin (which favor countries under NAFTA).

Christina-Vasiliki Kanellopoulou
Independent Scholar

See also Accounting Fraud; Tax Evasion; Value-Added Tax Fraud

Further Readings

Agiomirgianakis, G. M., M. Vlassis, and H. Thompson. *International Financial Relations* [in Greek]. Athens, Greece: Rosili, 2006.

Giannakopoulos, Nikolaos A. *Lessons in Pure International Trade Theory* [in Greek], 2nd ed. Athens, Greece: Stamoulis, 1994.

Salinger, Lawrence M. *Encyclopedia of White-Collar and Corporate Crime*. Thousand Oaks, CA: Sage, 2005.

Symeonidou-Kastanidou, E. and M. Kaiafa-Gbandi. *Special Penal Legislation* [in Greek]. Thessaloniki, Greece: Sakkoulas, 1998.

Todd, Edwin Ernest Enever. *The Case Against Tariff Reform*. London: J. Murray, 1911.

TAX EVASION

Tax evasion refers to illegal acts that reduce a government's revenues. These behaviors include subterfuge, concealment, and acts of deceit regarding income and profits. It differs from tax avoidance in that the latter involves such legal strategies as realizing losses, deferral of income, and allowable tax shelters, and while some may construe these to be immoral, they are not illegal. Tax evasion is a concern to people in many countries, because it can involve substantial inequities and may result in losses of expected and much-needed government revenue, which is especially harmful to developing countries. These inequalities mean that the tax burden is borne by local corporate entities with weak political ties and also by the local citizenry. Of course, this can be devastating to the local economy, as smaller businesses are often the main employers of their country's nationals. The inequities make it nearly impossible for smaller businesses to compete successfully with larger, multinational tax evaders that route their gains through foreign tax havens. In a number of African nations, such as Nigeria (where oil is a major export), as well as a number of European nations, local business elites are believed to effect tax evasion and avoidance to their advantage. The actors in tax evasion offenses include promoters of foreign banks and trusts, corporate managers, bankers, accountants, and attorneys.

Transnational tax evasion by wealthy individuals has existed for decades. In recent years, the activity has become increasingly common, concomitant with substantial growth in global economic ventures by multinational companies. These companies might engage in tax evasion to maximize profitability, especially given the gains of competitors. They do this largely by utilizing offshore financial institutions, tax havens, and vague aspects of the law. Specific schemes by businesses might include underreporting wages to reduce withholdings and underreporting of revenues or overreporting business costs to reduce reported profits. The managerial motive for these behaviors is simply to maximize profits. The outcome of this action is that countries rich in natural resources, such as oil, watch while their industry's profits get diverted into the accounts of wealthy tax evaders and local citizens remain in poverty with heavy taxes to pay.

The use of offshore financial institutions is also a common mechanism that the wealthiest individuals use to evade many of their tax obligations. In 2007, an estimated $12 trillion of the world's wealth was believed to be in tax havens. Some assets are in hedge funds that are not based in countries such as France, the United Kingdom, or the United States but in tax-haven countries. Tax havens, otherwise called "financial paradises," "financial refuges," or "special tax zones," are areas that have created laws specifically permitting persons who are nonresidents to avoid or to evade tax regulation by legalizing financial secrecy from outside interests. The tax rates in these areas are usually very low or nonexistent, and their financial institutions are generally greater than one would expect, given the local economy. Territories or countries known for facilitating tax evasion include Switzerland, Gabon, Guernsey, Jersey, Anguilla, Costa Rica, Bermuda, the British Virgin Islands, Luxembourg, Monaco, the Isle of Man, Andorra, Singapore, and Ireland. Fifty-two percent of hedge funds worldwide are based in Bermuda, the Bahamas, the Cayman Islands, and the British Virgin Islands. In 2008, the Cayman Financial Services Authority claimed that 35 percent of hedge funds were based in the Cayman Islands. Indeed, tax havens have proliferated with globalization and are now commonplace in business; their use has contributed to international fiscal instability.

Notably, the world financial crisis that began in 2008 was accentuated by the use of tax havens by the likes of Bear Stearns, Lehman Brothers, Long Term Capital Management, Enron, Parmalat, Refco, Northern Rock, and Bernard Madoff's $50 billion Ponzi scheme. Britain's Northern Rock Bank was the fifth largest mortgage provider in the United Kingdom in 2007. Its tax haven for tainted collaterized debt obligations (CDOs) was under a charitable trust in Jersey. In Jersey, tax evasion often involves the use of "orphan" companies. An orphan company is dependent upon a multinational corporation but is supposedly owned by a charitable trust in the tax haven territory. The trust is created so that bonds might be issued to fund its debt. This essentially gives the appearance that the debt has been purged from the company's accounts, which then allows the company to absorb new debt, such as fresh mortgages. The movement of funds to the orphan also gives the appearance that its activities are independent of the multinational company. Such activities became an integral part of Enron's demise. The collapse of the Bear Stearns investment bank involved the movement of funds to hedge funds based in Ireland and the Cayman Islands. Similarly, Joseph Cassano, the chief financial officer of American International Group (AIG), established tax havens around the world with phony companies to facilitate AIG's fraud. One of the world's biggest tax evasion scandals, however, was that of LGT Bank in Liechtenstein. The bank is owned by the country's royal family. In 2008, a former employee stole a disk with information on 4,000 customers. It was reportedly sold to the German government, which then shared it with other countries. This scandal struck at the core of transnational tax evasion: the element of secrecy.

Tax scholars Ronen Palan, Richard Murphy, and Christian Chavagneux estimated that by 2007 there were 46 to 60 active tax havens worldwide, serving approximately 2 million international business companies (IBCs) and thousands of hedge funds, mutual funds, trusts, and captive (risk-management) insurance companies. The tax haven territories will often attempt to justify their actions by denying tax haven status, by issuing false claims of cooperation with investigators, and by criticizing the regulatory systems of the countries in which their foreign clients reside.

At the forefront of the war against transnational tax evasion is the Organisation for Economic Co-operation and Development (OECD), which encourages nations to unite to address tax evasion and other fiscal concerns. The mission of the OECD is to promote the social and economic well-being of persons worldwide. The Tax Justice Network also advocates for fiscal transparency and tax compliance as a justice and equity issue. The European Union's Savings Tax Directive (STD) is a tool to reduce tax evasion in Europe. It is an agreement between European Union member states to share information about customers who earn savings in one member state but reside in another member state.

Pressure from the United States' Internal Revenue Service (IRS) has also had substantial impact in efforts to uncover tax evasion over the past decade. For example, in 2009, the Swiss bank UBS AG paid $780 million in fines and submitted the names of 4,500 U.S. account holders to the IRS. Tax haven countries that have made similar moves include the world's fifth largest financial center, the Cayman Islands (with more than $800 billion). In 2008, the Isle of Man signed a tax information exchange agreement with several countries, including the United States. Swiss banks like USB and Credit Suisse, however, have responded to international pressure to uncover tax evaders by expanding their tax evasion services to Asia.

Within the United States there are stiff penalties for persons who are caught not indicating ownership of foreign accounts and trusts, and each year in which this omission has occurred is treated as a separate offense. A report of foreign bank and financial accounts (FBAR) must be filed. The statute of limitations for a criminal charge may go back six years; under civil law, there is no time limit. Regarding trusts, not indicating interest, capital gains, or dividends on a return could result in a sentence of up to five years in prison for each incident. A financial penalty of up to a half of what is owed is possible, but the amount is commonly a third of what is owed, plus interest.

Although the pursuit of tax evaders has been common for decades in the United States, the IRS redoubled its efforts following the September 11, 2001, terrorist attacks. The U.S.A. Patriot Act, enacted shortly thereafter, required improved reporting of money transfers in and out of the United States. Individual tax evaders are often caught after an audit that has been triggered by a report from an angry former spouse or observable discrepancies in reported income and lifestyle. Tax evasion promoters are usually prosecuted after their clients have been caught and the latter accept a deal in exchange for providing details about the promoters.

To combat corporate tax evasion, multinational corporations are required to arrange their accounts to reflect the requirements of the International Accounting Standards Board (IASB). Corporations operating largely out of the United States are also required to follow the United States Federal Accounting Standards Board (FASB) requirements.

These initiatives reflect an audit-based paradigm with multiple layers of control and formalized accountability. The approach is two-pronged, with one side consisting of audits and the other surveillance. The former brings obtrusive layers of control for maintaining order; the latter monitors a primary object. To utilize institutions and their services, actors must agree to open themselves to surveillance (unobtrusive monitoring). To date, the trend has been to make use of persons in private business roles to conduct surveillance in the course of their work. This is usually encouraged as a public-private partnership for the greater good. In the United States, a substantial effort in this regard was the 2002 law known as the Sarbanes-Oxley Act. The law requires specific financial professionals to report accounting fraud such as tax evasion schemes.

Other movements to prevent tax evasion include new rules in the United Kingdom designed to prevent individuals from building untaxed income in offshore funds. In Liechtenstein, a tax evasion haven for wealthy Germans, several foundations keep the money in trusts. Germany's foreign intelligence agency now works with informants in this and other haven countries to fight tax evasion. In Sweden, the banking system is dominated by four banks: SEB, Swedbank, Handelsbanken, and Nordea. The Swedish response to tax evasion requires balancing business values and public accountability. The public-sector ministries that pursue tax evaders are those of justice, finance, and law enforcement. The Financial Police Unit in the Anti-Money-Laundering Department of Swedish law enforcement and the Swedish Economic Crime Authority work together to recover assets and to enforce tax evasion and money-laundering laws.

Although efforts to curtail tax evasion have increased, its vastness, popularity, and investigative challenges render responses insufficient to eradicating the problem in the near future. An effective response would likely involve the creation of a group of international auditors with the power to sanction violators severely. The certainty of being caught would also need to be evident.

Camille Gibson
Edward J. Schauer
Prairie View A&M University

See also Accounting Fraud; Financial Fraud; Money Laundering: History; Money Laundering: Methods; Money Laundering: Targeting Criminal Proceeds; Money Laundering: Vulnerable Commodities and Services

Further Readings

D'Souza, Jayesh. *Terrorist Financing, Money Laundering and Tax Evasion: Examining the Performance of Financial Intelligence Units.* Boca Raton, FL: CRC Press, 2011.

Palan, Ronen, Richard Murphy, and Christian Chavagneux. *Tax Havens: How Globalization Really Works.* Ithaca, NY: Cornell University Press, 2010.

Power, Michael. *The Audit Society: Rituals of Verification.* Oxford, UK: Oxford University Press, 1997.

Shaxson, Nicholas. *Treasure Islands: Uncovering the Damage of Offshore Banking and Tax Havens.* New York: Palgrave Macmillan, 2011.

Watson, Camilla. *Tax Procedure and Tax Fraud in a Nutshell.* St. Paul, MN: Thomson/West, 2006.

TECHNOLOGY

Technology is the development and application of devices for productive processes. As such, it has always been inseparably connected to all aspects of crime and its control, etiology, commission, and apprehension. No aspect has emphasized this more significantly than when crime crosses borders and becomes transnational. This happened long before Athenians used carts to bring back booty stolen from Megara. To use such an ancient example, involving Greek city-states, is to note that in dealing with transnational crime, the possibility always exists that the criminals are in some way receiving support from their domestic authorities or know that their domestic government looks the other way regarding crimes committed against foreigners. The bombing of Pan Am Flight 103, involving sophisticated technology, was supported at the highest levels of the Libyan government.

All that has happened since ancient Greece is that the technology has improved everyone's abilities. Technology makes it easier for criminals to commit offenses and for the authorities to catch them. It is an arms race. With the exception of a limited amount of very esoteric technology of a specific military nature, the arms race between villains and authorities is essentially a tie game. It was the commercially available technology of a commercial airliner that brought down the Twin Towers on September 11, 2001.

The cynicism of sales philosophies in capitalistic countries, with little concern given to the purchasers of technology, allows criminals to use the same items as the authorities. In many instances, the criminals may be more advanced than the authorities as to the latest technology; they are often able to purchase the equipment more quickly, not being subject to the delays inherent in the public budgeting constraints faced by the law-enforcement authorities.

Etiology

Theories of crime have popularity cycles as to the academic disciplines on which they are based, but one thing is clear. However crime is explained, technology may inspire a would-be criminal to go ahead and complete a crime, when that perpetration would have been difficult, if not impossible, without such technological aid.

The explanation for crime known as vulnerable target theory, for example, suggests that without such a device as a wireless network finder, legally available at any electronics store, a criminal cannot hack into a victim's unsecured network connection for harmful purposes. First he or she has to find the victim or target. Once the potential victim is identified, the opportunity is too good to resist.

By way of other examples, some theorists propose behavioral psychology, exemplified in Albert Bandura's influential argument for the influence of the mass media, always technological leaders, on the would-be criminal.

Edwin H. Sutherland's theory of differential association, a major sociological proposition, offers yet another theory of crime, in which one learns from others how to commit crime. Formerly on videotape, now on DVD, illustrated lessons are available on how to commit crimes with international significance, such as primers on how to smuggle items. This is an example of how technology is being used to show people how to use technology to commit crimes. Among these lessons are instructions, available on the Internet, for building a nuclear bomb.

Commission

Panniers on donkeys traversing the Khyber Pass have become pallets on jumbo jets overflying those same mountains. Opium is still being moved from Asia to Marseilles for processing into heroin. The technology has simply advanced.

Nowhere is the technological development currently more apparent than in the use of fast motorboats by Somali-based pirates, hijacking the enormous oil tankers and other commercial vessels that ply the Indian Ocean. Without that improved technology, the crime would not take place as easily, if at all. The "arms race" (those *developments* in technology) has allowed an ancient transnational crime to be committed in much more effective and convincing fashion. Surface-to-surface missiles have replaced cannon balls.

In 2006, attackers from the Lebanese-based Hezbollah political party used a Chinese Yingi 82 antiship missile in an assault on an Israeli corvette, the INS *Hanit*. The missile had been sold to them with the full approval of the Chinese government. When Hezbollah loyalists fired rockets at Israeli border towns, these acts were properly labeled as the crime of terrorism by the Israelis. Only later was the conflict generally acknowledged as a full-scale war.

The matter here becomes one of political classification. The question is, "When does a crime become an act of war?" By definition, that is a transnational issue. The coordinated attacks on September 11, 2001 (9/11), present ongoing, and self-imposed, legal challenges in the United States, even if the crime is nothing more than an enormous example of the long-established crime known in those same United States as malicious mischief, or something similar. Technology, wrongly used, can have the effect of bringing into question the definition of "ordinary" crimes, especially between countries.

At the margins, persuasive technology can also influence the status of violent conflict with transnational implications. In the Cold War environment, it was in the interests of the world's superpowers to use proxies. After the fall of the Soviet Union, with less control of the proxies, there is worldwide concern about the whereabouts of a significant amount of weapons-grade nuclear material, even the bombs themselves, formerly in the Soviet Union, that may now be in the hands of terrorists in various places in the world.

For some, war is the ultimate crime. During World War II, Germany's attempt to destabilize the economies of its enemies involved flooding Europe with convincing, fake English paper money. They came dangerously close to success, as portrayed in the Oscar-winning 2007 film *Die Fälscher* (*The Forgers*). At any time, forgery relies on the available printing technology. That part of the arms race has developed exponentially in recent years. Each country with a major economy must now exercise the utmost vigilance to protect its economy against those using modern imaging technology to produce extraordinarily good fakes of legitimate paper currency.

Modern printing technology is now heavily dependent on the computer and digital technologies. It would be simplistic to identify the computer as the deus ex machina for all concerned with transnational crime, both villains and law-enforcement officials. In the second decade of the 21st century, however, it is without dispute the dominant technological factor in transnational crime and its control. The uniqueness of the computer is that it can be both the target of transnational crime (where the target, the victim's property, may be stored in electronic, virtual form) and the medium by which the criminal accesses that target.

The computer has joined the Internet to make scams and other crimes much easier to perpetrate than in the past. These include the well-established Nigerian 419 scam, named for the section of the Nigerian Criminal Code that is being violated. It emphasizes the need for all responsible members of the international community to control crime within their own borders, when crimes such as the 419 scams have enormous international consequences. To be fair to Nigerians, this particular crime is now committed from bases all over the world. The particular challenges posed by those Somali pirates include the lack of any effective national government to prosecute them in Somalia, for the foreseeable future. Nigeria cannot fall back on that "excuse."

The Nigerian 419 scam relies on easily produced mass e-mailings, using a computer and a telephone-based Internet connection that is essentially free. This combination allows the miscreant to send out millions of tempting come-ons at the same time. While part of the success of these e-mails is a reliance on the financial greed for which capitalists are famous, the commission of the crime is utterly dependent on technology with a enormous international reach.

From the perspective of the transnational criminal, the cost-efficiency here is unquestioned. With the ability to send out millions of leads at the same time, the villain only has to have a couple of victims bite on his or her hook to succeed financially. By comparison, the supplanted technology of conventional mail was by no means free, with large up-front investments. It is certainly not instantaneous. Without Internet technology, 419 scams do not happen. While the concept behind the Nigerian 419 crime is not inherently international, it is much more effectively committed when it is international, because of the difficulty, as noted below, of tracking down criminals when they are based in another country.

Elsewhere, an even more elegant crime, the area code (AC) 809 fraud (which milks the monetary balance of people's telephone accounts), relies first on the telephone and, by extension, the highly automated nature of modern telephone technology and usage in North America. The AC 809 criminal takes advantage of the automated ease whereby telephone users in the United States, Canada, and some Caribbean countries, no longer needing the assistance of an operator, can make long-distance calls to any country involved in that telephone compact, which uses the North American Numbering Plan (NANP). Note that this transnational crime is localized to North America and the Caribbean basin, because the international access code is not required. While it is a transnational crime from the perspective of the residence of the criminal vis-à-vis that of the victim, it is difficult for international law-enforcement authorities to address; it is not seen as an international problem by the North American telephone companies, which are unwitting participants in the crime.

Offenders (often based in the Dominican Republic) commit their crimes knowing that they are outside the reach of law-enforcement authorities in the United States, where the overwhelming majority of the victims live. This crime relies on a unique artifact of the extraordinarily sophisticated, user-friendly North American telephone system. Even so, without the existence and constant development in (in this case telephone) technology, crimes such as these cannot exist.

Apprehension

Modern communications technology allows the authorities to communicate with one another instantly across borders in their efforts to catch miscreants attempting to cross those borders to commit their crimes and avoid apprehension.

One AWACS plane flying at 30,000 feet can survey an area of more than 120,000 square miles. Such surveillance planes overflying the vast Indian Ocean can alert shipping to the possibility that a small vessel approaching a large commercial vessel at high speed could be a Somali pirate vessel. If an enforcement vessel is near the potential victim, such information could allow an act of piracy to be thwarted, or at least reacted to in quick fashion.

Before the development of the computer, the International Criminal Police Organization (Interpol) was a classic example of an elegant, seemingly important, international law-enforcement agency with limited effectiveness. Now, improvements in communications technology and the information storage capabilities of computers enable Interpol to provide valuable assistance to a nation's authorities. It has changed for the better the role, reputation, and value of Interpol. Now that organization functions as a very useful linking agency for the world's police forces, thanks to technology.

Mere availability of the technology, however, does not guarantee success. It only serves to emphasize the need for authorities in neighboring countries and beyond literally to be on the same wavelength. The eruption of Eyjafjallajökull, a minor volcano in Iceland, in 2010 caused havoc in European air travel, and the domino effect quickly embraced the whole world. While the eruption precipitated a problem of public safety (law enforcement's other responsibility) as much as an opportunity for crime, it was a reminder of what could happen if an international air hijacking incident were to take place that involved the victim plane moving from one country's airspace to another's. On April 14, 2010, the air traffic control authorities in the various European countries were not on the same page. It is expected that this problem would be fixed by the creation of a Europe-wide air traffic control authority.

The constant threat of terrorism in the early 21st century illustrates the value of (computer) technology in allowing early collation of data to generate lists of likely suspects, in the event that the perpetrators of terrorist acts have not already identified themselves. Such identification invariably involves the awareness of the terrorists of the hunger of the modern world for immediate news and the existence of worldwide news services able to share news immediately. Both criminals and law-enforcement authorities now use the technologically sophisticated international media to great advantage.

The criminal uses technology to improve the efficiency of the commission of the crime. The authorities face the challenge of using the technology available to them to best advantage in countering it. Enormous amounts of information were available to the authorities prior to the attacks of 9/11. Coordinating the information became the problem. For the authorities, there is the dual risk of resorting to technological solutions in place of apparently less sophisticated methods. They may rely too much on the machines. In what is called "the paralysis of analysis," with enormous amounts of information, too easily recalled, the authorities sometimes need self-restraint. With that caveat, technology and crime will continue to coexist, especially across borders.

David Orrick
Norwich University

See also Communication Technologies; Computer-Generated Scams; Counterfeit Currency; Counterfeit Goods; Forgery; Identity Theft; Internet Crime; Telemarketing Fraud; Terrorism: Nuclear

Further Readings

Byrne, James M. and Donald J. Rebovich, eds. *The New Technology of Crime, Law and Social Control*. Monsey, NY: Criminal Justice Press, 2007.

Pattavina, April, ed. *Information Technology and the Criminal Justice System*. Thousand Oaks, CA: Sage, 2005.

Siegel, Larry. *Criminology*, 10th ed. Belmont, CA: Thomson, 2009.

TELEMARKETING FRAUD

Telemarketing frauds are innovative ways of committing crime that are not confined within national borders to any specific country. Such fraud is a significant problem internationally. Anyone located anywhere in the world can be victimized by this type of fraud. Telemarketing fraud may be defined as fraud typically perpetrated over the telephone by an individual who offers products for a seemingly good price to a potential consumer in exchange for a secure payment. The telemarketer (fraudster) promises the potential consumer that he or she will reap financial gains. It is one of the most deceptive marketing practices today and involves a wide range of deceptive acts. More important, telemarketing fraud is a "faceless" crime, in that it does not require any direct or physical contact with consumers. Consequently, telemarketing fraud presents unique challenges for investigators, because victims are not forced to give up money directly in person but are persuaded to do so under the impression that they are likely to gain a profit based on a sales pitch put forth by the fraudster.

Telemarketing frauds occur frequently, on a daily basis, from locations known as "boiler rooms" because they are often overcrowded, with many stations. The telemarketer often uses illegal tactics perpetrated on unsuspecting individuals. Telemarketing fraud has been around for a while but has become even more prominent since the 1990s. In the United States alone, consumers have experienced more than $40 billion in losses. An individual with a telephone or even a cell phone can become a victim at any time.

Telemarketing frauds may be accomplished in a variety of ways, but they typically employ one of three media: phone calls, physical or direct mail, or print advertisements. Telemarketing frauds may involve fake checks, advance loans, or offers of credit cards, scholarships, grants, prizes, sweepstakes, lotteries, jackpots, magazines, or buyer's club advantages. As noted by the Federal Trade Commission (FCC), fraudsters use phrases such as the following: "you've won one of five valuable prizes"; "you've been preapproved for an advance loan—bad credit, no problem"; and "the investment is low risk and the best available." The means whereby fraudsters operate may differ, but the objectives are the same, and the modus operandi typically involves money in exchange for products or services that often prove to have a low value or are nonexistent.

The fake check scam is perhaps one of the most popular ways of conducting a telemarketing fraud. The fake check scam usually involves the consumer being paid with a fake check for items said to have been sold or for work performed. The consumer is then asked to wire extra funds (overpayment) back to the fraudster. In another situation, a person may be notified of having won a prize, but in order to claim that prize a fee must be paid in advance. Of course, the prize never materializes. Another example of telemarketing fraud is an advance fee loan. This involves individuals being promised personal

Telemarketing fraud—a "faceless" crime in that it does not require any direct or physical contact with consumers—can be difficult to detect because telemarketing is a legitimate activity. (Photos.com)

or business loans irrespective of credit history, for a small fee. Payment of the small fee may involve divulging personal information, which is then used to charge the consumer an exorbitant amount for the loan; the information may also be used later to scam other unsuspecting parties. Another fraud involves promises to rebuild a poor credit history. Fraudsters even manipulate persons to contribute to bogus organizations by misrepresenting charity foundations. The fraudster, however, cares very little about actually helping the consumer, and after the consumer has complied with the fraudster, he or she may never hear about the product or organization.

Although anyone can be a victim of telemarketing fraud, senior citizens are prime targets. Seniors are more likely to listen, are often very interested in products that are deemed helpful for anti-aging, and often own their homes and have good credit. Consumers who are interested in specific products and are receptive by indicating a willingness to listen, persons desperate to escape poverty or debt, and those who may have limited cognitive abilities are also prime candidates for this type of fraud. Routinely, these consumers are urged to act immediately because the product is available for a limited time only; the only payment might be shipping and handling, which is represented as only a tiny fraction of the product's value; and the opportunity cannot be missed, as risks are very low. The victim may jump at the prospect and act without a clear understanding of future consequences. Often the individual is not aware that he or she is being victimized before the fraudster disappears. When victims realize they have been duped, they may not report the crime out of embarrassment and fear of appearing gullible.

The underlying reason for telemarketing fraud is monetary gain, which can include access to personal information for further financial gain. The fraudster may obtain victims' phone numbers from a telephone directory or from what is commonly known as a "sucker list," which generally contains information about individuals who have responded to other telemarketing solicitations. Fraudsters may operate from different locations, use a bank of telephones, and vacate their locations frequently to avoid being caught. Fraudsters commonly make increasingly sophisticated offers in order to appear legitimate.

Telemarketing fraud can be difficult to detect, because telemarketing in general is a legitimate activity, used by many legitimate companies and organizations to solicit sales and secure funding for their operations. However, pursuant to its authority to enforce the Telephone Consumer Protection Act, the FCC established a national Do Not Call Registry, which is intended to limit such fraudulent activities by allowing people to place their names and telephone numbers in a national database that limits unsolicited telephone calls. Additionally, there are warning signs that suggest when telemarketing is likely to be fraudulent, including the need for urgency in making an immediate decision about the offer, a request for payment of shipping and handling fees to trigger a "free gift," and the company's unfamiliarity. Those who become susceptible to such schemes not only may lose a great deal of money but also may become victims of identity theft, and it can take years to recover from the resulting damages.

Marika Dawkins
Prairie View A&M University

See also Identity Theft; Job Offer Scams; Nigerian Money Scams; Pyramid Schemes; Telemarketing Fraud

Further Readings

Federal Bureau of Investigation. "A Byte Out of History: Turning the Tables on Telemarketing Fraud." http://www.fbi.gov/news/stories/2010/december/telemarketing_120810/telemarketing_120810 (Accessed February 2011).

Federal Bureau of Investigation. "Common Fraud Schemes." http://www.fbi.gov/scams-safety/fraud (Accessed February 2011).

Federal Trade Commission. "Do Not Call Registrations Permanent and Fees Telemarketers Pay to Access Registry Set." http://www.ftc.gov/opa/2008/04/dncfyi.shtm (Accessed February 2011).

Miller, Thomas J. "Telemarketing: Reach Out and Cheat Someone." *The Journal of State Government*, v.61 (1988).

Read, Brendan B. "Ending Fraud, Misrepresentations, and Bad Practices." *Customer Interaction Solutions*, v.28 (2009).

Terrorism: Defined

Terrorism is typically defined as premeditated, politically motivated attacks or threats of attacks by substate actors (that is, groups that are smaller than states) against noncombatants. Terrorists are those people who carry out or aid and abet in such attacks. Still, no widely agreed-upon definition exists. Definitional debates center on two issues: first, whether states as well as substate actors should be called "terrorists," and second, whether the term is so misused and inexact that it should be discarded altogether.

It is remarkable that an agreed-upon definition does not exist for a term as widely used in the media, academe, and common parlance as *terrorism*. Indeed, some scholars even argue that the term is so imprecise that it should be dropped altogether. The U.S. Department of State presents the following definition of terrorism: "Premeditated, politically motivated violence perpetrated against noncombatant targets by subnational groups or clandestine agents, usually intended to influence an audience." Alternatively, the U.S. Department of Defense *Dictionary of Military Terms* defines terrorism as "the calculated use of unlawful violence or threat of unlawful violence to inculcate fear; intended to coerce or to intimidate governments or societies in the pursuit of goals that are generally political, religious, or ideological." The Federal Bureau of Investigation (FBI), drawing on the U.S. Code of Federal Regulations, lists yet another definition of terrorism, and the text of the U.S.A. Patriot Act contains a different one still.

Exact definitions may seem unimportant; after all, one can say, "I know it when I see it." However, it is plainly obvious that a phenomenon cannot be studied unless those who study it agree on its precise definition. In his book *Inside Terrorism*, Bruce

Hoffman examined 109 definitions of terrorism and found that most included elements of violence or force, and many included some element of psychological impact and methods of combat, strategy, or tactics. Brigitte Nacos sees terrorists as exploiters of the linkages between the media, public opinion, and government decision making.

That terrorists instill fear in populations is central to some definitions (ergo the use of the word *terror*), but just about any type of war making and propaganda can do the same. Definitions of terrorism that state that it induces fear lend themselves to definitional vagueness, since actions as varied as the second Iraq War's "shock and awe" bombing campaign, the Ku Klux Klan's lynchings and cross burnings, the Tamil Tigers' suicide bombings, the aerial bombing of Dresden during World War II, and the dropping of nuclear bombs on Hiroshima and Nagasaki were all intended to instill terror in target populations.

The problem of definitional vagueness has led some to conclude that, as a practical matter, the term terrorism cannot be defined. Jeffrey Simon contends that there is no point to advancing a formal definition of terrorism, since any definition is influenced by the definer's opinion of what constitutes a terrorist threat. Jenny Hocking takes things a step further by asserting that terrorism has no independent reality and that it exists in the mind's eye of Westerners, who refer to certain threats as "terrorist." If a term is so subjective that definitions are by their nature contentious, then perhaps, one might argue, it should not be used.

One point of agreement among terror scholars is that terrorism is a pejorative term, frequently placed on one's enemies and almost never on one's friends. Any act against society, from the 2007 fires in Olympia, Greece, to data theft by cybercriminals, can be, and frequently is, called terrorist. The accusations of "terrorism" and "state terrorism" volleyed between Israelis and Palestinians are an example of this point.

An issue with most extant definitions of terrorism is that they try to please too many groups. Those who believe that Hamas is a terrorist group are accused of being overly subjective, so they construct definitions that include Western governments' actions as well. This serves only to muddy the waters. While calling a group terrorist certainly constitutes a value judgment to some, the term needs a narrow definition if it is to be systematically examined.

A key component of terrorism is the concept of propaganda by deed advanced by the 19th-century socialist political philosopher Carlo Pisacane. Pisacane believed that actions are necessary to change the world; ideas alone cannot do the trick. Terrorists draw on this notion by using violence or the threat of violence to achieve their goals. These goals invariably are political. A clear distinction can be made between terrorists and mass murderers, because the latter do not have any obvious political motivations.

Although states and governments have been behind horrible atrocities, including genocides and saturation-bombing campaigns, it is important to delink the study of terrorism from the actions of state governments. Some will surely take issue with this, because calling an action "terrorist" implies a value judgment; however, narrowing the definition certainly does not need to mean that states are "off the hook." A state's actions can be condemnable, but calling states terrorists makes the term too universal. After all, if both governments and substate actors could be called rebels or insurgents, those terms, too, would lose their meaning.

If terrorism is to be studied as an independent phenomenon rather than as a lexical anomaly, it must be viewed as politically motivated violence or threats carried out by substate actors. Terrorism is also premeditated, in that it involves violence or threats that are carefully calibrated to draw the attention of large audiences. The terrorists' ideal is for these large publics to then push their political leaders to act in response to the terrorists' demands. It is for this reason that terrorists almost exclusively target democracies. The final component of terrorism is that usually it is employed against noncombatants, meaning either civilians or off-duty military personnel. Some groups that are called terrorist, for this reason, may be better labeled insurgents if they target military personnel frequently. This is the case with the disparate Iraqi groups that have targeted coalition forces in Iraq since 2003.

Definitions of terrorism vary, and there is much disagreement on usage of the term. In the media and public, certain groups or actions are called terrorist either because they involve certain types of attacks, such as suicide bombing, or because they are otherwise abhorrent. If terrorism is to be studied as a phenomenon, a definition that eschews value judgments and narrows the term needs to be employed. For this reason, terrorism is here defined as premeditated, politically motivated threats of violence or violence carried out by substate actors against noncombatants.

Gabriel Rubin
Montclair State University

See also Antiterrorist Financing; Narco-Terrorism; Securitization After Terror; Terrorism: Domestic; Terrorism: Financing; Terrorism: Nondomestic; Terrorism: Nuclear; Terrorism Versus Transnational Crime

Further Readings

Crenshaw, Martha. *Terrorism in Context*. State College: Pennsylvania State University Press, 1995.

Forst, Brian. *Terrorism, Crime, and Public Policy*. Cambridge, UK: Cambridge University Press, 2008.

Hocking, Jenny. *Terror Laws: ASIO, Counter-Terrorism and the Threat to Democracy*. Sydney, Australia: UNSW Press, 2004.

Hoffman, Bruce. *Inside Terrorism*, Rev. ed. New York: Columbia University Press, 2006.

Nacos, Brigitte L. *Terrorism and the Media: From the Iran Hostage Crisis to the Oklahoma City Bombing*. New York: Columbia University Press, 1994.

Rubin, Gabriel. *Freedom and Order: How Democratic Governments Restrict Civil Liberties After Terrorist Attacks—and Why Sometimes They Don't*. Lanham, MD: Lexington Books, 2011.

Simon, Jeffrey D. *The Terrorist Trap: America's Experience With Terrorism*, 2nd ed. Bloomington: Indiana University Press, 2001.

TERRORISM: DOMESTIC

Terrorism is a crime that everyone can recognize when it happens, yet few can agree on exactly how it is defined. While there is not a single and universally accepted definition of *terrorism*, the U.S. Code of Federal Regulations (CFR), in Section 0.85, defines it as "the unlawful use of force and violence against persons or property to intimidate or coerce a government, the civilian population, or any segment thereof, in furtherance of political or social objectives." Terrorism is "domestic terrorism" when the terrorist activity occurs within one country, by a group or individual operating within that country without foreign direction, to create fear and produce change within that same country. The effect of terrorist activity is most devastating when the violent acts are forced upon the civilian, noncombatant population. Domestic terrorists, often called home-grown terrorists, have historically been responsible for most of the terrorist activity within the United States.

Other Definitions of Terrorism

After the horrific events of September 11, 2001, the U.S. Congress responded with the passage of the U.S.A. Patriot Act (Public Law 107–52) to strengthen the authority of law-enforcement officers to pursue terrorists and prevent further terrorism in the United States. Section 802 of the act expanded the definition of terrorism in the U.S. Code. Title 18, Section 2331(5) of the U.S. Code defines domestic terrorism as any activity that involves

> (A) . . . acts dangerous to human life that are a violation of the criminal laws of the United States or of any State [and] appear to be intended—(i) to intimidate or coerce a civilian population; (ii) to influence the policy of a government by intimidation or coercion; or (iii) to affect the conduct of a government by mass destruction, assassination, or kidnapping; . . . and (C) occur primarily within the territorial jurisdiction of the United States.

The well-known scholar and terrorism expert Walter Laqueur (1987) defines terrorism as the "illegitimate use of force to achieve a political objective when innocent people are targeted."

The Lost Word

The word that is absent from most definitions of terrorism is *fear*, yet it is the key to understanding how terrorists operate. The term *terrorism* has its origin in the domestic terrorism that existed throughout France during its revolution in the 18th century. In the period following the French Revolution, Maximilien Robespierre created the Reign of Terror as he eliminated his enemies, killing more than 30,000 people from 1793 through 1794. Those who supported the monarchy or were suspected of opposing the new French liberty were executed. Robespierre created an environment of fear throughout the country; people would not voice opposition for fear that they would be next in line for the guillotine.

While fear is a key element in many other crimes, such as blackmail, threats, and extortion, it is the key tool of the terrorist. It is fear that may stop a logger from cutting down a tree that may contain a steel spike; it is fear that will push doctors and patients away from abortion clinics where patrons and practitioners have been killed; and it is fear that will cause the young starlet to think twice about wearing an expensive white fur coat to a gala event, only to have blood thrown at her by those with radical animal rights agendas.

Terrorism as Crime

First and foremost, terrorism is a crime. The crime of domestic terrorism is essentially any underlying criminal offense that has an increased penalty because the motivation or reason behind the commission of the crime meets the statutory definition of terrorism, under a federal or state statute. Under the law, use of the word *terrorism* carries a penalty enhancement to the appropriate crime. These terrorist-related offenses include, but are not limited to, homicide, kidnapping, maiming, assault, destruction of property, making threats, and conspiracy.

The Federal Bureau of Investigation (FBI) is the lead federal law-enforcement agency responsible for investigating criminal acts of domestic terrorism, and the charges are prosecuted by the U.S. attorney for the district where the crime occurred. Each investigation is conducted according to the *Attorney General's Guidelines on General Crimes, Racketeering Enterprise and Terrorism Enterprise Investigations*. On April 14, 2011, Mark Giuliano, assistant director in the FBI's Counterterrorism Division, stated that the "homegrown violent extremist threat is one of the serious terrorism threats we face inside the homeland outside of al Qaeda and its affiliates. Homegrown violent extremism (HVE) is very difficult to define. It is a rapidly evolving threat with characteristics that are constantly changing due to external experiences and motivational factors." The FBI is quick to acknowledge that, unlike those who may be involved in transnational terrorism, domestic terrorists are already in the United States, and they may well be next-door neighbors.

Terrorist Groups and Incidents

Domestic terrorist groups exist for many reasons and in many forms, with widely diverging objectives and motives. While some seek only to reform what they see as a system that ignores certain human, animal, or ecological rights, other groups attempt to destroy a system that they believe chokes their liberty and that of others. Various militia groups, also known as separatist groups or supremacy groups, seek to terrorize government officials and any other citizens who support the federal and state governments and the laws they create. Groups that have been involved in domestic terrorist activity include the Aryan Nation, Black Panthers, Weather Underground, Symbionese Liberation Army, Fuerzas Armadas de Liberación Nacional (FALN), Army of God, Ku Klux Klan, Posse Comitatus, Christian Identity, and various ecoterror and animal rights groups. There have also been numerous "lone-wolf" terrorists who have acted on their own to redirect the politics or religion of the nation.

The FBI and other law-enforcement organizations have been largely successful in minimizing the impact of domestic terrorists. In March 2011, five members of a right-wing militia group were arrested in Fairbanks, Alaska, on charges of conspiracy to commit murder, kidnapping, and arson, including numerous firearms charges. These individuals conspired to kidnap and kill police officers and judges. The group is known as the Alaska Peacemakers Militia (APM), and its members are also associated with similar groups and entities, such as the Liberty Bell Network, Alaska Citizens Militia, We the People (WTP), the Sovereign Citizen Movement, and the Second Amendment Task Force. APM's leader is known for saying that he is "not opposed to bloody force" in support of "sovereign citizen" rights. The Southern Poverty Law Center has reported that WTP sees the federal government as a threat to life, liberty, and property.

The Sovereign Citizen Movement is a right-wing antigovernment, white supremacist group that rejects federal and state authority. Group members consider themselves "sovereign citizens" and exhibit antigovernment philosophies similar to those espoused by Timothy McVeigh and Terry Nichols, the two individuals responsible for the terrorist bombing of the Alfred P. Murrah Federal Building in Oklahoma City. The FBI has indicated that members of the group commit murder and physical assault and threaten judges, law-enforcement officers, and government personnel. In May 2010, two Sovereign Citizens (a father and son) shot and killed two police officers during a traffic stop; the driver of the stopped vehicle had simply been asked to produce a valid state driver's license. In March 2009, four members of the Sovereign Citizen Movement were arrested for money laundering, tax evasion, and possession of unregistered machine guns. The group is the subject of an investigation conducted by a joint terrorism task force (JTTF). The Anti-Defamation League has stated that the "Sovereign Citizens wage war against the government and other forms of authority using 'paper terrorism' harassment and intimidation tactics, and occasionally resorting to violence."

In January 2011, a pipe bomb was discovered in a backpack left on the route of a Martin Luther King Day parade in Spokane, Washington. Although the device did not explode, it was built for remote detonation, meaning that it was designed to be detonated from a distance at an optimal time. Had the bomb exploded, the loss of life and personal injuries would have been devastating. Nevertheless, the discovery alone of such a threat is sufficient to create fear and to discourage people from celebrating a national holiday. Although in the Spokane incident the FBI's JTTF arrested an individual, there will be others who take a similar approach to political change.

"To instill fear" is the reason that Antonio Martinez said that he wanted to kill everyone at a military recruitment station in Maryland, detonate a car bomb, and then burn the building. In December 2010, Martinez, a recent convert to Islam using the name Muhammad Hussain, was arrested by the FBI and charged with attempted murder and the use of a weapon of mass destruction. Martinez also discussed the possibility of blowing up Andrews Air Force Base. A similar event was attempted in Portland, Oregon, the previous month; the FBI was also able to intercept that terrorist before anything could happen. The FBI and Oregon law-enforcement officers arrested Mohamed Osman Mohamud, a naturalized U.S. citizen, who planned to detonate a car bomb during the lighting of a Christmas tree, which would have resulted in the deaths of children and their families.

In March 2010, nine members of the Michigan-based Hutaree Militia, another domestic terrorist group, were indicted by a federal grand jury for their involvement in a plot to kill law-enforcement officers and judges. The Title 18 criminal charges in the indictment included violations identified in sections 842(p)(2), 924c(1), 2332a(a)(2), and 2384. As the indictment indicated, the militia group had planned various terrorist activities. Describing themselves as a "Christian warrior" group, they viewed all law enforcement as the enemy. The indictment stated that members planned a violent act to get the

attention of the police, possibly by killing an officer at a traffic stop, then attacking the funeral procession with explosives.

Ecoterrorists and animal rights extremists are described by the FBI as among the most serious domestic terrorism threats. These groups have been involved with more than 2,000 crimes and losses of more than $110 million since 1979. The Animal Enterprise Terrorism Act of 2006 (Public Law 109–374, Title 18, Section 43 of the U.S. Code) provided law-enforcement agents with additional authority to fight domestic terrorism. A key phrase in the act addresses those whose actions place a person in "fear" of death or serious bodily injury—fear being a key element of terrorism.

The Animal Liberation Front (ALF), Earth Liberation Front (ELF), and Stop Huntingdon Animal Cruelty (SHAC) are three examples of radical animal rights and environmental domestic terrorist groups that have been responsible for hundreds of terrorist acts and $100 million of damage. Their methods involve arson, bombing, vandalism, and other serious crimes. These groups have targeted medical research laboratories, auto dealerships, universities, and housing developments, to mention just a few targets. People for the Ethical Treatment of Animals (PETA) is an ALF supporter but is less violent and destructive in its methods. In 2004, ALF and ELF were described by the FBI as two of the most active extremist elements in the United States. In 2006, as part of Operation Backfire, the FBI charged 11 defendants in a 65-count indictment with acts of domestic terrorism, relating to conspiracy, arson, use of destructive devices, and destruction of an energy facility over a five-year period. The ecoterrorist acts included 17 attacks and $12 million in damage due to arson in Vail, Colorado.

The perfect example of the lone-wolf domestic terrorist is Ted Kaczynski, the so-called Unabomber. Kaczynski, an anarchist, operated for almost two decades setting bombs in a variety of places in his effort to reform what he saw as a technology-burdened industrial society. He would send letters to the press and private companies telling them about the bombs he was making in an effort to create a high level of fear; he saw himself as a revolutionary destined to reform society through destruction. In a lengthy manifesto, Kaczynski stated that "the industrial revolution and its consequences have been a disaster for the human race."

Another lone-wolf domestic terrorist is Eric Rudolph, another bomber. However, Rudolph's terrorist motivations were different from those of Kaczynski. Known as the Olympic Park bomber for the bomb he placed at the site of the 1996 Summer Olympics in Atlanta, Georgia, Rudolph hoped that the bomb would create such a high level of fear that the Olympics would be canceled, causing financial devastation to the local economy and the corporations who sponsored it. He was not successful. Other bombings by Rudolph involved a gay bar and abortion clinics. His actions were intended to strike a high level of fear in those who sought to socialize in gay bars or those who sought abortion clinic services. They would not know when or where the next bomb would explode and hence would, he expected, avoid those places. The bombs he planted resulted in both injury and death. His bombings reflected his rejection of the government, the gay lifestyle, and abortion, and he sought to impose his beliefs on others through the use of terrorism.

Domestic Terrorism Outside the United States

Unfortunately, domestic terrorism is not limited to any one country. The United Kingdom has extensive experience with domestic terrorism, dating back to the 1600s and the slaughter of thousands of Irish Catholics by Oliver Cromwell, who believed he was acting in the name of God. In the 20th century, the major domestic terrorism in the United Kingdom involved attacks against both civilian and military personnel (on and off duty) by Irish independence groups. The Irish Republican Army (IRA), Sinn Féin, and other groups have fought against the Crown and British citizens for Irish freedom. The long-standing conflict was also seen as a battle between the Catholics of Ireland and the Protestants of England and Northern Ireland. After years of battle, a peace agreement was reached. Today, domestic terrorism in the United Kingdom involves radical Muslim groups, some of whom are immigrants and others who were born in the United Kingdom, homegrown terrorists. The indiscriminate bombings and attempted bombings of planes, buses, shopping centers, subways, and other public areas have returned. These violent domestic terrorist acts by many Muslim groups are examples of both domestic and nondomestic terrorism.

In Russia, government-sponsored terrorism reached a high point during the 1950s under Joseph Stalin's rule. There were also numerous terrorist events as the Union of Soviet Socialist Republics evolved into the Russian Federation following the Soviet Union's dissolution in 1991. However, domestic terrorism now has a new face with the continuing conflict with the Chechens, who are mostly Muslim. Although Chechnya declared its independence from Russia, it was denied by the government. Since that time, there have been numerous domestic terrorist events involving innocent civilians and armed conflict with state forces; terrorist activities included suicide bombings in a Moscow theater, a school (in Beslan), trains, and subways. The bombing of Moscow's Domodedovo Airport in January 2011 was believed to be perpetrated by the same person responsible for several bombings, a native Russian who converted to Islam; this person was suspected of a failed attempt to detonate a bomb during Russian New Year's celebrations in Red Square (after the phone company sent an automated text message—ironically wishing recipients a happy new year—that detonated the device prematurely via her cell phone). Islamic terrorist successes have increased through the use of native Russian converts, with jihadist terrorism an ongoing domestic issue for the Russian Federation.

Domestic terrorism in China is also not new. The most notable instances involved executions and other killings during the Chinese Communist and Cultural Revolution. During his reign of terror, Mao Zedong was reportedly responsible for the deaths of between 700,000 and 2 million Chinese, his own countrymen and countrywomen. While he attempted to justify his actions as a necessity to institute reforms in China, the methods of the Maoist regime—of seizing and controlling power and instituting policies that strictly controlled expression and behavior among the Chinese populace—are the same as those used two centuries earlier during the French Revolution. Despite economic reforms, the Chinese government today still rules with an iron hand that maintains a high level of fear in its citizens. There is a constant questioning of what price a "dissident" must pay for an independent voice. Terrorism within China now comes from groups such as the East Turkestan Islamic Party, the Turkestan Islamic Party, and similar groups that are responsible for a series of bombings in Shanghai, Wenzhou, Guangzhou, and Kunming.

Conclusions

Domestic terrorism in democratic nations is not a product of the state but is directed at the state and its citizens in order to create fear and effect change. The biggest challenge to law enforcement is to identify homegrown terrorists, infiltrate their organizations, and stop them in their tracks. As indicated above, in the United States, JTTFs have been very successful; it is to be hoped that their success continues.

Keith Gregory Logan
Kutztown University

See also Terrorism: Nondomestic

Further Readings

Combs, Cindy C. *Terrorism in the Twenty-First Century*. New York: Pearson-Longman, 2009.

Dyson, William E. *Terrorism: An Investigator's Handbook*. Cincinnati, OH: Anderson, 2005.

Giuliano, Mark F. "The Post 9/11 FBI: The Bureau's Response to Evolving Threats." (April 14, 2011). http://www.fbi.gov/news/speeches/the-post-9-11-fbi-the-bureaus-response-to-evolving-threats (Accessed January 2012).

Howard, Russell D. and Reid L. Sawyer, ed. *Terrorism and Counterterrorism: Understanding the New Security Environment, Reading and Interpretations*. Dubuque, IA: McGraw-Hill, 2006.

Laqueur, Walter. *The Age of Terrorism*. Boston: Little, Brown, 1987.

Logan, Keith Gregory, ed. *Homeland Security and Intelligence*. Santa Barbara, CA: Praeger Security International, 2010.

Savage, David G. and Richard Fausset. "Militia Members Indicted on Conspiracy, Weapons Charges." *Los Angeles Times* (March 30, 2010). http://articles.latimes.com/2010/mar/30/nation/la-na-militia-raids30-2010mar30 (Accessed January 2012).

Terrorism: Financing

A central front in law enforcement's war on transnational terrorism is the fight to interdict the funding of terrorist operations. While there is a limited degree of cooperation in the international community, little progress has been made in stopping the flow of funds across borders via illegitimate or underground financial networks.

Terrorism can be financed in two ways. First, profits realized from criminal enterprises can be directed to terrorism. Middle Eastern terrorist groups have received funding from criminal activities such as bank robbery, kidnapping, drug trafficking, or online fraud and identity theft. In 2009, armed robbers attacked an armored bank van in Yemen, displaying a level of sophisticated organization that suggested an Al Qaeda operation. Opium poppies grown in Afghanistan fund Taliban actions in that country and have also been used to fund Islamic terrorists in other parts of the world.

Second, money obtained legitimately can be channeled to illegitimate terrorist activities. In this second mode, terrorist financing functions as money laundering in reverse—clean money is made dirty. Terrorist sympathizers have raised funds from Muslims making religious pilgrimages to Mecca. Saudi Arabian donors are the major source of contributions to Sunni terrorist groups. The United Arab Emirates, Qatar, and Kuwait are also significant sources of terrorist financing.

Terrorist groups also obtain significant funding from individuals, organizations, and mosques in Great Britain and Europe. A number of Arab charities are suspected of channeling money to terrorist groups. Lashkar-e-Taiba, a Pakistani terrorist group, received funds collected among the Pakistani expatriate community in Great Britain to aid victims of the 2005 Kashmir earthquake and used it instead to fund terrorism.

In the United States, federal agents raided and shut down the Islamic American Relief Agency (IARA) in 2004, after wiretaps indicated the charity was funneling money to people in Sudan and

In October 2001, Deputy Treasury Secretary Kenneth Dam (left) and U.S. Customs Commissioner Robert C. Bonner announced the launch of Operation Green Quest, an initiative that targeted current and future terrorist funding sources. (U.S. Department of Homeland Security)

Pakistan who had ties to the Taliban and Al Qaeda. IARA was also charged with illegally sending money to Iraq prior to the U.S. invasion and with stealing from a U.S. Agency for International Development grant that was intended to fund development efforts in Mali.

The list of governments alleged to have deliberately engaged in state-sponsored terrorism is long. Western governments have also funded terrorism, albeit sometimes unintentionally. For example, precursors to contemporary Middle Eastern terrorist groups were initially aided by Western governments. During the Soviet Union's occupation of Afghanistan, the United States funded and trained fighters who would later join the Taliban, some of whom may have joined Al Qaeda. Later, during the U.S. occupation of Afghanistan, the Taliban insurgency routinely took a cut of foreign assistance funds, via extortion or protection rackets, corruption, or donations from contractors sympathetic to the Taliban cause. Elements within the Pakistani government may have also funneled money from foreign aid donors to Taliban forces. Iran has funded terrorist groups such as al-Mahdi, Hamas, Hezbollah, and the Palestinian Islamic Jihad.

The earliest counterterrorism legislation outlawed terrorist actions, but more recently terrorist financing has also become a particular target of antiterrorist law, often bundled with anti-money-laundering legislation. The United States and several western European countries have successfully seized funds and tightened money-laundering regulations in response to the terrorist threat.

In the United States, the Treasury Department's Financial Crimes Enforcement Network (FinCEN), formed in 1990, is tasked with monitoring and investigating terrorist financing and money laundering in general. FinCEN functions as the nexus in a network of other law-enforcement agencies that have an interest in such crimes.

American law requires financial institutions to keep records of and report cash transactions that exceed $10,000. It also requires institutions to file "suspicious activity reports" with FinCEN on any customer who appears to be engaged in money laundering. American law criminalizes both money laundering and any attempts to evade reporting requirements. Car dealers and real estate agencies are defined as financial institutions subject to cash-transaction-reporting requirements. Identity verification is required for people who purchase monetary instruments valued in excess of $3,000. Banks are required to implement anti-money-laundering procedures. Bank examiners are trained in anti-money-laundering investigations.

In 1999, the United Nations (UN) produced the International Convention for the Suppression of the Financing of Terrorism (also known as the Terrorist Financing Convention), an international treaty that criminalizes transnational actions that involve terrorist financing. It mandates each nation to regulate terrorist financing within its national boundaries. It encourages international cooperation among legal and law-enforcement institutions to investigate, prevent, and sanction terrorist financing.

In 2001, the United States passed laws designed to give government more tools to interdict terrorist financing in the U.S.A. Patriot Act (Uniting and Strengthening America by Providing Appropriate Tools Required to Intercept and Obstruct Terrorism Act). The act gives law-enforcement agencies more leeway to investigate financial records and engage in other relevant intelligence gathering, and it gives the Treasury Department regulatory powers over financial transactions involving foreigners.

Title III of the Patriot Act is titled the International Money Laundering Abatement and Financial Anti-Terrorism Act of 2001. It requires interagency information sharing among government bodies and requires more due diligence and anti-money-laundering programs from the financial services industry. Most significant, the Patriot Act recognizes the transnational nature of terrorist financing and attempts to give U.S. agencies the means to monitor and regulate foreign financial transactions that are of potential concern to the United States, including informal transactions in the underground economy. Since 2001, most of the G20 countries have established similar regulatory structures designed to fight terrorist financing.

Terrorists evade money transfer regulations by moving amounts that do not exceed the reporting thresholds or by using couriers to move cash, moneygrams, and prepaid value cards. One strategy for bypassing regulatory scrutiny is to engage in "structuring" (also known in the banking industry as "smurfing")—breaking large transactions up into amounts less than $10,000. Financial regulators are aware of this strategy, and thus laws in the United States and many other countries criminalize structuring.

A legal alternative is to transfer gold, diamonds, or gemstones via couriers. Deposits of such goods do not trigger international reporting regulations. Dubai is one of the largest and least regulated gold markets. When the United States attacked Afghanistan, Al Qaeda is believed to have smuggled gold out through Pakistan and then to Dubai for deposit. While moving gold works well to legally evade reporting requirements, it is risky in the sense that gold can be stolen or appropriated from the couriers before it reaches its final destination. However, the rise of bullion-backed online e-currencies removes such risks.

Another technique is to use informal value transfer systems (IVTS's). These are commonly known as hawala systems, an informal economy of money brokers ensconced in a network that spans the Middle East, northern Africa and the Horn, and south Asia, with outposts in Europe and the United States. The institution of hawala dates back more than a thousand years. Brokers known as hawaladars transfer value from one location to another on an honor system by means of telephone conversations, leaving no traceable records. Because such transfers depend on honor instead of formal contracts, hawala functions as an underground banking and money transfer system. It remains largely outside legal and juridical controls.

Since the terrorist attacks of September 11, 2001 (9/11), larger hawala organizations have had their accounts frozen as a result of counterterrorist initiatives; their brokers have been indicted and the organizations have been named on UN terrorist watch lists. Al Barakat was a global hawala network run by an associate of Osama bin Laden, with nearly 200 offices in at least 40 countries. The United States froze its funds after labeling it a global terrorist organization.

Legitimate businesses can also obscure transnational fund transfers by engaging in countervaluing of goods they import or export, often in conjunction with a hawaladar. Using this technique, a business in the United States might import goods worth $10,000, but the offshore exporter would overvalue the goods at $20,000. The overvaluation permits the U.S. firm to send the extra $10,000 out of the country without attracting regulatory attention. Buying and selling nonexistent items on eBay is a simple way to accomplish the same end.

Anti-money-laundering tools are traditionally considered a means of interdicting money obtained illegitimately. However, they are also used to interdict clean money flowing to terrorists. Increasingly, regulatory and law-enforcement agencies have access to software tools for monitoring large currency movements. Data from these sources can be combined and analyzed by sophisticated software tools that create profiles of customers and accounts. Unusual transactions that do not fit a customer's normal profile can be flagged for extra scrutiny. Software tools can also comb the databases to seek out patterns of action that are characteristic of illegal transactions.

While the international community has developed more sophistication and more cooperation with regard to interdicting transnational terrorist financing, success has been limited. With each new law-enforcement tactic, terrorist groups develop new ways of evading scrutiny.

Thomas F. Brown
Virginia Wesleyan College

See also Accounting Fraud; Al Qaeda; Charities and Financing; Financial Action Task Force; Informal Value Transfer Systems; Money Laundering: Countermeasures

Further Readings

Comras, V. "Al Qaeda Finances and Funding to Affiliated Groups." *Strategic Insights*, v.4/1 (2005).
El Qorchi, Mohammed et al. *Informal Funds Transfer Systems: An Analysis of the Informal Hawala System.* Washington, DC: International Monetary Fund, 2003.
Elizur, Yuval and Lawrence Malkin. "Terrorism's Money Trail." *World Policy Journal*, v.19/1 (2002).
Farah, D. *Blood From Stones: The Secret Financial Network of Terror.* New York: Broadway Books, 2004.
Napoleoni, L. *Modern Jihad: Tracing the Dollars Behind the Terror Networks.* Sterling, VA: Pluto, 2003.

TERRORISM: NONDOMESTIC

Nondomestic terrorism, also known as international terrorism, foreign terrorism, and transnational terrorism, is premeditated, politically motivated criminal acts involving violence, destruction, and fear against civilian or other noncombatant targets of one country or nation by subnational groups or clandestine agents of another country or nation. Today most transnational terrorism concerns religion, homeland independence (national identity), or ethnic separatism.

Definitions of Terrorism

While it is relatively easy to establish the key elements of transnational terrorism, there is no agreement on a single definition or identifying term. Title 18 of the U.S. Code, Section 2331, defines *international terrorism* as activities that

> (1)(A) involve violent acts or acts dangerous to human life that are a violation of the criminal laws of the United States or any State; (B) appear to be intended—(i) to intimidate or coerce a civilian population; (ii) to influence the policy of a government by intimidation or coercion; or (iii) to affect the conduct of a government by mass destruction, assassination, or kidnapping; and (C) occur primarily outside the territorial jurisdiction of the United States, or transcend national boundaries in terms of the means by which they are accomplished, the persons they appear intended to intimidate or coerce, or the locale in which their perpetrators operate or seek asylum.

This is the definition that the Federal Bureau of Investigation (FBI) follows when conducting terrorism investigations. The investigations are for crimes under existing criminal statutes, such as homicide, arson, destruction of property, threats, and extortion, because there is no single federal statute making "terrorism" a crime. Terrorist acts are normally used as a sentence enhancement pursuant to the sentencing guidelines. There are, however, numerous state terrorism statutes.

Title 22 of the U.S. Code, Section 265f(d), defines *international terrorism* simply as "terrorism involving citizens or the territory of more than one country." It adds that terrorism is "premeditated, politically motivated violence perpetrated against non-combatant [civilian] targets by subnational groups or clandestine agents." According to Title 28 of the Code of Federal Regulations, Section 0.85, terrorism is the "unlawful use of force and violence against persons or property to intimidate or coerce a government, the civilian population or any segment thereof, in furtherance of political or social objectives."

In *Terrorism 2002–2005*, the FBI indicates that "international terrorism investigations are conducted in accordance with *The Attorney General Guidelines for FBI Foreign Intelligence Collection and Foreign Counterintelligence Investigations*. These guidelines set forth the level and limits for investigating U.S. persons or foreign nationals in the United States who are targeting national security interests on behalf of a foreign power."

The U.S. State Department's Office of the Coordinator for Terrorism's definition is the same

as that in Title 22, U.S. Code Section 2656f(d)(2) but adds that it is "usually intended to influence an audience." The Department of Defense's *Dictionary of Military Terms* defines terrorism as the "calculated use of unlawful violence or threat of unlawful violence to inculcate fear, intended to coerce or to intimidate governments or societies in the pursuit of goals that are generally political, religious, or ideological."

Section 219 of the Immigration and Nationality Act (Title 8, U.S. Code Section 1189) establishes the procedures for designating a foreign terrorist organization. It requires a finding, first, that the organization is foreign; second, that it engages in terrorist activity as defined in this section (1189) or section 2656f(d)(2) of Title 22; third, that it has intent to engage in terrorism; and fourth that such activity threatens the security of the United States or its nationals. Examples of terrorist activity are crimes, essentially the same crimes that are addressed in various sections of federal and state criminal codes. What distinguishes these acts from traditional criminal acts, however, is the purpose or motive behind these acts, which involves who the perpetrators of the crimes are and why are they committing the crimes. Essentially, the determination of whether the activity is terrorist is a matter of asking the question of why the activity occurred: for profit (money) or to create fear and destruction. The use of the designation "terrorist act" reflects the importance that the government has placed on the prevention of terrorism; such acts carry enhanced penalties and may "toll" (cause a pause and therefore extend) the statute of limitations. Some legislation—such as the U.S.A. Patriot Act of 2001 (which stands for Uniting and Strengthening America by Providing Appropriate Tools Required to Intercept and Obstruct Terrorism), the Antiterrorism and Death Penalty Act of 1996, and the Airport and Transportation Security Act of 2001—is specifically directed at providing law-enforcement officers with more authority to prevent and fight terrorism and to increase penalties for being involved in terrorist activities.

Every other nation has its own definitions of domestic and foreign terrorism. Depending on time, place, politics, religion, media, and social conditions, these definitions of terrorism may vary. The Arab Convention for the Suppression of Terrorism, for example, was adopted by the Council of Arab Ministers of the Interior and the Council of Arab

Ministers of Justice in Cairo, Egypt, in 1998. This body defines terrorism as

> any act or threat of violence, whatever its motives or purposes, that occurs in the advancement of an individual or collective criminal agenda and seeking to sow panic among people, causing fear by harming them, or placing their lives, liberty or security in danger, or seeking to cause damage to the environment or to public or private installations or property or to occupying or seizing them, or seeking to jeopardize a national resources.

Although the words from each of these definitions may vary slightly, the same standard elements exist: the creation of violence and fear, and the purpose of achieving a certain or definitive end.

In defining terrorism as the "premeditated use or threat of use of violence by individuals or subnational groups to obtain a political or social objective through intimidation of a large audience beyond that of the immediate victims," B. Peter Rosendorf and Todd Sandler also identified two essential elements related to the motives (whether political or social) of terrorists and their reliance on violence to create continuing fear, beyond "immediate victims." It is these elements that distinguish terrorism from standard criminal conduct. Rosendorf and Sandler also noted that their definition excludes state terror, that is, a government's use of terrorist tactics to control its citizens.

Responding to Nondomestic Terrorism

A key to understanding and responding to what is a terrorist activity is knowing whether the activities are state-sponsored or are initiated by large groups, small groups, or a particular individual (a lone-wolf terrorist) and are not part of a government program. Libya, for example, supported a Chicago street gang (El Rukns) in its acts of violence in and against the United States. This enabled Libya to distance itself from the terrorist activity.

All terrorists are criminals, but not all criminals are terrorists. The FBI is the federal law-enforcement agency responsible for fighting both domestic and nondomestic terrorism within the United States; the Central Intelligence Agency (CIA), along with several other agencies, is responsible for stopping transnational terrorism directed against the United States and its citizens, wherever it may appear in the world. It is the "long arm" of U.S. laws and power that enables America to conduct counterterrorism activities anywhere in the world and hold terrorists accountable for their acts. An exhaustive investigation by the FBI may be necessary to determine whether actors who seek to harm the United States and its interests are merely criminals out for personal gain or terrorists who have a political agenda and want to create fear. The same issues present themselves to other nations. In response to threats from Somali pirates against Russian Federation (Russian) citizens and ships, the Russian government deployed a commando unit to counter the terrorist violence. What is not known is whether those pirates are merely bands of thieves or terrorist groups operating in Somalia whose ransoms are used to fund either domestic or transnational terrorist activities. It is possible that they represent both groups.

The FBI treats terrorists as criminals, whether they are domestic or nondomestic (foreign, international, or transnational) terrorists. As noted, in the United States all terrorists (or alleged terrorists) are charged according to existing criminal statutes. All suspected terrorists placed under arrest are provided access to legal counsel and are tried pursuant to standard judicial procedures, including all constitutional guarantees. The need to provide several of these legal guarantees to alleged terrorists has been challenged in Congress and in court, as many Americans believe terrorists should be treated differently from criminals and instead should be processed through military criminal procedures, as prisoners of war. Whether there will be any changes in the process is still an open issue.

In addition, Congress still has the opportunity to pass laws that identify a series of terrorist crimes, not just penalty enhancements, much as it has done with regard to air piracy. However, the federal government and all of the states, as well as the District of Columbia, currently have "terroristic threat" laws with a wide range of penalties, from probation to life in prison. These laws prohibit making threats of violence and creating fear. The underlying federal offenses include threats involving weapons of mass destruction (WMDs) with such instruments as biological, chemical, or radiological hazards, which make these threats more than simple crimes.

The 2009 *National Counterterrorism Center Report on Terrorism* indicates that about "11,000 terrorist attacks occurred in 83 countries … resulting in more than 58,000 victims, including nearly 15,000 fatalities." Today, the largest number of terrorist acts involve religion. The victims are civilian (about 60 percent), with 14 percent being police officers, and about 50 percent were Muslim. In 2009, about 50 percent of the attackers were identified with Sunni extremists using bombs, and the three deadliest groups initiating the attacks were the Taliban, al-Shabaab, and Al Qaeda. Islamic extremists were responsible for only two nondomestic attacks in the United States that resulted in fatalities. (In compiling its data, the NCTC uses the definition of terrorism from Title 22, U.S. Code Section 2656f(d)(2).) It is readily apparent that most of these terrorist attacks were outside the United States and involved domestic struggles for control of power. What is not clear is how many of these events were truly the product of nondomestic, foreign terrorists whose mission it was to foment unrest that would lead to a terrorist event. Groups such as Al Qaeda have followers all over the world, and the conflict among Muslims (mostly between Sunnis and Shiites) dates back to the death of Muhammad in 632 C.E., when the boundaries of nations were far different from those of today. Today's borders in the Middle East were drawn by Western colonial powers for various reasons, few of which related to the ethnicity and desires of the indigenous populations.

The FBI investigative guidelines set forth the threshold and limits for terrorism investigations, distinguishing domestic from nondomestic (international) terrorism depending on the origin, base, and objectives of the terrorist organization as well as the nationality of the citizens involved in the activity. International terrorist acts can occur both within and outside the United States, transcending national boundaries. The September 11, 2001 (9/11), destruction of the World Trade Center in New York City, the same day's attacks on the Pentagon in Washington, D.C., the October 2000 bombing of the USS *Cole* in Yemen, and the 1983 Marine barracks bombing in Beirut, Lebanon, were all acts of nondomestic (transnational) terrorists and occurred in three different countries, only one of which was the United States. The key to each of these events went well beyond the physical devastation and the loss of life, and the acts raised the level of "fear" to new heights.

Bombings, assassinations, kidnappings, skyjackings, and threats intimidate the target audience and violate every nation's domestic laws. Like the United States, every nation has laws that ensure that the territorial jurisdiction extends to the locations of the terrorist acts against them. According to U.S. laws, terrorists who have attacked commercial aircraft have most often been prosecuted under U.S. Code Chapter 465 or its "air piracy" predecessor, 49 U.S.C. App. 1472 (1988 ed.). This is because the air piracy statute was one of the first federal laws that directly addressed terrorism aboard commercial airlines. However, the changes have not stopped there. In response to terrorist activities, the United States, like other nations, has generated or revised its laws to ensure that transnational terrorist activity is appropriately prosecuted by the home nation. In particular, there have been a series of crimes that involve terrorist attacks, such as crimes against mass-transit systems, aboard or against an aircraft, against protected individuals, involving destructive devices, specialized inchoate crimes, and so forth. Title 49 of the U.S. Code includes sections involving piracy (49 U.S.C. 46502) and prohibits *mala in se* crimes such as murder, manslaughter, and assault (49 U.S.C. 46503–6) when committed within the special aircraft jurisdiction of the United States. There are also numerous special sections within Title 18 (such as 31 and 32, 844, 924, 956, 1992, 2284, 2332, 2339, 3281, 3286, and 3290) that apply in this area as well.

Financing of Terrorist Activities

An underlying problem is identifying the source of funding for the transnational, nondomestic terrorism activities that take place around the world. To stop the terrorists, it is important to identify what groups or nation-states provide the resources that fund various terrorist activities and what activities these terrorist groups may use to generate funds for their acts. These enterprises can be very elaborate and expensive (operated by large, organized drug cartels) or very simple (such as a false "family relief fund"). While it is clear that funding comes from several oil-rich nations that are sympathetic to certain terrorists, particular Muslim extremist groups, they do not constitute the sources of all the money necessary for these diverse terrorist activities. Osama bin Laden had personal assets, some of which were used and others that were seized; as a result, he had, in part, to rely on friends and family in Saudi Arabia and other nations to support his terrorism.

The term *narco-terrorism* is often used to identify the narcotics trade as a source of terrorist financing; it also describes a method of seeking a community's compliance and support of illegal drug activities, as is the problem in Mexico in an ongoing fight with the drug cartels. In Mexico, there is outright warfare in many Mexican cities that border the United States (Juarez, Mexico, being one of the worst), as the Mexican federal police (*federales*) retake control of its cities, where many of its local law-enforcement personnel have been intimidated by drug traffickers or seduced by profits from the drug trade. Violence in these wars both among the different cartels and with government authorities has escalated to the point that general lawlessness threatens large areas of the country; innocent tourists, bystanders, and families have been killed in the streets and in their homes, and fear is rampant.

When the United States invaded Afghanistan in search of bin Laden, it was well known that Afghanistan was a major source of heroin and an Al Qaeda stronghold for training terrorists. Afghan locals had found that it was easier and more profitable to grow and sell poppies to buy food than it was to grow wheat or other such crops for consumption within the country. The Drug Enforcement Administration (DEA) and the FBI have linked Al Qaeda and Sunni extremists to elements associated with the Afghan drug trade. A 2003 investigation led to the arrest of Afghans and Pakistanis linked to Al Qaeda and the Taliban. The al-Ittihad al-Islami (AIAI), a Somalian militant Islamic organization, is believed to be smuggling an illegal narcotic, khat, into the United States and sending money back to terrorist organizations via a hawala network. Hezbollah, a successful political party and active anti-Israeli/U.S. terrorist group in Lebanon, is also known to have connections with drug groups and use funds from drug trafficking to fund many of its initiatives, according to the FBI.

In addition to drug trafficking, bartering of drugs for weapons, including ammunition and bombs, is used to support terrorism. Whether it is explosives, weapons, drugs, sexual slavery for sale, or other criminal activity, there are many sources of illegal money that can be used to finance terrorist activity. Many of the other crimes that occur overseas, such as kidnapping, money laundering, and piracy, may not be the acts of independent criminal entrepreneurs but the acts of nondomestic terrorists seeking to fund their operations.

Arrests and Convictions for Transnational Activities

Not all arrests for terrorist activities made in the United States involve terrorist acts against the U.S. government or populace. In the 1980s, a group of Sikhs was arrested within the United States for conspiring to assassinate Indian Prime Minister Rajiv Gandhi during a U.S. visit. This was clearly an Indian transnational terrorist event that was not initiated on Indian soil and involved individuals living in the United States.

David Headly (also known as Daood Sayed Gilani), a Pakistani American, planned attacks on a Danish newspaper that published cartoons showing images of the Prophet Muhammad; he was also involved in the 2008 attacks in Mumbai, India, and conspired with other terrorists to cause destruction in India. Headly received extensive terrorist training at a camp in Pakistan operated by the Pakistani military. Aside from his terrorist activities involving conspiracy to commit murder, he was also involved in the illegal smuggling and sale of drugs before becoming an informant for the U.S. Drug Enforcement Administration (DEA). In 2010, he pleaded guilty in the Northern District of Illinois to a multicounty plea agreement (No. 09 CR 830–3) and received a life sentence.

In 2009, Najibullah Zazi, an Afghan citizen and legal U.S. resident, was arrested for conspiring with Al Qaeda operatives Saleh al-Somali and Rashid Rauf to attack the New York City subway using suicide bombers. Zazi pleaded guilty in 2010 to providing material support to a terrorist organization (in violation of Title 18, Section 2339B, of the U.S. Code). Members of Zazi's family and others were also indicted.

In 1993, bombs were exploded in the basement of the North Tower of the World Trade Center. Mahmud Abouhalima, Ahmed Ajaj, Mohammed Salameh, and Ramzi Yousef conspired with Khalid Shaikh Mohammed (who provided financing) and others to bring the towers down, although they were unsuccessful. In addition to criminal conspiracy, criminal charges and convictions involved crimes such as murder (seven people died), attempted murder (thousands were injured), explosive destruction, and interstate transportation of explosives. To this day, not everyone involved has been brought to justice.

Keith Gregory Logan
Kutztown University

See also Terrorism: Domestic

Further Readings

Combs, Cindy C. *Terrorism in the Twenty-First Century.* New York: Pearson-Longman, 2009.

Council of Arab Ministers of the Interior and Council of Arab Ministers of Justice. Arab Convention for the Suppression of Terrorism, 1998. http://terrorism.about .com/gi/dynamic/offsite.htm?zi=1/XJ/Ya&sdn=terroris m&cdn=newsissues&tm=6&f=22&tt=14&bt=0&bts= 0&zu=http%3A//www.worldlii.org/catalog/52859. html (Accessed February 2011).

Dyson, William E. *Terrorism: An Investigator's Handbook,* 2nd ed. Cincinnati, OH: Anderson, 2005.

Howard, Russell D. and Reid L. Sawyer, ed. *Terrorism and Counterterrorism: Understanding the New Security Environment, Reading and Interpretations.* Dubuque, IA: McGraw-Hill, 2006.

Logan, Keith Gregory, ed. *Homeland Security and Intelligence.* Santa Barbara, CA: Praeger Security International, 2010.

National Counterterrorism Center. Office of the Director of National Intelligence. *2009 Report on Terrorism 30 April 2010.* http://www.nctc.gov/witsbanner/ docs/2009_report_on_terrorism.pdf (Accessed January 2011).

Nemeth, Charles C. *Homeland Security.* Boca Raton, FL: Taylor Francis Group, 2010.

Reichel, Philip, ed. *Handbook of Transnational Crime and Justice.* Thousand Oaks, CA: Sage, 2005.

Rosendorff, B. Peter and Todd Sandler. "The Political Economy of Transnational Terrorism." *Journal of Conflict Resolution,* v.49/2 (2005).

U.S. Department of State. *Patterns of Global Terrorism 1994.* April 1995. http://www.hri.org/docs/USSD -Terror/94 and http://www.state.gov/s/ct/rls/pgtrpt (Accessed February 2011).

Terrorism: Nuclear

Before nuclear terrorism can be examined, the phenomenon of terrorism must be understood. Terrorism is a fact of life in the modern world. It is present across the globe, in both modern, developed countries and countries that have not fully advanced into the technological age. Terrorism is the bogeyman of peaceful societies, a fact not lost on the leaders and politicians who use it to justify all types of social, political, religious, and even personal agendas.

Generally defined, terrorism is the threat or actual use of force to compel an individual, group, society, or nation to act or not act, usually to accomplish some social, political, or religious goal that cannot be accomplished through legitimate methods. This is a broad definition of terrorism. However, terrorism is not an easy concept to strictly define. The reason for this difficulty is that labeling an act a threat is often a matter of perspective. For example, when a group of people in society decide to revolt to gain their political independence, they are frequently labeled as terrorists by the parties in power. However, to the people who are trying to gain their political freedom, they are viewed as freedom fighters and heroes.

One of the essential problems with terrorism is that it targets not only the parties who commit the acts that are used to justify the terrorist activities (such as torture by police, religious suppression by theologians, or economic oppression by oligarchs). It also targets innocent people, in part because those who commit the acts used to justify the terrorism are usually protected by the police, the military, and security services. Thus, many terrorists attempt to effect change by terrorizing the general populace.

Terrorism can be accomplished by various means. Weapons such as personal firearms are used. These small arms are favored when terrorists are seeking to assassinate kidnap a specific individual. Explosives are favored by many terrorists seeking to inflict a greater amount of harm and damage.

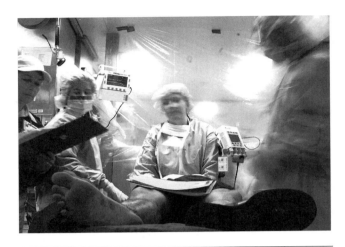

A small nuclear device that could spread nuclear radiation over a large population center is known as a "dirty bomb." U.S. Navy medical personnel assess a leg injury during a 2004 chemical, biological, and radiological mass casualty "dirty bomb" exercise aboard hospital ship USNS *Mercy*. (U.S. Navy/Johansen Laurel)

Although a single terrorist with a machine gun can fire into a crowded market and inflict a number of casualties, that terrorist would likely be swiftly caught and interrogated, revealing the identity and location of his compatriots. In contrast, explosives can be set and detonated remotely and at a later time, minimizing the chances of the perpetrators being caught and maximizing the potential harm and damage. Also, the fact that the general populace will not have any warning of the explosion only heightens the level of fear and terror as a result of this unpredictability. There are other methods that can raise the level of fear and terror to almost Olympian heights, involving weapons of mass destruction (WMDs). WMDs include biological, chemical, and nuclear weapons.

Nuclear weapons are probably the most feared WMDs, although they are not as insidious as biological weapons. The basic reason for this fear is the massive extent of physical damage that they wreak and the resulting radiation, which can kill thousands of people with radiation sickness and poison the environment for decades. Furthermore, the use of sufficient nuclear weapons would result in a "nuclear winter" during which the atmosphere, filled with debris, could block the sun, alter atmospheric activity, and contaminate and destroy all or a significant portion of life on the planet.

There are several types of nuclear weapons. Strategic nuclear weapons can be delivered by ground-based intercontinental ballistic missiles (ICBMs), airplanes, or orbital space platforms. Tactical nuclear weapons are usually delivered by artillery, ground- or sea-based rockets, or airplanes. Finally, nuclear weapons known as "backpack nuclear weapons" (or "backpack nukes") are small nuclear weapons that can be carried by a single person or transported in a small container, such as a suitcase. Their portability makes backpack nuclear weapons a serious danger to all societies and a much sought-after weapon by terrorists. The level of destruction that can be inflicted by backpack nuclear weapons is much less than a tactical or a strategic nuclear weapon, but it is still considerable. For example, a backpack nuclear weapon could have the destructive power of approximately 5 kilotons of TNT (dynamite). In comparison, the atomic bombs dropped by the United States on Hiroshima and Nagasaki, Japan, at the end of World War II had the destructive power of 16 to 21 kilotons of TNT. Modern thermonuclear warheads can attain the destructive yield of 5 megatons.

The portability of backpack nuclear weapons makes them very difficult to track and control. They can be transported across borders with relative ease. In 1997, it was reported that Russia had lost track of approximately 100 of its backpack nuclear weapons. The claim was immediately denied by Russia, but since the dissolution of the Soviet Union there have been other reports of the disappearance of nuclear material. Moreover, in recent years there have been numerous reports of other nations attempting to develop nuclear weapons. The best-known example is that of Iran, which has greatly expanded its nuclear program and is suspected of developing nuclear weapons. Many nations of the world are concerned about Iran, as Iran is suspected of engaging in and sponsoring numerous acts of terrorism and terrorist groups. Also, Pakistan, which became a nuclear power in 1998, is suspected of having close ties with various terrorist groups. There have been serious concerns about Pakistan transferring its nuclear technology to other nations. Given these realities, many authorities believe that terrorist groups might be able to obtain nuclear weapons from these nations or from their personnel.

Another danger involving nuclear terrorism is not that of a large nuclear weapon but a small nuclear device that could spread nuclear radiation over a large population center. Such nuclear devices are known as "dirty bombs." Even though such devices might be small and not cause much physical destruction, if packed with sufficient radioactive material the detonation of such a device could cause the spread of nuclear radiation over a large city. The impact, both physical and psychological, of such an event on a large civilian population would be devastating. Thus, a dirty bomb would be an ideal weapon for terrorists.

Prevention of such an occurrence is high on any list of national security. One of the best ways to prevent them from crossing borders is through the use of radiation detectors. However, it is much more effective to prevent them from being built. To accomplish this goal, many nations have entered into various treaties to coordinate their efforts. For example, the Nuclear Non-Proliferation Treaty, signed in 1968, prohibited the spread of nuclear weapons. Almost all the nations of the world have signed it, except for India, Israel, Pakistan, and North Korea. Pakistan and North Korea or some of their people are suspected of being involved in some form of nuclear weapons transfer to such nations as the former Iraq and Iran. Also, it is suspected that the United States is responsible for transferring nuclear weapons to Israel, but the Israelis have yet to verify this claim. The International Atomic Energy Agency and the United Nations (UN) Disarmament Commission work to limit the proliferation of and to reduce nuclear weapons in the world.

There is little doubt that a nuclear weapon would be a terrorist's weapon of choice. The destruction and terror that would be inflicted would be incalculable. As of this time, it could be tentatively assumed that the nations of the world have prevented the spread of nuclear weapons to terrorist groups as evidenced by the lack of their use. However, with the spread of technology, nuclear terrorism is still a very real possibility.

Wm. C. Plouffe Jr.
Independent Scholar

See also Jihad; Terrorism: Defined; Terrorism: Domestic; Terrorism: Nondomestic; Violence: Uses

Further Readings

Allison, Graham. *Nuclear Terrorism.* New York: Macmillan, 2005.

Dumas, Lloyd. *Lethal Arrogance.* New York: St. Martin's Press, 1999.

Frantz, Douglas and Catherine Collins. *The Nuclear Jihadist.* New York: Twelve, 2007.

Hoffman, Bruce. *Inside Terrorism.* New York: Columbia University Press, 2006.

Lake, Anthony. *Nightmares.* Boston: Little, Brown, 2000.

Mueller, John. *Overblown.* New York: Free Press, 2006.

Ray, Ellen and William Schaap, eds. *Covert Action: Roots of Terrorism.* Melbourne, Australia: Ocean Press, 2003.

Semler, Eric, James Benjamin, and Adam Gross. *The Language of Nuclear War.* New York: Harper and Row, 1987.

Terrorism Versus Transnational Crime

Transnational crime is generally organized crime. While organized crime might be found in most countries around the world, it does not in itself form a global network. Terrorism also operates on a transnational basis and, again, even though organizations such as Al Qaeda have global influence, there are no global terrorist networks. In the same way, there is no global nexus of transnational crime and terrorism. Instead, there are a number of transnational organized crime and terrorist nexuses. Terrorists have previously been included as part of an analysis of organized crime, as it is argued that they operate in a way similar to organized crime groups (OCGs). However, there is a distinction, in that organized criminals are motivated by financial gain and terrorists, although they may commit crime for financial gain to further their organization, are ultimately motivated by political or religious ideology.

Any bond, link, or third-party junction that connects transnational organized crime with terrorism is a nexus between the two. This includes any strategic or tactical connection between OCGs and terrorists formed by direct contact between the two or by way of a third-party facilitator. It also includes terrorists who, over time, evolve into organized crime groups, or vice versa, and terrorists who commit transnational crimes in preparation for the commission of a terrorist act.

Transnational crime and terrorism nexuses exist in a number of countries, in various forms. This entry will focus on nexuses connected to Northern Ireland, Afghanistan, and Colombia and how these are interlinked with each other. Terrorists native to Northern Ireland, specifically the Irish Republican Army (IRA), formed a nexus with organized crime by taking part in intellectual property crime (IPC). IPC is the manufacture, transportation, storage, and sale of pirated goods, and it operates on a transnational basis. At first terrorists in Northern Ireland controlled IPC in that country through links with OCGs, taking a cut of the profit to further their ideology. More recently, as a result of the implementation of the 1998 peace agreement, IRA terrorists and, on the other side of the divide, loyalist terrorists developed further nexuses with OCGs. Former terrorists have turned to organized crime activity of various types, including IPC and drug dealing, purely for financial gain.

Although many terrorists in Northern Ireland have evolved into OCGs, there are still some who are active terrorists. They have not followed the peace process. They still have political motivations and appear to be prepared to deal with OCGs on a transnational basis. In 2008 a Real Irish Republican Army (RIRA) member was arrested in Lithuania attempting to purchase firearms and explosives illegally from an undercover officer posing as an arms dealer. Such arms-purchasing nexuses also existed prior to the peace process. During the 1990s, loyalist terrorists from Northern Ireland became part of a nexus with an OCG in England. Firearms originating from the English OCG were recovered from loyalist terrorists. These included Uzi submachine guns, which had been purchased, deactivated, from an international arms dealer and then illegally reactivated and sold on the criminal market. An alleged Al Qaeda–influenced terrorist, operating in the United Kingdom and Bangladesh, used the same OCG as a source of firearms.

Al Qaeda is made up of a number of terrorist groups that operate independently but are influenced by religious fanaticism fueled by the preaching of the core leadership group, based in Afghanistan and Pakistan. Al Qaeda located its base in Afghanistan during the war with the Russians, who invaded the country in 1979. They fought alongside Afghan guerrillas, the mujahideen, who were supported by the United States; however, that

support was withdrawn when Russia withdrew from Afghanistan. The communist regime, left in power by the Russians, collapsed and the Taliban became the new rulers of Afghanistan. They allowed Al Qaeda leaders, including Osama bin Laden, to remain in the country. Al Qaeda then began to promote terrorism against their new enemy, the United States and its allies. The United States had angered many Muslims by using Saudi Arabia as a base to invade Iraq.

Forces led by the North Atlantic Treaty Organization (NATO) invaded Afghanistan following the terrorist attacks on the United States on September 11, 2001 (9/11), with the intention of dismantling the Al Qaeda terrorist organization and replacing the Taliban regime. However, even though some of their leaders were killed and others dispersed to remote regions of neighboring Pakistan, the Taliban and Al Qaeda remain as insurgents in Afghanistan fighting NATO forces. Al Qaeda fighters are not known to take a direct part in drug smuggling. However, the Taliban, who harbor Al Qaeda and who fight alongside members of Al Qaeda, raise funds for their fight by working in partnership with criminal groups in Afghanistan. They protect the transnational drug trade and keep open the heroin-smuggling routes out of the country.

Al Qaeda influence is global, as the leaders are able to preach through the media and the Internet. Many terrorists, acting in groups or alone, follow the teachings of the Al Qaeda leadership and take unilateral terrorist action. Although Al Qaeda leaders do not promote links with OCGs, many terrorists who follow their cause have to fund their terrorist acts by committing transnational crimes because they do not receive direct funding from the leadership. Because they do not receive direct supplies from the Al Qaeda leadership, they purchase firearms and explosives from OCGs. One such terrorist group that is influenced by Al Qaeda is Al Qaeda in Islamic Maghreb. They are developing a nexus that allows the transportation of cocaine through West and North Africa, where they operate. That cocaine originates from Colombia, where it is under the control of a terrorist group native to Colombia, the Revolutionary Armed Forces of Colombia (FARC), and it is destined for Europe, where it will be distributed by transnational OCGs.

The FARC have taken control of a large part of the cocaine business in the areas of Colombia that they control. They started by "taxing" those involved in the cocaine trade before eventually taking control of the OCGs involved, including their transnational drug-supply operations. To keep themselves supplied with weapons and other provisions, the FARC deal with various OCGs from eastern Europe and Jordan. In particular, they have worked with Croatian arms dealers. It is alleged that while the Provisional IRA (PIRA) in Northern Ireland was still active, it trained FARC members in handling explosives and firearms. In return, the FARC paid for a shipment of arms to PIRA from Croatian arms dealers using drugs supplied from Colombia.

Three transnational crimes are prevalent in crime-terror nexuses: drug dealing, arms dealing, and money laundering. The drug business generates large profits for OCGs and is seen as an easy source of income for terrorists who "tax" the dealers, or protect shipments in return for a share of the profits. Terrorists need firearms and explosives to commit acts of terror and OCGs see a good profit in supplying them to the terrorists. The profit from dealing in drugs and arms and the actual deals themselves need to be hidden by way of money laundering. Without access to money, terrorists and OCGs cannot operate. As most of their money cannot be declared as legitimate income, it has to be hidden or made to look legitimate. In the case of financing a terrorist act, the intended use of the money has to be disguised. Those who launder money and the methods used, such as hawala banking, form nexuses in themselves as they launder money for both terrorists and OCGs.

There are a number of reasons for when, why, and how nexuses between transnational crime and terrorism are formed. They include the lack of law and order in a particular fragile or corrupt state, the signing of peace accords that leads some terrorists to turn to organized crime to make a profit, the displacement and prioritization by law enforcement, the reduction in state sponsoring of terrorism, OCGs taking up a terrorist cause, terrorists exploiting easy profits made from transnational criminal activity, and terrorists purchasing firearms from OCGs because they have no other source. Generally, however, the nexus between transnational crime and terrorism involves nexuses between terrorists and OCGs formed because the terrorists have a need for what the OCG can supply: resources to further their cause. Usually those resources constitute equipment, such as arms and explosives, or money to purchase the equipment. The supply is then made either willingly, by donation of OCG profits to the cause or because the OCG sees a profit in the deal, or unwillingly, when the OCG is coerced into paying the terrorists so they can operate. Occasionally terrorists will commit their own transnational crimes, separate from the ultimate terrorist act. This activity, again, will be to meet their need for resources, such as money, and can include their own drug-smuggling explosives-smuggling operations.

There are those who argue that the crime-terror nexus is uncertain. However, the examples that have been given here from just three countries, together with a short analysis of the crimes involved and when, why, and how the nexuses are formed, show that the nexus is certain. Although there is no one global nexus of transnational crime and terrorism, there are clearly a number of individual nexuses that exist between transnational crime and terrorism.

Richard Severns
Sheffield Hallam University

See also Al Qaeda; Antiterrorist Financing; Cocaine; Drug Trade: Source, Destination, and Transit Countries; Failed States; Globalization; Heroin; Money Laundering: Countermeasures; Money Laundering: History; Money Laundering: Methods; Money Laundering: Targeting Criminal Proceeds; Money Laundering: Vulnerable Commodities and Services; Narco-Terrorism; Organized Crime: Defined; Terrorism: Defined; Terrorism: Domestic; Terrorism: Nondomestic; Transnational Crime: Defined; Weapons Smuggling

Further Readings

Clarke, Ryan and Stuart Lee. "The PIRA, D-Company, and the Crime Terror Nexus." *Terrorism and Political Violence*, v.20 (2008).
Harfield, Clive. "The Organization of Organized Crime Policing and Its International Context." *Criminology and Criminal Justice*, v.8/4 (2008).
Levi, Michael. "Organised Crime and Terrorism." In *The Oxford Book of Criminology*, Mike Maguire et al., eds., 4th ed. New York: Oxford University Press, 2007.
Makarenko, Tamara. "The Crime–Terror Continuum: Tracing the Interplay Between Transnational Organised Crime and Terrorism." *Global Crime*, v.6/1 (2004).
Rollins, John. "International Terrorism and Transnational Crime: Security Threats, U.S. Policy, and Considerations for Congress." http://www.fas.org/sgp/crs/terror/R41004.pdf (Accessed February 2011).

TOBACCO SMUGGLING

Tobacco smuggling can be defined as the clandestine importation of tobacco products from one jurisdiction to another. Tobacco smuggling includes the evasion of excise, customs, and sales taxes. Price disparities and differential taxation levels determine the likelihood of tobacco smuggling. Tobacco smuggling goes hand in hand with taxation systems and can be found whenever revenue duties are imposed. While no reliable estimate of the annual market value of smuggled cigarettes exists, some sources say the figure would be in excess of US$50 million. This is an economic and political reality that cannot be dissociated from tax laws and the development of national economies.

The illicit trade in tobacco products is one of the most profitable types of smuggling. The World Health Organization (WHO) has estimated that smuggling accounts for almost 12 percent of the nearly 6 trillion cigarettes sold around the globe each year, or about 657 billion cigarettes each year, which comes to roughly $40.5 billion of lost revenue annually.

Incentives for Tobacco Smuggling

The three major types of taxes levied on tobacco products consist of excise, customs, and sales taxes. Excise taxes are levied on tobacco products produced within a country. The excise tax is considered an indirect one, as the manufacturer or seller usually pays the tax and passes it on to buyers by raising purchase prices. Excise taxes can be collected from tobacco producers, manufacturers, wholesalers, importers, and retailers. This is a highly predictable and easily administered revenue source. It is also a more difficult tax to evade. Value-added taxes on tobacco products are typically collected at several points along the production process and thus are inherently more difficult to administer. Most jurisdictions impose sales taxes on the retail price; purchases on Native American reservations and online attempt to evade sales taxes. A custom duty is a tax or tariff placed usually on the importation, or rarely on the exportation, of tobacco products.

The profits potentially available to tobacco smugglers are dependent upon the differences between what they pay for tobacco products versus what they can sell them for. The greatest profit potential is in obtaining tax-free tobacco products and selling them in highly taxed and high-cost jurisdictions, but this strategy bears the greatest legal risks and usually necessitates high capital investments and large-scale operations. It is substantially less risky to purchase tobacco products in low-taxed jurisdictions and then transport them to more highly taxed ones, preferably with high purchase prices as well. Large price disparities between countries stimulate transnational smuggling.

Different governmental policies also contribute to tobacco smuggling. European Union laws, for instance, stipulate that the taxes on cigarettes must account for at least 70 percent of the retail price. Several countries have severe restrictions on the importation of tobacco products, such as quotas, tariffs, and other nontariff barriers. These practices lead to restrictions on availability, which results in price differentials; this fosters more incentive to engage in smuggling.

Measuring Tobacco Smuggling

Several methods have been used to measure tobacco smuggling. One approach relies on monitoring the producers and manufacturers of tobacco products; discrepancies between the volume of tobacco products produced and that reported legally sold suggest the degree of smuggling. Another tactic is to study tobacco users directly and query them as to how they obtained their tobacco products. Yet another method is to monitor the exporting and importing of tobacco products; analysis of these data, particularly at a transnational level, can indicate the amount of smuggling. Globally it has been observed that total tobacco exports reported exceed the amount of imports reported. The tobacco industry has been implicated for being in collusion with transnational crime organizations involved in smuggling. Since 1997, researchers have demonstrated that, comparing global cigarette exports with imports, about one third of all cigarettes entering global commerce annually could not be accounted for. This in-transit diversion accounts for wholesale smuggling but does not include bootlegging, cross-border shopping, and related activities. Another method is to compare reported sales of tobacco products with estimates of consumption, which can be obtained from survey data or by means of economic inference, such as regression analyses. It is estimated that tobacco smuggling accounts for between 6 and 10.7 percent of global cigarette use.

Efforts to Control Tobacco Smuggling

In 1794, Alexander Hamilton, the first secretary of the Treasury, introduced the first U.S. federal excise tax on tobacco, but it was soon repealed. The U.S. Congress on July 1, 1862, passed an excise tax on tobacco to help raise revenue to pay for the costs of the Civil War. In 1921, Iowa became the first U.S. state to impose a state excise tax on tobacco; other states soon followed this example. Some municipalities impose their own excise taxes on tobacco as well.

In 1978, the U.S. Congress passed the Contraband Cigarette Act (Public Law 95-575), which deemed as illegal shipments or purchases of more than 60,000 cigarettes that did not having the appropriate tax stamps for the state in question. In February 2005, the World Health Organization's Framework Convention on Tobacco Control took effect. President Barack Obama signed into law two major pieces of legislation impacting tobacco smuggling. On February 4, 2009, he signed the Children's Health Program Reauthorization Act (Public Law 111-3), which raised the federal excise tax on tobacco products to help subsidize healthcare for impoverished children. On March 31, 2010, he signed the Prevent All Cigarette Trafficking Act, intended to strengthen enforcement efforts against cigarette smuggling; it includes provisions prohibiting the U.S. Postal Service from delivering most types of tobacco products.

Tobacco smugglers, in addition to the risks of fines and possible imprisonment, often incur higher operating costs than those involved in legal commerce—other than, of course, paying the tax burden. In order to avoid detection, tobacco smugglers often must travel by more circuitous and less scrutinized routes. They often must pay extra costs to hide their products, as well as typically having to bribe customs officers and other authorities. These additional types of expenses have to be offset by the profit differentials between their cargo and that of legal operators. Policy makers can create conditions that would reduce the returns potentially available to tobacco smugglers, or else they can increase those for legal operations; either approach would likely reduce smuggling.

Tobacco smuggling makes less expensive tobacco products available, which directly results in higher levels of consumption and, in turn, leads to greater amounts of tobacco-related disease and death. This smuggling also circumvents various tobacco control policies intended to reduce use, such as those intended to curb consumption by youth. Reducing tobacco smuggling has been shown to result in increases in tax revenues and improved health. The stopping of tobacco smuggling globally now would immediately give governments at least $31 billion; and, from 2030 onward it would save more than 160,000 lives annually. Evidence also suggests that the illegal tobacco trade is conducted mainly by transnational criminal organizations, which use the proceeds to fund other criminal activities, including terrorist operations. The U.S. Bureau of Alcohol, Tobacco, Firearms and Explosives has found numerous cases of illicit cigarette trafficking linked to terrorist organizations such as Hamas, Hezbollah, and Al Qaeda. It is also believed that tobacco-smuggling rates are related to the level of corruption tolerated in respective countries.

Recommendations to Curtail Tobacco Smuggling

Many strategies have been suggested to curtail tobacco smuggling around the globe. High on any such list should be efforts to track and trace tobacco products. This approach could facilitate the identification of points along the supply chain where tobacco products are diverted from the legal to the illicit market. Such points could then be more directly targeted by legislative and enforcement efforts. Tobacco manufacturers must be encouraged to maintain better control of the supply chains for their products, with far stiffer penalties imposed upon those who fail to do so, including that they be liable for any unpaid taxes and duties on confiscated products. It has been suggested that licensing and other techniques to monitor and control the behavior of various parties along the supply and distribution chains for tobacco products be established. As long as there are financial incentives to the tobacco industry and insufficient disincentives, it should not be expected that efforts to curtail tobacco smuggling will be highly effective. Finally, it is recommended that law-enforcement and other mechanisms of international cooperation, such as conventions and protocols pertaining to the investigation and prosecution of transgressions, should be enhanced. Moreover, the establishment of more mutual legal assistance and extradition arrangements would reinforce the efficacy of international efforts directed at the illicit tobacco trade, including the manufacturing of both genuine tobacco products and those that are counterfeited.

Summary

Every year, about 6.6 billion cigarettes, which is more than one third of all cigarettes exported legally, are smuggled across global borders illegally. In fact, cigarettes are the most commonly smuggled legal consumer product in the world. Tobacco smuggling is fundamentally a criminal endeavor to avoid payment of tobacco taxation. This includes crimes to avoid excise taxes on tobacco products, which are collected primarily from tobacco producers; crimes to avoid customs taxes, which are collected mainly from tobacco distributors; and crimes to avoid sales taxes, which are collected primarily from tobacco retailers. Transnational tobacco smuggling is conducted primarily in the form of wholesale smuggling and is carried out mainly by transnational organized criminal organizations, several of which are linked to terrorist organizations. Bootlegging of tobacco products is conducted mainly along jurisdictional borders and does not require the organizational capabilities of wholesale tobacco smuggling.

Victor B. Stolberg
Essex County College

See also Legal and Illegal Economies; Sales Tax; Tariff Crimes

Further Readings

Jha, Prabhat and Frank J. Chaloupka. *Curbing the Epidemic: Governments and the Economics of Tobacco Control.* Washington, DC: World Bank, 1999.

Joossens, Luk, David Merriman, Hana Ross, and Martin Raw. *How Eliminating the Global Illicit Cigarette Trade Would Increase Tax Revenue and Save Lives.* Paris: International Union Against Tuberculosis and Lung Disease, 2009.

Merriman, David, Ayda Yurekli, and Frank J. Chaloupka. "How Big Is the Worldwide Cigarette Smuggling Problem?" In *Tobacco Control in Developing Countries*, Prabhat Jha and Frank J. Chaloupka, eds. Geneva: Oxford Medical Publications, 2000.

Thachuk, Kimberley L. *Transnational Threats: Smuggling and Trafficking in Arms, Drugs, and Human Life.* Westport, CT: Praeger Security International, 2007.

Van Duyne, P. C. and Georgios Antonopoulos. *The Criminal Smoke of Tobacco Policy Making: Cigarette Smuggling in Europe.* Nijmegen, Netherlands: Wolf Legal Publishers, 2009.

TOXIC DUMPING

Transnational toxic dumping involves the disposal of hazardous waste materials across national borders. These must be handled, stored, transported, and disposed of in a controlled manner. Typically, hazardous wastes are poisonous by-products of commerce and industrial manufacturing industries, which are harmful to humans, animals, and plant life in both the short and long terms. Hazardous wastes can be liquid, solid, or sludge, containing chemicals, heavy metals, radiation, dangerous pathogens, or other toxins. Additionally, the rapid emergence of global communication information technology has led to a growth in the last two decades of electronic waste, or e-waste: unwanted mobile phones, computers, and other electronic devices. If these are not disposed of properly, the chemicals in their components can poison natural habitats and kill wildlife.

This entry outlines how developed countries such as the United States, European nations, and Japan engage in waste dumping in landfill sites located mainly in developing Third World countries. Efforts to regulate the toxic dumping trade by the international community through the Basel Convention on the Control of Transboundary Movements of Hazardous Wastes and Their Disposal (1992) are outlined. It is noted that critics have argued that further cooperation is needed between member states to ensure that humans, animals, and natural environments are protected from illegal toxic dumping.

The management of toxic waste at a transnational level is inextricably linked to the nature of the relationship between the developed and developing world. It is estimated that between 500 and 600 million metric tons of toxic waste are discharged globally each year, the vast majority of which is produced by developed nations. The biggest exporter of toxic waste is the United States, and the most common destination is developing countries, such as India, Nigeria, Somalia, the Ivory Coast, and the Philippines. There are two reasons for this. First, within developed countries such as the United States and the United Kingdom, increasing public awareness of environmental issues and the dangers posed by toxic waste has increasingly led governments to export it to landfill sites abroad so it is "out of sight and out of mind," as well as introducing strict disposal regulations within their borders, which have made the disposal of toxic waste more expensive. Second, and related to this, poorer countries burdened by massive foreign debt find it financially attractive to offer their land as dumping sites for toxic and other forms of waste at a highly competitive business rate. Consequently, it can cost anywhere between $1,000 and $2,000 to dispose of a ton of toxic waste in the United States, but it can cost one tenth of that in a developing nation. For example, Japan currently exports a high proportion of its toxic waste to the Philippines, as it is significantly cheaper to do so than to treat that waste and dispose of it at home in accordance with its own environmental laws.

It has been noted that the legal trade in waste disposal is widespread and growing. It is argued that so-called dirty industries and dirty waste have been

The National Oceanic and Atmospheric Administration (NOAA) tested fish, water, and sediment samples in the Gulf of Mexico following Hurricane Katrina to determine the level of fish, water, and sediment exposure to pesticides and other contaminants, such as PCBs and DDTs. (NOAA)

transferred to the Third World by the processes of globalization since the 1980s. For example, plastic waste from Europe and the United States is buried in Egypt's Sahara Desert, and French and German radioactive waste is increasingly being disposed of in African countries such as the Ivory Coast. Illegal trade in toxic dumping is also on the increase. For example, one investigation into 17 European seaports examining more than 3,000 shipping certificates and documentation, as well as nearly 300 cargo holds, and found that 50 percent of the waste shipped abroad was illegal toxic waste.

A growing form of toxic waste is e-waste from computers and communications devices such as cellular phones. These contain chemical toxins such as mercury and lead, which can poison waterways, killing both human beings and livestock if not disposed of appropriately. A 2006 report by the United Nations (UN) Environment Programme estimated that 50 million tons of e-waste are generated globally on a yearly basis, most of which finds its way to landfill sites in the developing world, particularly in Nigeria.

Toxic dumping in developing countries may be favored by many developed world nations, but it has been argued by environmental campaigners and scientists that these countries are frequently vulnerable to environmental disaster brought about by toxic dumping, typically as a result of a mixture of local corruption and poorly resourced national regulatory and enforcement systems. For example, in 2006 more than 600 tons of toxic caustic soda and petroleum residues—which should have been securely dumped underground but instead had been dumped in the open at approximately a dozen public waste sites as well as a nearby ocean surrounding the city of Abidjan in the Ivory Coast—caused the deaths of at least 16 people, the hospitalization of more than 70 others, and more than 100,000 of the city's 5 million inhabitants needing medical attention. Cases such as these have led the African Union to argue that African nations lack the technology and financial means to address the problems generated by waste disposal, and they therefore require the help of developed nations, such as the United States and European countries.

Currently, transnational trade in toxic dumping is regulated by the 1992 Basel Convention on the Control of Transboundary Movements of Hazardous Wastes and Their Disposal. The Basel

Convention has been signed by 160 nations. The purpose of the Basil Convention is to control the import and export of hazardous waste. Items are shipped both nationally and internationally under one of three "lists." Green List items are categorized as nonhazardous and typically are shipped for commercial or recycling purposes. These do not require appropriate Basel Convention paperwork. Amber List items are mixed-material items that contain both nonhazardous and hazardous parts and can be manufactured or biological in nature. Shipping these items requires appropriate paperwork for transport between nations that be completed by each country's environmental and shipping authorities prior to movement. The Red List consists of solely hazardous materials. Shipping of these items internationally must follow a strict protocol developed by experts, and it is strictly illegal to move such items between nation-states without appropriate movement documentation.

A key aim of the Basel Convention is to make legal transnational movements of hazardous wastes for toxic dumping fully transparent for all parties involved and to leave a documentary audit trail to enable third-party investigation if need be. The transportation of toxic materials under the Basel Convention must be justifiable in terms of environmental safety and economic efficiency. This is particularly important, as sophisticated technologies are often required to dispose of some toxic materials. However, the Basel Convention has been criticized for failing to end illegal toxic dumping and failing to restrict the movement of toxic waste from developed to developing nations. It is argued by some commentators that scientific research and environmental disasters brought about by illegal and legal toxic dumping reinforce the need to ban the movement of all hazardous waste between developed and developing nations. Some scientists have even gone as far as to argue that if toxic dumping in developing nations continues, it will be impossible to create sustainable global solutions to address environmental climate change.

However, it is equally arguable that the Basel Convention has led to the introduction of a rigorous monitoring system, which, although it has not completely wiped out illegal toxic dumping, has nevertheless reduced it and furthermore has led nation-states to introduce more recycling technology within their borders as well as taking positive action to dispose of toxic waste more responsibly.

John Martyn Chamberlain
Loughborough University

See also Pollution: Air and Water

Further Readings

Bridgland, F. *Europe's New Dumping Ground: Fred Bridgland Reports on How the West's Toxic Waste Is Poisoning Africa.* 2006. http://www.ban.org/ban_news/2006/061001_dumping_ground.html (Accessed October 2010).

Chi, N. *Poor Countries Bear the Brunt of Toxic Burden.* 2006. http://vietnamnews.vnagency.com.vn/Opinion/Outlook/160116/Poor-countries-bear-brunt-of-toxic-burden.html (Accessed October 2010).

Iafrica.com. *West Should Pay for Ruining Africa.* 2007. http://www.iafrica.com/news/sa/752001.htm (Accessed October 2010).

Orloff, K. and F. Henry. "An International Perspective on Hazardous Waste Practices." *International Journal of Hygiene and Environmental Health*, v.206/4 (2003).

Schmidt, C. "Environmental Crimes: Profiting at the Earth's Expense." *Environmental Health Perspectives*, v.112/4 (2004).

Stinus-Remonde, M. "Mission Impossible: Address Our Serious Waste Problems First." *The Manila Times* (October 31, 2006).

United Nations Environment Programme. *Call for Global Action on E-Waste.* New York: Author, 2006.

White, R. "Toxic Cities: Globalising the Problem of Waste." *Social Justice*, v.35/3 (2008).

TRANSITIONAL JUSTICE

Transitional justice is a unique form of justice. It is implemented in societies changing forms of government and recovering from massive human rights violations. The concept was used in the late 1980s and the 1990s to describe the transitions occurring in eastern Europe and South Africa. Communism disintegrated in eastern Europe, and South Africa ended apartheid and became a democratized state. The question was what to do with the perpetrators of mass human rights violations over the previous 50–75 years. In order for South Africa to successfully transition, it had to reconcile its past through forgiveness or punishment. Hence, it had to complete a process of transitional justice.

The term *transitional justice* is often used to describe methods of justice put in place after a society has experienced extraordinary events, including, but not limited to, genocide, crimes against humanity, armed conflict, and revolutions. Several methods can be used to achieve transitional justice, including criminal prosecutions, truth and reconciliation commissions, memorialization efforts, reparations, gender justice, and security reform. Often the phrase "There can be no peace without justice" refers to criminal prosecutions. Victims who have lost family to genocide or have otherwise suffered oppression often demand that perpetrators be punished. Criminal prosecutions are the best means of imposing punishment; however, the prosecutions have to live up to international standards. This means that the accused must be treated according to minimum standards of due process, which are found in the United Nations' (UN's) Universal Declaration of Human Rights and the International Covenant on Civil and Political Rights, as well as many other authoritative international legal documents. Minimum standards of due process include the right to a defense attorney and the right to be judged by a competent and fair tribunal established by law.

Competent criminal tribunals include national criminal courts, international criminal courts, multinational criminal courts, or internationalized criminal courts. The International Criminal Tribunal at Nüremberg prosecuted 22 Nazis following World War II and imposed punishments on those convicted. According to Principle 5 of the 1950 Nüremberg Principles, anyone charged with an international crime has the right to a fair trial. It is believed that the prosecution of Nazis at Nüremberg contributed to the democratization of West Germany after World War II. The International Criminal Tribunal for the Far East, which prosecuted Japanese war criminals after World War II, decided not to prosecute the emperor of Japan. It was believed that prosecuting the emperor would result in subsequent hostilities by Japanese citizens. However, the position of emperor was stripped of significant power. This form of selective prosecution remains extremely controversial, but it allowed for smoother and more successful transitional justice.

National and internationalized criminal courts are the best forums for prosecutions since they allow justice to be institutionalized at the national level. As a result, victims, and the larger community as a whole, achieve justice within the victimized community. Article 6 of the Convention for Prevention and Punishment of the Crime of Genocide states that persons charged with genocide shall be prosecuted by a competent tribunal of the state in the territory in which the crime was committed or by an international penal tribunal. The current International Criminal Court requires that the state have the opportunity to achieve justice, and only if the state is either unable or unwilling to prosecute will the International Criminal Court's jurisdiction be triggered. Transitional justice is best achieved at the local level.

Alternatives to criminal prosecutions are truth and reconciliation commissions. The most popular commission was the South African Truth and Reconciliation Commission, established in 1995. After 40 years of apartheid, the attempt to prosecute all perpetrators of human rights abuses was a daunting task. Therefore, the Truth and Reconciliation Commission was established to allow the country to deal with the human rights abuses in the hope of enabling it to reconcile past wrongs. To earn amnesty, which was limited to political offenses, people accused of crimes must apply for it, honestly admit their offenses, and show remorse. The commission ultimately decides who is granted amnesty.

Another common method of achieving transitional justice is through memorialization efforts. Establishing memorials (such as monuments, plaques, or statues set in public gardens or parks) enables the crimes and their victims to be acknowledged and remembered in history. Too often throughout history, atrocities and victims have been forgotten. Memorialization can surpass memorials and include museums, which house artifacts (photographs, films, literature, testimonies of victims, and other social artifacts) surrounding the atrocities and other crimes that occurred during armed conflict. Museums not only allow victims to heal and to acknowledge the events of the past but also record history for the national and even world populace, offer resources for historians and other researchers, and help ensure that the crimes of the past will be understood in context and not repeated.

Harry M. Rhea
Richard Stockton College of New Jersey

See also International Criminal Court; War Crimes

Further Readings

Bassiouni, M. Cherif. *Post-Conflict Justice*. New York: Transnational, 2002.

Forst, Rainer. *Transnational Justice and Democracy*. Frankfurt am Main, Germany: Goethe-Universität Institut für Philosophie, 2011.

Jackson, Donald W., Michael Carlton Tolley, and Mary L. Volcansek. *Globalizing Justice: Critical Perspectives on Transnational Law and the Cross-Border Migration of Legal Norms*. Albany: State University of New York Press, 2010.

Reichel, Philip L. *Handbook of Transnational Crime and Justice*. Thousand Oaks, CA: Sage, 2005.

Roht-Arriaza, Naomi. *The Pinochet Effect: Transnational Justice in the Age of Human Rights*. Philadelphia: University of Pennsylvania Press, 2005.

TRANSNATIONAL CRIME: DEFINED

Before any topic can be adequately understood, it must be defined. There are many different ways of defining a term, which include explaining it, providing a demonstration of it, and experiencing it. In most academic fields, explanation is the most common way to define a concept (although in the natural sciences the preferred method is demonstration through experimentation). Transnational crime contains two distinct concepts: the adjective *transnational* and the noun *crime*.

Crime, as a practical matter, is relatively easy to define. Crime is generally considered to be a violation of a law, enacted by a legitimate sovereign political authority, prohibiting certain behavior for the protection of society, individuals, property, and government, the violation of which may be punishment by fines, probation, imprisonment, death, or a combination of these. The criminal law in question can either mandate or prohibit certain activities. Prohibition of an activity is the most common form of criminal law. The primary source of criminal law in most of the world is usually government, which

can create laws by legislative acts, administrative rule making, or judicial decisions. Although there are other sources of law, such as the philosophical concept of natural law or the theological concept of divine law, only enacted or accepted law as it relates to the social, economic, and political activities of humankind are employed when defining transnational law.

The term *transnational* is somewhat more difficult to define. Transnational contains two basic parts: the prefix *trans* and the root word *national*. National refers to the basic independent political unit in the world, that is, a particular country or nation-state. *Trans* usually denotes "above," "over," or "beyond." Thus the term transnational refers to a phenomenon that goes beyond what is national.

Although it would appear that transnational is synonymous with international, it is not, especially in the context of crime and law. The difference will be demonstrated by examining both law, which defines crime, and the nature of various crimes themselves.

National law is law that is enacted by and enforced by a nation, generally within its own geographical boundaries. It is frequently referred to as domestic law. Each nation and, at least in the United States, its political subdivisions have their own criminal codes. However, many nations and especially smaller nations have only a national criminal code. In contrast, international law consists of generally accepted principles of law, treaties, and judicial decisions that are accepted by all nations and considered to be applicable to all nations, although in practice the more powerful nations occasionally ignore certain international laws. International law is generally not the statutes enacted by a single nation, although some of the more powerful nations try to impose their own domestic laws on other nations of the world. International law can be applied outside the borders of nations, such as for acts of piracy committed on the high seas.

International law can be considered to be a form of transnational law, or at least to have transnational effects, but transnational law is not international law. The difference is illustrated by the definition of transnational law.

Transnational law is law that has effects or is applied across national geographic borders. In other words, if a law is enacted in one nation and a violation of that law committed in that country can or will have an effect across a national political border, then that law is considered to be transnational. Thus, even a domestic law can be transnational if it is committed or has an effect across a national border. For example, when a person stands on one side of a national border and shoots and kills a person on the other side of that same border, transnational law will be applied, in that the law prohibiting murder in the perpetrator's home nation will have an effect on the application of law in the victim's nation. This illustration shows how a domestic law can be considered transnational.

However, there are numerous examples of crimes that, although domestic in nature, are committed across borders or otherwise have transnational effects. One of the more common examples is smuggling. Most if not all developed nations in the world have laws against smuggling. The primary purposes of these laws, at least in the past, were to ensure that import and export taxes (tariffs) were collected and to prevent illegal items from being brought into the country. Some of the more popular items smuggled into nations include drugs, human beings, stolen works of art, and certain types of weapons. Another frequently occurring transnational crime is the smuggling of human beings for slavery and forced prostitution. Thus, smuggling is an example of a transnational crime that is committed across a national border.

Other forms of transnational crime include tax evasion, computer crime, copyright infringement, and organized crime. Tax evasion becomes a transnational crime when citizens of one country attempt to hide money in foreign banks to avoid paying domestic taxes. Computer crime, such as hacking, becomes transnational when people from a foreign country attempt to hack into computer databases in a different country. Copyright infringement is a transnational problem when intellectual property (such as films, music, and books) copyrighted and manufactured domestically are copied overseas and then shipped over domestic borders for sale at a much cheaper price. In many countries, organized criminal enterprises, such as the Mafia or the South American drug cartels, are illegal. However, when they operate across national borders, their actions become transnational crimes. These crimes are generally not addressed by international law (although there have been a number of treaties enacted to address such transnational crimes) and usually trigger domestic laws, but they become transnational when they have effects in more than one nation or are committed across national borders.

There are few crimes that are recognized by international law. Generally, international criminal law addresses such crimes as crimes against peace (such as initiating a war of aggression), crimes against humanity (such as the murder of civilian populations in war, as opposed to individual homicides), genocide (the deliberate annihilation of particular ethnic, religious, or national group as such), and war crimes (such as the use of poison gas, human experimentation, and enslavement during war). These crimes obviously also fall within the definition of transnational crimes. One of the most important transnational crimes today is terrorism. Although terrorist activities are illegal in most if not all of the nations of the world, terrorism is becoming more recognized as an international crime, too.

In conclusion, transnational crimes are those crimes that are committed across national borders or have an effect in other nations. Whether a crime is transnational or not does not depend on whether it is enacted as international law and may be a matter of domestic law.

Wm. C. Plouffe Jr.
Independent Scholar

See also Cigarette Smuggling; Cocaine; Heroin; Human Smuggling; Marijuana or Cannabis; Sex Slavery; Tariff Crimes; Tax Evasion; Terrorism: Nondomestic; War Crimes; Weapons Smuggling

Further Readings

Carter, Barry and Phillip Trimble. *International Law.* Boston: Little, Brown, 1991.

Madsen, Frank. *Transnational Organized Crime.* New York: Routledge, 2009.

United Nations. Charter of the United Nations, Chapter XIV, Article 92, Statute of the International Court of Justice. http://www.un.org/en/documents/charter/chapter14.shtml (Accessed February 2011).

TRANSNATIONAL CRIME: RESEARCH CENTERS

In this entry no attempt has been made to identify all transnational research centers in the world. In an arbitrary fashion, centers in Italy, the Netherlands, Asia, the United States, Australia, and Canada were selected to illustrate the range of activities.

Transcrime

Transcrime is an Italian research center operated by the University of Trento and the Catholic University of Milan. Each institution operates a Transcrime office staffed with a research coordinator, a group of researchers, a secretariat, and other administrative staff. Both offices are under the direction of the center's founder, Ernesto U. Savona, professor of criminology at the University of Trento, where the main administrative office is based. The center engages in research and evaluation activities covering a range of transnational crimes and crime reduction strategies, and it also provides expertise and assistance. Transcrime is funded through local authorities, national bodies, government departments, international corporations, and the European Union.

The center was established in November 1994 by the University of Trento and then consisted of only four undergraduates from the Faculty of Law serving as research assistants under Savona. Transcrime subsequently expanded in January 2000 to become an interdepartmental research center, allowing staff to collaborate with other departments, such as law, economics, sociology, and social research, and human and social sciences. In January 2004, the center officially entered a collaborative partnership with the Catholic University of Milan; now both that institution and the University of Trento are responsible for the overall operations and activities of Transcrime. Eight members from both universities appointed to four-year terms make up the Executive Council, which convenes meetings regularly to review and approve the annual agenda, identify budgetary resources, manage internal operations, and elect the executive and associate directors.

The center takes an integrated multidisciplinary approach in conducting research and evaluation activities by incorporating expertise from fields such as criminology, law, economics, statistics, sociology, and psychology. Using a range of scientific methods, Transcrime pursues three major objectives: (1) to analyze crime trends at the local, national, and transnational levels; (2) to evaluate crime reduction strategies; and (3) to develop solutions for improving these, with a focus on those dealing with aspects of economic and organized crime that have transnational dimensions. This information is then used to provide expertise and assistance to various levels of government, in the formulation and implementation of legislative reforms, and to provide specialized training to staff working in justice, policing, and regulatory agencies.

Transcrime is particularly interested in researching corruption; business crime; cybercrime; organized crime; disorder, insecurity, and urban crime; migration and illegal immigration; fraud; child pornography; money laundering; terrorism; and human trafficking for purposes of exploitation. Similarly, in conducting research on controlling these crimes, Transcrime is concerned with evaluating the following areas of crime reduction: anti-money-laundering, crime-proofing, psychosocial prevention, situational crime prevention, seizure and confiscation of crime proceeds, business security, and urban security. Transcrime also provides technical assistance at the local, national, and international levels. To date, Transcrime has conducted more than 90 research projects in these areas.

Transcrime provides a range of other services. Annually, it sponsors a number of conferences, lectures, and seminars on key topics and concerns in the study of transnational crime, which are attended by researchers and policy makers alike. Transcrime is also home to the *European Journal on Criminal Policy and Research* and produces a range of other research and policy publications, which are available on the center's Website. In partnership with associated institutions, Transcrime in 2005 launched two academic degree programs: a two-year master of science in applied social science with a specialization in crime sciences and security technologies, and a three-year international Ph.D. in criminology. Both degrees aim to prepare graduates for careers in either research or practice.

Transnational Institute

Transnational Institute (TNI) is a research and policy think tank and international network of scholars and activists engaged in critical analysis of global problems, such as transnational crime, in order help support social movements seeking to improve society, whether democratically, equitably, or environmentally. TNI was originally established in 1963 in Washington, D.C., as the Institute for Policy Studies and in 1973 moved to Amsterdam, in the Netherlands, where its headquarters are currently based. Broadly, TNI centers its activities in the areas of contested cultures, drug policies, environmental justice, global economic justice, peace and security, and resistance and alternatives. A range of sources, which include the European Commission, international organizations, private foundations, governments, and churches, help finance the institute.

TNI is particularly interested in a number of areas of relevance to transnational crime. Since 1988, the institute has been engaged with reforming drug policy, for example, by responding to drug abuse with hard reduction initiatives and by providing key information, competing perspectives, and policy recommendations in other areas, such as on drugs and conflict and the War on Drugs. Other areas of interest include environmental crimes and justice, militarism and Islamic extremism, globalization and the War on Terror, human rights, and competition over natural resources. TNI does not engage in work on transnational organized crime, money laundering, tax evasion, transfer pricing, or terrorism and civil liberties, but it does provide resources pertaining to these topics on its Website.

ASEAN Center for Combating Transnational Crime

In 1999, the inaugural meeting of the Association of Southeast Asian Nations (ASEAN) Ministerial Meeting on Transnational Crime (AMMTC) adopted the ASEAN Declaration on Transnational Crime, pledging both regional and international cooperation to further the fight against transnational crime. The second meeting, the following June, established specific mechanisms and identified particular crimes of concern, including the trafficking of women and children. One such mechanism was the ASEAN Center for Combating Transnational Crime (ACTC), a research center to promote the sharing of information among agencies in ASEAN nations; act as a repository of information on jurisprudence, legislation, and regulations; and conduct analysis of transnational crime in the region.

In 2006, ASEAN's transnational crime-fighting efforts advanced with the launch of the electronic ASEAN Chiefs of Police database system, e-ADS, a Web-based database replacing an earlier and outmoded crime database.

Terrorism, Transnational Crime and Corruption Center

The Terrorism, Transnational Crime and Corruption Center (TraCCC) is a research center in the School of Public Policy at George Mason University (GMU), the first center in the United States devoted to the study of the links between, and the formulation of policy on, terrorism, transnational crime, and corruption. Established in 1998 at American University, the center moved to GMU in 2007.

Specific areas of study at TraCCC include transnational crime, corruption, human trafficking, weapons smuggling, money laundering, security, terrorism, illicit trade, drug trafficking, environmental crime, and the crime-terror nexus. Courses offered through GMU address illicit trade; international migration, global governance, and the knowledge economy; transnational crime; weapons of mass destruction; arms control policy; international police operations; and corruption and public policy. Much of TraCCC's research has been undertaken in former Soviet states and Turkey, working with specialists from around the world. The center operates study centers in Russia, Ukraine, and the Republic of Georgia. TraCCC hosts visiting scholars throughout the year, through programs such as the Open World Leadership Program and Fulbright fellowships. The Open World Leadership Program is sponsored by the U.S. Congress, and TraCCC hosts delegations from Russia through the program on economic development and antitrafficking initiatives.

Centre for Transnational Crime Prevention (CTCP)

Located at the University of Wollongong in NSW Australia, research at the Centre for Transnational Crime Prevention (CTCP) examines the nature of organized cross-border criminal activities that affect regional and global security, including terrorism, human trafficking, money-laundering, cybercrime, and identity fraud. CTCP researchers represent a variety of disciplines, and their work seeks to improve global understanding of the causes, dynamics, and manifestations of these threats and to address detection and prevention strategies for governments, law-enforcement agencies, and nongovernmental organizations. The center is founded on the idea that the jurisdictional, operational, legal, and political complexities of countering transnational crime demand a unique, multidisciplinary response. The CTCP is within the Faculty of Law and was established in 2000 by the University of Wollongong to tackle the increasing threat of transnational crime.

(Jack & Mae) Nathanson Centre on Transnational Human Rights, Crime and Security

Located within Osgoode Hall Law School at York University, the focus of the Nathanson Centre on Transnational Human Rights, Crime and Security is the development and facilitation of a cross-disciplinary program of research. The Nathanson Centre began in 1997 with a mandate that concentrated on organized crime and corruption. By 2006 it was clear that those two topics were interwoven with broader issues of human rights and security concerns. Their expanded mandate was thus to enhance knowledge of the variety of transnational phenomena that is rapidly changing (and challenging) society, law, and governance. By focusing on three thematic pillars—human rights, crime, and security—the center seeks out the relationships among them as informed by transnational perspectives.

Michael J. Puniskis
Middlesex University

See also Globalization; Nongovernmental Organizations; Transparency International

Further Readings

Emmers, R. "ASEAN and the Securitization of Transnational Crime in Southeast Asia." *The Pacific Review*, v.16/3 (2003).

Savona, E. U. "Crime Institute Profile: Transcrime, Research Group on Transnational Crime." *European Journal on Criminal Policy and Research*, v.5/1 (1997).

TRANSPARENCY INTERNATIONAL

Transparency International (TI) is a global nongovernmental organization (NGO) and international movement working to identify and tackle domestic and transnational corruption in public and private sectors. The NGO is a worldwide coalition created to bring together key people in order to raise public attention, diminish tolerance, and devise strategies to respond to corruptive practices and behavior. Established in May 1993 by founding chairman Peter Eigen and a group of individuals who shared a common vision and have personally experienced corruption, TI aims to provide a world free of corruption and one in which the daily lives of people and various aspects of society can operate free from the devastating and far-reaching effects of corruption.

With headquarters in Berlin, Germany, TI operates a global network of more than 90 nationally established chapters, along with others under formation in countries where society is allowed to operate freely. These branches help to research, monitor, and publicize instances of corruption in their respective regions, and their findings and activities are regularly disseminated through a variety of official reports and publications.

Specifically, the global priorities of TI are to fight corruption in a number of key areas that affect everyday life, such as politics, public contracting, government organizations and agencies, private-sector companies, and areas involving work in poverty and development. TI also plans international conventions and conferences on corruption and works with governments to help introduce anticorruption reform measures. The NGO does not investigate instances of corruption or expose individual cases; rather, TI staff work with key players in government, politics, and business, along with experts and other volunteer specialists, to promote transparency in political elections, public administration, and business practices. Additionally, TI staff devote attention and resources to rights to access information and public services, protecting and advancing rights, advocacy and legal advice, health and humanitarian assistance during global crises, corruption in sectors involving natural resources, defense and security, education and the judiciary, anticorruption education and training, and the recognition of leaders and protection of whistleblowers. Politically nonpartisan, TI focuses all its work on its mission of promoting the following values: transparency, accountability, integrity, solidarity, courage, justice, and democracy. The efforts of TI have helped to place corruption on the global agenda and have improved standards in public life across many countries.

The work of TI is funded through a number of donors in order to maintain independence from any particular source. The main financial support comes from governments, with other funds from international organizations, private companies, honoraria, and publications. Each national chapter of TI is supported independently through funds by governments and public agencies, corporate and individual donors, charitable foundations, membership fees, and judicially imposed monetary sanctions. Policies are also in place to ensure that only legitimate funds are received and used. For example, financial statements are regularly published on the TI Website in order to ensure full transparency with regard to funding from various donors, and contributions are therefore not accepted from any donor that refuses to be listed publicly or from any individual or organization known to have engaged in any form of corruption. Additionally, TI does not allow companies to publicize that they have donated and will not accept funds with certain conditions attached by the donor.

TI is governed in two ways. The overall organization is centrally managed by a board of directors who are elected by national chapters and individual members at annual membership meetings. Second, an advisory council made up of prominent individuals, such as presidents and prime ministers, judges, professors, and other government representatives, also helps to advise the movement. The international secretariat in Berlin has a mutually supportive relationship with TI's 90 nationally established chapters around the globe. The headquarters help to provide skills, training, and support through tools and techniques—for example, by disseminating information on best practices and new strategies to fight corruption. Although individual chapters have their own forms of governance, all staff associated with TI must abide by a statement of vision, values, and guiding principles that provide the ethical framework for the organization and staff; these can be modified by chapters in light of certain conditions. Additionally, TI has a conflict-of-interest policy and codes of conduct, both of which establish standards to eliminate situations in which personal interests of staff may appear to be in conflict with organizational aims and objectives.

TI has developed a number of methods to research corruption globally, nationally, and locally. In order to evaluate the perceived level of corruption within a number of countries, the Corruption Perceptions Index (CPI) was developed in 1995 to survey business people and analysts in 180 countries on their perceptions of corruption. While a useful tool, the CPI has been criticized because definitions of corruption may vary among those surveyed and methods have varied each year, making it difficult to compare results across years. The Bribe Payers Index (BPI) is a ranking of 30 industrialized exporting countries and their engagement in accepting bribes when operating abroad, based on responses from business people and analysts to the Executive Opinion Survey administered by the World Economic Forum. The Global Corruption Barometer (GCB) surveys public attitudes and experiences of corruption in public services and key institutions, along with views on government efforts in responding to corruption.

These—among other official reports, research studies, working papers, policy position papers, and expert briefs—are regularly published by TI in a number of languages, which are available on TI's Website and are utilized by a variety of stakeholders. TI's annual reports highlight various problems and situations in a number of areas subject to corruption around the globe, as well as recognizing efforts and achievements of national chapters.

Michael J. Puniskis
Middlesex University

See also Nongovernmental Organizations; Transnational Crime: Research Centers

Further Readings

Galtung, Fredrik and Jeremy Pope. "The Global Coalition Against Corruption: Evaluating Transparency International." In *The Self-Restraining State: Power and Accountability in New Democracies*, A. Schedler, L. Diamond, and M. F. Plattner, eds. Boulder, CO: Lynne Rienner, 1999.

Hongying, Wang and James Rosenau. "Transparency International and Corruption as an Issue of Global Governance." *Global Governance*, v.7/1 (2001).

Transparency International. "Annual Report 2009." http://www.transparency.org (Accessed October 2010).

U

UN CONVENTION AGAINST TRANSNATIONAL ORGANIZED CRIME

The UN Convention Against Transnational Organized Crime (UNCATOC) is the first global agreement to address organized crime comprehensively. With its three protocols, it provides an international legal framework to improve the enforcement of laws against organized crime, particularly through international cooperation. Although this legal framework is a remarkable step toward better action on organized crime, the key definition of *organized criminal group* provided by Article 2 is extremely broad and may result in the excessive expansion of the scope of these legal instruments. As a result, efforts and resources may be dispersed and not concentrated on the most serious forms of organized crime.

The process of elaboration of the convention started in the first half of the 1990s and lasted several years. The convention was adopted by the UN General Assembly on November 15, 2000, with General Assembly Resolution 55/25, along with two protocols: the Protocol to Prevent, Suppress and Punish Trafficking in Persons, Especially Women and Children (General Assembly Resolution 55/25 annex II, hereinafter referred to as the Trafficking Protocol) and the Protocol Against the Smuggling of Migrants by Land, Sea and Air (General Assembly Resolution 55/25 annex III, hereinafter the Smuggling Protocol). The convention and the two protocols were opened for signature in Palermo, Italy, on December 12–15, 2000. The convention entered into force on September 29, 2003; as of February 2011, it had 159 parties. The Trafficking Protocol entered into force on December 25, 2003; as of February 2011, it had 143 parties. The Smuggling Protocol entered into force on January 28, 2004; as of February 2011, it had 127 parties. On May 31, 2001, the General Assembly adopted a third protocol. The Protocol Against the Illicit Manufacturing of and Trafficking in Firearms, Their Parts and Components and Ammunition (General Assembly Resolution 55/255, annex, hereinafter the Firearms Protocol) entered into force on July 3, 2005, and, as of February 2011, had 83 parties.

The convention and the three protocols provide an innovative solution in international criminal law. Indeed, the convention not only has specific provisions on transnational organized crime but also is a "parent treaty" enabling nations to accede to the three protocols and providing a common legal framework for their implementation. Other protocols may be drafted, enlarging the scope of the current international legal framework dealing with transnational organized crime. The existing protocols cover specific offenses and related measures whose inclusion in the convention proved very controversial; consequently, the drafting of separate protocols was the preferred option.

The convention can be divided into the following parts: definitions and scope (Articles 1–4); criminalization of specific offenses and establishment of penalties (Articles 5–12 and Article 23); investigative measures and international cooperation (Articles 13–22 and 26–27); protection and assistance to victims (Articles 24 and 25); information sharing, training, technical assistance, economic development, and prevention of organized crime (Articles 28–31); and implementation and other technical issues (Article 32–41).

The main goal of the convention was to facilitate international cooperation against transnational organized crime. Indeed, the first priority was the adoption of a toolbox of measures to fight organized crime and to support international cooperation. Accordingly, the majority of the 41 articles of the convention deal with investigative measures and international cooperation.

The definition of organized crime and its criminalization proved from the beginning to be among the most difficult obstacles. Some negotiators even argued that a definition was not fundamental and that there was no stringent necessity for it. This controversy reflects the difficulties in achieving a consensus among different political and legal traditions. Nevertheless, the final text of the convention contains a definition of organized criminal groups and the requirement to criminalize the participation in an organized criminal group. The influence of the European Union has been important in achieving a consensus on these topics. Indeed, the final definition of an organized criminal group is consistent with the joint action on making it a criminal offense to participate in a criminal organization (98/733/JHA), adopted by the European Union in 1998, which contained a similar definition of a criminal organization.

Given the difficulties in achieving a consensus on the definition of organized crime and the lower priority of this issue compared to the enhancement of international cooperation, the definition resulted in the most controversial provision. Indeed, definitions inevitably impact the whole architecture of the convention and its protocols. The definition is provided by Article 2 of the convention, which defines the concepts of "organized criminal group," "serious crime," and "structured group."

An *organized criminal group* is a structured group of at least three persons, existing for a period of time and acting in concert for the commission of one or more serious crimes to obtain a financial or other material benefit. The requirements of the existence for a period of time and of action in concert are spelled out in generic terms. The aim

of a material benefit has been broadly interpreted, including, for example, pedopornographic material (child pornography).

A *serious crime* is an offense punished with at least four years of maximum security. This selection technique applies to nearly 160 countries. Arguably, the crimes falling within this threshold are likely to vary significantly among different countries and legal cultures. Furthermore, governments may increase or decrease penalties purposely to have some specific crimes labeled as those of organized criminal groups.

A *structured association* is not a randomly formed group for the immediate commission of a crime, but it does not need to be a complex organization with formal roles and continuity of affiliation. This definition does not provide any positive definitional element. Rather, it states only what a structured organization is *not*.

The foregoing concepts provide a very broad definition of organized crime, encompassing a number of different groups and crimes. The broadness of the definition inevitably reflects on the scope of the convention and its protocols, which may trigger the application of serious measures on minor criminal activities that have nothing to do with organized crime, contrasting with the general principles of criminal law. Furthermore, the overextension of the scope of the convention could jeopardize the effective enforcement of the most serious cases of organized crime, wasting important human and financial resources to tackle less dangerous cases.

Francesco Calderoni
Università Cattolica/Transcrime

See also Conventions, Agreements, and Regulations; Organized Crime: Defined; Transnational Crime: Defined; United Nations

Further Readings

Albrecht, Hans-Jörg and Cyrille Fijnaut, eds. *The Containment of Transnational Organized Crime: Comments on the UN Convention of December 2000.* Freiburg im Breisgau, Germany: Edition Iuscrim, 2002.

McLean, David. *Transnational Organized Crime: A Commentary on the UN Convention and Its Protocols.* Oxford, UK: Oxford University Press, 2007.

Schloenhardt, Andreas. *Palermo on the Pacific Rim: Organized Crime Offences in the Asia Pacific Region.*

Bangkok, Thailand: UN Office on Drugs and Crime, Regional Centre for East Asia and the Pacific, 2009.

United Nations Office on Drugs and Crime. *Legislative Guides for the Implementation of the United Nations Convention Against Transnational Organized Crime and the Protocols Thereto.* New York: United Nations, 2004.

United Nations Office on Drugs and Crime. *Travaux Préparatoires of the Negotiations for the Elaboration of the United Nations Convention Against Transnational Organized Crime and the Protocols Thereto.* New York: United Nations, 2006.

UNDERGROUND BANKING REGULATIONS

Underground banking (also commonly referred to as alternative remittance systems or informal value transfer systems) is the movement of money outside the network of banks and money transfer institutions that make up the formal banking system. The term *underground banking* does not necessarily denote illegal activity. Underground banking can provide a number of legitimate benefits, such as avoiding the unstable financial systems of some countries, getting money to people in remote areas, and avoiding the inefficiency and cost of moving money through formal financial systems. However, national governments are very much concerned about the use of underground banking channels to facilitate a wide range of illegal activities—particularly terrorism but also drug smuggling and cybercrime—and many have enacted regulatory frameworks to deal with individuals and organizations engaged in underground banking.

A classic example of an underground banking system is hawala, which emerged from Arabic-speaking countries. The hawala system is an informal method of transferring money whereby the money to be transferred never physically moves. This system, along with formal financial channels, was used to fund the terrorist attacks of September 11, 2001 (9/11). If person A in Saudi Arabia wishes to transfer US$10,000 to a person B in Indonesia, then the person in Saudi Arabia would approach a hawaladar (a hawala broker or operator) in that country to initiate the exchange. The hawaladar in Saudi Arabia would contact a hawaladar in Indonesia and have the Indonesian hawaladar give the equivalent of $10,000 to person B. The two hawaladars would collect some sort of fee for their services and settle the balance between themselves by transferring money via formal money transfer systems. As a result, the formal transfer occurs not between persons A and B but instead between the two hawaladars.

Informal value transfer systems (IVTSs) are legal in the United States but are subject to strict licensing and regulation requirements as a money-transmitting business (MSB). This increased scrutiny began in earnest after the role that underground banking played in the 9/11 attacks was discovered. When the United States passed the U.S.A. Patriot Act in 2001, it amended Section 5330 of the Bank Secrecy Act to implement regulations placing new requirements on anyone operating an MSB. An MSB is any operation that transmits money within the United States or a foreign country by wire, check, draft, fax, or courier, and all states and the federal government have licensing requirements to which these businesses must adhere. All MSBs must be registered in the state in which they operate and with the U.S. Financial Crimes Enforcement Network (FinCEN). They must also establish an anti-money-laundering program and comply with record-keeping and reporting requirements. If a person or group operates an MSB without a license, that entity is subject to punishment under the various state laws and Title 18, Section 1960 of the U.S. Code.

The United States also carries out bilateral training and technical assistance activities with countries in order to share training and expertise with foreign governmental officials, so that they will be able to analyze and regulate financial systems to determine if formal or informal value transfer systems are being used for money laundering and terrorist financing. These bilateral programs are carried out by various U.S. governmental entities, such as the Department of State, the Federal Bureau of Investigation (FBI), and FinCEN. In addition, the United States has mutual legal assistance treaties (MLATs) with numerous countries. These MLATs allow for the exchange of evidence and information that may be of use in criminal investigations.

Other countries followed the United States' lead in creating stricter regulations governing IVTSs after the 9/11 attacks. India is a country that has been familiar with the hawala system for years; it was used to finance operations carried out by Kashmiri terrorists. It is suspected that the terrorist attacks carried out in the Indian city Mumbai on November 26, 2008, were funded in part through hawala merchants. In 2003, the Indian government passed the Prevention of Money Laundering Act, which requires people engaging in money-transfer businesses to register with the government, maintain records of their transactions, and identify the people involved in those transactions. India also created a Financial Intelligence Unit to track financial channels and identify suspicious financial transactions that may relate to terrorism financing or other criminal activity.

Australia is another country that has implemented legislation to regulate underground banking. Again, the impetus behind these regulations is the concern that IVTSs, particularly the hawala system, might be used for terrorist financing. The primary legal mechanism for regulating underground banking in Australia is the Anti-Money-Laundering and Counter-Terrorism Financing Act (AML-CTF), passed in 2006. This law requires entities that engage in money-transfer activities to register with the government. It also requires that those registered entities verify the identity of their customers, keep records of transactions, implement counterterrorism and anti-money-laundering measures, and conduct ongoing due diligence and reporting with respect to their activities. All of this is overseen by the Australian Transaction Reports and Analysis Center (AUSTRAC), which acts as the financial intelligence unit for Australia.

Many other countries, along with the United States, India, and Australia, have some sort of regulatory framework in place related to IVTSs. The Financial Action Task Force (FATF) is an international, intergovernmental body that is seeking to encourage countries to adopt strict rules with relation to money laundering and terrorist financing, including underground banking channels. The FATF has made a special recommendation (Special Recommendation VI) for all countries to impose rules regulating financial channels operating outside formal financial networks.

Because of the attempts by countries to regulate underground banking, there are more robust and enforceable regulatory frameworks governing formal financial networks. As more regulations are passed to govern the movement of money through formal banking systems, underground banking networks will likely become more and more popular, which, in turn, is likely to lead many nations to increase their scrutiny of underground banking networks in the future.

Matthew C. Dahl
Independent Scholar

See also Antiterrorist Financing; Black Market Peso Exchange; Charities and Financing; Financial Action Task Force; Informal Value Transfer Systems; Money Laundering: Countermeasures; Money Laundering: History; Money Laundering: Methods; Money Laundering: Targeting Criminal Proceeds; Money Laundering: Vulnerable Commodities and Services; Mutual Legal Assistance Treaties

Further Readings

Australian Institute of Criminology. "Underground Banking: Legitimate Remittance Network or Money Laundering System." http://www.aic.gov.au/documents/ A/0/C/%7BA0C5EAE8-9D4A-4BD6-8B6D -C65F46C3FBE8%7Dtandi300.pdf (Accessed January 2011).

U.S. Department of the Treasury, Financial Crimes Enforcement Network. "FinCEN Advisory: Subject: Informal Value Transfer Systems." http://www.fincen .gov/news_room/rp/advisory/pdf/advis33.pdf (Accessed January 2011).

Vidyasagar, S. V. Adithya. "Financing of Terrorism, Hawala and the Law." http://lawlib.wlu.edu/lexopus/works/ 927-1.pdf (Accessed January 2011).

United Nations

The United Nations (UN) is the most prominent international organization for fighting transnational crime. This entry outlines the origins of the UN, the evolution of its conventions and protocols related to transnational crime, and the role of the UN Office on Drugs and Crime (UNODC). Also considered are some of the central debates about the effectiveness of the UN, particularly UNODC.

Origins and Overview

Established in June 1945, the UN is an intergovernmental organization comprising 192 member states.

During World War II, the Allied powers held a series of conferences to establish an organization that would undertake a role similar to that of the failed League of Nations, an organization that had been established to manage and preserve international peace and security. The UN Charter was signed in June 1945 by 51 state representatives, and it entered into force on October 24, 1945.

The charter identifies four main purposes of the UN:

- to keep peace throughout the world;
- to develop friendly relations among nations;
- to help nations work together to improve the lives of poor people, to conquer hunger, disease and illiteracy, and to encourage respect for each other's rights and freedoms; and
- to be a centre for harmonizing the actions of nations to achieve these goals.

The main bodies of the UN are the General Assembly, the Security Council, the Economic and Social Council, the International Court of Justice, the Trusteeship Council, the Secretariat, and the Repertory of Practice of United Nations Organs. The UN also comprises a range of specialized

A view of the United Nations (UN) General Assembly room at the UN headquarters in New York City. The main bodies of the UN are the General Assembly, the Security Council, the Economic and Social Council, the International Court of Justice, the Trusteeship Council, the Secretariat, and the Repertory of Practice of United Nations Organs. (Wikimedia)

agencies, funds, and programs, many of which are pertinent to the UN's work regarding transnational crime and justice.

The UN, Transnational Crime, and Justice

Although today a wide range of transnational criminal and justice issues fall under the UN's jurisdiction, initially the organization was concerned primarily with the international control of illicit drugs and psychotropic substances. The UN's role as the international organization responsible for controlling organized crime began in 1946, when it assumed control of the international drug control regime from the League of Nations at the Lake Success Protocol. It continued upon a Western (primarily U.S.-endorsed) trajectory that assumed a predominantly prohibitionist and punitive position rather than a medical and rehabilitative approach to the supply and consumption of illicit drugs. The Geneva Protocol of 1946 resulted in the creation of the Commission on Narcotic Drugs (CND) by the Economic and Social Council (ECOSOC) as the UN's primary policymaking body regarding illicit drugs.

The UN's current legal framework for dealing with illicit drugs is governed by three prominent conventions: the Single Convention on Narcotic Drugs of March 30, 1961; the Convention on Psychotropic Substances of February 21, 1971; and the UN Convention Against Illicit Traffic in Narcotic Drugs and Psychotropic Substances of December 19, 1988.

The 1961 Single Convention was significant because it standardized all extant multilateral treaties on illicit drug control and also included cannabis on the list of controlled substances; previous treaties had been confined to coca and opium and their derivatives, such as cocaine and heroin. The Permanent Central Board and Drug Supervisory Board were also merged under the convention to create the Narcotics Control Board (NCB). Growing international concern about the heightened use of psychotropic substances (in particular amphetamines, methamphetamines, and LSD) in the 1960s led to the international prohibition of these substances through the 1971 convention. The UN Fund for Drug Abuse and Control, later the UN Drug Control Program (UNDCP), was also established under the 1971 convention. The 1961 and 1971 conventions mandate the World Health

Organization (WHO) to recommend which new substances should be controlled and the extent to which they should be restricted. Finally, the 1988 convention complements the previous two conventions and deals primarily with the transnational problem of trafficking (as the previous two conventions dealt primarily with cultivation, supply, and consumption). According to the UN, this convention's objective is to create and consolidate international cooperation between law-enforcement bodies such as customs, police, and judicial authorities and to provide them with the legal guidelines to interdict illicit trafficking effectively, to arrest and try drug traffickers, and to deprive them of their ill-gotten gains.

In 1997, the UN Office on Drugs and Crime (UNODC) was established through the merger of the UNDCP and the International Centre for Crime Prevention. Although international drug control features significantly, UNODC's activities reflect a broader understanding of and approach to organized crime, as it deals with a range of transnational organized criminal and justice issues. According to UNODC, the three central pillars of its work program are field-based technical cooperation projects to enhance the capacity of member states to counteract illicit drugs, crime, and terrorism; research and analytical work to increase knowledge and understanding of drugs and crime issues and expand the evidence base for policy and operational decisions; and normative work to assist states in the ratification and implementation of the relevant international treaties, the development of domestic legislation on drugs, crime, and terrorism, and the provision of secretariat and substantive services to the treaty-based and governing bodies.

The UN's primary international instrument to deal with transnational organized crime was adopted on November 15, 2000, by the UN General Assembly in the form of the UN Convention Against Transnational Organized Crime. The convention, which came into force on September 29, 2003 (after it was opened to signatures from member states at the December 2000 Palermo Conference), is supplemented by three protocols adopted by the General Assembly. If a state wishes to be party to any or all of the protocols, it must also be party to the convention. The protocols are the Protocol to Prevent, Suppress and Punish Trafficking in Persons, Especially Women

and Children; the Protocol Against the Smuggling of Migrants by Land, Sea and Air; and the Protocol Against the Illicit Manufacturing of and Trafficking in Firearms, Their Parts and Components and Ammunition. According to the UN, the protocols are particularly significant because they constitute the first global, legally binding instruments that address trafficking in persons, migrants, and firearms. However, despite the UN's and the international community's commitment to mitigating transnational organized crime and upholding justice, the approach and effectiveness of the UN as the main international organization to fight transnational organized crime has been subject to question.

Globalization has dramatically altered the shape of serious and organized crime; hence, a far more complex form of transnational organized crime has emerged. Advances in technology have allowed criminal organizations and networks to take advantage of time-space compressions whereby they can easily communicate with one another over long distances between states and regions. Furthermore, the new international division of labor has resulted in a significant increase in land, air, and sea transport, affording criminal organizations ample logistical opportunities to traffic their illegal commodities (including people) around the world. Furthermore, the structures of these criminal networks are more fragmented and diffused and no longer emulate the traditional organizational structure of the Mafia crime groups. Contrary to past experience, efforts to cut off the proverbial head of a criminal organization have not resulted in its dissolution, because either the head is immediately replaced or the flatter structure of the organization means that there was no head in the first place. The second challenge for the international community, particularly the UN, is the increasingly dependent relationship between conflict and crime that has occurred since the New Wars phenomenon of the post–Cold War period. Increasingly, those crimes that are labor-intensive, such as the drug-cultivation component of drug trafficking, rely on countries and regions with vulnerable civilian populations that may be coerced (financially or physically) into participating in such elements of the transnational organized crime supply chain. Yet the orthodox approach to fighting organized crime does not take into account these new contexts, and the blanket objective of punishing all parties involved has resulted in the subjection of many innocent civilians to punitive measures.

The UN's orthodox approaches to fighting transnational organized crime have been criticized for thus far falling short of the mark. In response to growing concern from the international community and commentators about the UN's ability to mitigate transnational organized crime, UNODC released a document titled *The Globalization of Crime: A Transnational Organized Crime Threat Assessment* (*TOCTA*), its first comprehensive report on the problem of transnational organized crime. This report maps the nine main types of transnational organized crime—trafficking in persons, smuggling of migrants, heroin trafficking, cocaine trafficking, firearms trafficking, environmental resource trafficking, product counterfeiting, maritime piracy, and cybercrime—and has produced important empirical data about the nature of such illicit flows. UNODC has also reflected on the complexity of transnational organized crime itself and the global environment in which it operates; hence, the report calls for "new ways of looking at—and fighting—transnational organized crime" and a further inquiry into understanding transnational criminal markets.

TOCTA is considered demonstrative of the UN's willingness to adopt a new approach to fighting transnational organized crime so that its operations and functions may be more effective. However, some central criticisms remain regarding both UNODC's approach to metrics and the accuracy of its statistical data. First, questions have been raised about the appropriate way to prioritize types of crimes and their impacts, as this affects the distribution of resources and finances, as well as the formulation of policy. UNODC typically lists drug trafficking as its largest concern, because drugs generate the greatest amount of money per annum, whereas crimes such as conflict-mineral trafficking do not generate as much money and thus are not as high in priority. Some commentators argue that harms and violence should play a role in the metrics of prioritization, pointing out that while the drug wars in Latin America have resulted in hundreds of thousands of deaths, the wars involving conflict minerals in West and Central Africa have resulted in millions of deaths. Thus, these commentators say, the UN priorities should account for both the size and the harms of the type of transnational organized crime being measured. Second, the reliability of UN statistical data has been questioned, as gathering data on illegal activities is inherently problematic. However, UNODC has stated that much of the data in *TOCTA* is preliminary and will be refined in later reports.

The International Criminal Court

Although the International Criminal Court (ICC) is an independent organization governed by the Rome Statute, it maintains a relationship with UN system under the Relationship Agreement Between International Criminal Court and the UN. Thus, despite their technical autonomy and independence from one another, the relationship between the UN and the ICC is highly cooperative. Article 13 of the Rome Statute mandates the UN to refer any of the crimes within the jurisdiction of the ICC under Article 5 to the ICC prosecutor. The prosecutor may also seek additional information and/or testimony from the UN in order to properly analyze any information received under Article 15 of the Rome Statute. Finally, the Security Council may request the suspension of any ICC investigation or prosecution for a period of 12 months under Article 16.

Georgia Lysaght
University of Wollongong

See also Conventions, Agreements, and Regulations; Globalization; International Criminal Court; UN Convention Against Transnational Organized Crime; United Nations: Typologies of Criminal Structures

Further Readings

McClean, David. *Transnational Organized Crime: A Commentary on the UN Convention and Its Protocols*. Oxford, UK: Oxford University Press, 2007.

United Nations Office on Drugs and Crime. "The Globalization of Crime: A Transnational Organized Crime Threat Assessment." http://www.unodc.org/unodc/en/data-and-analysis/tocta-2010.html (Accessed February 2011).

United Nations Office on Drugs and Crime. "Information About Drugs." http://www.unodc.org/unodc/en/illicit-drugs/definitions/index.html (Accessed February 2011).

United Nations Office on Drugs and Crime. "United Nations Convention Against Transnational Organized Crime and Its Protocols." http://www.unodc.org/unodc/en/treaties/CTOC/index.html (Accessed February 2011).

Williams, Phil and Ernesto U. Savona. *The United Nations and Transnational Organized Crime*. London: Frank Cass, 1996.

UNITED NATIONS: TYPOLOGIES OF CRIMINAL STRUCTURES

Typologies of transnational organized criminal structures or operations are used by the United Nations (UN) to help in the UN's efforts to reduce the influence of transnational organized crime structures. The typologies provide a useful framework for collecting data and information on trends of transnational organized crime. The data and information can be collected and grouped to allow the trends to be analyzed. In addition, the typologies may be revised as necessary where new types or categories are developed. Typologies of these organizations also provide an overview of the different types and provide a useful training tool for law-enforcement personnel. Using the typologies, law enforcement can study these groups and the information on the various typologies may be transmitted to member states. In addition, the activities of similar groups may be compared.

In 1998, the member states of the UN established a committee for the purpose of elaborating a comprehensive international convention against transnational organized crime. To enhance the committee's ability to monitor these organizations, the UN Office on Drugs and Crime in 2002 conducted a pilot survey of 40 selected organized criminal groups in 16 countries.

The survey report noted that the diversity of criminal actors and organizations made consensus about what constitutes "transnational organized crime" difficult. The survey report noted that the concept of transnational crime, which was defined as criminal activity that crosses national borders, was introduced in the 1990s. In 1995, the UN established 18 categories of transnational offenses. The offenses included money laundering, terrorists' activities, theft of art and cultural items, theft of intellectual property, insurance fraud, illicit weapons trafficking, trafficking in humans, trade in human body parts, drug trafficking, and corruption and bribery of public officials. Then the UN promoted a survey among the member states that failed to provide much information because of differences in definitions in the states' legislation and the blurred distinctions between the national and transnational nature of the offenses. The UN now uses typologies to help overcome these deficiencies.

After a review of the data obtained from the 2002 pilot survey, five typologies based on the structures of the groups were identified: standard hierarchy, regional hierarchy, clustered hierarchy, core groups, and criminal networks.

A *standard hierarchy* typology is the most common form identified by the UN. It is characterized by a single leader and a clearly defined hierarchal structure. Systems of discipline are very strict. Generally, strong social or ethnic identities are present. It is common for this form to have relatively clear allocations of tasks and an internal code of conduct. The size of standard hierarchy groups can range from a few individuals to several hundred, with 10 to 50 most common. Unlike some other types of groups, a standard hierarchy group generally has a name that is well known to both members and outsiders. Of the 40 groups analyzed by the pilot survey, 13 belonged to this typology. The use of violence is an essential characteristic of their activities. Their illegal activities include prostitution, illegal gambling, smuggling, and racketeering. In many cases, corrupt local officials and public representatives are used to secure influence and protection for the groups.

A *regional hierarchy* typology is a hierarchically structured group that has strong internal lines of discipline and control but operates with regional autonomy. Although this is a hierarchical group with clear lines of command from the center, the regional groups have some degree of autonomy. The level of regional autonomy varies and is usually restricted to day-to-day management issues. Often regional groups appear to operate according to a franchise model. The command structure at the center is generally duplicated at the regional level. The level of discipline is high, with instructions from the center overriding any regional initiatives. Such groups are likely to engage in multiple criminal activities.

Probably the most successful of the regional hierarchy groups are the outlaw motorcycle gangs. The basic element of the chapter operates with a president and under the direction of the center. The members live an outlaw lifestyle and are mostly males. Their frequent use of violence, especially against rival motorcycle gangs, is well known. The gangs are prominent in the production and distribution of amphetamines and cannabis. Asian organized crime groups such the Yamaguchi-Gumi in Japan, the Fuk Ching gang in the United States, and the Japanese Yakuza in Australia also belong to the regional hierarchy typology. In these groups, the day-to-day running of the businesses is generally left to managers. They have a variety of rules and norms based on ethnic groupings and operate with a high level of discipline. Most of the Italian organized crime groups have a hierarchical structure and are headed by a single crime boss.

The third typology is the *clustered hierarchy*. This form may be described as a set of criminal groups with an established system of coordination and control, which ranges from weak to strong, over all of their activities. The governing arrangement ranges from a flexible umbrella-type structure to the rigid, controlled body. Each cluster of the structure has a high degree of autonomy and often assumes an identity of its own. The clusters engage in a wide range of criminal activity and have a relatively broad membership. An example of the clustered hierarchy is the 28s prison gang in South Africa. The 28s started more than 100 years ago and consist of former prisoners. The gang, while dominant in the Western Cape, operates across South Africa.

Core groups are relatively tightly organized but unstructured groups that are surrounded in most cases by a network of individuals engaged in criminal activities. Often the criminal group in this typology consists of a limited number of individuals who have formed a relatively small, structured group to carry out criminal activities. Associated with this core group will be a large number of associates. Generally the core groups carry on a single or limited number of criminal enterprises. Discipline is maintained by the small size and by the use of violence. Generally these groups have no social identity and are run for the benefit of a small number of individuals. The gangs often are not known by any name or special label. Of the 40 groups tracked by the pilot survey, eight were identified as core groups.

The fifth typology used by the UN is the *criminal networks* typology. These are loose and fluid networks of individuals, often with particular skills, who constitute themselves around an ongoing series of criminal projects. The members of this group frequently do not consider themselves to be part of an organized group. They do, however, coalesce around a series of criminal projects. The nature and success of the group are determined largely by the individual characteristics and skills of those who are involved in the network. There are a large number of criminal networks in West Africa, especially Nigeria.

Cliff Roberson
Kaplan University
Elena Azaola
Centro de Investigaciones y Estudios Superiores
en Antropologia Social

See also Egmont Group of Financial Intelligence Units; Financial Action Task Force; Measuring Transnational Crime; Profit-Driven Crime: Naylor's Typology; Terrorism Versus Transnational Crime; Transnational Crime: Defined; UN Convention Against Transnational Organized Crime; United Nations

Further Readings

Gottschalk, Petter. "Management and Enterprise Development in Criminal Organizations." *International Journal of Management and Enterprise Development*, v.5/4 (2008).

United Nations Office on Drugs and Crime. "Global Programme Against Transnational Organizations: Results of a Pilot Survey of Forty Selected Organized Criminal Groups in 16 Countries." 2002. http://www .unodc.org/pdf/crime/publications/Pilot_survey.pdf (Accessed January 2011).

VALUE-ADDED TAX FRAUD

European value-added tax (VAT) fraud is growing exponentially, both in degree and in level of cultivation, to the point that it is adversely affecting the accuracy of trade statistics of member states of the Organisation for Economic Co-operation and Development (OECD). Although estimates of VAT losses vary, the International VAT Association brackets losses from 60 billion to 100 billion euros per annum for all member states. Whatever the actual quantum of fraud, the general amount of these losses indicates the urgent need for proactive reform of the European Union (EU) VAT system and for arresting the growth and influence of the "black," or underground, economy.

Value added can be defined as the market value of a firm's outputs less the inputs bought from others. At each stage, the difference between what a firm pays for a product and what it receives from selling the product is paid out as wages, rent, interest, and profit. A consumption tax is a broad category of tax that is levied on the consumption value of goods and services. Examples of consumption taxes include retail sales taxes, excise taxes, and value-added taxes. Consequently, a value-added tax, or VAT, is an excise tax based on the value added to a product at each stage of production or distribution. The value added is determined by subtracting from the total value of the product at the end of each stage of production, or along the distribution chain, the value of the goods bought at its initiation. Customarily, producers and distributors pass the cost of the VAT on to the end user or consumer in the form of a price increase. Taxes are added to the price of the product each time it transitions until it is delivered to the customer, at which time a final tax is paid.

VAT has become synonymous with a national sales tax. However, sales tax is levied on the total retail price of an item sold, whereas a VAT tax applies to the value added at each stage of production and distribution. Furthermore, VAT is more complex than sales tax; it carries more restraints against tax fraud because taxes are assessed at more than one point in the distribution process. Value-added taxes are a principal source of tax revenue in many European and other developed countries, including member countries of the OECD, which uses a VAT or similar tax on consumer expenditures, with the exception of the United States.

Several fraudulent tactics are employed by organized crime to exploit the way VAT is treated within multijurisdictional trading where the movement of goods between jurisdictions is VAT-free, resulting in the theft of VAT from a government. Missing trader fraud (also known as missing trader intra-community, MTIC, or carousel fraud) allows the defrauder to charge VAT on the sale of goods and then, rather than pay the monies collected to the appropriate government authority, simply abscond with the VAT—hence the term *missing trader*. The fraud exploits this reclamation of tax, obliging itself to small, high-value items, such as microchips and mobile telephones. The missing trader fraud is the simplest form of VAT fraud.

A situation in which the goods are made available for consumers in the importer's home market is often known as *acquisition fraud*. Within the EU VAT system, the defrauder imports the goods from an exporter in another member state. This allows the exporter to "zero-rate," which means that the exporter does not have to pay VAT. Concurrently, the defrauder reverse charges the VAT, and when the fraudster sells the goods to the vendor, the vendor pays the price of the goods and the VAT that the defrauder reverse charged. Primarily the defrauder/importer must pay over the reverse-charged VAT to his or her government, but not immediately, depending on the day of the month the transaction occurred. Therefore, the fraudster must sell the goods before turning in the reverse-charged VAT.

Carousel refers to a more complex type of fraud, in which VAT and goods are passed around between companies and jurisdictions, similar to the round-and-round motion of a carousel. Contratrading fraud is another form of carousel fraud, which evades government detection by using two carousels of traded goods, where one carousel is legitimate and the other is not, thereby allowing an accounting scheme in which the input and output VATs neutralize each other, ultimately concealing the fraud. Also, domestic sales disguised as exports are contrived. Under this subterfuge, traders sell goods and services in a domestic market but attest to having sold them in an export market. The purpose is to acquire fraudulent export invoices that contain claims about the amount of purchases greater than the actual amount made by traders. Apparently, such fabricated invoices legitimize their claims to greater VAT payments and therefore to greater VAT refunds.

A more complex carousel fraud example calls for several businesses to act in concert. In that scenario, the goods would be sold to a series of companies before being exported again. The goods go around in the "carousel," and each of the businesses would be described as a "buffer." Realistically, there can be many buffers, all helping to obscure the channel between the final reclamation and the original importer, which will disappear. An entire series of transactions can occur without the goods ever leaving the dock in a European port before being re-exported. Moreover, the same goods can be used again and again, passing through the various buffers, with each pass around the carousel bringing reclaimed VAT to the victimizers.

Inflated refund claims constitute a VAT fraud scheme through which traders acquire invoices for purchases not made. The intent is to claim more refunds from tax-collecting authorities than deserved. Such traders acquire fraudulent invoices because they are essential to refund claims, being proof of merchandise purchases made upon which refundable VAT has been paid. There exists an established crime network dealing in such fabricated invoices, which are purchased by people to defraud governments.

Finally, underreported sales fraud necessitates the traders' concealment of the actual amount of sales from domestic markets in order to evade obligation to charge VAT on those sales. This tactic enables them to claim more refunds (credits) than deserved. Additionally, the scheme has the natural potential of boosting the business of such traders, because it encourages patronage on account of the relatively cheap goods and services buyers are offered.

Ben F. Linton II
Independent Scholar

See also Money Laundering: History; Price-Fixing; Sales Tax

Further Readings

International VAT Association. "Combating VAT Fraud in the EU: The Way Forward." March 1, 2007. http://www.iva-online.org/documents/IVA_Paper_FINAL.pdf (Accessed February 2011).

McConnell, Campbell R. and Stanley L. Brue. *Economics: Principles, Problems, and Policies*, 16th ed. Boston: McGraw-Hill, 2005.

Mikesell, John L. "Major Tax Structures: Taxes on Goods and Services." In *Fiscal Administration: Analysis and Applications for the Public Sector*, 7th ed. Belmont, CA: Thomson-Wadsworth, 2006.

VIOLENCE: INTIMIDATION

Transnational intimidation by violence comprises threats of or actual violence that involves citizens or governments from various nation-states or the transfer of goods or people internationally. Although legal transnational interactions and migration certainly may involve violence, transnational crime particularly fosters violent abuses. Consequently, this entry will discuss organized crime and gangs, terrorism, human trafficking, hate crime, and violence based on gender or sexual identity. Technological developments have additionally facilitated transnational criminal communication, harassment, threats, and detection, so these will also be covered.

Transnational Crime

In the prior few decades, transnational crime has gone up as a result of globalization and the increased ease of moving goods, resources, and individuals around the world. Large economic disparities within and between countries, as well as political conflicts, facilitate and fund illegal trade. When the Cold War ended, many Third World states lost financial sources that provided economic and political stability. Nations previously under authoritarian rule have experienced years of intimidation, violence, and corruption that threaten the establishment of new democracies. Consequently, the United States' Institute for National Strategic Studies observes that criminals are more capable of manipulating government employees with bribery or threats, even forming shadow governments that grant the cover of a seemingly legitimate sovereign state. Through absorbing weak governments, criminals such as organized syndicates and terrorists can desolate state resources and the threat of such groups often compares to those of legitimate sovereign states. Although globalization has ushered in a novel time period of unprecedented migration of people and goods, this openness of global exchange has also facilitated criminal networks' abilities to control and exchange resources, placing both governments and citizens at risk for exposure to violence, coercion, and intimidation.

Terrorism

Terrorism is commonly considered to be the use of violence and threats for purposes of coercion, typically with a political intent. Walter Enders and Todd Sandler find that, although terrorism is fairly inexpensive to engage in, it is costly to prevent and combat, and its secretive nature further enables state actors to sponsor terrorism without fear of detection. Whereas leftist terrorism flourished during the Cold War, the post–Cold War period of globalization, tension between Islam and other religions, and the increase in secular governments have facilitated the rise of Islamic terrorist groups, according to Kristopher Robison, Edward Crenshaw, and Craig

Jenkins. Although during the Cold War terrorists were often trained and financed by governments, today terrorist groups are united under religious or political goals and not connected to an individual state; consequently, they are more challenging to locate. Earlier, leftist terrorist organizations aimed to find support among the people to combat inequalities, and consequently such organizations minimized citizen casualties. Alternatively, fundamentalist terrorist organizations intently pursue mass casualties. Although most terrorism is domestic, any incident involving victims from or representing another country is categorized as transnational and is a threat to international relations.

Organized Crime and Gangs

Organized crime organizations employ violence, corruption, and violation of laws as tools for profit, which may be funneled toward other illegal enterprises or covertly exchanged through legal markets. Drug trafficking, nuclear material trafficking, waste dumping, trafficking of illegal arms, car theft and smuggling, human trafficking, and trafficking of human body parts are typical illegal profit-making enterprises that organized crime organizations direct. Global organized crime takes advantage of divergent market opportunities and criminal justice standards. One of the features of organized crime involves the use of violence and intimidation, even against authorities, to usurp control of territories and markets in order to expand profits, according to Bruno Ristau, Ugjesa Zvekic, and Mary Ellen Warlow.

Street gangs are considered different from organized crime organizations. They generally lack the hierarchy, organization, resources, and workforce necessary to direct a complex criminal organization. Celinda Franco notes that, although most gangs are considered to be first- (localized and loosely organized) or second-generation (localized, with a business structure, centralized leadership, and a focus on drugs), some have evolved into what appear to be more like third-generation gangs: sophisticated, global, and potentially terroristic groups. These groups display violence, intimidation, and coercion that are borderless. Los Angeles gangs Mara Salvatrucha (MS-13) and the 18th Street Gang (M-18) have aroused concern over whether they have the capacity to become coordinated, transnational gangs, because of their spread to Central America and Mexico and their involvement in sophisticated organized crime and smuggling operations. Because of many gang members' targeted deportation to their home countries, these gangs have reestablished themselves and have attacked state sovereignty in Central America in order to defend their ability to engage in gang criminal activity and destabilizing violence such as murder and kidnapping, extortion, and the trafficking of drugs, weapons, and people. Government resources are consequently trained on combating these gangs, leaving citizens frustrated and fueling a culture that is supportive of insurgency.

Human Trafficking

As former socialist countries became democratized, globalization has dramatically increased both legal migration and migrant trafficking. Although during the 1950s and 1960s immigration was driven largely primarily by labor needs and postcolonial associations, currently immigration policy is tied to military conflicts, civil wars, and unstable cultural and economic climates. Immigration has been considered a prominent European concern during the prior two decades, as the borders between eastern and western Europe have opened. Specifically, Andreas Schloenhardt finds that the Asia-Pacific region is considered a source, transit point, and destination for greater numbers of migrants. As countries such as Australia, Canada, and the United States have increased restrictions on immigration and asylum and economic inequalities have increased, so has migrant trafficking.

The U.S. Department of State estimates that around 800,000 people are trafficked internationally each year, primarily for forced labor or sexual exploitation. The transport of migrants is often conducted under inhumane conditions that may include lack of air, water, food, and temperature control. Migrants in "safe houses," where they may be kept as hostages until they complete payment to traffickers, often face death threats as well as physical and sexual assault. Immigrants who enter destination countries illegally are vulnerable to victimization and must live with uncertainty and fear of government detection. The decline of industrial jobs in destination countries and increased demand for highly skilled labor to work in the service and information markets leave immigrants in a changed labor market, where shadow economies and black markets with an increased risk of violence may offer the most attractive work opportunities, as indicated by Hans-Jörg Albrecht.

Harsh conditions are common for migrants, but violence and intimidation may be especially brutal in sex trafficking. Charlotte Watts and Cathy Zimmerman estimate that most victims are believed to come from Asia, the former Soviet Union, central and eastern Europe, Latin America and the Caribbean, and Africa. Women and children are often manipulated into the hands of traffickers through offers of relatively high-paying foreign jobs; they may also, however, be coerced or kidnapped. Susan Tiefenbrun documents the concern that, although sex-trafficked women additionally face legal persecution in countries where prostitution is illegal, countries with legalized prostitution tend to be greater targets for trafficked women, particularly since policies protecting victims of forced prostitution are generally weak in these nations. (Notably, Sweden, where prostitution is legal but the purchase of sex is criminalized, has a low rate of sex trafficking.)

Hate crimes—crimes based on race, religion, sexual orientation, or ethnicity—are another threat migrants face upon arrival at the destination country. The 2000 European Commission Against Racism and Intolerance found hate crimes to be widespread throughout Europe. Common fears of immigrants involve the notion that they are "benefits tourists" and the belief that migrants are moving through Europe to access social security and healthcare. In addition to being motivated by economic prejudice, hate crimes against immigrants may be prompted by punctuating events. In the year following September 11, 2001, for example, there was a 1,600 percent increase in hate crimes against Muslims, as reported to the Federal Bureau of Investigation.

Violence Based on Gender or Sexual Identity

Although historically there was little consideration of the unique attributes of gender-based crimes, following the Cold War the United Nations (UN) integrated violence against women into the international agenda. Widespread examples of violence against women include female genital mutilation, dowry deaths, human trafficking, rape as a tool of war, acid throwing, honor killings, forced sexual initiation, and domestic and sexual violence. Watts and Zimmerman indicate that violence against men and women frequently varies in its origin and political response. Violence against women is unique in that the violence is often not isolated but involves repeated violence that recurs over time, the perpetrator is frequently known by the victim, and women and girls are often blamed with somehow having provoked or escalated their victimization. They may even come to believe wrongly that, in fact, they are responsible. It is, moreover, almost always underreported. Ironically, James Wilets points out, although domestic violence has frequently been categorized as a private concern, same-gender or sexual-minority consensual sexual activity is commonly categorized as a concern of the state. Although women have made limited advances in increasing international recognition of women's human rights, sexual minorities have made almost no progress in establishing protections against violence and rape, given the fact that, unlike women, sexual minorities are often considered to be nonexistent or, in many countries, criminals.

Because of legislative preferences for constructing laws related to the public rather than the private sphere and the respective gendered allocation, women are often highly vulnerable to violence without protection in the home. One prominent transnational domestic violence issue is the 1980 Hague Child Abduction Convention. The convention requires judicial proceedings regarding custody contests to take place in the country of habitual residence. However, as Carol Bruch documents, research has indicated that the majority of abductors are mothers, and frequently these women are kidnapping their children away from abusive husbands and fathers. Consequently, children returned to their habitual residence may face increased abuse.

The international marriage broker (IMB) industry additionally presents transnational domestic violence problems. Leslye Orloff and Hema Sarangapani discuss IMBs in the context of the United States, finding that typically the male applies for a temporary fiancée visa, which permits the woman to enter the United States. If they do not marry within 90 days, the fiancée becomes an undocumented immigrant, leaving the male in complete control with regard to the filing, or withdrawal of, a family-based visa petition. Large economic disparities between potential fiancées, women's lack of access to background information

on their potential husbands, and male expectations of a devoted wife have established a scenario in which abuses of power may easily take place, particularly when compounded by cultural perceptions of "mail-order brides" as less legitimate than American-born wives. Giselle Hass, Nawal Ammar, and Orloff have observed that when a male marries a foreign-born woman, the likelihood of abuse increases threefold compared to the average. In the reauthorization of the Violence Against Women Act (VAWA) in 2005, the International Marriage Broker Regulation Act was passed, mandating that foreign-born women be given information about their rights and the criminal and marital backgrounds of their U.S. fiancés at the beginning of the process.

Technology

Peter Margulies documents how the Internet presents a new capability to connect spatially distant individuals, and in the United States the Internet is not bound by filters similar to those used in other types of media and is protected by First Amendment rights. Through the lack of filtering and easy access to a greater proportion of citizenry, the Internet additionally provides a degree of specialization wherein individuals seek out political views that align with their own, and radical, violent political views may become even more polarized. Despite the international dispersal of supporters, electronic networks facilitate interaction among terrorists communicating plans for violence or resource exchange. Furthermore, the speed of the Internet allows asynchronous interactions to be conducted easily.

Regarding the ability of perpetrators of domestic violence to continue tracking and harassing their victims, even cross-nationally, technology can enable abusers to expand their span of control through cell phones, Internet communication, Global Positioning System (GPS) devices, and wireless digital video cameras, according to Cynthia Southworth and her colleagues. Abusers may read a victim's e-mail covertly through "sniffer" programs, use the victim's electronic identity to impersonate the victim in communications with others, or discover a victim's personal information and use it to make financial exchanges. Abusers may further tap phone lines and exploit the built-in GPS features of cellular phones to find information on victims. Caller ID, Internet telephone directories, and information left at the tops of faxes may also be used to locate victims. Stalkers may use prepaid calling cards to distort their identities. Abusers may also surreptitiously place GPS devices on their victims or their victims' property.

Conclusion

As globalization and the modernization of technology have opened up opportunities for international transit of goods and people, communication capabilities, criminal networks, and individual perpetrators of domestic violence have also taken advantage of the increased ease of illegal trafficking of goods and people, including the detection of victims who have attempted escape. Although nongovernmental organizations (NGOs) and agencies of the UN may be viable organizations for intervening in global inequalities and violence and facilitating collaboration between nation-states, national authorities must also address such inequalities and the need to collaborate in the extradition of criminals, in order to address intimidation by violence as perpetrated through globalized transit and communication.

Elizabeth A. Tomsich
Angela R. Gover
University of Colorado, Denver

See also Gender-Based Violence; Violence: Protection; Violence: Uses

Further Readings

Albrecht, H.-J. "Fortress Europe? Controlling Illegal Immigration." *European Journal of Crime, Criminal Law and Criminal Justice*, v.10/1 (2002).

Bruch, C. S. "The Unmet Needs of Domestic Violence Victims and Their Children in Hague Child Abduction Convention Cases." *Family Law Quarterly*, v.38/3 (2004).

Enders, W. and T. Sandler. "Transnational Terrorism in the Post–Cold War Era." *International Studies Quarterly*, v.43/1 (1999).

Franco, C. "The MS-13 and 18th Street Gangs: Emerging Transnational Gang Threats?" 2008. http://assets .opencrs.com/rpts/RL34233_20080130.pdf (Accessed February 2011).

Hass, G. A., N. Ammar, and L. Orloff. "Battered Immigrants and U.S. Citizen Spouses." *Legal Momentum*. 2006. http://www.mcadsv.org/webinars/ IR-2007-April/VI/BatteredImmigrantsUSCitizenSpouses. pdf (Accessed February 2011).

Margulies, P. "The Clear and Present Internet: Terrorism, Cyberspace, and the First Amendment." *UCLA Journal of Law and Technology*, v.8/2 (2004). http://www .lawtechjournal.com/articles/2004/04_041207_ margulies.pdf (Accessed February 2011).

Orloff, L. E. and H. Sarangapani. "Governmental and Industry Roles and Responsibilities With Regard to International Marriage Brokers: Equalizing the Balance of Power Between Foreign Fiancés and Spouses." *Violence Against Women*, v.13/5 (2007).

Ristau, B. A., U. Zvekic, and M. E. Warlow. "Are International Institutions Doing Their Job?" *American Society of International Law*, v.90 (1996).

Robison, K. K., E. M. Crenshaw, and J. C. Jenkins. "Ideologies of Violence: The Social Origins of Islamist and Leftist Transnational Terrorism." *Social Forces*, v.84/4 (2006).

Schloenhardt, A. "Migrant Trafficking and Regional Security." *Forum for Applied Research and Public Policy*, v.16/2 (2001).

Southworth, C. et al. "Intimate Partner Violence, Technology, and Stalking." *Violence Against Women*, v.13 (2007).

Tiefenbrun, S. "The Saga of Susannah, a U.S. Remedy for Sex Trafficking in Women: The Victims of Trafficking and Violence Protection Act of 2000." *Utah Law Review*, v.17 (2002).

Watts, C. and C. Zimmerman. "Violence Against Women: Global Scope and Magnitude." *Lancet*, v.359 (2002).

Wilets, J. D. "Conceptualizing Private Violence Against Sexual Minorities as Gendered Violence: An International and Comparative Law Perspective." *Albany Law Review*, v.60 (1997).

VIOLENCE: PROTECTION

According to the World Health Organization (WHO), each year more than 1.6 million people worldwide lose their lives to violence. In addition, WHO reports that for every person who dies as a result of violence, many more are injured and suffer from a range of physical, sexual, reproductive, and mental health problems. Violence places a massive burden on national economies, costing countries billions of U.S. dollars each year in healthcare, law enforcement, and lost productivity. WHO works with partners to prevent violence through scientifically credible strategies that are conceived and implemented in relation to causes at the levels of the individual, family, community, and society. WHO presented the first world report on violence in 2002. In 2007, the United Nations' (UN's) General

Assembly adopted a resolution declaring 2007 the UN Year for Violence Prevention. By 2011, more than 30 governments had organized national policy discussions on the prevention of violence.

The *World Report on Violence and Health* was the first comprehensive review of the problem of violence on a global scale. The report focused on what violence is, whom it affects, and what can be done about it. The report was the end product of three years' work and benefited from the participation of more than 160 experts from around the world, receiving both peer review from scientists and contributions and comments from representatives of all the world's regions.

The report noted that because of the huge, and often hidden, complexity of violence, it would take a wide range of actors to successfully implement violence-prevention programs. The report noted that assistance is needed from health professionals to community workers, from law-enforcement officials to school authorities, from urban planners to media campaigners—because violence prevention has to emanate from many alliances and takes various forms. The report concluded that most important of all, tackling violence prevention requires political and financial commitment. The engagement of governments and other stakeholders at all levels of decision making—local, national, and international—is crucial to the success of any program designed to prevent violence.

The World Health Organization (WHO) estimates that more than 1.6 million people worldwide lose their lives to violence per year. The results of violence cost nations billions of U.S. dollars each year in healthcare, law enforcement, and lost productivity. (Photos.com)

Using the WHO report as a guideline, many world governments have developed national injury prevention policies, strategies, and plans of action. Although the instruments used vary across nations in nature and scope, they provide a guide to the nations' efforts to prevent injury-related death and disability. For example, both WHO's *World Report on Road Traffic Injury Prevention* and its *World Report on Violence and Health* called upon nations to develop procedures for the prevention of road traffic injuries and violence. WHO recommended that such policies, strategies, and plans of action be definite and contain objectives, priorities, timetables, and mechanisms for evaluation. The *World Report on Violence and Health* suggests that responsibility be assigned for all stages of implementation and that the plans be developed in a participatory manner. In addition, the implementation should involve both government and nongovernment actors alike. Some policies were developed by and for a single sector, such as health, transport, justice, or education, but ideally they should be developed in a multisectoral fashion. It was also recommended that policy makers and planners take into account at an early stage the human and financial requirements necessary for implementation.

The WHO report concluded that national planning to prevent violence must be based on a consensus developed by a wide range of governmental and nongovernmental actors. The planning should include a timetable and evaluation mechanism and should enable collaboration between sectors that might contribute to preventing violence, such as the criminal justice, human rights, education, labor, health, and social welfare sectors.

The report noted that many countries do not have a national plan or a coordinating agency or department that deals with violence comprehensively. Moreover, in many countries the response is focused on law and order, with only limited strategic cooperation with other authorities to help reduce violence. The report asserts that the formulation and implementation of a coherent and multidisciplinary national plan is the first critical step toward violence prevention.

According to the report, most national injury prevention policies, strategies, and plans of action currently being used originated in high-income countries. Few low- and middle-income countries have developed such policies. Of those that currently exist, some are comprehensive, pertaining to all injury-related mortality and morbidity, while others focus on a particular type of injury, such as road traffic injuries or violence-related injuries, or a particular group of intended beneficiaries, such as children, youth, or women. The success of these policies, strategies, and plans depends on the burden posed by these public health concerns in the country and the county's willingness and ability to recognize these as issues that need to be addressed and to take action.

The WHO report concludes that the important primary prevention interventions for reducing violence include prenatal healthcare for mothers, as well as preschool enrichment and social development programs for children and adolescents; training for good parenting practices and improved family functioning; improvements to urban infrastructure, both physical and socioeconomic; measures to reduce firearm injuries and improve firearm-related safety; and media campaigns to change attitudes, behavior, and social norms. The report notes that the first two interventions are important for reducing child abuse and neglect as well as violence perpetrated during adolescence and adulthood. The latter three can have significant impacts on several types of violence, such as youth and collective violence or suicide.

Finally, the report notes that violence is not an intractable social problem or an inevitable part of the human condition. Nations and citizens can do much to address and prevent it, but the world has not measured the size of the task and does not yet have all the tools to carry it out. The report notes that the global knowledge base is growing and much useful experience has already been gained that needs to be implemented. Violence is associated with the majority of transnational crimes, particularly crimes such as human trafficking, child pornography, and gun smuggling. In addition, violence is frequently used as a weapon in international crimes such as rape as war strategy and child warriors.

Cliff Roberson
Kaplan University
Elena Azaola
Centro de Investigaciones y Estudios Superiores
en Antropologia Social

See also Gender-Based Violence; Violence: Intimidation; Violence: Uses

Further Readings

Herrenkohl, Todd Ian et al. *Violence in Context: Current Evidence on Risk, Protection, and Prevention.* New York: Oxford University Press, 2011.

Humphreys, Catherine and Nicky Stanley. *Domestic Violence and Child Protection: Directions for Good Practice.* Philadelphia: Jessica Kingsley, 2006.

Stanley, Janet and Chris Goddard. *In the Firing Line: Violence and Power in Child Protection Work.* New York: Wiley, 2002.

World Health Organization. *World Report on Violence and Health.* Geneva: Author, 2002. http://whqlibdoc.who.int/publications/2002/9241545615_eng.pdf (Accessed February 2011).

Violence: Uses

Violence may be broadly defined as the use of force to coerce, abuse, or injure an individual or a group of individuals. This force may include actual physical force or the threat of using physical force. In considering violent acts, the criminal justice system often considers the intent of the aggressor. Acts that are not intentional may be excused or punished to a lesser degree (as in some cases involving negligence). Violent acts vary in their scope, with regard not only to the number of offenders but also to the number of victims who are killed or injured as a result of the violence.

Violence may be considered on either a personal or a structural level. Personal forms of violence include acts such as homicide, sexual assault, and assault and are often criminalized by individual societies. Forms of punishment for individual violent acts vary, depending on the country and its prescribed norms and values, but common forms of punishment may range from imprisonment to capital punishment.

Structural forms of violence may include corporate-level violence (such as pollution), racial violence, war, and genocide. The frequency and types of structural violence vary greatly according to the acceptance of such forms of violence in individual nations, and thus the penalties for these also vary greatly by society. In some cultures, structural violence has become accepted, while in others extreme levels of structural violence may be penalized with criminal penalties. The norm in some societies, such as the United States, is to punish structural violence with civil penalties, such as through lawsuits, which hold the corporation or entity responsible for its wrongdoings. Some forms of structural violence, such as war, are not punishable because they are sanctioned by governments and are therefore seen as acceptable. Even though structural violence is committed by groups of people, it is important to note that the resulting violence has an impact both on society as a whole and on individuals.

Another form of violence that becomes increasingly important in discussing international violence is transnational violence. Transnational violence is organized by criminal groups and occurs across international boundaries. Some forms of transnational violence occur in the contexts of international terrorism, human trafficking, and drug or weapons trafficking. Violence in these arenas may occur in the process of smuggling weapons and drugs in and out of countries. An increase in the globalization of the world's economy has led to an increase in such illicit transnational markets and, hence, in transnational violence as nations interact with one another more than ever before.

Violence is perpetrated for a wide range of reasons. Homicide may be explained by the motivations to commit the homicide, such as for money, pleasure, or out of anger. Sexual violence is often perpetrated as a way of exerting power over another individual. Robbery is often committed for financial gain. Genocide is often committed as a way of displaying superiority of one race or group of races over another, as well as for political reasons. Violence that is incidental to war may be committed for the stated purposes of the war itself, for self-defense during battle, or as the result of a group mentality used to justify violence in a given situation.

Interestingly, many of those who commit violence may not view their actions as violent. This may especially be the case for those who commit structural violence. Those who commit political or religious acts of violence may believe that their violence is justified by the greater good of society or may view those who they are committing violence against as oppressors or society's enemies. In the case of international terrorism, those carrying out terrorist acts may view civilians in the same light as soldiers, essentially making no distinction between people who volunteer to be at war and those who do not. Even in the case of personal violence, it may be that perpetrators do not see their victims as injured by their wrongdoing, even possibly believing that the victims are less than human.

In viewing violence as an issue that crosses national boundaries, it becomes difficult to make cross-country comparisons in terms of rates of violence. What is considered a criminally violent act in one country may not be considered such in another country. Comparisons are often made between countries that share characteristics such as population size or degree of industrialization and technology. Two major data collection agencies are the United Nations (UN) and the International Criminal Police Organization (Interpol), both of which regularly collect crime data statistics from various nations.

The crimes that can be most easily compared across nations are homicides. Homicide has a relatively consistent definition cross-nationally. One of the most reliable international data sources is the World Health Organization (WHO), which has been collecting statistics on various forms of death since 1948. Data from more than 60 countries are included in WHO's data set. However, there are some flaws in this data source as a tool for accurate homicide information. For example, there are vast differences by country in terms of civil war and unrest, as well as how developed each country is. These factors can impact governments' ability to collect accurate statistics. Moreover, definitions of various forms of death that are included in WHO's reports have varied over time and may include deaths due to war. Also, although information is provided on both age and gender of the victims, there is no information collected on race or ethnicity. Another issue is that information is not given as to whether another crime was committed during the transaction in which a death occurred.

The United States has among the highest rates of violence of all industrialized nations. Many reasons have been provided for this, such as that U.S. citizens enjoy a great amount of individual freedom in comparison with citizens of other nations. Although many forms of violence are condemned and sanctioned in the United States, it may be that the country has a culture that inadvertently condones violence, perhaps even leading some individuals to be desensitized to violent activities. For example, some explain an individual's violent tendencies by citing the media's role in endorsing violence via television, movies, music, and video games. Others believe that the availability of lethal weapons, especially handguns, contributes to increased levels of violence. It may also be the quest for individualism itself that leads some people to become violent, encouraging certain individuals to express a sense of superiority over (or frustration with) others by committing violent or degrading acts against other individuals. It is notable that, within the United States, the prevalence of violence varies by region, with the southern and western regions experiencing higher levels of violence, especially fatal violence, than other regions, on average. Moreover, urban areas tend to display higher levels of violence than rural and suburban areas.

In most societies, forms of violence that are considered criminal are subject to criminal penalties. These criminal penalties often involve violence. In the United States, some instances of homicide may be punished by death. Islamic law also dictates that some types of offenses are punishable with violent penalties. Death may be imposed as a punishment for murder, assault, and maiming. Lesser violent punishments, such as hand amputation, may be used for thievery, and flogging may be used as a punishment for adultery. Some fault such instances of "state-sanctioned violence," carried out by governing authorities. The justifications for these corporal and capital punishments often include that the offenses committed are an affront either to collective society or to the primary established religion of the society.

Kristine Levan Miller
Plymouth State University

See also Impact of Transnational Crime; Violence: Protection

Further Readings

Alvarez, A. and R. Bachman. *Violence: The Enduring Problem*. Thousand Oaks, CA: Sage, 2008.

Eller, J. D. *Violence and Culture: A Cross-Cultural and Interdisciplinary Approach*. Belmont, CA: Thomson-Wadsworth, 2006.

Ember, C. R. and M. Ember. "Issues in Cross-Cultural Studies of Interpersonal Violence." *Violence and Victims*, v.8 (1993).

Frank, N. K. and M. J. Lynch. *Corporate Crime, Corporate Violence*. Guilderland, NY: Harrow and Heston, 1992.

Souryal, S. S., D. W. Potts, and A. I. Alobied. "The Penalty of Hand Amputation for Theft in Islamic Justice." *Journal of Criminal Justice*, v.22/3 (1994).

World Health Organization, Regional Office for Europe. *Mortality Indicators by Sixty Seven Causes of Death, Age and Sex*. Copenhagen: Author, 2010.

WAR CRIMES

War crimes are serious violations of international humanitarian law during an armed conflict. Armed conflicts may be either international or internal (noninternational). International armed conflicts are between two or more states; internal armed conflicts (such as a civil war) occur within one state.

International humanitarian law, which is also referred to as the law of war, developed over many centuries through customary international law, which is law established from customs, rather than conventional international law, which is law established by international treaties ratified by states. Two forms of law govern international humanitarian law. The first is *jus ad bellum*, which is the law that governs the legality of initiating an armed conflict. The second is *jus in bello*, which governs the legality of acts during an armed conflict. The two may be related but are definitely separate. For example, if a state unlawfully attacks another state in violation of *jus ad bellum*, then *jus in bello* is still applicable to belligerents participating in the armed conflict. Contrarily, if a state lawfully attacks another state, *jus in bello* is still applicable to prevent and punish those who may commit war crimes during the armed conflict.

Historically, international humanitarian law is based on three principles that govern the conduct of military personnel during armed conflicts. The first principle is necessity, which states that what is necessary to achieve a military objective may be done. The second principle is humanity, which states that acts that cause unnecessary harm and suffering are unlawful. While the principle of necessity states what may be done to achieve a military objective, the principle of humanity states what may not be done unless otherwise done by necessity. For example, it may be necessary to kill an enemy who is firing his weapon at you; however, it is unnecessary and inhumane to kill a prisoner of war or a person who has surrendered and is no longer a threat. The third principle is chivalry, which requires military personnel to fight honorably and respect each other during combat. This principle would dictate respecting military and religious symbols as well as signs of neutrality. For example, if military personnel use the white flag, which means surrender, to draw their enemies closer in order to attack them, chivalry has been violated. Chivalry is also violated when religious symbols and entities, such as the star, crucifix, sacred text, or a house of worship, are attacked or used to gain a military advantage. A sign of neutrality signifies nonparticipation in the armed conflict and therefore an entity that does not favor one side over the other. The red cross and red crescent, for example, are universal symbols of neutrality that are not to be attacked or used in favor of or against participants to achieve a military objective.

Argentine prisoners of war are marched through Port Stanley after the surrender of the Argentine governor ended the Falklands War. The principle of necessity defines what may be done to achieve a military objective and states that it is unnecessary and inhumane to kill a prisoner of war. (Wikimedia)

The first codification of international humanitarian law was the Lieber Code, named after its codifier Francis Lieber, in 1863. The Lieber Code was authorized by the U.S. War Department under President Abraham Lincoln in response to reports of atrocities committed during the American Civil War. The Lieber Code consisted of 157 articles defining how military personnel were to conduct themselves in the field. Since the Lieber Code, many international conventions have drafted treaties defining unlawful conduct and use of weapons during armed conflict. Most notable are the 1899 and 1907 Hague Conventions, which are referred as Hague Law, and the four 1949 Geneva Conventions, which confirmed Hague Law in addition to formulating other rules and principles based on or expanding upon customary international law.

After World War II, the Allied victors, including the United States, the United Kingdom, the Soviet Union, and France, established the International Military Tribunal to prosecute high-ranking Nazis for the atrocities they had committed both before and during the war. Article 6 of the Charter of the International Military Tribunal included war crimes in its jurisdiction and defined them as,

> namely, violations of the laws or customs of war. Such violations shall include, but not be limited to, murder, ill-treatment or deportation to slave labor or for any other purpose of civilian population of or in occupied territory, murder or ill-treatment of prisoners of war or persons on the seas, killing of hostages, plunder of public or private property, wanton destruction of cities, towns or villages, or devastation not justified by military necessity.

For the first time in history, government officials were prosecuted by another state for committing atrocities during war. The "Nüremberg momentum" was a result of the International Military Tribunal, which changed the law of war forever. Subsequently, Nazi war criminals were prosecuted at Nüremberg for their unlawful conduct during World War II in court proceedings now known as the Nüremberg Trials. In 1949, four Geneva Conventions were adopted protecting groups during armed conflicts. These include sick and wounded military personnel on land; sick, wounded, and shipwrecked military personnel at sea; prisoners of war; and civilians.

Shortly after the International Military Tribunal was completed in 1946, the United Nations (UN) General Assembly affirmed the Principles of International Law Recognized in the Charter of the Nüremberg Tribunal and in the Judgment of the Tribunal, which were adopted in 1950. They are as follows:

- *Principle I:* Any person who commits an act which constitutes a crime under international law is responsible therefor and liable to punishment.
- *Principle II:* The fact that international law does not impose a penalty for an act which constitutes a crime under international law does not relieve the person who committed the act from responsibility under international law.
- *Principle III:* The fact that a person who committed an act which constitutes a crime under international law acted as head of state or responsible government official does not relieve him from responsibility under international law.
- *Principle IV:* The fact that a person acted pursuant to order of his government or of a superior does not relieve him from responsibility under international law, provided a moral choice was in fact possible to him.
- *Principle V:* Any person charged with a crime under international law has the right to a fair trial on the facts and law.

- *Principle VI:* The crimes hereinafter set out are punishable as crimes under international law:
  - (a) Crimes against peace:
    - (i) Planning, preparation, initiation or waging of a war of aggression or a war in violation of international treaties, agreements or assurances;
    - (ii) Participation in a common plan or conspiracy for the accomplishment of any of the acts mentioned under (i).
  - (b) War crimes: Violations of the laws or customs of war include, but are not limited to, murder, ill-treatment or deportation to slave-labor or for any other purpose of civilian population of or in occupied territory, murder or ill-treatment of prisoners of war, of persons on the seas, killing of hostages, plunder of public or private property, wanton destruction of cities, towns or villages, or devastation not justified by military necessity.
  - (c) Crimes against humanity: Murder, extermination, enslavement, deportation and other inhuman acts done against any civilian population, or persecutions on political, racial or religious grounds, when such acts are done or such persecutions are carried on in execution of or in connection with any crime against peace or any war crime.
- *Principle VII:* Complicity in the commission of a crime against peace, a war crime, or a crime against humanity as set forth in Principle VI is a crime under international law.

The first international criminal tribunal to prosecute war crimes since the 1949 Geneva Conventions was the International Criminal Tribunal for the former Yugoslavia in 1993, which was established by the UN Security Council for the prosecution of genocide, crimes against humanity, and war crimes. In 1994, the UN Security Council established the International Criminal Tribunal for Rwanda for the prosecution of genocide, crimes against humanity, and war crimes by applying Common Article 3. Article 3 of all four Geneva Conventions of 1949 applies certain offenses to internal armed conflicts. The conflict in Rwanda was internal; therefore, Common Article 3 was necessary to prosecute certain violations of the Geneva Conventions of 1949.

The two basic elements for war crimes are that the violation is serious and that it occurs during an armed conflict. The latter is to include that the serious violation has a connection to the armed conflict; in other words, if there is no war (or connection to that war), then there is no war crime. For example, if a murder is committed in a state that is at war with another state but the murder has no connection to the war itself, then a war crime has not been committed and the result is a murder that is to be prosecuted as such by the state with jurisdiction of crimes. Conversely, if a crime is committed in connection with a war but does not constitute a serious violation (as when a soldier takes a loaf of bread from a village that has much food), then a war crime has not been committed, since the offense is not considered serious.

The International Criminal Tribunals for the former Yugoslavia and Rwanda are temporary courts that were established in response to particular conflicts and will eventually complete their work and disband. The International Criminal Court, established on July 1, 2002, is a permanent court established to prosecute genocide, crimes against humanity, war crimes, and the crime of aggression. The crime of aggression represents crimes against peace at the International Military Tribunal.

Harry M. Rhea
Richard Stockton College of New Jersey

See also Adjudicating International Crimes; International Criminal Court

Further Readings

Detter, Ingrid. *The Law of War*, 2nd ed. New York: Cambridge University Press, 2005.

Gutman, Roy and David Rieff, eds. *Crimes of War: What the Public Should Know*. New York: W. W. Norton, 1999.

McCormack, Timothy L. H. and Gerry J. Simpson, eds. *The Law of War Crimes: National and International Approaches*. Boston: Kluwer Law International, 1997.

Meron, Theodor. *War Crimes Law Comes of Age: Essays*. New York: Oxford University Press, 1998.

WAR CRIMES TRIBUNALS

War crimes tend to connote genocide, population transfers, prisoner-of-war abuse, and rape. Tribunals face the obstacle of seeking and administering justice under the ambiguities found in fluid rather than concrete international norms. Depending on the legal interpretation, war crimes could easily include the mass murder of Ukrainian political prisoners to save money or the mass suffocation of German prisoners of war while using a defective form of transportation between camps in France. In addition, tribunals range from military courts-martial to specially created tribunals under the auspices of the United Nations (UN).

Historical Context

The Hague Peace Conferences of 1899 and 1907 marked the beginning of the establishment of war crimes law. In addition, the signing of the Treaty of Versailles on June 28, 1919, following the end of World War I, marked a turning point in the legal history of war crimes, because it placed liability on heads of state, identifying them as sharing responsibility for crimes committed during the war. The successes and failures of the Treaty of Versailles served as the reference point for the construction of post–World War II international criminal law.

The establishment of war crimes judicial offices was motivated by the effects of the Nazis' 1939 attack on Poland. During the post–World War II era, the administration of justice faced challenges regarding mutual impartiality and trust that governments would unanimously refrain from withholding information regarding the defendants, despite cultural values of national honor, revenge, or a quest to settle old disputes. Common ground became easier to attain when the involved parties decided to seek justice for innocent civilians who had been victimized.

The 1949 Geneva Convention established fundamental policies for the treatment of prisoners of war. These rules forbid individuals from using torture and abuse to obtain information. Evidence of just such a practice surfaced in the case of detainees at the Abu Ghraib prison, near Baghdad, in 2003.

The initiation of war crimes trials at Nüremberg and Tokyo ushered in an era of international courts; at the time, these trials contrasted with global conventions for administering justice. Although the trials were experimental, they paved the way for the establishment of more efficient criminal courts at The Hague, while serving as a benchmark for the future International Criminal Tribunal for the former Yugoslavia (ICTY), International Criminal Tribunal for Rwanda (ICTR), and International Criminal Court (ICC).

In 1975, the UN Convention Against Torture provided reinforcement to the Geneva Convention

by extending the prohibition of torture on behalf of the government. The statement in Article 4 that "each State Party shall ensure that all acts of torture are offenses under its criminal law" provides a sense of legal assurance and international cooperation.

The year 1993 marked the establishment of the International Criminal Tribunal for the former Yugoslavia (ICTY), which sought restitution and retribution against war criminals of the Bosnia-Herzegovina dispute and other conflicts affiliated with the dismantling of the former Yugoslavia. As part of the first case of the International War Crimes Tribunal, Bosnian Serb Duško Tadić received convictions for both war crimes and crimes against humanity. Likewise, the formation of the International Criminal Tribunal for Rwanda (ICTR) in 1994 sought to prosecute offenders of international law within the context of the Rwandan Civil War.

The Label *Genocide*

Genocide consists of a systematic attempt to annihilate a population or a sector of its culture. The term was initially coined in the 1940s; however, the practice dates to ancient historical times. Because genocide has the connotation of "the ultimate evil," the use of this emotionally loaded term can prove problematic. A government's interchangeable use of the terms *population transfer* and *genocide* has often served to mask that government's use of state-sponsored atrocities but has also provoked social outrage in response to such emotional manipulation. Disputes over the definition of genocide are significant to critics of the international community, including the UN, since the international community is perceived as unresponsive to genocidal acts despite the international ban on the practice. Advocates for international accountability argue that seeking understanding of the events and the quest for clarity in defining genocide constitute a moral obligation.

Prisoner Abuse During Wartime

Forms of prisoner abuse include torture, forced nudity, sexual abuse (including the practice of coercing prisoners into sexual performances with other prisoners), sleep deprivation, forced contortionism (which prolongs suffering while interfering with normal circulation), intentional defilement of that which prisoners deem as sacred, and the use of "extraction techniques" as a means of entertainment for soldiers. A major obstacle in applying the Geneva

Conventions to the abuse at Abu Ghraib Prison stems from the fact that the prisoners were classified as detainees and were deliberately not classified as prisoners of war.

In the case of the Abu Ghraib trials, the soldiers' abuse of detainees had undergone neutralization through an argument that the soldiers' character was normal and noncriminal but that, when immersed in a tainted ambiance, they experienced temporary anomie and took on contrary personas, described as evil and sadistic. Accounts from the trials rationalized prisoner abuse as the result of soldiers becoming oblivious to the presence of continuous screaming from pain and as a reaction to a sense of desperation caused by long-term lack of necessities, which included statements of moral boundaries from superiors. The prisoner abuse of both Iraqi soldiers and innocent civilians, including women and children, received further support by an implied "code of silence" caused by fear of fellow soldiers and the lack of sanctions or investigation when prior incidents of abuse were reported. As an expert witness at the trial, Stjepan Meštrović acknowledged that protecting the U.S. Army's national sense of honor ranked as a high priority, at the expense of justice on behalf of the abused.

Exposing prisoner abuse in Abu Ghraib brought global attention to a breach of law, violations of human rights, and disavowing "the honor code." During 2003–04, the U.S. Army had filed approximately 100 cases against U.S. soldiers for alleged prisoner and civilian abuse of natives of Iraq and Afghanistan. However, the vast majority of those convicted for war crimes were low-ranking soldiers. Unlike the Nüremberg and other war crimes trials, the Abu Ghraib prosecutions did not invoke the doctrine of command responsibility. These trials presented the possibility of insufficient justice that might make exemptions from the Geneva Conventions' rules the norm rather than the exception. Second, insufficient accountability supports an ideology of defending national honor as more important than addressing the harm done to the victims.

Rape as a War Crime

Before rape was classified as a war crime, it was historically regarded as one of the spoils of war, as well as a means of causing terror among civilians. The conventional narrative of history truncates the common practice of sexual assault and rape as the epitome of war atrocities.

Mass rape with forced impregnation functioned as a genocidal attempts in the case of Bosnia-Herzegovina. Such actions have the potential to alter the genetic imprint of a nation, branding offspring with the lasting reminder of defeat. Serbian concentration camps were settings for Serbian soldiers raping Croatian and Muslim women. In the Muslim belief system, sexual purity ranks as a significant cultural value, and its defilement brings shame on both the individual and her family. Although the expulsion of non-Serbians was the immediate social and political goal of the genocide, rape and various forms of sexual violence beyond technical rape functioned to support the genocide.

When large numbers of the male population become killed or captured during war in a society with a highly patriarchal social order, women and children become especially vulnerable to sexual violence and rape. In the case of Rwanda in 1994, the mass slaughter resulted in the deaths of 10 percent of the Rwandan population. Hutus engaged in public gang rapes of Tutsi women, followed by torture prior to the killing the women. Several young Tutsi males were forced to rape their mothers.

Before rape was regarded as a criminal act, it was used to entice men to join the military, because laws against rape in the civilian world became less applicable during war. Rape symbolically functioned as an act of celebration of victory, affirmation of manhood, and expansion of territory through women's wombs at the expense of bringing shame to individual victims, their families, and the nation. Despite a long history of rape as a weapon of war and its dehumanizing effects, especially upon innocent civilians, it received minimal attention from the international community for most of history.

Early war crimes tribunals, such as the Nüremberg and Tokyo trials, failed to acknowledge cases of gender-based violence. However, rape eventually became classified as a war crime under the ICTR and ICTY statutes. Moreover, women served as judges and prosecutors in both Rwanda and the former Yugoslavia, which contributed significantly to the success of the ICTR and ICTY in indicting perpetrators of violent sex crimes.

Transnational Justice Challenges

Establishing evidence credibility standards in a court or tribunal poses an additional hurdle for international justice advocates. Various methods for collecting evidence include eyewitness accounts under oath, expert opinions, court-martial records, medical examination reports, and transcripts of prisoner-of-war interrogations. However, propaganda manipulation, appeals to populism, fabrications or exaggerations of witnesses with the intent of deception, biased judgments in the case of alliances, and inadequate witness protection rank among the leading areas of caution for international courts.

The establishment of the International Criminal Court (ICC) was intended to provide a standardized and normative legal environment with the capability of providing international justice while ideally avoiding local political involvement. Appealing to nation-state sovereignty has consistently served as a strategy for justifying repression and state-sponsored expulsion of minorities, resulting in national interests trumping the rights of a large number of human victims. The difficulty in determining the morally responsible individuals and groups contributes to the difficulties in achieving justice.

In the case of the former Yugoslavia, evidence shows that Serbia, Croatia, and Bosnia found that institutionalizing transitional justice was advantageous, helping them to secure European Union (EU) membership, and provided a bargaining tool for maneuvering through the local agendas of the elites. Postwar trials face further challenges, including the task of reconciling the potentially abrasive relationship between international norms and domestic demands.

During the 1990s, the Burundi government approached the UN to initiate an international commission as the death toll from its civil conflicts reached approximately 50,000. The assassination of Burundi's first ethnic Hutu president, Melchior Ndadaye, in 1993 set the stage for the overthrow of the government by a coup on July 25, 1996, and the details of the commission's report bear witness to acts of genocide.

Also during the 1990s, East Timor in Indonesia experienced a reign of terror that culminated in 1999 with atrocities committed against humanity in the form of a massacre. The establishment of the Commission of Truth and Friendship (CTF) led to confessions of collective guilt in Indonesia in reaction to the lack of prosecutions from the local courts. Individuals, however, were able to avoid prosecution.

The Khmer Rouge regime in Indonesia during the late 1970s resulted in approximately 1.5 million deaths, with little or no accountability for those responsible. The formation of the Extraordinary Chambers in the Courts of Cambodia (ECCC) in 2006—by which time a significant number of the leading perpetrators of the genocide had died—resulted in minuscule numbers of suspects facing custody and most perpetrators escaping indictment.

The religious sectarian group called the Lord's Resistance Army led a Ugandan massacre in Sudan and the Democratic Republic of the Congo that resulted in mass murders and allegedly large-scale abductions and brutal sexual enslavement. As a result of the direct attacks from the Janjaweed, a state-sponsored militia group of Sudan, an estimated 400,000 casualties have occurred in Darfur. In addition to direct attacks, such indirect genocidal means as starvation and diseases have contributed to the death tolls.

Impact on Transnational Crime and Justice

Support for investigation by tribunals relies on a broad international acceptance of the tribunal as legitimate. Tribunals, and the ICC specifically, face an ideological polarization between "legalists" and "realists." Legalists collectively support tribunals and the ICC, believing that adequate exposure of war crimes and crimes against humanity will have a deterrent effect at an international level. However, legalists acknowledge the imperativeness of a swift response in order overcome the hurdle of bureaucratically initiated delays. Realists tend to have concerns regarding the defense of sovereign states' rights within the international context. For example, realists are concerned about the constitutional rights of U.S. citizens within the context of a judicial system outside that of the United States. Moreover, the exposure of U.S. soldiers as war criminals poses a threat to the United States' national honor. In this scenario, the concept of national sovereignty lies at the heart of justifications for obstructing the timely prosecution of war crimes or genocide by international tribunals.

Michael D. Royster
Prairie View A&M University

See also Gender-Based Violence; Genocide; International Criminal Court; Internationalized Criminal Tribunals; World Court

Further Readings

Akhavan, Payam. "The International Criminal Tribunal for Rwanda: The Politics and Pragmatics of Punishment." *American Journal of International Law*, v.90/3 (1996).

Davis, Patricia H. "The Politics of Prosecuting Rape as a War Crime." *The International Lawyer*, v.34/4 (2002).

De Zayas, Alfred-Maurice. "The Wehrmacht Bureau on War Crimes." *The Historical Journal*, v.5/2 (1992).

Gutman, Roy. *Crimes of War: What the Public Should Know*. New York: W. W. Norton, 1999.

Hayden, Robert M. "The Tactical Use of Passion on Bosnia." *Current Anthropology*, v.38/5 (1997).

Hazan, Pierre. "Justice in a Time of War." *The True Story Behind the International Criminal Tribunal for the former Yugoslavia*. Austin: Texas A&M University Press, 2004.

Lilly, Carol S. "Amoral Realism of Immoral Obfuscation?" *Slavic Review*, v.55/4 (1996).

McKanna, Clare V., Jr. *Court-Martial of Apache Kid: Renegade of Renegades*. Lubbock: Texas Tech University Press, 2009.

Meron, Theodor. "Reflections on the Prosecution of War Crimes by International Tribunals." *American Journal of International Law*, v.100/3 (2006).

Meštrovi, Stjepan G. *The Trials of Abu Ghraib: An Expert Account of Shame and Honor*. Boulder, CO: Paradigm, 2005.

Pfiffner, James P. *Torture as Policy: Restoring U.S. Credibility on the World Stage*. Boulder, CO: Paradigm, 2010.

Ratner, Steven R. "Belgium's War Crimes Statute: A Postmortem." *A Journal of International Law*, v.97/4 (2003).

Stahn, Carster. "Responsibility to Protect: Political Rhetoric or Emerging Legal Norm." *American Journal of International Law*, v.101/1 (2007).

Subotic, Jelena. *Justice Hijacked: Dealing With the Past in the Balkans*. Ithaca, NY: Cornell University Press, 2009.

United Nations, Convention Against Torture and Other Cruel, Inhuman or Degrading Treatment or Punishment, December 9, 1975.

Wilkinson, Paul. "Can a State Be 'Terrorist'?" *International Affairs*, v.57/3 (1981). http://www.hrweb.org/legal/cat.html (Accessed January 2012).

WEAPONS SMUGGLING

The proliferation of illegal weapons has been likened to a cancer spreading across the developed and developing world. Development economist Paul Collier has referred to armed conflict as "social and economic development in reverse," and chronic patterns of armed conflict are fundamentally sustained, more than anything else, by (typically illicit) supplies of small arms and light weapons (SALW). Furthermore, international law-enforcement agencies suggest that the illicit trade in small arms and light weapons represents one of the major security threats facing the 21st century, contributing to problems of terrorism, regional instability, failed states, international drug trafficking, urban gang weaponization, and other organized crime.

Although poorer societies typically bear the brunt of these problems, more developed societies (among which are often the leading producers and exporters of SALW) are not immune to the problems of the gun. Indeed, it is in the very nature of weapons trafficking to use scarcity to drive up the price that trafficked weapons can command. Countries with relatively successful gun-control regimes but a demand for weapons can see their control efforts undermined by bad neighbors as weapon scarcity renders even small-scale smuggling fairly lucrative. For example, more than half of the illegal handguns recovered in Canada and around 80 percent of illegal firearms recovered in Mexico originate within the United States.

Generally speaking, illegal trafficking in weapons takes one or more of the following forms: leakage (theft and fraud) directly from points of production or military stockpiles; fake export arrangements, sometimes involving governments or other well-placed intermediaries (including ex-military or security personnel); conversion of nonlethal firearms; recycling of discarded or surplus weapons; theft, fraud, and leakage from legal dealers or private owners; and fraud by private owners. Differences of scale are clearly entailed here, from states to private individuals, but each plays a part.

So significant are the security issues posed by the proliferation of SALW that it might be expected that the whole question of international weapons smuggling and trafficking would be subject to the most comprehensive scrutiny and analysis. Unfortunately, until relatively recently, for a number of reasons—attributable to fragmentation of scrutiny, secrecy, politics, criminality, danger, and difficulty—this has not been the case. Even now that a number of powerful organizations have become engaged with the issue—not least the United Nations (UN), which commenced its Programme of Action on the Illicit

Small arms are cheap, light, easy to handle, transport, and conceal, and are illicitly circulated through distribution, theft, divergence, pilferage, or resale. (Photos.com)

Trade in Small Arms and Light Weapons in 2001— these difficulties remain, frustrating the efforts of researchers and law enforcement alike. To take the first issue, fragmentation of scrutiny, the applied social sciences' collective grasp on SALW smuggling tends to be divided between criminologists (whose interest primarily concerns the criminal misuse of firearms on the streets), defense and security studies (often preoccupied by the supply of weapons to terrorist or organized criminal groups), conflict and war studies (the role of weapons used by militias and armed groups to destabilize regions and perpetrate war crimes or genocide), international relations (the licit and illicit use of arms brokerage to sustain geopolitical alliances), and development and peace studies (the study of disarmament and demobilization processes). There are relatively few attempts to take in the whole picture, different disciplines have tended to tackle the issues from their own particular perspectives, and furthermore, these perspectives can often be very local or regional.

Weapons smuggling, gunrunning, and firearms trafficking have become increasingly globalized phenomena, typically keeping pace with the globalization of trade and of crime more generally and often closely reflecting important geopolitical patterns of influence within international relations. Relatively little consistent empirical evidence exists regarding the scale and nature of the problem at the national level, and despite sporadic efforts by international law-enforcement agencies, such as the International Criminal Police Organization (Interpol), there is even less clear and consistent evidence at the international level. What we do know tends to reflect

the work of a limited number of specialist security studies, research organizations, and nongovernmental organizations (NGOs), such as the Graduate Institute of International Studies in Geneva, which since 1999 has conducted an annual *Small Arms Survey* (a review of global small arms issues, including production, stockpiling, brokering, legal and illicit arms transfers, the impact of small arms, and national, bilateral, and multilateral strategies to tackle the problems associated with small arms); the Institute for Security Studies (originally established in South Africa but now networked across 17 African countries); the Stockholm International Peace Research Institute (SIPRI); the International Action Network on Small Arms (IANSA); and Saferworld. There are also a number of, generally smaller, research institutes attached to universities in different countries around the world. A great deal of the evidence of illegal weapons trafficking is particularistic and often anecdotal, coming to light, like the visible tip of an iceberg, when an illegal shipment, large or small, is discovered. Drawing largely upon the work of this limited range of research institutes and NGOs, it is possible to form some conclusions about the scale, structure, and nature of contemporary weapon smuggling.

There are important distinctions of scale and organization within the weapons-trafficking arena. Large-scale items such as tanks and military vehicles, planes, and even warships are generally traded, directly or indirectly, by governments—although often cloaked by the involvement of layers of brokerage companies and networks of contractors and subcontractors. Hugh Griffiths and Adrian Wilkinson, in their report on clandestine arms transfers for the South Eastern and Eastern Europe Clearinghouse for the Control of Small Arms and Light Weapons (SEESAC), point out that relatively few illegal weapons shipments have been detected or intercepted in transit and that this is often attributable to a combination of "inefficiency, lack of resources and high-level complicity and corruption." The systematic analysis and detection of clandestine arms shipments, they claim, remains "still in its infancy." Professional arms dealers often operate on the fringes of legality and financial accountability, perhaps rarely contravening the laws of their "base countries" but utilizing a range of covert connections, underregulated offshore banking systems, and contacts with military and governmental personnel to evade proper scrutiny (perhaps underpinned by bribes and other inducements to regulators). The expansion of global trade, changing international business practice, and, not least, the advent of private military companies, consultants, and trainers (who provide and deliver military services and supplies) have further complicated these complex and opaque international markets.

Alternatively, governmental arms transfers may be shielded by the systems of export licensing and "end-user certifications" (EUCs) that supposedly guarantee the legality and credibility of arms transfers between states. For example, in 1997 the Inter-American Convention Against the Illicit Manufacturing of and Trafficking in Firearms, Ammunition, Explosives, and Other Related Materials, of Organization of American States (OAS), emphasized the need for government-issued EUCs and related documentation in the weapons export licensing process, and this was endorsed by the 2001 UN Programme of Action to Prevent, Combat and Eradicate the Illicit Trade in Small Arms and Light Weapons, which encouraged states to employ "authenticated end-user certificates and effective legal and enforcement measures" when controlling the export of SALW.

Unfortunately, these systems of scrutiny and accountability have become subject to the same pressures of illegality and corruption as the original arms transactions. The problems with EUCs can fall into a number of types: EUCs can be forged, original documents can be altered and reused, misleading or incomplete information can be provided on them, weapons can be diverted in transit to putative "end users," and the "end user" described in the documentation can fail to comply with the agreements and resell the weapons to a third party. A study of end-user certification processes by SIPRI in 2010, conducted by M. Bromley and H. Griffiths, found examples of forged, fabricated, or altered EUCs issued in respect of arms transfers involving Equatorial Guinea, Chad, and Tanzania. The same study found examples of privately issued EUCs that have, since 1945, allowed considerable discretion and limited documentary regulation to British arms dealers presumed to be operating "on behalf of" government. Between 2003 and 2005, a series of private EUCs was used to permit the export of 200,000 AK-47 assault rifles from eastern European states, including 100,000 from Bosnia. The overall

purpose of the transaction is unspecified (but might have involved the intended destruction of the weapons), although at least one consignment of the Bosnian-sourced rifles, numbering between 25,000 and 30,000 weapons, was diverted to Iraqi government forces. A subsequent British parliamentary committee on arms export controls has since recommended that the arrangements for monitoring and controlling large-volume weapons transfers should be tightened.

Moving somewhat down the scale in terms of trafficked military hardware, the international community has become increasingly concerned with the proliferation of man-portable air defense systems (MANPADS) in the hands of nonstate and terrorist-aligned groups. The advantages of these light, ground-to-air missile systems (such as the U.S. Stinger missile) to small armed groups and terrorist cells are their relative ease of use and their transportability. A Federation of U.S. Scientists "Missile Watch" report of 2010 claimed that 45 civilian aircraft had been shot down by MANPADS since 1975. More than 100 states report stockpiling these weapons, and arms transfers of varying shades of illegality appear to be equipping the armed groups of the world (including rogue states, insurgents, terrorists, and rebel militias) with them. The Central Intelligence Agency (CIA) supplied approximately 1,000 Stinger missiles to the Afghan mujahideen in the 1980s, and up to a half of these remain unaccounted for. Eritrea was thought to have supplied Russian-sourced missiles to a warlord in Somalia; likewise, Iran is alleged to have supplied them to Hezbollah. In 2003, looters were said to have stolen as many as 5,000 of them from Iraqi arms depots following the collapse of Saddam Hussein's regime in Iraq. Finally, an arms shipment containing five crates of surface-to-air missiles from North Korea was intercepted in Thailand, as reported by Saferworld in 2010.

What the question of portable surface-to-air missile systems reaffirms concerns the varying layers of official secrecy and criminal conspiracy, rendering accountability and transparency of international arms transfers very limited. In addition to degrees of scale there are also important questions of nature, structure, and consequences to consider. Arms transfer analysts tend to refer to "licit" and "illicit" weapons transfers, and among the illicit transfers they distinguish between the "gray" and "black" markets. The black market, the major part of which involves SALW, concerns outright criminal sales and transfers of weapons, trade in which is thought to be worth around $3 billion per year. Arms transfers here can be both large- and small-scale. For example, among the latter is the notorious "trail of ants" (*trafico de la hormiga*) that routinely smuggles firearms across the Mexican border from the United States. Here a legally entitled or "straw" purchaser can make multiple gun purchases from gun stores and gun shows in Arizona, Texas, New Mexico, and California. The guns are then handed to traffickers who shift them across the border in small consignments hidden either in vehicles or among a variety of trade goods. Nearly 8,000 firearms sold in the United States during 2009–10 were traced to Mexico, a substantial increase over previous years. Another, essentially small-scale, dimension of this smuggling has seen British and American troops bringing home "battlefield souvenirs" from their tours of duty in Iraq and Afghanistan. Some of these weapons undoubtedly remain as trophies; others, however, are sold.

Moving upscale in the black market, it becomes clear how the supplies of arms during the Cold War years established durable international networks for the subsequent clandestine distribution of weapons to all manner of groups and organizations. Illegal gunrunning was often an aspect of covert foreign policy. For example, CIA involvement with the Air America airline allowed covert distribution of weapons throughout Vietnam, Laos, and Cambodia. Similar arrangements prevailed across the former Soviet Union, with agreements on weapons production and distribution forming an important dimension of Soviet trade as well as foreign and economic policy. Following the end of the Cold War, and particularly the deterioration of economic conditions in the region, small arms (especially the AK-47 assault rifle, which is perhaps the Soviet Union's best-selling product) became an important source of hard currency. There is a degree of irony in the fact that it took capitalist globalization and thriving illegal international economies, neither of which the Soviet Union could resist or control, to fully realize the potential of the AK-47 as the most prolific firearm of all time.

As the European Union expanded and trade and customs barriers were lowered, the weapons offloaded by former Soviet military, police, and security services trickled into western Europe as well as flowing south and east into conflict zones such as the former Yugoslavia (which in turn became a key supply route for small arms into western Europe), the Middle East, Asia, and Africa. As arms analysts remark, despite the illegal, typically covert, character of these transactions, certain basic market principles—supply and demand—dictate the flow of illegal weapons. Progress in tackling weapons proliferation requires that both elements of this equation be addressed. Weapons move to where they can command a price—either in bulk, toward rogue and failed states and conflict or civil war zones in the Third World, or in smaller numbers to criminal groups in more developed societies, where gun-control regimes, enforcement risks, and the resulting scarcity inflate prices. R. T. Naylor, one of the leading analysts of the modern black market in arms, has described a critical shift in the "new" international trafficking of weapons. Compared to the Cold War era, dominated by a few big suppliers who understood what their merchandise could do for their customers' political ambitions and who used arms transfers to cement political alliances, the new, fragmented, criminal weapons market has been overtaken by mercenaries and traffickers who are chiefly interested in what the merchandise might do for their own financial ambitions. As a result, according to the 2002 *Small Arms Survey*, firearm suppliers should now be seen as "independent variables" in conflict zones or "situational facilitators" of violence—including chronic levels of gender-based violence and abuse. Conflicts are driven and sustained by the supply of weapons, so durable solutions to these conflicts must focus on the tools of violence as well as the underlying causes.

Yet the vital point about the "black" market in weapons is that it would not exist at anything like its contemporary scale and seriousness were it not for an extensive "gray" market. This gray market comprises both the fringe stockpiles of surplus military equipment around the world and the extensive global civilian ownership of weapons. As of the 2003 *Small Arms Survey*, the world's supply of weapons in circulation was approaching 650 million, with close to 400 million of these estimated to be in civilian hands. The many forms of leakage and slippage, both small and large scale, from the gray to the black markets, establish the criminogenic international weapons-trafficking environment of the contemporary world. This explains, in part, why the UN Programme of Action on the Illicit Trade in Small Arms and Light Weapons, commencing in 2001, sought to target the civilian ownership of weapons as a priority. This was, and remains, undoubtedly controversial, and not just in the United States, where the ownership of firearms is taken to be a constitutional right.

Notwithstanding the scale of the problems posed by weapons proliferation in the world, the international arms control movements can certainly point to important progress, particularly on international treaties against cluster munitions and landmines. They would also point to better research, greater transparency and accountability, and improved information exchange and enforcement coordination on illicit arms transfers.

Peter Squires
University of Brighton

See also Eastern Europe and Russia; European Union; Failed States; Gender-Based Violence; Genocide; Globalization; Interpol; Legal and Illegal Economies; Military Industries; Nongovernmental Organizations; Terrorism Versus Transnational Crime; United Nations; War Crimes; Western Europe

Further Readings

Bromley, M. and H. Griffiths. "End-User Certificates: Improving Standards to Prevent Diversion." *SIPRI Insights on Peace and Security*, v.3 (March 2010).

Cukier, W. and V. Seidel. *The Global Gun Epidemic: From Saturday Night Specials to AK47s*. Westport CT: Praeger Security International, 2006.

Graduate Institute of International Studies. *Small Arms Survey: Profiling the Problem*. New York: Oxford University Press, 2001.

Griffiths, Hugh and Adrian Wilkinson. *Guns, Planes and Ships: Identification and Disruption of Clandestine Arms Transfers*. Belgrade, Serbia: South Eastern and Eastern Europe Clearinghouse for the Control of Small Arms and Light Weapons, United Nations Development Programme, 2007.

Lumpe, L., ed. *Running Guns: The Global Black Market in Small Arms*. New York: Zed Books, 2000.

Saferworld. "Controlling the Transfer of Man-Portable Air Defence Systems: A Guide to Best Practice." 2010.

http://www.saferworld.org.uk/manpads (Accessed February 2011).

Stohl, R., M. Schroeder, and D. Smith. *The Small Arms Trade*. Oxford: Oneworld Books, 2007.

West Asia

In the wake of the attacks on the United States on September 11, 2001 (9/11), an analytic spotlight has been focused on Afghanistan and, to a slightly lesser extent, its eastern neighbor Pakistan. Afghanistan has been a base for Al Qaeda, the transnational militant group behind the 9/11 attacks. Al Qaeda was provided a safe haven by the Taliban, a local Islamist group with which it has had a complicated relationship. Less attention, however, has been paid to Afghanistan's northern neighbors Turkmenistan, Uzbekistan, Tajikistan, and Kyrgyzstan. Collectively, for the purposes of this entry, these states, along with Nepal and Bhutan, comprise the region of West Asia.

Transnational criminal activity in West Asia is characterized by a range of often interconnected actors and illicit behavior, notably corruption, trafficking in weapons and drugs, organized crime, and militancy. Although there are peculiarities tied to each state's history, politics, demographics, and geopolitical importance, transnational crime in this region is linked by issues including governance challenges, varying levels of border control, and socioeconomic conditions.

Corruption

Corruption involves an abuse of power and can include criminal acts such as bribery and embezzlement. The United Nations (UN) promulgated a legally binding treaty, the UN Convention Against Corruption (UNCAC), which entered into force in December 2005. Afghanistan, Kazakhstan, Kyrgyzstan, Pakistan, Tajikistan, Turkmenistan, and Uzbekistan are all states parties; Bhutan and Nepal signed the UNCAC but have not yet ratified it.

Corruption in Turkmenistan and Uzbekistan is rooted in the countries' authoritarian political systems and connected lack of political and legal accountability. These factors combine to impact the functionality of the states and their provision of public services, integral to the socioeconomic well-being of their populations. Turkmenistan raises particular corruption concerns because of its large natural gas reserves and the risks for illicit exploitation involving bribery for access.

Afghanistan's corruption problems are caught up in a web of intertwined factors, which include the process of state building, the lack of a developed economy and the corresponding presence of an active informal economy, the production and trafficking of opium, the state's role in the international battle with the Taliban, and related efforts to thwart terrorism. This is all compounded by a legacy of conflict and weak center-periphery relations between the capital, Kabul (situated in the province of the same name) and the other Afghan provinces.

Overall, corrupt acts in West Asian states range from bribery for the provision of state services, such as utilities and education, to the payment of protection money to bribery for border access and passage to the embezzlement of state funds for private financial gain.

Weapons Trafficking

Several countries in West Asia either "host" violent conflicts or have gone through such conflict in recent history. Conflict zones raise numerous issues regarding the proliferation and trafficking of arms, including insecure stockpiles, the involvement of organized crime, weapons as commodities, arms purchases by militant actors, and state instability.

An international coalition of military forces led by the North Atlantic Treaty Organization (NATO) and the United States has been stationed in Afghanistan to quash Taliban-affiliated insurgents armed with a range of weapons and to stave off the threat posed by Al Qaeda. Neighboring Pakistan has battled with a combination of tribal militants and Taliban insurgents as well. Tajikistan survived a civil war that nearly tore apart the country in the 1990s. Uzbekistan has been challenged by Islamist militant groups. The porous borders between Afghanistan and Pakistan, to the east, and Afghanistan and the Central Asian states, to the north, have allowed trafficking into and out of those states as well as insecure stockpiles from the days of the Soviet Union. Afghanistan has been in a near-constant state of war since the 1970s; many of the weapons in the country today were originally provided by the United States to aid the resistance against the Soviets.

Nepal has been a battle zone where the monarchy has been pitted against Maoist rebels. In Nepal there have been concerns about the availability of weapons in conjunction with the rebel insurgency and ordinary criminality. The government of India was a major weapons supplier to the monarchy for part of the conflict, and questions have been raised about connections and trafficking between Indian militants and Maoist insurgents.

Notably, concerns about the interconnection between corruption, weapons, drug trafficking, and militancy abound and require complex solutions that can involve the military, police, justice, and development sectors.

Drug Trafficking

Much of the literature about drug trafficking in the West Asia region revolves around Afghanistan and the production and trafficking of opium noted above. Afghan opium production and trafficking involve a variety of unlikely characters: Islamist insurgents, rural farmers, Kabul-based government officials, secular organized criminals, and far-flung drug abusers.

Opium production and trafficking have numerous negative effects on Afghanistan and the surrounding states. Within Afghanistan, the illegal opium economy undermines efforts to construct licit and sustainable national and local economies, provides financial support for the Taliban, fuels domestic heroin addiction, and helps undermine efforts to create institutions that support good governance. The financial gains from the opium trade are also connected to the purchase of weapons and escalation of violence within the state. Gretchen Peters of the U.S. Institute for Peace (USIP) notes, "Taliban commanders on the village level have expanded their activities related to drugs from collecting extortion and charging protection fees to running heroin refineries and engaging in kidnapping and other smuggling schemes."

Outside Afghanistan, opium trafficking helps promote corruption as traffickers bribe border guards and security service personnel to facilitate moving the drugs. Drug trafficking also provides organized criminal and militant individuals with "jobs" and is said to fund militant groups in the region. Finally, Afghan opium growth and trafficking result in increased heroin addiction rates. The UN Office on Drugs and Crime reported in 2009 that more people die annually from opium produced in Afghanistan than any other drug. Further, addiction has risen specifically in Central Asia, Iran, and Russia.

Human Trafficking

The UN Convention Against Transnational Organized Crime (UNTOC) is supplemented by the Protocol to Prevent, Suppress, and Punish Trafficking in Persons, Especially Women and Children. Both entered into force in 2003. Afghanistan, Pakistan, Tajikistan, Turkmenistan, Uzbekistan, Kyrgyzstan, and Kazakhstan are all states parties. Nepal has signed, but not yet ratified, and Bhutan has neither signed nor ratified the UNTOC. Article 3 of the protocol defines human trafficking as "the recruitment, transportation, transfer, harbouring or receipt of persons, by means of the threat or use of force or other forms of coercion, of abduction, of fraud, of deception, of the abuse of power" to exploit another person for purposes including forced labor or slavery as well as sexual abuse. According to the U.S. Department of State's annual report on human trafficking, Afghanistan, Pakistan, Nepal, Tajikistan, Turkmenistan, Uzbekistan, Kyrgyzstan, and Kazakhstan all grapple with serious human trafficking issues and are addressing them to varying degrees. The states also have different roles in the human trafficking pipeline: For example, Nepal is a source country for persons who are trafficked out of the country, sometimes through organized criminal networks. Pakistan, on the other hand, functions as a source, transit, and destination country where young men may be sold into forced labor or girls into forced marriages.

Militancy

Conflict, often between nonstate actors and states, has wreaked havoc in the West Asia region. Violent conflict involving nonstate actors raises a range of issues; these include the organization and goals of the militant groups; the nexus between strategic goals and the violent acts they commit; the destabilization of states targeted by militant violence; groups' ability to cross porous borders because of corruption and a related lack of dedicated resources; the impact on nearby states; the methods by which militant groups raise, store, and move funds; and, their acquisition of weapons and the methods through which they pay for and traffic them.

Al Qaeda is a much discussed and debated transnational movement, whose key figures, in recent years, have based themselves in Afghanistan and Pakistan. Al Qaeda exploits localized Muslim grievances, often sociopolitical, from various conflicts around the world, seeking to advance its vision of a global Islamic caliphate. In promoting this vision, it encourages violence against those who do not agree with its agenda.

As noted above, Afghanistan was a safe haven for Al Qaeda until the United States attacked that country seeking to eliminate the terrorist threat and rout its state sponsors, the Taliban, from power. Ten years after that routing, many analysts believed Al Qaeda to be an operational shadow of its former self. However, it retains the ability to inspire and incite violence against those who stand in its way in regional conflicts—from Pakistan to Kashmir to Afghanistan to Uzbekistan. Al Qaeda leader Osama bin Laden was shot and killed by American forces in Pakistan in May 2011, and numerous key figures in the Al Qaeda organization are believed to reside in the Afghanistan-Pakistan border region, retaining relations with multiple Taliban organizations in both states.

Militancy has also taken its toll on neighbors to the north in central Asia, particularly Uzbekistan. Uzbekistan's most notorious group is the Islamist Union of Uzbekistan (IMU), founded in the late 1990s. Members have been involved in repeated attacks in Uzbekistan as well as in Kyrgyzstan, the latter most notably in the mid-1999 and again in 2000. IMU militants reportedly received training in Afghanistan and have been arrested in Pakistan. State security services and regional analysts connect them to the Afghan opium trade and believe it has been a significant source of financing.

Kimberly Jones
Northeastern University

See also Al Qaeda; Antiterrorist Financing; Drug Trade: Source, Destination, and Transit Countries; Failed States; Heroin; Human Smuggling; Human Trafficking; Legal and Illegal Economies; Narco-Terrorism; Terrorism: Nondomestic

Further Readings

Burke, Jason. *Al Qaeda: The True Story of Radical Islam.* New York: I. B. Tauris, 2004.

Freedom House. *Nations in Transit.* Washington, DC: Author, 2010.

Giustozzi, Antonio. *Decoding the New Taliban.* New York: Columbia University Press, 2009.

Olcott, Martha Brill. *Central Asia's Second Chance*. Washington, DC: Carnegie Endowment for International Peace, 2005.

Oxfam. "India and the Arms Trade Treaty." September 2006. http://www.oxfam.org.uk/resources/policy/ conflict_disasters/downloads/bn_india_att.pdf (Accessed February 2011).

Peters, Gretchen. "How Opium Profits the Taliban." Washington, DC: U.S. Institute for Peace, 2009.

Rashid, Ahmed. *Descent Into Chaos*. New York: Penguin, 2009.

Transparency International. "Corruption Perceptions Index 2010." http://www.transparency.org/content/ download/55725/890310 (Accessed February 2011).

United Nations Office on Drugs and Crime. "United Nations Convention Against Corruption." 2004. http:// www.unodc.org/documents/treaties/UNCAC/ Publications/Convention/08-50026_E.pdf (Accessed February 2011).

United Nations Office on Drugs and Crime. "United Nations Convention Against Transnational Organized Crime." http://www.unodc.org/documents/treaties/ UNTOC/Publications/TOC%20Convention/ TOCebook-e.pdf (Accessed April 2011).

United Nations Regional Centre for Peace and Disarmament in Asia and the Pacific. "Supporting the Arms Trade Treaty Negotiations Through Regional Discussions and Expertise Sharing" (November 2010). http://www.unidir.org/pdf/activites/pdf2-act561.pdf (Accessed February 2011).

U.S. Agency for International Development. *Assessment of Corruption in Afghanistan*. Washington, DC: Author, 2009. http://pdf.usaid.gov/pdf_docs/PNADO248.pdf (Accessed February 2011).

U.S. Department of State. "Trafficking in Persons Report 2010." June 2010. http://www.state.gov/g/tip/rls/ tiprpt/2010/index.htm (Accessed April 2011).

WESTERN EUROPE

Modern policing began in Europe, with law-enforcement agencies that originated in municipalities such as London and Paris serving as models for those in other locations. These institutions, with their rich traditions of preventing transnational crimes, have greatly affected how many nations perceive and administer justice. Recent trends and developments, however, have altered some of these practices. Globalization has caused a tremendous streamlining of many of the rules and regulations that traditionally impeded transnational business dealings. A similar change has occurred with regard to transnational crime, which is more sophisticated and multifaceted than ever before. Ways of conceptualizing law enforcement and administering justice have recently evolved to meet these challenges.

Traditional Law-Enforcement Approaches

Since the time of the ancient Greeks and Romans, Europeans have sought to establish effective ways of discouraging and punishing criminal behavior. The ancient Greeks used commonly owned slaves to enforce laws, while the Romans relied upon their army to combat crimes and other civil unrest. During the Middle Ages, feudal lords were responsible for maintaining the peace in areas they controlled, although many towns and cities hired watchmen to help with the prevention of crime. It was only during the 19th century that modern police forces originated, and their initial concern was with local crime. Various mechanisms were created within individual nations for dealing with transnational crime, and many of these exist to the present day. As the European Union has become more established, it has also created initiatives for dealing with transnational crime and means of punishing wrongdoers.

The Metropolitan Police Service (commonly known as "the Met" or "Scotland Yard") was established in London in 1829. One of the first modern police organizations extant, the Met was established by British home secretary Sir Robert Peel pursuant to the Metropolitan Police Act of 1829. The Met's first headquarters were located at 4 Whitehall Place, which backed onto a street known as Great Scotland Yard, which resulted in the organization's eponymous nickname. Officers from Scotland Yard were charged primarily with battling crime in the greater London area, but the organization's great size, expertise, and resources also meant that its know-how was often in demand for crimes that occurred in outlying areas. Scotland Yard also became frequently involved in matters involving transnational crimes that demanded greater resources to address. Scotland Yard officials have traditionally had responsibility for investigating and combating certain serious organized crimes, although this was shared with certain other groups, formed chiefly during the 1990s, including the National Crime Squad (NCS), the National Criminal Investigative Service (NCIS), and the National Hi-Tech Crime Unit (NHTCU). This situation changed with the Serious Organised Crime and Police Act of 2005 (SOCPA), which established a national Serious Organised Crime Agency (SOCA). SOCA merged the operations of a variety of investigative units—including the NCS, the NCIS, and the NHTCU—in an effort to create an investigative and intelligence unit that can fight transnational and other major crimes. SOCA does not deal with matters of national security, nor does it focus on counterintelligence measures. Instead, SOCA works to combat organized crime, especially that dealing with illegal narcotics, immigrants, and weapons trafficking. SOCA has not usurped Scotland Yard's Specialist Crime Directorate, which continues to deal with homicides, economic crimes, and vice and offers forensic and intelligence services.

France was another leader in developing modern policing services. Today, three major agencies provide policing services across France. The Police Nationale, founded in 1812 by Eugène François Vidocq, was known before 1966 as the Sûreté Nationale. The Police Nationale, a civilian force, has approximately 150,000 agents who are chiefly responsible for major municipalities and regions run by the Ministry of the Interior. The Gendarmerie Nationale is a paramilitary force charged with keeping the peace in small towns and rural areas. The Gendarmerie Nationale represents one of the oldest institutions in France, stemming from the Middle Ages, and has more than 100,000 members working under the auspices of the Ministry of Defense. The third branch is the Directorate-General of Customs and Indirect Taxes, which prevents smuggling, investigates counterfeiting, maintains border control, and levies indirect taxes. The Directorate-General of Customs and Indirect Taxes is an armed service, commonly known as La Douane, and under the supervision of the Ministry for Budget, Public Accounts and the Civil Service. While historically these three divisions were able to deal with crime, recent developments, including the opening of borders as part of the European Union's initiatives and the difficulties many eastern European governments have had in maintaining order, led many to believe that a new initiative was needed to combat transnational crime. To deal with the growing problem of transnational crime, in 2008 the Direction Centrale du Renseignement Intérieur (Central Directorate of Interior Intelligence, or DCRI) became operational. The DCRI has slightly more than 3,000 agents and is responsible for fighting cybercrime, surveillance of groups and individuals involved in organized crime, counterterrorism, and counterespionage. Headquartered in Levallois-Perret, a suburb of Paris, the DCRI attempts to coordinate and administer programs designed to combat transnational crime with the other three major police agencies.

German law enforcement is vested with its various states pursuant to the German constitution. Unlike other major European powers, such as Italy or France, Germany has no tradition of a national police force or agency, nor has it had a central investigative clearinghouse such as the United Kingdom's Scotland Yard. Part of this distinction is historical (because, since the time of German unification in 1871, policing was left in the hands of the state governments), and part is a reaction to the Nazi regime, which established an infamous national police force notorious for its gross abuse of power. Within this context, three minor national police forces do operate within Germany, including the Federal Police (Bundespolizei), the Federal Criminal Police Office (Bundeskriminalamt), and the Police of the Parliament (Polizei beim Deutschen Bundestag). Each of these three forces has distinct responsibilities. The Federal Police, with 40,000 agents, is largely responsible for border control and also handles hostage incidents, organized crime, and assassinations. The Federal Criminal Police Office, with 5,200 staff members, serves chiefly as a coordinating agency that assists with investigations involving transnational crimes. The Police of the Parliament, the smallest group with only a few hundred agents, is responsible for protection of the premises of the Bundestag in Berlin. Traditional fears of police power have slowed the movement to establish a more cohesive approach to transnational crime.

Although Italy did not become a unified nation until 1861, its national police force, the Corps of Carabinieri (Arma dei Carabinieri), was founded in 1814 by King Victor Emmanuel of Sardinia. The Corps of Carabinieri was organized so that one division was assigned to each province; each division was further divided into companies and lieutenancies, with local police stations commanded by an officer of the force. During the fascist rule of Benito Mussolini (1920–43), the Corps of Carabinieri was used to suppress opposition, although later opposition to the Nazi occupation restored the group's good standing. A separate branch of the Italian military since 2000, the Carabinieri are organized into territories that allows them to pursue their law-enforcement duties. The Carabinieri have several divisions that expressly fight transnational crime. The Special Operations Group (Raggruppamento Operativo Speciale, or ROS) was created in 1990 in the wake of the Corps' success against the Red Brigades. The ROS focuses on investigating organized crime, combating drug trafficking and kidnapping, and providing analysis to other divisions of the force. Twenty-six regional anticrime units exist, coordinated through the ROS command center located in Chieti. The ROS has a reputation for being extremely successful in apprehending those involved in transnational crimes such as money laundering, arms trafficking, narcotics smuggling, and kidnapping, in part because of its agents' willingness to infiltrate criminal organizations.

Other European nations have also developed rigorous means of dealing with transnational crime. In Spain, for example, cocaine importation is a serious problem, in part because of the nation's proximity to the sea, which facilitates easy smuggling of narcotics and other substances. Spain uses its three-part police force to address this issue—including the Civil Guard (Guardia Civil), the National Police Corps (Cuerpo Nacional de Policía), and the Customs Surveillance Service (Servicio de Vigilancia Aduanera)—to coordinate efforts to address drug-trafficking and other crimes, such as fraud, cyberattacks, and organized crime. Each of the Scandinavian nations has its own national police service, including the Norwegian Police Service (Politi- og lensmannsetaten) in Norway and the Swedish National Police Board (Rikspolisstyrelsen) in Sweden. These agencies coordinate local policing authorities and provide strategic, intelligence, and forensic support that assists in addressing transnational crimes. As in all of Europe, as border crossings become more frequent and less arduous, transnational crime has increased.

Collaborative Approaches

Although European police cooperation has historically tended to be a low priority, increasing transnational organized crime, especially that concerned with arms trafficking and narcotics, has provided the impetus to explore new ways to approach these challenges. A variety of institutions at the local, regional, and international levels have been created to confront and contain transnational organized criminal activities. These efforts have meant that at times, the traditional separation between intelligence organizations, law-enforcement agencies, and the military has been blurred. These initiatives are not all new. Since 1928, for example, the International Criminal Police Organization (Interpol) has worked to foster cooperation and collaboration between the police agencies of various nations. Based in Lyon, France, Interpol is an international organization, although it is especially active in western Europe. Interpol actively works to address transnational crime in Europe and around the globe. It possesses extensive databases related to past transnational criminal activity, and its analysts provide intelligence on trends and patterns that local law-enforcement agencies can use to formulate strategies and determine priorities. Criminal activity that is especially susceptible to Interpol's highly organized and scientific approach include corruption, counterfeiting, environmental misdeeds, illicit drug manufacture and transport, money laundering, organized crime, pornography, and a variety of other crimes.

Western European concerns regarding crime in the region have sometimes resulted in initiatives that are designed to fight transnational crime outside the region. For example, western European nations largely sponsored the Stability Pact Initiative Against Organized Crime (SPOC) in southeastern Europe, which was in place from 1999 until 2008, at which time it was replaced with the Regional Cooperation Council (ROC). Both the SPOC and the ROC aimed to strengthen peace, human rights, democracy, and economic development in the group of nations that includes Albania, Bosnia and Herzegovina, Bulgaria, Croatia, Macedonia, Moldova, Montenegro, Romania, and Serbia. Although the SPOC was largely successful, it was reorganized as the ROC chiefly because the many nations involved desired more local control than was afforded by the prior configuration, which included input from the nations of the European Union, Japan, Russia, and the United States. Similarly, the Southeastern Europe Cooperation Initiative (SECI), which includes the SPOC nations and Greece, Hungary, Slovenia, and Turkey, used Western aid to provide stability in a previously unstable region. This increased stability has greatly assisted western European nations in fighting transnational criminal activity that took place there. As transnational crime grows ever more complex, the distinctions between matters considered security and those thought of as law enforcement will continue to become less clear. Further actions might well be expected to attend to those problems that contribute to transnational crime.

Stephen T. Schroth
Jason A. Helfer
Angeles Garduño
Knox College

See also Anticorruption Legislation; Centralization; Joint Force Policing and Integrated Models; North America; Policing: Transnational; Racketeer Influenced and Corrupt Organizations Act

Further Readings

Davis, I., C. Hirst, and B. Mariani. *Organized Crime, Corruption and Illicit Arms Trafficking in an Enlarged EU: Challenges and Perspectives.* London: Saferworld, 2001.

Deflem, M. *Policing World Society: Historical Foundations of International Police Cooperation.* Oxford, UK: Clarendon Press, 2004.

Goldsmith, A. and J. Sheptycki. *Crafting Transnational Policing: State-Building and Global Policing Reform.* Oxford, UK: Hart Law Publishers, 2007.

Nadelmann, E. A. *Cops Across Borders: The Internationalization of U.S. Law Enforcement.* University Park: Pennsylvania State University Press, 1993.

WILDLIFE CRIME

Wildlife crime involves the illegal trade of protected species that are trafficked as foodstuff, pets, souvenirs, fashion items, trophies, and medicinal ingredients. Popular destinations for this trade include North America, Asia, and Europe. The following discussion outlines the main features of wildlife crime and its impact on endangered species. Links between wildlife crime and organized crime are noted and the response of the international community to tackle it at a transnational level outlined. It is concluded that although work still needs to be done to continue to address wildlife crime, moves to protect endangered species arguably represent one of the greater successes of the international community, in terms of both membership agreement and the measures implemented to govern wildlife trade and protect endangered species.

It is necessary to begin looking at wildlife crime at a transnational level by considering developments in the protection of endangered species. It is unfortunately the case that all biological organisms can (and indeed frequently do) become extinct for a number of reasons tied to biodiversity, evolution, and environmental change. Nevertheless, species can (and indeed frequently do) become threatened by the introduction of changes brought about by human beings. From a global perspective, the key development in the protection of endangered species was the creation in 1948 of the International Union for Conservation of Nature (IUCN). Based in Geneva, Switzerland, this organization is dedicated to identifying and protecting endangered species. Every five years it publishes the Red List. This is a comprehensive inventory of the global conservation status of animal and plant species. Based on key criteria such as population size, geographic distribution, and rate of population/geographic decline, species are classified into one of the following nine groups:

- *Extinct* (EX), with no population remaining (such as the Javan tiger)
- *Extinct in the wild* (EW), surviving only in captivity (such as the Alagoas curassow)
- *Critically endangered* (CR), at extreme risk of extinction in the wild (such as the mountain gorilla)
- *Endangered* (EN), at high risk for extinction in the wild (such as the blue whale)
- *Vulnerable* (VU), at high risk of endangerment in the wild (such as the cheetah)
- *Near threatened* (NT), likely in the near future to become endangered (such as the tiger shark)
- *Least concern* (LC), at lowest risk (such as the house mouse)
- *Data deficient* (DD), lacking enough data to make an assessment of the risk of extinction
- *Not evaluated* (NE), not yet evaluated against the criteria

The IUCN Red List is a critical measure by which nation-states internationally recognize species at risk of extinction. However, in addition to identifying and recognizing a species as being in danger of extinction, it is necessary to legislate for the legal trade in them (such as for scientific research purposes) as well as to police illegal trade both domestically and across international borders. Although each nation-state controls its own domestic arrangements, internationally the framework for such action comes from the Convention on International Trade in Endangered Species of Wild Fauna and Flora (CITES). Established in 1973, this convention subjects international trade in species to certain controls covering import, export, and re-export. Of the 192 nation-states recognized by the United Nations (UN), 175 have signed the convention. More than 6,000 species of animals and 30,000 species of plants are protected by CITES. International trade between nation-states is governed by the use of CITES permits, which are divided into three categories (known as appendices) based on the risk of extinction for the species in question. CITES has informed the development of legislation at the nation-state level. For example, CITES was incorporated into U.S. law via the Endangered Species Act (1973). In addition to regulating trade, this act seeks both to prevent the extinction of species at risk of extinction and to lessen threats to their survival in their natural habitat by restricting hunting and land development as well as creating specialist animal preserves and breeding programs.

CITES may well prohibit commercial international trade in plant and animal species threatened with extinction. However, this does not mean that domestic black markets and trafficking across national borders do not exist. Illegal exports of wildlife and protected items such as ivory, rhinoceros horns, shark fins, and exotic birds are estimated to earn criminals between $15 billion and $20 billion a year. Dealers range from individuals and businesses to organized crime syndicates. Indeed, many of the same routes used for transportation of illegal weapons, people, and drugs are used for wildlife trafficking. Demand can be said to be driven by a mixture of two factors: lifestyle and culture. In Europe and the United States, demand for illegal wildlife is typically driven by tourism, clothing fashions, and jewelry, alongside the exotic pet trade. In Asia, demand for illegal wildlife is also frequently driven by social status and the practices of traditional medicine.

Addressing wildlife crime at a local and global level can be a complex issue, given its link with cultural and spiritual practices within certain geographic areas. For example, traditional Chinese medicine requires many animal products (such as tiger meat) that are available only through the wildlife smuggling trade. Similarly, in Africa "bushmeat" in the form of wild animals (which includes endangered primates) is viewed as a delicacy and provides local hunters and traders with incomes and livelihoods that by and large could not be replaced without a considerable amount of investment well beyond the economic means currently available to African nation-states. Nevertheless it can be argued that it is vitally important for the international community to provide aid to help these nations continue to tackle wildlife crime, given that it promotes health threats to human beings in addition to the more obvious threat of extinction it poses to indigenous wildlife populations. Indeed, severe acute respiratory syndrome (SARS), monkeypox, and avian influenza are all believed by scientists to have been in part spread through the illegal trade in exotic pets from African and Asian countries into Europe and the United States.

It is impossible to know the true extent of illegal smuggling in protected wildlife. Furthermore, wildlife trafficking in the context of supplying Chinese medicine and African bushmeat brings to the foreground the need to address cultural as well as economic factors when attempting to stamp out illegal wildlife trade practices. This said, through international cooperation leading to developments such as IUCN, the Red List, and CITES, significant progress has been made in the last half century in protecting endangered wildlife from illegal domestic trade and export.

John Martyn Chamberlain
Loughborough University

See also Australia; East Asia; Pollution: Air and Water; Pollution: Corporate; Pollution: Shipping-Related; Toxic Dumping

Further Readings

Birnie, P. and A. Boyle. *International Law and the Environment*, 2nd ed. Oxford, UK: Oxford University Press, 2002.

South, N. and P. Beirne. *Issues in Green Criminology: Confronting Harms Against Environments, Humanity and Other Animals.* Devon, UK: Willan, 2007.

Wilcove, D. S. and L. L. Master. "How Many Endangered Species Are There in the United States?" *Frontiers in Ecology and the Environment*, v.3/8 (2008).

Women and Transnational Crime

Transnational crime has historically been dominated by men. However, there is a growing awareness of women's presence and participation. Women are most visible in research and literature on transnational crime as victims. This entry describes the role of gender among those who are active participants in transnational crime.

Women are present in most aspects of transnational crime, although research on the nature of women's involvement is in the early stages of development. Some researchers in the area have claimed that the numbers of women involved in transnational crime has increased in recent decades. There are three dominant hypotheses put forward to explain these changes. The first is that wider changes in the position of women in society have driven women's involvement in illegal activities. In other words, as women become "emancipated," access to better educational and employment opportunities in turn provides greater access to illegal power and opportunities. Second, it has been claimed that structural changes in crime have provided new opportunities for women. For example, it has been claimed that the drug trade expanded rapidly in the 1990s, which weakened existing (exclusive) drug distribution networks, thereby creating new opportunities for women. Similarly, prosecution of men in organized crime groups in Italy (or the Mafia) created new opportunities for women in the families to take over while their men were imprisoned. Finally, it has been argued that cultural changes have occurred in organized crime: Sexism and old boys' networks have been replaced by the logic of the market; thus, traditional barriers to women's involvement have been broken down or removed. In general, evidence to support the foregoing hypotheses is scant. Since research on transnational crime and justice is a relatively new field (and since research on women's involvement is a relatively recent field of research), it is almost impossible to know if there are more women involved, as there is no baseline against which to compare contemporary research. Existing research is outlined below. The final section discusses the criminal justice implications of women as offenders.

International Drug Trade

Although women are undoubtedly present in the international trade in drugs globally, research is most well developed in the area of the international cocaine trade. Research finds that women are present wherever cocaine is grown, processed, trafficked, sold, and consumed. It is not yet fully understood to what extent women are actively involved. Women's main role in the international cocaine trade is as drug mules. Although it is popularly thought that the majority of mules are women, research has shown that in fact 70 percent of people arrested at international borders with drugs are men (this group may include "mules" as well as independent traffickers). Nonetheless, the numbers of women involved is significant enough to have important implications for criminal justice institutions. Research has examined mules' motives for involvement. Julia Sudbury's research on Jamaican drug mules found that female "liberation" has little to do with their involvement. Rather, women's role as the head of the household combined with economic pressures result in women becoming involved in crime to make ends meet. Similarly, research by Howard Campbell into the drug trade on the U.S.-Mexican border suggests that involvement in the drug trade does not bring emancipation but further victimization. Little research has examined women's involvement in other aspects of the trade, such as recruiting mules or buying, selling, and trafficking drugs. Limited evidence suggests that the drug trade remains a male-dominated business where few women are able to progress. Nonetheless, anecdotal evidence suggests that in spite of this, a small number of women are successful in the international cocaine trade, but they remain the exception rather than the rule.

Organized Crime and the Mafia

It has long been presumed that the "macho" nature of Italian culture would exclude women from involvement in organized crime through the Mafia in Italy. Nonetheless, women have long been part of organized crime as part of the support system and as part of the family on which the Mafia is built. Although there is some variation across Italy and internationally, Mafia historians find that women could exercise power indirectly through their sons and husbands. In recent years, research has found that women have increasingly been present in organizational roles. In the 1980s and 1990s many important men were imprisoned and women were able to move into positions of power. Equally, women are also involved in anti-mafia campaigns in Italy.

Sex Trafficking

It bears mentioning that the international sex trade is a highly gendered phenomenon insofar as the overwhelming majority of those "consumers" who drive the trade are men, whereas those trafficked are almost exclusively women. Discourse about women's victimization in sex trafficking (and human trafficking, a crime that is often confused with sex trafficking) has obscured the possibility that women may choose to be smuggled. This echoes previous debates about whether women are involved in prostitution out of choice or necessity. Furthermore, although women may choose to be smuggled, they may be misled by their smugglers and find themselves doing a very different job from the one they agreed to do. This is an extremely difficult topic to research, and emerging research is contradictory. What is clear is that this complex topic is intertwined not only with gender relationships but also with globalization and migration.

Transnational Crime and Justice

The number of men and women imprisoned outside their country of birth has grown rapidly since the 1980s. This is attributable to a number of factors, including increased mobility of people as a result of globalization and in particular involvement in transnational crime. The implications of such imprisonments for criminal justice institutions are only just being explored. In England and Wales, 15 percent of people in prison are foreign nationals, compared to around 6 percent in the United States. The issue involves important gender dimensions: One in five women in prison in the United Kingdom is a foreign national. Across Europe this varies considerably. Although statistics must be interpreted with care, since the numbers of women prisoners are typically very low, foreign national women represent a significant portion of prisoners across Europe: 18 percent in Ireland, 16 percent in Germany, 45 percent in Italy, 26 percent in the Netherlands, and 28 percent in Portugal.

Being imprisoned in a foreign country is tough for both men and women. Both experience isolation and loneliness, and language difficulties mean that foreign nationals often have trouble understanding criminal justice procedures and prison regulations. These problems also form a serious barrier to participating in rehabilitation and education programs. Women have additional needs relating to their role as caregivers and heads of the household. In the United Kingdom, the charity Hibiscus/Female Prisoners Welfare Project has been leading the way since 1986 in advocating on behalf of women in prison to help them access services; it also helps women maintain contact with their families and children and supports women through resettlement in Jamaica. Women imprisoned in other parts of the world are much less fortunate. Although some women may be returned home to complete their sentences close to their families, most serve very long sentences thousands of miles from their families.

Jennifer Fleetwood
University of Kent

See also Cocaine; Gender-Based Violence; Globalization; Human Smuggling; Sex Slavery

Further Readings

Campbell, Howard. "Female Drug Smugglers on the U.S.-Mexico Border: Gender, Crime and Empowerment." *Anthropological Quarterly*, v.81/1 (2008).
Findaca, G. *Women and the Mafia: Female Roles in Organized Crime Structures.* New York: Springer, 2007.
Hibiscus/Female Prisoners Welfare Project. http://fpwphibiscus.org.uk (Accessed February 2011).
Sudbury, J., ed. *Global Lockdown: Race, Gender, and the Prison-Industrial Complex.* London: Routledge, 2005.

WORLD BANK

The World Bank, with headquarters in Washington, D.C., and with offices in more than 100 nations, is an international nongovernmental organization that provides financial and technical assistance to combat poverty around the world. The organization's motto is "Working for a World Free of Poverty." The World Bank accomplishes this through financial assistance by providing loans, credits, and grants to low- and middle-income nations for investments in government, social services, medicine, business, and environmental protection. It also provides considerable technical assistance, usually in the form of policy or legal advice on reforms needed to reach poverty reduction goals, as well as data, donor aid coordination, research and evaluation, data analysis, and research capacity building. In fiscal year 2009, the World Bank provided nearly $47 billion for its projects in developing nations.

The World Bank gets its money through a variety of mechanisms. It sells bonds in the world's financial markets and lends out its own capital. It also receives support from its 187 member nations, 40 of which support no-interest loans to the poorest of nations. Although praised for its antipoverty efforts, the World Bank has been the subject of criticism and protest. The criticisms are broad and considerable, but some focus on negative social and environmental implications of projects that the World Bank has funded, such as displacement of indigenous people.

The 187 member nations are represented by a board of governors (usually the member nations' development or economic leader) that sets policy for the organization and generally meets on a yearly basis. Specific duties and day-to-day operations are delegated to a team of executive directors, which meets once or twice per week. Every five years, the executive directors select a U.S. national as president to run the organization; this is because the United States is the largest contributor to the World Bank. The president is supported by a staff of more than 10,000 persons, including economists, engineers, financial analysts, public policy experts, and social scientists.

The historical roots of the World Bank can be found at the end of World War II, when world leaders discussed how to assist war-torn countries. In 1944, a meeting in New Hampshire established the World Bank to assist nations in postwar reconstruction efforts. Consequently, many of the World Bank's early efforts were focused on massive infrastructure development, including a first loan in 1947 to France for $250 million to support its efforts at postwar rebuilding and modernization.

The World Bank actually comprises two primary institutions, the International Bank for Reconstruction and Development (IBRD) and the International Development Association (IDA), which are owned by member countries. The IBRD and IDA are complemented by three branches (technically considered part of the World Bank Group rather than the World Bank): the International Finance Corporation (IFC), the Multilateral Investment Guarantee Agency (MIGA), and the International Centre for Settlement of Investment Disputes (ICSID).

Although the IBRD and IDA share the common goal of poverty alleviation, they do have at least one major difference, in terms of the nations to which they provide services. The IBRD focuses on reducing poverty and promoting sustainable growth in middle-income and creditworthy low-income countries, through loans and other financial products, as well as through analytical and advisory services. The IBRD is able to use its income to fund development projects and provide client countries with loans at good terms. The IBRD works closely with the IFC, the MIGA, and the International Monetary Fund (IMF) to strengthen deliverable products and services and to maximize their potential impacts.

The IDA, on the other hand, concentrates on the most impoverished nations. The IDA supports programs that aim to reduce poverty, typically through no-interest loans that are typically repaid over periods of 35 to 40 years or more. Some of the IDA's work has focused on helping poor countries recover from civil war and armed conflict, and the IDA often funds efforts to rebuild the nation's infrastructure and increase its resilience to future civil violence and war. One notable program is the IDA's support of efforts to reintegrate ex-combatants in civil strife into peaceable coexistence in their current nations.

Six strategic themes guide the World Bank's work. These are overcoming poverty and spurring sustainable growth in the poorest nations, addressing the challenges of postconflict and fragile nations, building a competitive menu of development solutions for middle-income countries, playing a more active role in global issues such as disease and trade, working with partners to strengthen opportunity in the Arab world, and promoting the use of knowledge to guide organizational policy and practice.

Crime and justice issues are addressed by the World Bank throughout all of these areas, particularly in financing programs designed to reduce political and judicial corruption, ameliorate the conditions that promote terrorism, provide opportunities for youth to get education or jobs, and develop safe roads and transit. For example, the Second Justice Services Improvement Project for Peru was funded to improve justice hiring practices, increase transparency of judicial and other justice agencies, enhance citizens' access to justice, and better the services provided by all of the Peruvian justice system's institutions.

The World Bank has many departments and subdivisions, and at least one is centrally focused on crime. The Social Development Department created the Conflict, Crime and Violence (CCV) cluster to focus on critical issues that plague those nations that are especially vulnerable to conflict and poststrife poverty, known as "fragile states." The CCV's central goal is to collect and distribute innovative ideas and methods for vulnerable nations to implement to address conflict, crime, and violence. The CCV plays an active role in providing information and solutions on political violence and civil war, forced displacement, urban crime and violence, and youth and gender-based violence. Low- or middle-income countries can be fragile states. Middle-income countries are particularly vulnerable in urban settings; countries in areas such as Latin America and East Asia see high levels of violence resulting in financial and political upheaval. The CCV also emphasizes the improvement of governance and increased accountability as critical factors in the reduction of violence and poverty.

Collectively, the World Bank and its subdivisions, such as the CCV, have implemented a large portfolio of programs to address crime and violence. The World Bank has supported the development of conflict resolution programs in Indonesia; has created databases and analysis techniques to track and analyze problems of homicide, drugs, and other crime affecting economic growth in Latin America; has implemented projects designed to address displacement and youth violence in eastern Europe; and has provided peace-building efforts in war-stricken regions such Afghanistan, Colombia, and Rwanda.

Consistent with its theme of being a learning organization, the World Bank since the 1990s has prioritized evaluation, particularly impact studies, to assess the effects of its projects. Increasingly, the World Bank has embraced rigorous research designs, including randomized experiments and sophisticated quasi-experiments, to analyze changes in the well-being of individuals, households, firms, and communities and to provide further feedback to improve the design of future programs and policies. The organization is also a renowned source for reports, data, and indicators on world development, and it has created a number of helpful software and other tools for analyzing data. Two journals, the *World Bank Economic Review* and the *World Bank Research Observer*, are academic publications that provide access to papers by World Bank as well as nonbank researchers.

Anthony Petrosino
Trevor Fronius
WestEd

See also Capital Flight; Egmont Group of Financial Intelligence Units; Globalization; Informal Value Transfer Systems; International Monetary Fund; Public Expenditure Tracking Systems (PETS); Recovery of Stolen Assets; Underground Banking Regulations; United Nations

Further Readings

Bretton Woods Project. "Critical Voices on the World Bank and the IMF." http://www.brettonwoodsproject.org/index.shtml (Accessed February 2011).

Marquette, Heather. *Corruption, Politics and Development: The Role of the World Bank*. New York: Palgrave Macmillan, 2003.

World Bank. *A Guide to the World Bank*. Washington, DC: Author, 2007.

WORLD COURT

The International Court of Justice (ICJ), or the World Court as it is more popularly known, is the highest court (at least in theory) in the world. Part of the United Nations (UN), the ICJ is based at The Hague. Its purpose is the pacific settlement of disputes between nations.

Human history is replete with situations—economic, political, and military—in which nations disagree, frequently resulting in war, with all of its attendant horrors of death and destruction. A number of attempts to address this situation were made, with some limited success, with the formation of temporary tribunals to handle specific situations. However, it was recognized that a permanent organization to address disputes between nations was needed.

In 1899, at the initiation of Czar Nicholas II of Russia, the Hague Peace Conference of 1899 convened. The primary purpose of the Hague Peace Conference was to discuss and address issues of peace and disarmament. Numerous nations, primarily from Europe, participated in it. The result of the conference was the adoption of the Convention on the Pacific Settlement of International Disputes. One of the main accomplishments of the convention was the establishment of the Permanent Court of Arbitration to provide a mechanism for the pacific settlement of disputes between nations.

The Permanent Court of Arbitration was not quite an actual court but rather a procedure for the settlement of disputes. The Permanent Court of Arbitration consisted of a panel of jurists who were appointed by each state that had accepted the Convention on the Pacific Settlement of International Disputes. Each member state was allowed to appoint four jurists. Whenever there was a dispute between member states, the dispute could be submitted to the Permanent Court of Arbitration for settlement, with the parties to the dispute selecting jurists from the panel. The convention also provided for an administrative apparatus known as the Bureau and a set of procedures for the conduct of arbitrations. The Permanent Court of Arbitration was formed in 1900 and began operations in 1902.

In 1907, the second Hague Peace Conference was held. Many nations from Central and South America were invited to attend. The United States was also a participant. At the 1907 Hague Peace Conference, the United States proposed a permanent court of international justice, with judges whose sole duty would be to hear cases. Unfortunately, there was not enough support for the creation of such a court. However, the 1907 Hague Peace Conference did result in an improvement of the procedures of the Permanent Court of Arbitration. The Permanent Court of Arbitration still operates today.

With the ending of World War I, the League of Nations was formed in 1919 with the goal of preventing such conflicts from occurring again. U.S. President Woodrow Wilson was a prime proponent of the League of Nations, for which he was awarded the Nobel Peace Prize. Unfortunately, because of Republican opposition in the Senate, the United States never ratified the Covenant of the League of Nations, although many other nations did.

The World Court (shown here in private session) is in theory the highest court in the world, charged with settling disputes between nations. The court is a division of the United Nations and is located in The Hague, Netherlands. (Wikimedia)

Article 14 of the Covenant of the League of Nations provided for the formation of an international court of justice. In 1920, the League of Nations formally adopted the Statute of the Permanent Court of International Justice. It provided for a permanent court, with a registry for the administration of the court and the election of the judges. By 1921, a majority of the members of the League of Nations had ratified it. The Permanent Court of International Justice began work in 1922.

Although the Permanent Court of International Justice was authorized by the Covenant of the League of Nations and was created by the League of Nations, it was separate from the League of Nations. Member states of the League of Nations were not automatically members of the Permanent Court of International Justice. All states had access to the Permanent Court of International Justice if they exercised their option to submit to its jurisdiction.

The Permanent Court of International Justice operated from 1922 until the start of World War II, when the court moved to Geneva, Switzerland. During the time before World War II, the court handled 29 disputed cases between nations and issued 27 advisory opinions and was, thus, firmly accepted in the international community as an authoritative body for the pacific handling of international disputes.

Toward the end of World War II, the Allied nations started negotiations for creation of the UN and the continuation of the Permanent Court of

International Justice. In 1945, the UN Charter was adopted, as was the new Statute of the International Court of Justice. On January 31, 1946, the judges of the Permanent Court of International Justice all resigned and on February 6, 1946, elections for the justices for the International Court of Justice were held.

The ICJ is based at The Hague. The purposes of the ICJ are to settle, in accordance with international law, legal disputes submitted to it by the states and to provide advisory legal opinions when so requested by the UN and its agencies.

The ICJ is composed of 15 judges who are elected by the UN Assembly and the UN Security Council. To be elected, each judge must receive an absolute majority separate vote from both entities. Also, no more than one judge may be a citizen of the same state. Judges are elected to nine-year terms. To ensure equal representation of the nations of the world on the ICJ, judges are usually elected from the following regions: Africa (three judges), Latin America and the Caribbean (two judges), eastern Europe (two judges), and western Europe and other states (five judges). While they hold office, judges are prohibited from engaging in any other activities except their duties as a judge for the ICJ. Only states that are parties to the Statute of the ICJ may nominate persons to be a judge.

The court is presided over by a president and a vice president. The president and the vice president are elected by the members of the court by secret ballot every three years. The president presides over all meetings of the ICJ and is responsible for and supervises the administration of the court. The president may cast a vote when there is a tie vote among the judges hearing a case. The vice president assumes the duties of the president in the absence of the president. The ICJ also has a registry. The registry is the administrative organ of the court. The registry is headed by the registrar and has an administrative staff to fulfill its functions.

Jurisdiction is the power and authority to hear and adjudicate a case. The ICJ has the jurisdiction to hear two types of cases: contentious cases between and submitted by states, and requests for advisory legal opinions submitted by the UN and its agencies. Only states that are parties to the Statute of the ICJ or that have agreed to submit to jurisdiction of the court, whether by specific agreement or by treaty, may submit cases to be heard by the court.

Generally, when states accept the jurisdiction of the ICJ, it is compulsory. However, when states submit declarations of submission to the ICJ, they may include reservations about certain types of disputes or limitations on the term of acceptance. The use of reservations and the power to withdraw from the compulsory jurisdiction of the ICJ have led to some unfortunate and embarrassing international situations.

The most infamous example of the use or abuse of the power to withdraw from the jurisdiction of the ICJ is the case of *Nicaragua v. United States*. During the 1980s and the Reagan administration, the United States was involved in the internal affairs of Nicaragua, specifically with aiding the Contras, who were attempting to overthrow the government of Nicaragua. The United States became involved in the illegal mining of the harbors of Nicaragua, which resulted in damage to not only Nicaraguan shipping but also the shipping of various other nations. At that time, both Nicaragua and the United States were parties to the Statute of the ICJ and subject to its jurisdiction, although the United States had filed an acceptance of jurisdiction that included a reservation to withdraw on six months' notice. In 1984, Nicaragua decided to take the United States to the ICJ to seek justice. The court decided to accept the case. In response, on January 18, 1985, the United States refused to participate in the suit and on October 7, 1985, the United States provided notice that it would withdraw from the ICJ after six months, as allowed by Article 36(2) of the Statute of the ICJ. International indignation and criticism as a result of the actions of the United States were enormous.

Situations such as this have led to significant criticism of the ICJ regarding its ability to effectively execute its duties. If the most powerful nations of the world thumb their noses at the ICJ, the criticism goes, it will lose its credibility and authority to issue binding rulings of law upon the parties appearing before it. If a court is to be truly international, then it must have power and authority over all of the international parties that participate in international affairs.

By contrast, when, in 1989, Iran brought the United States to the ICJ in 1989 after the U.S. guided missile cruiser the *Vincennes* shot down an Iranian civilian airliner with the loss of 290 lives (including 66 children), the United States did not unilaterally refuse to participate. The United States eventually settled with Iran, paying more than $60 million for the loss of life, although the United States refused to admit responsibility for the event and refused to apologize for the incident.

Another aspect of jurisdiction is the nature of the parties who appear before a court. The ICJ can only hear suits by nations as parties. Individual persons are not allowed to bring suit in the ICJ.

Proceedings in contentious matters can be instituted before the ICJ in one of two ways: Either one of the parties can submit to the court a copy of the agreement, provided that the matter is to be submitted to the court, or one of the parties may file an application with the court asking the court to hear its complaint against the other party. In the latter case, the court will decide if it has jurisdiction to hear the case. At that point, the parties will submit pleadings, explaining their respective positions, and the matter will be scheduled for oral argument before the court. Usually, a quorum of nine judges will hear each case. It is also possible to have matters heard by less than a full quorum of judges in a "chambers hearing," which is usually quicker and more efficient than a hearing before the full court. Requests for advisory opinions from the UN or its agencies are usually submitted in writing but may include oral proceedings, with the court asking interested nations to submit their positions on the issue in question. Bringing cases before the ICJ is expensive, and not all nations have the resources to do so, especially developing or Third World nations. An interesting aspect of the ICJ is that it maintains a fund to assist parties in their cases before the court.

The ICJ has peacefully resolved numerous international disputes and has gained wide acceptance in the international community as the legitimate international judicial power and authority. There have been serious problems when large and powerful nations ignore the court and its rulings. Essentially, neither the court nor the UN, of which the court is a part, has its own international police force to enforce its rulings. Likewise, the International Criminal Police Organization (Interpol), the international police force, has no powers of arrest or enforcement and is only advisory, educational, and administrative in nature. Furthermore, not all nations have agreed to submit to the ICJ's jurisdiction, although because most nations have submitted, it is likely merely a matter of time before the ICJ will have compulsory jurisdiction over all nations and thus all international disputes involving the nations of the world.

Wm. C. Plouffe Jr.
Independent Scholar

See also Adjudicating International Crimes; United Nations

Further Readings

Arend, Anthony Clark. *The United States and the Compulsory Jurisdiction of the International Court of Justice.* Lanham, MD: University Press of America, 1986.

Carter, Barry and Phillip Trimble. *International Law.* Boston: Little, Brown, 1991.

Falk, Richard. *Reviving the World Court.* Charlottesville: Virginia University Press, 1986.

Franck, Thomas. *Judging the World Court.* New York: Priority Press, 1986.

Gordon, Edward. "The World Court and the Interpretation of Constitutive Treaties." *American Journal of International Law,* v.59/4 (October 1965).

Maier, Harold G. "Appraisals of the International Court of Justice's Decision: Nicaragua v. United States." *American Journal of International Law,* v.81/106 (1987).

Rosenne, Shabtai. *The World Court and How It Works.* New York: Oceana, 1963.

Glossary

Alien: A person who is a citizen of a country other than the one in which he or she currently resides.

Amnesty International: An international organization founded in 1961 to protect human rights around the world. It focuses particularly on abolition of torture, regulation of the global arms trade, freedom for prisoners of conscience, and defense of the rights of refugees, migrants, women, and of those trapped in poverty.

Anti-Slavery International: An international charitable organization, founded in 1839 and based in the United Kingdom, that fights against slavery and associated abuses; it adopted its current name in 1990.

Arms trafficking: Smuggling or other illegal means of transporting and selling weapons and ammunition in violation of national and international law.

Asymmetrical political relations: A situation in which, as a result of their different levels of power, one country can dominate another and thus engage in unilateral (one-sided) decision making rather than bilateral decisions in which the two countries have approximately equal power.

Biological weapon: A biological agent, such as a virus or bacteria, that may be intentionally released in order to harm human life; examples include the anthrax bacterium and the smallpox virus.

Biometric identification technology: A type of computer technology that allows matching of fingerprints and facial features in digital photographs with people suspected of using false travel papers or who are suspected of being terrorists.

Black market: A market in which goods are sold in violation of national or international law; black markets may exist because the goods are prohibited in international trade (for instance, those made from ivory or tortoise shell), are prohibited in a particular country (for instance, firearms or certain drugs), or to avoid paying tariffs or duties on the goods.

Black September: A Palestinian terrorist group best known for kidnapping and killing eleven Israeli athletes and coaches during the Munich Olympics in September 1972.

Blue Blindfold: An international campaign, launched in 2007, of the United Kingdom Human Trafficking Centre (UKHTC), which is aimed to prevent human trafficking, share information about trafficking, and aid those victimized by it.

Bonded labor: Also called debt bondage, a system in which a person pledges his or her labor as security for a debt; it may be considered a modern form of slavery, as the person may be paid wages so low that the debt can never be repaid.

Border Patrol: An agency that monitors U.S. borders between ports of entry and is part of U.S. Customs and Border Protection.

Border security: Officials in charge of maintaining an orderly process of entry and exit at a nation's borders in order to prevent unauthorized entry, exit, and smuggling.

Bribery: Offering or accepting an undue advantage (such as money) to influence the decision of a public official or private person holding power.

Chemical agents: Chemicals that can be used as weapons of terrorism or converted for that purpose.

CITES: The Convention on International Trade in Endangered Species of Wild Fauna and Flora, drafted in 1963 at a meeting of the World Conservation Union (ICUN); the final text was approved in 1973 and entered into force in 1975. CITES is a voluntary international agreement regulating the trade in wild animals and plants and their products (such as ivory) in order to protect species that are endangered or may become endangered.

CND: The Commission on Narcotic Drugs, established in 1946 by the Economic and Social Council of the United Nations as the United Nations' central policy-making body in matters relating to drugs.

Convention Against Transnational Organized Crime: A multilateral treaty adopted by the United Nations in 2000, with two protocols: one against human trafficking, especially of women and children, and one against smuggling of migrants.

Convention on Combating Bribery of Foreign Public Officials in International Business Transactions: A convention that was adopted in 1997 by the Organisation for Economic Co-operation and Development and that came into force in 1999 to address bribery of foreign public officials.

Core Principles: Shorthand for the Core Principles for Effective Banking Supervision of the Basel Committee on Banking Supervision, the Insurance Supervisory Principles of the International Association of Insurance Supervisors, and the Objectives and Principles for Securities Regulation of the International Organization of Securities Commissions.

Council of Europe Criminal Law Convention on Corruption: A convention covering a broad range of offenses, including bribery in the public and private sectors and trading in influence; as of February 2007, it had 48 signatories.

Counterterrorism: Policies and actions aimed at identifying and eliminating terrorist groups or individual terrorists and preventing terrorist actions.

Cross-border crime: Another name for transnational (or transborder) crime, that is, illegal activities that straddle territorial boundaries.

CSEC: Commercial sexual exploitation of children, including procuring or offering a child for use as a prostitute or in the production of pornography or pornographic performances; signatories to the International Labour Organization's 1999 Worst Forms of Child Labour Convention have explicitly agreed to combat CSEC.

CUBAC: Children used by adults in the commission of a crime (often the production or trafficking of illegal drugs), a practice explicitly prohibited under the International Labour Organization's 1999 Worst Forms of Child Labour Convention.

Cyberterrorism: The use of technology for the purpose of disrupting information systems such as computer networks.

Debt bondage: Also known as bonded labor or peonage and considered by many a modern form of slavery, the practice of tricking or forcing an individual into a labor contract that does not pay enough to meet personal needs or to pay off past debts.

Deportation: The formal process of removing an alien who has violated immigration laws and returning that person to his or her home country.

Derogation: Partial revocation of a law; various international conventions specify that certain human rights may be derogated at times of public emergency that threaten the existence of a nation, while others may never be derogated.

Dirty bomb: An explosive device intended to spread radioactive material, considered a weapon of mass destruction because it could render large areas inhabitable.

Drug cartel: A sophisticated criminal organization involving multiple drug-trafficking organizations and cells with specific duties such as production, transport, and distribution.

Drug trafficking: The large-scale practice of transporting illegal drugs across a border so they may be sold (to be differentiated from drug dealing, which occurs on a smaller scale and involves street-level distribution).

ECPAT International: An organization founded in 1990 to combat commercial sexual exploitation of children; the organization's motto is "End Child Prostitution, Child Pornography and Trafficking in Children for Sexual Purposes."

Environmental crime: An act that is intended to secure a financial or other advantage for the actor and that also carries the potential or intention to harm ecological or biological systems or violate an existing environmental protection statute.

Ethnic cleansing: A policy intended to remove the civilian population of a particular religious or ethnic group from a geographic area, by means including force and intimidation as well as murder.

Europol: The European Police Office, founded in 1999 to improve cooperation and share information among the police forces of member states.

EWI: "Entered without inspection," a term applied to foreign nationals crossing a border (such as between Canada or Mexico and United States) without having their documents inspected by immigration officials.

FATF: The Financial Action Task Force (in French, Groupe d'Action Financière, or GAFI), an organization founded at the G7 summit in 1989 to combat money laundering.

Free the Slaves: An organization based in Washington, D.C., that conducts research into modern slavery, works with grassroots organizations, conducts educational campaigns, and generally works to end slavery throughout the world.

GRECO: The Group of States Against Corruption, founded in 1999 by the Council of Europe to monitor states' compliance with anti-corruption standards.

GTD: The Global Terrorism Database, a database maintained by the National Consortium for the Study of Terrorism and Responses to Terrorism at the University of Maryland; it contains information about terrorist events, worldwide, from 1970 to 2008 and is freely available the public through the Internet at http://www.start.umd.edu/gtd.

Hacking: Breaking into a computer or computer network, whether for purposes of committing a crime or for intellectual pleasure.

Human Rights Watch: An international organization founded in 1978 (as Helsinki Watch) to monitor the Soviet Union's compliance with the Helsinki Accords; today it is headquartered in New York City and conducts research and advocacy campaigns on many aspects of human rights.

Human smuggling: Also known as migrant smuggling, the practice of transporting or facilitating the entry of individuals across national borders in violation of immigration laws. Human smuggling is distinguished from human trafficking: Human smuggling involves the transport of individuals who have chosen to take part in the border crossing (for instance, moving from a poor to a rich country), although they may be exposed to harsh conditions that they did not anticipate, whereas human trafficking involves involuntary participation of the trafficked individuals.

Human trafficking: A modern form of slavery in which human beings are bought and sold for the purpose of forced labor or sexual exploitation; it is distinguished from human smuggling because in trafficking there is the element of force and coercion, in addition to fraud, and the human rights of the individuals trafficked are violated.

Humanitarian intervention: The use of force or the threat of force across national borders to prevent or end violations of fundamental human rights.

IAP: The Istanbul Action Plan, an anticorruption program endorsed by the Anti-Corruption Network (ACN) in 2003, which provides review, monitoring, and self-assessment of anticorruption activities in Armenia, Azerbaijan, Georgia, Kazakhstan, the Kyrgyz Republic, the Russian Federation, Tajikistan, and Ukraine.

Integration: The third and final stage of money laundering, in which the laundered funds reenter the legitimate economy—for instance, by being invested in real estate or business ventures.

Interdiction: The legal process of intercepting contraband or unauthorized migrants at a nation's border.

Interpol: The International Criminal Police Organization, established in 1923 (as the International Police Commission) to act as a liaison between the law-enforcement agencies of member countries, sharing information and promoting cooperation in order to combat criminal activity.

IOM: The International Organization for Migration, an intergovernmental organization established in 1951 in Brussels to aid resettlement of refugees, displaced persons and economic migrants, and which today helps ensure that human migrations takes place in an orderly and human manner.

Keystroke logging: Tracking the keys struck on a computer keyboard without the awareness of the person doing the typing, with the intention of stealing sensitive information such as a computer account username and password; also called key logging, this practice is often accomplished through a computer virus or worm installed on the computer of an unsuspecting individual.

Lacey Act: A law passed in the United States in 1900 to protect plants and wildlife by prohibiting the sale or trafficking of animals, fish, or plants acquired in a manner that violated the law in the region where they were acquired.

Layering: The second stage of money laundering: the process of moving money through a financial system—for instance, through shell companies or multiple identities—to make it more difficult to trace the money back to its illicit source.

Malware: Malicious software, a broad category including computer viruses, computer worms, spyware, and Trojan horses.

Money laundering: A crime that involves a variety of methods for concealing the proceeds of illegal activities: for instance, they may be combined with legitimate proceeds (such as those from a store or other business) or may be concealed through a company deliberately founded to conduct most transactions in cash and thus make the illegal gains difficult to monitor.

Nonintervention: A principle in international law in which one state respects the sovereignty and self-determination of other states and refrains from interfering in their internal politics.

Palermo Protocol: Also called the UN TIP Protocol, the Protocol to Prevent, Suppress and Punish Trafficking in Persons, Especially Women and Children, which supplemented the United Nations' Convention Against Transnational Organized Crime.

Placement: The first stage in money laundering: the introduction of illicit funds (obtained through criminal activity) into a financial system.

Poaching: Killing or taking wild animals or plants in a manner that contradicts conservation and wildlife management laws—for instance, hunting an animal out of season, without a permit or on land where hunting is not allowed.

Ports of entry: Locations at which individuals and cargo can legally enter a country via land, air, or sea.

Radiological agents: Radioactive materials that can harm people or animals when inhaled or ingested.

Refoulement: Forcible return of a refugee to his or her former homeland, where the person's life or freedom might be imperiled; this practice was prohibited by the 1951 United Nations Convention Relating to the Status of Refugees.

Refugee: A person who is unwilling or unable to return to his or her home country because of fear of persecution on the basis of religion, race, political opinion, or nationality.

Rogue state: A state that supports terrorist activity or terrorist groups.

SIS: The Schengen Information System, a database used by 27 European countries to share information relevant to law enforcement, national security, and border control.

SOCA: The Serious Organised Crime Agency, a national intelligence and law-enforcement agency created in the United Kingdom in 2006, which deals with matters including money laundering, child exploitation, and computer crime and is the United Kingdom's point of contact for Interpol.

START: The National Consortium for the Study of Terrorism and Responses to Terrorism, a program based at the University of Maryland and established in 2005 by the U.S. Department of Homeland Security. START conducts research and publishes information related to terrorism, radicalization, and community resistance to terrorism.

State terrorism: Acts of terror committed by a state against its own people or against a foreign state; the term is controversial because some scholars believe that terrorism can be committed only by nonstate actors.

Stateless person: A person who does not belong to or does not have a legally enforceable claim to citizenship in a recognized state; the problem of statelessness is addressed in the 1948 Universal Declaration of Human Rights adopted by the United Nations, which says that everyone has the right to a nationality and no one should arbitrarily be deprived of nationality or of the right to change nationality.

Stockholm Declaration: The Declaration of the United Nations Conference on the Human Environment, adopted in 1972 by the United Nations as the first international document to recognize the rights of human beings to a healthy environment.

TI: Transparency International, an organization founded in 1993 to monitor and expose corruption in international development; it publishes the annual Corruption Perceptions Index, which surveys of business people to rank countries according to how corrupt they are perceived to be.

TraCCC: The Terrorism, Transnational Crime and Corruption Center, located within the School of Public Policy at George Mason University, Virginia, established in 1998 as the first U.S. center devoted to studying terrorism and transnational crime.

Trading in influence: A crime that occurs when a person with real or apparent influence on the decision making of a public official accepts an undue advantage in exchange for exerting this influence.

TREVI: An intergovernmental network formed among members of the European Community in 1975 in response to terrorist acts, including the massacre of several Israeli athletes during the 1972 Munich Olympics; TREVI was integrated into the Justice and Home Affairs division of the European Union in 1992.

Trojan horse: A type of computer software that appears to perform a desirable function but in fact (or also) performs harmful functions such as stealing data, downloading files, or logging keystrokes on the computer where it is installed.

UNCAC: The United Nations Convention Against Corruption, adopted in 2003 as a global, legally binding instrument against corruption.

UNIDROIT: The International Institute for the Unification of Private Law, an independent organization created in 1926 to harmonize and coordinate international commercial and private law.

UNODC: The United Nations Office on Drugs and Crime, an agency established in 1997 (as the Office for Drug Control and Crime Prevention) to address drug trafficking, criminal justice, corruption, and international terrorism.

Virus: A type of computer software which can replicate itself and infect computers, often spreading on networks.

Sarah E. Boslaugh
Kennesaw State University

Resource Guide

Books

Agamben, Giorgio. *Means Without End: Notes on Politics.* Minneapolis: University of Minnesota Press, 2000.

Ain-Krupa, Julia. *Roman Polanski: A Life in Exile.* Santa Barbara, CA: Praeger, 2010.

Albrecht, Hans-Jörg and Cyrille Fijnaut, eds. *The Containment of Transnational Organized Crime: Comments on the UN Convention of December 2000.* Freiburg im Breisgau, Germany: Edition Iuscrim, 2002.

Arar, Mazigh. *Hope and Despair in My Struggle to Free My Husband, Maher Arar.* Toronto, ON: McClelland and Stewart, 2008.

Arendt, Hannah. *Eichmann in Jerusalem: A Report on the Banality of Evil.* New York: Viking, 1965.

Atwan, B. A. *The Secret History of Al Qaeda.* London: Saqi Books, 2006.

Baker, Thomas E. *Introductory Criminal Analysis: Crime Prevention and Intervention Strategies.* Upper Saddle River, NJ: Pearson/Prentice-Hall, 2005.

Bales, K. *Disposable People: New Slavery in the Global Economy.* Berkeley: University of California Press, 1999.

Bales, K. and B. Cornell. *Slavery Today.* Toronto, ON: Groundwork Books, 2008.

Batstone, David. *Not for Sale: The Return of the Global Slave Trade—and How We Can Fight It.* New York: HarperOne, 2007.

Bierne, P. and N. South. *Issues in Green Criminology: Confronting Harms Against Environments, Humanity and Other Animals.* Devon, UK: Willan Publishing, 2007.

Birnie, P. and A. Boyle. *International Law and the Environment.* New York: Oxford University Press, 2002.

Caplan, J. and J. Torpey. *Documenting Individual Identity.* Princeton, NJ: Princeton University Press, 2001.

Christensen, Peter. *The Decline of Iranshahr: Irrigation and Environments in the History of the Middle East, 500 B.C. to A.D. 1500.* Copenhagen, Denmark: Museum Tusculanum Press, 1993.

Clark, Robert. *Intelligence Analysis: A Target Centric Approach.* Washington, DC: CQ Press, 2007.

Clinard, Marshall. *Corporate Corruption.* New York: Praeger, 1990.

Clinard, Marshall and Peter Yeager. *Corporate Crime.* New York: Free Press, 1980.

DeStefano, Anthony M. *The War on Human Trafficking: U.S. Policy Assessed.* New Brunswick, NJ: Rutgers University Press, 2008.

Elias, Norbert. *The Civilizing Process.* Oxford, UK: Blackwell, 1978.

Eller, J. D. *Violence and Culture: A Cross-Cultural and Interdisciplinary Approach.* Belmont, CA: Thomson-Wadsworth, 2006.

Ericson, Richard and Kevin Haggerty. *Policing the Risk Society.* Toronto, ON: University of Toronto Press, 1997.

Farah, D. *Blood From Stones: The Secret Financial Network of Terror.* New York: Broadway Books, 2004.

Farr, Kathryn. *Sex Trafficking: The Global Market in Women and Children.* New York: Worth, 2005.

Findaca, G. *Women and the Mafia: Female Roles in Organized Crime Structures.* London: Springer, 2007.

Foucault, Michel. *Discipline and Punish: The Birth of the Prison.* New York: Random House, 1975.

Foucault, Michel. *The History of Sexuality.* Vol. 1, *The Will to Knowledge.* London: Penguin, 1976.

Frank, N. K. and M. J. Lynch. *Corporate Crime, Corporate Violence.* Guilderland, NY: Harrow and Heston, 1992.

Gerdes, L. I. *Endangered Oceans.* San Diego, CA: Greenhaven Press, 2004.

Gerges, F. *Journey of the Jihadist: Inside Muslim Militancy.* San Diego, CA: Harcourt, 2006.

Goode, E. *Drugs in American Society.* Boston: McGraw-Hill, 2008.

Gunaratna, R. *Inside Al Qaeda: Global Network of Terror.* New York: Berkley, 2002.

Habeck, M. *Knowing the Enemy: Jihadist Ideology and the War on Terror.* New Haven, CT: Yale University Press, 2006.

Harris, Robert. *Political Corruption: In and Beyond the Nation State.* London: Routledge, 2003.

Hazan, Pierre. *Justice in a Time of War: The True Story Behind the International Criminal Tribunal for the*

Former Yugoslavia. Austin: Texas A&M University Press, 2004.

Herzog, Arthur. *Vesco: From Wall Street to Castro's Cuba: The Rise, Fall, and Exile of the King of White Collar Crime.* New York: Doubleday, 1987.

Inciardi, J. *The War on Drugs IV.* Boston: Allyn and Bacon, 2008.

Jenkins, P. *Beyond Tolerance: Child Pornography on the Internet.* New York: New York University Press, 2001.

Kepel, G. *Jihad: The Trail of Political Islam.* New York: I. B. Tauris, 2004.

Khee-Jin Tan, A. *Vessel-Source Marine Pollution: The Law and Politics of International Regulation.* New York: Cambridge University Press, 2006.

LaFaive, Michael, Patrick Fleenor, and Todd Nesbit. *Cigarette Taxes and Smuggling: A Statistical Analysis and Historical Review.* Midland, MI: Mackinac Center for Public Policy, 2008.

Levinthal, C. *Drugs, Society and Criminal Justice.* Boston: Pearson, 2008.

Lyman, Michael D. and Gary W. Potter. *Organized Crime.* Upper Saddle River, NJ: Pearson/Prentice-Hall, 2009.

Mahan, Sue and Pamela L. Griset. *Terrorism in Perspective.* Thousand Oaks, CA: Sage, 2008.

Manning, Peter. *The Technology of Policing: Crime Mapping, Information Technology and the Rationality of Crime Control.* New York: New York University Press, 2008.

Marcus, R. and G. Hastings. *Identity Theft Inc.* London: Disinformation, 2008.

Mares, D. *Drug Wars and Coffeehouses: The Political Economy of the International Drug Trade.* Washington, DC: CQ Press, 2006.

Martha, Rutsel Silvestre J. *The Legal Foundation of Interpol.* Oxford: Hart, 2010.

Mayer, Jane. *The Dark Side: The Inside Story of How the War on Terror Became the War on American Ideals.* New York: Doubleday, 2009.

McKanna, Clare V., Jr. *Court Martial of Apache Kid, Renegade of Renegades.* Lubbock: Texas Tech University Press, 2009.

McLean, David. *Transnational Organized Crime: A Commentary on the UN Convention and Its Protocols.* New York: Oxford University Press, 2007.

Mestrovic, Stjepan G. *The Trials of Abu Ghraib: An Expert Account of Shame and Honor.* Boulder, CO: Paradigm, 2005.

Meyer, K. and T. Parssinen. *Webs of Smoke: Smugglers, Warlords, Spies and the History of the International Drug Trade.* New York: Rowman and Littlefield, 1998.

Mgbeoji, I. *Global Biopiracy: Patents, Plants and Indigenous Knowledge.* Vancouver: University of British Columbia Press, 2006.

Miles, Robert. *Racism After "Race Relations."* London: Routledge, 1993.

Musto, D. *The American Disease: Origins of Narcotic Control.* New York: Oxford University Press, 1999.

Napoleoni, L. *Modern Jihad: Tracing the Dollars Behind the Terror Networks.* Sterling, VA: Pluto, 2003.

Newman, J. Q. *Identity Theft: The Cybercrime of the Millennium.* Port Townsend, WA: Loompanics, 1999.

Nicholls, Clive, Clare Montgomery, and Julian B. Knowles. *The Law of Extradition and Mutual Assistance.* New York: Oxford University Press, 1987.

Peterson, Marilyn. *Applications in Criminal Analysis: A Sourcebook.* Westport, CT: Praeger, 1998.

Pfiffner, James P. *Torture as Policy: Restoring U.S. Credibility on the World Stage.* Boulder, CO: Paradigm, 2010.

Pyle, Christopher H. *Extradition, Politics, and Human Rights.* Philadelphia: Temple University Press, 2001.

Ratcliffe, Jerry. *Intelligence-Led Policing.* Portland, OR: Willan Publishing, 2008.

Roebuck, Julian and Stan Weeber. *Political Crime in the United States.* New York: Praeger, 1978.

Ross, Jeffrey Ian. *Dynamics of Political Crime.* Thousand Oaks, CA: Sage, 2003.

Sambei, Avinder and John R. W. D. Jones. *Extradition Law Handbook.* New York: Oxford University Press, 2008.

Shantz, Jeff, ed. *Racial Profiling and Borders: International, Interdisciplinary Perspectives.* Lake Mary, FL: Vandeplas, 2010.

Shiva, V. *Biopiracy.* Boston: South End Press, 1999.

Sigel, Lisa *International Exposure: Perspectives on Modern European Pornography, 1800–2000.* New Brunswick, NJ: Rutgers University Press, 2005.

Skinner, E. Benjamin. *A Crime So Monstrous: Face-to-Face With Modern-Day Slavery.* New York: Free Press, 2008.

South, N. and P. Beirne. *Issues in Green Criminology: Confronting Harms Against Environments, Humanity and Other Animals.* Devon, UK: Willan Publishing, 2007.

Spindlove, Jeremy R. and Clifford E. Simonsen. *Terrorism Today: The Past, the Players, the Future.* Upper Saddle River, NJ: Pearson/Prentice Hall, 2010.

Subotic, Jelena. *Justice Hijacked: Dealing With the Past in the Balkans.* Ithaca, NY: Cornell University Press, 2009.

Sudbury, J. *Global Lockdown: Race, Gender, and the Prison-Industrial Complex.* London: Routledge, 2005.

United Nations Office on Drugs and Crime. *Legislative Guides for the Implementation of the United Nations Convention Against Transnational Organized Crime and the Protocols Thereto.* New York: United Nations, 2004.

Wall, D. *Cybercrime*. Cambridge, UK: Polity Press, 2007.

Weber, Max. *The Protestant Ethic and the Spirit of Capitalism*. London: Penguin, 2002.

Whelan, R. *Al-Qaedaism: The Threat to Islam, the Threat to the World*. Dublin: Ashfield Press, 2005.

White, R. *Crimes Against Nature: Environmental Criminology and Ecological Justice*. Devon, UK: Willan Publishing, 2009.

Wright, L. *The Looming Tower: Al-Qaeda and the Road to 9/11*. New York: Knopf, 2006.

Youngers, C. and E. Rosin. *Drugs and Democracy in Latin America*. Washington, DC: Washington Office on Latin America, 2005.

Journals

American Journal of International Law
Anthropological Quarterly
British Journal of Clinical Pharmacology
British Journal of Criminology
Brown Journal of World Affairs
Crime, Law and Social Change
Criminology and Criminal Justice
European Journal of Crime, Criminal Law, and Criminal Justice
European Journal on Criminal Policy and Research
FBI Law Enforcement Bulletin
Global Crime
Global Governance
International Affairs
International Criminal Law Review
International Journal of Comparative and Applied Criminal Justice
International Journal of Law in Context
International Lawyer
Journal of Criminal Justice
Journal of Gang Research
Journal of International Law
Justice Quarterly
Policing
Science and Engineering Ethics
Social Justice
Social Problems
Strategic Insights
Terrorism and Political Violence
War Crimes, Genocide, and Crimes Against Humanity
World Policy Journal

Internet

Art Loss Register: http://www.artloss.com

ASEAN Center for Combating Transnational Crime: http://www.asean.org

Central Intelligence Agency: https://www.cia.gov

Egmont Group: http://www.egmontgroup.org

Europol: https://www.europol.europa.eu

Federal Bureau of Investigation: http://www.fbi.gov

Financial Action Task Force: http://www.fatf-gafi.org

International Association of Chiefs of Police: http://www.theiacp.org

International Court of Justice (World Court): http://www.icj-cij.org

International Criminal Court: http://www.icc-cpi.int

International Monetary Fund: http://www.imf.org

Interpol: http://www.interpol.int

National Consortium for the Study of Terrorism and Responses to Terrorism: http://www.start.umd.edu/start

National Institute of Justice: http://nij.gov

Office of the Director of National Intelligence: http://www.dni.gov

Piracy Under International Law (United Nations Division for Ocean Affairs and the Law of the Sea): http://www.un.org/depts/los/piracy/piracy.htm

Terrorism, Transnational Crime and Corruption Center: http://policy-traccc.gmu.edu

Transcrime: http://www.transcrime.unitn.it/tc/664.php

Transnational Institute: http://www.tni.org

United Nations Office on Drugs and Crime: http://www.unodc.org

U.S. Department of State, Office to Monitor and Combat Trafficking in Persons: http://www.state.gov/g/tip/index.htm

World Bank: http://www.worldbank.org

Appendix

The following selected Websites, along with editorial commentary, are provided for further research in transnational crime and justice.

International Criminal Court

www.icc-cpi.int

The International Criminal Court (ICC) is an independent international organization and the first permanent, treaty-based court established as a court of last resort to deal with serious crimes that are not prosecuted by a national judicial system. It is based in The Hague, the Netherlands, and was established in 1998 when 120 countries adopted the Rome Statute. The ICC is funded by contributions from State Parties and voluntary contributions from governments, individuals, international corporations, and other entities. Proceedings may be initiated by the United Nations Security Council, a State Party, or the Prosecutor.

The ICC Website is available in English or French and includes information about the court's history, structure, and rationale; information about situations and cases brought before the ICC; information about the Assembly of States Parties (the ICC's management and legislative body, consisting of representatives of the countries that have ratified the Rome Statute); and press materials, including press releases, video streaming of public hearings, and weekly updates of ICC activities.

As of November 2011, 11 cases in seven countries (Uganda, Democratic Republic of the Congo, Sudan, Central African Republic, Kenya, Libya, and Côte d'Ivoire) have been brought before the ICC. Each situation and case is summarized on the ICC Website. Within each section, links are provided to information about each case, including a timeline and materials, such as the text of the warrant of arrest and the decision. The *Official Journal of the ICC* is also available on the Website; this includes texts such as the Rome Statute, the Rules of Procedure and Evidence, the Code of Judicial Ethics, and the Agreement between the International Criminal Court and the United Nations.

The ICC is in the process of developing the ICC "Legal Tools," an electronic library about international criminal law and justice and four legal and reference tools meant to make the documents more useful. These documents, which are in process, are "Case Matrix," "Elements Digest," "Proceedings," and "Means of Proof Digest." The purpose of the Legal Tools is to "equip users with legal information, digests and an application to work more effectively with core international crimes cases (involving war crimes, crimes against humanity, genocide or aggression," according to the ICC Website. As of 2011, the library section of the ICC Legal Tools contains almost 50,00 documents, including ICC documents, international legal instruments, national implementing legislation, and national cases involving core international crimes; these documents may be read or downloaded in PDF format from the ICC Website.

INTERPOL: Connecting Police for a Safer World

www.interpol.int

INTERPOL is an international organization that works closely with a number of international partners, including the United Nations and the European Union, to facilitate mutual assistance between criminal law enforcement agencies, ensure global access to police data and information, and facilitate secure communication. INTERPOL also provides operational support for certain prime areas and fosters continuous development of the knowledge and skills required for effective international policing.

As of 2011, 188 countries have become members of INTERPOL. INTERPOL's strategic priorities for the years 2011–13 are to create and operate a secure global communication network, provide constant (24 hours a day, 7 days a week) support and operational assistance to member countries, raise the standards of training and infrastructure for international policing and security, assist member countries in identifying crimes and criminals, improve INTERPOL's own core infrastructure, and enhance the legal foundation for international police activities.

The INTERPOL Website is written in English, but parts of it are also available in French, Spanish, and Arabic, as are many of the documents available for download from the Website. The Website is divided into five main areas: general information about INTERPOL, news and media, areas of INTERPOL expertise, types of crimes, and member countries. Information about INTERPOL includes an overview of the organization, its structure and governance, its priorities, origin and meaning of the name and official symbols (logo and flag), history of the organization, legal materials relating to INTERPOL (general regulations, rules of procedure, etc.), and information about international partners (the United Nations, the European Union, the Group of Eight, the World Health Organization, and some private-sector companies). The news and media section includes press releases, texts of speeches, notices of events, publications, videos, and photos. The publications area is particularly substantial and includes downloadable fact sheets on different types of crimes (drug trafficking, maritime piracy, nuclear and radiological terrorism, etc.), annual reports from 1998 to 2010, and other types of publications, including guides, manuals, and brochures. All of these documents are available in English, and many are available in French, Arabic, and Spanish as well.

Specific areas of INTERPOL expertise documented on the Web page include training and capacity building, data exchange, databases, notices, the command and coordination center, response teams, forensics, and intelligence analysis. Within each area, an overview is provided on the Website with links to related information (for example, a history of fingerprints in the forensics section). The Website also organizes information according to type of crime, with each section containing an explanation

of INTERPOL's activities in this area, relevant news items, and links to further information. The 16 crime areas covered in this manner are corruption, crimes against children, cybercrime, drugs, environmental crime, financial crime, firearms, fugitive investigations, intellectual property crime and counterfeiting, maritime piracy, organized crime, pharmaceutical crime, terrorism, trafficking in human beings, vehicle crime, and works of art. Finally, the member countries section includes brief information about INTERPOL operations in that country and links to news reports, if relevant.

National Institute of Justice, International Center

wwow.nij.gov/nij/international

The National Institute of Justice (NIJ) is an agency within the U.S. Department of Justice, an executive agency within the U.S. federal government. The NIJ is dedicated to research, development, and evaluation for the purpose of "improving knowledge and understanding of crime and justice issues through science," according to its Website. In addition, the NIJ "is committed to being a transformative force in the criminal justice field" by meeting five challenges: fostering science-based criminal justice practice, translating knowledge into practice, advancing technology, working across disciplines, and adopting a global perspective.

The International Center of the NIJ focuses on research into terrorism, international organized crime, trafficking in persons, cybercrime, and forensics. Its goals include increasing awareness of transnational crimes; improving access to information about transnational crime; supporting global research partnerships; ensuring NIJ-funded research, including crime across national borders; and disseminating research, technology, and best practices for combating crime at all levels, from local to transnational. The International Center partners with international researchers, foreign governments, and other U.S. government agencies to aid in knowledge transfer across national boundaries, building international collaborations and partnerships, and constructing global networks of policy makers, practitioners, and researchers.

Three areas of particular interest within the NIJ Website are those devoted to transnational organized crime (http://nij.gov/topics/crime/transnational-organized-crime/welcome.htm), human trafficking (http://nij.gov/nij/topics/crime/human-trafficking/welcome.htm), and terrorism (http://nij.gov/nij/topics/crime/terrorism/welcome.htm). In each case, the NIJ Website provides an introduction to the topic, including links to references (e.g., section on human trafficking includes a link to the United Nations Web page summarizing the *Protocol to Prevent, Suppress, and Punish Trafficking in Persons, Especially Women and Children*, and the terrorism section includes a link to Title 22 of the U.S. Code, which defines terrorism), describes NIJ efforts to combat the crime in question, and provides an annotated bibliography with links to relevant publications published or sponsored by the NIJ. Most of these publications can be read on the Website and/or downloaded in PDF or text format.

The NIJ Website includes a search engine to search the Website or NIJ publications on all topics. The International Document Exchange (IDE; https://www.ncjrs.gov/intlide.html) facilitates sharing of information across national boundaries by providing access to publications of the National Criminal Justice Reference Service for organizations outside the United States. Those interested must register on the IDE Website; currently organizations in over 60 countries use this resource.

Piracy Under International Law (United Nations Division for Ocean Affairs and the Law of the Sea)

http://www.un.org/depts/los/piracy/piracy.htm

The Division for Ocean Affairs and the Law of the Sea is the secretariat of the United Nations Convention on the Law of the Sea (UNCLOS). Its mandate, according to its Website, is "to provide information and advice on the uniform and consistent application of the provisions of UNCLOS, including those relevant to the repression of piracy." The Website explains the rationale for the suppression of piracy and the obligations of states to cooperate in combating piracy and other threats to maritime security. This includes links to the UNCLOS articles that provide the legal framework to define piracy, the obligation of states to combat piracy, and the differentiation between piracy and armed robbery against ships. The entire Oceans and

Law of the Sea Website is also searchable by keyword, date, language, and file format.

This Website provides links to many United Nations documents concerning piracy, most of which are available in multiple languages in addition to English (e.g., French, Russian, Spanish, and Arabic). These include eight Security Council resolutions, from 2008 to 2011, on piracy off the coast of Somalia; a number of General Assembly resolutions on Oceans and the Law of the Sea; links to numerous reports of the Secretary-General addressing piracy (with the relevant page numbers noted); and two reports from the United Nations Open-ended Informal Consultative Process on Oceans and the Law of the Sea that focus on piracy.

Another section of the United Nations piracy Web page provides information from various countries and international national organizations regarding piracy and links to information about national legislation regarding piracy in over 50 member states of the United Nations. In about 30 cases, the links lead to the actual text of the legislation; in the remaining cases, information about the laws is provided. It also provides a link to a detailed 2011 letter from the International Maritime Organization (IMO), which includes a number of documents intended to assist members in implementing international antipiracy conventions.

One section of this Website is also devoted to links to other organizations and Websites involved in combating piracy. These include the IMO, the United Nations Office on Drugs and Crime, ReCAAP (Regional Cooperation Agreement on Combating Piracy and Armed Robbery against Ships in Asia, the Maritime Security Centre: Horn of Africa, the International Maritime Bureau of the International Chamber of Commerce, INTERPOL (international police organization), and UNPOS (United Nations Political Office for Somalia, created in 1995 to help advance peace and reconciliation within Somalia).

U.S. Department of State, Office to Monitor and Combat Trafficking in Persons

www.state.gov/g/tip/index.htm

The Department of State is the branch of the U.S. federal government that deals with issues of relations with other countries. The Under Secretary for Democracy and Global Affairs within the

Department of State deals with a number of issues, including human trafficking (trafficking in persons). The Office to Monitor and Combat Trafficking in Persons leads the U.S. global effort to combat human trafficking, an umbrella term describing a person obtained or held in compelled service. Types of human trafficking include sex trafficking, forced or bonded labor, debt bondage, child soldiers, and involuntary domestic servitude.

The Web page of the Office to Monitor and Combat Trafficking in Persons includes basic information about human trafficking, including a definition of the various types of activities included in that term (forced labor, sex trafficking, etc.) and information about the extent of each type of trafficking. The "Trafficking in Persons Report" provides much more detailed information about human trafficking. This annual report is available for the years 2001–11 in PDF and HTML format on the Website, and it is available in Arabic, Chinese, French, Persian, Russian, and Spanish as well as in English.

The Office to Monitor and Combat Trafficking in Persons administers a competitive grant program devoted to eradicating human trafficking. Information about applying for one of the grants in this program is available from the Website. The Website also includes a chart listing and describing research funded by the Office to Monitor and Combat Trafficking in Persons in the past, with clickable links leading to the reports for some of the projects. The entire Department of State Website can also be searched by keyword or browsed by topic, country, date, and several other options. More basic information on topics of special interest (e.g., "Optimal Regulatory Approach for Labor Recruiting," "Slavery and Food Security: The Fishing Fleet") is available on the Website in English, Chinese, French, Russian, Spanish, Arabic, and Persian. A number of press materials are also available on the Website, including fact sheets, press releases, speeches, interviews, and testimony (video and/or text) relevant to the subject of human trafficking.

Sarah E. Boslaugh
Kennesaw State University

Index

Entry titles and their page numbers are in **bold**.